The Editor

GORDON MCMULLAN is Reader in English at King's College London. His publications include *The Politics of Unease in the Plays of John Fletcher* (1994) and two edited collections of essays, *The Politics of Tragicomedy: Shakespeare and After* (edited with Jonathan Hope, 1992) and *Renaissance Configurations: Voices/Bodies/Spaces, 1580–1690* (1998). His Arden edition of Shakespeare and Fletcher's *Henry VIII* was published in 2000. He is currently working on a book about Shakespeare and the invention of late writing.

W. W. NORTON & COMPANY, INC.
Also Publishes

THE NORTON ANTHOLOGY OF AFRICAN AMERICAN LITERATURE
edited by Henry Louis Gates Jr. and Nellie Y. McKay et al.

THE NORTON ANTHOLOGY OF AMERICAN LITERATURE
edited by Nina Baym et al.

THE NORTON ANTHOLOGY OF CONTEMPORARY FICTION
edited by R. V. Cassill and Joyce Carol Oates

THE NORTON ANTHOLOGY OF ENGLISH LITERATURE
edited by M. H. Abrams and Stephen Greenblatt et al.

THE NORTON ANTHOLOGY OF LITERATURE BY WOMEN
edited by Sandra M. Gilbert and Susan Gubar

THE NORTON ANTHOLOGY OF MODERN AND CONTEMPORARY POETRY
edited by Jahan Ramazani, Richard Ellmann, and Robert O'Clair

THE NORTON ANTHOLOGY OF POETRY
edited by Margaret Ferguson, Mary Jo Salter, and Jon Stallworthy

THE NORTON ANTHOLOGY OF SHORT FICTION
edited by R. V. Cassill and Richard Bausch

THE NORTON ANTHOLOGY OF THEORY AND CRITICISM
erdited by Vincent B. Leitch et al.

THE NORTON ANTHOLOGY OF WORLD LITERATURE
edited by Sarah Lawall et al.

THE NORTON FACSIMILE OF THE FIRST FOLIO OF SHAKESPEARE
prepared by Charlton Hinman

THE NORTON INTRODUCTION TO LITERATURE
edited by Jerome Beaty, Alison Booth, J. Paul Hunter, and Kelly J. Mays

THE NORTON INTRODUCTION TO THE SHORT NOVEL
edited by Jerome Beaty

THE NORTON READER
edited by Linda H. Peterson, John C. Brereton, and Joan E. Hartman

THE NORTON SAMPLER
edited by Thomas Cooley

THE NORTON SHAKESPEARE, BASED ON THE OXFORD EDITION
edited by Stephen Greenblatt et al.

For a complete list of Norton Critical Editions, visit
www.wwnorton.com/college/english/nce/welcome.htm

A NORTON CRITICAL EDITION

William Shakespeare

1 HENRY IV

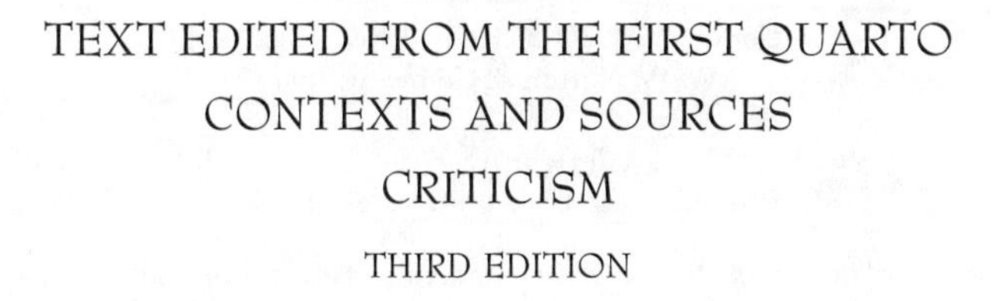

TEXT EDITED FROM THE FIRST QUARTO
CONTEXTS AND SOURCES
CRITICISM

THIRD EDITION

Edited by

GORDON McMULLAN

KING'S COLLEGE LONDON

W. W. NORTON & COMPANY
New York • London

W. W. Norton & Company has been independent since its founding in 1923, when William Warder and Mary D. Herter Norton first published lectures delivered at the People's Institute, the adult education division of New York City's Cooper Union. The Nortons soon expanded their program beyond the Institute, publishing books by celebrated academics from America and abroad. By mid-century, the two major pillars of Norton's publishing program—trade books and college texts—were firmly established. In the 1950s, the Norton family transferred control of the company to its employees, and today—with a staff of four hundred and a comparable number of trade, college, and professional titles published each year—W. W. Norton & Company stands as the largest and oldest publishing house owned wholly by its employees.

Printed in the United States of America.

The text of this book is composed in Fairfield Medium
with the display set in Bernhard Modern.
Composition by PennSet, Inc.
Manufacturing by the Maple-Vail Book Manfacturing Group.
Book design by Antonina Krass.

Library of Congress Cataloging-in-Publication Data

Shakespeare, William, 1564–1616.
[King Henry IV. Part 1]
1 Henry IV : text edited from the first quarto : contexts and sources, criticism / William Shakespeare ; edited by Gordon McMullan.— 3rd ed.
p. cm. — (A Norton critical edition)
Includes bibliographical references (p.).

ISBN 0-393-97931-8 (pbk.)

1. Henry IV, King of England, 1367–1413—Drama. 2. Great Britain—History—Henry IV, 1399–1413—Drama. 3. Shakespeare, William, 1564–1616. King Henry IV. Part 1. 4. Henry IV, King of England, 1367–1413—In literature. I. Title: One-Henry-Four. II. McMullan, Gordon, 1962– III. Title.

PR2810.A2 M39 2002
822.3′3—dc21

2002026529

W. W. Norton & Company, Inc., 500 Fifth Avenue, New York, N.Y. 10110
www.wwnorton.com

W. W. Norton & Company Ltd., Castle House,
75/76 Wells Street, London W1T 3QT

1 2 3 4 5 6 7 8 9 0

Contents

O'NEILL. But you'll tell the truth?

LOMBARD. If you're asking me will my story be as accurate as possible—of course it will. But are truth and falsity the proper criteria? I don't know. Maybe when the time comes my first responsibility will be to tell the best possible narrative. Isn't that what history is, a kind of story-telling?

O'NEILL. Is it?

LOMBARD. Imposing a pattern on events that were mostly casual and haphazard and shaping them into a narrative that is logical and interesting. Oh, yes, I think so.

O'NEILL. And where does the truth come into all this?

LOMBARD. I'm not sure that 'truth' is a primary ingredient. . . .

— Brian Friel, *Making History* (1989)

Preface

You recognize Henry VIII and Elizabeth I when you see them in portraits, I'm sure. Of all the other English kings and queens, I imagine you have slightly more of a sense of Henry V than of the rest—assuming, that is, that you have seen one or the other of the two highly successful twentieth-century film adaptations of Shakespeare's *Henry V*, starring Laurence Olivier and Kenneth Branagh respectively—and you will surely know more about him than you do about his father, Henry IV. If so, and if you haven't encountered *1 Henry IV* before, then you should know that it is also a play about Henry V, charting a stage of his development from irresponsible youth to heroic national leader. But this play—perhaps the finest of all of the Shakespearean history plays (quite a feat, this, bearing in mind that the competition includes *Richard III* as well as *Henry V*)—is about much more than one character. It is a dramatic study of the establishment and maintenance of power, of kinship and the negotiation of identity, of the relationship between official life and the alternative world of carnival, and of the fundamental instability of masculinity, of hereditary monarchy, and of British geography. Above all, it is a powerful and engaging stage play that has thrived in the theater ever since it was first performed, probably in 1596.

The History of King Henry the Fourth, Part I (or *One-Henry-Four*, as it is generally called) was, in published form, an early modern best-seller, appearing in seven editions prior to the Shakespeare First Folio of 1623, a status that underlines the play's immediate success on the stage, a success that has never waned. Bearing in mind the prominence of Hal/Henry V in recent productions, the title page of the First Quarto—the earliest authoritative text—suggests a more complex and multiple focus: "The History of Henrie the Fovrth; With the battell at Shrewsburie, *betweene the King and Lord* Henry Percy, surnamed Henrie Hotspur of the North. *With the humorous conceits of Sir* Iohn Falstalffe." Hal doesn't get a look in: the named characters are the King, Hotspur, and Falstaff. And for the first three hundred and fifty years of the play's life, in fact, productions focused sometimes on Hotspur but mainly on Falstaff, the "Manningtree ox with the pudding in his belly," the Lord of

Misrule who, as "Monsieur Remorse," manages somehow also both to partake of and to parody the melancholy of Lent. Physically originated in direct response to the chronicles' descriptions of Prince Hal as unusually tall and skinny, Falstaff began dramatic life as someone ostensibly quite different—as Lollard martyr Sir John *Oldcastle*, not Sir John *Falstaff* (within "Contexts and Sources," see the section "Composition/Publication"); but, origins notwithstanding, he rapidly became the most popular and memorable figure in the play (the Elizabethans seem to have quoted his lines as we might quote "Blackadder," say), spawning not only *2 Henry IV* and (in memory, at least) *Henry V*, but also, as a kind of reprise, *The Merry Wives of Windsor* (though "the greasy philanderer who assumed the part of Sir John in Windsor," as J. Dover Wilson delicately phrased it, is different in several ways from the Falstaff of the *Henry IV* plays).

It was not until the twentieth century that the theatrical and critical focus switched to Hal and to questions of the acquisition and maintenance of political power. This necessitated presenting *1 Henry IV* not on its own—as it had certainly been presented in Shakespeare's time—but as part of a sequence of plays from *Richard II* to *Richard III*, a tendency that culminated in large-scale theatrical cycles after the mid-century, beginning with the 1951 productions at Stratford. *1 Henry IV* also developed a cinematic life around this time, most notably in Orson Welles's magnificent but neglected *Chimes at Midnight* (1965), the best of Shakespearean films, which rearranges the Hal/Falstaff material from *1* and *2 Henry IV* into an intense sequence. The Hal/Falstaff story is also briefly summarized in flashback at the beginning of Branagh's *Henry V* (1989), but its principal large-screen manifestation in the late twentieth century was Gus Van Sant's cult film *My Own Private Idaho* (1991), which juxtaposed the surreal narrative of a young narcoleptic male prostitute with the story of his poor-little-rich-boy friend whose plot is based directly on the Hal/Falstaff scenes from *1 Henry IV.* Though the film is, as it happens, more successful in its non-Shakespearean scenes, it remains the most interesting attempt to rework the play for a contemporary American audience.

The theatrical insistence on treating *1 Henry IV* as part of the overall scheme of Shakespearean history echoed twentieth-century criticism's assessment of the play not as a fine dramatic achievement in its own right, but as part of a set of four plays, each component part of which is seen to make more chronological sense in the company of the others. These plays—*Richard II, 1* and *2 Henry IV*, and *Henry V*—are known as the "Second Tetralogy" because Shakespeare had already produced four historically contiguous plays—the three parts of *Henry VI* and *Richard III*—which, though earlier in terms of Shakespearean chronology, are later in terms of the history they represent. The First Tetralogy thus maps the violent and messy civil wars that followed after the death of Henry V, while the Second Tetralogy maps the violent and messy civil wars out of which the heroic Henry V emerged. This sense—developed in hindsight—of a broader historical and dramatic logic has largely controlled the way in which the individual plays have been read, despite the fact that an Elizabethan playgoer turning up at the Theatre in 1597 who had not seen *Richard II* (and who could not have seen *Henry V* for the simple reason that it had not yet been written) would not have thought in terms of such overarching groupings. "Tetralogy-think" was sufficiently ingrained in Shakespeareans in the twentieth century, however, that it is impossible now to provide a representative set of essays on *1 Henry IV* without a certain amount of engagement with *Richard II* and *2 Henry IV*; and, because of this, you will find working on *1 Henry IV* easier if you have read the other plays. What you *do* at least need to know of *2 Henry IV* in order to make sense of this engagement is that it ends (apologies if you have not read it yet) with Hal's—or, rather, the newly crowned Henry V's—rejection of Falstaff. "I know thee not, old man," he says to Falstaff's face just after he has been crowned, adding that he has "long dreamt of such a kind of man, / So surfeit-swelled, so old and so profane, / But being awaked,' he says, 'I do despise my dream" (*2 Henry IV*, 5.5.43–47).

Critically, analysis of *1 Henry IV* since the Second World War has struggled with one influence in particular: that of E. M. W. Tillyard in his books *The Elizabethan World Picture* (1943) and *Shakespeare's History Plays* (1944). Tillyard's argument that Elizabethans shared a wholehearted belief in a fixed, ordered universe and, by analogy, in an unchallenged, firmly hierarchical social order and that Shakespeare's history plays were a grand illustration of this order as it had manifested itself in English history provided an intellectual underpinning for theatrical history cycles, continues to exert a remarkable hold over the theatergoer's psyche, and is still held as Shakespearean orthodoxy by a surprising number of theater professionals. Yet critics have persistently demonstrated the flaws in Tillyard's argument, noting, for instance, that his emphasis on the influence of the chronicler Edward Hall underplays the much more complex representation of history offered by Shakespeare's main source, the collaboratively written chronicles published under the name Raphael Holinshed. Recent critics, looking at the same materials as Tillyard, have tended to reach the opposite conclusion: where Tillyard saw the weight of sixteenth-century publications pressing home the fixity of spiritual and political hierarchy as support for his claim that this constituted a universal belief at the time, later critics have seen these same publications as evidence of the determination of the elite to instill this belief in a recalcitrant English public—a very different reading of the situation. As Graham Holderness phrases it, "Not every Elizabethan could have accepted the state's official explanation of things: there were within the culture intellectual divisions over matters of religion, politics, law, ethics; there were Catholics and Protestants and Puritans, monarchists and republicans, believers in the divine right of kings and defenders of the common law and the rights of the subject" (see p. 274). In other words, recent critics see what for Tillyard were statements of a universally held world view as a form of propaganda attempting to inculcate that world view into a public much less organic and consensual than Tillyard and his disciples wanted to acknowledge.

For the first audiences, the play provides a narrative of events that had taken place in the past, but not the impossibly distant past. For us now, an equivalent play would perhaps portray the First World War, recognizably "modern" in some ways (air raids, tanks), surprisingly archaic in others (cavalry charges, the sight of men advancing upright into heavy fire). In other words, these were events that the audiences would have heard of and read about—events, perhaps, in which their great-grandparents had been caught up—and they would have at least a vague sense of the shape of things, even if their grasp of detail might be a bit limited. It is not history that would either have been immediate for them, as you might be tempted to assume, or wholly remote, as it is for us now. And it helps, I think, to remember that anachronism abounds throughout the plays. There is no doubt at all, for instance, that the Eastcheap scenes are Elizabethan scenes, entirely recognizable as contemporary to those first audiences; indeed, the whole set of "history plays" has been understood as representing a theatrical attempt to legitimize the Tudor line and to exorcise the fears of English people living under a childless monarch, fears of the possibility of civil war in the absence of a firm line of succession; the plays are, then, as much about Elizabethan England as they are about the England of the various Richards, Edwards, and Henries portrayed. For us, though—certainly for anyone coming for the first time to *1 Henry IV* without a thorough knowledge of English history in the fifteenth century (that is, pretty much everyone)—one of the hardest things to deal with is the intricacy of events, of family ties, and especially of the rules for inheritance and the complex interfamilial connections that led all too easily to royal claims and counterclaims. I hope the family tree on page xvii, together with the extracts from Peter Saccio's *Shakespeare's English Kings* on pages 167–83, will help readers new to this history to make sense of the overall picture.

What is important, whether or not you are sure you have fully grasped the ins and outs of deposition and rebellion, of military and ecclesiastical history, of alliance and counteralliance, is that you have a sense of the ephemeral nature of legitimacy represented in this fragmented history, the ease with which confusion over the place of the female line within the patrilineal system of inheritance could lead to a series of conflicting claims, none of which can be said irrefutably to be the one true claim. Feminist criticism has recently excavated much that has not been said about the role of women in these plays, generally held in the past to be at best secondary, noting that their presence in certain key scenes "calls attention to the gap between official history and the social domains it must exclude to constitute itself" (Howard and Rackin, p. 429). Moreover, a glance back at the title of the First Quarto suggests that geography plays a powerful role both in constituting and in resisting the official version of history. It is abundantly clear that, as Howard and Rackin note, in this play "England is no longer a kingdom, but an aggregate of heterogeneous people and places" (pp. 413–14). The fragmentation and fluidity of kinship and inheritance in the world of *1 Henry IV* thus have their counterpart in the fragmentation of the physical land and the fluidity of the borders between England and Wales, between England and Scotland, as well as in the ongoing legacy of colonialism, physical and linguistic, in both Ireland and Wales and in the debilitating opposition between north and south within England itself. Over the centuries, the protagonist of *1 Henry IV* has been variously identified as Falstaff, as Hotspur, as Hal. Yet in the end, it is the nation itself that arguably furnishes the play's principal role, a nation that is as impossible to define as it is to control.

James L. Sanderson's fine Norton Critical Edition of 1962 (revised in 1969) offered a clear picture of the state of the art in *1 Henry IV* studies at that time and has been a boon to students for decades. A great deal of work has, however, been done on the play since then, and it was time to bring the edition up to date. I am grateful to Carol Bemis at W. W. Norton for asking me to perform the revision and for overseeing the process. My instructions were to keep Professor Sanderson's text (except for one or two minor corrections), to write a brief introduction, to revise the notes to the text, and to select a new set of essays representative both of the history and of the current state of play in critical analysis. I am grateful to Michael Bristol, Stephen Greenblatt, Barbara Hodgdon, Pat Parker, and Sue

Wiseman for their generosity, to Sylvia Morris at the Shakespeare Centre Library, Stratford, for her help with the jacket photo, to Jim Shapiro and Lucy Munro for reading the draft preface, and to David Scott Kastan for suggesting my name to Carol and for providing helpful suggestions as I worked on the play. If sales of this edition affect David's Arden royalties, I promise to buy him a pint or two (but not a curry, since I don't always succeed in choosing a venue which matches up to his exacting standards).

GORDON MCMULLAN
London, 2002

A Note on the Text

The present text, with few departures, follows that of the First Quarto (1598) edition of the play. Act and scene divisions are not indicated in the Quarto; those of the First Folio have been incorporated here with one exception: scene ii of Act V has been divided into two scenes and the concluding scenes renumbered accordingly. Stage directions supplemental to those in the Quarto have been placed in brackets. Aside from the adoption of modern conventions of spelling and punctuation, I have made only a few textual emendations. Words added have been placed in brackets; the other emendations are as follows:

I.ii.69. *similes:* smiles Q 137. *thou:* the Q 141. *Bardolph, Peto:* Haruey, Rossill Q 166. *to-night:* to morrow night Q I.iii.233. *I will:* ile Q II.ii.45. *Bardolph. What news?:* [Printed as part of Poins' preceding lines] Q 46–48. *assigned to Gadshill:* [assigned to Bard.] Q II.iii.3. *respect:* the respect Q II.iv.29. *precedent:* present Q 32. *Assigned to Poins:* [assigned to Prince] Q 157–60. *Parts assigned to Prince, Gadshill, Falstaff, Gadshill:* Gad, Ross., Falst., Ross. [respectively] Q 164–65. *Gadshill:* Ross Q 220. *eel-skin:* elsskin Q 271. *Tell:* Faith tell Q 303. *Owen:* O Q 350. *tristful:* trustfull Q 357. *yet:* so Q 404. *reverend:* reverent Q III.i.100. *cantle:* scantle Q 116. *I will:* Ile Q 192. *She will:* sheele Q III.iii.29. *that's:* that Q 48. *tithe:* tight Q 89. *lose:* loose Q 175. *Poins:* Peto Q 182. *they or we:* we or they Q IV.i.20. *bear:* beares Q; *lord:* mind Q 108. *dropped:* drop Q 126. *cannot:* can Q 127. *yet:* it Q IV.ii.29. *that* (1): *as* Q 67. *on:* in Q IV.iii.21. *horse:* horses Q 82. *country's:* Countrey Q V.i.2. *busky: bulky* Q V.ii.3. *undone:* vnder one Q 10. *ne'er:* neuer Q 70. *Upon:* On Q V.iv.33. *So:* and Q 67. *Nor:* Q 153. *ours:* our Q 154. *let's:* let us Q

JAMES L. SANDERSON

ABBREVIATED GENEALOGY OF THE MORTIMERS AND THE HOUSE OF LANCASTER

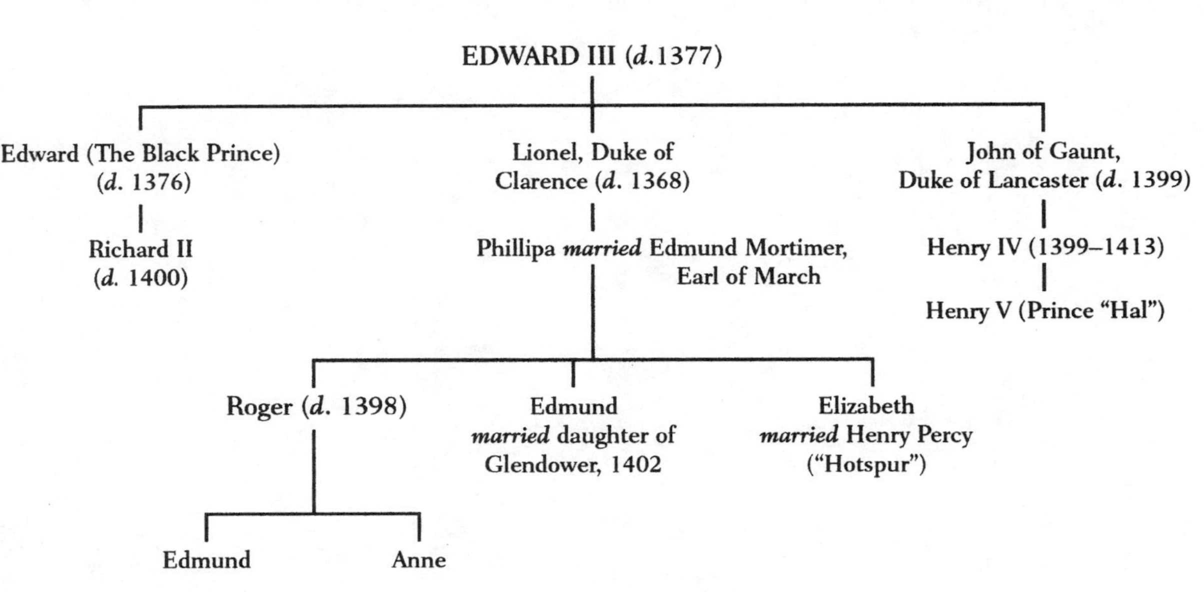

THE HISTORY OF HENRIE THE FOVRTH;

With the battell at Shrewsburie, *betweene the King and Lord* Henry Percy, surnamed Henrie Hotspur of the North.

With the humorous conceits of Sir Iohn Falstalffe.

AT LONDON,
Printed by *P. S.* for *Andrew Wise*, dwelling in Paules Churchyard, at the signe of the Angell. 1598.

Dramatis Personae

KING *Henry the Fourth*
Henry ("Hal"), PRINCE *of Wales*
Lord JOHN *of Lancaster*
Earl of WESTMORELAND
Sir Walter BLUNT

Thomas Percy, Earl of WORCESTER
Henry Percy, Earl of NORTHUMBERLAND
Henry Percy (HOTSPUR), *his son*
LADY PERCY (*"Kate"*), *wife of* HOTSPUR *and sister of* MORTIMER
Edmund MORTIMER, *Earl of March*
LADY *Mortimer, wife of* MORTIMER *and daughter of* GLENDOWER
Archibald, Earl of DOUGLAS
Owen GLENDOWER
Sir Richard VERNON
Richard Scroop, ARCHBISHOP *of York*
SIR MICHAEL, *friend of the* ARCHBISHOP

Sir John FALSTAFF
POINS
GADSHILL
PETO
BARDOLPH
Mistress Quickly, HOSTESS *of the Boar's Head Tavern*

Lords, Carriers, Ostler, Chamberlain, Travellers, Vintner, Drawers, Officers, Messengers, Sheriff, and Attendants

The First Part of King Henry the Fourth

[ACT I. SCENE I. *London. The Palace.*]

Enter the KING, LORD JOHN OF LANCASTER, EARL OF WEST-MORELAND, [SIR WALTER BLUNT], *with others.*

KING. So shaken as we are, so wan with care,
Find we a time for frighted peace to pant,
And breathe short-winded accents of new broils
To be commenced in stronds afar remote.
No more the thirsty entrance of this soil 5
Shall daub her lips with her own children's blood,
No more shall trenching war channel her fields,
Nor bruise her flow'rets with the armed hoofs
Of hostile paces; those opposed eyes
Which, like the meteors of a troubled heaven, 10
All of one nature, of one substance bred,
Did lately meet in the intestine shock
And furious close of civil butchery,
Shall now, in mutual well-beseeming ranks,
March all one way and be no more opposed 15
Against acquaintance, kindred, and allies.
The edge of war, like an ill-sheathed knife,
No more shall cut his master. Therefore, friends,
As far as to the sepulchre of Christ,

1. **wan:** pale.
2. **pant:** get its breath back.
3. **accents:** words, speech; **broils:** arguments, battles.
4. **stronds:** strands, shores.
5. **entrance:** mouth.
7. **trenching:** plowing; **channel:** furrow.
8. **armed:** i.e., with horseshoes.
12. **intestine:** internal.
13. **close:** encounter.
14. **mutual:** united.
18. **his:** its.
19. **sepulchre . . . Christ:** i.e., Jerusalem.

Whose soldier now, under whose blessed cross 20
We are impressed and engaged to fight,
Forthwith a power of English shall we levy,
Whose arms were moulded in their mother's womb
To chase these pagans in those holy fields
Over whose acres walked those blessed feet 25
Which fourteen hundred years ago were nailed
For our advantage on the bitter cross.
But this our purpose now is twelve month old,
And bootless 'tis to tell you we will go;
Therefore we meet not now. Then let me hear 30
Of you, my gentle cousin Westmoreland,
What yesternight our council did decree
In forwarding this dear expedience.

WESTMORELAND. My liege, this haste was hot in question
And many limits of the charge set down 35
But yesternight; when all athwart there came
A post from Wales, loaden with heavy news,
Whose worst was that the noble Mortimer,
Leading the men of Herefordshire to fight
Against the irregular and wild Glendower, 40
Was by the rude hands of that Welshman taken,
A thousand of his people butchered;
Upon whose dead corpse there was such misuse,
Such beastly shameless transformation,
By those Welshwomen done as may not be 45
Without much shame retold or spoken of.

KING. It seems then that the tidings of this broil
Brake off our business for the Holy Land.

WESTMORELAND. This matched with other did, my gracious lord;
For more uneven and unwelcome news 50
Came from the north, and thus it did import:
On Holy-rood Day the gallant Hotspur there,

21. **impressed:** conscripted; **engaged:** pledged.
22. **power:** army.
29. **bootless:** pointless.
30. **Therefore . . . now:** that's not the reason for today's meeting.
31. **cousin:** Westmoreland's wife was Henry's half-sister.
33. **dear expedience:** important undertaking.
34. **liege:** sovereign; **hot . . . question:** being urgently discussed.
35. **limits . . . charge:** responsibilities allocated.
36. **athwart:** across (the plans being made).
37. **post:** messenger; **heavy:** depressing.
40. **irregular:** i.e., to fight a guerrilla war.
41. **rude:** uncivilized.
43. **corpse:** plural—i.e., corpses.
44. **transformation:** mutilation.
47. **broil:** quarrel, battle.
49. **other:** i.e., other news.
50. **uneven:** unsettling.
52. **Holy-rood Day:** September 14.

Young Harry Percy, and Brave Archibald,
That ever-valiant and approved Scot,
At Holmedon met, 55
Where they did spend a sad and bloody hour;
As by discharge of their artillery
And shape of likelihood the news was told;
For he that brought them, in the very heat
And pride of their contention did take horse, 60
Uncertain of the issue any way.

KING. Here is [a] dear, a true industrious friend,
Sir Walter Blunt, new lighted from his horse,
Stained with the variation of each soil
Betwixt that Holmedon and this seat of ours, 65
And he hath brought us smooth and welcome news.
The Earl of Douglas is discomfited.
Ten thousand bold Scots, two and twenty knights,
Balked in their own blood, did Sir Walter see
On Holmedon's plains. Of prisoners, Hotspur took 70
Mordake Earl of Fife and eldest son
To beaten Douglas, and the Earl of Athol,
Of Murray, Angus, and Menteith.
And is not this an honorable spoil?
A gallant prize? Ha, cousin, is it not? 75

WESTMORELAND. In faith,
It is a conquest for a prince to boast of.

KING. Yea, there thou mak'st me sad, and mak'st me sin
In envy that my Lord Northumberland
Should be the father to so blest a son, 80
A son who is the theme of honor's tongue,
Amongst a grove the very straightest plant,
Who is sweet fortune's minion and her pride;
Whilst I, by looking on the praise of him,
See riot and dishonor stain the brow 85
Of my young Harry. O that it could be proved
That some night-tripping fairy had exchanged
In cradle clothes our children where they lay,
And called mine Percy, his Plantagenet!
Then would I have his Harry, and he mine. 90

55. Holmedon: place in Northumberland.
58. shape . . . likelihood: probability.
60. pride . . . contention: height of their battle.
61. issue: outcome.
62. true industrious: zealous in his loyalty.
66. smooth: agreeable.
69. Balked: heaped up in ridges, thwarted.
83. minion: favorite.
85. riot: wasteful living.
89. Plantagenet: surname of the English royal family.

But let him from my thoughts. What think you, coz,
Of this young Percy's pride? The prisoners
Which he in this adventure hath surprised
To his own use he keeps, and sends me word
I shall have none but Mordake Earl of Fife. 95

WESTMORELAND. This is his uncle's teaching, this is Worcester,
Malevolent to you in all aspects,
Which makes him prune himself and bristle up
The crest of youth against your dignity.

KING. But I have sent for him to answer this; 100
And for this cause awhile we must neglect
Our holy purpose to Jerusalem.
Cousin, on Wednesday next our council we
Will hold at Windsor. So inform the lords;
But come yourself with speed to us again, 105
For more is to be said and to be done
Than out of anger can be uttered.

WESTMORELAND. I will, my liege.

Exeunt.

[SCENE II. *London. An apartment of the* PRINCE'S.]

Enter PRINCE OF WALES *and* SIR JOHN FALSTAFF.

FALSTAFF. Now, Hal, what time of day is it, lad?

PRINCE. Thou art so fat-witted with drinking of old sack, and unbuttoning thee after supper, and sleeping upon benches after noon, that thou hast forgotten to demand that truly which thou wouldest truly know. What a devil hast thou to do with 5 the time of the day? Unless hours were cups of sack, and minutes capons, and clocks the tongues of bawds, and dials the signs of leaping houses, and the blessed sun himself a fair hot wench in flame-colored taffeta, I see no reason why thou shouldst be so superfluous to demand the time of the day. 10

FALSTAFF. Indeed, you come near me now, Hal; for we that take

91. **coz:** cousin.
93. **surprised:** taken prisoner.
94. **To . . . use:** i.e., for ransom.
96. **Worcester:** (two syllables: *wus-ter*).
97. **Malevolent . . . aspects:** hostile in every way (an astrological expression comparing Worcester to a star exerting an evil influence on the king).
98. **prune:** preen.
101. **neglect:** leave incomplete.
2. **sack:** Spanish white wine.
7. **capons:** chickens (specifically, castrated cocks).
8. **leaping houses:** brothels.
9. **taffeta:** silken cloth associated with prostitutes.
10. **superfluous:** unnecessarily inquisitive, luxurious.
11. **come . . . me:** get close to the point.

purses go by the moon and the seven stars, and not by Phoebus, he, that wand'ring knight so fair. And I prithee, sweet wag, when thou art a king, as, God save thy grace—majesty I should say, for grace thou wilt have none— 15

PRINCE. What, none?

FALSTAFF. No, by my troth, not so much as will serve to be prologue to an egg and butter.

PRINCE. Well, how then? Come, roundly, roundly.

FALSTAFF. Marry, then, sweet wag, when thou art king let not 20 us that are squires of the night's body be called thieves of the day's beauty. Let us be Diana's foresters, gentlemen of the shade, minions of the moon; and let men say we be men of good government, being governed as the sea is, by our noble and chaste mistress the moon, under whose countenance we steal. 25

PRINCE. Thou sayest well, and it holds well too; for the fortune of us that are the moon's men doth ebb and flow like the sea, being governed, as the sea is, by the moon. As, for proof now: a purse of gold most resolutely snatched on Monday night and most dissolutely spent on Tuesday morning; got with swearing 30 "Lay by," and spent with crying "Bring in"; now in as low an ebb as the foot of the ladder, and by and by in as high a flow as the ridge of the gallows.

FALSTAFF. By the Lord, thou say'st true, lad. And is not my hostess of the tavern a most sweet wench? 35

PRINCE. As the honey of Hybla, my old lad of the castle. And is not a buff jerkin a most sweet robe of durance?

FALSTAFF. How now, how now, mad wag? What, in thy quips and thy quiddities? What a plague have I to do with a buff jerkin? 40

PRINCE. Why, what a pox have I to do with my hostess of the tavern?

FALSTAFF. Well, thou hast called her to a reckoning many a time and oft.

12. **go by:** (1) tell time by, (2) navigate by; **seven stars:** the Pleiades; **Phoebus:** the sun.
13. **wag:** habitual joker.
17. **troth:** faith.
18. **prologue . . . butter:** brief prayer before an inadequate meal.
19. **roundly:** get to the point.
20. **Marry:** indeed.
22. **Diana:** Roman goddess of the moon and the hunt.
23–24. **government:** behavior.
25. **steal:** (1) move stealthily, (2) rob.
26. **it . . . well:** the image is appropriate.
31. **"Lay by":** highwayman's command; **"Bring in":** order for drinks in a tavern.
32. **ladder:** i.e., to the gallows.
36. **Hybla:** a town in Sicily famous for its honey; **old . . . castle:** (1) a ruffian, (2) a pun on Oldcastle, the original name for the character Falstaff.
37. **buff jerkin:** leather jacket worn by arresting officers; **durance:** (1) durable material, (2) imprisonment.
39. **quiddities:** subtleties of wit.
43. **reckoning:** (1) totaling of a bill, (2) giving an account of herself, probably sexually.

PRINCE. Did I ever call for thee to pay thy part? 45
FALSTAFF. No, I'll give thee thy due; thou hast paid all there.
PRINCE. Yea, and elsewhere, so far as my coin would stretch; and where it would not, I have used my credit.
FALSTAFF. Yea, and so used it that, were it not here apparent that thou art heir apparent—But I prithee, sweet wag, shall there 50 be gallows standing in England when thou art king? and resolution thus fubbed as it is with the rusty curb of old father antic the law? Do not thou, when thou art king, hang a thief.
PRINCE. No; thou shalt.
FALSTAFF. Shall I? O rare! By the Lord, I'll be a brave judge. 55
PRINCE. Thou judgest false already. I mean, thou shalt have the hanging of the thieves and so become a rare hangman.
FALSTAFF. Well, Hal, well; and in some sort it jumps with my humor as well as waiting in the court, I can tell you.
PRINCE. For obtaining of suits? 60
FALSTAFF. Yea, for obtaining of suits, whereof the hangman hath no lean wardrobe. 'Sblood, I am as melancholy as a gib cat or a lugged bear.
PRINCE. Or an old lion, or a lover's lute.
FALSTAFF. Yea, or the drone of a Lincolnshire bagpipe. 65
PRINCE. What sayest thou to a hare, or the melancholy of Moor Ditch?
FALSTAFF. Thou hast the most unsavory similes, and art indeed the most comparative, rascalliest, sweet young prince. But, Hal, I prithee trouble me no more with vanity. I would to God 70 thou and I knew where a commodity of good names were to be bought. An old lord of the council rated me the other day in the street about you, sir, but I marked him not; and yet he talked very wisely, but I regarded him not; and yet he talked wisely, and in the street too. 75
PRINCE. Thou didst well, for wisdom cries out in the streets, and no man regards it.
FALSTAFF. O, thou hast damnable iteration, and art indeed able

51–52. resolution: courage.
52. fubbed: cheated.
53. antic: buffoon.
55. brave: fine.
58–59. jumps . . . humor: suits my temperament.
60. suits: (1) petitions, (2) clothes.
61–62. hangman . . . wardrobe: The hangman retained the clothing of his victims.
62. 'Sblood: by God's blood.
62–63. gib cat: tomcat.
63. lugged: led with a chain.
66. hare: considered a melancholy animal.
66–67. Moor Ditch: an open sewer outside the walls of London.
69. comparative: given to making (insulting) comparisons.
70. commodity: quantity; **names:** reputations.
72. rated: chided.
76–77. wisdom . . . it: echo of Proverbs 1:20–24: "Wisdom crieth . . . in the streets . . . , saying . . . 'I have stretched out my hand, and no man regarded.' "
78. iteration: repetition (of passages from the Bible).

to corrupt a saint. Thou hast done much harm upon me, Hal; God forgive thee for it! Before I knew thee, Hal, I knew nothing; and now am I, if a man should speak truly, little better than one of the wicked. I must give over this life, and I will give it over! By the Lord, an I do not, I am a villain! I'll be damned for never a king's son in Christendom. 80

PRINCE. Where shall we take a purse to-morrow, Jack? 85

FALSTAFF. 'Zounds, where thou wilt, lad! I'll make one. An I do not, call me villain and baffle me.

PRINCE. I see a good amendment of life in thee: from praying to purse-taking.

FALSTAFF. Why, Hal, 'tis my vocation, Hal. 'Tis no sin for a man to labor in his vocation. 90

Enter POINS.

Poins! Now shall we know if Gadshill have set a match. O, if men were to be saved by merit, what hole in hell were hot enough for him? This is the most omnipotent villain that ever cried "Stand!" to a true man. 95

PRINCE. Good morrow, Ned.

POINS. Good morrow, sweet Hal. What says Monsieur Remorse? What says Sir John Sack and Sugar? Jack, how agrees thedevil and thee about thy soul, that thou soldest him on Good Friday last for a cup of Madeira and a cold capon's leg? 100

PRINCE. Sir John stands to his word, the devil shall have his bargain; for he was never yet a breaker of proverbs. He will give the devil his due.

POINS. Then art thou damned for keeping thy word with the devil. 105

PRINCE. Else he had been damned for cozening the devil.

POINS. But, my lads, my lads, to-morrow morning, by four o'clock early at Gad's Hill, there are pilgrims going to Canterbury with rich offerings, and traders riding to London with fat purses. I have vizards for you all; you have horses for yourselves. Gadshill lies to-night in Rochester. I have bespoke sup- 110

79. saint: one of the (self-proclaimed) godly.
83. an: if.
86. 'Zounds: by God's wounds; **make one:** take part.
87. baffle: disgrace.
92. set a match: planned a robbery.
93. by merit: according to one's own efforts, rather than through God's grace.
95. "Stand": highwayman's command; **true:** honest.
100. Madeira: sweet wine.
107. cozening: cheating.
109. pilgrims: The pilgrims are taking gifts to the famous shrine of St. Thomas à Becket at Canterbury.
112. Gadshill: the name of one of the thieves and also the location (near Rochester on the road from London to Canterbury) for the robbery; **Rochester:** a town thirty-three miles east of London; **bespoke:** booked.

per to-morrow night in Eastcheap. We may do it as secure as sleep. If you will go, I will stuff your purses full of crowns; if you will not, tarry at home and be hanged! 115

FALSTAFF. Hear ye, Yedward; if I tarry at home and go not I'll hang you for going.

PRINCE. You will, chops?

FALSTAFF. Hal, wilt thou make one?

PRINCE. Who, I rob? I a thief? Not I, by my faith. 120

FALSTAFF. There's neither honesty, manhood, nor good fellowship in thee, nor thou cam'st not of the blood royal if thou darest not stand for ten shillings.

PRINCE. Well then, once in my days I'll be a madcap.

FALSTAFF. Why, that's well said. 125

PRINCE. Well, come what will, I'll tarry at home.

FALSTAFF. By the Lord, I'll be a traitor then, when thou art king.

PRINCE. I care not.

POINS. Sir John, I prithee, leave the prince and me alone; I will lay him down such reasons for this adventure that he shall go. 130

FALSTAFF. Well, God give thee the spirit of persuasion and him the ears of profiting, that what thou speakest may move and what he hears may be believed, that the true prince may (for recreation sake) prove a false thief; for the poor abuses of the time want countenance. Farewell; you shall find me in East- 135 cheap.

PRINCE. Farewell, thou latter spring! farewell, All-hallown summer!

[*Exit* FALSTAFF.]

POINS. Now, my good sweet honey lord, ride with us to-morrow. I have a jest to execute that I cannot manage alone. Falstaff, 140 Bardolph, Peto, and Gadshill shall rob those men that we have already waylaid; yourself and I will not be there, and when they have the booty, if you and I do not rob them, cut this head off from my shoulders.

PRINCE. How shall we part with them in setting forth? 145

POINS. Why, we will set forth before or after them and appoint them a place of meeting, wherein it is at our pleasure to

113. Eastcheap: a London street.
116. Yedward: Edward.
118. chops: fat face.
121. honesty: honor.
122. royal: a play on the name of a coin worth 10 shillings.
123. stand: fight for.
124. madcap: one who acts on impulse.
135. want countenance: lack encouragement.
137. latter spring: old man with youthful drive.
137–38. All-hallown summer: a period of fine weather in autumn.
142. waylaid: ambushed.
147–48 at . . . fail: our choice to avoid.

fail; and then will they adventure upon the exploit themselves, which they shall have no sooner achieved, but we'll set upon them. 150

PRINCE. Yea, but 'tis like that they will know us by our horses, by our habits, and by every other appointment to be ourselves.

POINS. Tut, our horses they shall not see—I'll tie them in the wood; our vizards we will change after we leave them; and, sirrah, I have cases of buckram for the nonce, to immask our 155 noted outward garments.

PRINCE. Yea, but I doubt they will be too hard for us.

POINS. Well, for two of them, I know them to be as true-bred cowards as ever turned back; and for the third, if he fight longer than he sees reason, I'll forswear arms. The virtue of 160 this jest will be the incomprehensible lies that this same fat rogue will tell us when we meet at supper: how thirty, at least, he fought with; what wards, what blows, what extremities he endured; and in the reproof of this lives the jest.

PRINCE. Well, I'll go with thee. Provide us all things necessary 165 and meet me to-night in Eastcheap; there I'll sup. Farewell.

POINS. Farewell, my lord.

Exit POINS.

PRINCE. I know you all, and will awhile uphold
The unyoked humor of your idleness.
Yet herein will I imitate the sun, 170
Who doth permit the base contagious clouds
To smother up his beauty from the world,
That, when he please again to be himself,
Being wanted, he may be more wondered at
By breaking through the foul and ugly mists 175
Of vapors that did seem to strangle him.
If all the year were playing holidays,
To sport would be as tedious as to work;
But when they seldom come, they wished-for come,
And nothing pleaseth but rare accidents. 180

152. **habits:** clothes; **appointment:** equipment.
155. **sirrah:** a form of address usually applied to inferiors, here expressing familiarity; **buckram:** clothing of coarse linen; **for . . . nonce:** for the occasion; **immask:** cover with a mask.
156. **noted:** recognizable.
157. **doubt:** fear; **be . . . hard:** i.e., fight too well.
159. **turned back:** i.e., turned their backs and ran away.
160. **forswear:** give up.
161. **incomprehensible:** boundless.
163. **wards:** defensive postures.
164. **the . . . this:** demonstrating this to be false.
169. **unyoked . . . idleness:** undisciplined tendency of your frivolous behavior.
171. **base:** low-lying; **contagious:** noxious.
174. **wanted:** missed.
180. **rare accidents:** unusual events.

So, when this loose behavior I throw off
And pay the debt I never promised,
By how much better than my word I am,
By so much shall I falsify men's hopes;
And like bright metal on a sullen ground, 185
My reformation, glitt'ring o'er my fault,
Shall show more goodly and attract more eyes
Than that which hath no foil to set it off.
I'll so offend to make offense a skill,
Redeeming time when men think least I will. 190

Exit.

[SCENE III. *London. The Palace.*]

Enter the KING, NORTHUMBERLAND, WORCESTER, HOTSPUR, SIR WALTER BLUNT, *with others.*

KING. My blood hath been too cold and temperate,
Unapt to stir at these indignities,
And you have found me, for accordingly
You tread upon my patience; but be sure
I will from henceforth rather be myself, 5
Mighty and to be feared, than my condition,
Which hath been smooth as oil, soft as young down,
And therefore lost that title of respect
Which the proud soul ne'er pays but to the proud.
WORCESTER. Our house, my sovereign liege, little deserves 10
The scourge of greatness to be used on it;
And that same greatness, too, which our own hands
Have holp to make so portly.
NORTHUMBERLAND. My lord,—
KING. Worcester, get thee gone; for I do see 15
Danger and disobedience in thine eye.
O, sir, your presence is too bold and peremptory,
And majesty might never yet endure
The moody frontier of a servant brow.

184. **hopes:** expectations.
185. **sullen ground:** dark background.
188. **foil:** thin sheet of metal set beneath a jewel to enhance its brightness.
189. **skill:** effective strategy.
190. **Redeeming time:** buying back time—i.e., making up for lost time.
2. **Unapt:** uninclined, slow.
3. **found me:** i.e., found me to be so.
6. **condition:** disposition (to be restrained in response to injury).
10. **Our house:** i.e., the Percy family.
13. **holp:** helped; **portly:** stately, substantial.
16. **Danger:** menace, defiance.
17. **peremptory:** imperious.
19. **moody . . . brow:** frowning forehead of a disloyal subject.

You have good leave to leave us; when we need 20
Your use and counsel, we shall send for you.

Exit WORCESTER.

You were about to speak. [*to* NORTHUMBERLAND]
NORTHUMBERLAND. Yea, my good lord.
Those prisoners in your highness' name demanded
Which Harry Percy here at Holmedon took,
Were, as he says, not with such strength denied 25
As is delivered to your majesty.
Either envy, therefore, or misprision
Is guilty of this fault, and not my son.
HOTSPUR. My liege, I did deny no prisoners.
But I remember, when the fight was done, 30
When I was dry with rage and extreme toil,
Breathless and faint, leaning upon my sword,
Came there a certain lord, neat and trimly dressed,
Fresh as a bridegroom, and his chin new reaped
Showed like a stubble land at harvest home. 35
He was perfumed like a milliner,
And 'twixt his finger and his thumb he held
A pouncet box, which ever and anon
He gave his nose, and took't away again;
Who therewith angry, when it next came there, 40
Took it in snuff; and still he smiled and talked;
And as the soldiers bore dead bodies by,
He called them untaught knaves, unmannerly,
To bring a slovenly unhandsome corse
Betwixt the wind and his nobility. 45
With many holiday and lady terms
He questioned me, amongst the rest demanded
My prisoners in your majesty's behalf.
I then, all smarting with my wounds being cold,
To be so pestered with a popingay, 50

20. **good leave:** full permission.
26. **delivered:** reported.
27. **envy:** malice; **misprision:** misunderstanding.
31. **rage:** excitement of battle.
34. **new reaped:** just shaved.
35. **Showed:** looked; **harvest home:** the close of harvesting.
36. **milliner:** seller of gloves and other fashion accessories.
38. **pouncet box:** small container for perfume.
39. **gave:** put up to.
40. **Who:** i.e., the nose.
41. **Took . . . snuff:** (1) breathed it in (and implying sneezing it out), (2) took offense; **still:** continually.
43. **untaught:** uneducated.
44. **corse:** i.e., corpse.
46. **holiday . . . terms:** expressions appropriate for a festive occasion and for a woman.
50. **popingay:** parrot.

Out of my grief and my impatience
Answered neglectingly—I know not what—
He should, or he should not; for he made me mad
To see him shine so brisk, and smell so sweet,
And talk so like a waiting gentlewoman 55
Of guns and drums and wounds,—God save the mark!—
And telling me the sovereignest thing on earth
Was parmaceti for an inward bruise,
And that it was great pity, so it was,
This villainous saltpetre should be digged 60
Out of the bowels of the harmless earth,
Which many a good tall fellow had destroyed
So cowardly, and but for these vile guns,
He would himself have been a soldier.
This bald unjointed chat of his, my lord, 65
I answered indirectly, as I said,
And I beseech you, let not his report
Come current for an accusation
Betwixt my love and your high majesty.

BLUNT. The circumstance considered, good my lord, 70
Whate'er Lord Harry Percy then had said
To such a person, and in such a place,
At such a time, with all the rest retold,
May reasonably die, and never rise
To do him wrong, or any way impeach 75
What then he said, so he unsay it now.

KING. Why, yet he doth deny his prisoners,
But with proviso and exception,
That we at our own charge shall ransom straight
His brother-in-law, the foolish Mortimer, 80
Who, on my soul, hath willfully betrayed
The lives of those that he did lead to fight
Against that great magician, damned Glendower,
Whose daughter, as we hear, that Earl of March

51. **grief:** pain.
52. **neglectingly:** without thinking what I was saying.
54. **brisk:** smartly dressed.
57. **sovereignest:** most excellent.
58. **parmaceti:** spermaceti, a fatty substance found in the head of the sperm whale and used as an ointment.
60. **saltpetre:** the main ingredient of gunpowder; also used as a medicine.
62. **tall:** brave.
65. **bald:** trivial; **unjointed:** incoherent.
68. **Come current:** be accepted as genuine.
75. **impeach:** call into question the loyalty of.
76. **so:** provided that.
77. **yet:** still; **deny:** refuse to give up.
78. **But . . . exception:** except on the condition.
79. **straight:** instantly.

Hath lately married. Shall our coffers, then, 85
Be emptied to redeem a traitor home?
Shall we buy treason? and indent with fears
When they have lost and forfeited themselves?
No, on the barren mountains let him starve!
For I shall never hold that man my friend 90
Whose tongue shall ask me for one penny cost
To ransom home revolted Mortimer.

HOTSPUR. Revolted Mortimer!
He never did fall off, my sovereign liege,
But by the chance of war. To prove that true 95
Needs no more but one tongue for all those wounds,
Those mouthèd wounds, which valiantly he took
When on the gentle Severn's sedgy bank,
In single opposition hand to hand,
He did confound the best part of an hour 100
In changing hardiment with great Glendower.
Three times they breathed, and three times did they drink,
Upon agreement, of swift Severn's flood,
Who then, affrighted with their bloody looks,
Ran fearfully among the trembling reeds 105
And hid his crisp head in the hollow bank,
Bloodstained with these valiant combatants.
Never did bare and rotten policy
Color her working with such deadly wounds,
Nor never could the noble Mortimer 110
Receive so many, and all willingly.
Then let not him be slandered with revolt.

KING. Thou dost belie him, Percy, thou dost belie him!
He never did encounter with Glendower.
I tell thee, 115
He durst as well have met the devil alone
As Owen Glendower for an enemy.
Art thou not ashamed? But, sirrah, henceforth
Let me not hear you speak of Mortimer.
Send me your prisoners with the speediest means, 120

87. indent . . . fears: enter into a compact with those we have reason to fear.
92. revolted: rebellious.
94. fall off: withdraw his allegiance.
97. mouthèd: gaping.
98. sedgy: covered in reeds.
100. confound: consume.
101. changing hardiment: exchanging blows.
102. breathed: rested in order to get their breath back.
106. crisp: rippled.
108. policy: trickery.
109. Color: disguise.
112. revolt: the accusation that he rebelled.
113. belie: lie about.
116. alone: in single combat.

Or you shall hear in such a kind from me
As will displease you. My Lord Northumberland,
We license your departure with your son.
Send us your prisoners, or you will hear of it.

Exeunt KING, [BLUNT, *and* TRAIN].

HOTSPUR. An if the devil come and roar for them, 125
I will not send them. I will after straight
And tell him so, for I will ease my heart,
Albeit I make a hazard of my head.

NORTHUMBERLAND. What, drunk with choler? Stay, and pause awhile.
Here comes your uncle.

Enter WORCESTER.

HOTSPUR. Speak of Mortimer? 130
'Zounds, I will speak of him, and let my soul
Want mercy if I do not join with him!
Yea, on his part I'll empty all these veins,
And shed my dear blood drop by drop in the dust,
But I will lift the downtrod Mortimer 135
As high in the air as this unthankful king,
As this ingrate and cankered Bolingbroke.

NORTHUMBERLAND. Brother, the king hath made your nephew mad.

WORCESTER. Who struck this heat up after I was gone?

HOTSPUR. He will, forsooth, have all my prisoners; 140
And when I urged the ransom once again
Of my wife's brother, then his cheek looked pale,
And on my face he turned an eye of death,
Trembling even at the name of Mortimer.

WORCESTER. I cannot blame him. Was not he proclaimed 145
By Richard that dead is, the next of blood?

NORTHUMBERLAND. He was; I heard the proclamation.
And then it was when the unhappy king
(Whose wrongs in us God pardon!) did set forth
Upon his Irish expedition; 150
From whence he intercepted did return
To be deposed, and shortly murdered.

128. make . . . of: risk.
129. choler: anger.
132. Want: lack.
137. ingrate: ungrateful; **cankered:** corrupt; **Bolingbroke:** i.e., Henry IV (but not calling him king).
140. forsooth: in truth.
143. eye . . . death: fearful look.
145–46. proclaimed . . . blood: specified as the successor to the throne.
148. unhappy: unfortunate.
149. in: done by.

WORCESTER. And for whose death we in the world's wide mouth
Live scandalized and foully spoken of.
HOTSPUR. But soft, I pray you. Did King Richard then 155
Proclaim my brother Edmund Mortimer
Heir to the crown?
NORTHUMBERLAND. He did; myself did hear it.
HOTSPUR. Nay, then I cannot blame his cousin king,
That wished him on the barren mountains starve.
But shall it be that you, that set the crown 160
Upon the head of this forgetful man,
And for his sake wear the detested blot
Of murtherous subornation—shall it be
That you a world of curses undergo,
Being the agents or base second means, 165
The cords, the ladder, or the hangman rather?
O, pardon me that I descend so low
To show the line and the predicament
Wherein you range under this subtle king!
Shall it for shame be spoken in these days, 170
Or fill up chronicles in time to come,
That men of your nobility and power
Did gage them both in an unjust behalf
(As both of you, God pardon it! have done)
To put down Richard, that sweet lovely rose, 175
And plant this thorn, this canker, Bolingbroke?
And shall it in more shame be further spoken
That you are fooled, discarded, and shook off
By him for whom these shames ye underwent?
No! yet time serves wherein you may redeem 180
Your banished honors and restore yourselves
Into the good thoughts of the world again;
Revenge the jeering and disdained contempt
Of this proud king, who studies day and night
To answer all the debt he owes to you 185
Even with the bloody payment of your deaths.
Therefore, I say—
WORCESTER. Peace, cousin, say no more;
And now I will unclasp a secret book,
And to your quick-conceiving discontents

154. scandalized: defamed.
156. brother: brother-in-law.
163. murtherous subornation: incitement to murder.
165. second: subordinate.
168. line: degree; **predicament:** dangerous position.
169. range: are classified; **subtle:** cunning.
173. gage: pledge; **behalf:** cause.
176. canker: (1) wild rose, (2) corrupt growth.
185. answer: repay.
189. to . . . discontents: to you, quick to understand because of your frustrations.

I'll read you matter deep and dangerous, 190
As full of peril and adventurous spirit
As to o'erwalk a current roaring loud
On the unsteadfast footing of a spear.

HOTSPUR. If he fall in, good night, or sink or swim!
Send danger from the east unto the west, 195
So honor cross it from the north to south,
And let them grapple. O, the blood more stirs
To rouse a lion than to start a hare!

NORTHUMBERLAND. Imagination of some great exploit
Drives him beyond the bounds of patience. 200

[HOTSPUR.] By heaven, methinks it were an easy leap
To pluck bright honor from the pale-faced moon,
Or dive into the bottom of the deep,
Where fathom-line could never touch the ground,
And pluck up drowned honor by the locks, 205
So he that doth redeem her thence might wear
Without corrival all her dignities;
But out upon this half-faced fellowship!

WORCESTER. He apprehends a world of figures here,
But not the form of what he should attend. 210
Good cousin, give me audience for a while.

HOTSPUR. I cry you mercy.

WORCESTER. Those same noble Scots
That are your prisoners—

HOTSPUR. I'll keep them all!
By God, he shall not have a Scot of them!
No, if a Scot would save his soul, he shall not. 215
I'll keep them, by this hand!

WORCESTER. You start away
And lend no ear unto my purposes.
Those prisoners you shall keep.

HOTSPUR. Nay, I will! That's flat!
He said he would not ransom Mortimer,
Forbade my tongue to speak of Mortimer, 220
But I will find him when he lies asleep,

194. he: i.e., the man trying to cross the river.
196. So: as long as; **it:** i.e., its path.
198. start: hunting term, meaning to force the hare to leave its lair.
204. fathom-line: depth tester.
206. redeem: rescue.
207. corrival: anyone with an equal claim; **dignities:** favors.
208. out upon: away with; **half-faced fellowship:** imperfect partnership.
209. apprehends: grasps at; **figures:** i.e., of speech.
210. form . . . attend: issue on which he should be focusing.
212. cry . . . mercy: beg your pardon.
214. Scot: (1) Scottish person, (2) minor payment.
217. my purposes: the point of what I am saying.

And in his ear I'll holla "Mortimer!"
Nay, I'll have a starling shall be taught to speak
Nothing but "Mortimer," and give it him
To keep his anger still in motion. 225
WORCESTER. Hear you, cousin, a word.
HOTSPUR. All studies here I solemnly defy,
Save how to gall and pinch this Bolingbroke;
And that same sword-and-buckler Prince of Wales,
But that I think his father loves him not 230
And would be glad he met with some mischance,
I would have him poisoned with a pot of ale.
WORCESTER. Farewell, kinsman. I will talk to you
When you are better tempered to attend.
NORTHUMBERLAND. Why, what a wasp-stung and impatient fool 235
Art thou to break into this woman's mood,
Tying thine ear to no tongue but thine own!
HOTSPUR. Why, look you, I am whipped and scourged with rods,
Nettled, and stung with pismires when I hear
Of this vile politician, Bolingbroke. 240
In Richard's time—what do you call the place?—
A plague upon it! it is in Gloucestershire;
'Twas where the madcap duke his uncle kept,
His uncle York—where I first bowed my knee
Unto this king of smiles, this Bolingbroke— 245
'Sblood!—when you and he came back from Ravenspurgh—
NORTHUMBERLAND. At Berkeley Castle.
HOTSPUR. You say true.
Why, what a candy deal of courtesy
This fawning greyhound then did proffer me! 250
Look, "when his infant fortune came to age,"
And "gentle Harry Percy," and "kind cousin"—
O, the devil take such cozeners! God forgive me!
Good uncle, tell your tale, [for] I have done.
WORCESTER. Nay, if you have not, to it again. 255
We will stay your leisure.
HOTSPUR. I have done, i' faith.
WORCESTER. Then once more to your Scottish prisoners.

222. holla: holler, shout.
223. starling: small bird with the ability to imitate sounds.
225. still: continually.
227. studies: activities; **defy:** renounce.
229. sword-and-buckler: blustering, ungentlemanly.
239. Nettled: stung by nettles, irritated; **pismires:** ants.
240. politician: schemer.
243. kept: lived.
249. candy deal: sweet load.
253. cozeners: cheats (punning on "cousin").
256. stay . . . leisure: wait until you're ready (ironic).

Deliver them up without their ransom straight,
And make the Douglas' son your only mean
For powers in Scotland—which, for divers reasons 260
Which I shall send you written, be assured
Will easily be granted. You, my lord,

[*to* NORTHUMBERLAND]

Your son in Scotland being thus employed,
Shall secretly into the bosom creep
Of that same noble prelate well—beloved, 265
The archbishop.

HOTSPUR. Of York, is it not?

WORCESTER. True; who bears hard
His brother's death at Bristow, the Lord Scroop.
I speak not this in estimation,
As what I think might be, but what I know 270
Is ruminated, plotted, and set down,
And only stays but to behold the face
Of that occasion that shall bring it on.

HOTSPUR. I smell it. Upon my life, it will do well.

NORTHUMBERLAND. Before the game is afoot thou still let'st slip. 275

HOTSPUR. Why, it cannot choose but be a noble plot.
And then the power of Scotland and of York
To join with Mortimer, ha?

WORCESTER. And so they shall.

HOTSPUR. In faith, it is exceedingly well aimed.

WORCESTER. And 'tis no little reason bids us speed 280
To save our heads by raising of a head;
For, bear ourselves as even as we can,
The king will always think him in our debt,
And think we think ourselves unsatisfied,
Till he hath found a time to pay us home. 285
And see already how he doth begin
To make us strangers to his looks of love.

HOTSPUR. He does, he does! We'll be revenged on him!

WORCESTER. Cousin, farewell. No further go in this

258. Deliver . . . up: set them free.
259–60. mean . . . powers: means for conscripting soldiers.
260. divers: diverse, various.
264. into . . . creep: become a confidant of.
268. Bristow: Bristol, southwestern city and port; **Lord Scroop:** William Scrope, earl of Wiltshire, executed by Henry IV in 1399.
269. estimation: guesswork.
275. Before . . . slip: an expression from hunting: you always loose the dogs before the game animal has started.
279. aimed: planned.
281. head: army.
282. even: carefully.
285. pay . . . home: (1) discharge the debt, (2) punish us severely.

Than I by letters shall direct your course. 290
When time is ripe, which will be suddenly,
I'll steal to Glendower and Lord Mortimer,
Where you and Douglas, and our pow'rs at once,
As I will fashion it, shall happily meet,
To bear our fortunes in our own strong arms, 295
Which now we hold at much uncertainty.

NORTHUMBERLAND. Farewell, good brother. We shall thrive, I trust.

HOTSPUR. Uncle, adieu. O, let the hours be short
Till fields and blows and groans applaud our sport!

Exeunt.

[ACT II, SCENE I. *Rochester. An inn yard.*]

Enter a CARRIER *with a lantern in his hand.*

1 CARRIER. Heigh-ho! an it be not four by the day, I'll be hanged. Charles' wain is over the new chimney, and yet our horse not packed.—What, ostler!

OSTLER. [*within*] Anon, anon.

1 CARRIER. I prithee, Tom, beat Cut's saddle, put a few flocks in the point. [The] poor jade is wrung in the withers out of all cess. 5

Enter another CARRIER.

2 CARRIER. Peas and beans are as dank here as a dog, and that is the next way to give poor jades the bots. This house is turned upside down since Robin Ostler died. 10

1 CARRIER. Poor fellow never joyed since the price of oats rose. It was the death of him.

2 CARRIER. I think this be the most villainous house in all London road for fleas. I am stung like a tench.

291. **suddenly:** very soon.
293. **pow'rs . . . once:** united forces.
294. **happily:** fortunately.
299. **fields:** battlefields.
SD. **Carrier:** a transporter of goods.
1. **by the day:** in the morning.
2. **Charles' wain:** the constellation Ursa Major.
3. **ostler:** groom.
4. **Anon:** right away; I'm just coming.
5. **flocks:** tufts of wool (for padding).
6. **point:** pommel; **jade:** worn-out horse; **wrung:** chafed; **withers:** the juncture of the shoulder bones and neck.
6–7. **out . . . cess:** beyond measure.
9. **next:** nearest, quickest; **bots:** intestinal worms.
13. **house:** inn.
14. **tench:** a fish with red spots.

1 CARRIER. Like a tench? By the mass, there is ne'er a king christen could be better bit than I have been since the first cock. 15
2 CARRIER. Why, they will allow us ne'er a jordan, and then we leak in your chimney, and your chamber-lye breeds fleas like a loach.
1 CARRIER. What, ostler! come away and be hanged! come away! 20
2 CARRIER. I have a gammon of bacon and two razes of ginger, to be delivered as far as Charing Cross.
1 CARRIER. God's body! the turkeys in my pannier are quite starved. What, ostler! A plague on thee! hast thou never an eye in thy head? Canst not hear? An 'twere not as good deed 25 as drink to break the pate on thee, I am a very villain. Come, and be hanged! Hast no faith in thee?

Enter GADSHILL.

GADSHILL. Good morrow, carriers. What's o'clock?
1 CARRIER. I think it be two o'clock.
GADSHILL. I prithee lend me thy lantern to see my gelding in the 30 stable.
1 CARRIER. Nay, by God, soft! I know a trick worth two of that, i' faith.
GADSHILL. I pray thee lend me thine.
2 CARRIER. Ay, when? canst tell? Lend me thy lantern, quoth he? 35 Marry, I'll see thee hanged first!
GADSHILL. Sirrah carrier, what time do you mean to come to London?
2 CARRIER. Time enough to go to bed with a candle, I warrant thee. Come, neighbor Mugs, we'll call up the gentlemen. They 40 will along with company, for they have great charge.

Exeunt [CARRIERS].

Enter CHAMBERLAIN.

GADSHILL. What, ho! chamberlain!
CHAMBERLAIN. At hand, quoth pickpurse.

15–16. **king christen:** Christian king.
16. **first cock:** midnight.
17. **jordan:** chamberpot.
18. **leak:** urinate; **chamber-lye:** urine.
19. **loach:** fish thought to breed prolifically.
20. **come away:** hurry up.
21. **gammon . . . bacon:** ham; **razes:** roots.
22. **Charing Cross:** a village the other side of London from Rochester.
23. **pannier:** basket carried by a horse.
25–26. **as . . . thee:** as satisfying to hit you on the head as to take a drink.
27. **Hast . . . thee?:** are you not trustworthy?
35. **canst tell?:** i.e., never.
39. **Time enough:** i.e., in time; **warrant:** assure.
41. **charge:** baggage.
43. **At . . . pickpurse:** proverbial, meaning "right here."

GADSHILL. That's even as fair as "at hand, quoth the chamberlain"; for thou variest no more from picking of purses than giving direction doth from laboring; thou layest the plot how. 45

CHAMBERLAIN. Good morrow, Master Gadshill. It holds current that I told you yesternight. There's a franklin in the Wild of Kent hath brought three hundred marks with him in gold. I heard him tell it to one of his company last night at supper; a kind of auditor, one that hath abundance of charge too, God knows what. They are up already and call for eggs and butter. They will away presently. 50

GADSHILL. Sirrah, if they meet not with Saint Nicholas' clerks, I'll give thee this neck. 55

CHAMBERLAIN. No, I'll none of it. I pray thee keep that for the hangman; for I know thou worshippest Saint Nicholas as truly as a man of falsehood may.

GADSHILL. What talkest thou to me of the hangman? If I hang, I'll make a fat pair of gallows; for if I hang, old Sir John hangs with me, and thou knowest he is no starveling. Tut! there are other Trojans that thou dream'st not of, the which for sport sake are content to do the profession some grace; that would, if matters should be looked into, for their own credit sake make all whole. I am joined with no foot land-rakers, no long-staff six-penny strikers, none of these mad mustachio purple-hued maltworms; but with nobility and tranquillity, burgomasters and great oneyers, such as can hold in, such as will strike sooner than speak, and speak sooner than drink, and drink sooner than pray; and yet, 'zounds, I lie; for they pray continually to their saint, the commonwealth, or rather, not pray to her, but prey on her, for they ride up and down on her and make her their boots. 60 65 70

44. even: just; **fair:** plausible.
45–47. thou . . . how: there is no more difference between you and a pickpocket than there is between a laborer and a foreman: you give the instructions that others carry out.
48. holds current: is still true.
49. that: what; **franklin:** landowner.
50. marks: each mark is valued at 13 shillings 4 pence.
52. auditor: accountant.
54. presently: immediately.
55. Saint Nicholas' clerks: highwaymen.
57. I'll: I want.
60. What: why.
63. Trojans: roisterers; **the which:** who.
66. make . . . whole: insure everything goes well; **joined:** associated with; **foot land-rakers:** horseless highwaymen.
66–67. long-staff . . . strikers: thieves using a long staff to pull people down and rob them of sixpence.
68. maltworms: drunkards.
68–69. burgomasters: mayors.
69. oneyers: ones; **hold in:** keep a secret.
74. boots: booty, spoils.

CHAMBERLAIN. What, the commonwealth their boots? Will she hold out water in foul way? 75

GADSHILL. She will, she will! Justice hath liquored her. We steal as in a castle, cocksure; we have the receipt of fernseed, we walk invisible.

CHAMBERLAIN. Nay, by my faith, I think you are more beholding to the night than to fernseed for your walking invisible. 80

GADSHILL. Give me thy hand. Thou shalt have a share in our purchase, as I am a true man.

CHAMBERLAIN. Nay, rather let me have it, as you are a false thief.

GADSHILL. Go to; *homo* is a common name to all men. Bid the ostler bring my gelding out of the stable. Farewell, you muddy knave. 85

[*Exeunt.*]

[SCENE II. *The Highway, near Gadshill.*]

Enter PRINCE, POINS, PETO, *and* [BARDOLPH].

POINS. Come, shelter, shelter! I have removed Falstaff's horse, and he frets like a gummed velvet.

PRINCE. Stand close.

[*They step back.*]

Enter FALSTAFF.

FALSTAFF. Poins! Poins, and be hanged! Poins!

PRINCE. [*coming forward*] Peace, ye fat-kidneyed rascal! What a brawling dost thou keep! 5

FALSTAFF. Where's Poins, Hal?

PRINCE. He is walked up to the top of the hill; I'll go seek him.

[*Steps aside.*]

FALSTAFF. I am accursed to rob in that thief's company. The rascal hath removed my horse and tied him I know not where. If I travel but four foot by the squire further afoot, I shall break my wind. Well, I doubt not but to die a fair death for all this, 10

76. **hold . . . way:** keep feet dry on muddy roads—i.e., provide protection.
77. **liquored:** waterproofed.
78. **as . . . castle:** i.e., safely; **receipt:** recipe; **fernseed:** thought to make you invisible.
83. **purchase:** booty.
86. **muddy:** dull.
2. **frets:** chafes; **gummed velvet:** gum used to stiffen velvet peeled off ("fretted") when it became hardened.
3. **close:** hidden.
6. **keep:** keep up.
11. **squire:** square (a foot rule).
11–12. **break . . . wind:** (1) run out of breath, (2) fart.
12. **for:** despite.

if I 'scape hanging for killing that rogue. I have forsworn his company hourly any time this two and twenty years, and yet I am bewitched with the rogue's company. If the rascal have not 15 given me medicines to make me love him, I'll be hanged. It could not be else; I have drunk medicines. Poins! Hal! A plague upon you both! Bardolph! Peto! I'll starve ere I'll rob a foot further. An 'twere not as good a deed as drink to turn true man and to leave these rogues, I am the veriest varlet 20 that ever chewed with a tooth. Eight yards of uneven ground is threescore and ten miles afoot with me, and the stony-hearted villains know it well enough. A plague upon it when thieves cannot be true one to another! (*They whistle.*) Whew! A plague upon you all! Give me my horse, you rogues! give me 25 my horse and be hanged!

PRINCE. [*coming forward*] Peace, ye fat-guts! Lie down, lay thine ear close to the ground, and list if thou canst hear the tread of travellers.

FALSTAFF. Have you any levers to lift me up again, being down? 30 'Sblood, I'll not bear mine own flesh so far afoot again for all the coin in thy father's exchequer. What a plague mean ye to colt me thus?

PRINCE. Thou liest; thou art not colted, thou art uncolted.

FALSTAFF. I prithee, good Prince Hal, help me to my horse, good 35 king's son.

PRINCE. Out, ye rogue! Shall I be your ostler?

FALSTAFF. Hang thyself in thine own heir-apparent garters! If I be ta'en, I'll peach for this. An I have not ballads made on you all, and sung to filthy tunes, let a cup of sack be my poison. 40 When a jest is so forward, and afoot too, I hate it.

Enter GADSHILL.

GADSHILL. Stand!

FALSTAFF. So I do, against my will.

POINS. [*coming forward*] O, 'tis our setter; I know his voice.

BARDOLPH. What news? 45

GADSHILL. Case ye, case ye! On with your vizards! There's money of the king's coming down the hill; 'tis going to the king's exchequer.

FALSTAFF. You lie, ye rogue! 'Tis going to the king's tavern.

16. medicines: love potions.
20. veriest varlet: most complete rascal.
33. colt: trick.
34. uncolted: i.e., deprived of your horse.
38. heir-apparent garters: double reference to Hal's being next in line to the throne (as heir apparent, he had been installed into the Order of the Garter).
39. peach: turn king's evidence—i.e., become an informer in return for amnesty.
41. forward: (1) well advanced, (2) presumptuous; **afoot:** (1) well advanced, (2) on foot.
44. setter: one who decoys persons to be robbed.
46. Case ye: put on your disguises.

GADSHILL. There's enough to make us all. 50

FALSTAFF. To be hanged.

PRINCE. Sirs, you four shall front them in the narrow lane; Ned Poins and I will walk lower. If they 'scape from your encounter, then they light on us.

PETO. How many be there of them? 55

GADSHILL. Some eight or ten.

FALSTAFF. 'Zounds! will they not rob us?

PRINCE. What, a coward, Sir John Paunch?

FALSTAFF. Indeed, I am not John of Gaunt, your grandfather, but yet no coward, Hal. 60

PRINCE. Well, we leave that to the proof.

POINS. Sirrah Jack, thy horse stands behind the hedge; when thou need'st him, there thou shalt find him. Farewell and stand fast.

FALSTAFF. Now cannot I strike him, if I should be hanged.

PRINCE. [*aside to* POINS] Ned, where are our disguises? 65

POINS. [*aside to* PRINCE] Here, hard by. Stand close.

[*Exeunt* PRINCE *and* POINS.]

FALSTAFF. Now, my masters, happy man be his dole, say I. Every man to his business.

Enter the TRAVELLERS.

TRAVELLER. Come, neighbor. The boy shall lead our horses down the hill; we'll walk afoot awhile and ease our legs. 70

THIEVES. Stand!

TRAVELLER. Jesus bless us!

FALSTAFF. Strike! down with them! cut the villains' throats! Ah, whoreson caterpillars! bacon-fed knaves! they hate us youth. Down with them! Fleece them! 75

TRAVELLER. O, we are undone, both we and ours for ever!

FALSTAFF. Hang ye, gorbellied knaves, are ye undone? No, ye fat chuffs; I would your store were here! On, bacons, on! What, ye knaves! young men must live. You are grandjurors, are ye? We'll jure ye, 'faith! 80

Here they rob them and bind them. Exeunt.

Enter the PRINCE *and* POINS [*in buckram*].

50. **make:** i.e., our fortunes (also "cause," as Falstaff takes it in next line).
52. **front:** confront.
53. **lower:** lower down.
61. **proof:** test.
66. **hard:** near.
67. **happy . . . dole:** good luck.
74. **whoreson:** vile, detestable; **caterpillars:** parasites.
75. **Fleece:** strip of property.
77. **gorbellied:** fat-bellied.
78. **chuffs:** churls, misers; **your store:** all your possessions; **bacons:** fat men.
79. **grandjurors:** people of sufficient importance to be selected as jurors.
80. **jure:** nonce word, ostensibly meaning "make jurors of you," but serving as a threat.

PRINCE. The thieves have bound the true men. Now could thou and I rob the thieves and go merrily to London, it would be argument for a week, laughter for a month, and a good jest for ever.

POINS. Stand close! I hear them coming. 85

Enter the THIEVES *again.*

FALSTAFF. Come, my masters, let us share, and then to horse before day. An the prince and Poins be not two arrant cowards, there's no equity stirring. There's no more valor in that Poins than in a wild duck.

As they are sharing, the PRINCE *and* POINS *set upon them. They all run away, and* FALSTAFF, *after a blow or two, runs away too, leaving the booty behind them.*

PRINCE. Your money! 90

POINS. Villains!

PRINCE. Got with much ease. Now merrily to horse. The thieves are all scattered, and possessed with fear so strongly that they dare not meet each other; each takes his fellow for an officer. Away, good Ned. Falstaff sweats to death and lards the lean 95 earth as he walks along. Were't not for laughing, I should pity him.

POINS. How the [fat] rogue roared!

Exeunt.

[SCENE III. *Warkworth Castle.*]

Enter HOTSPUR *solus, reading a letter.*

HOTSPUR. "But, for mine own part, my lord, I could be well contented to be there, in respect of the love I bear your house." He could be contented: why is he not then? In respect of the love he bears our house! He shows in this he loves his own barn better than he loves our house. Let me see some more. 5 "The purpose you undertake is dangerous"—why, that's certain! 'Tis dangerous to take a cold, to sleep, to drink; but I tell you, my lord fool, out of this nettle, danger, we pluck this flower, safety. "The purpose you undertake is dangerous,

83. **argument:** subject for conversation.
87. **arrant:** out-and-out.
88. **equity stirring:** sound judgment anywhere.
95. **lards:** greases, bastes.
S.D. ***solus:*** alone.
2. **house:** family.

the friends you have named uncertain, the time itself unsorted, and your whole plot too light for the counterpoise of so great an opposition." Say you so, say you so? I say unto you again, you are a shallow, cowardly hind, and you lie. What a lack-brain is this! By the Lord, our plot is a good plot as ever was laid; our friends true and constant: a good plot, good friends, and full of expectation; an excellent plot, very good friends. What a frosty-spirited rogue is this! Why, my Lord of York commends the plot and the general course of the action. "Zounds, an I were now by this rascal, I could brain him with his lady's fan! Is there not my father, my uncle, and myself; Lord Edmund Mortimer, my Lord of York, and Owen Glendower? Is there not, besides, the Douglas? Have I not all their letters to meet me in arms by the ninth of the next month, and are they not some of them set forward already? What a pagan rascal is this! an infidel! Ha! you shall see now, in very sincerity of fear and cold heart, will he to the king and lay open all our proceedings. O, I could divide myself and go to buffets for moving such a dish of skim milk with so honorable an action! Hang him, let him tell the king! We are prepared. I will set forward to-night. 10 15 20 25 30

Enter his LADY.

How now, Kate? I must leave you within these two hours.

LADY. O my good lord, why are you thus alone?
For what offense have I this fortnight been
A banished woman from my Harry's bed?
Tell me, sweet lord, what is't that takes from thee 35
Thy stomach, pleasure, and thy golden sleep?
Why dost thou bend thine eyes upon the earth,
And start so often when thou sit'st alone?
Why hast thou lost the fresh blood in thy cheeks
And given my treasures and my rights of thee 40
To thick-eyed musing and cursed melancholy?
In thy faint slumbers I by thee have watched,
And heard thee murmur tales of iron wars,
Speak terms of manage to thy bounding steed,

10–11. unsorted: unsuitable.
11. for . . . counterpoise: to counterbalance.
13. hind: rustic.
16. expectation: promise.
17–18. Lord of York: Richard le Scrope, archbishop of York.
23. letters . . . meet: i.e., letters promising to meet.
25. pagan, infidel: unbelieving.
27–28. divide . . . buffets: split myself in two and pick a fight with myself.
36. stomach: appetite.
41. thick-eyed: dim-sighted; **cursed:** bad-tempered.
42. faint: light; **watched:** stayed awake.
44. manage: manège, horsemanship.

Cry "Courage! to the field!" And thou hast talked 45
Of sallies and retires, of trenches, tents,
Of palisadoes, frontiers, parapets,
Of basilisks, of cannon, culverin,
Of prisoners' ransom, and of soldiers slain,
And all the currents of a heady fight. 50
Thy spirit within thee hath been so at war,
And thus hath so bestirred thee in thy sleep,
That beads of sweat have stood upon thy brow
Like bubbles in a late-disturbed stream,
And in thy face strange motions have appeared, 55
Such as we see when men restrain their breath
On some great sudden hest. O, what portents are these?
Some heavy business hath my lord in hand,
And I must know it, else he loves me not.

HOTSPUR. What, ho!

[*Enter a* SERVANT.]

Is Gilliams with the packet gone? 60

SERVANT. He is, my lord, an hour ago.

HOTSPUR. Hath Butler brought those horses from the sheriff?

SERVANT. One horse, my lord, he brought even now.

HOTSPUR. What horse? [A] roan, a crop-ear, is it not?

SERVANT. It is, my lord.

HOTSPUR. That roan shall be my throne. 65
Well, I will back him straight. O esperance!
Bid Butler lead him forth into the park.

[*Exit* SERVANT.]

LADY. But hear you, my lord.

HOTSPUR. What say'st thou, my lady?

LADY. What is it carries you away? 70

HOTSPUR. Why, my horse, my love, my horse!

LADY. Out, you mad-headed ape!
A weasel hath not such a deal of spleen

46. sallies: sorties; **retires:** retreats.
47. palisadoes: defenses made of stakes; **frontiers:** outlying defenses; **parapets:** banks of earth in front of trenches.
48. basilisks: large cannon; **culverin:** small cannon.
50. currents: ebbs and flows; **heady:** headlong.
54. late-disturbed: recently stirred up.
57. hest: command, determination.
58. heavy: serious.
60. packet: parcel of letters.
62. sheriff: county official with juridical responsibilities.
64. roan: a horse in whose coat the principal color is thickly interspersed with another.
66. back: mount, ride; **esperance:** hope (the Percy family motto).
68. hear you: listen.
73. spleen: nervous energy.

As you are tossed with. In faith,
I'll know your business, Harry; that I will! 75
I fear my brother Mortimer doth stir
About his title and hath sent for you
To line his enterprise; but if you go—

HOTSPUR. So far afoot, I shall be weary, love.

LADY. Come, come, you paraquito, answer me 80
Directly unto this question that I ask.
In faith, I'll break thy little finger, Harry,
An if thou wilt not tell me all things true.

HOTSPUR. Away, away, you trifler! Love? I love thee not;
I care not for thee, Kate. This is no world 85
To play with mammets and to tilt with lips.
We must have bloody noses and cracked crowns,
And pass them current too. God's me, my horse!
What say'st thou, Kate? What wouldst thou have with me?

LADY. Do you not love me? do you not indeed? 90
Well, do not then, for since you love me not,
I will not love myself. Do you not love me?
Nay, tell me if you speak in jest or no.

HOTSPUR. Come, wilt thou see me ride?
And when I am a-horseback, I will swear 95
I love thee infinitely. But hark you, Kate:
I must not have you henceforth question me
Whither I go, nor reason whereabout.
Whither I must, I must, and to conclude,
This evening must I leave you, gentle Kate. 100
I know you wise, but yet no farther wise
Than Harry Percy's wife; constant you are,
But yet a woman; and for secrecy,
No lady closer, for I well believe
Thou wilt not utter what thou dost not know, 105
And so far will I trust thee, gentle Kate.

LADY. How! so far?

HOTSPUR. Not an inch further. But hark you, Kate:
Whither I go, thither shall you go too;
To-day will I set forth, to-morrow you. 110

74. tossed with: agitated by.
76. stir: cause commotion.
77. title: claim to the throne.
78. line: strengthen.
80. paraquito: parakeet, small parrot.
86. mammets: dolls; **tilt . . . lips:** compete at kissing, in a kind of lovers' tournament.
87. crowns: (1) heads, (2) coins valued at 5 shillings.
88. pass . . . current: place them in circulation; **God's me:** God save me.
98. reason whereabout: ask why I am going.
104. closer: better at keeping a secret.
106. so far: to that extent.

Will this content you, Kate?
LADY. It must of force.

Exeunt.

[SCENE IV. *The Boar's Head Tavern in Eastcheap.*]

Enter PRINCE *and* POINS.

PRINCE. Ned, prithee, come out of that fat room and lend me thy hand to laugh a little.
POINS. Where hast been, Hal?
PRINCE. With three or four loggerheads amongst three or four-score hogsheads. I have sounded the very bass-string of hu- 5 mility. Sirrah, I am sworn brother to a leash of drawers and can call them all by their christen names, as Tom, Dick, and Francis. They take it already upon their salvation that, though I be but Prince of Wales, yet I am the king of courtesy, and tell me flatly I am no proud Jack like Falstaff, but a Corin- 10 thian, a lad of mettle, a good boy (by the Lord, so they call me!), and when I am King of England I shall command all the good lads in Eastcheap. They call drinking deep, dyeing scarlet; and when you breathe in your watering, they cry "hem!" and bid you play it off. To conclude, I am so good a 15 proficient in one quarter of an hour that I can drink with any tinker in his own language during my life. I tell thee, Ned, thou hast lost much honor that thou wert not with me in this action. But, sweet Ned—to sweeten which name of Ned, I give thee this pennyworth of sugar, clapped even now into 20 my hand by an under-skinker, one that never spake other English in his life than "Eight shillings and sixpence," and "You are welcome," with this shrill addition, "Anon, anon, sir! Score a pint of bastard in the Half-moon," or so. But, Ned, to drive away the time till Falstaff come, I prithee do 25

111. **of force:** through lack of alternative.
1. **fat:** stuffy.
4. **loggerheads:** blockheads.
5. **hogsheads:** barrels.
5–6. **humility:** baseness of degree (not meekness).
6. **leash:** three (the usual number of hounds coupled to one leash); **drawers:** tapsters, those who draw and serve the beer in a tavern.
8. **take . . . salvation:** are as certain about it as they are of Christian redemption.
10. **Jack:** (1) Jack (i.e., John) Falstaff, (2) knave.
10–11. **Corinthian:** a festive drinking companion.
14. **breathe . . . watering:** pause for breath while drinking.
15. **play it off:** drink it up.
19. **action:** battle, heroic exploit.
21. **under-skinker:** junior drawer.
24. **Score:** charge, tally; **bastard:** sweet Spanish wine; **Half-moon:** name of a room in the inn.

thou stand in some by-room while I question my puny drawer to what end he gave me the sugar; and do thou never leave calling "Francis!" that his tale to me may be nothing but "Anon!" Step aside, and I'll show thee a precedent.

POINS. Francis! 30

PRINCE. Thou art perfect.

POINS. Francis!

[*Exit* POINS.]

Enter [FRANCIS, *the*] DRAWER.

FRANCIS. Anon, anon, sir. Look down into the Pomgarnet, Ralph.

PRINCE. Come hither, Francis.

FRANCIS. My lord? 35

PRINCE. How long hast thou to serve, Francis?

FRANCIS. Forsooth, five years, and as much as to—

POINS. [*within*] Francis!

FRANCIS. Anon, anon, sir.

PRINCE. Five year! by'r Lady, a long lease for the clinking of 40 pewter. But, Francis, darest thou be so valiant as to play the coward with thy indenture and show it a fair pair of heels and run from it?

FRANCIS. O Lord, sir, I'll be sworn upon all the books in England I could find in my heart— 45

POINS. [*within*] Francis!

FRANCIS. Anon, sir.

PRINCE. How old art thou, Francis?

FRANCIS. Let me see—about Michaelmas next I shall be—

POINS. [*within*] Francis! 50

FRANCIS. Anon, sir. Pray stay a little, my lord.

PRINCE. Nay, but hark you, Francis: for the sugar thou gavest me—'twas a pennyworth, was't not?

FRANCIS. O Lord, I would it had been two!

PRINCE. I will give thee for it a thousand pound. Ask me when 55 thou wilt, and thou shalt have it.

POINS. [*within*] Francis!

FRANCIS. Anon, anon.

PRINCE. Anon, Francis? No, Francis; but to-morrow, Francis; or,

26. **by-room:** side room; **puny:** novice.
29. **precedent:** a performance that will set the tone for later mirth.
31. **Thou . . . perfect:** you have learned your lines.
33. **Pomgarnet:** Pomegranate (the name of a room).
36. **serve:** i.e., as an apprentice drawer.
40. **by'r Lady:** by Our Lady.
41. **pewter:** metal out of which tankards were made.
42. **indenture:** a contract between an apprentice and his master.
49. **Michaelmas:** September 29.
51. **stay a little:** wait a moment.

Francis, a Thursday; or indeed, Francis, when thou wilt. But, Francis— 60

FRANCIS. My lord?

PRINCE. Wilt thou rob this leathern-jerkin, crystal-button, not-pated, agate-ring, puke-stocking, caddis-garter, smooth-tongue, Spanish-pouch— 65

FRANCIS. O Lord, sir, who do you mean?

PRINCE. Why then, your brown bastard is your only drink; for look you, Francis, your white canvas doublet will sully. In Barbary, sir, it cannot come to so much.

FRANCIS. What, sir? 70

POINS. [*within*] Francis!

PRINCE. Away, you rogue! Dost thou not hear them call?

Here they both call him. The DRAWER *stands amazed, not knowing which way to go.*

Enter VINTNER.

VINTNER. What! stand'st thou still, and hear'st such a calling? [Lo]ok to the guests within. [*Exit* FRANCIS.] My lord, old Sir John, with half-a-dozen more, are at the door. Shall I let them in? 75

PRINCE. Let them alone awhile, and then open the door.

[*Exit* VINTNER.]

Poins!

POINS. [*within*] Anon, anon, sir.

Enter POINS.

PRINCE. Sirrah, Falstaff and the rest of the thieves are at the door. Shall we be merry? 80

POINS. As merry as crickets, my lad. But hark ye; what cunning match have you made with this jest of the drawer? Come, what's the issue?

PRINCE. I am now of all humors that have showed themselves 85

63. **rob:** i.e., rob your master of your services as apprentice; **leathern-jerkin:** leather-jacketed (Hal gives an apparently typical picture of an innkeeper).

63–64. **not-pated:** short-haired.

64. **puke:** good quality wool; **caddis:** worsted.

65. **Spanish-pouch:** a pouch made of Spanish leather.

67–69. **Why . . . much:** Hal deliberately confuses Francis with a nonsense speech that plays on the offer of a place in his household he was apparently, but not really, making.

67. **your . . . drink:** sweet wine is the only one worth drinking.

68. **your . . . sully:** your apprentice apron will get dirty (i.e., you are better off staying here).

69. **it:** i.e., the sugar Francis gave Hal.

72 S.D. ***amazed:*** deeply confused.

83. **match:** game.

84. **issue:** outcome, point.

85–87. **I . . . midnight:** i.e., the effect of making a fool of the drawer is to make me ready for anything.

humors since the old days of goodman Adam to the pupil age of this present twelve o'clock at midnight.

[*Enter* FRANCIS.]

What's o'clock, Francis?

FRANCIS. Anon, anon, sir.

[*Exit*.]

PRINCE. That ever this fellow should have fewer words than a parrot, and yet the son of a woman! His industry is upstairs and downstairs, his eloquence the parcel of a reckoning. I am not yet of Percy's mind, the Hotspur of the North, he that kills me some six or seven dozen of Scots at a breakfast, washes his hands, and says to his wife, "Fie upon this quiet life! I want work." "O my sweet Harry," says she, "how many hast thou killed to-day?" "Give my roan horse a drench," says he, and answers, "Some fourteen," an hour after; "a trifle, a trifle." I prithee call in Falstaff. I'll play Percy, and that damned brawn shall play Dame Mortimer his wife. "Rivo!" says the drunkard. Call in ribs, call in tallow. 90 95 100

Enter FALSTAFF, [GADSHILL, BARDOLPH, *and* PETO; *followed by* FRANCIS *with wine*].

POINS. Welcome, Jack! Where hast thou been?

FALSTAFF. A plague of all cowards, I say, and a vengeance too! Marry and amen! Give me a cup of sack, boy. Ere I lead this life long, I'll sew netherstocks, and mend them and foot them too. A plague of all cowards! Give me a cup of sack, rogue. Is there no virtue extant? 105

He drinketh

PRINCE. Didst thou never see Titan kiss a dish of butter, pitiful-hearted Titan, that melted at the sweet tale of the sun's? If thou didst, then behold that compound. 110

FALSTAFF. You rogue, here's lime in this sack too! There is nothing but roguery to be found in villainous man; yet a coward is worse than a cup of sack with lime in it—a villainous cow-

86. goodman: yeoman, farmer; **pupil age:** youth.
92. parcel . . . reckoning: items on a bill.
93–94. kills me: i.e., kills.
97. drench: dose of medicine.
99. brawn: boar
100. Rivo: a drinker's shout.
101. ribs: beef roast; **tallow:** dripping.
103. of: on.
105. netherstocks: stockings; **foot:** make new feet for.
108. Titan: the sun.
110. compound: mass of melted butter—i.e., Falstaff.
111. lime: an additive used to clarify wine.

ward! Go thy ways, old Jack, die when thou wilt; if manhood, good manhood, be not forgot upon the fact of the earth, 115
then am I a shotten herring. There lives not three good men unhanged in England; and one of them is fat and grows old. God help the while! A bad world, I say. I would I were a weaver; I could sing psalms or anything. A plague of all cowards, I say still! 120

PRINCE. How now, wool-sack? What mutter you?

FALSTAFF. A king's son! If I do not beat thee out of thy kingdom with a dagger of lath and drive all thy subjects afore thee like a flock of wild geese, I'll never wear hair on my face more. You Prince of Wales! 125

PRINCE. Why, you whoreson round man, what's the matter?

FALSTAFF. Are not you a coward? Answer me to that, and Poins there?

POINS. 'Zounds, ye fat paunch, an ye call me coward, by the Lord, I'll stab thee. 130

FALSTAFF. I call thee coward? I'll see thee damned ere I call thee coward, but I would give a thousand pound I could run as fast as thou canst. You are straight enough in the shoulders; you care not who sees your back. Call you that backing of your friends? A plague upon such backing! Give me them 135
that will face me. Give me a cup of sack. I am a rogue if I drunk to-day.

PRINCE. O villain! thy lips are scarce wiped since thou drunk'st last.

FALSTAFF. All is one for that. (*He drinketh.*) A plague of all 140
cowards, still say I.

PRINCE. What's the matter?

FALSTAFF. What's the matter? There be four of us here have ta'en a thousand pound this day morning.

PRINCE. Where is it, Jack? where is it? 145

FALSTAFF. Where is it? Taken from us it is. A hundred upon poor four of us!

PRINCE. What, a hundred, man?

FALSTAFF. I am a rogue if I were not at half-sword with a dozen of them two hours together. I have 'scaped by miracle. I 150
am eight times thrust through the doublet, four through the hose; my buckler cut through and through, my sword hacked

116. **shotten herring:** herring that has shed its roe (and is thus thin).
118. **the while:** the present time.
119. **weaver . . . psalms:** weavers were noted for their singing while working at their looms.
123. **dagger . . . lath:** comic weapon in morality plays, wielded by the Vice.
134. **backing:** supporting.
140. **All . . . that:** it doesn't matter.
149. **at half-sword:** at close quarters.
151. **doublet:** close-fitting jacket.
152. **hose:** breeches; **buckler:** small shield.

like a handsaw—*ecce signum!* [*Shows his sword.*] I never dealt better since I was a man. All would not do. A plague of all cowards! Let them speak. If they speak more or less than truth, they are villains and the sons of darkness. 155

PRINCE. Speak, sirs. How was it?

GADSHILL. We four set upon some dozen—

FALSTAFF. Sixteen at least, my lord.

GADSHILL. And bound them. 160

PETO. No, no, they were not bound.

FALSTAFF. You rogue, they were bound, every man of them, or I am a Jew else, an Ebrew Jew.

GADSHILL. As we were sharing, some six or seven fresh men set upon us— 165

FALSTAFF. And unbound the rest, and then come in the other.

PRINCE. What, fought you with them all?

FALSTAFF. All? I know not what you call all, but if I fought not with fifty of them, I am a bunch of radish! If there were not two or three and fifty upon poor old Jack, then am I no two-legged creature. 170

PRINCE. Pray God you have not murdered some of them.

FALSTAFF. Nay, that's past praying for. I have peppered two of them. Two I am sure I have paid, two rogues in buckram suits. I tell thee what, Hal, if I tell thee a lie, spit in my face, call me horse. Thou knowest my old ward. Here I lay, and thus I bore my point. Four rogues in buckram let drive at me. 175

PRINCE. What, four? Thou saidst but two even now.

FALSTAFF. Four, Hal. I told thee four.

POINS. Ay, ay, he said four. 180

FALSTAFF. These four came all afront and mainly thrust at me. I made me no more ado but took all their seven points in my target, thus.

PRINCE. Seven? Why, there were but four even now.

FALSTAFF. In buckram? 185

POINS. Ay, four, in buckram suits.

FALSTAFF. Seven, by these hilts, or I am a villain else.

153. ***ecce signum:*** behold the sign, here's the proof.
154. **dealt:** fought.
163. **Ebrew:** Hebrew.
166. **other:** others.
173. **peppered:** given the death blow.
174. **paid:** killed.
176. **horse:** i.e., a senseless animal; **ward:** parry.
176–77. **Here . . . point:** this is the posture I adopted, and this is the angle at which I held my sword.
178. **even:** just.
181. **mainly:** strongly.
182. **I made me:** I made.
183. **target:** shield.
187. **by . . . hilts:** Falstaff swears by the crosslike shape made by the hilt and the blade of his sword.

PRINCE. [*aside to* POINS] Prithee let him alone. We shall have more anon.

FALSTAFF. Dost thou hear me, Hal? 190

PRINCE. Ay, and mark thee too, Jack.

FALSTAFF. Do so, for it is worth the listening to. These nine in buckram that I told thee of—

PRINCE. So, two more already.

FALSTAFF. Their points being broken— 195

POINS. Down fell their hose.

FALSTAFF. Began to give me ground; but I followed me close, came in, foot and hand, and with a thought seven of the eleven I paid.

PRINCE. O monstrous! Eleven buckram men grown out of two! 200

FALSTAFF. But, as the devil would have it, three misbegotten knaves in Kendal green came at my back and let drive at me, for it was so dark, Hal, that thou couldst not see thy hand.

PRINCE. These lies are like their father that begets them—gross as a mountain, open, palpable. Why, thou clay-brained guts, thou 205 knotty-pated fool, thou whoreson, obscene, greasy tallow-catch—

FALSTAFF. What, art thou mad? art thou mad? Is not the truth the truth?

PRINCE. Why, how couldst thou know these men in Kendal green when it was so dark thou couldst not see thy hand? 210 Come, tell us your reason. What sayest thou to this?

POINS. Come, your reason, Jack, your reason.

FALSTAFF. What, upon compulsion? 'Zounds, an I were at the strappado or all the racks in the world, I would not tell you on compulsion. Give you a reason on compulsion? If reasons 215 were as plentiful as blackberries, I would give no man a reason upon compulsion, I.

PRINCE. I'll be no longer guilty of this sin. This sanguine coward, this bed-presser, this horseback-breaker, this huge hill of flesh—

FALSTAFF. 'Sblood, you starveling, you eel-skin, you dried neat's- 220 tongue, you bull's pizzle, you stockfish! O for breath to utter what is like thee! you tailor's yard, you sheath, you bowcase, you vile standing tuck!

191. **mark:** pay attention.
195. **points:** (1) sword points, (2) laces supporting the hose.
197. **followed me:** followed.
202. **Kendal green:** Kendal is a town in Cumbria, then noted for textiles.
206. **knotty-pated:** thick-headed; **tallow-catch:** lump of fat.
211. **reason:** explanation.
214. **strappado:** a torture machine.
215. **reasons:** pronounced *raisins*, allowing a punning contrast with blackberries.
218. **this sin:** i.e., concealing the truth; **sanguine:** red-faced.
220. **neat's:** ox's.
221. **pizzle:** dried penis; **stockfish:** dried cod.
222. **yard:** yardstick.
223. **standing tuck:** rapier standing on end.

PRINCE. Well, breathe awhile, and then to it again; and when thou hast tired thyself in base comparisons, hear me speak but this. 225

POINS. Mark, Jack.

PRINCE. We two saw you four set on four, and bound them and were masters of their wealth. Mark now, how a plain tale shall put you down. Then did we two set on you four and, with a word, outfaced you from your prize, and have it; yea, and can show it you here in the house. And, Falstaff, you carried your guts away as nimbly, with as quick dexterity, and roared for mercy, and still run and roared, as ever I heard bullcalf. What a slave art thou to hack thy sword as thou hast done, and then say it was in fight! What trick, what device, what starting hole canst thou now find out to hide thee from this open and apparent shame? 230 235

POINS. Come, let's hear, Jack. What trick hast thou now?

FALSTAFF. By the Lord, I knew ye as well as he that made ye. Why, hear you, my masters: Was it for me to kill the heir apparent? Should I turn upon the true prince? Why, thou knowest I am as valiant as Hercules, but beware instinct. The lion will not touch the true prince. Instinct is a great matter. I was now a coward on instinct. I shall think the better of myself, and thee, during my life; I for a valiant lion, and thou for a true prince. But, by the Lord, lads, I am glad you have the money. Hostess, clap to the doors. Watch to-night, pray to-morrow. Gallants, lads, boys, hearts of gold, all the titles of good fellowship come to you! What, shall we be merry? Shall we have a play extempore? 240 245 250

PRINCE. Content—and the argument shall be thy running away.

FALSTAFF. Ah, no more of that, Hal, an thou lovest me!

Enter HOSTESS.

HOSTESS. O Jesu, my lord the Prince!

PRINCE. How now, my lady the hostess! What say'st thou to me? 255

HOSTESS. Marry, my lord, there is a noble man of the court at door would speak with you. He says he comes from your father.

PRINCE. Give him as much as will make him a royal man, and send him back again to my mother. 260

231. outfaced you: scared you away.
236. starting hole: refuge.
237–38. apparent: manifest.
248. Watch: stay awake.
251. extempore: off the cuff, impromptu.
252. argument: plot.
256–59. noble . . . royal: puns on court terms and names of coins: noble (6 shillings 8 pence) and royal (10 shillings).
260. send . . . mother: i.e., send him to oblivion (Hal's mother was dead by this time).

FALSTAFF. What manner of man is he?
HOSTESS. An old man.
FALSTAFF. What doth gravity out of his bed at midnight? Shall I give him his answer?
PRINCE. Prithee do, Jack. 265
FALSTAFF. Faith, and I'll send him packing.

Exit.

PRINCE. Now, sirs, by'r Lady, you fought fair; so did you, Peto; so did you, Bardolph. You are lions too: you ran away upon instinct, you will not touch the true prince; no, fie!
BARDOLPH. Faith, I ran when I saw others run. 270
PRINCE. Tell me now in earnest, how came Falstaff's sword so hacked?
PETO. Why, he hacked it with his dagger, and said he would swear truth out of England but he would make you believe it was done in fight, and persuaded us to do the like. 275
BARDOLPH. Yea, and to tickle our noses with speargrass to make them bleed, and then to beslubber our garments with it and swear it was the blood of true men. I did that I did not this seven years before. I blushed to hear his monstrous devices.
PRINCE. O villain! thou stolest a cup of sack eighteen years ago 280 and wert taken with the manner, and ever since thou hast blushed extempore. Thou hadst fire and sword on thy side, and yet thou ran'st away. What instinct hadst thou for it?
BARDOLPH. My lord, do you see these meteors? [*pointing to his own face*] Do you behold these exhalations? 285
PRINCE. I do.
BARDOLPH. What think you they portend?
PRINCE. Hot livers and cold purses.
BARDOLPH. Choler, my lord, if rightly taken.

Enter FALSTAFF.

PRINCE. No, if rightly taken, halter. Here comes lean Jack; here 290 comes bare-bone. How now, my sweet creature of bombast? How long is't ago, Jack, since thou sawest thine own knee?
FALSTAFF. My own knee? When I was about thy years, Hal, I was not an eagle's talon in the waist; I could have crept into

274. but . . . would: if he did not.
278. that: something.
281. wert . . . manner: caught in the act.
284–85. meteors . . . exhalations: Bardolph is describing the eruptions on his face as if his face were the heavens.
288. Hot . . . purses: i.e., drunkenness and poverty.
289 Choler: anger.
290. taken: (1) construed, (2) arrested; **halter:** the hangman's noose—i.e., a "collar," with a pun on "choler" above.
291. bombast: cotton padding.

any alderman's thumb-ring. A plague of sighing and grief! It 295
blows a man up like a bladder. There's villainous news abroad.
Here was Sir John Bracy from your father. You must to the
court in the morning. That same mad fellow of the north,
Percy, and he of Wales that gave Amamon the bastinado, and
made Lucifer cuckold, and swore the devil his true liegeman 300
upon the cross of a Welsh hook—what a plague call you him?

POINS. Owen Glendower.

FALSTAFF. Owen, Owen, the same; and his son-in-law Mortimer,
and old Northumberland, and that sprightly Scot of Scots,
Douglas, that runs a-horseback up a hill perpendicular— 305

PRINCE. He that rides at high speed and with his pistol kills a
sparrow flying.

FALSTAFF. You have hit it.

PRINCE. So did he never the sparrow.

FALSTAFF. Well, that rascal hath good metal in him; he will not 310
run.

PRINCE. Why, what a rascal art thou then, to praise him so for
running!

FALSTAFF. A-horseback, ye cuckoo! but afoot he will not budge
a foot. 315

PRINCE. Yes, Jack, upon instinct.

FALSTAFF. I grant ye, upon instinct. Well, he is there too, and
one Mordake, and a thousand bluecaps more. Worcester is
stolen away to-night; thy father's beard is turned white with
the news; you may buy land now as cheap as stinking mackerel. 320

PRINCE. Why then, it is like, if there come a hot June, and this
civil buffeting hold, we shall buy maidenheads as they buy
hobnails, by the hundreds.

FALSTAFF. By the mass, lad, thou sayest true; it is like we shall
have good trading that way. But tell me, Hal, art not thou 325
horrible afeared? Thou being heir apparent, could the world
pick thee out three such enemies again as that fiend Douglas,
that spirit Percy, and that devil Glendower? Art thou not horribly afraid? Doth not thy blood thrill at it?

PRINCE. Not a whit, i' faith. I lack some of thy instinct. 330

FALSTAFF. Well, thou wilt be horribly chid to-morrow when
thou comest to thy father. If thou love me, practice an answer.

299. Amamon: the name of a devil; **bastinado:** beating.
300. made . . . cuckold: gave the devil his horns; **liegeman:** vassal sworn to the service of his lord.
301. Welsh hook: a pike with a curved blade ending in a hook.
314. afoot: i.e., when fighting on foot.
318. bluecaps: Scottish soldiers, who wore blue caps.
320. you . . . mackerel: economic uncertainty caused by war will reduce land values.
329. thrill: tingle with fear.

PRINCE. Do thou stand for my father and examine me upon the particulars of my life. 335

FALSTAFF. Shall I? Content. This chair shall be my state, this dagger my sceptre, and this cushion my crown.

PRINCE. Thy state is taken for a joined-stool, thy golden sceptre for a leaden dagger, and thy precious rich crown for a pitiful bald crown. 340

FALSTAFF. Well, an the fire of grace be not quite out of thee, now shalt thou be moved. Give me a cup of sack to make my eyes look red, that it may be thought I have wept; for I must speak in passion, and I will do it in King Cambyses' vein.

PRINCE. Well, here is my leg. 345

FALSTAFF. And here is my speech. Stand aside, nobility.

HOSTESS. O Jesu, this is excellent sport, i' faith!

FALSTAFF. Weep not, sweet queen, for trickling tears are vain.

HOSTESS. O, the Father, how he holds his countenance!

FALSTAFF. For God's sake, lords, convey my tristful queen! For 350 tears do stop the floodgates of her eyes.

HOSTESS. O Jesu, he doth it as like one of these harlotry players as ever I see!

FALSTAFF. Peace, good pintpot. Peace, good tickle-brain. Harry, I do not only marvel where thou spendest thy time, but also 355 how thou art accompanied. For though the camomile, the more it is trodden on, the faster it grows, yet youth, the more it is wasted, the sooner it wears. That thou art my son I have partly thy mother's word, partly my own opinion, but chiefly a villainous trick of thine eye and a foolish hanging of thy 360 nether lip that doth warrant me. If then thou be son to me, here lies the point: why, being son to me, art thou so pointed at? Shall the blessed sun of heaven prove a micher and eat blackberries? A question not to be asked. Shall the son of England prove a thief and take purses? A question to be 365

334. stand for: act as if you were.
336. state: chair of state.
338. joined-stool: stool made by a joiner—i.e., by a professional craftsman.
340. crown: i.e., head.
344. in . . . vein: in a loud, bombastic, and theatrically old-fashioned manner, like the title character in a 1570 play by Thomas Preston, *Cambyses, King of Persia.*
345. leg: a particular kind of bow.
349. the Father: in God's name; **holds . . . countenance:** keeps a straight face.
350. convey: escort away; **tristful:** sad.
351. stop: fill.
352. harlotry: scurvy.
354. pintpot: nickname for someone who sells beer; **tickle-brain:** a highly alcoholic drink.
356. camomile: an aromatic plant.
360. trick: characteristic expression.
361. nether: lower; **warrant:** assure.
362–63. pointed at: i.e., in mockery or disapproval.
363. micher: truant.
363–64. eat blackberries: i.e., wander here and there.
365. England: i.e., the king of England.

asked. There is a thing, Harry, which thou hast often heard of, and it is known to many in our land by the name of pitch. This pitch, as ancient writers do report, doth defile; so doth the company thou keepest. For, Harry, now I do not speak to thee in drink, but in tears; not in pleasure, but in passion; not 370 in words only, but in woes also; and yet there is a virtuous man whom I have often noted in thy company, but I know not his name.

PRINCE. What manner of man, an it like your majesty?

FALSTAFF. A goodly portly man i' faith, and a corpulent; of a 375 cheerful look, a pleasing eye, and a most noble carriage; and, as I think, his age some fifty, or, by'r Lady, inclining to threescore; and now I remember me, his name is Falstaff. If that man should be lewdly given, he deceiveth me; for, Harry, I see virtue in his looks. If then the tree may be known by the fruit, 380 as the fruit by the tree, then, peremptorily I speak it, there is virtue in that Falstaff. Him keep with, the rest banish. And tell me now, thou naughty varlet, tell me where hast thou been this month?

PRINCE. Dost thou speak like a king? Do thou stand for me, and 385 I'll play my father.

FALSTAFF. Depose me? If thou dost it half so gravely, so majestically, both in word and matter, hang me up by the heels for a rabbit-sucker or a poulter's hare.

PRINCE. Well, here I am set. 390

FALSTAFF. And here I stand. Judge, my masters.

PRINCE. Now, Harry, whence come you?

FALSTAFF. My noble lord, from Eastcheap.

PRINCE. The complaints I hear of thee are grievous.

FALSTAFF. 'Sblood, my lord, they are false! Nay, I'll tickle ye for 395 a young prince, i' faith.

PRINCE. Swearest thou, ungracious boy? Henceforth ne'er look on me. Thou art violently carried away from grace. There is a devil haunts thee in the likeness of an old fat man; a tun of man is thy companion. Why dost thou converse with 400 that trunk of humors, that bolting hutch of beastliness, that

369–71. **now . . . also:** a parody of the style of John Lyly's *Euphues* (1578).
370. **passion:** sorrow.
375. **portly:** (1) stately, (2) fat.
379. **lewdly given:** inclined to wicked, lustful behavior.
380. **tree . . . fruit:** cf. Matthew 12:33.
381. **peremptorily:** clearly, boldly.
383. **naughty varlet:** bad boy.
389. **rabbit-sucker:** unweaned rabbit; **poulter's hare:** hare sold by a poulterer.
390. **set:** seated.
395–96. **I'll . . . prince:** I'll entertain you by playing the part of a prince (an aside).
399. **tun:** (1) barrel, (2) ton weight.
400. **converse:** associate.
401. **humors:** bodily fluids that determine temperament; **bolting hutch:** miller's sifting bin.

swollen parcel of dropsies, that huge bombard of sack, that stuffed cloakbag of guts, that roasted Manningtree ox with the pudding in his belly, that reverend vice, that grey iniquity, that father ruffian, that vanity in years? Wherein is he good, but to taste sack and drink it? wherein neat and cleanly, but to carve a capon and eat it? wherein cunning, but in craft? wherein crafty, but in villainy? wherein villainous, but in all things? wherein worthy, but in nothing? 405

FALSTAFF. I would your grace would take me with you. Whom means your grace? 410

PRINCE. That villainous abominable misleader of youth, Falstaff, that old white-bearded Satan.

FALSTAFF. My lord, the man I know.

PRINCE. I know thou dost. 415

FALSTAFF. But to say I know more harm in him than in myself were to say more than I know. That he is old, the more the pity, his white hairs do witness it; but that he is, saving your reverence, a whoremaster, that I utterly deny. If sack and sugar be a fault, God help the wicked! If to be old and merry be a sin, then many an old host that I know is damned. If to be fat be to be hated, then Pharaoh's lean kine are to be loved. No, my good lord: banish Peto, banish Bardolph, banish Poins; but for sweet Jack Falstaff, kind Jack Falstaff, true Jack Falstaff, valiant Jack Falstaff, and therefore more valiant being, as he is, old Jack Falstaff, banish not him thy Harry's company, banish not him thy Harry's company. Banish plump Jack, and banish all the world! 420 425

PRINCE. I do, I will.

[*A great knocking heard. Exeunt* HOSTESS, FRANCIS, *and* BARDOLPH.]

Enter BARDOLPH, *running.*

BARDOLPH. O, my lord, my lord! the sheriff with a most monstrous watch is at the door. 430

FALSTAFF. Out, ye rogue! Play out the play. I have much to say in the behalf of that Falstaff.

402. dropsies: diseases that make the sufferer swell up; **bombard:** leather jug for wine.
403. cloakbag: large bag for clothes; **Manningtree:** town in Essex at whose annual fairs oxen, famous for their size, were roasted.
404. pudding: sausage; **vice:** mischievous character in morality plays; **iniquity:** sin.
406. cleanly: adroit.
407. cunning: skillful.
410. take . . . you: let me understand you.
418–19. saving . . . reverence: forgive me if I use an offensive word.
421. host: innkeeper.
422. Pharaoh's . . . kine: *kine* are cattle (see Genesis 41:19–21).
431. watch: posse of constables.

Enter the HOSTESS.

HOSTESS. O Jesu, my lord, my lord!

PRINCE. Heigh, heigh, the devil rides upon a fiddlestick! What's the matter? 435

HOSTESS. The sheriff and all the watch are at the door. They are come to search the house. Shall I let them in?

FALSTAFF. Dost thou hear, Hal? Never call a true piece of gold a counterfeit. Thou art essentially made without seeming so. 440

PRINCE. And thou a natural coward without instinct.

FALSTAFF. I deny your major. If you will deny the sheriff, so; if not, let him enter. If I become not a cart as well as another man, a plague on my bringing up! I hope I shall as soon be strangled with a halter as another. 445

PRINCE. Go hide thee behind the arras. The rest walk up above. Now, my masters, for a true face and good conscience.

FALSTAFF. Both which I have had; but their date is out, and therefore I'll hide me.

[*Exit.*]

PRINCE. Call in the sheriff. 450

[*Exeunt all but the* PRINCE *and* PETO.]

Enter SHERIFF *and the* CARRIER.

Now, master sheriff, what is your will with me?

SHERIFF. First, pardon me, my lord. A hue and cry
Hath followed certain men into this house.

PRINCE. What men?

SHERIFF. One of them is well known, my gracious lord, 455
A gross fat man.

CARRIER. As fat as butter.

PRINCE. The man, I do assure you, is not here,
For I myself at this time have employed him.
And, Sheriff, I will engage my word to thee
That I will by to-morrow dinner time 460
Send him to answer thee, or any man,

435. **devil . . . fiddlestick:** much ado about nothing (proverbial).
440. **essentially made:** the real thing—i.e., a genuine prince.
442. **deny . . . deny:** (1) reject, (2) refuse to let in; **your major:** the principal premise of your argument.
443. **become:** suit, adorn; **cart:** used to transport prisoners to their execution.
444. **bringing up:** (1) upbringing, (2) trial and conviction.
446. **arras:** tapestry, wall hanging; **walk . . . above:** go upstairs.
447. **true:** honest.
448. **date is out:** term has expired.
452. **hue and cry:** posse of citizens.
459. **engage:** pledge.
460. **dinner time:** i.e., noon.

For anything he shall be charged withal;
And so let me entreat you leave the house.
SHERIFF. I will, my lord. There are two gentlemen
Have in this robbery lost three hundred marks. 465
PRINCE. It may be so. If he have robbed these men,
He shall be answerable; and so farewell.
SHERIFF. Good night, my noble lord.
PRINCE. I think it is good morrow, is it not?
SHERIFF. Indeed, my lord, I think it be two o'clock. 470

Exeunt [SHERIFF *and* CARRIER].

PRINCE. This oily rascal is known as well as Paul's. Go call him forth.
PETO. Falstaff! Fast asleep behind the arras, and snorting like a horse.
PRINCE. Hark how hard he fetches breath. Search his pockets. 475

He searcheth his pocket[s] *and findeth certain papers.*

What hast thou found?
PETO. Nothing but papers, my lord.
PRINCE. Let's see what they be. Read them.
[PETO.] [*reads*]
"Item, A capon...2s. 2d.
Item, Sauce 4d. 480
Item, Sack two gallons.....................................5s. 8d.
Item, Anchovies and sack after supper............2s. 6d.
Item, Bread.. ob."
[PRINCE.] O monstrous! but one halfpennyworth of bread to this intolerable deal of sack! What there is else, keep close; we'll 485 read it at more advantage. There let him sleep till day. I'll to the court in the morning. We must all to the wars, and thy place shall be honorable. I'll procure this fat rogue a charge of foot, and I know his death will be a march of twelve score. The money shall be paid back again with advantage. Be with 490 me betimes in the morning, and so good morrow, Peto.
PETO. Good morrow, good my lord.

Exeunt.

462. **withal:** with.
469. **morrow:** morning.
471. **Paul's:** St. Paul's Cathedral, a huge building.
483. **ob.:** halfpenny.
485. **intolerable deal:** unacceptably large quantity; **close:** secret.
486. **more advantage:** a more convenient time.
488–89. **charge of foot:** command of a company of infantry.
489. **his . . . score:** marching 240 paces will kill him.
490. **advantage:** interest.
491. **betimes:** early.

[ACT III. SCENE I. *Wales.* GLENDOWER'S *Castle.*]

Enter HOTSPUR, WORCESTER, LORD MORTIMER, OWEN GLENDOWER.

MORTIMER. These promises are fair, the parties sure,
And our induction full of prosperous hope.
HOTSPUR. Lord Mortimer, and cousin Glendower,
Will you sit down?
And uncle Worcester,—a plague upon it! 5
I have forgot the map.
GLENDOWER. No, here it is.
Sit, cousin Percy; sit, good cousin Hotspur,
For by that name as oft as Lancaster
Doth speak of you, his cheek looks pale and with
A rising sigh he wisheth you in heaven. 10
HOTSPUR. And you in hell, as oft as he hears Owen
Glendower spoke of.
GLENDOWER. I cannot blame him. At my nativity
The front of heaven was full of fiery shapes
Of burning cressets, and at my birth 15
The frame and huge foundation of the earth
Shaked like a coward.
HOTSPUR. Why, so it would have done at the same
season if your mother's cat had but kittened,
though yourself had never been born. 20
GLENDOWER. I say the earth did shake when I was born.
HOTSPUR. And I say the earth was not of my mind,
If you suppose as fearing you it shook.
GLENDOWER. The heavens were all on fire, the earth did tremble.
HOTSPUR. O, then the earth shook to see the heavens on fire, 25
And not in fear of your nativity.
Diseased nature oftentimes breaks forth
In strange eruptions; oft the teeming earth
Is with a kind of colic pinched and vexed
By the imprisoning of unruly wind 30
Within her womb, which, for enlargement striving,
Shakes the old beldame earth and topples down
Steeples and mossgrown towers. At your birth
Our grandam earth, having this distemp'rature,
In passion shook.

2. **induction:** initial step; **prosperous hope:** hope of prospering.
8. **Lancaster:** i.e., Henry IV.
14. **front:** face, forehead.
15. **cressets:** fire baskets used as beacons—i.e., meteors.
31. **enlargement:** release from confinement.
32. **beldame:** grandmother (same as *grandam*, line 34).
34. **distemp'rature:** disease.
35. **passion:** suffering.

GLENDOWER. Cousin, of many men 35
I do not bear these crossings. Give me leave
To tell you once again that at my birth
The front of heaven was full of fiery shapes,
The goats ran from the mountains, and the herds
Were strangely clamorous to the frighted fields. 40
These signs have marked me extraordinary;
And all the courses of my life do show
I am not in the roll of common men.
Where is he living, clipped in with the sea
That chides the banks of England, Scotland, Wales, 45
Which calls me pupil or hath read to me?
And bring him out that is but woman's son
Can trace me in the tedious ways of art
And hold me pace in deep experiments.

HOTSPUR. I think there's no man speaks better Welsh. 50
I'll to dinner.

MORTIMER. Peace, cousin Percy; you will make him mad.

GLENDOWER. I can call spirits from the vasty deep.

HOTSPUR. Why, so can I, or so can any man;
But will they come when you do call for them? 55

GLENDOWER. Why, I can teach you, cousin, to command
The devil.

HOTSPUR. And I can teach thee, coz, to shame the devil
By telling truth. Tell truth and shame the devil.
If thou have power to raise him, bring him hither, 60
And I'll be sworn I have power to shame him hence.
O, while you live, tell truth and shame the devil!

MORTIMER. Come, come, no more of this unprofitable chat.

GLENDOWER. Three times hath Henry Bolingbroke made head
Against my power; thrice from the banks of Wye 65
And sandy-bottomed Severn have I sent him
Bootless home and weather-beaten back.

HOTSPUR. Home without boots, and in foul weather too?
How 'scapes he agues, in the devil's name?

GLENDOWER. Come, here is the map. Shall we divide our right 70

36. bear . . . crossings: tolerate these interruptions.
44. clipped . . . with: encircled by.
45. chides: lashes, chafes.
46. Which: who; **read to:** lectured, taught.
47. bring . . . out: produce anyone.
48. trace . . . art: follow me in the laborious practice of magic.
49. hold . . . pace: keep up with me; **deep:** secret.
53. call: summon; **vasty deep:** lower world.
64. made head: raised an army.
65. power: army.
67. Bootless: without profit, unsuccessful.
69. agues: fevers and chills.
70. our right: the land that belongs to us.

According to our threefold order ta'en?
MORTIMER. The archdeacon hath divided it
Into three limits very equally:
England, from Trent and Severn hitherto,
By south and east is to my part assigned; 75
All westward, Wales beyond the Severn shore,
And all the fertile land within that bound,
To Owen Glendower; and, dear coz, to you
The remnant northward lying off from Trent.
And our indentures tripartite are drawn, 80
Which being sealed interchangeably
(A business that this night may execute),
To-morrow, cousin Percy, you and I
And my good Lord of Worcester will set forth
To meet your father and the Scottish power, 85
As is appointed us, at Shrewsbury.
My father Glendower is not ready yet,
Nor shall we need his help these fourteen days.
Within that space you may have drawn together
Your tenants, friends, and neighboring gentlemen. 90
GLENDOWER. A shorter time shall send me to you, lords;
And in my conduct shall your ladies come,
From whom you now must steal and take no leave,
For there will be a world of water shed
Upon the parting of your wives and you. 95
HOTSPUR. Methinks my moiety, north from Burton here,
In quantity equals not one of yours.
See how this river comes me cranking in
And cuts me from the best of all my land
A huge half-moon, a monstrous cantle out. 100
I'll have the current in this place dammed up,
And here the smug and silver Trent shall run
In a new channel fair and evenly.
It shall not wind with such a deep indent
To rob me of so rich a bottom here. 105
GLENDOWER. Not wind? It shall, it must! You see it doth.

71. **order ta'en:** arrangements made.
73. **limits:** areas marked by a boundary.
74. **hitherto:** to this point.
80. **indentures tripartite:** three-party compact.
81. **interchangeably:** i.e., sealed in triplicate by the three parties.
82. **execute:** see completed.
87. **father:** i.e., father-in-law.
92. **conduct:** escort.
96. **moiety:** share; **Burton:** Burton-on-Trent.
98. **comes . . . in:** comes winding in.
100. **cantle:** piece.
102. **smug:** smoothy.
103. **fair . . . evenly:** i.e., in a straight line.
105. **bottom:** valley.

MORTIMER. Yea, but
Mark how he bears his course, and runs me up
With like advantage on the other side,
Gelding the opposed continent as much 110
As on the other side it takes from you.
WORCESTER. Yea, but a little charge will trench him here
And on this north side win this cape of land;
And then he runs straight and even.
HOTSPUR. I'll have it so. A little charge will do it. 115
GLENDOWER. I will not have it altered.
HOTSPUR. Will not you?
GLENDOWER. No, nor you shall not.
HOTSPUR. Who shall say me nay?
GLENDOWER. Why, that will I.
HOTSPUR. Let me not understand you then; speak it in Welsh.
GLENDOWER. I can speak English, lord, as well as you; 120
For I was trained up in the English court,
Where, being but young, I framed to the harp
Many an English ditty lovely well,
And gave the tongue a helpful ornament,
A virtue that was never seen in you. 125
HOTSPUR. Marry, and I am glad of it with all my heart!
I had rather be a kitten and cry mew
Than one of these same metre ballet-mongers.
I had rather hear a brazen canstick turned
Or a dry wheel grate on the axletree, 130
And that would set my teeth nothing on edge,
Nothing so much as mincing poetry.
'Tis like the forced gait of a shuffling nag.
GLENDOWER. Come, you shall have Trent turned.
HOTSPUR. I do not care. I'll give thrice so much land 135
To any well-deserving friend;
But in the way of bargain, mark ye me,
I'll cavil on the ninth part of a hair.
Are the indentures drawn? Shall we be gone?
GLENDOWER. The moon shines fair; you may away by night. 140
I'll haste the writer, and withal

110. Gelding . . . continent: cutting off from the opposite bank.
112. charge: expense; **trench:** i.e., divert by way of a trench.
122. framed . . . harp: set to the music of the harp.
123. ditty: lyrics of a song.
124. gave . . . ornament: gave musical expression to the words.
128. ballet-mongers: i.e., balladmongers, singers and sellers of ballads.
129. canstick: candlestick; **turned:** shaped on a lathe.
130. axletree: axle.
131. nothing: not a bit.
133. forced . . . nag: awkward paces of a hobbled horse.
138. cavil: make objections.
139. drawn: drawn up.
141. withal: at the same time.

Break with your wives of your departure hence.
I am afraid my daughter will run mad,
So much she doteth on her Mortimer.

Exit.

MORTIMER. Fie, cousin Percy! how you cross my father! 145
HOTSPUR. I cannot choose. Sometimes he angers me
With telling me of the moldwarp and the ant,
Of the dreamer Merlin and his prophecies,
And of a dragon and a finless fish,
A clip-winged griffin and a moulten raven, 150
A couching lion and a ramping cat,
And such a deal of skimble-skamble stuff
As puts me from my faith. I tell you what:
He held me last night at least nine hours
In reckoning up the several devils' names 155
That were his lackeys. I cried "hum," and "Well, go to!"
But marked him not a word. O, he is as tedious
As a tired horse, a railing wife;
Worse than a smoky house. I had rather live
With cheese and garlic in a windmill far 160
Than feed on cates and have him talk to me
In any summer house in Christendom.
MORTIMER. In faith, he is a worthy gentleman,
Exceedingly well read, and profited
In strange concealments, valiant as a lion, 165
And wondrous affable, and as bountiful
As mines of India. Shall I tell you, cousin?
He holds your temper in a high respect
And curbs himself even of his natural scope
When you come 'cross his humor. Faith, he does. 170
I warrant you that man is not alive
Might so have tempted him as you have done

142. **Break with:** break the news to.
145. **cross:** irritate by disagreeing with.
147. **moldwarp:** mole.
148. **Merlin:** magician and prophet of Arthurian legend.
150. **griffin:** mythical animal, half lion and half eagle; **moulten raven:** a raven that has molted.
151. **couching:** lying down; **ramping:** rearing up.
152. **skimble-skamble:** nonsensical.
153. **puts . . . faith:** makes me forget I am a Christian.
155. **several:** various.
156. **go to:** expression of polite amazement.
161. **cates:** delicacies.
164–65. **profited . . . concealments:** skilled in magic.
167. **India:** i.e., East or West Indies.
168. **temper:** temperament.
169. **scope:** freedom of expression.
170. **come 'cross:** contradict.
172. **tempted:** defied.

Without the taste of danger and reproof;
But do not use it oft, let me entreat you.
WORCESTER. In faith, my lord, you are too willful-blame, 175
And since your coming hither have done enough
To put him quite besides his patience.
You must needs learn, lord, to amend this fault.
Though sometimes it show greatness, courage, blood—
And that's the dearest grace it renders you— 180
Yet oftentimes it doth present harsh rage,
Defect of manners, want of government,
Pride, haughtiness, opinion, and disdain;
The least of which haunting a nobleman
Loseth men's hearts, and leaves behind a stain 185
Upon the beauty of all parts besides,
Beguiling them of commendation.
HOTSPUR. Well, I am schooled. Good manners be your speed!
Here come our wives, and let us take our leave.

Enter GLENDOWER *with the* LADIES.

MORTIMER. This is the deadly spite that angers me: 190
My wife can speak no English, I no Welsh.
GLENDOWER. My daughter weeps; she will not part with you;
She'll be a soldier too, she'll to the wars.
MORTIMER. Good father, tell her that she and my aunt Percy
Shall follow in your conduct speedily. 195

GLENDOWER *speaks to her in Welsh, and she answers him in the same.*

GLENDOWER. She is desperate here. A peevish self-willed harlotry,
One that no persuasion can do good upon.

The LADY *speaks in Welsh.*

MORTIMER. I understand thy looks. That pretty Welsh
Which thou pourest down from these swelling heavens
I am too perfect in; and, but for shame, 200

175. willful-blame: obstinately culpable.
179. blood: mettle.
182. want of government: lack of self-control.
183. opinion: arrogance.
187. Beguiling: depriving.
188. be . . . speed: give you success.
190. spite: irritation.
194. my . . . Percy: This Mortimer is a composite of two Edmund Mortimers, one nephew to, the other younger brother of, Hotspur's wife.
196. desperate here: determined on this point; **peevish . . . harlotry:** stubborn and disobedient woman.
198. That . . . Welsh: i.e., those eloquent tears.
199. heavens: i.e., eyes.
200. am . . . in: understand only too well.

In such a parley should I answer thee.

The LADY *again in Welsh.*

I understand thy kisses, and thou mine,
And that's a feeling disputation.
But I will never be a truant, love,
Till I have learnt thy language; for thy tongue 205
Makes Welsh as sweet as ditties highly penned,
Sung by a fair queen in a summer's bow'r,
With ravishing division, to her lute.

GLENDOWER. Nay, if you melt, then will she run mad.

The LADY *speaks again in Welsh.*

MORTIMER. O, I am ignorance itself in this! 210

GLENDOWER. She bids you on the wanton rushes lay you down
And rest your gentle head upon her lap,
And she will sing the song that pleaseth you
And on your eyelids crown the god of sleep,
Charming your blood with pleasing heaviness, 215
Making such difference 'twixt wake and sleep
As is the difference betwixt day and night
The hour before the heavenly-harnessed team
Begins his golden progress in the east.

MORTIMER. With all my heart I'll sit and hear her sing. 220
By that time will our book, I think, be drawn.

GLENDOWER. Do so,
And those musicians that shall play to you
Hang in the air a thousand leagues from hence,
And straight they shall be here. Sit, and attend.

HOTSPUR. Come, Kate, thou art perfect in lying down. 225
Come, quick, quick, that I may lay my head in thy lap.

LADY PERCY. Go, ye giddy goose.

The music plays.

HOTSPUR. Now I perceive the devil understands Welsh.
And 'tis no marvel he is so humorous,

201. such a parley: i.e., the language of tears.
203. disputation: conversation, debate.
206. highly penned: written in a lofty style.
208. division: melody.
209. melt: i.e., in tears.
211. wanton: luxuriant; **rushes:** used for floor covering.
215. blood: mood; **heaviness:** sleepiness.
218. heavenly-harnessed team: i.e., the sun.
219. progress: official journey of monarch.
221. book: i.e., the rebel compact.
224. attend: listen.
225. perfect in: expert at.
229. humorous: capricious.

By'r Lady, he is a good musician. 230

LADY PERCY. Then should you be nothing but musical, for you are altogether governed by humors. Lie still, ye thief, and hear the lady sing in Welsh.

HOTSPUR. I had rather hear Lady, my brach, howl in Irish.

LADY PERCY. Wouldst thou have thy head broken? 235

HOTSPUR. No.

LADY PERCY. Then be still.

HOTSPUR. Neither! 'Tis a woman's fault.

LADY PERCY. Now God help thee!

HOTSPUR. To the Welsh lady's bed. 240

LADY PERCY. What's that?

HOTSPUR. Peace! she sings.

Here the LADY *sings a Welsh song.*

Come, Kate, I'll have your song too.

LADY PERCY. Not mine, in good sooth.

HOTSPUR. Not yours in good sooth? Heart, you swear like a 245
comfit-maker's wife. "Not you in good sooth!" and "as true as I live!" and "as God shall mend me!" and "as sure as day!"
And givest such sarcenet surety for thy oaths
As if thou never walk'st further than Finsbury.
Swear me, Kate, like a lady as thou art, 250
A good mouth-filling oath, and leave "in sooth"
And such protest of pepper gingerbread
To velvet guards and Sunday citizens.
Come, sing.

LADY PERCY. I will not sing. 255

HOTSPUR. 'Tis the next way to turn tailor or be redbreast-teacher.
An the indentures be drawn, I'll away within these two hours; and so come in when ye will.

Exit.

GLENDOWER. Come, come, Lord Mortimer. You are as slow
As hot Lord Percy is on fire to go. 260
By this our book is drawn; we'll but seal,

232. humors: whims.
234. brach: bitch.
235. head broken: i.e., the skin on the head ruptured, not the actual skull.
244. sooth: truth.
246. comfit-maker's: confectioner's (renowned for puritanism).
248. sarcenet: a finely woven silk—i.e., flimsy.
249. Finsbury: a popular place of recreation near London.
253. velvet guards: wearers of clothing trimmed with velvet; **Sunday citizens:** citizens in their Sunday best.
256. tailor: a profession known for singing while working; **redbreast-teacher:** one who teaches caged birds to sing.
261. this: this time.

And then to horse immediately.
MORTIMER. With all my heart. *Exeunt.*

[SCENE II. *London. The Palace.*]

Enter the KING, PRINCE OF WALES, *and others.*

KING. Lords, give us leave: the Prince of Wales and I
Must have some private conference; but be near at hand,
For we shall presently have need of you.

Exeunt LORDS.

I know not whether God will have it so
For some displeasing service I have done, 5
That, in his secret doom, out of my blood
He'll breed revengement and a scourge for me;
But thou dost in thy passages of life
Make me believe that thou art only marked
For the hot vengeance and the rod of heaven 10
To punish my mistreadings. Tell me else,
Could such inordinate and low desires,
Such poor, such bare, such lewd, such mean attempts,
Such barren pleasures, rude society,
As thou art matched withal and grafted to, 15
Accompany the greatness of thy blood
And hold their level with thy princely heart?
PRINCE. So please your majesty, I would I could
Quit all offenses with as clear excuse
As well as I am doubtless I can purge 20
Myself of many I am charged withal.
Yet such extenuation let me beg
As, in reproof of many tales devised,
Which oft the ear of greatness needs must hear
By smiling pickthanks and base newsmongers, 25
I may, for some things true wherein my youth
Hath faulty wandered and irregular,

6. **doom:** judgment; **blood:** family.
8. **passages:** actions.
9–10. **marked for:** appointed as an instrument of.
12. **inordinate:** (1) intemperate, (2) unworthy of your status.
13. **bare:** wretched; **lewd:** base.
14. **rude society:** socially inappropriate friends.
15. **withal:** with.
17. **hold . . . level:** treat themselves as equal.
19. **Quit:** acquit myself of.
20. **doubtless:** certain.
23. **in . . . of:** in order to refute.
25. **pickthanks:** flatterers, informers; **newsmongers:** spreaders of gossip.

Find pardon on my true submission.
KING. God pardon thee! Yet let me wonder, Harry,
At thy affections, which do hold a wing 30
Quite from the flight of all thy ancestors.
Thy place in council thou hast rudely lost,
Which by thy younger brother is supplied,
And art almost an alien to the hearts
Of all the court and princes of my blood. 35
The hope and expectation of thy time
Is ruined, and the soul of every man
Prophetically do forethink thy fall.
Had I so lavish of my presence been,
So common-hackneyed in the eyes of men, 40
So stale and cheap to vulgar company,
Opinion, that did help me to the crown,
Had still kept loyal to possession
And left me in reputeless banishment,
A fellow of no mark nor likelihood. 45
By being seldom seen, I could not stir
But like a comet I was wondered at;
That men would tell their children, "This is he!"
Others would say, "Where? Which is Bolingbroke?"
And then I stole all courtesy from heaven, 50
And dressed myself in such humility
That I did pluck allegiance from men's hearts,
Loud shouts and salutations from their mouths
Even in the presence of the crowned king.
Thus did I keep my person fresh and new, 55
My presence like a robe pontifical,
Ne'er seen but wondered at; and so my state,
Seldom but sumptuous, showed like a feast
And won by rareness such solemnity.
The skipping king, he ambled up and down 60
With shallow jesters and rash bavin wits,

28. submission: confession.
30. affections: inclinations.
30–31. hold . . . from: fly in a very different direction from (a term from falconry).
32. rudely: by violent behavior.
33. supplied: filled.
36. time: youth, life.
38. forethink: predict.
40. common-hackneyed: vulgarized.
42. Opinion: public opinion.
43. Had . . . possession: i.e., had remained loyal to the then king, Richard II.
44. reputeless: inglorious.
45. mark: significance; **likelihood:** prospect of success.
56. pontifical: belonging to a bishop.
57. state: appearance on public occasions.
60. skipping: flighty.
61. bavin: brushwood.

Soon kindled and soon burnt; carded his state;
Mingled his royalty with cap'ring fools;
Had his great name profaned with their scorns
And gave his countenance, against his name, 65
To laugh at gibing boys and stand the push
Of every beardless vain comparative;
Grew a companion to the common streets,
Enfeoffed himself to popularity;
That, being daily swallowed by men's eyes, 70
They surfeited with honey and began
To loathe the taste of sweetness, whereof a little
More than a little is by much too much.
So, when he had occasion to be seen,
He was but as the cuckoo is in June, 75
Heard, not regarded; seen, but with such eyes
As, sick and blunted with community,
Afford no extraordinary gaze
Such as is bent on sunlike majesty
When it shines seldom in admiring eyes; 80
But rather drowsed and hung their eyelids down,
Slept in his face, and rendered such aspect
As cloudy men use to their adversaries,
Being with his presence glutted, gorged, and full.
And in that very line, Harry, standest thou; 85
For thou hast lost thy princely privilege
With vile participation. Not an eye
But is a-weary of thy common sight,
Save mine, which hath desired to see thee more,
Which now doth that I would not have it do: 90
Make blind itself with foolish tenderness.

[*Weeping*]

PRINCE. I shall hereafter, my thrice gracious lord,
Be more myself.

KING. For all the world,
As thou art to this hour was Richard then

62. **carded:** mixed with something base; **state:** status as king.
64. **with . . . scorns:** by the scornful attitudes of his associates.
65. **gave . . . name:** authorized, to the detriment of his status as king.
66. **gibing:** jeering.
66–67. **stand . . . comparative:** tolerate the insolence of every youth who makes offensive comparisons.
69. **Enfeoffed:** surrendered; **popularity:** favor with the lowest classes.
77. **community:** commonness.
82. **Slept . . . face:** insulted him by going to sleep in his presence; **aspect:** look.
83. **cloudy:** sullen.
85. **line:** i.e., line of descent.
87. **vile participation:** spending time with the lowest class of people.
90. **that:** that which.
91. **tenderness:** i.e., tears.

When I from France set foot at Ravenspurgh; 95
And even as I was then is Percy now.
Now, by my sceptre, and my soul to boot,
He hath more worthy interest to the state
Than thou, the shadow of succession;
For of no right, nor color like to right, 100
He doth fill fields with harness in the realm,
Turns head against the lion's armed jaws,
And, being no more in debt to years than thou,
Leads ancient lords and reverend bishops on
To bloody battles and to bruising arms. 105
What never-dying honor hath he got
Against renowned Douglas! whose high deeds,
Whose hot incursions, and great name in arms
Holds from all soldiers chief majority
And military title capital 110
Through all the kingdoms that acknowledge Christ.
Thrice hath this Hotspur, Mars in swathling clothes,
This infant warrior, in his enterprises
Discomfited great Douglas; ta'en him once,
Enlarged him, and made a friend of him, 115
To fill the mouth of deep defiance up
And shake the peace and safety of our throne.
And what say you to this? Percy, Northumberland,
The Archbishop's grace of York, Douglas, Mortimer
Capitulate against us and are up. 120
But wherefore do I tell these news to thee?
Why, Harry, do I tell thee of my foes
Which art my nearest and dearest enemy?
Thou that art like enough, through vassal fear,
Base inclination, and the start of spleen, 125
To fight against me under Percy's pay,
To dog his heels and curtsy at his frowns,
To show how much thou art degenerate.

97. **to boot:** also.
98. **interest:** claim.
99. **shadow:** name without substance.
100. **color:** substance.
101. **harness:** men in armor.
102. **Turns head:** directs an army.
103. Historically, Hal was twenty-three years younger than Hotspur.
108. **hot:** violent.
109. **majority:** superiority.
110. **capital:** chief.
112. **swathling:** i.e., swaddling.
115. **Enlarged:** set free.
116. **To . . . up:** make defiance more vociferous.
120. **Capitulate:** draw up articles of agreement; **up:** i.e., in arms.
123. **dearest:** (1) most loved, (2) direst—i.e., bitterest.
124. **like:** likely; **vassal:** servile.
125. **start . . . spleen:** vicious impulse.

PRINCE. Do not think so. You shall not find it so.
And God forgive them that so much have swayed 130
Your majesty's good thoughts away from me.
I will redeem all this on Percy's head,
And in the closing of some glorious day
Be bold to tell you that I am your son,
When I will wear a garment all of blood, 135
And stain my favors in a bloody mask,
Which, washed away, shall scour my shame with it.
And that shall be the day, whene'er it lights,
That this same child of honor and renown,
This gallant Hotspur, this all-praised knight, 140
And your unthought-of Harry chance to meet.
For every honor sitting on his helm,
Would they were multitudes, and on my head
My shames redoubled! For the time will come
That I shall make this northern youth exchange 145
His glorious deeds for my indignities.
Percy is but my factor, good my lord,
To engross up glorious deeds on my behalf;
And I will call him to so strict account
That he shall render every glory up, 150
Yea, even the slightest worship of his time;
Or I will tear the reckoning from his heart.
This in the name of God I promise here;
The which if He be pleased I shall perform,
I do beseech your majesty, may salve 155
The long-grown wounds of my intemperance.
If not, the end of life cancels all bands,
And I will die a hundred thousand deaths
Ere break the smallest parcel of this vow.
KING. A hundred thousand rebels die in this! 160
Thou shalt have charge and sovereign trust herein.

Enter BLUNT [*hastily*].

How now, good Blunt? Thy looks are full of speed.
BLUNT. So hath the business that I come to speak of.

132. redeem: make up for.
136. favors: facial features.
138. lights: dawns.
141. unthought-of: disregarded.
146. indignities: unworthy traits.
147. factor: agent.
148. engross: buy up.
151. worship: honor; **time:** lifetime.
152. reckoning: account.
156. intemperance: immoderate behavior.
157. bands: bonds, debts.
159. parcel: part.
161. charge: command of soldiers; **sovereign:** (1) royally granted, (2) supreme.

Lord Mortimer of Scotland hath sent word
That Douglas and the English rebels met 165
The eleventh of this month at Shrewsbury.
A mighty and a fearful head they are,
If promises be kept on every hand,
As ever offered foul play in a state.

KING. The Earl of Westmoreland set forth to-day, 170
With him my son, Lord John of Lancaster,
For this advertisement is five days old.
On Wednesday next, Harry, you shall set forward;
On Thursday we ourselves will march. Our meeting
Is Bridgenorth; and, Harry, you shall march 175
Through Gloucestershire; by which account,
Our business valued, some twelve days hence
Our general forces at Bridgenorth shall meet.
Our hands are full of business. Let's away;
Advantage feeds him fat while men delay. 180

Exeunt.

[SCENE III. *Eastcheap. The Boar's Head Tavern.*]

Enter FALSTAFF *and* BARDOLPH.

FALSTAFF. Bardolph, am I not fallen away vilely since this last action? Do I not bate? Do I not dwindle? Why, my skin hangs about me like an old lady's loose gown. I am withered like an old apple-john. Well, I'll repent, and that suddenly, while I am in some liking. I shall be out of heart shortly, and then I shall 5 have no strength to repent. An I have not forgotten what the inside of a church is made of, I am a peppercorn, a brewer's horse. The inside of a church! Company, villainous company, hath been the spoil of me.

BARDOLPH. Sir John, you are so fretful you cannot live long. 10

FALSTAFF. Why, there is it; come, sing me a bawdy song; make me merry. I was as virtuously given as a gentleman need to be,

167. **head:** army.
171. **Lord John of Lancaster:** Henry IV's third son.
172. **advertisement:** information.
174. **meeting:** rendezvous.
175. **Bridgenorth:** a market town in Shropshire, twenty miles from Shrewsbury.
176–77. **by . . . valued:** carefully estimating the time it will take to do what is necessary.
180. **Advantage . . . delay:** We will allow our opponents to capitalize if we waste time.
1. **fallen away:** shrunk.
1–2. **last action:** i.e., the robbery at Gad's Hill.
2. **bate:** shrink, decrease.
4. **apple-john:** a kind of apple that can be kept and eaten after its skin has shriveled; **suddenly:** right now.
5. **in . . . liking:** in the mood; **out . . . heart:** uninclined.
7–8. **brewer's horse:** old, emaciated horse.

virtuous enough: swore little, diced not above seven times a week, went to a bawdy house not above once in a quarter of an hour, paid money that I borrowed three or four times, lived 15 well, and in good compass; and now I live out of all order, out of all compass.

BARDOLPH. Why, you are so fat, Sir John, that you must needs be out of all compass, out of all reasonable compass, Sir John.

FALSTAFF. Do thou amend thy face, and I'll amend my life; thou 20 art our admiral: thou bearest the lantern in the poop, but 'tis in the nose of thee. Thou art the Knight of the Burning Lamp.

BARDOLPH. Why, Sir John, my face does you no harm.

FALSTAFF. No, I'll be sworn; I make as good use of it as many a man doth of a death's-head or a *memento mori*. I never see 25 thy face but I think upon hellfire and Dives that lived in purple, for there he is in his robes, burning, burning. If thou wert any way given to virtue, I would swear by thy face; my oath should be "By this fire, that's God's angel." But thou art altogether given over, and wert indeed, but for the light in thy 30 face, the son of utter darkness. When thou ran'st up Gad's Hill in the night to catch my horse, if I did not think thou hadst been an *ignis fatuus* or a ball of wildfire, there's no purchase in money. O, thou art a perpetual triumph, an everlasting bonfire-light! Thou hast saved me a thousand marks in 35 links and torches, walking with thee in the night betwixt tavern and tavern; but the sack that thou has drunk me would have bought me lights as good cheap at the dearest chandler's in Europe. I have maintained that salamander of yours with fire any time this two and thirty years. God reward me for it! 40

BARDOLPH. 'Sblood, I would my face were in your belly!

FALSTAFF. God-a-mercy! so should I be sure to be heartburned.

Enter HOST[ESS].

How now, Dame Partlet the hen? Have you inquired yet who picked my pocket?

16. **compass:** order.
19. **compass:** circumference.
21. **admiral:** flagship; **poop:** stern.
22. **Knight . . . Lamp:** parodying heroic names in medieval romance.
25. **death's-head:** skull; ***memento mori:*** reminder of death.
26. **Dives:** for the parable of Dives and Lazarus, see Luke 16:19–31.
26–27. **purple:** expensive clothing.
29. **By . . . angel:** Cf. Exodus 3:2: "And the Angel of the Lord appeared unto him in a flame of fire out of the midst of a bush."
30. **given over:** i.e., to evil.
33. ***ignis fatuus:*** will-o'-the-wisp (natural phosphorescence over wetlands).
33–34. **purchase:** value.
34. **triumph:** public festivity by torchlight.
35. **marks:** unit of currency worth two-thirds of a pound.
36. **links:** torches.
37. **me:** i.e., at my expense.
38. **good cheap:** cheaply; **chandler:** seller of candles.
39. **salamander:** a kind of lizard believed to be able to live in fire.
43. **Dame Partlet:** a talkative, advice-giving hen in Chaucer's "Nun's Priest's Tale."

HOSTESS. Why, Sir John; what do you think, Sir John? Do you think I keep thieves in my house? I have searched, I have inquired, so has my husband, man by man, boy by boy, servant by servant. The tithe of a hair was never lost in my house before. 45

FALSTAFF. Ye lie, hostess. Bardolph was shaved and lost many a hair, and I'll be sworn my pocket was picked. 50
Go to, you are a woman, go!

HOSTESS. Who, I? No; I defy thee! God's light, I was never called so in mine own house before!

FALSTAFF. Go to, I know you well enough. 55

HOSTESS. No, Sir John; you do not know me, Sir John. I know you, Sir John; you owe me money, Sir John, and now you pick a quarrel to beguile me of it. I bought you a dozen of shirts to your back.

FALSTAFF. Dowlas, filthy dowlas. I have given them away to bakers' wives; they have made bolters of them. 60

HOSTESS. Now, as I am a true woman, holland of eight shillings an ell. You owe money here besides, Sir John, for your diet and by-drinkings, and money lent you, four and twenty pound.

FALSTAFF. He had his part of it; let him pay. 65

HOSTESS. He? Alas, he is poor; he hath nothing.

FALSTAFF. How? Poor? Look upon his face. What call you rich? Let them coin his nose; let them coin his cheeks. I'll not pay a denier. What, will you make a younker of me? Shall I not take mine ease in mine inn but I shall have my pocket picked? I have lost a seal-ring of my grandfather's worth forty mark. 70

HOSTESS. O Jesu, I have heard the prince tell him, I know not how oft, that that ring was copper!

FALSTAFF. How? the prince is a Jack, a sneak-up.
'Sblood, an he were here, I would cudgel him like a dog if he would say so. 75

Enter the PRINCE [*and* POINS], *marching, and* FALSTAFF *meets* [*them*], *playing upon his truncheon like a fife.*

How now, lad? Is the wind in that door, i' faith? Must we all march?

48. tithe: tenth part.
50. shaved: (1) had a haircut, (2) contracted venereal disease (baldness was considered a symptom of syphilis).
60. Dowlas: a coarse linen.
61. bolters: flour sieves.
62. holland: fine linen fabric.
63. ell: a cloth measure of 45 inches.
64. by-drinkings: drinks between meals.
69. denier: a French coin worth a tenth of a penny; **younker:** novice.
71. seal-ring: a ring bearing a seal, often an heirloom.
74. Jack: knave; **sneak-up:** sneak.
76 S.D. ***truncheon:*** cudgel, officer's staff; ***fife:*** military flute.
77. Is . . . door?: Is the wind blowing that way?

BARDOLPH. Yea, two and two, Newgate fashion.
HOSTESS. My lord, I pray you hear me. 80
PRINCE. What sayest thou, Mistress Quickly? How doth thy husband? I love him well; he is an honest man.
HOSTESS. Good my lord, hear me.
FALSTAFF. Prithee let her alone and list to me.
PRINCE. What sayest thou, Jack? 85
FALSTAFF. The other night I fell asleep here behind the arras and had my pocket picked. This house is turned bawdy house; they pick pockets.
PRINCE. What didst thou lose, Jack?
FALSTAFF. Wilt thou believe me, Hal, three or four bonds of forty 90 pound apiece and a seal-ring of my grandfather's.
PRINCE. A trifle, some eight-penny matter.
HOSTESS. So I told him, my lord, and I said I heard your grace say so; and, my lord, he speaks most vilely of you, like a foul-mouthed man as he is, and said he would cudgel you. 95
PRINCE. What? he did not.
HOSTESS. There's neither faith, truth, nor womanhood in me else.
FALSTAFF. There's no more faith in thee than in a stewed prune, nor no more truth in thee than in a drawn fox; and for womanhood, Maid Marian may be the deputy's wife of the ward to 100 thee. Go, you thing, go!
HOSTESS. Say, what thing? what thing?
FALSTAFF. What thing? Why, a thing to thank God on.
HOSTESS. I am no thing to thank God on, I would thou shouldst know it! I am an honest man's wife, and, setting thy knight- 105 hood aside, thou art a knave to call me so.
FALSTAFF. Setting thy womanhood aside, thou art a beast to say otherwise.
HOSTESS. Say, what beast, thou knave, thou?
FALSTAFF. What beast? Why, an otter. 110
PRINCE. An otter, Sir John? Why an otter?
FALSTAFF. Why, she's neither fish nor flesh; a man knows not where to have her.
HOSTESS. Thou art an unjust man in saying so. Thou or any man knows where to have me, thou knave, thou! 115
PRINCE. Thou say'st true, hostess, and he slanders thee most grossly.

79. **two . . . fashion:** two by two, like prisoners on their way to the city gaol at Newgate.
90. **bonds:** papers documenting money owed to the bearer.
98. **stewed prune:** associated with brothels (implying that the Hostess is a bawd).
99. **drawn fox:** fox lured out of his hole by hunters and, therefore, needing all his cunning to escape.
100. **Maid Marian:** disreputable woman character in morris dances, traditionally associated with Robin Hood; **deputy's . . . ward:** i.e., the wife of a respectable and probably puritanical local official.
100–01. **to thee:** compared to you.
110. **otter:** mammal equally at home in the water or on land.

HOSTESS. So he doth you, my lord, and said this other day you ought him a thousand pound.

PRINCE. Sirrah, do I owe you a thousand pound? 120

FALSTAFF. A thousand pound, Hal? A million! Thy love is worth a million; thou owest me thy love.

HOSTESS. Nay, my lord, he called you Jack and said he would cudgel you.

FALSTAFF. Did I, Bardolph? 125

BARDOLPH. Indeed, Sir John, you said so.

FALSTAFF. Yea, if he said my ring was copper.

PRINCE. I say 'tis copper. Darest thou be as good as thy word now?

FALSTAFF. Why, Hal, thou knowest, as thou art but man, I dare; but as thou art prince, I fear thee as I fear the roaring of the 130 lion's whelp.

PRINCE. And why not as the lion?

FALSTAFF. The king himself is to be feared as the lion. Dost thou think I'll fear thee as I fear thy father? Nay, an I do, I pray God my girdle break. 135

PRINCE. O, if it should, how would thy guts fall about thy knees! But, sirrah, there's no room for faith, truth, nor honesty in this bosom of thine. It is all filled up with guts and midriff. Charge an honest woman with picking thy pocket! Why, thou whore-son, impudent, embossed rascal, if there were anything 140 in thy pocket but tavern reckonings, memorandums of bawdy houses, and one poor pennyworth of sugar candy to make thee long-winded, if thy pocket were enriched with any other injuries but these, I am a villain. And yet you will stand to it; you will not pocket up wrong. Art thou not ashamed? 145

FALSTAFF. Dost thou hear, Hal? Thou knowest in the state of innocency Adam fell, and what should poor Jack Falstaff do in the days of villainy? Thou seest I have more flesh than another man, and therefore more frailty. You confess then, you picked my pocket? 150

PRINCE. It appears so by the story.

FALSTAFF. Hostess, I forgive thee. Go make ready breakfast, love thy husband, look to thy servants, cherish thy guests. Thou shalt find me tractable to any honest reason. Thou seest I am pacified still. Nay, prithee be gone. 155

130–31. fear . . . whelp: Cf. Proverbs, 20:2: "The fear of a king is as the roaring of a lion."

138. bosom: belly; **midriff:** diaphragm (associated with laughter).

140. embossed: swollen.

141. memorandums: keepsakes.

142–43. make . . . long-winded: give you energy.

144. stand to it: insist you are telling the truth.

144–45. you . . . wrong: proverbial: you will not accept it without protest.

148–49. flesh . . . frailty: playing with the biblical idea that "the flesh is weak" (e.g., Matthew 26:41).

153. cherish: entertain kindly.

155. still: always.

Exit HOSTESS.

Now, Hal, to the news at court: for the robbery, lad—how is that answered?

PRINCE. O my sweet beef, I must still be good angel to thee; the money is paid back again.

FALSTAFF. O, I do not like that paying back; 'tis a double labor. 160

PRINCE. I am good friends with my father and may do anything.

FALSTAFF. Rob me the exchequer the first thing thou doest and do it with unwashed hands too.

BARDOLPH. Do, my lord.

PRINCE. I have procured thee, Jack, a charge of foot. 165

FALSTAFF. I would it had been of horse. Where shall I find one that can steal well? O for a fine thief of the age of two and twenty or thereabouts! I am heinously unprovided. Well, God be thanked for these rebels. They offend none but the virtuous. I laud them, I praise them. 170

PRINCE. Bardolph!

BARDOLPH. My lord?

PRINCE. Go bear this letter to Lord John of Lancaster,
To my brother John; this to my Lord of Westmoreland.

[*Exit* BARDOLPH.]

Go Poins, to horse, to horse; for thou and I 175
Have thirty miles to ride yet ere dinner time.

[*Exit* POINS.]

Jack, meet me to-morrow in the Temple Hall
At two o'clock in the afternoon.
There shalt thou know thy charge, and there receive
Money and order for their furniture. 180
The land is burning; Percy stands on high;
And either they or we must lower lie.

[*Exit.*]

FALSTAFF. Rare words! brave world! Hostess, my breakfast, come.
O, I could wish this tavern were my drum! [*Exit.*]

157. answered: dealt with.
158. sweet beef: unsalted beef.
163. with . . . hands: quickly, without taking time to wash your hands.
165. charge of foot: an infantry command.
168. heinously: dreadfully; **unprovided:** underequipped.
170. laud: praise.
177. Temple Hall: hall of one of the Inns of Court (societies of lawyers), a popular rendezvous.
180. furniture: equipment.
183. brave: impressive.
184. I . . . drum: I wish I could stay here rather than go to war.

[ACT IV, SCENE I. *The Rebel camp near Shrewsbury.*]

[*Enter* HOTSPUR, WORCESTER, *and* DOUGLAS.]

HOTSPUR. Well said, my noble Scot. If speaking truth
In this fine age were not thought flattery,
Such attribution should the Douglas have
As not a soldier of this season's stamp
Should go so general current through the world. 5
By God, I cannot flatter; I do defy
The tongues of soothers; but a braver place
In my heart's love hath no man than yourself.
Nay, task me to my word; approve me, lord.
DOUGLAS. Thou art the king of honor. 10
No man so potent breathes upon the ground
But I will beard him.

Enter one with letters.

HOTSPUR. Do so and 'tis well.—
What letters hast thou there?—I can but thank you.
MESSENGER. These letters come from your father.
HOTSPUR. Letters from him? Why comes he not himself? 15
MESSENGER. He cannot come, my lord; he is grievous sick.
HOTSPUR. 'Zounds! how has he the leisure to be sick
In such a justling time? Who leads his power?
Under whose government come they along?
MESSENGER. His letters bear his mind, not I, my lord. 20
WORCESTER. I prithee tell me, doth he keep his bed?
MESSENGER. He did, my lord, four days ere I set forth,
And at the time of my departure thence
He was much feared by his physicians.
WORCESTER. I would the state of time had first been whole 25
Ere he by sickness had been visited.
His health was never better worth than now.
HOTSPUR. Sick now? droop now? This sickness doth infect
The very life blood of our enterprise.

2. fine: refined.
4–5. not . . . world: Nobody else coined at this time with the stamp of soldier could be so universally valuable.
6. defy: despise.
7. soothers: flatterers; **braver:** better.
9. task . . . word: challenge me to be as good as my word; **approve:** try.
12. beard: defy boldly.
18. justling: i.e., jostling, contentious.
19. government: command.
21. keep: stay in.
24. feared: i.e., feared for.
25. state . . . time: present state of affairs.

'Tis catching hither, even to our camp. 30
He writes me here that inward sickness—
And that his friends by deputation could not
So soon be drawn; nor did he think it meet
To lay so dangerous and dear a trust
On any soul removed but on his own. 35
Yet doth he give us bold advertisement
That with our small conjunction we should on
To see how fortune is disposed to us;
For, as he writes, there is no quailing now,
Because the king is certainly possessed 40
Of all our purposes. What say you to it?

WORCESTER. Your father's sickness is a maim to us.

HOTSPUR. A perilous gash, a very limb lopped off.
And yet, in faith, it is not! His present want
Seems more than we shall find it. Were it good 45
To set the exact wealth of all our states
All at one cast? to set so rich a main
On the nice hazard of one doubtful hour?
It were not good, for therein should we read
The very bottom and the soul of hope, 50
The very list, the very utmost bound
Of all our fortunes.

DOUGLAS. Faith, and so we should.
Where now remains a sweet reversion,
We may boldly spend upon the hope
Of what is to come in. 55
A comfort of retirement lives in this.

HOTSPUR. A rendezvous, a home to fly unto,
If that the devil and mischance look big
Upon the maidenhead of our affairs.

WORCESTER. But yet I would your father had been here. 60
The quality and hair of our attempt
Brooks no division. It will be thought

32. **by deputation:** through Northumberland's agents.
33. **drawn:** brought together; **meet:** appropriate.
35. **removed:** not immediately concerned.
36. **advertisement:** advice.
37. **conjunction:** united force; **on:** go ahead.
40. **possessed:** informed.
44. **His . . . want:** his current absence.
46. **set:** stake; **exact:** entire.
47. **cast:** i.e., of the dice; **main:** wager.
48. **nice:** precarious.
51. **list:** limit.
53. **reversion:** hope of future inheritance.
56. **comfort . . . retirement:** refuge.
58. **big:** haughty, threatening.
59. **maidenhead:** i.e., very beginning.
61. **hair:** nature.
62. **Brooks:** allows.

By some that know not why he is away,
That wisdom, loyalty, and mere dislike
Of our proceedings kept the earl from hence. 65
And think how such an apprehension
May turn the tide of fearful faction
And breed a kind of question in our cause.
For well you know we of the off'ring side
Must keep aloof from strict arbitrement, 70
And stop all sight-holes, every loop from whence
The eye of reason may pry in upon us.
This absence of your father's draws a curtain
That shows the ignorant a kind of fear
Before not dreamt of.

HOTSPUR. You strain too far. 75
I rather of his absence make this use:
It lends a lustre and more great opinion,
A larger dare to our great enterprise,
Than if the earl were here; for men must think,
If we, without his help, can make a head 80
To push against a kingdom, with his help
We shall o'erturn it topsy-turvy down.
Yet all goes well; yet all our joints are whole.

DOUGLAS. As heart can think. There is not such a word
Spoke of in Scotland as this term of fear. 85

Enter SIR RI[CHARD] VERNON.

HOTSPUR. My cousin Vernon! welcome, by my soul.

VERNON. Pray God my news be worth a welcome, lord.
The Earl of Westmoreland, seven thousand strong,
Is marching hitherwards; with him Prince John.

HOTSPUR. No harm. What more?

VERNON. And further, I have learned, 90
The king himself in person is set forth,
Or hitherwards intended speedily,
With strong and mighty preparation.

HOTSPUR. He shall be welcome too. Where is his son,
The nimble-footed madcap Prince of Wales, 95

64. **loyalty:** i.e., to the king; **mere:** downright.
66. **apprehension:** (1) understanding, (2) fear.
67. **fearful faction:** nervous conspiracy.
69. **off'ring:** taking the offensive.
70. **strict arbitrement:** impartial investigation.
71. **loop:** loophole.
75. **strain too far:** exaggerate.
77. **opinion:** reputation.
78. **dare:** daring.
80. **make a head:** raise an army.
83. **joints:** limbs.
92. **intended:** purposed to come.

And his comrades, that daffed the world aside
And bid it pass?

VERNON. All furnished, all in arms;
All plumed like estridges that with the wind
Bated like eagles having lately bathed;
Glittering in golden coats like images; 100
As full of spirit as the month of May
And gorgeous as the sun at midsummer;
Wanton as youthful goats, wild as young bulls.
I saw young Harry with his beaver on,
His cushes on his thighs, gallantly armed, 105
Rise from the ground like feathered Mercury,
And vaulted with such ease into his seat
As if an angel dropped down from the clouds
To turn and wind a fiery Pegasus
And witch the world with noble horsemanship. 110

HOTSPUR. No more, no more! Worse than the sun in March
This praise doth nourish agues. Let them come.
They come like sacrifices in their trim,
And to the fire-eyed maid of smoky war
All hot and bleeding will we offer them. 115
The mailed Mars shall on his altar sit
Up to the ears in blood. I am on fire
To hear this rich reprisal is so nigh,
And yet not ours. Come, let me taste my horse,
Who is to bear me like a thunderbolt 120
Against the bosom of the Prince of Wales.
Harry to Harry shall, hot horse to horse,
Meet, and ne'er part till one drop down a corse.
O that Glendower were come!

VERNON. There is more news.
I learned in Worcester, as I rode along, 125
He cannot draw his power this fourteen days.

96. **daffed:** thrust.
98. **estridges:** ostriches.
99. **Bated:** flapped their wings.
100. **coats:** coats of armor; **images:** statues.
103. **Wanton:** frolicsome.
104. **beaver:** helmet.
105. **cushes:** cuisses, thigh armor.
106. **Mercury:** Roman messenger of the gods; he has winged feet.
109. **wind:** wheel, turn round; **Pegasus:** winged horse of Greek mythology.
110. **witch:** bewitch.
112. **agues:** fevers.
113. **trim:** fine trappings.
114. **maid:** Bellona, Roman goddess of war.
116. **mailed:** armored; **Mars:** Roman god of war.
118. **reprisal:** prize; **nigh:** near.
119. **taste:** try.
123. **corse:** corpse.
125. **Worcester:** cathedral city on the Severn, south of Shrewsbury.
126. **draw:** gather together; **power:** army.

DOUGLAS. That's the worst tidings that I hear of yet.
WORCESTER. Ay, by my faith, that bears a frosty sound.
HOTSPUR. What may the king's whole battle reach unto?
VERNON. To thirty thousand.
HOTSPUR. Forty let it be. 130
My father and Glendower being both away,
The powers of us may serve so great a day.
Come, let us take a muster speedily.
Doomsday is near. Die all, die merrily.
DOUGLAS. Talk not of dying. I am out of fear 135
Of death or death's hand for this one half-year.

Exeunt.

SCENE II. *A public road near Coventry.*

Enter FALSTAFF [*and*] BARDOLPH.

FALSTAFF. Bardolph, get thee before to Coventry; fill me a bottle of sack. Our soldiers shall march through. We'll to Sutton Cophill to-night.
BARDOLPH. Will you give me money, captain?
FALSTAFF. Lay out, lay out. 5
BARDOLPH. This bottle makes an angel.
FALSTAFF. An if it do, take it for thy labor; and if it make twenty, take them all; I'll answer the coinage. Bid my lieutenant Peto meet me at town's end.
BARDOLPH. I will, captain. Farewell. 10

Exit.

FALSTAFF. If I be not ashamed of my soldiers, I am a soused gurnet. I have misused the king's press damnably. I have got, in exchange of a hundred and fifty soldiers, three hundred and odd pounds. I press me none but good householders, yeomen's sons; inquire me out contracted bachelors, such as had 15

129. battle: army.
132. powers . . . us: forces we have available; **serve:** prove enough for.
2. Sutton Cophill: (pronounced Co'fil) Sutton Coldfield, a town in northern Warwickshire on the road to Shrewsbury.
5. Lay out: pay for it yourself.
6. makes an angel: brings the total I have spent to an angel (10 shillings).
7. An . . . labor: Falstaff puns on "make," saying if the bottle can be made into an angel, Bardolph may keep the money for his efforts.
8. I'll . . . coinage: I'll take responsibility for the illegality of such profiteering.
11–12. soused gurnet: pickled fish.
12. press: conscription—Falstaff has accepted money from the one hundred and fifty *not* to draft them.
14. good: wealthy.
14–15. yeomen's sons: sons of comfortably-off smallholders.
15–16. contracted . . . banns: i.e., those on the very verge of marriage.

been asked twice on the banns, such a commodity of warm slaves as had as lieve hear the devil as a drum, such as fear the report of a caliver worse than a struck fowl or a hurt wild duck. I pressed me none but such toasts-and-butter, with hearts in their bellies no bigger than pins' heads, and they 20
have bought out their services; and now my whole charge consists of ancients, corporals, lieutenants, gentlemen of companies—slaves as ragged as Lazarus in the painted cloth, where the glutton's dogs licked his sores; and such as, indeed, were never soldiers, but discarded unjust serving-men, younger 25
sons to younger brothers, revolted tapsters, and ostlers trade-fallen; the cankers of a calm world and a long peace; ten times more dishonorable ragged than an old fazed ancient; and such have I to fill up the rooms of them that have bought out their services that you would think that I had a hundred 30
and fifty tattered prodigals lately come from swine-keeping, from eating draff and husks. A mad fellow met me on the way, and told me I had unloaded all the gibbets and pressed the dead bodies. No eye hath seen such scarecrows. I'll not march through Coventry with them, that's flat. Nay, and the villains 35
march wide betwixt the legs, as if they had gyves on, for indeed I had the most of them out of prison. There's not a shirt and a half in all my company, and the half-shirt is two napkins tacked together and thrown over the shoulders like a herald's coat without sleeves; and the shirt, to say the truth, stolen 40
from my host at Saint Albans, or the red-nose innkeeper of Daventry. But that's all one; they'll find linen enough on every hedge.

Enter the PRINCE [*and the*] LORD OF WESTMORELAND.

16. **banns:** general requests for reasons why two people should not be wed, which are read on three successive Sundays in church prior to the wedding; **commodity:** parcel; **warm:** wealthy.
17. **had . . . lieve:** would just as well.
18. **caliver:** musket; **struck:** wounded.
19. **toasts-and-butter:** men of delicate constitution.
21. **bought . . . services:** bribed me to let them avoid conscription; **charge:** company.
22. **ancients:** ensigns, standard-bearers.
22–23. **gentlemen . . . companies:** soldiers above the rank of regular enlisted men.
23. **Lazarus:** see Luke 16:19–31; **painted cloth:** decorative hanging.
25. **discarded:** discharged; **unjust:** dishonest.
26. **revolted:** runaway.
26–27. **trade-fallen:** unemployed.
28. **fazed ancient:** ragged flag.
32. **draff:** pig swill.
33. **gibbets:** gallows.
35. **that's flat:** that's for sure.
36. **gyves:** shackles.
41. **my host:** the innkeeper.
41–42. **Saint Albans . . . Daventry:** towns north of London, on the road to Coventry.
42. **that's . . . one:** it doesn't matter.
42–43. **they'll . . . hedge:** i.e., they will steal laundry placed on hedges to dry.

PRINCE. How now, blown Jack? How now, quilt?
FALSTAFF. What, Hal? How now, mad wag? What a devil dost thou in Warwickshire? My good Lord of Westmoreland, I cry you mercy. I thought your honor had already been at Shrewsbury. 45
WESTMORELAND. Faith, Sir John, 'tis more than time that I were there, and you too, but my powers are there already. The king, I can tell you, looks for us all. We must away all night. 50
FALSTAFF. Tut, never fear me; I am as vigilant as a cat to steal cream.
PRINCE. I think, to steal cream indeed, for thy theft hath already made thee butter. But tell me, Jack, whose fellows are these that come after? 55
FALSTAFF. Mine, Hal, mine.
PRINCE. I did never see such pitiful rascals.
FALSTAFF. Tut, tut! good enough to toss; food for powder, food for powder. They'll fill a pit as well as better. Tush, man, mortal men, mortal men. 60
WESTMORELAND. Ay, but, Sir John, methinks they are exceeding poor and bare, too beggarly.
FALSTAFF. Faith, for their poverty, I know not where they had that, and for their bareness, I am sure they never learned that of me. 65
PRINCE. No, I'll be sworn, unless you call three fingers on the ribs bare. But, sirrah, make haste. Percy is already in the field.

Exit.

FALSTAFF. What, is the king encamped?
WESTMORELAND. He is, Sir John. I fear we shall stay too long. 70
FALSTAFF. Well, to the latter end of a fray and the beginning of a feast fits a dull fighter and a keen guest.

Exeunt.

[SCENE III. *The rebel camp near Shrewsbury.*]

Enter HOTSPUR, WORCESTER, DOUGLAS, VERNON.

HOTSPUR. We'll fight with him to-night.
WORCESTER. It may not be.

44. blown: (1) inflated, (2) short of breath; **quilt:** i.e., thickly padded.
46–47. cry you mercy: beg your pardon (for not having greeted him promptly).
50. powers: soldiers.
51. away: march.
52. fear: doubt; **vigilant:** wakeful.
59. toss: carry aloft on the point of a pike; **food . . . powder:** cannon fodder.
60. pit: mass grave.
67. three fingers: three-finger thicknesses of fat.

DOUGLAS. You give him then advantage.
VERNON. Not a whit.
HOTSPUR. Why say you so? Looks he not for supply?
VERNON. So do we.
HOTSPUR. His is certain, ours is doubtful.
WORCESTER. Good cousin, be advised; stir not to-night. 5
VERNON. Do not, my lord.
DOUGLAS. You do not counsel well.
You speak it out of fear and cold heart.
VERNON. Do me no slander, Douglas. By my life,
And I dare well maintain it with my life,
If well-respected honor bid me on, 10
I hold as little counsel with weak fear
As you, my lord, or any Scot that this day lives.
Let it be seen to-morrow in the battle
Which of us fears.
DOUGLAS. Yea, or to-night.
VERNON. Content.
HOTSPUR. To-night, say I. 15
VERNON. Come, come, it may not be. I wonder much,
Being men of such great leading as you are,
That you foresee not what impediments
Drag back our expedition. Certain horse
Of my cousin Vernon's are not yet come up. 20
Your uncle Worcester's horse came but to-day;
And now their pride and mettle is asleep,
Their courage with hard labor tame and dull,
That not a horse is half the half of himself.
HOTSPUR. So are the horses of the enemy 25
In general journey-bated and brought low.
The better part of ours are full of rest.
WORCESTER. The number of the king exceedeth ours.
For God's sake, cousin, stay till all come in.

The trumpet sounds a parley. Enter SIR WALTER BLUNT.

BLUNT. I come with gracious offers from the king, 30
If you vouchsafe me hearing and respect.
HOTSPUR. Welcome, Sir Walter Blunt; and would to God
You were of our determination.
Some of us love you well; and even those some

2. **then:** if you delay.
3. **supply:** reinforcements.
10. **well-respected:** carefully considered.
17. **leading:** experience as generals.
19. **expedition:** haste; **horse:** cavalry.
26. **journey-bated:** travel-wearied.
31. **respect:** attention.
33. **determination:** way of thinking.

Envy your great deservings and good name, 35
Because you are not of our quality,
But stand against us like an enemy.

BLUNT. And God defend but still I should stand so.
So long as out of limit and true rule
You stand against anointed majesty. 40
But to my charge. The king hath sent to know
The nature of your griefs, and whereupon
You conjure from the breast of civil peace
Such bold hostility, teaching his duteous land
Audacious cruelty. If that the king 45
Have any way your good deserts forgot,
Which he confesseth to be manifold,
He bids you name your griefs, and with all speed
You shall have your desires with interest,
And pardon absolute for yourself and these 50
Herein misled by your suggestion.

HOTSPUR. The king is kind, and well we know the king
Knows at what time to promise, when to pay.
My father and my uncle and myself
Did give him that same royalty he wears; 55
And when he was not six and twenty strong,
Sick in the world's regard, wretched and low,
A poor unminded outlaw sneaking home,
My father gave him welcome to the shore;
And when he heard him swear and vow to God 60
He came but to be Duke of Lancaster,
To sue his livery and beg his peace,
With tears of innocency and terms of zeal,
My father, in kind heart and pity moved,
Swore him assistance, and performed it too. 65
Now when the lords and barons of the realm
Perceived Northumberland did lean to him,
The more and less came in with cap and knee,
Met him in boroughs, cities, villages,
Attended him on bridges, stood in lanes, 70
Laid gifts before him, proffered him their oaths,
Gave him their heirs as pages, followed him
Even at the heels in golden multitudes.

35. **Envy:** begrudge.
36. **of . . . quality:** on our side.
38. **defend:** forbid; **still:** always.
39. **limit:** accepted bounds of loyalty; **true rule:** obedience.
42. **griefs:** grievances; **whereupon:** on what basis.
51. **suggestion:** instigation.
58. **unminded:** ignored.
62. **sue . . . livery:** seek possession of his inheritance.
63. **zeal:** ardent affection.
68. **The . . . knee:** Those of high and low status came to offer allegiance.

He presently, as greatness knows itself,
Steps me a little higher than his vow 75
Made to my father, while his blood was poor,
Upon the naked shore at Ravenspurgh;
And now, forsooth, takes on him to reform
Some certain edicts and some strait decrees
That lie too heavy on the commonwealth; 80
Cries out upon abuses, seems to weep
Over his country's wrongs; and by this face,
This seeming brow of justice, did he win
The hearts of all that he did angle for;
Proceeded further, cut me off the heads 85
Of all the favorites that the absent king
In deputation left behind him here
When he was personal in the Irish war.

BLUNT. Tut! I came not to hear this.

HOTSPUR. Then to the point.
In short time after, he deposed the king, 90
Soon after that deprived him of his life,
And in the neck of that tasked the whole state;
To make that worse, suffered his kinsman March
(Who is, if every owner were well placed,
Indeed his king) to be engaged in Wales, 95
There without ransom to lie forfeited,
Disgraced me in my happy victories,
Sought to entrap me by intelligence,
Rated mine uncle from the council board,
In rage dismissed my father from the court, 100
Broke oath on oath, committed wrong on wrong,
And in conclusion drove us to seek out
This head of safety, and withal to pry
Into his title, the which we find
Too indirect for long continuance. 105

BLUNT. Shall I return this answer to the king?

HOTSPUR. Not so, Sir Walter. We'll withdraw awhile.

74. **as . . . itself:** i.e., as someone in authority comes to recognize his own power.
76. **while . . . poor:** while he was still humble.
79. **strait:** strict.
81. **Cries . . . upon:** denounces.
82. **face:** pretense.
87. **In deputation:** as his deputies.
88. **personal:** in person.
92. **in . . . that:** immediately after; **tasked:** taxed.
94. **if . . . placed:** if everyone has his due.
95. **engaged:** held as hostage.
96. **forfeited:** unredeemed.
97. **Disgraced . . . victories:** used even my victories on his behalf as ways to disgrace me.
98. **intelligence:** espionage.
99. **Rated:** drove out by scolding.
103. **head . . . safety:** self-defense force; **withal:** at the same time.

Go to the king; and let there be impawned
Some surety for a safe return again,
And in the morning early shall mine uncle 110
Bring him our purposes; and so farewell.

BLUNT. I would you would accept of grace and love.

HOTSPUR. And may be so we shall.

BLUNT. Pray God you do.

[*Exeunt.*]

[SCENE IV. *York, The Archbishop's palace.*]

Enter ARCHBISHOP OF YORK [*and*] SIR MICHAEL.

ARCHBISHOP. Hie, good Sir Michael; bear this sealed brief
With winged haste to the lord marshal;
This to my cousin Scroop; and all the rest
To whom they are directed. If you knew
How much they do import, you would make haste. 5

SIR MICHAEL. My good lord,
I guess their tenor.

ARCHBISHOP. Like enough you do.
To-morrow, good Sir Michael, is a day
Wherein the fortune of ten thousand men
Must bide the touch; for, sir, at Shrewsbury, 10
As I am truly given to understand,
The king with mighty and quick-raised power
Meets with Lord Harry; and I fear, Sir Michael,
What with the sickness of Northumberland,
Whose power was in the first proportion, 15
And what with Owen Glendower's absence thence,
Who with them was a rated sinew too
And comes not in, overruled by prophecies—
I fear the power of Percy is too weak
To wage an instant trial with the king. 20

SIR MICHAEL. Why, my good lord, you need not fear;
There is Douglas and Lord Mortimer.

ARCHBISHOP. No, Mortimer is not there.

SIR MICHAEL. But there is Mordake, Vernon, Lord Harry Percy,
And there is my Lord of Worcester, and a head 25

108. impawned: pledged.
111. Bring . . . purposes: report our terms.
1. Hie: hurry; **brief:** letter.
7. tenor: import.
10. bide . . . the touch: stand the test.
15. in . . . proportion: larger than those of his co-conspirators.
17. rated sinew: dependable support.
25. head: troop.

Of gallant warriors, noble gentlemen.
ARCHBISHOP. And so there is; but yet the king hath drawn
The special head of all the land together:
The Prince of Wales, Lord John of Lancaster,
The noble Westmoreland and warlike Blunt, 30
And many mo corrivals and dear men
Of estimation and command in arms.
SIR MICHAEL. Doubt not, my lord, they shall be well opposed.
ARCHBISHOP. I hope no less, yet needful 'tis to fear;
And, to prevent the worst, Sir Michael, speed. 35
For if Lord Percy thrive not, ere the king
Dismiss his power, he means to visit us,
For he hath heard of our confederacy,
And 'tis but wisdom to make strong against him.
Therefore make haste. I must go write again 40
To other friends; and so farewell, Sir Michael.

Exeunt.

[ACT V, SCENE I. *The King's camp near Shrewsbury.*]

Enter the KING, PRINCE OF WALES, LORD JOHN OF LANCASTER, SIR WALTER BLUNT, FALSTAFF.

KING. How bloodily the sun begins to peer
Above yon busky hill! The day looks pale
At his distemp'rature.
PRINCE. The southern wind
Doth play the trumpet to his purposes
And by his hollow whistling in the leaves 5
Foretells a tempest and a blust'ring day.
KING. Then with the losers let it sympathize,
For nothing can seem foul to those that win.

The trumpet sounds. Enter WORCESTER [*and* VERNON].

How now, my Lord of Worcester! 'Tis not well
That you and I should meet upon such terms 10
As now we meet. You have deceived our trust
And made us doff our easy robes of peace
To crush our old limbs in ungentle steel.

28. **special head:** best commanders.
31. **mo:** more; **corrivals:** associates; **dear:** worthy.
32. **estimation:** value.
36. **thrive:** succeed.
2. **busky:** bushy.
3. **his:** the sun's; **distemp'rature:** discomposure.
4. **Doth . . . purposes:** acts as a trumpeter announcing what the sun portends by its unusual appearance.
12. **easy:** comfortable.

This is not well, my lord; this is not well.
What say you to it? Will you again unknit 15
This churlish knot of all-abhorred war,
And move in that obedient orb again
Where you did give a fair and natural light,
And be no more an exhaled meteor,
A prodigy of fear, and a portent 20
Of broached mischief to the unborn times?

WORCESTER. Hear me, my liege.
For mine own part, I could be well content
To entertain the lag-end of my life
With quiet hours, for I [do] protest 25
I have not sought the day of this dislike.

KING. You have not sought it! How comes it then?

FALSTAFF. Rebellion lay in his way, and he found it.

PRINCE. Peace, chewet, peace!

WORCESTER. It pleased your majesty to turn your looks 30
Of favor from myself and all our house;
And yet I must remember you, my lord,
We were the first and dearest of your friends.
For you my staff of office did I break
In Richard's time, and posted day and night 35
To meet you on the way and kiss your hand
When yet you were in place and in account
Nothing so strong and fortunate as I,
It was myself, my brother, and his son
That brought you home and boldly did outdare 40
The dangers of the time. You swore to us,
And you did swear that oath at Doncaster,
That you did nothing purpose 'gainst the state,
Nor claim no further than your new-fall'n right,
The seat of Gaunt, dukedom of Lancaster. 45
To this we swore our aid. But in short space
It rained down fortune show'ring on your head,
And such a flood of greatness fell on you,

16. **all-abhorred:** hated by everyone.
17. **orb:** sphere of action.
19. **exhaled meteor:** meteors were believed to be formed by vapors exhaled (drawn up from) the earth.
20. **prodigy . . . fear:** ill omen.
21. **broached:** set running.
24. **entertain:** fill up; **lag-end:** latter part.
26. **dislike:** discord.
29. **chewet:** chough (a kind of crow), chatterer.
32. **remember:** remind.
35. **posted:** rode fast.
38. **Nothing so:** not at all as.
40. **outdare:** defy.
42. **Doncaster:** town in Yorkshire.
44. **new-fall'n:** recently-come-about.

What with our help, what with the absent king,
What with the injuries of a wanton time, 50
The seeming sufferances that you had borne,
And the contrarious winds that held the king
So long in his unlucky Irish wars
That all in England did repute him dead;
And from this swarm of fair advantages 55
You took occasion to be quickly wooed
To gripe the general sway into your hand;
Forgot your oath to us at Doncaster;
And, being fed by us, you used us so
As that ungentle gull, the cuckoo's bird, 60
Useth the sparrow, did oppress our nest;
Grew by our feeding to so great a bulk
That even our love durst not come near your sight
For fear of swallowing; but with nimble wing
We were enforced for safety sake to fly 65
Out of your sight and raise this present head;
Whereby we stand opposed by such means
As you yourself have forged against yourself
By unkind usage, dangerous countenance,
And violation of all faith and troth 70
Sworn to us in your younger enterprise.

KING. These things, indeed, you have articulate,
Proclaimed at market crosses, read in churches,
To face the garment of rebellion
With some fine color that may please the eye 75
Of fickle changelings and poor discontents,
Which gape and rub the elbow at the news
Of hurlyburly innovation.
And never yet did insurrection want
Such water colors to impaint his cause, 80
Nor moody beggars, starving for a time

50. **injuries**: abuses; **wanton**: ill-governed.
51. **sufferances**: distresses.
52. **contrarious**: adverse.
57. **gripe**: grasp firmly; **general sway**: overall control.
60. **ungentle gull**: the fledgling cuckoo in the sparrow's nest.
63. **our love**: those of us who loved you.
64. **swallowing**: being swallowed.
67. **opposed . . . means**: forced into opposition for such reasons.
69. **unkind**: unnatural; **dangerous**: threatening.
70. **troth**: truth, pledged word.
71. **in . . . younger**: at the beginning of your.
72. **articulate**: spelled out.
74. **face**: trim.
76. **changelings**: turncoats.
77. **rub . . . elbow**: show yourself pleased (by crossing your arms and rubbing your elbows).
78. **hurlyburly**: tumultuous; **innovation**: rebellion.
79. **want**: lack.
80. **water colors**: weak excuses; **impaint**: portray.

Of pell-mell havoc and confusion.
PRINCE. In both your armies there is many a soul
Shall pay full dearly for this encounter,
If once they join in trial. Tell your nephew 85
The Prince of Wales doth join with all the world
In praise of Henry Percy. By my hopes,
This present enterprise set off his head,
I do not think a braver gentleman,
More active-valiant or more valiant-young, 90
More daring or more bold, is now alive
To grace this latter age with noble deeds.
For my part, I may speak it to my shame,
I have a truant been to chivalry;
And so I hear he doth account me too. 95
Yet this before my father's majesty—
I am content that he shall take the odds
Of his great name and estimation,
And will, to save the blood on either side,
Try fortune with him in a single fight. 100
KING. And, Prince of Wales, so dare we venture thee,
Albeit considerations infinite
Do make against it. No, good Worcester, no!
We love our people well; even those we love
That are misled upon your cousin's part; 105
And, will they take the offer of our grace,
Both he, and they, and you, yea, every man
Shall be my friend again, and I'll be his.
So tell your cousin, and bring me word
What he will do. But if he will not yield, 110
Rebuke and dread correction wait on us,
And they shall do their office. So be gone.
We will not now be troubled with reply.
We offer fair; take it advisedly.

Exit WORCESTER [*and* VERNON].

PRINCE. It will not be accepted, on my life. 115
The Douglas and the Hotspur both together

82. pell-mell: chaotic.
88. set . . . head: taken off the charge sheet.
89. braver: finer.
92. latter: modern.
94. chivalry: the duties of knighthood.
98. estimation: reputation.
102. Albeit: despite the fact that.
105. cousin's: i.e., nephew's.
106. grace: pardon.
111. wait . . . us: are in our service.
112. office: duty.
114. take . . . advisedly: accept because it is the sensible thing to do.

Are confident against the world in arms.
KING. Hence, therefore, every leader to his charge;
For, on their answer, will we set on them,
And God befriend us as our cause is just! 120

Exeunt. Manent PRINCE, FALSTAFF.

FALSTAFF. Hal, if thou see me down in the battle and bestride me, so! 'Tis a point of friendship.
PRINCE. Nothing but a colossus can do thee that friendship. Say thy prayers, and farewell.
FALSTAFF. I would 'twere bedtime, Hal, and all well. 125
PRINCE. Why, thou owest God a death.

[*Exit.*]

FALSTAFF.. 'Tis not due yet: I would be loath to pay him before his day. What need I be so forward with him that calls not on me? Well, 'tis no matter; honor pricks me on. Yea, but how if honor prick me off when I come on? How then? Can honor 130 set to a leg? No. Or an arm? No. Or take away the grief of a wound? No. Honor hath no skill in surgery then? No. What is honor? A word. What is in that word honor? What is that honor? Air. A trim reckoning! Who hath it? He that died a Wednesday. Doth he feel it? No. Doth he hear it? No. 'Tis 135 insensible then? Yea, to the dead. But will [it] not live with the living? No. Why? Detraction will not suffer it. Therefore I'll none of it. Honor is a mere scutcheon—and so ends my catechism.

Exit.

[SCENE II. *The rebel camp.*]

Enter WORCESTER [*and*] SIR RICHARD VERNON.

WORCESTER. O no, my nephew must not know, Sir Richard,
The liberal and kind offer of the king.

119. on . . . answer: when they give their response (presumed to be negative).
122. so: good.
123. colossus: Colossus, an immense statue and one of the wonders of the ancient world, was thought to have stood astride the entrance to the harbor at Rhodes.
126. death: punning on "debt."
128–29. forward . . . me: keen to pay a creditor who has not yet called in the debt.
129. pricks: spurs.
130. prick . . . off: check my name off his list as a casualty.
131. set . . . leg: set a broken leg; **grief:** pain.
134. trim reckoning: fine final account.
136. insensible: not perceptible to the senses.
137. Detraction: slander; **suffer:** permit.
138. scutcheon: escutcheon, a painted representation of a shield bearing a coat of arms, typically exhibited at funerals.
139. catechism: statement of belief in question-and-answer form.

VERNON. 'Twere best he did.
WORCESTER. Then are we all undone.
It is not possible, it cannot be,
The king should keep his word in loving us. 5
He will suspect us still and find a time
To punish this offense in other faults.
Supposition all our lives shall be stuck full of eyes;
For treason is but trusted like the fox,
Who, ne'er so tame, so cherished and locked up, 10
Will have a wild trick of his ancestors.
Look how we can, or sad or merrily,
Interpretation will misquote our looks,
And we shall feed like oxen at a stall,
The better cherished still the nearer death. 15
My nephew's trespass may be well forgot;
It hath the excuse of youth and heat of blood
And an adopted name of privilege,
A hare-brained Hotspur, governed by a spleen.
All his offenses live upon my head 20
And on his father's. We did train him on;
And, his corruption being ta'en from us,
We, as the spring of all, shall pay for all.
Therefore, good cousin, let not Harry know,
In any case, the offer of the king. 25

Enter HOTSPUR [*and* DOUGLAS].

VERNON. Deliver what you will, I'll say 'tis so.
Here comes your cousin.
HOTSPUR. My uncle is returned.
Deliver up my Lord of Westmoreland.
Uncle, what news?
WORCESTER. The king will bid you battle presently. 30
DOUGLAS. Defy him by the Lord of Westmoreland.
HOTSPUR. Lord Douglas, go you and tell him so.
DOUGLAS. Marry, and shall, and very willingly.

Exit.

3. **undone:** ruined.
6. **still:** always.
8. **Supposition:** suspicion.
10. **ne'er so:** however.
12. **or . . . merrily:** either serious or happy.
18. **adopted . . . privilege:** a nickname ("Hotspur") that licenses impulsiveness.
19. **spleen:** impulse.
21. **train:** lure.
22. **his . . . us:** since we are viewed as the source of his guilt.
23. **spring:** source.
26. **Deliver:** report.
28. **Deliver up:** release; **Westmoreland:** the hostage given by the king.
30. **presently:** immediately.
33. **Marry, . . . shall:** I certainly will.

WORCESTER. There is no seeming mercy in the king.
HOTSPUR. Did you beg any? God forbid! 35
WORCESTER. I told him gently of our grievances,
Of his oath-breaking, which he mended thus,
By now forswearing that he is forsworn.
He calls us rebels, traitors, and will scourge
With haughty arms this hateful name in us. 40

Enter DOUGLAS.

DOUGLAS. Arm, gentlemen, to arms! for I have thrown
A brave defiance in King Henry's teeth,
And Westmoreland, that was engaged, did bear it;
Which cannot choose but bring him quickly on.
WORCESTER. The Prince of Wales stepped forth before the king 45
And, nephew, challenged you to single fight.
HOTSPUR. O, would the quarrel lay upon our heads,
And that no man might draw short breath to-day
But I and Harry Monmouth! Tell me, tell me,
How showed his tasking? Seemed it in contempt? 50
VERNON. No, by my soul. I never in my life
Did hear a challenge urged more modestly,
Unless a brother should a brother dare
To gentle exercise and proof of arms.
He gave you all the duties of a man; 55
Trimmed up your praises with a princely tongue;
Spoke your deservings like a chronicle;
Making you ever better than his praise
By still dispraising praise valued with you;
And, which became him like a prince indeed, 60
He made a blushing cital of himself,
And chid his truant youth with such a grace
As if he mastered there a double spirit
Of teaching and of learning instantly.
There did he pause; but let me tell the world, 65

34. **seeming:** evidence of.
37. **mended:** atoned for.
38. **forswearing . . . forsworn:** falsely denying that he has broken his word.
42. **brave:** haughty.
43. **engaged:** pledged as a hostage.
44. **cannot . . . but:** must certainly.
49. **Harry Monmouth:** i.e., Hal, taking his name from the place of his birth in Wales.
50. **tasking:** challenge.
52. **urged:** proposed.
54. **gentle:** noble; **proof:** trial.
55. **duties of:** respect due to.
56. **Trimmed . . . praises:** adorned his praise of you
59. **dispraising:** disparaging; **valued . . . you:** compared with you in respect of worth.
61. **blushing . . . himself:** modest and frank account of the way he has behaved.
64. **instantly:** at the same time.

If he outlive the envy of this day,
England did never owe so sweet a hope,
So much misconstrued in his wantonness.
HOTSPUR. Cousin, I think thou art enamored
Upon his follies. Never did I hear 70
Of any prince so wild a liberty.
But be he as he will, yet once ere night
I will embrace him with a soldier's arm,
That he shall shrink under my courtesy.
Arm, arm with speed! and, fellows, soldiers, friends, 75
Better consider what you have to do
Than I, that have not well the gift of tongue,
Can lift your blood up with persuasion.

Enter a MESSENGER.

MESSENGER. My lord, here are letters for you.
HOTSPUR. I cannot read them now. 80
O gentlemen, the time of life is short!
To spend that shortness basely were too long
If life did ride upon a dial's point,
Still ending at the arrival of an hour.
An if we live, we live to tread on kings; 85
If die, brave death, when princes die with us!
Now for our consciences, the arms are fair,
When the intent of bearing them is just.

Enter another [MESSENGER].

MESSENGER. My lord, prepare. The king comes on apace.
HOTSPUR. I thank him that he cuts me from my tale, 90
For I profess not talking. Only this—
Let each man do his best; and here draw I
A sword whose temper I intend to stain
With the best blood that I can meet withal
In the adventure of this perilous day. 95

66. envy: malice.
67. owe: own.
68. wantonness: youthful excesses.
71. so . . . liberty: such unrestrained behavior.
73–74. I . . . courtesy: (1) I will embrace him and show myself even more courteous, (2) I will defeat him in battle and prove myself the more accomplished.
76–78. Better . . . persuasion: thinking about the task ahead will put you into a better fighting spirit than any words I could speak, since I am not much of an orator.
83–84. If . . . hour: even if life lasted no more than one hour and concluded at the end of that hour.
86. brave: glorious.
87. for: as for; **fair:** just.
89. apace: speedily.
90. cuts . . . tale: stops me from talking.
91. I . . . talking: talking is not my occupation.
95. adventure: chance.

Now, Esperance! Percy! and set on.
Sound all the lofty instruments of war,
And by that music let us all embrace;
For, heaven to earth, some of us never shall
A second time do such a courtesy. 100

Here they embrace. The trumpets sound. [*Exeunt.*]

[SCENE III. *A Plain between the camps.*]

The KING *enters with his power* [*and passes over*]. *Alarum to the battle. Then enter* DOUGLAS *and* SIR WALTER BLUNT.

BLUNT. What is thy name, that in battle thus
Thou crossest me? What honor dost thou seek
Upon my head?
DOUGLAS. Know then my name is Douglas,
And I do haunt thee in the battle thus
Because some tell me that thou art a king. 5
BLUNT. They tell thee true.
DOUGLAS. The Lord of Stafford dear to-day hath bought
Thy likeness, for instead of thee, King Harry,
This sword hath ended him. So shall it thee,
Unless thou yield thee as my prisoner. 10
BLUNT. I was not born a yielder, thou proud Scot;
And thou shalt find a king that will revenge
Lord Stafford's death.

They fight. DOUGLAS *kills* BLUNT. *Then enter* HOTSPUR.

HOTSPUR. O Douglas, hadst thou fought at Holmedon thus,
I never had triumphed upon a Scot. 15
DOUGLAS. All's done, all's won. Here breathless lies the king.
HOTSPUR. Where?
DOUGLAS. Here.
HOTSPUR. This, Douglas? No. I know this face full well.
A gallant knight he was, his name was Blunt; 20
Semblably furnished like the king himself.
DOUGLAS. Ah fool, go with thy soul, whither it goes!
A borrowed title hast thou bought too dear:
Why didst thou tell me that thou wert a king?
HOTSPUR. The king hath many marching in his coats. 25

96. **Esperance:** motto of the Percy family, used here as a battle cry.
97. **lofty . . . war:** i.e., drums and trumpets.
99. **heaven . . . earth:** heaven bet against earth.
S.D. ***power:*** army; ***Alarum:*** call to arms.
7. **dear:** dearly.
7–8. **bought . . . likeness:** paid for resembling you.
16. **breathless:** i.e., dead.
21. **Semblably furnished:** similarly dressed.
25. **coats:** garments worn over armor and embroidered with coats of arms.

DOUGLAS. Now, by my sword, I will kill all his coats;
I'll murder all his wardrobe, piece by piece,
Until I meet the king.
HOTSPUR. Up and away!
Our soldiers stand full fairly for the day.

[*Exeunt.*]

Alarum. Enter FALSTAFF *solus.*

FALSTAFF. Though I could 'scape shot-free at London, I fear the shot here. Here's no scoring but upon the pate. Soft! who are you? Sir Walter Blunt. There's honor for you! Here's no vanity! I am as hot as molten lead, and as heavy too. God keep lead out of me. I need no more weight than mine own bowels. I have led my ragamuffins where they are peppered. There's not three of my hundred and fifty left alive, and they are for the town's end, to beg during life. But who comes here? 30 35

Enter the PRINCE.

PRINCE. What, stand'st thou idle here? Lend me thy sword.
Many a nobleman lies stark and stiff
Under the hoofs of vaunting enemies, 40
Whose deaths are yet unrevenged. I prithee
Lend me thy sword.
FALSTAFF. O Hal, I prithee give me leave to breathe awhile. Turk Gregory never did such deeds in arms as I have done this day. I have paid Percy; I have made him sure. 45
PRINCE. He is indeed, and living to kill thee.
I prithee lend me thy sword.
FALSTAFF. Nay, before God, Hal, if Percy be alive, thou get'st not my sword; but take my pistol, if thou wilt.
PRINCE. Give it me. What, is it in the case? 50
FALSTAFF. Ay, Hal. 'Tis hot, 'tis hot. There's that will sack a city.

The PRINCE *draws it out and finds it to be a bottle of sack.*

PRINCE. What, is it a time to jest and dally now?

He throws the bottle at him. Exit.

29. **stand . . . day:** are in a good position to gain the victory.
30. **shot-free:** without having to pay the bill.
31. **scoring:** (1) reckoning up a bill, (2) cutting.
32–33. **Here's . . . vanity!:** If this doesn't prove I'm right about the emptiness of honor, nothing will.
35. **I . . . peppered:** I have led my company to where they have all been killed (perhaps in order to collect their pay).
37. **town's end:** the edge of town, where the destitute would gather to beg from travelers.
43–44. **Turk Gregory:** possibly Pope Gregory XIII, who had promised immunity to anyone who murdered Queen Elizabeth; "Turk" was synonymous with cruelty and savagery.
45. **paid:** killed; **made . . . sure:** made certain of him.
51. **hot:** i.e., from firing; **sack:** ransack (punning on wine).

FALSTAFF. Well, if Percy be alive, I'll pierce him. If he do come in my way, so; if he do not, if I come in his willingly, let him make a carbonado of me. I like not such grinning honor as Sir Walter hath. Give me life; which if I can save, so; if not, honor comes unlooked for, and there's an end. 55

[*Exit.*]

[SCENE IV. *Another part of the field.*]

Alarum. Excursions. Enter the KING, *the* PRINCE, LORD JOHN OF LANCASTER, EARL OF WESTMORELAND.

KING. I prithee, Harry, withdraw thyself; thou bleedest too much.
Lord John of Lancaster, go you with him.
JOHN. Not I, my lord, unless I did bleed too.
PRINCE. I [do] beseech your majesty make up,
Lest your retirement do amaze your friends. 5
KING. I will do so.
My Lord of Westmoreland, lead him to his tent.
WESTMORELAND. Come, my lord, I'll lead you to your tent.
PRINCE. Lead me, my lord? I do not need your help;
And God forbid a shallow scratch should drive 10
The Prince of Wales from such a field as this,
Where stained nobility lies trodden on,
And rebels' arms triumph in massacres!
JOHN. We breathe too long. Come, cousin Westmoreland,
Our duty this way lies. For God's sake, come! 15

[*Exeunt* PRINCE JOHN *and* WESTMORELAND.]

PRINCE. By God, thou has deceived me, Lancaster!
I did not think thee lord of such a spirit.
Before, I loved thee as a brother, John;
But now, I do respect thee as my soul.
KING. I saw him hold Lord Percy at the point 20
With lustier maintenance than I did look for
Of such an ungrown warrior.
PRINCE. O, this boy
Lends mettle to us all!

Exit.

56. carbonado: meat scored across and grilled.
58. an end: i.e., to Falstaff's catechism and to life.
4. make up: bring up your troops.
5. retirement: retreat; **amaze:** bewilder.
12. stained: with blood and dishonor.
14. breathe: pause for breath.
21. lustier maintenance: more vigorous endurance.

[*Enter* DOUGLAS.]

DOUGLAS. Another king? They grow like Hydra's heads.
I am the Douglas, fatal to all those 25
That wear those colors on them. What art thou
That counterfeit'st the person of a king?
KING. The king himself, who, Douglas, grieves at heart
So many of his shadows thou hast met,
And not the very king. I have two boys 30
Seek Percy and thyself about the field;
But seeing thou fall'st on me so luckily,
I will assay thee. So defend thyself.
DOUGLAS. I fear thou art another counterfeit;
And yet, in faith, thou bearest thee like a king. 35
But mine I am sure thou art, whoe'er thou be,
And thus I win thee.

They fight. The KING *being in danger, enter* PRINCE OF WALES.

PRINCE. Hold up thy head, vile Scot, or thou art like
Never to hold it up again. The spirits
Of valiant Shirley, Stafford, Blunt are in my arms. 40
It is the Prince of Wales that threatens thee,
Who never promiseth but he means to pay.

They fight. DOUGLAS *flieth.*

Cheerly, my lord, how fares your grace?
Sir Nicholas Gawsey hath for succor sent,
And so hath Clifton. I'll to Clifton straight. 45
KING. Stay and breathe awhile.
Thou hast redeemed thy lost opinion,
And showed thou mak'st some tender of my life
In this fair rescue thou hast brought to me.
PRINCE. O God, they did me too much injury 50
That ever said I hearkened for your death.
If it were so, I might have let alone
The insulting hand of Douglas over you,
Which would have been as speedy in your end
As all the poisonous potions in the world, 55

24. **Hydra:** the nine-headed monster of Greek mythology that grew two new heads for each one cut off.
26. **colors:** i.e., the king's coat of arms.
29. **shadows:** likenesses.
32. **luckily:** by chance.
33. **assay thee:** put you to the test.
36. **mine:** my prize.
43. **Cheerly:** a cry of encouragement.
46. **breathe:** get my breath back.
47. **redeemed:** recovered; **opinion:** reputation.
48. **thou . . . of:** you have some regard for.
51. **hearkened for:** hoped to hear of.
53. **insulting:** scornfully triumphing.

And saved the treacherous labor of your son.
KING. Make up to Clifton; I'll to Sir Nicholas Gawsey.

Exit.

Enter HOTSPUR.

HOTSPUR. If I mistake not, thou art Harry Monmouth.
PRINCE. Thou speak'st as if I would deny my name.
HOTSPUR. My name is Harry Percy.
PRINCE. Why, then I see 60
A very valiant rebel of the name.
I am the Prince of Wales, and think not, Percy,
To share with me in glory any more.
Two stars keep not their motion in one sphere,
Nor can one England brook a double reign 65
Of Harry Percy and the Prince of Wales.
HOTSPUR. Nor shall it, Harry, for the hour is come
To end the one of us; and would to God
Thy name in arms were now as great as mine!
PRINCE. I'll make it greater ere I part from thee, 70
And all the budding honors on thy crest
I'll crop to make a garland for my head.
HOTSPUR. I can no longer brook thy vanities.

They fight.

Enter FALSTAFF.

FALSTAFF. Well said, Hal! to it, Hal! Nay, you shall find no boy's
play here, I can tell you. 75

Enter DOUGLAS. *He fighteth with* FALSTAFF, [*who*] *falls down as if he were dead.* [*Exit* DOUGLAS.] *The* PRINCE *killeth* PERCY.

HOTSPUR. O Harry, thou hast robbed me of my youth!
I better brook the loss of brittle life
Than those proud titles thou hast won of me.
They wound my thoughts worse than thy sword my flesh.
But thoughts the slaves of life, and life time's fool, 80
And time, that takes survey of all the world,
Must have a stop. O, I could prophesy,
But that the earthy and cold hand of death
Lies on my tongue. No, Percy, thou art dust,
And food for— 85

57. Make up: advance.
65. brook: endure.
71. budding . . . crest: feathers or other mark of honor on his helmet.
73. vanities: idle boasts.
74–75. boy's play: child's play.
82. prophesy: dying men were thought to have the gift of prophecy.

[*Dies.*]

PRINCE. For worms, brave Percy. Fare thee well, great heart;
Ill-weaved ambition, how much art thou shrunk!
When that this body did contain a spirit,
A kingdom for it was too small a bound;
But now two paces of the vilest earth 90
Is room enough. This earth that bears thee dead
Bears not alive so stout a gentleman.
If thou wert sensible of courtesy,
I should not make so dear a show of zeal.
But let my favors hide thy mangled face; 95
And, even in thy behalf, I'll thank myself
For doing these fair rites of tenderness.
Adieu, and take thy praise with thee to heaven.
Thy ignominy sleep with thee in the grave,
But not remem'b'red in thy epitaph. 100

He spieth FALSTAFF *on the ground.*

What, old acquaintance? Could not all this flesh
Keep in a little life? Poor Jack, farewell!
I could have better spared a better man.
O, I should have a heavy miss of thee
If I were much in love with vanity. 105
Death hath not struck so fat a deer to-day,
Though many dearer, in this bloody fray.
Embowelled will I see thee by and by;
Till then in blood by noble Percy lie.

Exit.

FALSTAFF *riseth up.*

FALSTAFF. Embowelled? If thou embowel me to-day, I'll give 110
you leave to powder me and eat me too to-morrow. 'Sblood, 'twas time to counterfeit, or that hot termagant Scot had paid me scot and lot too. Counterfeit? I lie; I am no counterfeit. To die is to be a counterfeit, for he is but the counterfeit of a man who hath not the life of a man; but to counterfeit dying 115 when a man thereby liveth is to be no counterfeit, but the

92. stout: valiant.
93. sensible . . . courtesy: able to hear these compliments.
94. dear: heartfelt; **zeal:** admiration.
95. favors: feathers or material worn as a badge of honor; Hal is giving Hotspur the honor he has just won by killing him.
104. have . . . thee: miss you terribly (punning on Falstaff's weight).
105. vanity: foolishness.
108. Embowelled: disemboweled and ready for embalming.
111. powder: salt.
112. termagant: violent; **paid:** killed.
113. scot . . . lot: thoroughly, in a final reckoning.

true and perfect image of life indeed. The better part of valor is discretion, in the which better part I have saved my life. 'Zounds, I am afraid of this gunpowder Percy, though he be dead. How if he should counterfeit too and rise? By my faith, 120 I am afraid he would prove the better counterfeit. Therefore I'll make him sure; yea, and I'll swear I killed him. Why may not he rise as well as I? Nothing confutes me but eyes, and nobody sees me. Therefore, sirrah [*stabbing him*], with a new wound in your thigh, come you along with me. 125

He takes up HOTSPUR *on his back. Enter* PRINCE [*and*] JOHN OF LANCASTER.

PRINCE. Come, brother John; full bravely hast thou fleshed
Thy maiden sword.

JOHN. But, soft! whom have we here?
Did you not tell me this fat man was dead?

PRINCE. I did; I saw him dead,
Breathless and bleeding on the ground. Art thou alive? 130
Or is it fantasy that plays upon our eyesight?
I prithee speak. We will not trust our eyes
Without our ears. Thou art not what thou seem'st.

FALSTAFF. No, that's certain, I am not a double man; but if I be not Jack Falstaff, then am I a Jack. There is Percy 135

[*throwing the body down*].

If your father will do me any honor, so; if not, let him kill the next Percy himself. I look to be either earl or duke, I can assure you.

PRINCE. Why, Percy I killed myself, and saw thee dead!

FALSTAFF. Didst thou? Lord, Lord, how this world is given to 140 lying. I grant you I was down, and out of breath, and so was he; but we rose both at an instant and fought a long hour by Shrewsbury clock. If I may be believed, so; if not, let them that should reward valor bear the sin upon their own heads. I'll take it upon my death, I gave him this wound in the 145 thigh. If the man were alive and would deny it, 'zounds! I would make him eat a piece of my sword.

JOHN. This is the strangest tale that ever I heard.

PRINCE. This is the strangest fellow, brother John.
Come, bring your luggage nobly on your back. 150

126–27. fleshed . . . sword: used your sword for the first time in battle.
134. double man: (1) a ghost, (2) two men (i.e., with Hotspur on his shoulder).
135. Jack: knave.
141. lying: (1) telling lies, (2) playing dead.
142. at . . . instant: at the same moment.
145. I'll . . . death: I'll swear as I would on my deathbed, with my soul in the balance.

For my part, if a lie may do thee grace,
I'll gild it with the happiest terms I have.

A retreat is sounded.

The trumpet sounds retreat; the day is ours.
Come, brother, let's to the highest of the field,
To see what friends are living, who are dead. 155

Exeunt [PRINCE HENRY *and* PRINCE JOHN].

FALSTAFF. I'll follow, as they say, for reward. He that rewards me, God reward him. If I do grow great, I'll grow less; for I'll purge, and leave sack, and live cleanly, as a nobleman should do.

Exit [*dragging off the body*].

[SCENE V. *Another part of the field.*]

The trumpets sound. Enter the KING, PRINCE OF WALES, LORD JOHN OF LANCASTER, EARL OF WESTMORELAND, *with* WORCESTER *and* VERNON *prisoners.*

KING. Thus ever did rebellion find rebuke.
Ill-spirited Worcester, did not we send grace,
Pardon, and terms of love to all of you?
And wouldst thou turn our offers contrary?
Misuse the tenor of thy kinsman's trust? 5
Three knights upon our party slain to-day,
A noble earl, and many a creature else
Had been alive this hour,
If like a Christian thou hadst truly borne
Betwixt our armies true intelligence. 10
WORCESTER. What I have done my safety urged me to;
And I embrace this fortune patiently,
Since not to be avoided it falls on me.
KING. Bear Worcester to the death, and Vernon too;
Other offenders we will pause upon. 15

[*Exeunt* WORCESTER *and* VERNON, *guarded.*]

151. **do . . . grace:** reflect credit on you.
152. **happiest:** most favorable.
154. **highest:** i.e., highest point, best vantage point.
158. **purge:** (1) lose weight, (2) repent.
S.D. ***trumpets sound:*** marking the king's entrance.
2. **grace:** good will.
5. **Misuse . . . trust:** Misreport the message from us to Hotspur and thus abuse his trust in you.
10. **true intelligence:** accurate information.
15. **pause upon:** delay action on.

How goes the field?
PRINCE. The noble Scot, Lord Douglas, when he saw
The fortune of the day quite turned from him,
The noble Percy slain, and all his men
Upon the foot of fear, fled with the rest; 20
And falling from a hill, he was so bruised
That the pursuers took him. At my tent
The Douglas is, and I beseech your grace
I may dispose of him.
KING. With all my heart.
PRINCE. Then, brother John of Lancaster, to you 25
This honorable bounty shall belong.
Go to the Douglas and deliver him
Up to his pleasure, ransomless and free.
His valors shown upon our crests to-day
Have taught us how to cherish such high deeds, 30
Even in the bosom of our adversaries.
JOHN. I thank your grace for this high courtesy,
Which I shall give away immediately.
KING. Then this remains, that we divide our power.
You, son John, and my cousin Westmoreland, 35
Towards York shall bend you with your dearest speed
To meet Northumberland and the prelate Scroop,
Who, as we hear, are busily in arms.
Myself and you, son Harry, will towards Wales
To fight with Glendower and the Earl of March. 40
Rebellion in this land shall lose his sway,
Meeting the check of such another day;
And since this business so fair is done,
Let us not leave till all our own be won.

Exeunt.

16. **How . . . field?:** What is the overall outcome of the battle?
20. **upon . . . fear:** panicking and running away.
26. **bounty:** act of generosity.
27–28. **deliver . . . Up:** release him.
29. **crests:** i.e., helmets.
33. **give away:** grant.
36. **bend you:** proceed; **dearest:** quickest.
41. **his:** its.
42. **check:** reversal.
43. **fair:** successfully.
44. **leave:** stop.

CONTEXTS AND SOURCES

Composition and Publication

From the 1598 Quarto

Editing an early modern dramatic text is never straightforward. In order to see the kinds of decision that editors make when creating a modern-spelling edition of a play such as *1 Henry IV*, readers are encouraged to compare the Quarto opening, which follows, with 1.2.145–190 and 1.3.1–28 of the edited text and to think about the processes involved in the way the former is represented in the latter.

Twentieth-century editors of *1 Henry IV* faced two particular issues in the editing process—the question of the relationship between *1* and *2 Henry IV*, and the question of Sir John's surname. The essays that follow the Quarto opening provide a brief overview of both debates. I have reproduced two essays on each topic, the second of each pair engaging with the first. However, this does not imply that the second essays are the last word on the subject.

The question of the relationship of *1* and *2 Henry IV* is simple: are the two plays really one play divided into (or elongated into) two parts, or are they distinct and separate plays? Harold Jenkins summarizes centuries of debate and then halves the matter, arguing that the two plays are both complementary and incompatible. Paul Yachnin maintains that the question itself is the product of an inadequate critical understanding of the nature of theatrical art, thereby dissolving rather than resolving the argument.

The question of Sir John's surname came into public consciousness when, in 1986, the editors of the groundbreaking Oxford *Complete Works* chose to call the character everyone knew as "Falstaff" in *1 Henry IV* by a different name, "Oldcastle." Gary Taylor, one of the Oxford editors, offers a history of the issues involved and a defense of "Oldcastle," arguing that this name, as Shakespeare's original choice, should be used in modern editions and that the lampooning of a man considered a proto-Protestant martyr suggests Shakespeare's sympathies with Catholicism. David Kastan responds by noting both that Oldcastle, as a Lollard, would be more likely to be associated with Puritan sectarianism than with mainstream English Protestantism and that to privilege a presumed original authorial intention in "restoring" a character's name is to deny the material nature of the socialized early modern play text.

In each case, it is clear that questions that might appear to be only of interest to editors in fact impinge fundamentally on questions of critical interpretation.

Prin. How ſhall we part with them in ſetting forth?

Po. Why, we wil ſet forth before or after them, and appoint them a place of meeting, wherein it is at our pleaſure to faile: and then wil they aduenture vpõ the exploit themſelues, which they ſhal haue no ſooner atchieued but weele ſet vpon them.

Prin. Yea but tis like that they wil know vs by our horſes, by our habits, and by euery other appointment to be our ſelues.

Po. Tut, our horſes they ſhal not ſee, ile tie them in the wood, our vizards wee wil change after wee leaue them: and ſirrha, I haue caſes of Buckrom for the nonce, to immaske our noted outward garments.

Prin. Yea, but I doubt they wil be too hard for vs.

Po. Wel, for two of them, I know them to bee as true bred cowards as euer turnd backe: and for the third, if he fight longer then he ſees reaſon, ile forſweare armes. The vertue of this ieaſt wil be the incomprehenſible lies, that this ſame fat rogue wil tel vs when we meet at ſupper, how thirtie at leaſt he fought with, what wardes, what blowes, what extremities he indured, and in the reproofe of this liues the ieſt.

Prin. Well, ile goe with thee, prouide vs all thinges neceſſarie, and meete me to morrow night in Eaſtcheape, there ile ſup: farewell.

Po. Farewel my Lord. *Exit Poines*.

Prin, I know you all, and wil a while vphold
The vnyokt humour of your idlenes,
Yet herein wil I imitate the ſunne,
Who doth permit the baſe contagious clouds
To ſmother vp his beautie from the world,
That when he pleaſe againe to be himſelfe,
Being wanted he may be more wondred at
By breaking through the foule and ougly miſts
Of vapours that did ſeeme to ſtrangle him.
If all the yeere were playing holly-dayes,
To ſport would be as tedious as to worke;
But when they ſeldome come, they wiſht for come,
And nothing pleaſeth but rare accidents:
So when this looſe behauiour I throw off,
And pay the debt I neuer promiſed,

By

By how much better then my word I am,
By ſo much ſhall I falſifie mens hopes,
And like bright mettal on a ſullein ground,
My reformation glittring ore my fault,
Shal ſhew more goodly, and attract more eyes
Then that which hath no foile to ſet it off.
Ile ſo offend, to make offence a skill,
Redeeming time when men thinke leaſt I wil. *Exit.*

Enter the King, Northumberland, Worceſter, Hotſpur, ſir Walter blunt, with others.

King. My blood hath bin too colde and temperate,
Vnapt to ſtir at theſe indignities,
And you haue found me, for accordingly
You tread vpon my patience, but be ſure
I will from henceforth rather be my ſelfe
Mightie, and to be fearde, then my condition
Which hath bin ſmooth as oile, ſoft as yong downe,
And therefore loſt that title of reſpect,
Which the proud ſoule neare payes but to the proud.

Wor. Our houſe (my ſoueraigne liege) little deſerues
The ſcourge of greatnes to be vſd on it,
And that ſame greatneſſe to, which our owne hands
Haue holpe to make ſo portly. *Nor.* My Lord.

King. Worceſter get thee gone, for I do ſee
Danger, and diſobedience in thine eie:
O ſir, your preſence is too bold and peremptorie,
And Maieſtie might neuer yet endure
The moodie frontier of a ſeruant browe,
You haue good leaue to leaue vs, when we need
Your vſe and counſel we ſhall ſend for you. *Exit Wor.*
You were about to ſpeake.

North. Yea my good Lord.
Thoſe priſoners in your highnes name demanded,
Which Harry Percy here at Holmedon tooke,
Were as he ſaies, not with ſuch ſtrength denied
As is deliuered to your maieſtie.
Either enuie therefore, or miſpriſion,
Is guiltie of this fault, and not my ſonne.

One Play or Two?

HAROLD JENKINS

The Structural Problem in Shakespeare's *Henry the Fourth*†

* * *

The first problem that confronts one in approaching *Henry IV*, and the one about which I propose to be particular, has inevitably introduced itself already. Is it one play or two? Some of you will dismiss this as an academic question * * *. But it is also, surely, a practical question: how satisfactorily can either the first part or the second be shown in the theatre without the other? What is gained, or indeed lost, by presenting the two parts * * * on successive evenings? And thus of course the question becomes a problem of literary criticism. Until it has been answered, how can the dramatic quality of *Henry IV* be fully appreciated, or even defined? Yet the numerous literary critics who have attempted an answer to the question have reached surprisingly opposite conclusions.

Answers began more than two hundred years ago in the *Critical Observations on Shakespeare* by John Upton, a man who deserves our regard for trying to scotch the notion so strangely current in the eighteenth century that "Shakespeare had no learning". Far from accepting that Shakespeare's plays were the happy, or the not so happy, products of untutored nature, Upton maintained that they were constructed according to some principles of art; and his examination of *Henry IV* suggested to him that each of its two parts had, what Aristotle of course demanded, its own beginning, middle, and end. Upton held it to be an injury to Shakespeare even to speak of a first and second *part* and thus conceal the fact that there were here two quite independent plays.[1] To this Dr Johnson retorted that these two plays, so far from being independent, are "two only be-

† Harold Jenkins, *The Structural Problem in Shakespeare's "Henry the Fourth": An Inaugural Lecture Delivered at Westfield College, University of London, on 19 May 1955* (London: Methuen, 1956), 2–27. Reprinted by permission of the publisher. The original notes have been emended by the editor except where indicated.

1. John Upton, *Critical Observations on Shakespeare* (London, 1746), 11, 41–42, 70–71.

cause they are too long to be one". They could appear as separate plays, he thought, only to those who looked at them with the "ambition of critical discoveries". In these tart words Johnson shrewdly defined what if not one of the deadly sins, is still a vice and one to which universities are prone. The "ambition of critical discoveries" * * * has been responsible for many interpretations of Shakespeare whose merit is in their being new rather than their being true. Yet one must not always accept the accepted. Dr Johnson's contemporaries did not all find it as plain as he did that *Henry IV* was just one continuous composition. It seemed probable to Malone that Part 2 was not even "conceived"[2] until Part 1 had been a roaring success. Capell, on the other hand, thought that both parts were "planned at the same time, and with great judgment".[3]

Among present-day scholars Professor Dover Wilson is on Johnson's side. He insists that the two parts of *Henry IV* are "a single structure" with the "normal dramatic curve" stretched over ten acts instead of five. Professor R. A. Law, however, declares that *Henry IV* is "not a single ten-act play", but two organic units "written with different purposes in view". On the contrary, says Dr Tillyard, "The two parts of the play are a single organism." Part 1 by itself is "patently incomplete". "Each part is a drama complete in itself", says Kittredge flatly.[4] In short, some two centuries after Upton and Johnson, scholars are still about equally divided as to whether *Henry IV* was "planned" as "one long drama" or whether the second part was, as they put it, an "unpremeditated sequel". A new professor, his ambition already dwindling at Johnson's warning, might well lapse into melancholy, or even modesty. Modest or not, he can hardly escape the conclusion, reached by another eighteenth-century dignitary in a somewhat different situation, that "much might be said on both sides". Like Sir Roger de Coverley, he "would not give his judgment rashly", yet like the late R. W. Chambers, * * * he may think that the modesty which forbears to make a judgment is disastrous.[5]

Words like "planned" and "unpremeditated" figure largely in this controversy; and of course they imply intention or the lack of it, and will therefore be suspect in those circles which denounce what is called "the intentional fallacy".[6] I am far from belonging to that

2. Edmond Malone, "An Attempt to Ascertain the Order in which the Plays Attributed to Shakespeare were Written," in Samuel Johnson and George Steevens (eds.), *The Plays of William Shakespeare*, 10 vols. (London, 1778), I. 300.
3. Edward Capell, *Notes and Various Readings to Shakespeare* [London, 1775], 164.
4. George L. Kittredge, ed., *The First Part of "King Henry the Fourth," by William Shakespeare* (Boston and New York, 1940), viii.
5. See R. W. Chambers, *Beowulf, an Introduction to the Study of the Poem . . .*, 2d ed. (Cambridge, Eng., 1932), 390.
6. This is actually the title of an article by W. K. Wimsatt and M. C. Beardsley in the *Sewanee Review* 54 (1946): 468 ff.; repr. in Wimsatt's *The Verbal Icon* (Lexington, Ky., 1954.

school of criticism which holds that an author's own intention is irrelevant to our reading of his work; yet, as Lascelles Abercrombie says, aesthetic criticism must ultimately judge by results: a man's work is evidence of what he did, but you can never be sure what he intended.[7] This position, with the coming of the Freudian psychology, is finally inescapable, but in its extreme form it seems to me unnecessarily defeatist. When I find *Much Ado About Nothing* beginning with talk of a battle in which those killed are "few of any sort, and none of name", I may infer that Shakespeare intended to write a comedy and not a realistic one at that. But if I wish to play for safety, I may use a phrase of Lascelles Abercrombie's own and speak—not of what Shakespeare intended, but of what he "warned his audience to expect" (Abercrombie, 22). If we leave aside for the present all question of Shakespeare's intention, what does *Henry IV* itself, as it begins and proceeds along its course, warn us to expect?

The short first scene, filled with reports of wars—wars this time in which multitudes are "butchered"—makes an apt beginning for a history play. But its dialogue announces no main action. Yet certain topics, brought in with apparent casualness, naturally engage our interest. There is talk of two young men who do not yet appear, both called "young Harry", yet apparently unlike. The first of them, Hotspur, is introduced as "gallant", an epithet which is very soon repeated when he is said to have won "a gallant prize". The prisoners he has taken are, we are told, "a conquest for a prince to boast of". Already, before Prince Hal is even named, a contrast is being begun between a man who behaves like a prince though he is not one and another who is in fact a prince but does not act the part. The King makes this explicit. Hotspur, who has gained "an honourable spoil", is "a son who is the theme of Honour's tongue", while the King's own son is stained with "riot and dishonour". In the second and third scenes the two Harries in turn appear. First, the Prince, already associated with dishonour, instead of, like Hotspur, taking prisoners in battle, plans to engage in highway robbery. Then, when he has arranged to sup next night in a tavern, he is followed on the stage by Hotspur telling how, when he took his prisoners, he was "dry with rage and extreme toil". This practice of juxtaposing characters who exhibit opposite codes of conduct is a common one in Shakespeare's drama. After the "unsavoury similes" that Hal swaps with Falstaff, in which a squalling cat and a stinking ditch are prominent, there is Hotspur's hyperbole about plucking "bright honour from the pale-faced moon". It may not be a classical construction, but there is enough suggestion here of arrangement

7. Lascelles Abercrombie, *A Plea for the Liberty of Interpreting*, British Academy Shakespeare Lecture (London, 1930), 6.

to justify Upton's claim for Shakespeare's art. We expect that central to the play will be the antithesis between these two young men and the lives they lead. And we shall find that this antithesis precipitates a moral contest which is an important aspect of the historical action of the drama.

The historical action presents Hotspur's rebellion. It is an action which develops with a fine structural proposition throughout Part 1. The act divisions, although they are not Shakespeare's of course, being first found in the Folio, may serve nevertheless as a convenient register of the way the action is disposed. In the first act the rebel plot is hatched, in the second Hotspur prepares to leave home, in the third he joins forces with the other rebel leaders, in the fourth the rebel army is encamped ready to give battle, in the fifth it is defeated and Hotspur is killed. Meantime, along with the military contest between Hotspur and the King, the moral contest between the Prince and Hotspur proceeds with an equally perfect balance. The opposition of honour and riot established in the first act is intensified in the second, where a scene of Hotspur at home preparing for war is set against one of Hal revelling in the tavern. The revelry even includes a little skit by Hal on Hotspur's conversation with his wife, which serves not only to adjust our view of Hotspur's honour by subjecting it to ridicule, but also to emphasize that the Prince is—with gleeful understatement—"not yet of Percy's mind". That he is not of Percy's mind leads the King in the third act to resume his opening plaint: it is not the Prince but Percy, with his "never-dying honour", who is fit to be a king's son. At this point the Prince vows to outshine his rival. He will meet "this gallant Hotspur"—the words echo the opening scene—this "child of honour", and overcome him. And so, when the rebels see the Prince in Act 4, he is "gallantly arm'd"—Hotspur's word is now applied to him—and he vaults upon his horse "as if an angel dropp'd down from the clouds"—with a glory, that is, already beyond Hotspur. All that then remains is that the Prince shall demonstrate his new chivalry in action, which of course he does in the fifth act, first saving his father's life and finally slaying Hotspur in single combat. Opposed to one another throughout the play, constantly spoken of together, these two are nevertheless kept apart till the fifth act, when their first and last encounter completes in the expected manner the pattern of their rivalry that began in the opening words. The two have exchanged places. Supremacy in honour has passed from Hotspur to the Prince, and the wayward hero of the opening ends by exhibiting his true princely nature.

What then is one to make of the view of Professor Dover Wilson that the Battle of Shrewsbury, in which the Prince kills Hotspur, is not an adequate conclusion but merely the "nodal point we expect in a third act"? If we do expect a "nodal point" in a third act, then *Henry IV* Part 1 will not disappoint us. For there *is* a nodal point, and—I am tempted to say this categorically—it is in the third act of Part 1 that it occurs. In this third act, when the King rebukes his son, the Prince replies, "I will redeem all this . . ."; in the fifth act he fulfils this vow at Shrewsbury, as is signalized by the King's admission that the Prince has "redeem'd" his "lost opinion". Again, in the third act, the prince swears that he will take from Hotspur "every honour sitting on his helm"; in the fifth act Hotspur is brought to confess that the Prince has won "proud titles" from him.[8] More significantly still, the third act ends with the Prince saying,

Percy stands on high;
And either we or they must lower lie;

and then the fifth act shows us the spectacle of the hero looking down upon his rival's prostrate form. The curve of the plot could hardly be more firmly or more symmetrically drawn. It does not seem easy to agree with Dr Johnson and Professor Dover Wilson that *Henry IV* Part 1 is only the first half of a play.

If this were all there were to *Henry IV* Part 1, the matter would be simple. But the Prince's conquest of honour is only one aspect of his progress; the other is his break with the companions of his riots. Interwoven with the story of the Prince and Hotspur are the Prince's relations with Falstaff, and these, from Falstaff's first appearance in the second scene of the play, are presented in a way which leads us to expect a similar reversal. The essential thing about Hal is that, scapegrace that he is, he is the future king—the "true prince", the "sweet young prince", the "king's son", the "heir apparent", as Falstaff variously calls him, with whatever degree of mockery, in their first dialogue together. More than that, this dialogue is constantly pointing forward to the moment when he will come to the throne. "When thou art king"—Falstaff uses these words four times in the first seventy lines and yet again before the scene is over. "Shall there be gallows standing in England when thou art king?" "Do not thou, when thou art king, hang a thief." And so on. With these words ringing in our ears, then, we are continually being reminded of what is to come. These words seem, however, to refer to some vague time in the distant future. The Prince's reign will inescapably become reality, but it is at present apprehended as a dream. Falstaff's irrepressible fancy blows up a vast gaily-coloured bubble, and as Bradley recognized,[9] it is because

8. The connection here is reinforced by the Prince's use of his earlier image: "all the budding honours on thy crest I'll crop" [*Author's note*].
9. A. C. Bradley, "The Rejection of Falstaff," *Oxford Lectures on Poetry* (London: 1909), 262–63.

this bubble encloses the dreams of all of us that we feel for Falstaff so much affection. In our dreams we all do exactly as we like, and the date of their realization is to be when Hal is king. Then, everything will be changed—except of course ourselves. *We* shall go on as before, our friend Falstaff will continue his nocturnal depredations, but highwaymen will not be regarded as thieves and punishments will be abolished. Unfortunately, in the real world outside the bubble, it is not the law but we ourselves that should change, as Falstaff recognizes when he says, "I must give over this life, and I will give it over . . . I'll be damned for never a king's son in Christendom." The joke of this is that we know that Falstaff will never give over, nor means to; but the joke does not quite conceal the seriousness of the alternatives—give over or be damned; and the idea of damnation continues to dance before us, now and later, in further jests about Falstaff's selling his soul to the devil, wishing to repent, and having to "give the devil his due". What Falstaff's eventual doom is to be could be discerned more than dimly by a mind that came to this play unfurnished by literature or folk-lore. And none of us is quite as innocent as that. We cannot help being aware of an archetypal situation in which a man dallies with a diabolical tempter whom he either renounces or is destroyed by; and to the first audience of *Henry IV* this situation was already familiar in a long line of Christian plays, in some of which man's succumbing to temptation was symbolized in his selling his soul to the devil and being carried off to Hell. It is because it is so familiar that it is readily accepted as matter for jesting, while the jests give a hint of Falstaff's role in the play. I merely pick out one or two threads in the very complex fabric of the dialogue: you will be good enough, I trust, to believe that, in spite of some dubious precedents in the recent criticism of other plays, I am not seeking to interpret *Henry IV* as an allegory of sin and damnation. Falstaff is not a type-figure, though within his vast person several types are contained. And one of them is a sinner and provokes many piquant allusions to the typical fate of sinners, whether on the earthly gallows or in the infernal fire. There is also an ambiguity, to use the modern jargon, which permits Falstaff to be not only the sinner but the tempter as well. The jokes of a later scene will call him indeed a devil who haunts the Prince, a "reverend vice", an "old white-bearded Satan". What I think the play makes clear from the beginning is that neither as sinner nor as tempter will Falstaff come to triumph. Even as we share his dream of what will happen when Hal is king, we confidently await the bursting of his bubble.

To strengthen our expectation even further is what we know of history, or at least of that traditional world where the territories of history and legend have no clear boundaries. The peculiarity of the history play is that while pursuing its dramatic ends, it must also obey history and steer a course reasonably close to an already known pattern of events. The story of Prince Hal was perfectly familiar to the Elizabethan audience before the play began, and it was the story of a prince who had a madcap youth, including at least one escapade of highway robbery, and then, on succeeding to the throne, banished his riotous companions from court and became the most valorous king England had ever had. Not only was this story vouched for in the chronicles, but it had already found its way on to the stage, as an extant play, *The Famous Victories of Henry the Fifth*, bears witness, in however garbled a text. It is hardly open to *our* play, then, to depart from the accepted pattern, in which the banishment of the tavern friends is an essential feature. Moreover, that they are to be banished the Prince himself assures us at the end of his first scene with Poins and Falstaff in that soliloquy which generations of critics have made notorious.

> *I know you all, and will awhile uphold*
> *The unyoked humour of your idleness.*

The word "awhile" plants its threat of a different time to come when a "humour" now "unyoked" will be brought under restraint. The soliloquy tells us as plain as any prologue what the end of the play is to be.

Yet although *Henry IV* Part 1 thus from its first act directs our interest to the time when Hal will be king, it is not of course until the last act of Part 2 that Pistol comes to announce, "Sir John, thy tender lambkin now is king." It is not until the last act of Part 2 that the Prince is able to institute the new régime which makes mock of Falstaff's dream-world. And it is not of course till the final scene of all that the newly crowned king makes his ceremonial entrance and pronounces the words that have threatened since he and Falstaff first were shown together. "I banish thee." To all that has been said about the rejection of Falstaff I propose to add very little. The chief of those who objected to it, Bradley himself, recognized the necessity of it while complaining of how it was done. Granted that the new king had to drop his former friend, might he not have spared him the sermon and parted from him in private (Bradley, 253)? Yet Professor Dover Wilson is surely right to maintain that the public utterance is the essential thing.[1] From the first, as I have shown, interest is concentrated on the prince as the future sovereign and Falstaff builds hopes on the nature of his rule. Their separation, when it comes, is not then a reluctant parting between friends, but a royal decree promulgated with due solemnity. This is also the per-

1. John Dover Wilson, *The Fortunes of Falstaff* (Cambridge, Eng.: Cambridge University Press, 1943), 120–21.

fect moment for it, when the crown that has hovered over the hero from the beginning is seen, a striking symbol in the theatre, fixed firmly on his head. The first words of the rejection speech elevate him still further—"I know thee not"—for the scriptural overtones here[2] make the speaker more than a king. The situation presents many aspects, but one of them shows the tempter vanquished and another the sinner cast into outer darkness. In either case the devil, we may say, gets his due.

The last act of Part 2 thus works out a design which is begun in the first act of Part 1. How then can we agree with Kittredge that each part is a complete play? Such a pronouncement fits the text no better than the opposite view of Johnson and Dover Wilson that Part 1, though it ends in Hotspur's death and the Prince's glory, is yet only the first half of a play. If it were a question of what Shakespeare intended in the matter, the evidence provided by what he wrote would not suggest either that the two parts were planned as a single drama or that Part 2 was an "unpremeditated sequel".

An escape from this dilemma has sometimes been sought in a theory, expounded especially by Professor Dover Wilson and Dr Tillyard, that what *Henry IV* shows is one action with two phases. While the whole drama shows the transformation of the madcap youth into the virtuous ruler, the first part, we are told, deals with the chivalric virtues, the second with the civil. In the first part the hero acquires honour, in the second he establishes justice. But I see no solution of the structural problem here. For though it is left to Part 2 to embody the idea of justice in the upright judge, the interest in justice and law is present from the start. On Falstaff's first appearance in Part 1 he jibes at the law as "old father antic". And he goes further. Included within his bubble is a vision of his future self not simply as a man freed from "the rusty curb" of the law but as a man who actually administers the law himself. "By the Lord, I'll be a brave judge", he says, making a mistake about his destined office which provokes Hal's retort, "Thou judgest false already." It is in the last act of Part 2 that we have the completion of this motif. Its climax comes when on Hal's accession Falstaff brags, "The laws of England are at my commandment", and its resolution when the true judge sends the false judge off to prison. But it begins, we see, in the first act of Part 1. The Prince's achievement in justice cannot, then, be regarded simply as the second phase of his progress. Certainly he has two contests: in one he outstrips Hotspur, in the other he puts down Falstaff. But these contests are not distributed at the rate of one per part. The plain fact is that in *Henry IV* two actions, each with the Prince as hero, begin together in the first act

2. Cf. Luke 13:25–27 [*Author's note*].

of Part 1, though one of them ends with the death of Hotspur at the end of Part 1, the other with the banishment of Falstaff at the end of Part 2.

Now, since the Falstaff plot is to take twice as long to complete its course, it might well be expected to develop from the beginning more slowly than the other. Certainly if it is to keep symmetry, it must come later to its turning-point. But is this in fact what we find? Frankly it is not. On the contrary, through the first half of Part 1 the Hotspur plot and the Falstaff plot show every sign of moving towards their crisis together.

Both plots, for example, are presented, though I think both are not usually observed, in the Prince's soliloquy in the first act which I have already quoted as foretelling the banishment of his tavern companions. It is unfortunate that this speech has usually been studied for its bearing on Falstaff's rejection; its emphasis is really elsewhere. It is only the first two lines, with the reference to the "unyoked humour" of the Prince's companions, that allude specifically to them, and what is primarily in question is not what is to happen to the companions but what is to happen to the Prince. In the splendid image which follows of the sun breaking through the clouds we recognize a royal emblem and behold the promise of a radiant king who is to come forth from the "ugly mists" which at present obscure the Prince's real self. Since Falstaff has just been rejoicing at the thought that they "go by the moon . . . and not by Phœbus", it is apparent that his fortunes will decline when the Prince emerges like Phœbus himself. It is equally apparent, or should be, that the brilliant Hotspur will be outshone.[3] There is certainly no clue at this stage that the catastrophes of Hotspur and Falstaff will not be simultaneous.

Our expectation that they will be is indeed encouraged as the two actions now move forward. While Hotspur in pursuit of honour is preparing war, Falstaff displays his cowardice (I use the word advisedly) at Gadshill. While Hotspur rides forth from home on the journey that will take him to his downfall, the exposure of Falstaff's makebelieve in the matter of the men in buckram is the foreshadowing of his. The news of Hotspur's rebellion brings the Falstaffian revels to a climax at the same time as it summons the Prince to that interview with his father which will prove, as we have seen, the crisis of his career and the "nodal point" of the drama. That this interview is to be dramatically momentous is clear enough in advance: before we come to it, it is twice prefigured by the Prince and Falstaff in burlesque. But not only do the two mock-interviews

3. I.e., this first-act soliloquy looks forward not only to the rejection of Falstaff but also to Vernon's vision of the Prince and his company before Shrewsbury, "gorgeous as the sun at midsummer."

excite our interest in the real one to come; the mock-interviews are in the story of the Prince and Falstaff what the real interview is in the story of the Prince and Hotspur. First, Falstaff, whose dream it is that he may one day govern England, basks in the makebelieve that he is king; and then Hal, who, as we have so often been reminded, is presently to be king, performs in masquerade his future part. The question they discuss is central to the play: "Shall the son of England prove a thief and take purses?" Shall he in fact continue to associate with Falstaff? One should notice that although the two actors exchange roles, they do not really change sides in this debate. Whether he acts the part of king or prince, Falstaff takes the opportunity of pleading for himself. When he is king he instructs the prince to "keep with" Falstaff; as prince he begs, "Banish not him thy Harry's company, banish not him thy Harry's company: banish plump Jack, and banish all the world." Falstaff's relations to the future king, a theme of speculation since the opening of the play, now come to a focus in this repeated word "banish". And when the Prince replies, "I do, I will", he anticipates in jest the sentence he is later to pronounce in earnest. If it were never to be pronounced in earnest, that would rob the masquerade of the dramatic irony from which comes its bouquet: those who accept Part 1 as a play complete in itself wrongly surrender their legitimate expectations. In this mock-interview the Prince declares his intentions towards Falstaff just as surely as in his real interview with his father he declares his intentions towards Hotspur. One declaration is a solemn vow, the other a glorious piece of fun, but they are equally prophetic and structurally their function is the same. We now approach the turning-point not of one, but of both dramatic actions. Indeed we miss the core of the play if we do not perceive that the two actions are really the same. The moment at the end of the third act when the Prince goes off to challenge Hotspur is also the moment when he leaves Falstaff's favourite tavern for what we well might think would be evermore. It is at the exit from the tavern that the road to Shrewsbury begins; and all the signposts I see indicate one-way traffic only. There should be no return.

The various dooms of Hotspur and Falstaff are now in sight; and we reasonably expect both dooms to be arrived at in Act 5. What we are not at all prepared for is that one of the two will be deferred till five acts later than the other. The symmetry so beautifully preserved in the story of Hotspur is in Falstaff's case abandoned. Statistics are known to be misleading, and nowhere more so than in literary criticism; but it is not without significance that in *Henry IV* Part 1 Falstaff's speeches in the first two acts number ninety-six and in the last two acts only twenty-five. As for Falstaff's satellites, with the exception of a single perfunctory appearance on the part of Bardolph, the whole galaxy vanishes altogether in the last two acts, only to reappear with some changes in personnel in Part 2. Falstaff, admittedly, goes on without a break, if broken in wind; and his diminished role does show some trace of the expected pattern of development. His going to war on foot while Hal is on horseback marks a separation of these erstwhile companions and a decline in Falstaff's status which was anticipated in jest when his horse was taken from him at Gadshill. When he nevertheless appears at one council of war his sole attempt at a characteristic joke is cut short by the Prince with "Peace, chewet, peace!" A fine touch, this, which contributes to the picture of the Prince's transformation: the boon companion whose jests he has delighted in is now silenced in a word. There is even the shadow of a rejection of Falstaff; over his supposed corpse the Prince speaks words that, for all their affectionate regret, remind us that he has turned his back on "vanity". But these things, however significant, are details, no more than shorthand notes for the degradation of Falstaff that we have so confidently looked for. What it comes to is that after the middle of Part 1 *Henry IV* changes its shape. And that, it seems to me, is the root and cause of the structural problem.

Now that this change of shape has been, I hope I may say, demonstrated from within the play itself, it may at this stage be permissible to venture an opinion about the author's plan. I do not of course mean to imply that *Henry IV*, or indeed any other of Shakespeare's plays, ever had a plan precisely laid down for it in advance. But it has to be supposed that when Shakespeare began a play he had some idea of the general direction it would take, however ready he may have been to modify his idea as art or expediency might suggest. Though this is where I shall be told I pass the bounds of literary criticism into the province of biography or worse, I hold it reasonable to infer from the analysis I have given that in the course of writing *Henry IV* Shakespeare changed his mind. I am compelled to believe that the author himself foresaw, I will even say intended, that pattern which evolves through the early acts of Part 1 and which demands for its completion that the hero's rise to an eminence of valour shall be accompanied, or at least swiftly followed, by the banishment of the riotous friends who hope to profit from his reign. In other words, hard upon the Battle of Shrewsbury there was to come the coronation of the hero as king. This inference from the play is not without support from other evidence. The prince's penitence in the interview with his father in the middle of Part 1 corresponds to an episode which, both in Holinshed and in the play of *The Famous Victories of Henry the Fifth*, is placed only shortly before the old king's death. And still more remarkable is the sequence of events in a poem which has been shown to be one of

Shakespeare's sources.[4] At the historical Battle of Shrewsbury the Prince was only sixteen years old, whereas Hotspur was thirty-nine. But in Samuel Daniel's poem, *The Civil Wars*, Hotspur is made "young" and " rash" and encounters a prince of equal age who emerges like a "new-appearing glorious star".[5] It is Daniel, that is to say, who sets in opposition these two splendid youths and so provides the germ from which grows the rivalry of the Prince and Hotspur which is structural to Shakespeare's play. And in view of this resemblance between Daniel and Shakespeare, it is significant that Daniel ignores the ten years that in history elapsed between the death of Hotspur and the Prince's accession. Whereas in Holinshed the events of those ten years fill nearly twenty pages, Daniel goes straight from Shrewsbury to the old king's deathbed. This telescoping of events, which confronts the Prince with his kingly responsibilities directly after the slaying of Hotspur, adumbrates the pattern that Shakespeare, as I see it, must have had it in mind to follow out. The progress of a prince was to be presented not in two phases but in a single play of normal length which would show the hero wayward in its first half, pledging reform in the middle, and then in the second half climbing at Shrewsbury the ladder of honour by which, appropriately, he would ascend to the throne.

The exact point at which a new pattern supervenes I should not care to define. But I think the new pattern can be seen emerging during the fourth act. At a corresponding stage the history play of *Richard II* shows the deposition of its king, *Henry V* the victory at Agincourt, even *Henry IV* Part 2 the quelling of its rebellion in Gaultree Forest. By contrast *Henry IV* Part 1, postponing any such decisive action, is content with preparation. While the rebels gather, the Prince is arming and Falstaff recruiting to meet them. Until well into the fifth act ambassadors are going back and fourth between the rival camps, and we may even hear a message twice over, once when it is despatched and once when it is delivered. True, this is not undramatic: these scenes achieve a fine animation and suspense as well as the lowlier feat of verisimilitude. But the technique is obviously not one of compression. Any thought of crowding into the two-hour traffic of one play the death of the old king and the coronation of the new has by now been relinquished, and instead the Battle of Shrewsbury is being built up into a grand finale in its own right. In our eagerness to come to this battle and our gratification at the exciting climax it provides, we easily lose sight of our previous expectations. Most of us, I suspect, go from the theatre well satisfied with the improvised conclusion. It is not,

4. See F. W. Moorman, "Shakespeare's History Plays and Daniel's 'Civile Wars,' " *Shakespeare Jahrbuch* 40 (1904): 77–83.
5. Book III, stanzas 97, 109–10 [*Author's note*].

of course, that we cease to care about the fate of individuals. On the contrary, the battle succeeds so well because amid the crowded tumult of the fighting it keeps the key figures in due prominence. Clearly showing who is killed, who is rescued, and who shams dead, who slays a valiant foe and who only pretends to, it brings each man to a destiny that we perceive to be appropriate. We merely fail to notice that the destiny is not in every case exactly what was promised. There is no room now in Part 1 to banish Falstaff. A superb comic tact permits him instead the fate of reformation, in fact the alternative of giving over instead of being damned. It is a melancholy fate enough, for it means giving over being Falstaff: we leave him saying that if he is rewarded, he will "leave sack, and live cleanly as a nobleman should do". But since this resolution is conditional and need in any case be believed no more than Falstaff has already taught us to believe him, it has the advantage that it leaves the issue open, which, to judge from the outcry there has always been over the ending of Part 2, is how most people would prefer to have it left. Shakepeare's brilliant improvisation thus provides a dénouement to Part 1 which has proved perfectly acceptable, while it still leaves opportunity for what I hope I may call the original ending, if the dramatist should choose to add a second part. I refrain, however, from assuming that a second part was necessarily planned before Part 1 was acted.

* * *

It has sometimes been objected that Falstaff runs away with Part 2. In truth he has to shoulder the burden of it because a dead man and a converted one can give him small assistance. Part 2 has less opportunity for the integrated double action of Part 1. To be sure, it attempts a double action, and has often been observed to be in some respects a close replica of Part 1—"almost a carbon copy", Professor Shaaber says. At exactly the same point in each part, for example, is a little domestic scene where a rebel leader contemplates leaving home, and in each part this is directly followed by the big tavern scene in which revelry rises to a climax. And so on. An article in a recent number of *The Review of English Studies* has even called *Henry IV* a diptych, finding the "parallel presentation of incidents" in the two parts the primary formal feature. I do not wish to deny the aesthetic satisfaction to be got from a recognition of this rhythmic repetition; yet it is only the more superficial pattern that can be thus repeated. With history and Holinshed obliging, rebellion can break out as before; yet the rebellion of Part 2, though it occupies our attention, has no significance, nor can have, for the principal characters of the play. The story of the Prince and Hotspur is over, and the King has only to die.

The one thing about history is that it does not repeat itself. Hotspur, unlike Sherlock Holmes, cannot come back to life. But there are degrees in all things; conversion has not quite the same finality as death. And besides, there is a type of hero whose adventures always can recur. Robin Hood has no sooner plundered one rich man than another comes along. It is the nature of Brer Fox, and indeed of Dr Watson, to be incapable of learning from experience. In folklore, that is to say, though not in history, you can be at the same point twice. And it seems as if Prince Hal may be sufficient of a folk-lore hero to be permitted to go again through the cycle of riot and reform. In Part 2 as in Part 1 the King laments his son's unprincely life. Yet this folk-lore hero is also a historical, and what is more to the point, a dramatic personage, and it is not tolerable that the victor of Shrewsbury should do as critics sometimes say he does, relapse into his former wildness and then reform again. The Prince cannot come into Part 2 unreclaimed without destroying the dramatic effect of Part 1. Yet if Part 2 is not to forgo its own dramatic effect, and especially its splendid last-act peripeteia, it requires a prince who is unreclaimed. This is Part 2's dilemma, and the way that it takes out of it is a bold one. When the King on his deathbed exclaims against the Prince's "headstrong riot", he has not forgotten that at Shrewsbury he congratulated the Prince on his redemption. He has not forgotten it for the simple reason that it has never taken place. The only man at court who believes in the Prince's reformation, the Earl of Warwick, believes that it will happen, not that it has happened already. Even as we watch the hero repeating his folk-lore cycle, we are positively instructed that he has not been here before:

The tide of blood in me
Hath proudly flow'd in vanity till now.

In the two parts of *Henry IV* there are not two princely reformations but two versions of a single reformation. And they are mutually exclusive. Though Part 2 frequently recalls and sometimes depends on what has happened in Part 1, it also denies that Part 1 exists. Accordingly the ideal spectator of either part must not cry with Shakespeare's Lucio, "I know what I know." He must sometimes remember what he knows and sometimes be content to forget it. This, however, is a requirement made in some degree by any work of fiction, or as they used to call it, feigning. And the feat is not a difficult one for those accustomed to grant the poet's demand for "that willing suspension of disbelief . . . which constitutes poetic faith".

Henry IV, then, is both one play and two. Part 1 begins an action which it finds it has not scope for but which Part 2 rounds off. But with one half of the action already concluded in Part 1, there is danger of a gap in Part 2. To stop the gap Part 2 expands the unfinished story of Falstaff and reduplicates what is already finished in the story of the Prince. The two parts are complementary, they are also independent and even incompatible. What they are, with their various formal anomalies, I suppose them to have become through what Johnson termed "the necessity of exhibition". Though it would be dangerous to dispute Coleridge's view that a work of art must "contain in itself the reason why it is so", that its form must proceed from within,[6] yet even works of art, like other of man's productions, must submit to the bondage of the finite. Even the unwieldy novels of the Victorians, as recent criticism has been showing, obey the demands of their allotted three volumes of space; and the dramatic masterpieces of any age * * * must acknowledge the dimensions of time. * * *

PAUL YACHNIN†

History, Theatricality, and the "Structural Problem" in the *Henry IV* Plays

The question of whether Shakespeare's *Henry IV* plays constitute one ten-act play or two separate plays of five acts each is one of those embarrassments literary criticism has brought on itself by its investment in the notion of organic form.[1] The fact that the two plays were never performed together in Shakespeare's time should have constituted definitive evidence against the view that the two plays are in fact one play with two parts—but it has not, and the

6. This is a synthesis of several passages in Coleridge. The words in quotation marks are said of whatever can give permanent pleasure; but the context shows Coleridge to be thinking of literary composition [author's note]. See *Biographia Literaria*, ed. J. Shawcross, 2 vols. (London, 1817), II, 9. Also relevant are "On Poesy or Art," *ibid.*, II, p. 262; and *Coleridge's Shakespearean Criticism*, ed. T. M. Raysor, 2 vols. (London, 1930), I, 223–24.

† Paul Yachnin, "History, Theatricality, and the 'Structural Problem' in the *Henry IV* Plays," *Philological Quarterly* 70 (1991): 163–79. Reprinted by permission of the author.

1. I will refer to what are normally called "*1 & 2 Henry IV*" as "the *Henry IV* plays" throughout this essay. My designation reflects a theatrical rather than a literary emphasis, and is in conformity with the practice of designating the first *Henry IV* play in the quarto editions, whereas the received "unifying" designation derives from the single quarto edition of the second play and from the First Folio, which, as Leah S. Marcus has recently argued (in *Puzzling Shakespeare: Local Reading and its Discontents* [U. of California Press, 1988], pp. 2–32), itself marks the inception of the movement to turn Shakespeare into a stable iconic figure, to transform (according to Marcus, p. 26) "the playtexts from records of performance to a form of literature in its own right, part of the realm called Art." A related case is *Tamburlaine*, where the second play's prologue explicitly states that the playwright wrote the second play in response to the success of the first, but where the title page of the first edition (1590) unifies the two plays as one work "divided into two Tragicall Discourses, as they were sundrie times shewed upon Stages in the Citie of London."

view is still current.[2] Indeed, the entire controversy concerning the relationship of the plays—on both sides of the issue—has arisen from what I believe is the mistaken attempt to force the idea of aesthetic unity upon the genre of Shakespeare's Histories. In this essay, therefore, I want to argue that the "structural problem in *Henry IV*" lies not in the plays themselves, but rather in the "structural" approach which has both created the problem and has gone on to produce a range of correspondingly problematic solutions. I want to suggest that the seeming puzzle of the two *Henry IV* plays can be solved merely by replacing the term "structure" with the term "sequence." Moreover, as I shall argue, this rethinking of the *Henry IV* plays in terms of sequence rather than structure allows us to see how the two plays develop Shakespeare's critique of Renaissance historiography, and enact the revisionist, open-ended nature of historical change which provides one of their two central thematic interests (the other being the operations of political power).

Of course, there is no novelty in referring to the second *Henry IV* play as the "sequel" to the first: Dr. Johnson called the second play a "sequel," as has Sherman H. Hawkins (and both Johnson and Hawkins hold that the two *Henry IV* plays are one play).[3] However, neither of these critics develops the idea of sequence into an interpretive approach. On the contrary, most, if not all, critics assume that the *Henry IV* plays constitute either one or two *literary* texts, that the meaning of a literary text subsists outside the movement of time, and that literary meaning is, by its nature, structural and synchronic; whereas if one takes seriously the theatrical idea of sequence, then one will assume that meaning is produced in time, that therefore meaning is either cumulative or revisionist, and, specifically, that the meaning of the *Henry IV* plays is changeable as well as contingent upon one's temporal position with respect to the sequence.

The very terms of the question of the "structural problem in *Henry IV*" point to a kind of thinking at odds with the emphases

2. Of course, my point that the two *Henry IV* plays were never presented in a single performance is unexceptional. In addition, see Mary Thomas Crane, "The Shakespearean Tetralogy," *SQ* 36 (1985): 282–99, for an analysis of Elizabethan multiple-part drama which concludes that there is little evidence for the consecutive performance, on successive days, of the *Henry IV* plays. For a brief account of the "structural" controversy up to 1983 see Dennis H. Burden, "Shakespeare's History Plays: 1952–1983," *Shakespeare Survey* 38 (1985): 13–14. Recent studies which depend upon a structural account of the relationship between the two plays include Catherine M. Shaw, "The Tragic Substructure of the *Henry IV* Plays," *Shakespeare Survey* 38 (1985): 61–67; and Robert B. Bennett, "Four Stages of Time: The Shape of History in Shakespeare's Second Tetralogy," *Shakespeare Studies* 19 (1987): 61–85 (Bennett's study depends upon the structural coherence of all four plays from *Richard II* to *Henry V*).
3. Samuel Johnson, *Selections from Johnson on Shakespeare*, ed. Bertrand H. Bronson and Jean M. O'Meara (Yale U. Press, 1986), 178; Sherman H. Hawkins, "*Henry IV*: The Structural Problem Revisited," *SQ* 33 (1982): 282.

of theatricality. The central question about the relationship between the two plays, in Harold Jenkins's formulation, has been: "is *Henry IV* one play or two?"[4] The question can be elaborated—as Jenkins recognizes (3)—in metaphysical terms: is *Henry IV* one unity or two, one "structure" of stable meanings or two distinct "structures"? It is easy to see that the "structural problem in *Henry IV*" is a consequence of the desire to render Shakespeare's meaning full, stable, and permanent, since interpretive stability depends upon the construction of a unified text in which all meaningful relations between parts will be fully present "all at once." Such a network of synchronically related meanings can be achieved only in terms of an interpretive model which excludes change as a condition of the text. In contrast, the interpretive model I will apply to the *Henry IV* plays *includes* change as the central condition of the production of meaning. From this point of view, meaning is never stable or full, but rather is constantly changing and revising itself. This model dissolves rather than resolves the "structural problem in *Henry IV*." Since, as I shall argue, neither play is a structure, there is no logical dilemma attendant upon their relationship—the second play merely follows the first, in basically the same way as scene follows scene within the individual plays.

The eighteenth century was the first great age of Shakespeare editing (as opposed to Shakespeare performance), and it was, not surprisingly, in the context of this shift from theater to text that the "structural problem" first appeared.[5] John Upton was the first to raise the relationship between the *Henry IV* plays as a problem in need of a solution. In his *Critical Observations on Shakespeare* (1746), Upton argued that both the *Henry IV* plays had what Aristotle demanded of a unified work—a beginning, a middle, and an ending—that each was therefore an independent play, and that it was an error to speak of a first and second part.[6] Dr. Johnson responded to this claim by insisting that the "two plays will appear to every reader, who shall peruse them without ambition of critical discoveries, to be so connected that the second is merely a sequel to the first; to be two only because they are too long to be one."[7] In spite of Johnson's use of the word "sequel," it is clear that both his response and the Upton's original claim depend upon seeing the *Henry IV* plays as literature rather than as performance-texts (so

4. Harold Jenkins, *The Structural Problem in Shakespeare's* Henry the Fourth (London: Methuen, 1956), 2.
5. For a stimulating discussion of the eighteenth-century redefinition of Shakespeare as a literary artist (as opposed to a player and playwright), see Gary Taylor, *Reinventing Shakespeare: A Cultural History from the Restoration to the Present* (New York: Weidenfeld and Nicolson, 1989), 52–99.
6. See *Henry the Fourth, Part I*, ed. S. B. Hemingway, New Variorum (Philadelphia and London: J. B. Lippincott, 1936), 11, 41–42, 70–71.
7. *Johnson on Shakespeare*, 178.

Johnson assumes that the plays are for readers rather than for audiences). This local dispute is in turn an effect of the larger eighteenth-century cultural project which sought to recuperate the player Shakespeare as an icon of conservative values by arresting and hypostatizing the traffic of the stage. The controversy that, since the eighteenth century, has swirled intermittently around the *Henry IV* plays has obscured the overall purpose, shared on both sides, of rescuing Shakespeare from the instability and temporality of theatricality. While the structural approach has changed Shakespeare's plays from their original nature as theatrical events, and while it has worked efficiently in terms of the critical privileging of synchronic over diachronic elements in the Comedies and Tragedies, it has nonetheless broken down with respect to the *Henry IV* plays since time-charged theatricality is crucial to those plays' production of meaning.

None of the attempts to impose structure upon the *Henry IV* plays has been entirely successful. Sherman Hawkins's recent argument for seeing the plays as a single unified structure succeeds in rebutting many points of Jenkins's influential *Structural Problem in Shakespeare's* Henry the Fourth; but fails, we shall see, to validate its own position. Moreover, in spite of Hawkins' strictures, Jenkins's argument—of all the attempts to solve the "structural problem"—still comes closest to being entirely satisfactory, although only by describing the relationship between the two plays in terms of a paradox—that "*Henry IV* . . . is both one play and two. . . . The two parts are complementary, they are also independent and even incompatible" (26). Further, if Jenkins's paradox is the right answer to the structural problem (and it has won wide acceptance),[8] then it seems to follow that the structural approach to the *Henry IV* plays—since it produces a paradoxical conclusion—must itself be inherently illogical. It would even suggest that Jenkins's argument could be seen as a *reductio ad absurdum* which demonstrates the inadequacy of the structural approach.

Sherman Hawkins's argument against Jenkins represents the most sustained attempt to prove the single-play theory. If Hawkins's argument fails (as I think it does), it is probably not the fault of the advocate, but rather the necessary consequence of attempting to apply structural terms to material whose meaning is produced temporally and sequentially.

Following the general views of Dr. Johnson, Dover Wilson, and E. M. W. Tillyard, Hawkins argues that "Part 1" looks ahead to, and is incomplete without, "Part 2," and that the "double conversion" of Prince

8. See, for example, James L. Calderwood, *Metadrama in Shakespeare's Henriad:* Richard II *to* Henry V (U. of California Press, 1979), 114; A. R. Humphreys, "Introduction," *King Henry IV, Part II*, Arden Shakespeare (London: Methuen, 1966), xxvi.

Hal does not contradict the single-play theory.[9] According to Hawkins, the ending of the first play, as well as the presence of the Archbishop of York within the play, anticipates and necessitates the second:

> Part I ends in a battle that establishes the house of Lancaster as the present and probably future victor in the civil war. But again triumph is blended with precaution: Northumberland and the Archbishop are "busily in arms" and Westmoreland and Lancaster must set off to meet then with "dearest speed."
>
> Rebellion in this land shall lose his sway,
> Meeting the check of such another day;
> And since this business so far is done,
> Let us not leave till all our own be won.
> (5.5.41–44)
>
> Could Shakespeare say more plainly that while Hotspur's business is done, he does not mean to leave his story yet? Shrewsbury is not its ending end: the King, the Archbishop, and the audience all look forward to "such another day" (pp. 280–81).

It is true that the ending of the first play looks ahead to the future. However, the first play's anticipations of the second do not constitute proof that the two are one work; rather, the point is that such cues as the King's "such another day" or the presence of the Archbishop in act 4, scene 4 will strike us as anticipatory of a sequel only when they are in fact fulfilled by a sequel.[1] As every storyteller knows, narrative is written backwards as well as forwards: links with earlier parts in the story are "discovered" as later parts are invented, unity is seldom planned out from the beginning (on the contrary, it is normally a product of the ending); more to the point, sequels (or continuations) are usually produced by opening up points of entry in the already written story, and sequels always change the meanings of the points of entry they create in the original. Therefore the ending of the first play means one thing in itself, and another from the viewpoint of its sequel; and the same is true of Hal's soliloquy in part 1, act 1, scene 1, of Falstaff's references, in the same scene, to Hal's eventual accession to the throne, and of the appearance of the Archbishop in act 4, scene 4.[2]

9. See John Dover Wilson, "Introduction," *The First Part of King Henry IV*, New Cambridge Shakespeare (Cambridge U. Press, 1946), vii–xiii; E. M. W. Tillyard, *Shakespeare's History Plays* (1944; rpt. Harmondsworth: Peregrine, 1964), 264–68.
1. This point does not apply to the Epilogue of the second play, since it explicitly promises a sequel.
2. Cf. Hawkins, 285–86. These two basic points—that a sequel changes the meaning of the play it follows; and that it creates, in the play it follows, the signposts which then are seen to anticipate it—can be illustrated by reference either to the revisionist relationship between *The Return of the Jedi* and *Star Wars*, or to the typological relationship between the New and Old Testaments.

If, as Hawkins wants to argue, the *Henry IV* plays constitute a unified two-part play, then he must explain the fact that Hal redeems himself in the first play, but then must redeem himself again in the second. Hawkins argues that the two conversions are "stages in a single process" on the basis of a series of claims about the psychological realism of the portrayal of Hal, the nature of Hal's conversation, the relationship between Hal and Henry, and the nature of history in the plays. However, none of these can substantiate the central claim that Hal's double conversion is a single process, since neither the King nor Worcester seems to think that Hal's delinquency in the second play is anything other than a continuous and uninterrupted state of lawlessness (*2H4* 4.4.54–80; 4.5.92–137); they do not seem to think Hal has relapsed after having been converted because neither seems able to remember that Hal has already redeemed himself in the first play. Finally, Hawkins seems unable to account for this crucial discontinuity between the plays he wishes to see as an unified structure.

Once we dispense with the desire to render Shakespeare's meaning stable and "structured," and replace the term "structure" with the term "sequence," the relationship between the two plays can be seen to be straightforward and coherent. Hal's interview with his father in the first play provides an illustration. For most critics, this scene, containing Hal's promise to vanquish Hotspur or to die trying, has seemed decisive, a moment around which Hal's story is organized and in whose terms it can be hypostatized as a structure of chivalric reformation.[3] Jenkins calls the scene a "nodal point": "when the King rebukes his son, the Prince replies, 'I will redeem all this . . .'; in the fifth act he fulfils this vow at Shrewsbury, as is signalized by the King's admission that the Prince has 'redeem'd his lost opinion.' . . . The curve of the plot could hardly be more firmly or more symmetrically drawn" (9).

It is true that, at the moment we witness Hal's interview with his father, we are likely to agree that the scene is crucial. More than that, we are likely to feel that Hal's promise to his father is the emotional fulfillment of the promise he made himself to "redeem all this" in soliloquy in act 1, scene 2, and (if we are thinking of the play in terms of structure) that the promise to his father links up with the earlier soliloquy and with the upcoming victory at Shrewsbury in order to provide the dramatic action with a solid interpretive framework. However, what this structural analysis overlooks is not merely that Hal returns to the tavern in act 3, scene 3 (a minor derogation which in any case is easily assimilated into the proposed

3. See, for example, Derek Traversi, *Shakespeare from* Richard II *to* Henry V (Stanford U. Press, 1957), 84; John W. Blanpied, *Time and the Artist in Shakespeare's English Histories* (U. of Delaware Press, 1983), 155–64.

pattern), but more importantly that Hal revises the meaning of the interview with his father in such a way as to destabilize it and to disable it as the "nodal point" in the proposed pattern of reformation. "O, my sweet beef," Hal says to Falstaff after the apparently decisive interview with his father, "I must still be good angel to thee.—The money is paid back again. . . . I am good friends with my father and may do any thing" (*1H4* 3.3.158–61).[4]

Hal's revisionist glance backwards to his interview with his father forces a revaluation of that apparently decisive turning-point in terms of Hal's apparent desire to persist in delinquency. Further, Hal's conduct at Shrewsbury in turn invites a revision of his revision of his interview with his father, so that Hal's remark to Falstaff can then be seen to be inconsequential, and his promise to his father can be restored—but now only provisionally—to its former authenticity. Revisionism, as I have said, the way the meaning of actions and words is changed and destabilized by subsequent actions and words, constitutes the central condition of the production of meaning in the plays. The first speech of the first play breaks between Henry's expression, on the one hand, of his intention immediately to mount a crusade ("No more the thirsty entrance of this soil / Shall daub her lips with her own children's blood, / . . . those opposed eyes, / Which . . . Did lately meet in the intestine shock / . . . Shall now . . . March all one way" [1.1.5–15]) and his statement, on the other, that a crusade is out of the question at this time: "But this our purpose now is twelve months old, / And bootless 'tis to tell you we will go; / Therefor we meet not now" (1.1.28–30). The second part of the speech revises the first part as largely Henry's actorly performance of zeal rather than as his authentic expression of zeal. In this respect, of course, the revisionism of the play's production of meaning persistently reveals the actorly nature of characters' actions and words, in the sense that the characters are shown, not merely performing historically significant actions and speaking historically significant words, but rather that actions and words constitute the characters' attempts to crystallize their own meanings in the face of the fluidity of meaning. That is, that which is defined as authentic is constitutive of its own meaning; it may be interpreted subsequently, but there will remain in the authentic action itself a core of meaning which is stable by virtue of being prior to interpretation.[5] On the other hand, an actorly performance of an action is already an interpretation; conse-

4. All quotations are from A. R. Humphreys's Arden editions, *King Henry IV, Part I* (London: Methuen, 1961) and *King Henry IV, Part II* (London: Methuen, 1967).

5. The conversion of the Prince in *Famous Victories* provides an excellent example of an authentic action which retains a stable core of meaning. The ideological difference between the *Famous Victories* Prince and Shakespeare's Hal consists in the fact that the self in Shakespeare (Hal himself) remains radically interiorized and maintains its hege-

quently, a performance of an action has no stable core of meaning. In this view, Hal's soliloquy, "I know you all," constitutes Hal's attempt to predetermine the meaning of his own history. In the course of the two plays, Hal's initial construction of his history—his self-construction—is revised several times, repudiated and confirmed by turns; however, once revealed to be not a speech from the heart, but rather the performance of a speech from the heart, the soliloquy remains actorly, or theatrical, and thus radically changeable in meaning rather than authentic and permanent.[6] The revisionism attendant upon the dramatic movement thus disables Hal's soliloquy from standing as a reference point which might be construed as stable by virtue of its externality to Hal's self-conscious construction of his history.

The relationship between the two *Henry IV* plays is also revisionist in that the second play constitutes a critique—even an undoing—of the first. The central problem in the relationship between the two plays, as we have seen, consists in the fact that Hal must redeem himself twice. Jenkins claims to see no problem in this repeated pattern. He bases his explanation of Hal's double conversion on his idea that Shakespeare intended to write only one play, but then found he had sufficient material for two.[7] However, according to Jenkins, the sequel also required an unreclaimed prince in order to achieve the desired dramatic effect: "The Prince cannot come into Part 2 unreclaimed without destroying the dramatic effect of Part 1. Yet if Part 2 is not to forego its own dramatic effect . . . it requires a prince who is unreclaimed. This is Part 2's dilemma, and the way it takes out of it is a bold one. When the King on his deathbed exclaims against the Prince's 'headstrong riot,' he has not forgotten that at Shrewsbury he congratulated the Prince on his redemption. He has not forgotten it for the simple reason that it has never taken place. . . . Accordingly the ideal spectator of either part must . . . sometimes remember what he knows and sometimes be content to forget it" (25–26).

As Sherman Hawkins has remarked, it is incredible to suppose that Shakespeare expected his audience to forget the main action of a play in that play's immediate sequel (300). Indeed, far from expecting us to forget Hal's first reformation, Shakespeare seems to want us to remember it: the first scene of the second play provides a lengthy account of Shrewsbury, and Poins recalls Hal's reforma-

---

mony over action and expression whereas action and expression in the earlier play are authentic by virtue of their power to determine character.

6. For a related discussion of the hero as provisionally self-constructed, see Mikhail Bakhtin, *Problems of Dostoevsky's Poetics*, ed. and trans. Caryl Emerson, Theory and History of Literature, 8 (U. of Minnesota Press, 1984), 47–77, 101–2, passim.
7. Hawkins, 282–84, decisively rebuts Jenkins' argument that Shakespeare wrote two *Henry IV* plays because he had too much material for one.

tion the first time Hal is onstage in the second play (Hawkins, 294).

What, then, is the nature of the relationship between Hal's reformation in the first play and the apparent requirement that he reform again in the second? I suggest that the second play relates to the first in basically the same way as the second part of Henry's "pilgrimage" speech relates to its first part, or as Hal's radically destabilizing comment ("I am good friends with my father and may do anything") relates to the interview with his father. That is, Hal's unreclaimed state in the second play contradicts the apparent reclamation in the first. In the light of this contradiction, Hal's actions at Shrewsbury are recast as an actorly performance of a reformation rather than a reformation itself; the meaning of Hal's actions is not then constituted in itself as a stable and permanent point in a changeless text, but rather is destabilized and made subject to the revisionist interpretations that come with the future.

The revision of Shrewsbury engineered by the second play brings into different focus Hal's rescue of his father. Whereas from the point of view of the first play, the moment of rescue authenticates the reconciliation between father and son, from the viewpoint of the sequel, the moment is burdened by continued mutual distrust and resentment—the father's praise is grudging and the son's response is uncomfortably defensive:[8]

> *King.* Thou has redeem'd thy lost opinion,
> And show'd thou mak'st some tender of my life,
> In this fair rescue thou has brought to me.
> *Prince.* O God, they did me too much injury
> That ever said I hearken'd for your death.
> If it were so, I might have let alone
> The insulting hand of Douglas over you,
> Which would have been as speedy in your end
> As all the poisonous options in the world,
> And sav'd the treacherous labour of your son.
> (*1H4* 5.4.47–56)

The revisionist relationship between the two plays explains why the first play is complete in itself until it is brought into juxtaposition with the second; the second play, that is, undoes the first, revises its meaning in order to appropriate it to its own darker view of political life.[9] The difference between the revisionist relationship

8. For readings which interpret the Shrewsbury reconciliation between Hal and Henry as strained and ironic in its immediate context, see Robert Ornstein, *A Kingdom for a Stage: The Achievement of Shakespeare's History Plays* (Harvard U. Press, 1972), 150–51; and Hawkins, 293–94. Of course, I would agree that this reading is valid, but only from the revisionist perspective of the second play.

9. Anthony B. Dawson, *Watching Shakespeare: A Playgoer's Guide* (London: Macmillan, 1988), 88–89, discusses the ways in which the two plays together are different from the first on its own.

between the plays and the revisionist movement within each of the plays consists, then, only in the fact that the latter is necessary and inescapable whereas the former is optional—was optional initially for the playwright himself, and has been subsequently for Shakespeare's audiences.

In the *Henry IV* plays, Shakespeare's idea of history is implicit in both the revisionist dramatic movement and the ironic undercutting of the characters' historiographical assumptions. Shakespeare's version of history as revisionist and open-ended (and therefore not providentialist)[1] seems to be a product of his sceptical engagement with conflicting Renaissance models of history. In the broadest terms, these historiographical models are divisible according to two patterns (linear and cyclical) and two modalities (providentialist and humanist). (While it is not always the case, there is nonetheless a strong tendency for linear models of history to be providentialist and cyclical models to be humanist.)[2] Thus Shakespeare had available to him a wide variety of combinations, all sharing the basic assumption that history is explicable in terms of a particular pattern and a particular modality.[3]

It should also be noted that while the *Henry IV* plays do critique the idea of history as patterned and hence as grounded in the transhistorical, Shakespeare does not develop an exclusively materialist account of history, since—in spite of their tendency to ascribe the causes of historical change to the level of nature—the plays do preserve an atmosphere of the uncanny. The dramatic irony of Henry IV's death in a room called "Jerusalem" in fulfillment of the prophecy that he would die in Jerusalem or the persuasive, but unauthoritative, "fatefulness" of Hal's meeting-up with Hotspur at Shrewsbury both suggest the persistent operation of the uncanny in spite of Shakespeare's generally sceptical representations of history.

Shakespeare was able to find the two principal Renaissance patternings of history in two of his favorite authors—Holinshed and Plutarch. In spite of his intermittent expressions of scepticism, Holinshed's construction of history as a linear causative chain represents merely a post-Reformation softening, rather than a repudiation, of Augustinian apocalyptic history, an historiographical model given a harder and more political turn by Reformation

1. For a persuasive critique of the providentialist view of the *Henry IV* plays, see H. A. Kelly, *Divine Providence in the England of Shakespeare's Histories* (Harvard U. Press, 1970), 109–60; for a good discussion of both the question of Shakespeare's providentialism and the open-endedness of history in Shakespeare, see David Scott Kastan, *Shakespeare and the Shapes of Time* (London: Macmillan, 1982), 9–33.
2. See Tom F. Driver, *The Sense of History in Greek and Shakespearean Drama* (Columbia U. Press, 1960), 19–66, for an extensive discussion of these historiographical models.
3. For a brief account of the various linear and cyclical models of time which were available to Renaissance historiography, see Bennett, "Four Stages of Time," 61–67.

polemicists such as John Bale and John Foxe.[4] Holinshed's linear historiography remains basically providentialist in conception (especially in the 1587 second edition which was used by Shakespeare), and therefore progressivist, figuring the "great perplexitie and little pleasure" of Henry IV's reign as the necessary consequence of the usurpation of Richard II and as the precondition of Henry V's victorious reign, all of which events are seen in turn as contributing to the accession of the Tudors.[5] In contrast, North's translation of Amyot's translation of Plutarch (which Shakespeare was getting to know when writing *Julius Caesar*, c. 1599)[6] emphasizes the basic repetitiveness of history, the cyclical structuring of time which underlies Plutarch's paralleling of famous Greeks and Romans, and which allows Amyot's conventional recommendation of the educational value of history so conceived—"it is a certain rule and instruction, which by examples past, teacheth us to judge of things present, and to foresee things to come: so as we may know what to like of, and what to follow, what to mislike, and what to eschew."[7] Further, Plutarch's late classical model of cyclical history was renewed in Renaissance humanist versions of historical recurrence such as that of Machiavelli.[8]

The conventional Christian response to the apparent circularity of history (and, implicitly, to the model of history as cyclical) was to assimilate repetition into the overarching linearity of Providence. Thus the Tudor historians routinely dovetail the retributive cycles following upon the usurpation of Richard II with the overall linear movement towards the accession of Henry VII, an ideological maneuver which may be epitomized by Thomas Browne's statement that the operations of Fortune constitute in fact "that serpentine and crooked line [whereby God] draws those actions that his wisdom intends in a more unknown and secret way."[9] In contrast, Shakespeare's history is openended because Shakespeare conflates, and thereby cancels, the two principal Renaissance patternings of

4. For an account of Holinshed's historiography, see F. J. Levy, *Tudor Historical Thought* (San Marino: Huntington Library, 1967), 182–86.
5. For the differences between the 1577/78 and 1587 editions of Holinshed with respect to their providentialism, see Kelly, *Divine Providence*, 138–60.
6. Shakespeare seems to be sending up Plutarch's historiographical model in Fluellen's comparison of Alexander and King Henry. See "Introduction," *Shakespeare's Plutarch*, ed. T. J. B. Spencer (Harmondsworth: Penguin, 1964), 11–12.
7. *Plutarch's Lives Englished by Sir Thomas North*, 10 vols. (1579; rpt. London: Dent, 1908), 1: 8–9. For an account of the relationship between linear and providentialist history on the one hand and cyclical and (what he calls) "exemplary" history on the other, see Kastan, 12–23.
8. On Machaivelli's construction of history as recurrent, see G. W. Trompf, *The Idea of Historical Recurrence in Western Thought: From Antiquity to the Reformation* (U. of California Press, 1979), 250–312.
9. Quoted in Herschel Baker, *The Race of Time: Three Lectures on Renaissance Historiography* (U. of Toronto Press, 1967), 65. Also see Baker's brief discussion of the Christian appropriation of the cyclical model of history, 59–66.

history—history as linear and progressive (or regressive); history as cyclical and repetitive—so that we simply cannot know where we are or even what kind of "where" we are in. In other words, the crowning of Henry IV might feel like a moment of real progress, but might merely be a step in a cyclical movement which will return us to where we have already been—civil disharmony and feuding over the throne. On the other hand, the delinquency of Hal might seem a mere repetition of Richard II's "skipping" trespasses (*1H4* 3.2.60–128), but might turn out to be a step in a progress towards the recuperation of royal authority (a recuperation which itself might be assimilated into a cycle of national expansion and senescence). The revisionist nature of historical change has the effect of persistently altering the basic shape of history, and so depriving history of basic shape altogether. History's consequent failure to resolve itself into a determinate shape means, then, that the full significance of events is unknowable at any time.

In the face of the open-endedness and "unpatterning" of history, the characters in the *Henry IV* plays undertake to adapt one or the other of the basic conventional constructions of historical movement, if only to explain their own meanings to themselves. Hastings, Warwick, and Henry IV construct history as repetitive and cyclical; each invests cyclical history with a different modality—Hastings adopts a secularized retributive cycle (*2H4*, 4.2.44–49), Warwick a pragmatic analysis of personality types (past behavior determines future behavior [*2H4* 3.1.80–92]), and Henry a fatalistic nihilism (*1H4* 3.2.93–128; *2H4* 3.1.45–65). In each case, the historiographical model is revealed as a rationalizing attempt to shape time by the measure of either the character's sense of defeat (Hastings and Henry) or the character's sense of present political requirements (Warwick needs to bolster the King's confidence); and in all cases the model fails to provide an adequate account of events.

In repudiation of Hastings's prophecy of ongoing civil war "Whiles England shall have generation" (*2H4* 4.2.49) is the audience's plain awareness that Gaultree Forest did not spawn such an endless civil war and Prince John's assertion of the open-endedness of history and the impenetrable depth of the future: "You are too shallow, Hastings, much too shallow, / To sound the bottom of the after-times" (*2H4* 4.2.50–51). In Henry's despairing speech in the middle of the second play (3.1.45–79), "the revolution of the times" acquires its root meaning of a "turning of the times," in telling opposition to Henry's earlier view (in *Richard II*) of his own revolutionary role in history, then conceived as linear, progressive, and avowedly providential. Henry's fatalistic and inadequate construction of history in the second *Henry IV* play, and in his interview with Hal in the first play, implies a critique of history (as record of events) as fundamentally a misdirected and covert legitimation of the present.[1] In this sense, the past is revealed to be a product of the present, a history (as record of events) as well as history (as the events themselves) is shown to be constructed in terms of revisionism. Moreover, as I have already suggested, history as record and history as the events themselves are tightly linked in the *Henry IV* plays, for the reason that interpretation begins with and is integral to the event. Finally, Warwick's account of history as recurrent by virtue of the predictability of human behavior remains unable to explain or to predict the change which takes place when Hal becomes Henry V.[2]

While, however, all constructions of history as cyclical are weakened by the bad motives of their advocates and vitiated by the actual unpredictability of events, all attempts to conceive history as linear—or to act as if history were linear—are equally undermined by the second play's patterned duplication of scenes from the first play, an effect which is especially prominent in the early scenes of the second play.[3] For example, the conspirators in *2 Henry IV*, act 1, scene 3 construct their role as political revolutionaries in terms of linear and progressive history: "in this great work," Lord Bardolph says, "Which is almost to pluck a kingdom down / And set another up" (48–50). However, while the conspirators believe they are making progress, it is difficult for us to escape the impression that they are merely repeating the previous conspiracy between Hotspur, Northumberland, and Worcester, which took place at the same point in the previous play. The duplication of scenes, then, has the effect of making the characters in the second play appear to be merely time's fools, and, by virtue of their seemingly inevitable repetitions of the past, of repudiating their construction of history as linear and progressive. The "unpatterning" of history within the world of the plays, then, parallels the thwarting of structure in the plays themselves; the *Henry IV* plays thus recast both history and

1. In *1H4* 3.2, Henry draws a parallel between Hal and Richard II which assumes a cyclical view of history. Henry's reasons for seeing history in this way are far from disinterested: he seems to desire a repetition of the original regicide, this time with Hal as Richard and Hotspur as Henry Bolingbroke, as expiation for his own crime. However, Hal is not like Richard for a number of reasons, the most immediate being that Hal is not king, that even if he were, he would not have Richard's *de jure* claim to the crown, and that Hal will not be overthrown.
2. Bennett, 74, has noted that while Warwick predicts Hal's transformation, he does not in fact believe his own prediction.
3. Needless to say, the plays do not resolve into a "diptych" structure (as G. K. Hunter has argued, "*Henry IV* and the Elizabethan Two-Part Play," *English Studies*, n.s. 5 [1954]: 236–48), for the reason that the duplications serve to contradict a linear account of history and so to problematize rather than to validate the attempt to structure history. Further, as Hawkins has pointed out (298), the pattern of duplication dwindles and disappears in the later acts of the second play.

literature in terms of the mind's provisional attempts to order the unstructured movement of time.

Finally, the unpatterning of history in the *Henry IV* plays, achieved by conflating and cancelling the two principal models of history, is folded into Shakespeare's sceptical representation of Hal's construction of his own history. In terms of the first play on its own, Hal's history seems linear: in his interview with his father, Hal acknowledges the open-endedness and unpredictability of time; and at the moment of victory over Hotspur, he seems the beneficiary of a quasi-providential "destiny" to which he has submitted his will. On the other hand, Hal, from the viewpoint of the end of the second play, seems merely to have circled around to where he began (in his soliloquy in *1H4* 1.2), so that Hal's conversion—at the very moment of its fulfillment—is brought under a sceptical analysis which is empowered to see Hal's history as cyclical rather than as linear (so that the last scene constitutes merely the *public* rejection of the man whom Hal has, from the outset, already secretly cast off), as occasioned by Hal's manipulative will to power rather than by "destiny," and, consequently, as no conversion at all. Or not. That is, Hal's story can be seen as consistently linear and providential in spite of the availability of a sceptical viewpoint, since the second play empowers, but does not authorize, scepticism. Further, at this moment in the second play and in terms of the story of Hal (who is both the thematic focal point and, in Bakhtinian terms, a "semantic position" by virtue of his self-conscious production of his own meaning), questions about the shape of history merge with questions about the operations of political power, and in both cases all possible answers are revealed to be the always provisional and partial (in both senses) positions produced by the mind in the face of the fluidity of meaning and in its attempts to wrest the Real from the merely actual—by Hal's mind and by the minds of the individual members of the audience with respect to Hal. In this regard, the nature of history becomes, in a full sense, a matter of interpretation.

In most of his plays, Shakespeare seems to be developing what I have characterized elsewhere as a Sidneian mystification of literary discourse.[4] In the *Apology for Poetry*, Philip Sidney set the poet above the historian by virtue of the poet's freedom from the constraints of Nature. Sidney crystallized an ideology of literature as opposed to historical and other mundane discourses, as separate, self-enclosed, and expressive of permanent Truth (in contrast to history's mere facticity) and—most importantly—as removed from the flow of time by virtue of poetry's connection with the transcen-

4. "The Powerless Theater," *English Literary Renaissance* 21.1 (1991): 49–74.

dent, and hence as productive of stable and unified meaning. To a large degree, Shakespeare shared Sidney's ideology of literary discourse. However, as I would like to suggest, in Shakespeare's time, and particularly in Shakespeare's theatrical milieu, the idea that a theatrical performance might be seen as both unified and separate from the world must have seemed *avant-garde* if not downright presumptuous. In this view, then, the "structural problem in *Henry IV*" is a consequence of the interpretation of the *Henry IV* plays in terms of a Sidneian theory of poetry; and that kind of interpretation has generated confusion, I suggest, because the *Henry IV* plays represent Shakespeare's critique of Sidney's, and his own, attempts to remove dramatic literature from both the context of theatrical performance and the day-to-day world of time.[5]

5. This article represents a version of a paper given at the Tri-Universities Conference on Literature and History at the U. of British Columbia in 1990. I am grateful to the members of the conference for their insightful and helpful comments, especially Ed Berry, Tony Dawson, Terry Sherwood, and Kay Stockholder.

Falstaff or Oldcastle?

GARY TAYLOR

The Fortunes of Oldcastle†

All Shakespeare's plays were subjected to political censorship. Every play had to be licensed before it could be performed or published; even after that, it could get its author or actors into trouble, if objection was subsequently taken to its performance.[1] Editors recognize these facts, and can sometimes retrospectively save a writer from the censor. When a play survives in an early quarto, set from Shakespeare's own draft, we can sometimes restore material excised in the First Folio. When a Jacobean text of an Elizabethan play shows little or no sign of authorial revision, but does omit an insulting reference to the Scots, it seems reasonable enough to infer that the change was made because the sensibility of William Shakespeare had in this instance to bow to that of James Stuart.[2] We infer that the text has been censored, and we act on that inference. But in one play we can do more than 'infer' that political interference has occurred. In one case we possess abundant contemporary evidence that the text was changed, we know what Shakespeare originally wrote, what his company originally performed, and that political pressure was applied in order to force him to alter his text. Nevertheless, no editor has ever restored the original reading—despite the fact that in this case the censor's intervention makes more difference to the meaning of the play than in any other known or suspected instance.

We all know that the character called 'Falstaff' in every modern edition of *Henry IV, Part 1* was originally called 'Oldcastle'. The for-

† Gary Taylor, "The Fortunes of Oldcastle," *Shakespeare Survey* 38 (1985), 85–100. Reprinted by permission of Cambridge University Press.

1. See G. E. Bentley, *The Profession of Dramatist in Shakespeare's Time, 1590–1642* (Princeton, 1971), 145–96; and, for a more thorough survey, Janet Clare, 'Art made tongue-tied by authority: a study of the relationship between Elizabethan and Jacobean drama and authority and the effect of censorship on the plays of the period' (unpublished Ph.D. thesis, University of Birmingham, 1981).
2. See *The Merchant of Venice*, 1.2.77, where 'the Scottish Lorde' in the Quarto (B1^{v}) becomes 'the other lord' in the Folio (TLN 267).

midable textual and historical evidence for this fact is ably marshalled in S. B. Hemingway's New Variorum edition, and in A. R. Humphreys's new Arden one.[3] The text itself punningly alludes to 'My old lad of the castle' (*Part 1*, 1.2.37); the only verse line in which the character's surname appears would be metrical if a three-syllable name had originally stood in place of the two-syllable 'Falstaff' [*2H4*, 2.2.103]; a speech-prefix identifies Sir John as *'Old.'* (*Part* 2, 1.2.138). The Epilogue to *Part* 2 goes out of its way explicitly to deny that 'Falstaffe' is 'Olde-castle' (ll. 31–2)—a denial surely unnecessary unless the previous play had given audiences good reason to make just that identification. This 'internal evidence' is confirmed by extensive external evidence. Thomas Middleton (1604), Nathan Field (*c.* 1611), the anonymous author of *Wandering-Jew, Telling Fortunes to Englishmen* (*c.* 1628), George Daniel (1647), Thomas Randolph (1651), and Thomas Fuller (1655, 1662) all testify to the character's original designation as 'Oldcastle'.[4]

The most explicit deposition comes from Dr Richard James (1592–1638), friend of Ben Jonson and librarian to Sir Robert Cotton, in an autograph epistle addressed "To my Noble friend S^r henry Bourchier', and prefixed to James's own manuscript edition of Hoccleve's 'The legend and defence of ye Noble knight and Martyr Sir Jhon Oldcastel' (Bodleian Library, James MS 34; also British Library, Add. MS 33785).[5] Halliwell-Phillipps, who first printed this epistle, dated it '*c.* 1625'; it cannot be earlier than 1625, and more probably dates from *c.* 1634. In it, James refers to *Henry IV, Part 1* as 'Shakespeares first shewe of Harrie ye fift':

> A young Gentle Ladie of your acquaintance having read ye works of Shakespeare, made me this question. How Sir Jhon Falstaffe, ⌈or Fastollf as he is written in ye statute book of Maudlin Colledge in Oxford where everye daye y^t societie were bound to make memorie of his soule⌉ could be dead in ^{ec} Harrie ye fifts time and againe liue in ye time of Harrie ye sixt to be banisht for cowardize. Whereto I made answeare that this was one of those humours and mistakes for which Plato banisht all poets out of his commonwealth.

After a thumbnail biography of the historical Sir John Fastolfe, James continues

3. Hemingway (Philadelphia, 1936), pp. 447–57; Humphreys (1960), xv–xviii. Line references follow Humphreys's text.
4. Hemingway, 447–57; Humphreys, xv–xvii. * * * Neither Hemingway nor Humphreys mentions the allusion in Randolph's *Hey for Honesty*, 28; this is quoted and discussed by Alice-Lyle Scoufos, *Shakespeare's Typological Satire: A Study of the Falstaff-Oldcastle Problem* (Athens, Ohio, 1979), 38, as part of her full survey of the allusions (32–43).
5. This dedication was first noted and transcribed by J. O. Halliwell[-Phillipps] in *On the Character of Sir John Falstaff, as originally exhibited by Shakespeare in the two parts of King Henry IV* (1841), 18–20; the entire manuscript was transcribed in *The Poems Etc., of Richard James, B.D.*, ed. A. B. Grosart (1880), where the dedication occurs on 137–8. * * *

> That in Shakespeares first shewe of Harrie ye fift, ye person with which he vndertook to playe a buffone was not Falstaffe, but Sr Jhon Oldcastle, and that offence beinge worthily taken by personages descended from his ⌜title,⌝ as peradventure by manie others allso whoe ought to haue him in honourable memorie, the poet was putt to make an ignorant shifte of abusing Sr Jhon ~~Falstaffe or~~ Fastolphe, a man not inferior ⌜of⌝ Vertue though not so famous in pietie as the other, whoe gaue witneſse vnto the truth of our reformation with a constant and resolute martyrdom, vnto which he was pursued by the Priests, Bishops, Moncks, and Friers of those dayes.

Dr James not only confirms that the change was made: he tells us why, and testifies that the poet was 'putt to . . . an ignorant shifte'. James's literary and court connections make his evidence impossible to dismiss. The 'personages descended from [Oldcastle's] title' can be readily identified as Sir William Brooke, Lord Cobham, Lord Chamberlain from August 1596 to March 1597, and his son, Sir Henry Brooke; one of Sir William's daughters was married to Sir Robert Cecil. The Lord Chamberlain was of course the master of the Master of the Revels, who licensed plays; moreover, *Part 1* was almost certainly written in 1596 or early 1597, when Lord Cobham was Lord Chamberlain. Thus, the character's name was changed as the result of the intervention of a peer of the realm, member of the Privy Council, intimate friend of Lord Burghley, and father-in-law of Sir Robert Cecil.[6] These historical facts have long been appreciated; Nicholas Rowe, Shakespeare's first editor, knew of the change, and provides independent confirmation that the Cobhams were responsible for it. As Humphreys bluntly says, 'Falstaff was certainly once Oldcastle'. No one now disputes this conclusion. But no one has acted upon it either. No one has restored the name Shakespeare intended for the character, before he was forced to change it. Why not?

Editors might be inhibited by the fact that in changing 'Falstaff' back to 'Oldcastle' in *Part 1* they would 'create' an inconsistency in the canon: Prince Hal's companion, identified as 'Oldcastle' in *Part 1*, must have been firmly identified as 'Falstaff' by the time Shakespeare wrote *Henry V* and *Merry Wives*—not to mention *Part 2*. But in fact editors are also left with inconsistencies if they retain 'Falstaff'. The 'young Gentle Ladie' who accosted Dr James was bewildered by one such inconsistency, 350 years ago: the reappearance, in *Henry VI*, of the character who apparently died in *Henry V*.[7] Everyone recognizes that the Sir John of the *Merry Wives*

6. The most thorough account of the Elizabethan Cobhams is the late David McKeen's unpublished doctoral dissertation, '"A Memory of Honour": A study of the House of Cobham of Kent in the Reign of Elizabeth I' (University of Birmingham, 1966).
7. George Walton Williams argues—in 'Fastolf or Falstaff', *English Literary Renaissance*,

differs from his counterpart in other plays; the character in *Henry V* does not fulfil the role promised by the Epilogue to *Part 2*; almost all critics since A. C. Bradley have accepted that there are substantial differences in the character even between the two parts of *Henry IV*.[8] Such inconsistencies bother us less if we respond to *Henry IV, Part 1* and its successors not as fragments of a 'tetralogy' but as whole, individual plays, written over the course of several years and never in Shakespeare's lifetime performed—so far as we know—as a cycle.

As for the fictive unity of the character himself, the old reprobate who appears in three different plays, that can be recognized by using the designation 'Sir John' for all his speech-prefixes in *Part 1*, *Part 2*, and *Merry Wives*. In fact, 'Sir John' is how the dialogue most often identifies him: the linked title and Christian name occur on their own 120 times in the four plays, whereas the surname on its own is used only 57 times, and never in any single play more often than 'Sir John'. The character could remain, in speech-prefixes and hence in critical discussion, 'Sir John with all Europe'—thus retaining a single designation which neither falsifies Shakespeare's intention nor robs the character of what unity he does possess; but in the dialogue and in stage directions he would be either 'Sir John Oldcastle' (in *Part 1*) or 'Sir John Falstaff' (elsewhere)—thereby restoring Shakespeare's original intention and recognizing the disparity between *Part 1* and the later plays.

The inconsistency 'created' by an editor's reversion to 'Oldcastle' in *Part 1* is created not by the modern editor, but by the sixteenth-century censor. Shakespeare wrote and produced *Part 1* using the surname 'Oldcastle'; he wrote—or at least finished—*Merry Wives*, *Henry V*, and (I believe) *Part 2* after he had been forced to change the surname to 'Falstaff'. An editor who restored the original surname would thus be preserving inconsistencies in Shakespeare's own writing—just as we preserve inconsistencies of time, place, and action. In 1.3 and 2.1 of *Merry Wives* Shakespeare confuses the characters of Ford and Brooke in ways no editor can untangle; in *Henry V* Pistol begins married to Nell (2.1), but apparently ends married to Doll (5.1); in *The Two Gentlemen of Verona* Silvia's father is both a duke and an emperor, living simultaneously in both Milan and Verona. If Shakespeare was so careless of elementary consistency even within a single play, we can hardly presume that he would have been offended by an inconsistency *between* plays.

5 (1975), 308–12, and 'Second Thoughts on Falstaff's Name', *Shakespeare Quarterly*, 30 (1979), 82–4—that 'Falstaff' in *Henry VI, Part 1* is a sophistication, and that the original name 'Fastolf' has in the Folio been contaminated, under the influence of his more famous counterpart. If Williams is right, then someone else had confused the two characters, even before Dr James's young lady.

8. 'The Rejection of Falstaff', in *Oxford Lectures on Poetry* (1909), 247–75.

Sopocles' three plays on the myth of Oedipus, though often spoken of as a 'trilogy' (with no less and no more justice than Shakespeare's histories are grouped into 'tetralogies'), are on many points mutually incompatible in their account of events. Consistency of this kind worries editors more than it does artists. In the matter of Sir John's surname, history produced an inconsistency, which we have no right to tidy up. The change of name was forced upon Shakespeare after he had completed *Part 1*, and had it performed; we can therefore restore *Part 1* to the form it took in Shakespeare's original conception. The other plays cannot be 'restored', because by the time he finished them Shakespeare had been forced to change his conception of the role.

It might be objected that, even in *Part 1*, Shakespeare's original conception is beyond recall. What if the change of name was accompanied by other, more substantial changes of dialogue, character, or structure? Dover Wilson believed—for this play as for most others—that the extant text represents a wholesale revision of an earlier lost Shakespearian original, written entirely in verse. No one now takes this speculation seriously. But Wilson's elaborate hypothesis has had the unfortunate effect of making even those editors who reject it continue to talk about the problem of Sir John's surname as a question of 'revision'. Wilson, following A. E. Morgann, supposed that Shakespeare had extensively revised his whole play;[9] for this conjecture there is no external evidence and no credible internal evidence. The historical record and the internal evidence instead testify that, because of complaints in high places, Shakespeare was compelled to change at least one character's name. The change of name is not an instance of revision but of censorship. But what if the censor also objected to other aspects of the original? If he did so, then those other features are lost beyond recovery. But we have no evidence that such additional changes were ever made. None of the many extant witnesses refers to lost episodes or actions—though we do know of lost material in less famous plays, like *Tamburlaine* and *Pericles* and *The Merry Devil of Edmonton* and *The Conspiracy and Tragedy of Charles, Duke of Byron*.[1] The fact that the extant texts of *Part 1* do not even remove the pun on Oldcastle's name, or attempt to smooth the metre of the only verse line in which the new name was substituted, or change his Chris-

9. A. E. Morgann, *Some Problems of Shakespeare's 'Henry IV'* (1924), and Wilson, 'The Origins and Development of Shakespeare's *Henry IV*', *The Library*, IV, 26 (1945), 2–16.
1. The omissions from *Tamburlaine* are allowed to in the printer's preface to the first edition; for *Byron*, see E. K. Chambers, *The Elizabethan Stage*, 4 vols. (Oxford, 1923), vol. 3, 257–8. For *Pericles* and *Merry Devil*, prose pamphlets clearly influenced by the play suggest that some material has been omitted: see *Pericles Prince of Tyre*, ed. Philip Edwards (Harmondsworth, 1976), 21–6, and *The Merry Devil of Edmonton*, ed. W. A. Abrams (Durham, North Carolina, 1942), 257–8. (For this last reference I am indebted to G. R. Proudfoot.)

tian name, or change his social rank, or take out of the character's mouth the many religious allusions so hypocritically appropriate to his original identity, do not suggest that the 'revision' was overly painstaking. Shakespeare seems—like many another writer in this situation—to have done the bare minimum demanded by his masters. Those who took offence at the portrayal of Oldcastle could insist either that the portrait of his character be reformed, or that the unreformed character not be identified with Oldcastle. Obviously, the easier of these two options was elected. Once the name was changed, there would be no need to alter the character. There is no reason to believe that the play has suffered more than a reformation of nomenclature; the censorship seems to have been literally 'nominal'. But even if we could be absolutely positive that the censor did enforce other changes, which we cannot now identify or undo, that impotence would not relieve us of the responsibility to undo those depredations which we can identify. Not all textual corruption is detectable; editors nevertheless correct whatever corruption they can detect. In the case of Sir John's surname, there can be absolutely no doubt that interference has occurred, and no doubt either about what should be restored.

In fact, such considerations have probably not influenced editors at all. Humphreys, for instance, does not raise them. So far as the printed text of his edition accurately reflects the progress of his textual decision-making, he seems never even to have considered the possibility of reverting to the original name. Partly, perhaps, this silence results from the fact that in this case rectification of censorship does not require the time-honoured practice of editorial conflation, but calls instead for something which radically departs from time-honoured practice. Falstaff vies with Hamlet as Shakespeare's most famous character. How can an editor *possibly* change his name, in the very play which first made him famous? Editors have not simply recoiled in horror from this thought; they have, apparently, failed even to think it. The idea is unthinkable—one might say, heretical. It may be worth remembering that Sir John Oldcastle was himself burned as a heretic. In some sense the Protestant Reformation may be characterized as an exceptionally acrimonious dispute between textual critics. The works of Shakespeare are now treated with some of the veneration usually reserved for Holy Writ, and—as in all idolatries—believers vociferously object to any tampering with the particular text of Holy Writ to which they are accustomed. Indeed, the priesthood of an idolatry—those persons entrusted with the institutional authority to teach and interpret it—is the group most likely to be most offended by any change to the received text. In Shakespearian terms, a proposal to change Falstaff's name back to Oldcastle is as heretical as Oldcastle's own opinion that the Eucharist was not literally transformed into the body and blood of Jesus Christ Our Lord.

Of course, what I am proposing is not really a heresy, but simply a single emendation, based on unimpeachable historical evidence. So far as I can see, the chief, indeed the only objection to restoring the original reading (Oldcastle) is that the substituted reading (Falstaff) has become famous: an entire tradition of criticism and performance has only based upon it. In response to this objection I can only reply, 'So much the worse for tradition; it is time the tradition was abandoned.' After all, in forty or at most fifty years every current critic and teacher of Shakespeare will be retired or dead; for a whole new generation of readers 'Oldcastle' could become as familiar as 'Falstaff' is now to us. What shocks us will not shock them. If I may quote Sir Walter Greg:[2]

RULE I

> The aim of a critical edition should be to present the text, so far as the available evidence permits, in the form in which we may suppose that it would have stood in a fair copy, made by the author himself, of the work as *he* finally intended it.

When Shakespeare finished *Part 1*, when it was performed by his own company, the name of his fat knight was undoubtedly Oldcastle.

But is Greg right? In the 'final' version of *Part 1*, the version being performed for most of Shakespeare's career, the character's name was 'Falstaff', and an editor might decide that the *reasons* for a particular change of nomenclature are none of our business: Shakespeare acquiesced in the alteration, and so should we. This is an intellectually respectable editorial position, much favoured by modern German textual scholarship;[3] but I think it is wrong in theory, and in Shakespeare's case deeply undesirable in practice. If a colleague suggests changes to a play, Shakespeare is at liberty to accept or reject those suggestions, and since he determines which changes to incorporate he becomes intentionally and voluntarily responsible for the final result. By contrast, if the Master of the Revels or the Lord Chamberlain says, 'Change this character's name', Shakespeare cannot ignore that advice—or, if he does so, he accepts that the play can no longer be performed, or ever printed. Theoretically, even this liberty might be denied him: the authorities might insist that the play be publicly performed or printed with the new name, in order to demonstrate to everyone the change of iden-

2. *The Editorial Problem in Shakespeare: A Survey of the Foundations of the Text*, 3rd edn. (Oxford, 1954), x (emphasis mine).
3. See Hans Zeller, 'A New Approach to the Critical Constitution of Literary Texts', *Studies in Bibliography*, 28 (1975), 245–9.

tity—just as heretics were forced to recant publicly.[4] In such cases, an author 'acquiesces' in alterations only to the extent that he wishes to avoid imprisonment or imposed silence, and as a result the author effectively ceases to be responsible for such changes, which might be made without even consulting him. If an editor nevertheless chose to accept the change of name as an alteration Shakespeare passively endorsed, then the same policy must be applied to such changes throughout the canon: all the Folio's excisions of politically sensitive or profane material must also be accepted, since they can be justified on exactly the same grounds as the change to 'Falstaff'. Of course, two of the plays most seriously misrepresented by such a policy would be the two parts of *Henry IV*, which suffered considerable pruning in the Folio. An editor can hardly reject those politically imposed changes while accepting the politically imposed change to Sir John's surname.

Nor is it clear that Shakespeare or his company did entirely acquiesce in the change. In the absence of a private diary or letter, or a report of his conversation, we simply do not know (and never will) what Shakespeare's 'final' thoughts were. We do know what Shakespeare originally intended, and why that intention was abandoned; what we know is more important than what we imagine or speculate about thought processes never committed to paper. Moreover, since only *Part 1* was composed with 'Oldcastle' in mind, the later intentions of Shakespeare and his company only matter in relation to a single question: would he (or they) have restored 'Oldcastle' to *Part 1*, if given the chance, even after *Part 2*, *Henry V*, and *Merry Wives* were written? Of course, Shakespeare and his colleagues might have harboured such a wish, even if they could never translate it into reality. But as it happens, considerable evidence exists that the play was, even after 1597, sometimes privately performed with the original designation intact.

On 6 March 1600 Rowland Whyte referred to a private performance of 'Sir Iohn Old Castell' by the Chamberlain's Men for their patron the Lord Chamberlain, before the visiting Austrian ambassador Verreiken, in England to negotiate peace with Spain;[5] on 6 January 1631 the same company (by then the King's Men) performed 'Old Castle' at court 'At the Cock-pitt';[6] on 29 May 1639 they again performed 'ould Castel' at court, on 'the princes berthnyght'.[7] The

4. Since Chambers made the suggestion—*William Shakespeare: A Study of Facts and Problems*, 2 vols. (Oxford, 1930), vol. 1, 382—it has been generally assumed that *Part 1*'s publication early in 1598 was required, in order to publicize the change of names: the company would normally have resisted publication of so recent and popular a play.
5. Arthur Collins, *Letters and Memorials of State*, 2 vols. (1746), vol. 2, 175; abstracted in *HMC De L'Isle and Dudley Papers*, vol. 2, 443. * * *
6. James G. McManaway, 'A New Shakespeare Document', *Shakespeare Quarterly*, 2 (1951), 119–22.
7. Chambers, *William Shakespeare*, vol. 1, 382; vol. 2, 353.

first of these cannot be a reference to Henslowe's *Oldcastle* play, which stayed in his possession from October 1599 until at least September 1602, and could hardly have been performed by a rival company at that time;[8] nor is it probable that Shakespeare's company would wish to perform a play which so clearly represents an attack on one of their own; they would, on the contrary, probably be asked to perform one of their own most successful plays, and that they did so is suggested by the ambassador's 'great Contentment' with what he saw. Moreover, since *Part 1* was sometimes referred to as 'Falstaff', it could evidently be identified by means of its chief comic character [Hemingway, 477], so it should not surprise us if the uncensored version were identified as 'Oldcastle'. Finally, since the Lord Chamberlain was the chief censor, and since in 1600 the Lord Chamberlain was no longer a Cobham but instead the patron of Shakespeare's company, he was obviously in a position to allow a private performance of the original version. It therefore seems probable that Shakespeare was able to change the name back to 'Oldcastle' at least once after 1597—and that he did so, despite the fact that *Part 2*, *Merry Wives*, and *Henry V*, which identify the character as 'Falstaff', had by 1600 all been written. This apparent reversion to the original surname constitutes fairly reliable external evidence that (as we would expect) Shakespeare was not happy with the enforced change and was willing to have the character in *Part 1* identified as 'Oldcastle' even after the alternative designation 'Falstaff' had become current in other plays.

It seems intrinsically likely that the later court performances of '*Oldcastle*' also involve Shakespeare's play. The fact that one of these took place on the birth-night of the Prince of Wales makes this particularly probable: Henslowe's play has no noticeable pertinence to such an occasion, but *Part 1* would be remarkably appropriate fare for the young prince. Moreover, Queen Henrietta Maria—notorious for her interest in the theatre—was an avowed and fervent Catholic; Charles I himself was often suspected of Catholic inclinations. The list noting the 1630 performance may well be, according to McManaway, in the hand of the actor John Lowin. The well-informed and generally reliable James Wright, writing in 1699, claimed that Lowin (1576–1653) actually played '*Falstaffe*'; he was certainly, on the basis of a variety of much earlier, reliable evidence, a huge, overweight man who regularly played gruff soldiers, either as comedians or villains.[9] The fact that this actor apparently identified the play—and hence the character—as

8. *Henslowe's Diary*, ed. R. A. Foakes and R. T. Rickert (Cambridge, 1961), 125, 126, 129, 132, 213, 214, 216.
9. Wright, *Historia Histrionica*, 4; Chambers, *Elizabethan Stage*, vol. 2, 328–9; Bentley, vol. 2, 499–506.

'Olde Castle' is therefore especially intriguing. But even if these Caroline court performances did not restore the original name, the two documents do suggest that, even in the 1630s, some people continued to identify Sir John as Oldcastle. Knowledgeable spectators restored Shakespeare's intention mentally, even if it could not be restored in print or on stage. And it may even have been restored in the theatre on more occasions than the one documented in 1600. Thomas Fuller's 1655 allusion to the play claims that Falstaff's name 'of late is substituted' for Oldcastle—an explicit statement difficult to reconcile with the assumption that all performances after 1597 accepted the change of name.[1]

In addition to such evidence that 'Oldcastle' was sometimes restored in performance, modern bibliographical analysis of the sequence of printing of the First Folio suggests that Heminges and Condell may have attempted to restore the original name. Henry Brooke, Lord Cobham, was arrested in July 1603, convicted of treason in November, and spent the rest of his life in the Tower, where he died in 1619; the title lapsed until 1645, when it was conferred on Henry's second cousin. Hence, from 1619 to 1645 the Cobham barony was vacant, and in no position to exert the political pressure it could have brought to bear in 1596–7. As a result, after 1619 Shakespeare's fellow-actors, who were also the editors of the First Folio, may have hoped that a restoration of the original surname was possible. Certainly, during the setting of *Richard II* there was an unexplained change in the sequence of composition, skipping over both *Henry IV* plays, so that *Henry V* and most of the three parts of *Henry VI* were set into type before the compositors returned to *Henry IV*. It has usually been assumed that difficulty in securing copyright caused this delay; that difficulty may then have been overcome by acquisition of a new manuscript, enabling the Folio editors to supply variant readings, and hence to claim that they were publishing a new or different version of the play, not covered by the existing copyright.[2] But this conjecture is speculative: we do not *know* that there was any difficulty over the copyright to *Part 1*. On the other hand we *do* know that there had been difficulty over the name of an important character in *Part 1*, and that a key figure in that controversy had recently died, without a successor. The delay in printing Folio *Henry IV* could easily have arisen because of an attempt to secure permission from the new Master of the Revels (who by then also licensed the publication of plays) to

1. *The Church-History of Britain: From the Birth of Jesus Christ, until the year 1648*, Book 4, 168.
2. See Charlton Hinman, *The Printing and Proof-Reading of the First Folio of Shakespeare*, 2 vols. (Oxford, 1963), vol. 1, 27–8 (on copyright), 159–60; vol. 2, 14–106, 489–503 (on the sequence of setting).

restore the original surname. Indeed, this explanation could easily coexist with the other, for the change of Sir John's surname would surely circumvent copyright as effectively as the introduction of a few score of insignificant verbal variants. If Heminges and Condell did attempt to restore 'Oldcastle', they obviously failed, presumably because religious objections to the name remained, even after the family objections of the Cobhams had lost their force: publication of the play with 'Oldcastle' restored, especially in an impressive folio volume 'printed in the best Crowne paper, far better than most Bibles', would have looked like an official public endorsement of its scurrilous portrayal of a 'martyr'.[3] The failure of their attempt would then have forced Heminges and Condell either to come to some arrangement with the copyright holder, or to provide the publishers with a variant manuscript. Such complications could easily account for the postponement of printing.

My reconstruction remains speculative too, of course, but at least it uses known events to account for known events, and illustrates the folly of assuming too readily that Heminges and Condell, as Shakespeare's literary executors, were happy enough to perpetuate 'Falstaff' in *Part 1*. It is possible that Heminges and Condell tried unsuccessfully to restore 'Oldcastle' in print in 1623; it is probable that the name was, as Fuller implies, actually used in some private performances in the 1630s. If so, then the players—as well as the playwright—demonstrated their dissatisfaction with the imposed change of name, when they could. Final acquiescence was only secured when Puritans ruled England and theatres were closed. The editorial concept of 'final intention' can have little value in a case like this, where social restraints only successfully finalized their domination of the author's meaning decades after his death.

Some readers may be willing to concede that, in principle, Oldcastle should be restored, and yet still protest that the change is impracticable: 'however right it may be, it would cause too much trouble'. Such arguments have also been heard recently in relation to *King Lear*, and they expose a fundamental contradiction in critical attitudes toward textual scholarship.[4] Critics do not object when an edition like *The Riverside Shakespeare* departs from its predecessors in hundreds of individual readings, because such scholarly labours increase one's confidence in the text, while at the same time making no difference to its interpretation. But when the same labours lead an editor to propose restoring both early versions

3. William Prynne, *Histrio-Mastix. The Players Scourge or Actors Tragœdie* (1633), 'To the Christian Reader', fol. 1ᵛ. * * *
4. Andrew Gurr, 'The Once and Future *King Lears*', *Bulletin of the Society for Renaissance Studies*, 2 (1984), 7–19. * * *

of *King Lear*, or the original name of Shakespeare's most famous comic character, then some critics will object that the changes are impractical simply because they make so much difference. This attitude creates a situation in which the results of textual scholarship are always trivial, because if the results are *not* trivial they will be disregarded. It also creates the paradox that minor authors will always be better edited than major ones—because the perceived imperative of 'practicality' exists only in so far as an author is already widely read and interpreted. Hence, Shakespeare's editors continue to produce texts which, in one way or another, they do not believe in; each succumbs to the weight of tradition, and thereby adds to the weight on any subsequent editor. At some point this vicious cycle must be broken, and Shakespeare edited with as much care as Robert Sidney or Edward Fairfax.

Even if it made no difference whatever to the play's meaning, the restoration of the character's original name would be, editorially, the proper thing to do. But reverting to Oldcastle does more than restore the tag by which Shakespeare identified a role: it restores the meaning and the shape which that identification gave to the character and the play. Oldcastle really was a soldier, who had fought for Henry IV in France and Wales: 'this valiant Knight', John Foxe called him; 'that thrice valiant Capitaine', in John Weever's words; 'a meetely good man of war', wrote John Stow; 'a valiaunt capitain and an hardy gentleman', according to Edward Hall.[5] The title-page of John Bale's influential, popular apologia actually portrays Oldcastle, described as a 'moste valyaunt warryour', with sword and shield.[6] Sir John's appearance at the King's side, in the council before the battle of Shrewsbury (5.1), would therefore not have seemed as incongruous with 'Oldcastle' as it does with 'Falstaff'. All the chroniclers agree that Oldcastle was 'well liked' by and 'highly in the . . . fauor' of Henry V, before his disgrace.[7] Aside from his appropriate presence at Shrewsbury, Shakespeare's Sir John takes no part in the major political events of the play; nor would this surprise anyone familiar with Foxe's description of him as 'but a priuate subject, and a poore Knight' [Foxe, 573b]. Oldcastle was also hanged on the gallows, before being burned—an unusual form of execution gruesomely illustrated by a large woodcut

5. Foxe, *Actes and Monuments of Martyrs, Newly revised and inlarged by the Author* (1583), 643b; Weever, *The Mirror of Martyrs, or The life and death of that thrice valiant Capitaine, and most godly Martyre* Sir John Old-castle knight, *Lord Cobham* (1601); Stow, *The Annales of England* (1592), 550–1; Hall, *The Union of the Two Noble and Illustre Families of Lancastre and Yorke* (1548), a.ii^{v} (of 'The Victorious actes of kyng Henry the V').
6. *A brefe Chronycle concernynge the Examinacyon and death of the blessed Martyr of Christ Syr Johan Oldecastell the lorde Cobham* (1544; repr. 1545? 1548?).
7. Hall, a.ii^{v}; Foxe, 566a, 568b; Raphael Holinshed, *The Third Volume of Chronicles* (1587), 544a.

in Foxe's influential 'Book of Martyrs' [Foxe, 643]. *Part 1* alludes half a dozen times to Sir John's anticipated death on the gallows. Shakespeare's Oldcastle also has affinities with the character of that name in the anonymous *Famous Victories of Henry the Fifth*, which Shakespeare undoubtedly knew: he participates in a robbery, swears profusely, and looks forward to being a hangman when Hal is king. Shakespeare's Sir John recognizably reflects features of the earlier historical and dramatic portrayals of Oldcastle.

But the historical Oldcastle was also the subject of one of the sixteenth century's running religious controversies: 'whether this foresayd sir John Oldcastle', as Foxe put it, 'is rather to be commēded for a Martyr, or to be reproued for a traytor' [Foxe, 568b]. In these relatively ecumenical times it may seem unlikely that Shakespeare intended Sir John to represent a man incinerated for his religious convictions. But the polemicists of the sixteenth century were not inhibited by such tender decorums. Foxe, for instance, describes the portrait of Oldcastle drawn by the 'English Chroniclers'—Fabian, Hall, Polydore Vergil, Cooper, Grafton—as 'malicious railing, virulent slanders, manifest vntruths, opprobrious contumelies, & stinking blasphemies, able almost to corrupt & infect ye aire'. Matthew Sutcliffe called Walsingham 'a lying Monke' and claimed that '*Stow* hath the most part of his lyes concerning the Lord *Cobham* out of *Walsingham*, which notwithstanding he vnderstood not being Latine, and he a meere English Taylor'.[8]

The historical tradition which so irritated these divines was first documented by Wilhelm Baeske in 1905 and, more thoroughly, by Alice-Lyle Scoufos in 1979; it characterizes Oldcastle as a robber, traitor, heretic and hypocrite.[9] Even Bale admitted that 'his youthe was full of wanton wildenesse'; Tyndale, Bale, and Foxe all quoted Oldcastle's confession, during his trial, that 'in my frayle youth I offended thee (Lord) most greuously in pride, wrath, and gluttony: in couetousnes, and in lechery. Many men haue I hurt in mine anger, and done many other horrible sinnes.'[1] Hall introduces his discussion of Oldcastle and other Lollards with a reference to 'certayne persones callyng themselfes spirituall fathers, but in deede carnall coueteous and gredy glottons'. Foxe devotes twenty folio pages of his revised edition to 'A defence of the Lord Cobham, agaynst Nich. Harpsfield'.[2] Shakespeare need not have read Harpsfield, or Walsingham, or the fifteenth-century histories, because their ver-

8. Foxe, 576b; Sutcliffe, *A Threefold Answer vnto the third part of a certain triobolar treatise* (1606), 24.
9. Baeske, *Oldcastle-Falstaff in der englischen Literatur bis zu Shakespeare*, Palaestra, 50 (Berlin, 1905); Baeske is summarized by Hemingway, 453–5. * * *
1. Foxe, 561a; Bale, 26–26^v. For Tyndale see *The examinacion of master William Thorpe . . . The examinacion of Syr J. Oldcastell* (Antwerp, 1530; STC 24045). * * *
2. Hall, a.ii^v; Foxe, 568–88. * * *

sion of Oldcastle is expounded in considerable detail by Foxe himself—as well as Hall, Holinshed, and Stow, all readily available and clearly consulted by Shakespeare when writing his history plays.

According to these authors, Oldcastle's 'intent was to destroy his soueraigne Lord the king' and 'to destroy Gods law' and 'to destroy all maner of policie, & finally the lawes of ye land' [Foxe, 572b, 573a, 573b]. Shakespeare's character, in outline and detail, has a good deal in common with this archetypal champion of moral chaos, and the presence of Oldcastle emphasizes the play's religious themes. The first speech in *Part 1* is devoted—irrelevantly, so far as the traditional text is concerned—to Henry IV's intended crusade to Jerusalem:

> those holy fields,
> Ouer whose acres walkt those blessed feet,
> Which 1400. yeares ago were naild
> For our aduantage on the bitter crosse.
> (1.1.24–7)

Sir John's moralizing, swearing, threats of repentance, and mimicry of Puritan idiom would have been especially delicious, and satirical, in the mouth of Oldcastle. At Gad's Hill Oldcastle and his companions plan to rob, of all people, 'pilgrims going to Canturburie' (1.2.109). Bale and Foxe—and later Matthew Sutcliffe, and Dr Richard James himself—contrasted Oldcastle with Thomas à Becket, to Becket's disadvantage.[3] When Hal at first declines to accompany them, Oldcastle swears, 'By the Lord, ile be a traitor then, when thou art king' (1.2.127). The historical Oldcastle did become a traitor when Hal became king. In what is perhaps his most famous speech, Oldcastle claims that he was 'a cowarde on instinct'; as he asks, 'was it for me to kill the heire apparent? should I turne vpon the true prince?' (2.4.247, 243–4). The historical Oldcastle did indeed allegedly turn upon the true prince, joining in a plot to kill him. Historically, Henry V made a considerable personal effort to persuade his friend to renounce his heresies; Oldcastle would not relent. Shakespeare's Sir John declares, 'ile be damnd for neuer a kings sonne in Christendom' (1.2.84–5); as Hal says, 'Sir John stands to his word, the diuell shall haue his bargain, for . . . he will giue the diuell his due' (1.2.103–4).

The two contrasted portraits of Hal's companion given in the play scene—as 'a vertuous man' with 'vertue in his lookes' (2.4.370, 380), or as 'a diuell . . . in the likenesse of an olde fat man . . . that reuerent vice, that gray iniquity . . . That villanous abhominable misleader of youth' (2.4.399, 404)—correspond to the two oppos-

3. Bale, 52–55^{v}; Foxe, 579b. * * *

ing conceptions of Oldcastle current in the sixteenth century. Hal even envisages Oldcastle as 'a rosted Manningtre Oxe' (2.4.403): the many members of the audience familiar with Oldcastle's historical fate must have considered this one of Hal's—and Shakespeare's—most unsavoury similes. At Shrewsbury, Shakespeare's fat knight rises, apparently, from the dead; Oldcastle allegedly said, just before his execution, that he would 'rise from death to life again, the third day'.[4] And in his final speech Sir John, looking forward to the reward he expects for having 'killed' Hotspur, promises 'If I do growe great, ile growe lesse, for ile purge and leaue Sacke, and liue cleanlie as a noble man should do' (5.4.157–9). This is not a speech many of us remember, or credit with much importance. But the historical Oldcastle did undergo a religious conversion, abandoning what Bale had conceded to be a certain wantonness 'in his youth': in the last years of Henry IV's reign, he did—according to the Protestants—both 'growe great . . . and liue cleanlie'. For many of the original audience to *Part 1*, these words would have clearly hinted—even if only parodically—at Oldcastle's subsequent career. But in the mouth of a fictional character called Falstaff, the words lose their historicity and ambiguity. To some extent, this is what happens to the whole character. The name 'Falstaff' fictionalizes, depoliticizes, secularizes, and in the process trivializes the play's most memorable character. It robs the play of that tension created by the distance between two available interpretations of one of its central figures.

The change of name affects the interpretation of other characters, too. Many of the original audience of *Part 1* would have known that the historical Oldcastle was eventually executed on the orders of the historical Henry V. The outcome of the relationship between Hal and his pal was never in doubt; the death of 'Falstaff' in *Henry V* was not an artistic accident, as some have claimed, an unfortunate change of plan forced upon Shakespeare by the departure of Will Kemp[5] from the company, but part of his conception of Henry's character from the beginning. But Oldcastle was indicted for heresy soon after Henry V was crowned; Henry intervened in order to save his old friend from the ecclesiastical authorities, delayed his trial and punishment, and personally attempted to save his soul. Oldcastle, unconvinced, escaped from the Tower, and was implicated in an uprising and a conspiracy to assassinate Henry. In the sequel that Shakespeare eventually wrote (under the eye of the censor), the sequel we all know, Hal rejects Sir John only because his old friend has become a political embarrassment: Henry's sense

4. Stow, *Annales*, 72. Stow's account is taken from Walsingham.
5. Kemp was a famous clown in Shakespeare's company [*Editor's note*].

of his own destiny, his responsibility as monarch, demands their separation. The motivation lies entirely within Henry. But when he wrote *Part 1*, Shakespeare was anticipating a sequel with a different 'Sir John in it'—a sequel in which Henry's rejection of his old friend might easily have been based, in part at least, on that friend's own treachery (like Scrope's). Th change of Oldcastle's name may have changed Prince Hal's role in * * * *Part 2*. * * *

* * *

* * * Consider Sir John's rebuke by the Lord Chief Justice, in the first scene in which either appears: 'Do you set down *your name* in the scroll of youth, that are *written down 'old'* with all the characters of age?' (1.3.177–9; my italics). Or the opening of Sir John's letter to Prince Hal, with the satirical comment it evokes: ' "John Falstaff, Knight"—every man must know that, as oft as he has occasion to name himself' (2.2.103–5). Just as passages of *Part 1* lose some of their significance if Sir John is not called 'Oldcastle', so passages in three other plays lose some of their significance if 'Falstaff' is not a new, and potentially confusing, surname.

Even in *Part 1*, of course, Shakespeare's Sir John is much more than a dramatic amalgamation of certain elements in sixteenth-century attitudes toward a fourteenth-century Lollard. He is a comic character of genius, who owes as much to the Vice of morality drama[6] as to the chronicles of Henry IV's reign. But Shakespeare's decision to conflate the historical Oldcastle with the theatrical Vice was itself a daring and provocative inspiration—moreover, an inspiration obscured for centuries by the imposed change of name. Because of Falstaff's false association with the allegedly cowardly soldier Fastolf, most critics before John Dover Wilson believed that Sir John's key literary antecedent was the *miles gloriosus* of Roman comedy; not until 1943 did any critic elaborate on his much more important similarities to the allegorical Vice.[7] Bad texts do not encourage good criticism.

Many of the parallels between the dramatic and the historical Sir John have been noticed before, but they have never been discussed in terms of the editorial issue they raise. Such details are not important as 'proof' that Falstaff was once Oldcastle; we already *know* that. Instead, the parallels demonstrate that the name of the character, his historical identity, forms a part of the meaning of the extant text. They confirm that little if anything of the nature of the original character has been altered: 'only the names have been changed, to protect the innocent'. And in this case the parallels cannot be dismissed as a bizarre growth nurtured in the hothouse

6. Like Vice, the recurrent allegorical character in morality plays from the 15th and 16th centuries, Sir John tries to lure a hero from the path of virtue [*Editor's note*].
7. Wilson, *The Fortunes of Falstaff* (Cambridge, 1943), 17–35.

of a twentieth-century imagination in search of tenure. Undeniably, many of Shakespeare's contemporaries took Shakespeare's character as a portrayal of and comment upon the historical Oldcastle. It is not surprising that the Jesuit Robert Parsons alluded to Shakespeare's play in his own attack, in 1604, upon Oldcastle as 'a Ruffian-knight . . . commonly brought in by comediants in their stages: he was put to death for robberyes and rebellion'.[8] But John Speed, in 1611, replying to Parsons, also assumed that the 'poet' and the 'stage-plaiers' meant to calumniate the martyr.[9] The team of playwrights who in 1599 produced Henslowe's derivative potboiler, 'The first part of the true and honorable historie, of the life of *Sir Iohn Old-castle, the good* Lord Cobham', specifically contrasted their play, which presents 'faire Truth', with the 'forg'de inuention' of Shakespeare's—just as Foxe had contrasted his pietistic interpretation with that of earlier chroniclers.[1] John Weever, in 1601, in a verse hagiography of Oldcastle demonstrably indebted to Shakespeare, claims to reveal 'of [his] life and death the veritie', in contrast to what 'thousands flocke to heare'.[2] This cannot be a complaint about Henslowe's play, which presented an entirely favourable picture of Oldcastle, comparable to Weever's own; moreover, the stanza in which it occurs is immediately followed by one in which all scholars recognize an allusion to Shakespeare's *Julius Caesar*.[3] Weever complains,

> O time vntaught, men scorners of sound teaching, Louers of playes, and loathers of good preaching.
>
> (D2)

Oldcastle's ghost goes out of his way to deny charges of 'cowardize' and of having fraternized with 'meane *Cumrades*' and 'base associates' (A6). Neither of these accusations is brought against Oldcastle by sixteenth-century historians, even the hostile ones; yet they have an obvious pertinence to Shakespeare's *Part 1*.

Most explicitly of all, of course, the very suppression of the name 'Oldcastle' from Shakespeare's play testifies to the influential and offended reactions of 'personages descended from his title'—and 'manie others allso whoe ought to have him in honorabe memorie'. Right-minded Protestants can hardly have been pleased by the fact that Shakespeare's 'buffone' bore the name—and some of the al-

8. N. D. (= Nicholas Dolman, pseudonym of Robert Parsons), *Examen of the Calender or Catalogue of Protestant Saints: The last six months* (1604) 31.
9. *The Theatre of the Empire of Great Britaine*, 2 vols. (1611), vol. 2, 637a.
1. The most helpful edition is in Michael Drayton, *Works*, ed. J. William Hebel, 4 vols. (rev. edn. Oxford, 1961), vol. 1, 393–468, with Notes and Introductions in volume 5, ed. Kathleen Tillotson and Bernard H. Newdigate, 44–52.
2. *Mirror of Martyrs*, A3v. * * *
3. Halliwell-Phillips first spotted the reference to *Casesar*: see his edition of Shakespeare's *Works*, 16 vols. (1853–65), vol. 13 (1865), 365. * * *

leged characteristics—of a revered Lollard martyr. James testifies explicitly to the hostility of such people, and Shakespeare himself implicitly recognizes it in the Epilogue to *Part 2*, promising that his next play will dramatize Henry V's adventures in France—'where (for any thing I knowe) Falstaffe shall die of a sweat, vnlesse already a be killd with your harde opinions; for Olde-Castle died Martyre, and this is not the man'. No one seems to have remarked upon the syntactical role of 'for' in this unusual sentence, perhaps because its implication is obvious. In worrying that Falstaff might already be 'killd with your harde opinions', Shakespeare may merely be allowing, humbly and conventionally, for the possibility that his new play has failed to please its audience; but the immediate change of subject, and the assertion of a casual link between the two statements, makes it seem to me probable that Shakespeare here alluded to the displeasure of *some* spectators at the original identification of the character as Oldcastle.

The traditional modern assumption is that the Cobhams, James, Weever, Parsons, Speed, Munday, Drayton *et al.* were all wrong; that Shakespeare's contemporaries woefully misunderstood, glibly assuming that 'Oldcastle' meant 'Oldcastle'; that we alone, centuries later, can see that there was—as Hamlet assures Claudius—'no offence i'th' world' intended by these apparent parallels between the play and the past. Geoffrey Bullough sums up this view when he claims that Shakespeare used the name Oldcastle 'without *arrière pensée* and without linking his Sir John with the martyr' [Bullough, 4:171]. Not surprisingly, this hypothesis of innocent inadvertence was first advanced by an Anglican bishop, who also happened to be an editor of Shakespeare, the Right Reverend William Warburton: 'I believe there was no malice in the matter. *Shakespear* wanted a droll name to his character, and never considered whom it belonged to.'[4]

Warburton's faith-saving fantasy has been perpetuated partly because of a confusion between two kinds of inadvertence. Shakespeare might not have expected or intended to offend the Cobham family; * * * it seems to me intrinsically improbable that any dramatist would deliberately satirize the Lord Chamberlain, the one official who could do a theatrical company most good or harm. Noticeably, neither *Famous Victories* nor *Part 1* ever identifies Oldcastle by his alternative title, Lord Cobham, though all the chroniclers and divines habitually mix the titles; equally important, neither play gives him a wife. The absence of the name from the extant texts might of course be due to censorship, but there seem to

4. *The Works of Shakespear*, 8 vols. (1747), vol. 4, 103. Warburton ignores the long, learned, intelligent note by Lewis Theobald on this matter: see *The Works of Shakespeare*, 8 vols. (1733), vol. 3, 348–9. * * *

be no puns on or allusions to the title either. Moreover, since Oldcastle acquired his title by marriage, and since the Elizabethan Cobhams descended not from Oldcastle himself but from his wife, the absence of Lady Cobham from both plays—and her corresponding presence in Henslowe's hagiographic rejoinder, and Weever's poem—is probably significant. Shakespeare, like the author of *Famous Victories*, might naturally have assumed that it was safe to bring Oldcastle on to the stage so long as he was never connected with the Cobhams or their ancestress. But Shakespeare's innocence of any intentional libel on the living Cobhams by no means exonerates him from responsibility for a deliberate and brilliant caricature of the dead Oldcastle. You do not call a hypocrite 'Sir John Oldcastle' without giving any thought to the fact that a 'Sir John Oldcastle'—who lived in the period in which your play is set—was famous as, depending on your taste, a martyr or a heretic. Moreover, Shakespeare clearly did 'link' his character and the historical one.

The controversy over whether Shakespeare intended to satirize the Cobhams has obscured the much more important fact that he portrayed a Protestant martyr as a jolly hypocrite. That is the inconvenient truth Warburton wishes to ignore. Warburton's reasoning was articulated much more openly, five years later, by a certain 'P.T.', who may have been Warburton himself, and who was certainly indebted to Warburton's arguments: 'What, I say, could *Shakespeare* make a pampered glutton, a debauched monster, of a noble personage, who stood foremost on the list of *English* reformers and Protestant martyrs . . . ? 'Tis absurd to suppose, 'tis impossible for any man to imagine.'[5] England's national poet could not be guilty of such treasonable heresy. And there the matter rested for almost a century: not until 1841, when Halliwell printed Dr James's epistle, did anyone dare again maintain that Shakespeare had ever called his character 'Oldcastle'.

Editors must of course disabuse themselves of any devotion other than allegiance to their author. Shakespeare might in this instance be usefully contrasted with Thomas Middleton. In the second-most-famous instance of censorship in English Renaissance drama, Middleton got into trouble for his caricature of prominent Roman Catholics; Shakespeare, by contrast, got into trouble for his caricature of a famous proto-Protestant. John Speed (in 1611) and Richard Davies (*c.* 1660) both alleged or assumed that Shakespeare was a 'papist'. There is documentary evidence that both Shakespeare's father and one of his daughters may have been popishly inclined.[6] In *Hamlet* Shakespeare exploited the Catholic belief in

5. 'Observations on Shakespeare's Falstaff', *Gentleman's Magazine*, 22 (1752), 459–61.
6. See S. Schoenbaum, *Shakespeare: A Compact Documentary Life* (Oxford, 1977), 45–62.

Purgatory; in *Richard III* he exploited Catholic beliefs about All Souls' Eve;[7] in both *Twelfth Night* and *Measure for Measure* he mocked the hypocrisy of Puritans. In 1609–10 both *Pericles* and *King Lear* were performed by a band of English recusant players with—in other respects—an obviously papist repertoire.[8] *Pericles* was also included in a continental Jesuit book-list of 1619, and twice performed before visiting Catholic ambassadors (in 1607–8 and 1619).[9] *King Lear*, as is well known, draws upon passages in Samuel Harsnet's *Declaration of Egregious Popish Impostures* (1603); what is perhaps not so well known is that Harsnet's book quotes extensively from a Catholic manuscript account of the same events, 'The Booke of Miracles'.[1] Virtually everything which Shakespeare allegedly took from Harsnet could have been taken, instead, from the lost manuscript; at the very least, Shakespeare's interest in Harsnet's pamphlet may have been stimulated by the fact that it made available, in print, excerpts from a proscribed account. What Shakespeare's treatment ignores entirely is Harsnet's own contribution: his ceaseless mockery of the whole idea of demonic possession. Edgar's performance as Poor Tom—whatever else it may be—does not seem designed to provoke cynical laughter; although he announces an intention to disguise himself as a bedlam beggar, he does not specifically promise to be possessed by devils; nor does his professed intention 'to put an antic disposition on' allow us to infer, in his case any more than in Hamlet's, that the resulting mental disequilibrium is entirely feigned. In 3.4 especially, where he never steps out of his 'role', Edgar's tortured hallucinations can be, in performance, triumphantly and disturbingly real. *King Lear* exploits dramatically a series of incidents in recent English recusant history, just as clearly as *Hamlet* and *Richard III* exploit elements of Catholic belief. And in *King John*—as in *Part 1*—Shakespeare tells the story of an early proto-Protestant 'martyr', whose life had been celebrated earlier in the century by both Bale and Foxe; but again, as in *Part 1*, Shakespeare's account of this figure is not very flattering. Such evidence does not prove that Shakespeare was a secret Catholic, but it does demonstrate, at the very least, his willingness to exploit a point of view which many of his contemporaries would have regarded as 'papist'. In such circumstances, the possibility that Shakespeare deliberately lampooned Oldcastle can hardly be denied.

I do not know whether Shakespeare meant to satirize the Cob-

7. Emrys Jones, *The Origins of Shakespeare* (Oxford, 1977), 227–9.
8. C. J. Sisson, 'Shakespeare's Quartos as Prompt-copies', *Review of English Studies*, 18 (1942), 129–43.
9. Willem Schrickx, '*Pericles* in a Book-List of 1619 from the English Jesuit Mission and Some of the Play's Special Problems', *Shakespeare Survey* 29 (Cambridge, 1976), 21–32.
1. Harsnet's use of 'The Booke of Miracles' is noted by Murphy, 7, 22–3, 36, 205.

hams, though I rather doubt it. I do not know whether Shakespeare was ever 'a papist', though I rather suspect it.[2] But I do know that Oldcastle is what Shakespeare wrote; that Oldcastle is what Shakespeare meant; and that Oldcastle is what his contemporaries understood. If editors nevertheless refuse to restore Shakespeare's name for the character, then they might as well confess that they care more about an artificial *post hoc* consistency than they do about the integrity of the individual work of art; that they care more about the preservation and intellectual authority of a cultural tradition than about the recovery and restoration of the original authoritative *logos*. In other words, they must join defenders of the corrupt and derivative Vulgate, against the reforms of Erasmus. We all know who won that argument.

DAVID SCOTT KASTAN

[Reforming Falstaff]†

No doubt, as has long been recognized, Shakespeare did not originally intend Hal's fat tavern companion to be named "Falstaff." As early as the 1630s, Richard James had noted that

> in Shakespeares first shewe of Harrie ye fift, ye person with which he vndertook to playe a buffone was not Falstaffe, but Sr Jhon Oldcastle, and that offence beinge worthily taken by personages descended from his title, as peradventure by manie others allso whoe ought to haue him in honourable memorie, the poet was putt to make an ignorant shifte of abusing Sr Jhon Fastolphe, a man not inferior of Vertue though not so famous in pietie as the other, whoe gaue witnesse vnto the truth of our reformation with a constant and resolute martyrdom, vnto which he was pursued by the Priests, Bishops, Moncks, and Friers of those dayes.[1]

Apparently objecting to the defamation of the well-known Lollard martyr, the fourth Lord Cobham (as Oldcastle became

2. Since this essay was written E. A. J. Honigmann, in *Shakespeare: The Lost Years* (Manchester, 1985), has provided new evidence of Shakespeare's early links with recusants in Lancashire.

† David Scott Kastan, " 'Killed with Hard Opinions': Oldcastle and Falstaff and the Reformed Text of *1 Henry IV*" in Kastan, *Shakespeare After Theory* (New York: Routledge, 1999), 93–106. Reprinted by permission of Routledge, Inc., part of the Taylor & Francis Group.

1. S. Schoenbaum, *William Shakespeare: A Documentary Life* (Oxford: Oxford Univ. Press, 1975), 143. James's account appears in the dedicatory epistle to his manuscript edition of Thomas Hoccleve's "The legend and defence of y^e Noble knight and Martyr Sir Jhon Oldcastel" (Bodleian Library, MS James 34). The epistle was first published in 1841 by James Orchard Halliwell [=Phillipps], and the entire manuscript was printed in *The Po-*

through his marriage to Joan Cobham in 1408), William Brooke, the tenth holder of the title,[2] seemingly compelled Shakespeare to alter the name of Sir John, acting either in his own right as Lord Chamberlain (as Brooke was from 8 August 1596 until his death on 5 March 1597) or through the intervention and agency of the Queen (as Rowe claims: "some of the Family being then remaining, the Queen was pleas'd to command him [Shakespeare] to alter it"[3]).

Pale traces of the original name, of course, seem to remain in the modified text. Hal refers to Falstaff as "my old lad of the castle" (1.2.37), the colloquial phrase for a roisterer seemingly taking its point from the name of its original referent; and a line in act two—"Away, good Ned. Falstaff sweats to death" (2.2.95)—is metrically irregular with Falstaff's name but arguably not with the trisyllabic "Oldcastle"[4] (and the image itself is grotesquely appropriate for a man who notoriously did virtually sweat to death, being hanged in chains and burned at St. Giles Fields, the spectacular martyrdom grimly memorialized in one of the woodcuts in Foxe's *Acts and Monuments*). Also, in the quarto of *2 Henry IV*, a speech prefix at 1.2.114 has "Old" for "Falstaff," a residual mark somewhat like phantom pain in an amputated limb[5]; and the Epilogue insists that "Oldcastle died a martyr, and this is not the man" (l. 32), a disclaimer that is meaningful only if it might reasonably have been assumed on the contrary that "this" might well have been "the man."

I do not have any substantive quarrel with this familiar argu-

---

ems Etc., of Richard James, B.D., ed. Alexander B. Grosart (London: Chiswick Press, 1880). In his "William Shakespeare, Richard James and the House of Cobham," *RES*, n.s. 38 (1987), Gary Taylor dates the manuscript in "late 1633 or early 1634" (p. 341).

2. Following the DNB [*Dictionary of National Biography*], most commentators identify William Brooke and his son Henry as the seventh and eighth Lords Cobham, but see *The Complete Peerage of England, Scotland, and Ireland*, by G. E. C[ockayne], rev. ed. by Vicary Gibbs (London: St. Catherine Press, 1913), vol. 3, 341–51, where they are identified as the tenth and eleventh holders. See also the genealogical tables in David McKeen's *A Memory of Honour: The Life of William Brooke, Lord Cobham* (Salzburg: Universität Salzburg, 1986), vol. 2, 700–2.
3. Nicholas Rowe, "Some Account of the Life, &c. of Mr. William Shakespear," *The Works of Mr. William Shakespeare* (London: Jacob Tonson, 1709), vol. 1, ix.
4. Stanley Wells says that this is "the only verse line in which [Falstaff's] name occurs" and notes that it "is restored to a decasyllable if 'Oldcastle' is substituted for 'Falstaff'," in his "Revision in Shakespeare's Plays," in *Editing and Editors: A Retrospect*, ed. Richard Landon (New York: AMS Press, 1988), 72. But it is worth observing that at least in the early editions this is not "a verse line" at all. The line appears as verse only following Pope. In all the early quartos, as well as in the folio, the line appears in a prose passage. In " 'This is not the man': On Calling Falstaff Falstaff," in *Analytical and Enumerative Bibliography*, n.s. 4 (1990): 59-71, Thomas A. Pendleton contests the assertion that the missing syllable argues for a merely perfunctory revision, pointing out how metrically rough the entire section is (and recognizing that it is printed as prose in the earliest editions), and how many simple ways there are to regularize the line if one only sought to substitute "Falstaff" for "Oldcastle" (62–63).
5. The text's "Old" could, however, stand for "Old man" ("I know thee not, old man") rather than "Oldcastle."

ment.[6] I have no new evidence that would confute it nor indeed any to confirm it. It seems certain that Shakespeare, in *1 Henry IV*, originally named his fat knight "Oldcastle" and under pressure changed it. The printing of the quarto in 1598 was perhaps demanded as proof of Shakespeare's willingness to respond to the concerns of the authorities.[7] Oldcastle thus disappeared from the printed texts of the play, though it is less certain that he disappeared in performance: Rowland White, for example, reports a production by the Lord Chamberlain's company in March of 1600 for the Flemish ambassador, apparently at Lord Hunsdon's house, of a play referred to as *Sir John Old Castell*. Though some have thought this to be *The First Part of the True and Honorable History of the Life of Sir John Oldcastle* by Drayton, Hathaway, Munday, and Wilson, it is almost certainly Shakespeare's *1 Henry IV* rather than the play belonging to the Admiral's men, which was unquestionably still in that company's possession (and so unavailable to the Lord Chamberlain's men) at least as late as September 1602, when Henslowe paid Dekker ten shillings "for his adicions."[8]

Yet whatever play was performed for the ambassador, clearly the character we know as Falstaff was sometimes known as Oldcastle. In Nathan Field's *Amends for Ladies*, published in 1618, Seldon asks, obviously referring to Falstaff's catechizing of honor in act five of *1 Henry IV*: "Did you never see / The Play, where the fat knight hight *Old-Castle*, / Did tell you truly what this honor was?" (sig. G1^{r}). Presumably Field, for one, did see that play with "Falstaff's" catechism in Oldcastle's mouth, seemingly did Jane Owen, who in 1634 similarly recalled "Syr Iohn Oldcastle, being expro-

6. There has, of course, been much discussion of the name change, most notably Gary Taylor's "The Fortunes of Oldcastle," *Shakespeare Survey* 38 (1985): 85–100; Taylor's "William Shakespeare, Richard James and the House of Cobham," *RES*, n.s. 38 (1987): 334–54; E. A. J. Honigmann, "Sir John Oldcastle: Shakespeare's Martyr," in *"Fanned and Winnowed Opinions": Shakespearean Essays Presented to Harold Jenkins*, ed. John W. Mahon and Thomas A. Pendleton (London: Routledge, 1987), 118–32; Pendleton's '"This is not the man': On Calling Falstaff Falstaff"; Jonathan Goldberg, "The Commodity of Names: 'Falstaff' and 'Oldcastle' in *1 Henry IV*" in *Reconfiguring the Renaissance: Essays in Critical Materialism*, ed. Jonathan Crewe (Lewisburg: Bucknell Univ. Press, 1992), 76–88; and Eric Sams, "Oldcastle and the Oxford Shakespeare," *Notes and Queries*, n.s. 40 (1993): 180–85. See also Rudolph Fiehler, "How Oldcastle Became Falstaff," *MLQ* 16 (1955): 16–28; and Alice-Lyle Scoufos, *Shakespeare's Typological Satire: A Study of the Falstaff-Oldcastle Problem* (Athens: Univ. of Ohio Press, 1978).
7. See E. K. Chambers, *William Shakespeare: A Study of Facts and Problems* (Oxford: Oxford Univ. Press, 1930), vol. 1, 382. Though it is perhaps worth noting that *The Famous Victories of Henry the fifth*, in which Oldcastle appears, was published by Thomas Creede also in 1598.
8. See *Henslowe's Diary*, ed. R. A. Foakes and R. T. Rickert (Cambridge: Cambridge Univ. Press, 1961), 216. Gary Taylor (in "Fortunes," 90) has similarly suggested that the performance for the ambassador [reported in a letter of 8 March 1599/1600 to Robert Sydney, *Letters and Memorials of State*, ed. Arthur Collins (London, 1746), vol. 2, 175] must be Shakespeare's play, but Eric Sams ("Oldcastle and the Oxford Shakespeare") has, energetically if not entirely convincingly, argued that "there is no objective reason to suppose that the text was not copied, or borrowed, or indeed commandeered, by the court company, the Lord Chamberlain's men" (182).

bated of his Cowardlynes" and responding: "If through my persusyte of Honour, I shall fortune to loose an Arme, or a Leg in the wars, can Honour restore to me my lost Arme, or legge?"[9]

I am concerned here with what Oldcastle's elimination from the subsequent haunting of *1 Henry IV* means—both for a critic of the play interested in its religio-political valences in the late 1590s, and for an editor of the text, necessarily concerned with questions of composition and transmission. Gary Taylor has recently argued that at very least what this history means is that editions of *1 Henry IV* should return "Oldcastle" to the play, restoring "an important dimension of the character as first and freely conceived."[1] And, notoriously, the complete Oxford text does just that; although somewhat oddly the individual edition of *1 Henry IV* in the Oxford Shakespeare, edited by David Bevington, pointedly retains Falstaff's name, arguing sensibly that as Falstaff reappears in other plays, depending on familiarity with the name and character of the fat knight in *1 Henry IV*, he must be considered, as Bevington writes, "a fictional entity, requiring a single name. Since that name could no longer be 'Oldcastle,' it had to be 'Falstaff,' in *1 Henry IV* as in the later plays."[2]

I share Bevington's resistance to Taylor's provocative editorial decision (though for reasons somewhat different than Bevington's and on grounds that he might not accept), and hope that my argument here, which attempts to reconsider the historical circumstances, both ideological and textual, of the act of naming, will lend it support. Nonetheless, Taylor's position has at least one solid stanchion. It cannot be denied that the name of Shakespeare's knight was initially "Oldcastle"; and therefore it may be helpful to consider that original act of naming. Critics who have commented on the "Oldcastle" name have usually focused on the perceived slight to the honor of the Cobham title and speculated either that Shakespeare intended an insult to William Brooke (usually, it is argued, because of Brooke's putative hostility to the theater[3]); or that Shakespeare intended no insult but unluckily chose his character's

9. The reference from Jane Owen's *An Antidote Against Purgatory* (1634) is reported by R. W. F. Martin in "A Catholic Oldcastle," *Notes and Queries*, n.s. 40 (1993): 185–86.

1. Stanley Wells and Gary Taylor, *William Shakespeare: A Textual Companion* (Oxford: Clarendon Press, 1987), 330. John Jowett has argued, on somewhat similar grounds, that Peto and Bardolph were names "introduced at the same time as Falstaff," and that their original names, Harvey and Russell (present in Q1 at 1.2.158), like Falstaff's, should be restored in modern editions. See his "The Thieves in *1 Henry IV*," *RES* 38 (1987): 325–33.

2. *Henry IV, Part 1*, ed. David Bevington (Oxford: Oxford Univ. Press, 1987), 108.

3. See, for example, J. Dover Wilson, "The Origin and Development of Shakespeare's *Henry IV*," *Library* 26 (1945): 13, who argues that Cobham was "a man puritanically inclined and inimical to the theatre." See also E. K. Chambers, *The Elizabethan Stage* (Oxford: Oxford Univ. Press, vol. 1, 297. William Green, however, in *Shakespeare's "Merry Wives of Windsor"* (Princeton: Princeton Univ. Press, 1962), has demonstrated that dur-

name, as Warburton argued in 1752: "I believe there was no malice in the matter. *Shakespear* wanted a droll name to his character, and never considered whom it belonged to."[4]

It seems to me unlikely that Shakespeare set out to mock or goad Lord Cobham, not least because, if the play was written, as most scholars assume, in late 1596 or early 1597, Cobham, who became Lord Chamberlain in August of 1596, was a dangerous man to offend; and no one has put forth any credible motive for the pragmatic Shakespeare to engage in such uncharacteristically imprudent behavior.[5] But Warburton's formulation can't be quite right either: that Shakespeare "*never* considered" to whom the name "Oldcastle" belonged. If the play does not use the fat knight to travesty the Elizabethan Lord Cobham, certainly it does use Sir John to travesty Cobham's medieval predecessor. Contemporaries seemed to have no doubt that Shakespeare's character referred to the Lollard knight. The authors of the 1599 *Sir John Oldcastle* consciously set out to correct the historical record Shakespeare had distorted: "It is no pampered glutton we present, / Nor aged Councellour to youthfull sinne, / But one whose vertue shone above the rest, / A Valiant Martyr, and a vertuous Peere" (Prologue, ll. 6–9). Thomas Fuller similarly lamented the travestying of the Lollard martyr by "Stage poets," and was pleased that "Sir John Falstaff hath relieved the memory of Sir John Oldcastle, and of late is substituted buffoon in his place."[6] George Daniel, in 1649, was another who saw through Shakespeare's fiction, like Fuller commending "The Worthy S^r whom Falstaffe's ill-us'd Name / Personates on the Stage, lest Scandall might / Creep backward & blott Martyr."[7]

If Shakespeare's fat knight, however named, is readily understood to "personate" the historical Oldcastle and "blott martyr," one might well ask what is at stake in his presentation as a "buffoon." Whatever Oldcastle was, he was hardly that.[8] Oldcastle had served the young Prince Henry in his Welsh command but had remained a

---

ing Cobham's term as Lord Chamberlain "not one piece of legislation hostile to the theater was enacted" and, in fact, between 1592 and his death in 1597, Lord Cobham "was absent from every meeting of the Council at which a restraining piece of theatrical legislation was passed" (113–14).

4. William Warburton, *The Works of Shakespear* (1747), vol. 4, 103.
5. See Robert J. Fehrenbach, "When Lord Cobham and Edmund Tilney 'were att odds': Oldcastle, Falstaff, and the Date of *1 Henry IV*," *Shakespeare Studies* 18 (1986): 87–101. But see also E. A. J. Honigmann, "Sir John Oldcastle: Shakespeare's Martyr," who argues that the play was intended "to annoy the Cobhams" and "to amuse Essex" (127–28), and suggests that the play "was written—or at least begun" in the first half of 1596 "before Lord Cobham became Lord Chamberlain" (122).
6. *The Church History of Britain* (London, 1655), book 4, 168.
7. George Daniel, *Trinarchodia*, in *The Poems of George Daniel, esq. of Beswick, Yorkshire*, ed. Alexander B. Grosart (privately printed, 1878), vol. 4, 112.
8. The best account of the life of Oldcastle's life is still W. T. Waugh's "Sir John Oldcastle," *English Historical Review* 20 (1905): 434–56, 637–58. See also the entry on Oldcastle in the DNB written by James Tait. The following paragraphs are indebted to both.

relatively undistinguished Herefordshire knight until his marriage, his third, to Joan Cobham, the heiress of the estate of the third Baron Cobham. At last wiving wealthily, Oldcastle became an influential landowner with manors and considerable land holdings in five counties. He was assigned Royal commissions and was called to sit in the House of Lords.

However, for all his new-found political respctability, Oldcastle remained theologically "unsound." Clearly, he held heterodox views. He was widely understood to be a protector of heretical preachers, and was himself in communication with Bohemian Hussites and possibly sent Wycliffite literature to Prague. Perhaps inspired by the decision of the council at Rome early in 1413 to condemn Wycliff's work as heretical and certainly encouraged by the newly crowned Henry V's need for ecclesiastical support, the English Church began vigorously to prosecute the Lollard heterodoxy, and Oldcastle himself was tried before Archbishop Arundel in September of 1413 and declared a heretic. Oldcastle was, however, given forty days to recant his heresy, no doubt because of his long friendship with the King, and during this period of confinement he succeeded in escaping from the Tower. Following his escape, a rebellion was raised in his name and an attack on the King was planned for Twelfth Night. The King learned of the uprising and surprised and scattered the insurgent troops mustered at Ficket Field. Oldcastle fled and remained at large for three years, hiding in the Welsh marches. On 1 December 1417, news of his capture reached London. Oldcastle was carried to the capital, brought before parliament, indicted and condemned. He was drawn through London to the newly erected gallows in St. Giles Field. Standing on the scaffold, Oldcastle, it was "popularly believed,"[9] promised that on the third day following his death he would rise again, whereupon he was hanged in chains and burned, as Francis Thynne writes, "for the doctrine of wiclyffe and for treasone (as that age supposed)."[1]

Although it took considerably longer than three days, Oldcastle was finally resurrected. As the English Reformation sought a his-

9. See DNB, vol. 14, 986. Stow, in his *Annals of England* (1592), reports that "the last words that he spake, was to sir Thomas of Erpingham, adjuring him, that if he saw him rise from death to life again, the third day, he would procure that his sect might be in peace and quiet" (572).

1. Quoted in David McKeen, *A Memory of Honour: The Life of William Brooke, Lord Cobham*, vol. 1, p. 22. Thynne's "treatise of the lord Cobhams" was written to honor Lord Cobham's admission to the Privy Council on 2 February 1586 for inclusion in the 1586/87 edition of Holinshed's *Chronicles*, but was excised from the edition along with other parts that touched on contemporary political events. Thynne presented an elegant manuscript version (British Museum MS add. 37666) to William's son, Henry, in December of 1598. See David Carlson, "The Writings and Manuscript Collections of the Elizabethan Alchemist, Antiquary, and Herald Francis Thynne," *Huntington Library Quarterly* 52 (1989), esp. 210–11 and 235–36.

tory, Oldcastle was rehabilitated and restored to prominence by a Protestant martyrology that found in his life and death the pattern of virtuous opposition to a corrupt clergy that underpinned the godly nation itself. Most powerfully, in the five Elizabethan editions of Foxe's *Acts and Monuments* (1563–96), Oldcastle emerged, as Foxe writes, as one "so faithful and obedient to God, so submiss[ive] to his king, so sound in his doctrine, so constant in his cause, so afflicted for the truth, so ready and prepared for death" that he may "worthily be adorned with the title of martyr, which is in Greek as much as a witnessbearer."[2]

Foxe, however, must explain away the charge of treason if Oldcastle's life is to bear compelling witness to the truth of the emerging Protestant nation. For Oldcastle to serve not just as a martyr whose life testifies to the perpetual struggle of "the true doctrine of Christ's gospel" against the "proud proceedings of popish errors" (vol. 2, 265) but also as the saving remnant on which the godly nation is built, his spiritual faith cannot be in conflict with his political loyalties. The heresy of his proto-Protestant Lollardy is easily dismissed by an emergent Protestant historiography but, since the Protestant cause in sixteenth-century England was inevitably tied to the monarchical claims of authority over the Church, the charge of treason is less easily accommodated. Oldcastle's putative participation in a rebellion against the King puts at risk what Peter Lake has called "the Foxian synthesis" of "a view of the church centered on the Christian prince and one centered on the godly community."[3]

Foxe, of course, successfully locates Oldcastle within this synthesis. He erases the tension produced by the insurrection by erasing from the chronicle accounts of Oldcastle's involvement in it.[4] Indeed, the erasure is literal, though Edward Hall rather than Foxe is the agent. Foxe reports how Hall had echoed earlier chroniclers in writing of Oldcastle's conspiracy "against the king" and was preparing to publish his account, but, when a servant brought him "the book of John Bale, touching the story of the lord Cobham," which had "newly come over" from the continent, Hall, "within two nights after . . . rased and cancelled all that he had written before against sir John Oldcastle and his fellows" (vol. 3, 377–78). For Foxe, the account of Hall's erasure of Oldcastle's treason is a con-

2. John Foxe, *Acts and Monuments*, ed. Josiah Pratt, in *The Church Historians of England* (London: Seeleys, 1855), vol. 3, 350.
3. "Presbyterianism, the Idea of a National Church and the Argument from Divine Right," in *Protestantism and the National Church in Sixteenth Century England*, ed. Peter Lake and Maria Dowling (London: Croom Helm, 1987), 195.
4. See Annabel Patterson, "Sir John Oldcastle as a Symbol of Reformation Historiography," in *Religion and Literature in Post-Reformation England, 1540–1658*, ed. Donna B. Hamilton and Richard Stie (Cambridge: Cambridge Univ. Press, 1996), 6–26.

version narrative that serves to guarantee Foxe's own debunking of the chronicle accounts of the Oldcastle rebellion.

Oldcastle's rebellion is finally for Foxe not an inconvenient fact but an outright invention of biased historians. He shows the inconsistencies and contradictions in the earlier accounts and concludes that it is merely "pretensed treason . . . falsely ascribed unto [Oldcastle] in his indictment, rising upon wrong suggestion and false surmise, and aggravated by rigour of words, rather than upon any ground of due probation." The invention, continues Foxe, is ideologically motivated, the charge rising "principally of his [Oldcastle's] religion, which first brought him in hatred of the bishops; the bishops brought him to hatred of the king; the hatred of the king brought him to his death and martyrdom" (vol. 3, 543).

But even if Oldcastle is innocent of treason, Foxe still must inconveniently admit "the hatred of the king," thus exposing the fault line in a historiography that would appropriate Lollardy as the precursor of the national Church. If Oldcastle is, as a Lollard, a martyr of the Protestant faith, he is, also, as one hated by the King, an uncomfortable hero of the Protestant nation. The unavoidable tension between Oldcastle's faith and Royal authority makes impossible the identity of the True Church and the godly nation that Elizabethan England officially demanded.

Perhaps it is on this note that one can begin to assess the question of why it is that Shakespeare should ever have chosen to portray the historical Oldcastle as the irresponsible knight of his play. In 1752, an article in *Gentleman's Magazine*, signed only P. T., asked, "could *Shakespeare* make a pampered glutton, a debauched monster, of a noble personage, who stood foremost on the list of *English* reformers and Protestant martyrs, and that too at a time when reformation was the Queen's chief study? 'Tis absurd to suppose, 'tis impossible for any man to imagine."[5] P. T. undertakes to explain away the evidence that Falstaff ever was Oldcastle in Shakespere's play, but since that evidence seems as incontrovertible as the evidence that Oldcastle, as P. T. says, "stood foremost on the list of *English* reformers and Protestant martyrs," one must assume that Shakespeare deliberately engaged in the very character assassination P. T. finds impossible to imagine.

Gary Taylor, committed to the original and the restored presence of Oldcastle in the play, has argued that Oldcastle's notoriety as a proto-Protestant hero is precisely that which demanded Shakespeare's travesty. John Speed, in *The Theatre of the Empire of Great*

5. P. T., "Observations on Shakespeare's Falstaff," *Gentleman's Magazine* 22 (October 1752): 459–61. Rudolph Fiehler, in "How Oldcastle Became Falstaff," has suggested that it is "not inconceivable" that P. T. was actually William Warburton (19).

Britaine (1611), had objected to the presentation of Oldcastle as "a Ruffian, a Robber, and a Rebell" by the Jesuit Robert Parsons (writing as N. D.), complaining that his evidence was "taken from the Stage-plaiers" and railing against "this Papist and his Poet, of like conscience for lies, the one euer faining, and the other euer falsifying the truth" (637). Marshalling evidence that purports to establish Shakespeare's sympathy to Catholic positions if not Shakespeare's commitment to the Catholic faith itself, Taylor, like Speed, takes the caricature of Oldcastle to suggest at very least Shakespeare's "willingness to exploit a point of view that many of his contemporaries would have regarded as 'papist.' " Noting other dramatic fact that admit of such an interpretation, Taylor concludes: "In such circumstances, the possibility that Shakespeare deliberately lampooned Oldcastle can hardly be denied" ("Fortunes," 99).

It can hardly be denied that Shakespeare has deliberately lampooned Oldcastle, but I think Taylor has somewhat misjudged the "circumstances" in which Shakespeare was writing and in which his play would be received. Whether or not Shakespeare was a Catholic or Catholic sympathizer, Shakespeare's audience in 1596 or 1597 was far more likely to see the lampooning of Oldcastle as the mark of a Protestant bias rather than a papist one, providing evidence of the very fracture in the Protestant community that made the accommodation of the Lollard past so problematic. Lollardy increasingly had become identified not with the godly nation but with the more radical Puritans, the "godly brotherhood," as some termed themselves, that had tried and failed to achieve a "further reformation" of the Church of England. If in the first decades of Elizabeth's rule the Lollards were seen (with the encouragement of Foxe) as the precursors of the national Church, in the last decades they were seen (with the encouragement of Bancroft and other voices of the Anglican polity) as the precursors of the nonconforming sectaries who threatened to undermine it.

No doubt recognizing that the radical Protestants were the inheritors of the doctrine and the discipline of the Lollards, as well as their reputation for sedition, John Hayward, in his *Life and Raigne of King Henrie IIII*, notes, as Daniel Woolf has observed, "with some regret the growth of Lollardy." The nonconformist community, the "favourers and followers of Wickliffes opinions," were consistently at odds with the crown, "which set the favour of the one and the faith of the other at great separation and distance." The political tensions existing at the end of Richard's reign and continuing through Henry's insure that Lollardy does not, in Hayward's history, comfortably anticipate the Protestant nation. "For Hayward," writes Woolf, "quite unlike John Foxe, Lollards were not early protestants but progenitors of Elizabethan Brownists, violators of the Reformation principle *cuius regio, eius religio*."[6]

But if Hayward recognized the nonconformist genealogy, he was not alone in doing so. In 1591, an almanac, written by a conforming astrologer identifying himself as "Adam Foulweather," predicted that "out of the old stock of heresies" would soon "bloom new schismatical opinions and strange sects, as Brownists, Barowists and such balductum devises, to the great hindrance to the unitie of the Church and confusion of the true faith."[7] And the separatist leader, Francis Johnson, writing defiantly from the Clink in 1593, himself confirmed his ties to "the old stock of heresies," proudly asserting that his opinions were identical to those that "were accounted Lollardye and heresye in the holy servants and martirs of Christ in former ages," like "the Lord Cobham (who was hanged and burnte hanging). . . ."[8]

Under the leadership of John Field (the father of Nathaniel Field, the author of *Amends for Ladies*), nonconforming Protestants had in the 1580s attempted the establishment of Presbyterianism by parliamentary authority, but by the mid-1590s, the government, led by Whitgift's rigorous promotion of uniformity and the Queen's continuing insistence "upon the truth of the reformation which we have already,"[9] had succeeded in its campaign against the radicals. Christopher Hatton's appointment as Lord Chancellor, as Thomas Digges remembered, marked a change of policy whereby not merely papists but "puritans were trounced and traduced as troublers of the state,"[1] and by the early 1590s, radical Protestantism, conceived of by the government as a threat to the polity, was in retreat, at least as a political movement. The "seditious sectaries," as the 1593 "Act to retain the Queen's subjects in obedience"[2] termed the nonconformists, were driven underground or abroad; and advanced

6. D. R. Woolf, *The Idea of History in Early Stuart England* (Toronto: Univ. of Toronto Press, 1990), 109. The two parts of Hayward's *Life and Raigne of King Henri IIII* have recently been published by the Camden Society, ed. John J. Manning (London: Royal Historical Society, 1991), and the quoted material is on 90–91. For an account of the association of Lollards with sedition, see Margaret Aston's "Lollardy and Sedition 1381–1431," *Past and Present* 17 (1960): 1–44.
7. Quoted in John Booty, "Tumult in Cheapside: The Hacket Conspiracy," *Historical Magazine of the Protestant Episcopal Church* 42 (1973): 293.
8. "That Fraunces Johnson For His Writing Is Not Under The Danger Of The Statute Of 35 Elizabeth, Chapter I . . . ", in *The Writings of John Greenwood and Henry Barrow*, ed. Leland H. Carlson (London: George Allen and Unwin, 1970), 463. An incomplete version of the document (Lansdowne MSS. 75, item 25, ff. 52–53) appears in John Strype, *Annals of the Reformation* (Oxford: Clarendon Press, 1824), vol. 4, 192–94.
9. See J. E. Neale, *Elizabeth I and her Parliaments 1584–1601* (New York: Norton, 1966), esp. 58–83; and Patrick Collinson, "John Field and Elizabethan Puritanism," in *Godly People: Essays on English Protestantism and Puritanism* (London: Hambledon Press, 1983), 335–70. The quotation from Elizabeth appears in Neale, 163.
1. Quoted in Patrick Collinson, *The Elizabethan Puritan Movement* (1967; rpt. Oxford: Clarendon Press, 1990), 388.
2. 35 Eliz. c. 1; in J.R. Tanner, *Tudor Constitutional Documents* (1922; Cambridge: rpt. Cambridge Univ. Press, 1951), 197–200. Neale sees the harsh turn against the Protes-

Protestantism, even as its evangelical impulse thrived, was, in its various sectarian forms, thoroughly "discredited," as Claire Cross has written, "as a viable alternative to the established Church in the eyes of most of the influential laity who still worked actively to advance a further reformation." Whatever Shakespeare's own religious leanings, then, certainly most members of his audience in 1596 would most likely have viewed the travesty of a Lollard martyr not as a crypto-Catholic tactic but an entirely orthodox gesture, designed to reflect upon the nonconformity that the Queen herself had termed "prejudicial to the religion established, to her crown, to her government, and to her subjects."[3]

Yet even if Taylor has mistaken the probable political implications of the lampooning of Oldcastle in 1596, what is for Taylor the most central bibliographic argument in favor of restoring the censored name "Oldcastle" to the text of *1 Henry IV* seemingly remains unaffected. Taylor argues that "[t]he name 'Falstaff' fictionalizes, depoliticizes, secularizes, and in the process trivializes the play's most memorable character" (95), and that argument would hold regardless of what the political valence of the suppressed "Oldcastle" actually is. Taylor's insistence that restoring "Oldcastle" effectively rehistoricizes the character of Sir John is compelling (even if I would rehistoricize it differently). However, what is to me troubling about the editorial implications of this argument is that restoring "Oldcastle," if it rehistoricizes the character, effectively *de*historicizes and in the process dematerializes the text in which he appears.[4]

Whether or not the travesty of Oldcastle would have shocked what Taylor calls "right-minded Protestants" ("Fortunes," 97)—and the answer clearly must depend upon what is understood to make a Protestant "right-minded"—whatever meanings attach to Shakespeare's fat knight, as Taylor's own argument shows, are not functions of an autonomous and self-contained text but are produced by the intersection of Shakespeare's text with something that lies outside it, a surrounding cultural text, what Roland Barthes calls "the volume of sociality,"[5] that the literary text both mediates and transforms. Yet if Taylor's critical response to the censored name "Old-

tant sectaries, equating schism with sedition, "as a revolution in parliamentary policy" accomplished by Whitgift and his party. See *Elizabeth I and her Parliaments, 1584–1601*, 280–97.

3. Quoted in Neale, *Elizabeth I and her Parliaments*, vol. 2, 163. For a different account of Falstaff/Oldcastle's relation to contemporary religious anxieties, see Kristen Poole's "Saints Alive! Falstaff, Martin Marprelate, and the Staging of Puritanism," *Shakespeare Quarterly* (1995): 47–75.
4. Jonathan Goldberg, in his essay in *Reconfiguring the Renaissance*, similarly argues that the restoration of the name "Oldcastle" works to "remove the traces of the history that produced the earliest texts of *1 Henry IV*" (83).
5. "The Theory of the Text," in *Untying the Text: A Post-Structural Reader*, ed. Robert Young (Boston and London: Routledge, 1981), 39.

castle" ingeniously acknowledges the interdependency of the literary and social text, his reintroduction of "Oldcastle" to the printed text paradoxically works to deny it.

Taylor insists that we should restore the name "Oldcastle" to the play since the change "was forced upon Shakespeare," and the restoration allows us to return to "Shakespeare's original conception" ("Fortunes," 88). "Oldcastle" is what Shakespeare initially intended and, therefore, argues Taylor, what modern editions should print. "So far as I can see," Taylor writes, "the chief, indeed the *only* objection to restoring the original reading (Oldcastle) is that the substituted reading (Falstaff) has become famous" ("Fortunes," 89, emphasis mine). But there is at least one other substantive objection to the restoration: that is, that all the authoritative texts print "Falstaff" and none prints "Oldcastle." "Oldcastle" may return us to "Shakespeare's original conception," but literally "Oldcastle" is not a "reading" at all.[6]

To disregard this fact is to idealize the activity of authorship, removing it from the social and material mediations that permit intentions to be realized in print and in performance. It is to remove the text from its own complicating historicity.[7] The restoration of "Oldcastle" enacts a fantasy of unmediated authorship paradoxically mediated by the Oxford edition itself. Taylor here privileges "what Shakespeare originally intended" ("Fortunes," 90) over the realized text that necessarily preserves multiple (and sometimes contradictory) intentions. While Taylor's commitment here to authorial intention is obviously not in itself an unknown nor unproductive theoretical position,[8] what is undeniably odd about this particular exercise of it is that it seemingly rejects what is the central achievement of the Oxford Shakespeare, which differentiates itself from its predecessors by acknowledging the fact that dramatic production in Shakespeare's England was never an autonomous authorial achievement but a complex social and theatrical activity in which authorship was only one determinant. The Oxford Shakespeare is, in Taylor's words, "an edition conspicuously committed to

6. In this regard it is notably different from the expurgation of profanity in the folio text. The uncensored forms exist in the 1598 quarto as readings that can be *restored*.

7. James Thorpe, in a seminal essay, "The Aesthetics of Textual Criticism," *PMLA* 80 (1965): 465–82, argued that in every work of art "the intentions of the person we call the author . . . become entangled with the intentions of all the others who have a stake in the outcome." Jerome J. McGann offers perhaps the most influential and sustained account of the literary text as a "social product," first in *A Critique of Modern Textual Criticism* (Chicago: Univ. of Chicago Press, 1983) and later in his *The Textual Condition* (Chicago: Univ. of Chicago Press, 1983) and later in his *The Textual Condition* (Princeton: Princeton Univ. Press, 1991). See, however, the essay by G. Thomas Tanselle, "Historicism and Critical Editing," *Studies in Bibliography* 39 (1986): 1–6, esp. 20–27.

8. See G. Thomas Tanselle, "The Editorial Problem of Final Authorial Intention," *Studies in Bibliography* 32 (1979): 309–54.

the textual and critical implications of the recognition that Shakespeare was a theatre poet, whose work found its intended fruition only in the collaborative theatrical enterprise for which he wrote."[9]

Obviously, Gary Taylor understands better than most editors that dramatic texts are produced by multiple collaborations, and the Oxford edition uniquely attempts to register these, presenting not "the literary, pretheatrical text" but a text as it appears "in the light of theatrical practice."[1] Yet what allows him in the case of the disputed name of Falstaff/Oldcastle to privilege Shakespeare's original intention over the operations of "the collaborative theatrical enterprise," the necessarily multiple and dispersed intentionalities of Renaissance playmaking, is Taylor's certainty that the change from "Oldcastle" in *1 Henry IV* was "forced upon" the playwright; that is, the replacement of "Oldcastle" is taken as evidence of an unsolicited and irresistible interference with the author's intentions rather than as a symptom of the inevitable compromise and accommodation that allow a play to reach the stage or the book shop. For Taylor the issue is clear: "The change of name is not an instance of revision but of censorship" ("Fortunes," 88). And as an instance of censorship it is a "depredation" to be editorially undone.

Indeed, it does seem certain that Shakespeare originally intended to call his character "Oldcastle," and it seems equally obvious that Shakespeare was, in some fashion, compelled to change the name. But the necessary vagueness of that "in some fashion" suggests a problem with the appeal to intention. If Taylor is correct to say that we "know what Shakespeare originally intended," his secondary premise is more vulnerable: that we know "why that intention was abandoned" ("Fortunes," 90). In fact we do not. If it does seem clear that political pressure was applied, it is less so in what form it was exerted. Taylor speaks confidently of "the censor's intervention" ("Fortunes," 85), but there is no record of any such action. It seems probable that Richard James's account is largely correct, that the Elizabethan Lord Cobham took "offence" at the travesty of a former holder of the title. But it is worth remembering that the scholarly James is writing well after the fact that with no obvious connection to any of the participants; and, although Nicholas Rowe's testimony is offered as "independent confirmation that the Cobhams were responsible" for the censorship ("Fortunes," 87), Rowe is writing at an even further remove from the events, and Rowe, as we've seen, actually says that "the Queen," not the Cobhams, commanded the

9. Gary Taylor and John Jowett, *Shakespeare Reshaped: 1606–1623* (Oxford: Clarendon Press, 1993), 237.

1. Gary Taylor, *Reinventing Shakespeare: A Cultural History from the Restoration to the Present* (New York: Weidenfeld & Nicolson, 1989), 311.

alteration, suggesting another source of pressure and muddying our sense of the nature of the interference with Shakespeare's text.[2]

My point is not to deny that governmental authorities were unhappy with the parody of the Lollard martyr, Oldcastle, but only to indicate that the available evidence does not allow us to say precisely why "Oldcastle" disappeared from the text of *1 Henry IV*. An influential family seems unquestionably to have objected to the name "Oldcastle," but it is less certain that the elimination of that name was a result of the operations of a process we can confidently and precisely identify as censorship. This is not to split hairs but to move to the heart of the bibliographic argument. If we have an example of the external domination of authorship, any edition of *1 Henry IV* that was committed to the recovery of Shakespeare's artistic intentions might well introduce—though certainly not *re*introduce—"Oldcastle" into the printed text; although an edition, like Oxford's, that insists "that Shakespeare was a theater poet" could plausibly, even in the case of such censorship, have found "Falstaff" to be the appropriate reading, since censorship was one of the inescapable conditions of a theater poet's professional existence.

But we do not in fact know that the replacement of "Oldcastle" with "Falstaff" was an effect of governmental imposition rather than an example of the inevitable, if arguably undesirable, compromises that authors make with and within the institutions of dramatic production. In the absence of documentation, we cannot tell whether we have a text marred by forces beyond the author's control or a text marked by the author's effort to function within the existing conditions in which plays were written and performed. It does seem certain that Lord Cobham objected to the scurrilous treatment of Oldcastle in the play, but we do not have the evidence that would tell us whether "Falstaff" is evidence of Shakespeare's subsequent loss of control over his text or of his effort to keep control of it; that is, we cannot be certain whether "Falstaff" resulted from the play's censorship or from its revision.

But the very uncertainty is as revealing as it is frustrating, suggesting that often no rigid distinction between the two can be maintained. Authority and authorship were usually not discrete and opposed sources of agency but instead were interdependent activities that helped constitute the drama in Elizabethan England.[3] No

2. It is worth wondering about how much weight to attach to Rowe's "confirmation." Rowe follows Richard Davies in recording the apocryphal story about Shakespeare's "frequent practice of Deer-stealing" in "a Park that belong'd to Sir *Thomas Lucy* of *Cherlecot*"; and the very passage that comments on the alteration of the name of "Oldcastle" includes the probably fanciful account, derived from John Dennis, of Queen Elizabeth's delight with the "Character of Falstaff" and her order to Shakespeare to write "one Play more, and to shew him in Love" ("Some Account of the Life, &c. of Mr. William Shakespear," *Works*, vol. 1, v, viii–ix).
3. T. H. Howard-Hill has claimed, for example, that Tilney's "relationship with the players

doubt some form of interference from above led Shakespeare to change Oldcastle's name to "Falstaff," but scrutiny and regulation were among the determining circumstances of playmaking no less than were boy actors in the theater or casting off copy in the printing house. Playwrights worked with and around censors to get their texts to the stage and into the shops. Finding what was acceptable to the censor was as necessary as finding out from the actors what played well. We cannot then say that "Falstaff" represents the "domination of the author's meaning" ("Fortunes," 92). "Falstaff" seems rather the evidence of the author's desire to have his meanings realized on stage and in print. Certainly, the use of "Falstaff" in subsequent plays suggests that Shakespeare, however happily, accepted the compromise of his artistic integrity, brilliantly incorporating it into his own intentionality.

Obviously we do not know what Shakespeare and his company thought about the change of name in *1 Henry IV*, but, claims Taylor, "the later intentions of Shakespeare and his company only matter in relation to a single question: would he (or they) have restored 'Oldcastle' to *Part 1*, if given the chance" ("Fortunes," 90). For Taylor the answer is "yes," confirming his decision to print "Oldcastle" in the edited text of the play. The stage history that apparently shows *1 Henry IV* occasionally performed "with the original designation intact," even after *2 Henry IV*, *The Merry Wives of Windsor*, and *Henry V* were written with the character of Sir John named "Falstaff," serves for Taylor as evidence that Shakespeare or Shakespeare's company continued to imagine the fat knight of *1 Henry IV* as "Oldcastle" ("Fortunes," 91).

But the argument from the stage history is at best inconclusive. Even ignoring the fact that intentions other than those of Shakespeare or his company might determine the choice of name, especially in a private performance, simply on the basis of the frequency of allusions to Falstaff in the seventeenth century (more than to any other Shakespearean character[4]), it seems clear that the play

although ultimately authoritarian was more collegial than adversarial," in "Buc and the Censorship of *Sir John Olden Barnavelt* in 1619," *RES*, n.s. 39 (1988): 43. For a full account of the mechanisms of dramatic censorship, see Richard Dutton, *Mastering the Revels: The Regulation and Censorship of English Renaissance Drama* (Iowa City: Univ. of Iowa Press, 1991). See also Annabel Patterson, *Censorship and Interpretation; The Conditions of Writing and Reading in Early Modern England* (Madison: Univ. of Wisconsin Press, 1984), who, while less interested in the processes of control than in its effects, sees the necessity for "assuming some degree of cooperation and understanding on the part of the authorities themselves" (11); and Janet Clare, *"Art made tongue-tied by authority": Elizabethan and Jacobean Dramatic Censorship* (Manchester and New York: Univ. of Manchester Press, 1990), who similarly understands that censorship "is perhaps the most potent external force which interacts with the creative consciousness" (215).

4. Gerald Bentley writes: "Falstaff was clearly most famous of all the characters of Shakespeare and Jonson in the seventeenth century. This fact ought to surprise no reader familiar with the literature of the time, but the overwhelming dominance of his position has perhaps not been so obvious." *Shakespeare and Jonson: Their Reputations in the Sev-*

was far more frequently played with the new name in place than with the residual "Oldcastle." The popularity of the character known as Falstaff was virtually proverbial. Sir Thomas Palmer remarks Falstaff's ability to captivate an audience as one benchmark of theatrical renown: *"I could . . . tell how long* Falstaff *from cracking nuts hath kept the throng,"* he says in a prefatory poem to the 1647 Beaumont and Fletcher folio, to indicate a standard against which to measure the collaborators' putatively greater success.[5] And Leonard Digges writes: "When let but *Falstaffe* come / *Hall* [*sic*], *Poines*, the rest—you shall scarce have a roome / All is so pester'd."[6] Sir Henry Herbert's office-book registers Falstaff's impressive cultural currency, referring to the play itself, as performed by the King's men at Whitehall on "New-years night" of 1624–25, as *The First Part of Sir John Falstaff.*[7]

Nonetheless, a bibliographic argument against Taylor's claim that Shakespeare or at least his company continued to think of Sir John as "Oldcastle" seems finally more compelling even than the theatrical one: his friends and fellow sharers were in fact "given the chance" to restore the censored name and manifestly decided *not* to return "Oldcastle" to the play. With the decision to collect and publish Shakespeare's plays in a folio edition, Heminges and Condell had the perfect opportunity to reinstate "Oldcastle." Indeed * * * they advertise the virtue of the 1623 Folio as repairing the defects of the earlier quartos, curing texts previously "maimed, and deformed" and printing them now "as he [Shakespeare] conceiu'd the[m]."[8] At the time of the printing of the First Folio, no Cobham was around to enforce the change of name demanded by the tenth Lord's sensitivity in 1596: Henry Brooke, the eleventh Lord Cobham, had been found guilty of treason in 1603 for his activity in a plot to place Arabella Stuart on the throne, and he remained confined in the Tower until his death in 1619. The Cobham title then remained unfilled until 1645. Yet in 1623, with the Cobham title discredited and vacant, Heminges and Condell did not see the restoration of "Oldcastle" to the text of *1 Henry IV* as a necessary

---

venteenth Century Compared (1945; rpt. Chicago and London: Univ. of Chicago Press, 1969), vol. 1, 119; see also 120 and 126.

5. Thomas Palmer, "Master John Fletcher his dramaticall Workes now at last printed," in *Comedies and Tragedies, written by Francis Beaumont and John Fletcher, Gentlemen* (London, 1647), sig. f2^v.
6. "Upon Master William Shakespeare, the Deceased Authour, and his Poems," in *Poems. written by Wil. Shake-speare. Gent.* (London, 1640), sig.*4^r.
7. Joseph Quincy Adams, ed., *The Dramatic Records of Sir Henry Herbert, 1623–1673* (New Haven: Yale Univ. Press, 1917), p. 52. That this was not an entirely anomalous practice is revealed by a notation on a scrap of paper from the Revels Office that has been dated *ca.* 1619: "nd part of Falstaff . . . " See Bentley, *Shakespeare and Jonson*, vol. 2, 1.
8. "To the great Variety of Readers," *The Norton Facsimile: The First Folio of Shakespeare*, ed. Charlton Hinman (New York: Norton, 1968), 7.

emendation to return the text to the uncontaminated form in which it was first "conceiu'd."

Taylor offers a conjectural argument that perhaps they "tried unsuccessfully" to reinstate the "Oldcastle" name: "The delay in printing Folio *Henry IV* could easily have risen because of an attempt to secure permission from the new Master of the Revels . . . to restore the original surname." Taylor, however, is forced to concede: "If Heminges and Condell did attempt to restore 'Oldcastle,' they obviously failed. . . ." Yet in the abence of any evidence that they in fact did try to restore the name or any that they were likely to have failed had they so tried, it is hard to resist the all-too-obvious conclusion that Taylor strenuously works to avoid: "that Heminges and Condell, as Shakespeare's literary executors, were happy enough to perpetuate 'Falstaff' in *Part 1*" (92). But so it seems they were. With no obvious impediment to reinstating "Oldcastle," Heminges and Condell retained the name "Falstaff," providing evidence not of Shakespeare's original intention, no doubt, but of the complex interplay of authorial and nonauthorial intentions that allowed *1 Henry IV* to be produced (and that allows any text to be produced), providing evidence, that is, that the play is not autonomous and self-defined but maddeningly alive in and to the world. "Falstaff" is the mark of the play's existence in history, and, perhaps in their most telling bibliographic decision, Heminges and Condell wisely left his "rejection" to Hal.

Origins

The selections that follow provide a range of contexts and sources which will, I hope, give readers access to some of the knowledge that the first audiences would have brought to the play and thus help them make sense of what is going on in *1 Henry IV*.

I begin with short extracts from Peter Saccio's *Shakespeare's English Kings*, a book which has for decades helped students to grasp the basics of the period portrayed in the Shakespearean history plays. It would be helpful for students to read the other plays, or at least *Richard II*, before working on *1 Henry IV*, but Saccio's summaries are a good place to begin, since they explain in brief the political arguments and events that precede the action of the play (though readers are advised to weigh certain of his underlying historical assumptions against the arguments of Graham Holderness later in this volume).

I then provide brief extracts from texts likely to have been familiar to playgoers in the 1590s: Hall's *Union of the Families of Lancaster and York*, the Holinshed *Chronicles*, and the 'Homily against Disobedience and Wilful Rebellion.' These selections offer a sense of early attitudes to Prince Hal, to the role of Elizabeth I in embodying national unity, and to the actions of the Percies (and, arguably, of Henry Bolingbroke in deposing Richard II).

Finally, I provide brief selections from three major sources for *1 Henry IV*: Holinshed again, Samuel Daniel's long poem *The Civil Wars*, and the anonymous play *Famous Victories*. Readers wishing to find out more about the nature of the deployment of these resources in the construction of the play are directed to the commentaries in recent critical editions of the play (notably David Scott Kastan's Arden edition), to Geoffrey Bullough's *Narrative and Dramatic Sources*, and to Peter Corbin and Douglas Sedge's Revels edition of *The Famous Victories* in their volume on *The Oldcastle Controversy*. On the nature and impact of the Holinshed *Chronicles*, Annabel Patterson's *Reading Holinshed's Chronicles* is very helpful.

PETER SACCIO

[Shakespearean History and the Reign of Henry IV]†

Shakespeare wrote eight plays on the later Plantagenets. Oddly, he did not write them in chronological order. He started with a tetralogy on the events from 1422 to 1485—the three parts of *Henry VI*, *Richard III*—and then, dovetailing into the previous work, composed a tetralogy whose story runs from 1398 to 1422—*Richard II*, the two parts of *Henry IV*, *Henry V*. Although the plays vary in quality, the first set being prentice work compared to the second, and although the reverse-chronological order of writing suggests that he started with an incomplete vision of the whole, the series of eight has high coherence as a history of fifteenth-century England. Indeed, far more than any professional historian, and despite the fact that the professionals have improved upon him in historical accuracy, Shakespeare is responsible for whatever notions most of us possess about the period and its political leaders. It is he who has etched upon the common memory the graceful fecklessness of Richard II, the exuberant heroism of Henry V, the dazzling villainy of Richard III.

Unfortunately, such central characterizations are often all that we retain from Shakespeare's history plays. Sometimes they are all a reader or playgoer ever firmly grasps. Not that Shakespeare neglected the exposition of surrounding circumstances: the problem lies in us. The characteristic complexity of Elizabethan plays suggests that Elizabethan audiences were more accustomed to comprehending a large cast and an intricate plot than modern drama has trained us to be. In the history plays, moreover, Shakespeare could rely upon a measure of prior knowledge in his audience. * * * The Elizabethans frequently derived from the reign of Richard II analogies to their own political problems. To a modern audience the question seems less than pressing. Editors of Shakespeare, of course, write explanatory introductions and footnotes. Introductions, however, are usually brief, and footnotes, by nature fragmentary, are awkward vehicles for conveying any quantity of historical information as well as distracting interruptions for a reader concerned with the dramatic values of a scene. As a teacher

† From Peter Saccio, *Shakespeare's English Kings: History, Chronicles and Drama* (New York: Oxford University Press, 1977), 4–5, 6–12, 13–15, 38–51. Reprinted by permission of the publisher.

of Shakespeare and an inveterate eavesdropper on lobby conversation at the various Stratfords, I find that many people let most of the history slip, consigning much of the dialogue about past relationships, present claims, and future intentions to a dimly perceived penumbra uneasily labelled "political complication." The process is understandable but unfortunate: it robs the playgoer of a good deal of the theatrical experience, and it places in the way of the student a considerable barrier to intelligent criticism of the plays. * * *

I aim to provide a brief coherent account of English history in the reigns concerned, concentrating on the persons and the issues that Shakespeare dramatized. I hope that it will serve as a clear introduction and a useful work of reference for the complicated story told by the plays, so that the reader and playgoer may enjoy Shakespeare more fully and more swiftly. * * *

Since students and playgoers may be thrust into the double tetralogy at any number of different points, it would be well, before plunging into detailed narration, to sketch the main lines of fifteenth-century English history. * * * Different accounts and interpretations of the fifteenth century have of course prevailed at different times. Distinguishing them is one of the tasks of this book. Since Shakespeare's version is dominated by a struggle within the royal house, the following summary stresses the dynastic issue.

We must begin with Edward III, seventh of the Plantagenet kings and ruler of England for the middle half of the fourteenth century (1327–1377). This monarch's extraordinary capacity for begetting offspring lies at the root of subsequent internecine strife. Of his twelve legitimate children, five sons grew up, were endowed with extensive powers and possessions within the kingdom, and passed these on to their issue. As long as the royal family itself remained united, Edward's generosity to his sons constituted an effective policy for governing England. In the absence of family harmony, the kingdom was almost sure to follow the Plantagenets into disorder.

Family harmony hinged largely upon the strength of the king. Unfortunately, Edward III's eldest son and heir, Edward the Black Prince, predeceased his father. Consequently, upon Edward III's death the crown went to a boy ten years old, the Black Prince's son Richard II. Although Richard stayed on the throne for twenty-two years, distinguishing himself in several crises by great personal courage, his reign never fully recovered from the circumstances of its inception. Surrounded as he was by powerful, not to say greedy, uncles and cousins, Richard the child was perforce submissive and Richard the adult tyrannically vengeful. Finally, in 1399, he overreached himself. After the death of his most powerful uncle, John of Gaunt duke of Lancaster, he seized the Lancastrian estates. Gaunt's son Henry of Bolingbroke, exiled in Paris, returned to England and gathered an army. Although Bolingbroke's professed aim was merely the recovery of his inheritance, he soon pushed Richard off the throne, into prison, and (some months later) into his grave, there being little else to do with a deposed medieval king.

As Henry IV, first king of the Lancaster branch, Bolingbroke was a ruler with obvious liabilities: a flawed title to his crown, blood on his hands, and debts in his pocket. Of the three, the debts were the most immediately important. Various noblemen had helped him to his precarious height. As soon as he displeased them (and no king can afford continual complaisance), it occurred to them to help him down again. For most of his reign, Henry's energies were consumed in meeting rebellions. As he was a shrewd politician and a competent soldier, he contrived to defeat the dissidents and die in his bed (1413). The record of his son was more spectacular. Henry V was another shrewd politician and probably the best general ever to sit on the English throne. Reviving an old claim of the English kings to the crown of France, he united his nobles by leading an expeditionary army across the Channel. At the end of two campaigns he was the acknowledged master of both kingdoms.

At this climactic moment history began to repeat itself. In 1422 Henry V died of dysentery at the age of thirty-five. The heir to two crowns, his son Henry VI, was nine months old. The house of Lancaster, having won its throne out of the turmoils of a royal minority, came to grief two generations later by producing a similar vacuum at the center of power.

Henry VI remained king of England for nearly forty years, but only nominally. The royal child became an adult saintly in personal character, incompetent in politics, and subject to occasional mental derangement. The royal uncles and cousins, in concert and in rivalry, asserted themselves. Driven out of France, which had been reinvigorated by Joan of Arc, they retired to England to bicker with each other. By the 1450s, their quarrelling had become armed conflict. In 1460, one of the royal cousins went so far as to claim superior right to Henry's crown. This was Richard duke of York, descended on both sides from sons of Edward III. Since his mother was heiress of the Mortimer family, the line springing from John of Gaunt's elder brother Lionel, Richard did indeed have a powerful claim, although it depended upon the principle that the royal succession could pass through a female—a controversial notion. The civil war thereupon became the dynastic struggle conventionally known as the Wars of the Roses: the Yorkists (white rose), led by Richard, versus the Lancastrians (red rose), led nominally by Henry but actually by his remarkable wife, the energetic Margaret of Anjou. When the dust finally settled, Richard, Henry, and Henry's son Edward were all dead, and occupying the throne was the house of York in the person of Richard's eldest son, Edward IV.

Except for a brief Lancastrian restoration in 1470–1471, Edward ruled competently for twenty-two years. Indeed, according to the arguments of recent historians, the reorganization of government that created the strong monarchy of the next century was in good part Edward's work. Dynastically, however, he created two serious difficulties for his house. First, instead of marrying the usual foreign princess, he wed an English widow named Elizabeth Woodville, a lady with an extraordinary quantity of relatives who promptly took advantage of their new royal connection by securing for themselves an abundance of titles, posts, and wealthy spouses. The inevitable quarrels between the older nobility and the upstart Woodvilles boded ill for the house of York. All might have been well but for the other dynastic difficulty: Edward died at the age of forty, when his two sons, Edward V and Richard, were but twelve and nine years old.

The familiar script was acted out once more, but this time at top speed. When Edward died in April 1483, the Woodvilles had custody of the young princes, whereas by the king's will authority was to reside in his brother Richard duke of Gloucester, who had no use at all for Woodvilles. Within three months and without a battle, the Woodvilles were out, the princes had disappeared forever, and Gloucester was crowned Richard III.

Richard's bold stroke, however, gave him only a two-year reign. In August 1485, one Henry Tudor invaded England from France, and the treachery of some of Richard's followers cost the last Plantagenet king his life at the battle of Bosworth. Henry claimed the crown by right of conquest and by Lancastrian inheritance: his mother was descended from the Beaufort family, John of Gaunt's bastard offspring who had been legitimated when Gaunt made his mistress his third wife. This rather feeble dynastic claim was strengthened by parliamentary confirmation and by Henry's subsequent marriage to Elizabeth of York, eldest daughter to Edward IV and sister to the missing princes. York and Lancaster were united in the new house of Tudor. The claim was made impregnable by Henry's efficiency as a king and by his and his son Henry VIII's thoroughness in disposing of the remaining Plantagenet heirs. The dynastic quarrel was over.

The preceding summary of fifteenth-century English history makes the dynastic issue paramount. Royal persons argue over who has the right to the crown; laws of inheritance and precise family relationships appear to control events altogether. To rest there, however, would be to falsify the picture. For example, given female succession, Richard duke of York did have a better claim than his cousin Henry VI. He refrained, however, from pressing that claim for many years; even after he asserted it, he was content at one point to be declared Henry's heir rather than his replacement. The original usurpation, that of Henry IV in 1399, was accomplished without much thought being given to the superior rights of the Mortimer line that was later to prove so troublesome. There was in the fifteenth century no written law governing inheritance of the crown, not even any established practice beyond the first principle that the eldest son of a king should succeed. Even the case of a grandson, as with Richard II, could raise some question, let alone circumstances involving more than two generations or descent through a woman. The various acts of parliament confirming monarchical titles in this period did little more than ratify accomplished fact, producing the genealogical justification appropriate to the case at hand and conveniently omitting whatever else might be said about the family tree. Whether parliament even had the right to declare who was king was a very delicate matter, debated then, and still under discussion by constitutional historians. This does not mean that anybody with sufficient influence, military capacity, and luck could have secured the crown for himself. The blood royal was necessary. Henry Tudor's promise to join his Lancastrian claim to the Yorkist claim by marrying a Yorkist princess brought him significant support. Given *some* dynastic justification, however, other factors determined the outcome.

Of other factors there was abundance. International politics played a role. Edward IV's recovery from the brief Lancastrian restoration of 1470–1471 was made possible by the assistance of the duke of Burgundy. Henry Tudor's attack on Richard III received aid from the king of France. Needless to say, these continental rulers were not acting out of disinterested charity. England, France, and Burgundy were engaged in ceaseless diplomatic maneuvering, each power fearful of alliance between the other two.

Probably more important than external pressures were social and economic conditions within England. The original Lancastrian usurpation was for many people vindicated by the success of the first two Lancastrian kings. Only in the social chaos of Henry VI's time, when the incompetence and the injustice of Henry's government were exacerbated by chagrin at the loss of France, did the York-Mortimer claim receive significant support. Edward IV's hold on the crown was in turn made acceptable to most people by his strenuous effort to correct local abuses and stabilize the royal finances. The usurpation of his brother Richard III was welcomed by some who feared another prolonged royal minority and who respected Richard as an energetic administrator.

Possibly even more important influences upon events—at least at any given moment—were the ambitions of individual noblemen outside the royal family. The immediate success of a royal claimant depended very largely upon his ability to attract support from nobles who could call up a fighting force, and these nobles were not driven by abstract passions for the rights of Lancaster or York. They aimed to secure properties or protect rights of their own; an alliance with a Henry or an Edward arose from temporarily congruent interests. Much betrayal and side-switching resulted. In 1455–1461, for example, the house of York had no greater ally than the earl of Warwick, who was the duchess of York's nephew; yet in 1470 Warwick betrothed his daughter to the Lancastrian heir and drove Edward IV temporarily from the throne. Perhaps influenced by modern civil wars fought on fundamental ideological issues, we are likely to imagine the York-Lancaster strife as an affair of more massive, coherent, and irreconcilable parties than was the case. Our inclination is reinforced by the romantic label, the Wars of the Roses, evoking as it does a vision of England divided into two camps whose members proudly flourished their red or white badges. In fact, there was almost no ideology involved, the armies were very small, and England went unscathed by any general destruction of life or property. As for the roses, they were made prominent by the Tudor historians rather than the Plantagenet combatants, popularized by Shakespeare, and turned into the standard formal name for the war only in the nineteenth century.

Just what did happen in the fifteenth century remains in many respects a puzzle. * * * First, there is a modern understanding of what happened in the fifteenth century, incomplete and full of questions though it be, built up by research historians. Secondly, there is a Tudor understanding. Henry VII commissioned an Italian humanist, Polydore Vergil, to write an official history of England. Vergil's book is the foundation of a lively tradition of Tudor historiography, culminating in two works that were Shakespeare's principal sources of information: Edward Hall's *The Union of the Two Noble and Illustre Families of Lancaster and York* (1548) and Raphael Holinshed's *The Chronicles of England, Ireland, and Scotland* (1578; Shakespeare used the second edition, 1587). Basic to these Tudor accounts is a belief in Henry VII as the savior of England. In part this belief sprang from the necessity to justify the Tudor acquisition of the throne: Richard III, for example, is made more spectacularly villainous than any man could possibly be, so that Tudor monarchy may appear the more desirable. In part the belief arose from the widespread sixteenth-century conviction that secular history displays patterns reflecting God's providential guidance of human affairs. Thus the deposition of Richard II is seen as a sacrilegious act interrupting the succession of God's anointed kings, a kind of original sin for which England and her rulers must suffer. The Lancastrians are then punished for their usurpation by the Yorkists, and the Yorkists by their own last king, until, England having atoned in blood, redemption may come in the form of Henry Tudor and his union of the rival houses. Thirdly, there is a Shakespearean perspective. This is, of course, still largely Tudor, since Shakespeare is writing during the reign of Henry's granddaughter, Queen Elizabeth, and drawing his material from Hall and Holinshed. Nonetheless, despite their large areas of agreement, the Tudor chroniclers, poets, and playwrights who dealt with historical matters (there were many) were certainly capable of individual interpretations of men and events. Shakespeare especially deviates from the received accounts because he is translating relatively formless chronicles into drama, taking historical liberties out of artistic necessity. Although there are limits on the liberties he can take—there is no point at all in writing a history play about Richard III if you have him *win* at Bosworth—he can, and does, change the personalities of historical figures, invent characters, compress the chronology, alter the geography, devise confrontations that never took place, commit anachronisms, and so forth. * * * Above all, Shakespeare personalizes. Whether or not history is really governed by the characters and the choices of individual men and women, the dramatist can only write as if it were. Social conditions, cultural habits, economic forces, justice and the lack of it, all that we mean by "the times," must be translated into persons and passions if they are to hold the stage.

* * *

[Saccio then provides a more detailed account of the deposition of Richard II and the reign of Henry IV.]

* * *

Henry IV was born Henry of Bolingbroke, only surviving son of the first marriage of John of Gaunt duke of Lancaster, who was in turn the third surviving son of Edward III. By his early thirties he had acquired a distinguished international reputation. He was famous as a jouster in tournaments; he had become an experienced campaigner while on crusade in Lithuania; he was noted for courtesy and generosity in the European courts that he had visited when returning from a pilgrimage to the Holy Land. He was energetic, learned, pious in an orthodox way, and popular among his own people. He was also a widower and the father of four sons. From time to time he had played a significant role in English politics.

Since the circumstances of Bolingbroke's usurpation provide some of the issues over which the characters of *Henry IV* wrangle, they must be related briefly here. In 1398, * * * mutual accusations of treason brought Bolingbroke and Thomas Mowbray duke of Norfolk to the point of trial by combat. The duel, however, never took place. [Richard II], presiding over the ceremony, threw down his staff of office to interrupt the proceedings, and, after consultation with his council, exiled both men. Early in the following year, when Bolingbroke's father died, Richard seized the Lancastrian estates. Bolingbroke thereupon broke exile, returning from France in July to regain his inheritance. Landing in the north, he was joined by various powerful noblemen who volunteered their assistance in the recovery of his rights and the reform of Richard's erratic behavior and financially exacting government. He proceeded to secure the capitulation of Richard's officials and to execute some who were held particularly responsible for misleading the king (the so-called caterpillars of the commonwealth). Richard himself, meanwhile, was in Ireland, attempting to crush rebellion there, and thus found himself badly placed to deal with the threat of Bolingbroke. He was, moreover, held there for some time by contrary winds and poor communications. Upon his return to Wales, his mismanagement of his troops, the treachery of some of his supporters, and the stratagems of Bolingbroke's friends resulted in his capture. Although Bolingbroke originally appeared to be seeking only the duchy of Lancaster, the unpopularity and collapse of the king allowed him to seize the throne of England as well. Richard was deposed and Henry crowned. After certain earls loyal to Richard attempted to restore him in January 1400, Richard himself died a mysterious death in prison. It was widely thought that he was murdered on Henry's orders, or at least by Henry's friends on his behalf.

The subsequent challenges to Henry's rule came both from persons who had assisted him and from those he had offended by taking the throne. Chief among his assistants was a family of border lords, the house of Percy. The Percies were the most powerful magnates in the northern counties of England, holding important castles and tracts of land in Yorkshire, Cumberland, and Northumberland. At the time of the usurpation, thanks in part to Richard's recent destruction of various other nobles, they were probably the most powerful subjects in the realm after Henry himself. They had repeatedly held the wardenships of the east and west marches (the areas on the Scottish border), thus directing border policies and receiving crown revenue to guard against Scottish invasion. In the raids and skirmishes common to the region, they gained much military experience and earned the intense loyalty of the people of the north. The head of the family was Henry Percy, upon whom Richard had bestowed the earldom of Northumberland in

(Born in 1341, Northumberland was a generation older than Henry IV; in Shakespeare, however, the king and the earl appear to be about the same age, and their sons are rivals in youthful chivalry.) Active in most of the political and military affairs of his time, Northumberland raised his family from the position of merely local northern influence it had enjoyed since the Norman Conquest, and from the barony it had held since 1314, into an earldom of national importance. His son, also named Henry Percy but known in his own time and ever since by the nickname Hotspur, was born in 1364. A soldier from his early teens, he led a distinguished career in the border warfare of the last decades of the fourteenth century. There was also a third significant Percy, Thomas, younger brother to Northumberland and uncle to Hotspur. Thomas eschewed the northern raids for service in the French wars under Edward III and in John of Gaunt's attempt to win the crown of Castile. Subsequently he rose in royal service at the court of Richard II, becoming steward of the household in 1393 and earl of Worcester in 1397.

Northumberland and Hotspur had been foremost among the nobles who flocked to Bolingbroke upon the latter's return to England in July 1399. They gave him valuable military support, and Northumberland carried out the essential maneuver of that summer, the capture of Richard himself in Wales. Worcester, having gone with Richard to Ireland, played a less central role. Nonetheless he significantly weakened Richard's position by deserting him, breaking his steward's staff and dismissing the royal household. One chronicler further reports Worcester to have been the first to acclaim Bolingbroke as king during the parliament that deposed Richard. If any besides Bolingbroke himself acted as kingmaker in the events of 1399, it was the house of Percy. By way of reward, the new king increased the Percies' already extensive power by granting them additional offices, revenues, and lands. Northumberland himself was made constable of England.

In 1403 this dangerous trio revolted against the king they had made. The causes moving them to insurrection are somewhat obscured by the biases of later chroniclers. Writers favoring the Lancastrians present the revolt as a proud and ambitious outbreak on the part of turbulent and ungrateful lords. Writers favoring Richard or the later Yorkist kings, committed to the belief that Henry's usurpation was unjust and disastrous in itself, see the Percies as rightfully opposing an unlawful king whom they had never intended to crown: they had willingly helped Henry when they believed that he sought only his stolen inheritance, after which events and Henry's cunning outstripped them. The heart of the matter is still a historical question: did Henry swear to the Percies, when he was gathering troops at Doncaster for his march south in July 1399, that he had no designs upon the throne? In 1403 the Percies claimed that he had so sworn, and that now they intended to rectify a wrong they had been tricked into abetting. Lancastrian chronicles either make no mention of such a vow or palliate its terms. To most modern historians it appears that no one as capable and experienced as the Percies undoubtedly were could have helped Henry to the extent they undoubtedly did without some perception of what the outcome might be; and that if they protested against that outcome when, with Richard locked up, Henry was openly arranging his own accession in September 1399, it is certainly strange that he should have loaded them with honors and powers once the crown was on his head. That is, if Henry did perjure himself at Doncaster, the Percies do not seem to have minded nearly so much in 1399 as they claimed they did four years later.

Money also caused trouble between Henry and the Percies. The latter were subject to heavy expenses as wardens of the marches, and the crown revenues assigned to them to meet these expenses were slow in coming. Here the Percies undoubtedly had a point. Henry IV had financial trouble throughout his reign; anxiety over money probably contributed to his premature aging and comparatively early death. As the heir of Lancaster, he had been a very rich young man who could and did spend lavishly and give generously. As king he had an even larger income, but far greater responsibilities. At one point his treasurer anxiously reported that, far from being able to obey Henry's orders to pay certain lords, he had no money in the coffers to pay even the messengers who were to bear summonses to members of the council. A particular difficulty lay in the late medieval system of royal finance, which was poorly designed for military expenditure. The regular crown revenue from crown lands, prerogatives, customs, and levies was barely sufficient to meet the king's ordinary expenses. Military campaigns were considered extraordinary expenses, requiring taxation in the form of subsidies voted by parliament. (There was no standing army.) Such subsidies entailed bargaining with parliament over each instance, and were moreover subject to long delays in collection and disbursement. Unfortunately for Henry, military campaigns were not in the least extraordinary in themselves. He was continually faced with border warfare in Scotland and Wales, and skirmishes with the French, as well as civil uprisings. The Percies had a just complaint, but it seems only fair to add that their financial arrears did not result from malicious or personally abusive designs on Henry's part. Hal, the king's own son, trying to govern Wales, and his brother Thomas, posted in Ireland, similarly complained about their inability to pay their garrisons. Everyone dependent upon crown funds, most of all the king himself, had the same problem.

Henry and the Percies were also at odds over the ransom of prisoners. In September 1402, at Homildon Hill in Yorkshire, Northumberland and Hotspur met a Scottish army led by their counterpart, the Scottish warden of the marches, Archibald earl of Douglas. The Percies inflicted a crushing defeat, capturing Douglas and a large number of other Scottish nobles. (A short list is given when the victory is reported in the first scene of Shakespeare's *1 Henry IV.*) As was customary with high-ranking captives, the king claimed the prisoners for himself, and Northumberland accordingly surrendered some. Hotspur, however, refused to surrender his (they included Douglas), arguing that their ransoms were due him in place of the crown revenues Henry had not paid him. The subsequent quarrel was entangled by another matter of ransom. Three months earlier Hotspur's brother-in-law, Sir Edmund Mortimer, had been captured by rebels in central Wales. the king refused to ransom Mortimer, a refusal that outraged Hotspur and hardened him in his resolution to keep his Scots.

The argument about the usurpation, the money problem, and the quarrel over ransoms all contributed to the worsening relationship between the king and his former allies. To what extent the Percies' grievances were just is still debatable. As a dramatist with an extraordinary ability to balance his characters against each other, Shakespeare does not decide which party has the better case: in *1 Henry IV* each side is allowed occasionally to make sound points, occasionally to bluster, and occasionally to fall victim to undermining ironies.

Perhaps the most significant cause of the Percy rebellion was a dynastic matter not yet mentioned: the rebels had a rival candidate, the earl of March, to place on Henry's throne. Henry IV's father, John of Gaunt, was the third son of Edward III. In seizing the crown after the deposition of Richard II, Henry had bypassed the issue of Edward's second son, Lionel duke of Clarence. This prince had died in 1368, leaving only a daughter, Philippa, wife to Edmund Mortimer third earl of March. (The Mortimer lands lay in the Welsh marches, that is, the border areas of western England and eastern Wales: hence the name of the earldom.) Both Philippa and her husband were dead by 1381, so that for the bulk of his reign Richard II's heir presumptive (formally so designated by the king) was their son Roger Mortimer, the fourth earl. His murder by the Irish in 1398 was the immediate cause of Richard's ill-timed trip to Ireland the next year. He in turn left a son, Edmund Mortimer the fifth earl, aged six at the time of his father's death. He was also survived by a brother, Sir Edmund Mortimer, a man in his twenties, and a sister Elizabeth, wife to Hotspur. (Holinshed calls her Elianor; Shakespeare changes the name to Kate.) If inheritance of the crown could pass through a female, Edmund the fifth earl of March, was, strictly speaking, the right inheritor of Richard's crown. Bolingbroke's swiftness in arranging his own accession and March's tender years prevented any significant claim being made on March's behalf in September 1399, but the existence of the Mortimers constituted an obvious threat to Henry thereafter. Accordingly, Henry kept young March in semicaptivity at Windsor from the beginning of his reign and, when Sir Edmund fell into Welsh hands in 1402, Henry was only too delighted to leave him there.

In the rebellion of 1403 the Percies aimed to put young March, now aged eleven, on the throne. From him they could expect greater power and less frustration than from Henry. Indeed, with Hotspur as his uncle by marriage, they must have expected to control the government altogether. Unfortunately, some confusion attends this dynastic issue for readers of Shakespeare. Shakespeare's sources (the historians Hall and Holinshed, the poet Daniel) mixed up the Mortimers, conflating into one person the youthful earl who was heir to the throne with his adult uncle who was Hotspur's brother-in-law and a Welsh captive. Shakespeare follows in this confusion: his "Mortimer" is an adult, Hotspur's brother-in-law, and a prisoner of the Welsh, and he is also the earl of March whom Henry's usurpation has deprived of his royal rights. (It is possible that, even if Shakespeare's authorities had not misled him, he would have conflated the Mortimers anyway, simply out of dramatic expediency. But it must be admitted that Shakespeare is not entirely consistent in the conflation: his Lady Percy at one point refers to "my brother Mortimer," and yet elsewhere she is called by him "aunt Percy.")

Discontent with Henry's rule sprang, not only from the houses of Percy and Mortimer, but also from Wales. During the late Middle Ages the English dominion over Wales, like the attempt to rule Ireland and the occasional assertions of overlordship in Scotland, inspired from time to time the actively expressed resentment of the local population. Throughout Henry IV's reign flourished Owen Glendower, the most pertinacious Welsh rebel since Edward I's thirteenth-century conquest of Wales. Glendower was a landowner of considerable position in north Wales, holding properties that his ancestors had ruled as independent Welsh princes. About forty at the time of Henry's coronation, he was a polished and educated gentleman. In his youth he had been an apprentice-at-law in one of the London Inns of Court and had married the daughter of a justice of the King's Bench. (Shakespeare combines this educated background with an expansion of Holinshed's hint that supernatural portents occurred at Glendower's birth: thus his Glendower becomes a remarkable union of English civilization and Welsh mysticism.) Glendower was not at first a revolutionary starry-eyed with the prospect of Welsh independence: only after several years of fighting did he pursue such goals. Initially he merely sought recognition of his rights as landowner.

The Welsh revolt originated in a petty quarrel between Glendower and a neighboring English magnate, Reginald Lord Grey of Ruthin. In the summer of 1400, Grey occupied some property whose ownership both men claimed. Shortly after, when Henry led an army into Scotland to demand the homage of Robert III, Grey may also have prevented Glendower from receiving the king's call to military duty, thus making Glendower look like a traitor. In September Glendower retaliated by burning Ruthin. He also sacked other English settlements in north Wales, his relatives (including the powerful family of Tudor in Anglesey) joining the outbreak. Responding upon his return from Scotland, Henry marched through north Wales, confiscating property and receiving submissions from some of the Welsh. There was no pitched battle, however, and Glendower himself eluded capture. Plagued by supply problems and unable to cope with guerrilla warfare in a difficult and unfamiliar landscape, Henry withdrew.

Every summer for the next eight years Glendower was on the attack. By the end of 1401 he was master of much of north Wales. In 1402 he captured Grey (who was ransomed) and Mortimer (who was not). That fall Mortimer threw in his lot with the Welsh, marrying Glendower's daughter and urging his friends by letter to join the Welsh cause. Thus Henry lost the allegiance of the Mortimer districts in the Welsh marches. Risings on Glendower's behalf also occurred that year in south Wales, and the royal armies were again prevented by difficulties of supply and by bad weather from coming to grips with him. In 1403, although he could not get to Shrewsbury in time to aid the Percy revolt, Glendower's successes continued in the same pattern. During the first half of 1404 he took the fortresses of Harlech and Aberystwyth in western Wales, part of the great chain of castles Edward I had built to secure his conquest. By this time he was leading a full-fledged national revolution: a Welsh parliament declared him prince of Wales and he concluded a treaty for assistance with the French. Although Glendower's aims concerned Welsh independence, not Henry's crown, a curious episode in this year reveals the direct threat Glendower posed to the new dynasty. The sister of the duke of York (Richard II's Aumerle), Lady Despenser, whose husband had been beheaded for his participation in the earls' plot of 1400, kidnapped young March and attempted to deliver him to Glendower. (The fugitives were overtaken before reaching Wales; York himself was probably privy to the conspiracy.)

The year 1405 marked the high point of Glendower's efforts. With French reinforcements, he invaded the west of England as far as Worcester. Here he in his turn experienced the difficulty of maintaining supply lines, and Henry, always at his best when speed was requisite, prevented him from getting to the city gates. The failure of two English rebellions, and the withdrawal of his French allies in 1406, severely damaged Glendower's cause. He lost Aberystwyth in 1408 and Harlech in early 1409. In the fall of Harlech to the English, Sir Edmund Mortimer was killed and most of Glendower's family, including Mortimer's children, were captured. Glendower himself seems to have returned to north Wales. He tried once again in 1410 and then disappeared into the Welsh mists. He probably died around 1415. Holinshed, however, reports that he perished of starvation in 1409, information that Shakespeare uses in *2 Henry IV*.

English control over Wales was largely the responsibility of the king's eldest son. The title "prince of Wales," bestowed upon the English heir apparent since Edward I's conquest, was no idle decoration. Those portions of Wales not held by marcher lords like Grey and Mortimer were ruled as a principality from Chester, albeit under the close supervision of the king at Westminster. Hal, aged twelve in 1399, could at first only be the nominal head of the governing council. As part of his reward for his assistance in crowning Henry, Hotspur was given chief authority. Hotspur resigned his post in 1401, complaining of the administrative difficulties and wishing to pursue his northern interests. His successor died not long after taking on the responsibility, and by 1403 Hal himself, at the age of sixteen, was king's lieutenant for Wales. Until the fall of Harlech he was principally occupied with the Welsh rebellion. If there is any truth behind the stories of his youthful profligacy in London that Shakespeare inherited from late Plantagenet and Tudor legend and used in *Henry IV*, Hal must have squeezed a great deal of self-indulgence into his winter trips to the capital. During campaign season he was otherwise occupied.

The Battle of Shrewsbury

1 Henry IV actually begins in 1402, with Mortimer's capture by Glendower (June) and Hotspur's victory at Homildon (September) as the latest news. The triple threat of Glendower, Percy, and the Mortimer claim, bound together by the Percy-Mortimer and Mortimer-Glendower marriages and by their common enmity to the new Lancastrian king, is emerging into the open. Neither in history nor in Shakespeare, however, does Henry lack support against the threat. Many lords remained loyal. Among them three require mention here.

The young earl of Arundel was son to the Arundel whom Richard II had executed in 1397 and nephew to Henry's archbishop of Canterbury. He had fled England after the execution of his father, returned with Bolingbroke in 1399, and regained his confiscated estates in 1400. Since these estates included extensive lands in the north of Wales, he was active in the conflict with Glendower and became friendly with Hal. In Shakespeare he is much less important than he was historically, appearing briefly and wordlessly in *2 Henry IV* under his other title as earl of Surrey.

Henry was also helped by a renegade Scotsman, George Dunbar the Scottish earl of March. In Shakespeare Dunbar receives only a single confusing allusion as having sent Henry a message about the rebels' movements. (The allusion—to "Lord Mortimer of Scotland"—is confusing because Shakespeare was confused. He refers to the Scottish earl of March as "Mortimer" because that was the family name of the English earls of March. The families had nothing to do with each other, and Dunbar's "march" was of course the northern border, not the Welsh.) Historically, however, he played a much larger role. After a quarrel with Robert III and the earl of Douglas, Dunbar had thrown his allegiance to the English crown and had helped the Percies at Homildon. Despite this comradeship in arms, his relationship with the Percies was fragile. Seeking under his new king control over border areas that he had held or threatened when loyal to the Scottish crown, he naturally came into competition with their territorial ambitions. Apparently it was he who first alerted Henry to the Percy conspiracy; certainly he urged Henry to deal with it swiftly and forcefully.

Another territorial rival to the Percies, and one who appears frequently in both parts of *Henry IV*, was Ralph Neville earl of Westmorland. In many respects Westmorland resembled Northumberland. Each was descended of a distinguished baronial family with northern properties; each had served as warden on the Scottish marches; each raised his family to an earldom; each was among the lords who first supported Bolingbroke in 1399. Unlike Northumberland, however, Westmorland remained loyal to the Lancastrian king, thus earning from Henry extensive gifts of land, offices, wardships, and pensions. Westmorland further married two heiresses, the second of whom was no less a person than Henry's half-sister, Joan Beaufort, John of Gaunt's daughter by Catherine Swynford. With the assistance of these wives he managed to rival Edward III's record for begetting influential offspring: of his sixteen children surviving infancy, four of the sons became peers, another became a bishop, and seven of the daughters married into noble families. The dynastic connections of the Nevilles made them one of the most powerful forces in fifteenth-century politics. Over half the people to be mentioned later in this book were the issue of or otherwise related to the first earl of Westmorland.

Shakespeare depicts the Percy rebellion as occurring swiftly but not so unexpectedly that the king lacks contingency plans or the time to send three armies out of London, led respectively by Westmorland, Hal, and himself. Actually, it occurred much more suddenly than that, and the royal family was not in London. The king was taken quite by surprise, and indeed the pace of events proved fatal to the rebels who initiated them. In the early summer of 1403, Hotspur raised an army in Cheshire. With him were three major confederates: his uncle Worcester, who had brought money from Hal's treasury in London to pay the rebel troops (he was officially Hal's governor); the earl of Douglas, who, like Mortimer, had become his captor's ally; and Sir Richard Vernon, a major Cheshire landowner. Hotspur had further concerted plans with Glendower and Mortimer in Wales. (Hotspur seems to have been on good terms with Glendower for some time: in 1401, when he was charged with the English defense in Wales, he had endeavored to secure a pardon for Glendower.) Northumberland, meanwhile, was still writing Henry letters from the north demanding money and reinforcements to meet the threat of a Scottish invasion. He told the king he feared revenge for the victory at Homildon. Henry started north, having decided first to aid his warden and then to move against the Welsh. On 13 July, while in Nottingham, he received news of the Percy revolt: Hotspur had issued proclamations renouncing his allegiance to Henry and was marching upon Shrewsbury, where Hal and his army were quartered. Persuaded by Dunbar not to return to London, Henry got to Shrewbury with remarkable speed, not only reaching the town before Hotspur but arriving well before Hotspur could expect reinforcement from his father in the north or from Glendower.

Battle was joined on 21 July two miles north of Shrewsbury. A parley preceded the battle, but the rebels rejected Henry's offers of reconciliation. According to one chronicle, Worcester, who served as the rebels' spokesman, deliberately misrepresented Henry's mercy when reporting back to Hotspur, thus causing Hotspur indignantly to refuse it. It is not certain that this was so: Worcester and Hotspur may genuinely have disagreed about the value of Henry's promises. That Worcester was treacherous even to his own nephew, however, was the tradition that came down to Shakespeare. In Holinshed, Worcester's aim "was ever (as some write) to procure malice and set things in a broil." That is, he was a born agent of chaos, something like a witch out of *Macbeth*. Shakespeare's Worcester is similarly malign, "malevolent to [the king] in all respects"; he is the evil genius of rebellion who, fearing that the king may later secure revenge upon him while forgiving Hotspur, deliberately suppresses the king's offers.

The battle itself was long and unusually bloody. Some combatants were still struggling at nightfall and casualties were very high. The earl of Stafford, who commanded one wing of the royal army, was killed; Hal, commanding the other in his first full-scale engagement, was shot in the face with an arrow but continued fighting. Inability to distinguish friend from foe led to much confused slaughter. Douglas and Hotspur made determined attempts to kill the king, during which many about him were cut down, including his standard-bearer Sir Walter Blunt. (Blunt, or Blount, had long been a retainer to John of Gaunt. After serving as Gaunt's executor, he naturally transferred his loyalty to Gaunt's son; he died at Shrewsbury at least partly because his armor greatly resembled that of his master.) Dunbar eventually withdrew the king from the forefront of the melee. Finally Worcester, Douglas, and Vernon were captured, and Hotspur perished, it is not known by whose hand. (Students of Shakespeare's sources have rightly pointed out that an ambiguous sentence in Holinshed makes it possible to suppose that Hal killed Hotspur. Hall's chronicle, however, which was Holinshed's own source at this point and was possibly consulted by Shakespeare, does not convey this false suggestion, and surely Shakespeare, having arranged Hotspur's age, the king's anxieties about his son, and many passages of dialogue to bring Hal and Hotspur into competing contrast, could have invented the climactic duel of *1 Henry IV* without the aid of stray ambiguities.) Much of the rebel army then fled. After the battle, Douglas was kept in captivity, from which he was not finally released until 1408. Worcester and Vernon, however, were immediately executed for treason. Portions of their bodies and of Hotspur's were then placed on public display in various cities, the customary manner of advertising the fate of rebels.

* * *

EDWARD HALL

Henry, Prince of Wales†

Henry Prince of Wales, sonne and heire to kyng Henry the. iiii. borne at Monmouth on the Riuer of Wye, after the obsequies of his noble parent solemply celebrate and sumpteously finished, toke vpon him the high power & regiment of this realme of Englande the. xx. daie of Marche in the yere after that Christ our sauior had entered into the immaculate wombe of the holy Uirgin his naturall mother a thousande foure hundred and. xii. and was crouned the. ix. daie of Aprill then next ensuyng, and proclaimed kyng by the name of kyng Henry the fifth. . . .

THIS kyng, this man was he, whiche (accordying to the olde Prouerbe) declared and shewed that honors ought to change maners, for incontinent after that he was stalled in the siege royall, and had receiued the croune and scepter of the famous and fortunate region, determined with hymself to put on the shape of a new man, and to vse another sorte of liuyng, turnyng insolencie and wildnes into grauitie and sobernes, and wauerying vice into constant vertue. And to thentent that he would so continue without goying backe, & not therunto bee allured by his familier compaignions, with whom he had passed his young age and wanton pastime & riotous misorder (insomuche that for imprisonmente of one of his wanton mates and vnthriftie plaifaiers he strake the chiefe Justice with his fiste on the face. For whiche offence he was not onely commited to streight prison, but also of his father put out of the preuy counsaill and banished the courte, and his brother Thomas duke of Clarence elected president of the kynges counsaill to his great displeasure and open reproche) he therfore banished and seperated from hym all his old flatterers and familier compaignions, (not vnrewarded nor yet vnpreferred) inhibityng them vpon a greate pain not once to approche ether to his speche or presence, nor yet to lodge or soiourne within ten miles of his courte or mansion. And in their places he elected and chose men of grauitee, men of witte, and men of high policy, by whose wise counsaill and prudente instruccion he myghte at all tymes rule to his honor and gouerne to his profite. This prince was almost the Arabical Phenix, and emongest his predecessors a very Paragon. . . .

† From Edward Hall, *The Union of the Two Noble and Illustrious Families of Lancaster and York* (London, 1548), fol.1r.

RAPHAEL HOLINSHED

Elizabeth and the Uniting of the Two Houses†

Upon the lowest stage was made one seat roiall, wherein were placed two personages, representing king Henrie the seuenth, and Elizabeth his wife, daughter of king Edward the fourth; either of these two princes sitting vnder one cloth of estate in their seates, none otherwise diuided, but that the one of them which was king Henrie the seuenth, proceeding out of the house of Lancaster, was inclosed in a red rose, and the other which was queene Elizabeth, being heire to the house of Yorke, inclosed with a white rose, each of them roiallie crowned. . . . And these personages were so set, that the one of them ioined hands with the other, with the ring of matrimonie perceiued on the finger. Out of the which two roses sprang two branches gathered into one, which were directed vpward to the second stage or degree, wherein was placed one representing the valiant & noble prince king Henrie the eight, which sproong out of the former stocke, crowned with a crowne imperiall, and by him sat one representing the right woorthie ladie queene Anne, wife to the said king Henrie the eight, and mother to our most souereigne ladie queene Elizabeth that now is, both apparelled with scepters and diadems, and other furniture due to the state of a king and queene. . . . From their seat also proceeded vpwards one branch, directed to the third and vppermost stage or degree, wherein likewise was planted a seat roiall, in the which was set one representing the queenes most excellent maiestie Elizabeth, now our most dread souereigne ladie. . . . The two sides of the same were filled with lowd noises of musicke. And all emptie places thereof were furnished with sentences concerning vnitie, and the whole pageant garnished with red roses and white. And in the fore front of the same pageant, in a faire wreath, was written the name and title of the same, which was; The vniting of the two houses of Lancaster and Yorke. This pageant was grounded vpon the queens maiesties name. For like as the long warre betweene the two houses of Yorke and Lancaster then ended, when Elizabeth daughter to Edward the fourth matched in mariage with Henrie the seuenth, heire to the house of Lancaster: so sith that the queenes maiesties name was Elizabeth, & for somuch as she is the onelie heire of Henrie the eight, which came of both the houses, as the knitting vp of concord: it was deuised, that like as Elizabeth was the first occasion of

† From Raphael Holinshed, *The Third Volume of Chronicles* (London, 1587), 5T3v.

concord, so she another Elizabeth, might mainteine the same among hir subiects, so that vnitie was the end whereat the whole deuise shot, as the queenes maiesties name moued the first ground.

ANONYMOUS

An Homilee agaynst disobedience and wylful rebellion†

. . . Thus you do see, that neither heauen nor paradise coulde suffer anye rebellion in them, neyther be places for any rebels to remayne in. Thus became rebellion, as you see, both the first and greatest, and the verye roote of all other sinnes, and the first and principall cause both of all worldlye and bodyly miseries, sorowes, diseases, sicknesses, and deathes, and whiche is infinitely worse then all these, as is sayde, the very cause of death and dampnation eternall also. After this breache of obedience to God, and rebellion agaynst his maiestie, all mischeefes and miseries breaking in therewith, and ouerflowying the worlde, lest all thinges shoulde come vnto confusion and vtter ruine, GOD forthwith by lawes geuen vnto mankynde, repayred agayne the rule and order of obedience thus by rebellion ouerthrowen, and besides the obedience due vnto his maiestie, he not onlye ordayned that in families and housholdes, the wyfe should be obedient vnto her husbande, the chyldren vnto their parentes, the seruauntes vnto their maisters: but also when mankynde increased, and spread it selfe more largely ouer the worlde, he by his holye worde did constitute and or[d]ayne in Cities and Countreys seuerall and speciall gouernours and rulers, vnto whom the residue of his people shoulde be obedient.

As in readyng of the holye scriptures, we shall finde in very many and almost infinite places, as well of the olde Testament, as of the newe, that kynges and princes, as well the euill as the good, do raigne by Gods ordinaunce, and that subiectes are bounden to obey them: that God doth geue princes wysdome, great power, and aucthoritie: that God defendeth them agaynst their enemies, and destroyeth their enemies horribly: that the anger and displeasure of the prince is as the roaring of a Lion, and the very messenger of death: and that the subiect, that prouoketh hym to displeasure, sin-

† From "An Homilee agaynst disobedience and wylful rebellion," in *The Second Tome of Homilees* (London, 1571), Sermon XXI, pp. 546–47, 549–51, 552, 554–55, 573–74, 594–95. Marginal glosses have been omitted. This homily was added in 1571 to those authorized for use in the English church in connection with the unsuccessful uprising in the North in 1569 and ends with a "thanksgiving for the suppression of the last rebellion."

neth agaynst his owne soule: With many other thinges, concernying both the aucthoritie of princes, and the duetie of subiectes.

. . . It commeth therfore neyther of chaunc and fortune (as they tearme it) nor of thambition [sic] of mortal men and women climing vp of theyr owne accorde to dominion, that there be Kynges, Queenes, princes, and other gouernours ouer men beyng theyr subiectes: but al Kinges, Queenes, and other gouernours are specially appoynted by the ordinaunce of GOD. And as GOD him selfe, beyng of an infinite maiestie, power, and wysdome, ruleth and gouerneth all thynges in heauen and in earth, as the vniuersal Monarche & onlye Kyng and Emperour ouer all, as beyng onlye able to take and beare the charge of all: so hath he constituted, ordayned, and set earthly princes ouer particuler kyngdomes and dominions in earth, both for the auoydyng of all confusion, whiche els woulde be in the worlde if it should be without such gouernours, and for the great quiet and benefite of earthly men theyr subiectes, and also that the princes them selues in aucthoritie, power, wysdome, prouidence, and ryghteousnes in gouernment of people and countreys, committed to their charge, shoulde resemble his heauenly gouernaunce, as the maiestie of heauenly thinges may by the bacenes of earthly thinges be shadowed and resembled: And for that similitude that is betweene the heauenly Monarchie, and earthly kyngdomes wel gouerned, our sauiour Christe in sundry parables, sayth that the kyngdome of heauen is resembled vnto a man a kyng, and as the name of the kyng is very often attributed and geuen vnto GOD in the holy scriptures, so doth GOD hym selfe in the same scriptures sometyme vouchsafe to communicate his name with earthly princes, tearming them gods: Doubtles for that similitude of gouernment which they haue or should haue not vnlike vnto GOD their king. Unto the which similitude of heauenly gouernment, the nearer and nearer that an earthly prince doth come in his regiment, the greater blessing of Gods mercie is he vnto that countrey and people ouer whom he raigneth: and the further and further that an earthlye prince doth swarue from the example of the heauenly gouernment, the greater plague he is of Gods wrath, and punishment by Gods iustice, vnto that countrey & people, ouer whom God for their sinnes hath placed suche a prince and gouernour.

. . . What shall subiectes do then? shall they obeye valiaunt, stout, wyse, and good Princes, and contempne, disobey, and rebel agaynst chyldren being theyr Princes, or against vndiscrete and euill gouernours: GOD forbid. For fyrst what a perilous thing were it to commit vnto the subiectes the iudgement whiche Prince is wyse and godly, and his gouernmẽt good, and which is otherwyse: as though the foote must iudge of the head: an enterprise very haynous, and must needes breede rebellion. For who els be they that are moste enclined to rebellion, but suche hautie spirites? From whom springeth suche foule ruine of Realmes? Is not rebellion the greatest of all mischeefes? And who are most readye to the greatest mischeefes, but the worste men? Rebelles therefore the worst of all subiectes are most redye to rebellion, as beyng the worst of all vices, and furthest from the duetie of a good subiect: as on the contrary part, the best subiectes are moste firme and constant in obedience, as in the speciall and peculier vertue of good subiectes. . . .

But what yf the prince be vndiscrete, and euil in deede, and it also euident to all mens eyes, that he so is? I aske agayne, what yf it be long of the wickedness of the subiectes, that the prince is vndiscrete and euyll? Shal the subiectes both by their wickednesse prouoke God for their deserued punishment to geue them an vndiscrete or euyll prince, and also rebell agaynst hym, and withall agaynst God, who for the punishment of their sinnes dyd geue them suche a prince? Wyll you heare the scriptures concernyng this poynt? God (say the holy scriptures) maketh a wicked man to raigne for the sinnes of the people. Agayne, God geueth a prince in his anger (meaning an euill one) and taketh away a good prince in his displeasure, meaning speciallye when he taketh away a good prince, for the sinnes of the people: as in our memorie he toke away our good Iosias kyng Edwarde in his young and good yeres for our wickednesse. And contrarilye the scriptures do teache that God geueth wysdome vnto princes, and maketh a wyse and good kyng to raigne ouer that people whom he loueth, and who loueth hym. Agayne, yf the prople obey God, both they and theyr kyng shall prosper and be safe, els both shall perishe, sayth God by the mouth of Samuel.

Here you see, that GOD placeth as well euyll princes as good, and for what cause he doth both. If we therefore wyll haue a good prince, eyther to be geuen vs, or to continue, nowe we haue suche a one, let vs by our obedience to God and to our prince, moue God thereunto. If we wwyll haue an euyll prince (when God shall sende such a one) taken away, and a good in his place, let vs take away our wickednesse whiche prouoketh God to place such a one ouer vs, & God wyll eyther displace hym, or if an euyll prince, make hym a good prince: so that we first wyll chaunge our euyll into good.

. . . How horrible a sinne agaynst God and man rebellion is, cannot possible be expressed accordyng vnto the greatnesse thereof. For he that nameth rebellion, nameth not a singuler, or one onely sinne, as is theft, robbery, murther, & such lyke: but he nameth the whole puddle and sinke of all sinnes agaynst God and man, agaynst his prince, his countrey, his countreymen, his parentes, his children, his kinsfolkes, his frendes, and agaynst all men vniuersally, all sinnes I say agaynst God and al men heaped together nameth he, that nameth rebellion.

. . . Wherefore to conclude, let all good subiectes consydering how horrible a sinne agaynst God, theyr prince, their countrey, and countreymen, agaynst all Gods and mans lawes rebellion is, beyng in deede not one seuerall sinne, but all sinnes agaynst God and man heaped together, consydering the mischeuous life and deedes, and the shamefull endes and deathes of all rebels hitherto, and the pitifull vndoyng of their wyues, chyldren, and families, and disheriting of theyr heyres for euer, and aboue all thinges consydering the eternall dampnation that is prepared for all impenitent rebels in hell with Satan the first founder of rebellion, and graunde captayne of all rebels, let all good subiectes I say, consyderyng these thinges, auoide and flee all rebellion, as the greatest of all mischeefes, and embrace due obedience to God and our prince, as the greatest of all vertues, that we may both escape all euils and miseries that do folowe rebellion in this worlde, and eternall dampnation in the world to come and enioye peace, quietnesse, and securities, with all other Gods benefites and blessinges, which folowe obedience in this life, and finally may enjoy the kyngdome of heauen the peculier place of all obedient subiects to God and their prince, in the world to come: which I beseche God the kyng of all kynges, graunt vnto vs for the obedience of his sonne our Sauiour Jesus Christe, vnto whom with the father and the holy ghost, one God and kyng immortall, all honour, seruice, and obedience of all his creatures is due for euer and euer. Amen.

RAPHAEL HOLINSHED

The Chronicles of England†

[Anno 1402]: . . . Owen Glendouer, according to his accustomed manner, robbing and spoiling within the English borders, caused all the forces of the shire of Hereford to assemble togither against them, vnder the conduct of Edmund Mortimer earle of March. But cōming to trie the matter by battell, whether by treason or otherwise, so it fortuned, that the English power was discomfited, the

† From *The Chronicles of England, from William the Conqueror . . . Faithfullie gathered and compiled by Raphaell Holinshed* (Second edition, 1587), III, 520, 521–24, 538–39.

earle taken prisoner, and aboue a thousand of his people slaine in the place. The shamefull villainie vsed by the Welshwomen towards the dead carcasses, was such, as honest eares would be ashamed to heare, and continent toongs to speake thereof. The dead bodies might not be buried, without great summes of monie giuen for libertie to conueie them awaie.

The king was not hastie to purchase the deliuerance of the earle March, bicause his title to the crowne was well inough knowen, and therefore suffered him to remaine in miserable prison, wishing both the said earle, and all other of his linage out of this life, with God and his saincts in heauen, so they had beene out of the waie, for then all had beene well inough as he thought. . . . About mid of August, the king to chastise the presumptuous attempts of the Welshmen, went with a great power of men into Wales, to pursue the capteine of the Welsh rebell Owen Glendouer, but in effect he lost his labor; for Owen conueied himself out of the waie, into his knowen lurking places, and (as was thought) through art magike, he caused such foule weather of winds, tempest, raine, snow, and haile to be raised, for the annoiance of the kings armie, that the like had not beene heard of; in such sort, that the king was constreined to returne home, hauing caused his people yet to spoile and burne first a great part of the countrie. . . . The Scots vnder the leding of Patrike Hepborne, of the Hales the yoonger, entring into England, were ouerthrowen at Nesbit, in the marches, as in the Scotish chronicle ye may find more at large. This battell was fought the two and twentith of Iune, in this yeare of our Lord 1402.

Archembald earle Dowglas sore displeased in his mind for this ouerthrow, procured a commission to inuade England, and that to his cost, as ye may likewise read in the Scotish histories. For at a place called Homildon, they were so fiercelie assailed by the Englishmen, vnder the leading of the lord Persie, surnamed Henrie Hotspur, and George earle of March, that with violence of the English shot they were quite vanquished and put to flight, on the Rood daie in haruest, with a great slaughter made by the Englishmen. . . . There were slaine of men of estimation, sir Iohn Swinton, sir Adam Gordon, sir Iohn Leuiston, sir Alexander Ramsie of Dalehousie, and three and twentie knights, besides ten thousand of the commons: and of prisoners among other were these, Mordacke earle of Fife, son to the gouernour Archembald earle Dowglas, which in the fight lost one of his eies, Thomas erle of Murrey, Robert earle of Angus, and (as some writers haue) the earles of Atholl & Menteith, with fiue hundred other of meaner degrees.

[Anno 1403] Edmund Mortimer earle of March, prisoner with Owen Glendouer, whether for irkesomnesse of cruell captiuitie, or feare of death, or for what other cause, it is vncerteine, agreed to take part with Owen, against the king of England, and tooke to wife the daughter of the said Owen.

Strange wonders happened (as men reported) at the natiuitie of this man, for the same night he was borne, all his fathers horsses in the stable were found to stand in bloud vp to the bellies. . . .

Henrie earle of Northumberland, with his brother Thomas earle of Worcester, and his sonne the lord Henrie Persie, surnamed Hotspur, which were to king Henrie in the beginning of his reigne, both faithfull freends, and earnest aiders, began now to enuie his wealth and felicitie; and especiallie they were greeued, bicause the king demanded of the earle and his sonne such Scotish prisoners as were taken at Homeldon and Nesbit: for of all the captiues which were taken in the conflicts foughten in those two places, there was deliuered to the kings possession onelie Mordake earle of Fife, the duke of Albanies sonne, though the king did diuers and sundrie times require deliuerance of the residue, and that with great threatnings: wherewith the Persies being sore offended, for that they claimed them as their owne proper prisoners, and their peculiar preies, by the counsell of the lord Thomas Persie earle of Worcester, whose studie was euer (as some write) to procure malice, and set things in a broile, came to the king vnto Windsore (vpon a purpose to prooue him) and there required of him, that either by ransome or otherwise, he would cause to be deliuered out of prison Edmund Mortimer earle of March, their cousine germane, whome (as they reported) Owen Glendouer kept in filthie prison, shakled with irons, onelie for that he tooke his part, and was to him faithfull and true.

The king began not a little to muse at the request, and not without cause: for in deed it touched him somewhat neere, sith this Edmund was sonne to Roger earle of March, sonne to the ladie Philip, daughter of Lionell duke of Clarence, the third sonne of king Edward the third; which Edmund at king Richards going into Ireland, was proclamed heire apparant to the crowne and realme, whose aunt called Elianor, the lord Henrie Persie had married; and therefore king Henrie could not well heare, that anie man should be earnest about the aduancement of that linage. The king when he had studied on the matter, made answer, that the earle of March was not taken prisoner for his cause, nor in his seruice, but willinglie suffered himselfe to be taken, bicause he would not withstand the attempts of Owen Glendouer, and his complices, & therefore he would neither ransome him, nor releeue him.

The Persies with this answer and fraudulent excuse were not a little fumed, insomuch that Henrie Hotspur said openlie: Behold, the heire of the relme is robbed of his right, and yet the robber with his owne will not redeeme him. So in this furie the Persies departed, minding nothing more than to depose king Henrie from the high type of his roialtie, and to place in his seat their cousine Edmund earle of March, whom they did not onlie deliuer out of captiuitie, but also (to the high displeasure of king Henrie) entered in league with the foresaid Owen Glendouer. Heerewith, they by their deputies in the house of the archdeacon of Bangor, diuided the realme amongst them, causing a tripartite indenture to be made and sealed with their seales, by the couenants whereof, all England from Seuerne and Trent, south and eastward, was assigned to the earle of March: all Wales, & the lands beyond Seuerne westward, were appointed to Owen Glendouer: and all the remnant from Trent northward, to the lord Persie.

This was doone (as some haue said) through a foolish credit giuen to a vaine prophesie, as though king Henrie was the moldwarpe, curssed of Gods owne mouth, and they three were the dragon, the lion, and the woolfe, which should diuide this realme betweene them. Such is the deuiation (saith Hall) and not diuination of those blind and fantasticall dreames of the Welsh prophesiers. King Henrie not knowing of this new confederacie, and nothing lesse minding than that which after happened, gathered a great armie to go againe into Wales, whereof the earle of Northumberland and his sonne were aduertised by the earle of Worcester, and with all diligence raised all the power they could make, and sent to the Scots which before were taken prisoners at Homeldon, for aid of men, promising to the earle of Dowglas the towne of Berwike, and a part of Northumberland, and to other Scotish lords, great lordships and seigniories, if they obteined the vpper hand. The Scots in hope of gaine, and desirous to be reuenged of their old greefes, came to the earle with a great companie well appointed.

The Persies to make their part seeme good, deuised certeine articles, by the aduise of Richard Scroope, archbishop of Yorke, brother to the lord Scroope, whome king Henrie had caused to be beheaded at Bristow. These articles being shewed to diuerse noblemen, and other states of the realme, mooued them to fauour their purpose, in so much that manie of them did not onelie promise to the Persies aid and succour by words, but also by their writings and seales confirmed the same. Howbeit when the matter came to triall, the most part of the confederates abandoned them, and at the daie of the conflict left them alone. Thus after that the conspirators had discouered themselues, the lord Henri Persie desirous to proceed in the enterprise, vpon trust to be assisted by Owen Glendouer, the earle of March, & other, assembled an armie of men of armes and archers foorth of Cheshire and Wales. Incontinentlie his vncle

Thomas Persie earle of Worcester, that had the gouernement of the prince of Wales, who as then laie at London in secret manner, conueied himselfe out of the princes house, and comming to Stafford (where he met his nephue) they increased their power all by waies and meanes they could deuise. The earle of Northumberland himselfe was not with them, but being sicke, had promised vpon his amendement to repaire vnto them (as some write) with all conuenient speed.

These noble men, to make their conspiracie to seeme excusable, besides the articles aboue mentioned, sent letters abroad, wherein was conteined, that their gathering of an armie tended to none other end, but onlie for the safegard of their owne persons, and to put some better gouernment in the commonwealth. For whereas taxes and tallages were dailie leuied, vnder pretense to be imploied in defense of the realme, the same were vainlie wasted, and vnprofitablie consumed: and where through the slanderous reports of their enimies, the king had taken a greeuous displeasure with them, they durst not appeare personallie in the kings presence, vntill the prelats and barons of the realme had obteined of the king licence for them to come and purge themselues before him, by lawfull triall of their peeres, whose iudgement (as they pretended) they would in no wise refuse. Manie that saw and heard these letters, did commend their diligence, and highlie praised their assured fidelitie and trustinesse towards the commonwealth.

But the king vnderstanding their cloaked drift, deuised (by what meanes he might) to quiet and appease the commons, and deface their contriued forgeries; and therefore he wrote an answer to their libels, that he maruelled much, sith the earle of Northumberland, and the lord Henrie Persie his sonne, had receiued the most part of the summes of monie granted to him by the cleargie and communaltie, for defense of the marches, as he could euidentlie prooue what should mooue them to complaine and raise such manifest slanders. And whereas he vnderstood, that the earles of Northumberland and Worcester, and the lord Persie had by their letters signified to their freends abroad, that by reason of the slanderous reports of their enimies, they durst not appeare in his presence, without the mediation of the prelats and nobles of the realme, so as they required pledges, whereby they might safelie come afore him, to declare and alledge what they had to saie in proofe of their innocencie, he protested by letters sent foorth vnder his seale, that they might safelie come and go, without all danger, or anie manner of indamagement to be offered to their persons.

But this could not satisfie those men, but that resolued to go forwards with their enterprise, they marched towards Shrewesburie, vpon hope to be aided (as men thought) by Owen Glendouer, and his Welshmen, publishing abroad throughout the countries on each side, that king Richard was aliue, whome if they wished to see, they willed them to repaire in armour vnto the castell of Chester, where (without all doubt) he was at that present, and redie to come forward. This tale being raised, though it were most vntrue, yet it bred variable motions in mens minds, causing them to wauer, so as they knew not to which part they should sticke; and verelie, diuers were well affected towards king Richard, speciallie such as had tasted of his princelie bountifulnes, of which there was no small number. And to speake a truth, no maruell it was, if manie enuied the prosperous state of king Henrie, sith it was euident inough to the world, that he had with wrong vsurped the crowne, and not onelie violentlie deposed king Richard, but also cruellie procured his death, for the which vndoubtedlie, both he and his posteritie tasted such troubles, as put them still in danger of their states, till their direct succeeding line was quite rooted out by the contrarie faction, as in Henrie the sixt and Edward the fourth it may appeare.

But now to returne where we left. King Henrie aduertised of the proceedings of the Persies, foorthwith gathered about him such power as he might make, and being earnestlie called vpon by the Scot, the earle of March, to make hast and giue battell to his enimies, before their power by delaieng of time should still too much increase, he passed forward with such speed, that he was in sight of his enimies, lieng in campe neere to Shrewesburie, before they were in doubt of anie such thing, for the Persies thought that he would haue staied at Burton vpon Trent, till his councell had come thither to him to giue their aduise what he were best to doo. But herein the enimie was deceiued of his expectation, sith the king had great regard of expedition and making speed for the safetie of his owne person, wherevnto the earle of March incited him, considering that in delaie is danger, & losse in lingering. . . .

By reason of the kings sudden cõming in this sort, they staied from assaulting the towne of Shrewesburie, which enterprise they were readie at that instant to haue taken in hand, and foorthwith the lord Persie (as a capteine of high courage) began to exhort the capteines and souldiers to prepare themselues to battell, sith the matter was growen to that point, that by no meanes it could be auoided, so that (said he) this daie shall either bring vs all to aduancement & honor, or else if it shall chance vs to be ouercome, shall delieuer vs from the kings spitefull malice and cruell disdaine: for plaieng the men (as we ought to doo) better it is to die in battell for the commonwealths cause, than through cowardlike feare to prolong life, which after shall be taken from vs, by sentence of the enimie.

Herevpon, the whole armie being in number about fourteene

thousand chosen men, promised to stand with him so long as life lasted. There were with the Persies as chiefteines of this armie, the earle of Dowglas a Scotish man, the baron of Kinderton, sir Hugh Browne, and sir Richard Vernon knights, with diuerse other stout and right valiant capteins. Now when the two armies were incamped, the one against the other, the earle of Worcester and the lord Persie with their complices sent the articles (whereof I spake before) by Thomas Caiton, and Thomas Saluain esquiers to king Henrie, vnder their hands and seales, which articles in effect charged him with manifest periurie, in that (contrarie to his oth receiued vpon the euangelists at Doncaster, when he first entred the realme after his exile) he had taken vpon him the crowne and roiall dignitie, imprisoned king Richard, caused him to resigne his title, and finallie to be murthered. Diuerse other matters they laid to his charge, as leuieng of taxes and tallages, contrarie to his promise, infringing of lawes & customes of the realme, and suffering the earle of March to remaine in prison, without trauelling to haue him delieuered. All which things they as procurors & protectors of the common-wealth, tooke vpon them to prooue against him, as they protested vnto the whole world.

King Henrie after he had read their articles, with the defiance which they annexed to the same, answered the esquiers, that he was readie with dint of sword and fierce battell to prooue their quarrell false, and nothing else than a forged matter, not doubting, but that God would aid and assist him in his righteous cause, against the disloiall and false forsworne traitors. The next daie in the morning earlie, being the euen of Marie Magdalene, they set their battels in order on both sides, and now whilest the warriors looked when the token of battell should be giuen, the abbat of Shrewsburie, and one of the clearks of the priuie seale, were sent from the king vnto the Persies, to offer them pardon, if they would come to any reasonable agreement. By their persuasions, the lord Henrie Persie began to giue eare vnto the kings offers, & so sent with them his vncle the earle of Worcester, to declare vnto the king the causes of those troubles, and to require some effectuall reformation in the same.

It was reported for a truth, that now when the king had condescended vnto all that was resonable at his hands to be required, and seemed to humble himselfe more than was meet for his estate, the earle of Worcester (vpon his returne to his nephue) made relation cleane contrarie to that the king had said, in such sort that he set his nephues hart more in displeasure towards the king, than euer it was before, driuing him by that meanes to fight whether he would or not: then suddenlie blew the trumpets, the kings part crieng S. George vpon them, the aduersaries cried *Esperance Persie*, and so the two armies furiouslie ioined. The archers on both sides shot for the best game, laieng on such load with arrowes, that manie died, and were driuen downe that neuer rose againe.

The Scots (as some write) which had the fore ward on the Persies side, intending to be reuenged of their old displeasures doone to them by the English nation, set so fiercelie on the kings fore ward, led by the earle of Stafford, that they made the same draw backe, and had almost broken their aduersaries arraie. The Welshmen also which before had laine lurking in the woods, mounteines, and marishes, hearing of this battell toward, came to the aid of the Persies, and refreshed the wearied people with new succours. The king perceiuing that his men were thus put to distresse, what with the violent impression of the Scots, and the tempestuous stormes of arrowes, that his aduersaries discharged freely against him and his people, it was no need to will him to stirre: for suddenlie with his fresh battell, he approched and relieued his men; so that the battell began more fierce than before. Here the lord Henrie Persie, and the earle Dowglas, a right stout and hardie capteine, not regarding the shot of the kings battell, nor the close order of the ranks, pressing forward togither bent their whole forces towards the kings person, comming vpon him with speares and swords so fiercelie, that the earle of March the Scot, perceiuing their purpose, withdrew the king from that side of the field (as some write) for his great benefit and safegard (as it appeared) for they gaue such a violent onset vpon them that stood about the kings standard, that slaieng his standard-bearer sir Walter Blunt, and ouerthrowing the standard, they made slaughter of all those that stood about it, as the earle of Stafford, that daie made by the king constable of the realme, and diuerse other.

The prince that daie holpe his father like a lustie yoong gentleman: for although he was hurt in the face with an arrow, so that diuerse noble men that were about him, would haue conueied him foorth of the field, yet he would not suffer them so to doo, least his departure from amongst his men might happilie haue striken some feare into their harts: and so without regard of his hurt, he continued with his men, & neuer ceassed, either to fight where the battell was most hot, or to incourage his men where it seemed most need. This battell lasted three long houres, with indifferent fortune on both parts, till at length, the king crieng saint George victorie, brake the arraie of his enimies, and aduentured so farre, that (as some write) the earle Dowglas strake him downe, & at that instant slue sir Walter Blunt, and three other, apparelled in the kings sute and clothing, saieng: I maruell to see so many kings thus suddenlie arise one in the necke of an other. The king in deed was raised, & did that daie manie a noble feat of armes, for as it is written, he slue that daie with his owne hands six and thirtie persons of his enimies. The other on his part incouraged by his doings, fought valiantlie, and slue the lord Persie, called sir Henrie Hotspurre. To conclude, the kings enimies were vanquished, and put to flight, in which flight, the earle of Dowglas, for hast, falling from the crag of an hie mounteine, brake one of his cullions, and was taken, and for his valiantnesse, of the king frankelie and freelie deliuered.

There was also taken the earle of Worcester, the procuror and setter foorth of all this mischeefe, sir Richard Vernon, and the baron of Kinderton, with diuerse other. There were slaine vpon the kings part, beside the earle of Stafford, to the number of ten knights, sir Hugh Shorlie, sir Iohn Clifton, sir Iohn Cokaine, sir Nicholas Gausell, sir Walter Blunt, sir Iohn Caluerleie, sir Iohn Massie of Podington, sir Hugh Mortimer, and sir Robert Gausell, all the which receiued the same morning the order of knighthood: sir Thomas Wendesleie was wounded to death, and so passed out of this life shortlie after. There died in all vpon the kings side sixteene hundred, and foure thousand were greeuouslie wounded. On the contrarie side were slaine, besides the lord Persie, the most part of the knights and esquiers of the countie of Chester, to the number of two hundred, besides yeomen and footmen, in all there died of those that fought on the Persies side, about fiue thousand. This battell was fought on Marie Magdalene euen, being saturdaie. Vpon the mondaie folowing, the earle of Worcester, the baron of Kinderton, and sir Richard Vernon knights, were condemned and beheaded. The earles head was sent to London, there to be set on the bridge.

[Anno 1412] . . . [T]he lord Henrie prince of Wales, eldest sonne to king Henrie, got knowledge that certeine of his fathers seruants were busie to giue informations against him, whereby discord might arise betwixt him and his father: for they put into the kings head, not onelie what euill rule (according to the course of youth) the prince kept to the offense of manie: but also what great resort of people came to his house, so that the court was nothing furnished with such a traine as dailie followed the prince. These tales brought no small suspicion into the kings head, least his sonne would presume to vsurpe the crowne, he being yet aliue, through which suspicious gelousie, it was perceiued that he fauoured not his sonne, as in times past he had doone.

The Prince sore offended with such persons, as by slanderous reports, sought not onelie to spot his good name abrode in the realme, but to sowe discord also betwixt him and his father, wrote his letters into euerie part of the realme, to reprooue all such slanderous deuises of those that sought his discredit. And to cleare himself the better, that the world might vnderstand what wrong he had to be slandered in such wise: about the feast of Peter and Paule, to wit, the nine and twentith daie of Iune, he came to the court with such a number of noble men and other his freends that wished him well, as the like traine had beene sildome seene repairing to the court at any one time in those daies. He was apparelled in a gowne of blew satten, full of small oilet holes, at euerie hole the needle hanging by a silke thred with which it was sewed. About his arme he ware an hounds collar set full of SS of gold, and the tirets likewise being of the same metall.

The court was then at Westminster, where he being entred into the hall, not one of his companie durst once aduance himselfe further than the fire in the same hall, notwithstanding they were earnestlie requested by the lords to come higher: but they regarding what they had in commandement of the prince, would not presume to doo in any thing contrarie therevnto. He himselfe onelie accompanied with those of the kings house, was streight admitted to the presence of the king his father, who being at that time greeuouslie diseased, yet caused himselfe in his chaire to be borne into his priuie chamber, where in the presence of three or foure persons, in whome he had most confidence, he commanded the prince to shew what he had to saie concerning the cause of his comming.

The prince kneeling downe before his father said: "Most redoubted and souereigne lord and father, I am at this time come to your presence as your liege man, and as your naturall sonne, in all things to be at your commandement. And where I vnderstand you haue in suspicion my demeanour against your grace, you know verie well, that if I knew any man within this realme, of whome you should stand in feare, my duetie were to punish that person, thereby to remooue that greefe from your heart. Then how much more ought I to suffer death, to ease your grace of that greefe which you haue of me, being your naturall sonne and liege man: and to that end I haue this daie made my selfe readie by confession and receiuing of the sacrament. And therefore I beseech you most redoubted lord and deare father, for the honour of God, to ease your heart of all such suspicion as you haue of me, and to dispatch me heere before your knees, with this same dagger [and withall he deliuered vnto the king his dagger, in all humble reuerence; adding further, that his life was not so deare to him, that he wished to liue one daie with his displeasure] and therefore in thus ridding me out of life, and your selfe from all suspicion, here in presence of these lords, and before God at the daie of the generall iudgement, I faithfullie protest clearlie to forgiue you."

The king mooued herewith, cast from him the dagger, and imbracing the prince kissed him, and with shedding teares confessed, that in deed he had him partlie in suspicion, though now (as he perceiued) not with iust cause, and therefore from thencefoorth no misreport should cause him to haue him in mistrust, and this he promised of his honour. So by his great wisedome was the wrongfull suspicion which his father had conceiued against him remooued, and he restored to his fauour. And further, where he could not but greeuouslie complaine of them that had slandered him so greatlie, to the defacing not onelie of his honor, but also putting him in danger of his life, he humblie besought the king that they might answer their vniust accusation; and in case they were found to haue forged such matters vpon a malicious purpose, that then they might suffer some punishment for their faults, though not to the full of that they had deserued. The king seeming to grant his resonable desire, yet told him that he must tarrie a parlement, that such offendors might be punished by iudgement of their peeres: and so for that time he was dismissed, with great loue and signes of fatherlie affection.

Thus were the father and the sonne reconciled, betwixt whom the said pickthanks had sowne diuision, insomuch that the sonne vpon a vehement conceit of vnkindnesse sproong in the father, was in the waie to be worne out of fauour. Which was the more likelie to come to passe, by their informations that priuilie charged him with riot and other vnciuill demeanor vnseemelie for a prince. Indeed he was youthfullie giuen, growne to audacitie, and had chosen him companions agreeable to his age; with whome he spent the time in such recreations, exercises, and delights as he fansied. But yet (it should seeme by the report of some writers) that his behauiour was not offensiue or at least tending to the damage of anie bodie; sith he had a care to auoid dooing of wrong, and to tedder his affections within the tract of vertue, whereby he opened vnto himselfe a redie passage of good liking among the prudent sort, and was beloued of such as could discerne his disposition, which was in no degree so excessiue, as that he deserued in such vehement maner to be suspected. In whose dispraise I find little, but to his praise verie much. . . .

SAMUEL DANIEL

The Ciuile Wars†

<Book III>

<86>

And yet new *Hydraes* lo, new heades appeare
T'afflict that peace reputed then so sure,
And gaue him much to do, and much to feare,
And long and daungerous tumults did procure,
And those euen of his chiefest followers were
Of whom he might presume him most secure,
Who whether not so grac'd or so preferd
As they expected, these new factions stird.

<87>

The *Percyes* were the men, men of great might,
Strong in alliance, and in courage strong
That thus conspired, vnder pretence to right
The crooked courses they had suffered long:
Whether their conscience vrgd them or despight,
Or that they saw the part they tooke was wrong,
Or that ambition hereto did them call,
Or others enuide grace, or rather all.

<88>

What cause soeuer were, strong was their plot,
Their parties great, meanes good, th'occasion fit:
Their practice close, their faith suspected not,
Their states far off and they of wary wit:
Who with large promises draw in the Scot
To ayde their cause, he likes, and yeeldes to it,
Not for the loue of them or for their good,
But glad hereby of meanes to shed our bloud.

† From Samuel Daniel, *The First Fowre Bookes of the Ciuile Wars Between the Two Houses of Lancaster and Yorke* (London, 1595), 59–64.

<89>

Then ioyne they with the *Welsh*, who fitly traind
And all in armes vnder a mightie head
Great *Glendowr*, who long warr'd, and much attaind,
Sharp conflicts made, and many vanquished:
With whom was *Edmond Earle* of *March* retaind
Being first his prisoner, now confedered,
A man the king much fear'd, and well he might
Least he should looke whether his Crown stood right.

<90>

For *Richard*, for the quiet of the state
Before he tooke those *Irish* warres in hand
About succession doth deliberate,
And finding how the certaine right did stand,
With full consent this man did ordinate
The heyre apparent in the crowne and land:
Then iudge if this the king might nerely touch,
Although his might were smal, his right being much.

<91>

With these the *Percyes* them confederate,
And as three heades they league in one intent,
And instituting a Triumuirate
Do part the land in triple gouerment:
Deuiding thus among themselues the state,
The *Percyes* should rule all the *North* from *Trent*
And *Glendowr Wales*: the *Earle* of *March* should bee
Lord of the *South* from *Trent*; and thus they gree.

<92>

Then those two helpes which still such actors find
Pretence of common good, the kings disgrace
Doth fit their course, and draw the vulgar mind
To further them and aide them in this case:
The king they accusd for cruell, and vnkind
That did the state, and crowne, and all deface;
A periurde man that held all faith in skorne,
Whose trusted othes had others made forsworne.

<93>

Besides the odious detestable act
Of that late murdered king they aggrauate,
Making it his that so had will'd the fact

That he the doers did remunerate:
And then such taxes daily doth exact
That were against the orders of the state,
And with all these or worse they him assaild
Who late of cthers with the like preuaild.

<94>

Thus doth contentious proud mortality
Afflict each other and itselfe torment:
And thus o thou mind-tortring misery
Restles ambition, borne in discontent,
Turn'st and retossest with iniquity
The vnconstant courses frailty did inuent:
And fowlst faire order and defilst the earth
Fostring vp warre, father of bloud and dearth.

<95>

Great seemd the cause, and greatly to, did ad
The peoples loue thereto these crimes rehearst,
That manie gathered to the troupes they had
And many more do flocke from costs disperst:
But when the king had heard these newes so bad,
Th'vnlookt for dangerous toyle more nearly perst;
For bẽt t'wards *Wales* t'appease those tumults there,
H'is for'st diuert his course, and them forbeare.

<96>

Not to giue time vnto th'increasing rage
And gathering fury, forth he hastes with speed,
Lest more delay or giuing longer age
To th'euill growne, it might the cure exceed:
All his best men at armes, and leaders sage
All he prepard he could, and all did need;
For to a mighty worke thou goest ô king,
To such a field that power to power shall bring.

<97>

There shall young *Hotespur* with a fury lead
Meete with thy forward sonne as fierce as he:
There warlike *Worster* long experienced
In forraine armes, shall come t'incounter thee:
There *Dowglas* to thy *Stafford* shall make head:
There *Vernon* for thy valiant *Blunt* shalbe:
There shalt thou find a doubtfull bloudy day,
Though sicknesse keepe *Northumberland* away.

<98>

Who yet reseru'd, though after quit for this,
Another tempest on thy head to raise,
As if still wrong reuenging *Nemesis*
Did meane t'afflict all thy continuall dayes:
And yet this field he happely might misse
For thy great good, and therefore well he staies:
What might his force haue done being ioynd thereto
When that already gaue so much to do?

<99>

The swift approch and vnexpected speed
The king had made vpon this new-raisd force
In th' vnconfirmed troupes much feare did breed,
Vntimely hindring their intended course;
The ioyning with the *Welsh* they had decreed
Was hereby stopt, which made their part the worse,
Northumberland with forces from the *North*
Expected to be there, was not set forth.

<100>

And yet undaunted *Hotspur* seeing the king
So nere approch'd, leauving the worke in hand
With forward speed his forces marshalling,
Sets forth his farther comming to withstand:
And with a cheerfull voice incouraging
By his great spirit his well imboldened band,
Bringes a strong host of firme resolued might,
And plac'd his troupes before the king in sight.

<101>

This day (saith he) ô faithfull valiaunt frendes,
What euer it doth giue, shall glorie giue:
This day with honor frees our state, or endes
Our misery with fame, that still shall liue,
And do but thinke how well this day he spendes
That spendes his bloud his countrey to relieue:
Our holie cause, our freedome, and our right,
Sufficient are to moue good mindes to fight.

<102>

Besides th' assured hope of victory
That wee may euen promise on our side
Against this weake-constrained companie,

Whom force & feare, not will, and loue doth guide
Against a prince whose foule impiety
The heauens do hate, the earth cannot abide,
Our number being no lesse, our courage more,
What need we doubt if we but worke therefore.

<103>

This said, and thus resolu'd euen bent to charge
Vpon the king, who well their order viewd
And carefull noted all the forme at large
Of their proceeding, and their multitude:
And deeming better if he could discharge
The day with safetie, and some peace conclude,
Great proffers sendes of pardon, and of grace
If they would yeeld, and quietnes imbrace.

<104>

But this refusd, the king with wrath incensd
Rage against fury doth with speed prepare:
And ô saith he, though I could haue dispensd
With this daies bloud, which I haue sought to spare
That greater glory might haue recompensd
The forward worth of these that so much dare,
That we might honor had by th' ouerthrown
That th' wounds we make, might not haue bin our own.

<105>

Yet since that other mens iniquity
Calles on the sword of wrath against my will,
And that themselues exact this cruelty,
And I constrained am this bloud to spill:
Then on my maisters, on couragiously
True-harted subiects against traitors ill,
And spare them not who seeke to spoile vs all,
Whose fowle confused end soone see you shall.

<106>

Straight moues with equall motion equall rage
The like incensed armies vnto blood,
One to defend, another side to wage
Foule ciuill war, both vowes their quarrell good:
Ah too much heate to bloud doth nowe inrage
Both who the deed prouokes and who withstood,
That valor here is vice, here manhood sin,
The forward'st hands doth ô least honor win.

<107>

But now begin these fury-mouing soundes
The notes of wrath that musicke brought from hell,
The ratling drums which trumpets voice cõfounds,
The cryes, th' incouragements, the shouting shrell:
That all about the beaten ayre reboundes,
Thundring confused, murmurs horrible,
To rob all sence except the sence to fight,
Well handes may worke, the mind hath lost his sight.

<108>

O war! begot in pride and luxury,
The child of wrath and of dissention,
Horrible good; mischiefe necessarie,
The fowle reformer of confusion,
Vniust-iust scourge of our iniquitie,
Cruel recurer of corruption:
O that these sin-sicke states in need should stand
To be let bloud with such a boystrous hand!

<109>

And ô how well thou hadst been spar'd this day
Had not wrong counsaild *Percy* bene peruers,
Whose yong vndanger'd hand now rash makes way
Vpon the sharpest fronts of the most fierce:
Where now an equall fury thrusts to stay
And rebeat-backe that force and his disperse,
Then these assaile, then those chace backe againe,
Till staid with new-made hils of bodies slaine.

<110>

There lo that new-appearing glorious starre
Wonder of Armes, the terror of the field
Young *Henrie*, laboring where the stoutest are,
And euen the stoutest forces backe to yeild,
There is that hand boldned to bloud and warre
That must the sword in woundrous actions weild:
But better hadst thou learnd with others bloud
A lesse expence to vs, to thee more good.

<111>

Hadst thou not there lent present speedy ayd
To thy indaungerde father nerely tyrde,
Whom fierce incountring *Dowglas* ouerlaid,
That day had there his troublous life expirde:

Heroycall Couragious *Blunt* araid
In habite like as was the king attirde
And deemd for him, excusd that fate with his,
For he had what his Lord did hardly misse.

<112>

For thought a king he would not now disgrace
The person then supposd, but princelike shewes
Glorious effects of worth that fit his place,
And fighting dyes, and dying ouerthrowes:
Another of that forward name and race
In that hotte worke his valiant life bestowes,
Who bare the standard of the king that day,
Whose colours ouerthrowne did much dismaie.

<113>

And deare it cost, and ô much bloud is shed
To purchase thee this loosing victory
O trauayld king: yet hast thou conquered
A doubtfull day, a mightie enemy:
But ô what woundes, what famous worth lyes dead!
That makes the winner looke with sorrowing eye,
Magnanimous *Stafford* lost that much had wrought,
And valiant *Shorly* who great glory gote.

<114>

Such wracke of others bloud thou didst behold
O furious *Hotspur*, ere thou lost thine owne!
Which now once lost that heate in thine waxt cold,
And soone became thy Armie ouerthrowne;
And ô that this great spirit, this courage bold,
Had in some good cause bene rightly showne!
So had not we thus violently then
Haue termd that rage, which valor should haue ben.

<115>

But now the king retires him to his peace,
A peace much like a feeble sicke mans sleepe,
(Wherein his waking paines do neuer cease
Though seeming rest his closed eyes doth keepe)
For ô no peace could euer so release
His intricate turmoiles, and sorrowes deepe,
But that his cares kept waking all his life
Continue on till death conclude the strife.

ANONYMOUS

The Famous Victories of Henry the Fifth†

Enter the yoong PRINCE, NED, *and* TOM.
HENRY THE FIFTH.

Come away *Ned* and *Tom*.
BOTH. Here my Lord.
HENR. 5. Come away my Lads
Tell me sirs, how much gold haue you got?
NED. Faith my Lord, I haue got fiue hundred pound.
HEN. 5. But tell me *Tom*, how much hast thou got?
TOM. Faith my Lord, some foure hundred pound.
HEN. 5. Foure hundred pounds, brauely spoke Lads.
But tell me sirs, thinke you not that it was a villainous part of me to rob my fathers Receiuers?
NED. Why no my Lord, it was but a tricke of youth.
HEN. 5. Faith *Ned* thou sayest true.
But tell me sirs, whereabouts are we?
TOM. My Lord, we are now about a mile off *London*.
HEN. 5. But sirs, I maruell that sir *Iohn Old-castle*
Comes not away: Sounds see where he comes.

Enters IOCKEY.

How now *Iockey*, what newes with thee?
IOCKEY. Faith my Lord, such newes as passeth,
For the Towne of *Detfort* is risen,
With hue and crie after your man,
Which parted from vs the last night,
And has set vpon, and hath robd a poore Carrier.
HEN. 5. Sownes, the vilaine that was wont to spie
Out our booties.
IOCK. I my Lord, euen the very same.
HEN. 5. Now base minded rascal to rob a poore carrier,
Wel it skils not, ile saue the base vilaines life:
I, I may: but tel me *Iockey*, whereabout be the Receiuers?
IOC. Faith my Lord, they are hard by,
But the best is, we are a horse backe and they be a foote,
So we may escape them.
HEN. 5. Wel, I[f] the vilaines come, let me alone with them.
But tel me *Iockey*, how much gots thou from the knaues?

† From *The Famous Victories of Henry the fifth: Containing the Honourable Battell of Agincourt: As it was plaide by the Queenes Maiesties Players* (1598).

For I am sure I got something, for one of the vilaines
So belamd me about the shoulders,
As I shal feele it this moneth.

IOCK. Faith my Lord, I haue got a hundred pound.

HEN. 5. A hundred pound, now brauely spoken *Iockey*:
But comes sirs, laie al your money before me,
Now by heauen here is a braue shewe:
But as I am true Gentleman, I wil haue the halfe
Of this spent to night, but sirs take vp your bags,
Here comes the Receiuers, let me alone.

Enters two Receiuers.

ONE. Alas good fellow, what shal we do?
I dare neuer go home to the Court, for I shall be hangd.
But looke, here is the yong Prince, what shal we doo?

HEN. 5. How now you vilaines, what are you?

ONE RECEI. Speake you to him.

OTHER. No I pray, speake you to him.

HEN. 5. Why how now you rascals, why speak you not?

ONE. Forsooth we be. Pray speake you to him.

HEN. 5. Sowns, vilains speak, or ile cut off your heads.

OTHER. Forsooth he can tel the tale better then I.

ONE. Forsooth we be your fathers Receiuers.

HEN. 5. Are you my fathers Receiuers?
Then I hope ye haue brought me some money.

ONE. Money, Alas sir we be robd.

HEN. 5. Robd, how many were there of them?

ONE. Marry sir, there were foure of them:
And one of them had sir *Iohn Old-Castles* bay Hobbie,
And your blacke Nag.

HEN. 5. Gogs wounds how like you this *Iockey*?
Blood you vilaines: my father robd of his money abroad,
And we robd in our stables.
But tell me, how many were of them?

ONE RECEI. If it please you, there were foure of them,
And there was one about the bignesse of you:
But I am sure I so belambd him about the shoulders,
That he wil feele it this month.

HEN. 5. Gogs wounds you lamd them faierly,
So that they haue carried away your money.
But come sirs, what shall we do with the vilaines?

BOTH RECEI. I beseech your grace, be good to vs.

NED. I pray you my Lord forgiue them this once.

[HEN. 5.] Well stand vp and get you gone,
And looke that you speake not a word of it,
For if there be, sownes ile hang you and all your kin.

Exit Purseuant[*s*].

HEN. 5. Now sirs, how like you this?
Was not this brauely done?
For now the vilaines dare not speake a word of it,
I haue so feared them with words.
Now whither shall we goe?
ALL. Why my Lord, you know our old hostes
At *Feuersham.*
HEN. 5. Our hostes at *Feuersham*, blood what shal we do there?
We haue a thousand pound about vs,
And we shall go to a pettie Ale-house.
No, no: you know the olde Tauerne in Eastcheape,
There is good wine: besides, there is a pretie wench
That can talke well, for I delight as much in their toongs,
As any part about them.
ALL. We are readie to waite vpon your grace.
HEN. 5. Gogs wounds wait, we will go altogither,
We are all fellowes, I tell you sirs, and the King
My father were dead, we would be all Kings,
Therefore come away.
NED. Gogs wounds, brauely spoken Harry.

[*Exeunt omnes.*]

[In the scene which follows, the night-watch, John Cobler, Robin Pewterer, and Lawrence Costermonger, assisted by Dericke, a clown, apprehend a "Theefe" (Gadshill), who had taken part in the robbery of the carriers. A "Vintners boy" closes the scene with a report on a tavern escapade of the Prince.]

BOY. How now good man Cobler?
COB. How now *Robin*, what makes thou abroad
At this time of night?
BOY. Marrie I haue beene at the Counter,
I can tells uch newes as neuer you haue heard the like.
COBLER. What is that *Robin*, what is the matter?
BOY. Why this night about two houres ago, there came the young Prince, and three or foure more of his companions, and called for wine good store, and then they sent for a noyse of Musitians, and were very merry for the space of an houre, then whether their Musicke liked them not, or whether they had drunke too much Wine or no, I cannot tell, but our pots flue against the wals, and then they drew their swordes, and went into the streete and fought, and some tooke one part, & some tooke another, but for the space of halfe an houre, there was such a bloodie fray as passeth, and none coulde part them vntill such time as the Maior and Sheriffe were sent for, and then at the last with much adoo, they tooke them, and so the yong Prince was carried to the Counter, and then about one houre after, there came a Messen-

ger from the Court in all haste from the King, for my Lord Maior and the Sheriffe, but for what cause I know not.

[Gadshill is then taken to Newgate Prison to await his appearance before the Lord Chief Justice. In the following scene Henry IV receives an account from the Lord Mayor of London of his imprisoning the young Prince. Henry IV replies:]

HEN. 4. Stand aside vntill we haue further deliberated on your answere.

Exit Maior.

HEN. 4. Ah *Harry, Harry*, now thrice accursed *Harry*,
That hath gotten a sonne, which with greefe
Will end his fathers dayes.
Oh my sonne, a Prince thou art, I a Prince indeed,
And to deserue imprisonment,
And well haue they done, and like faithfull subiects:
Discharge them and let them go.

[The next episode is the trial of Gadshill before the Lord Chief Justice. The Prince appears and demands custody of Gadshill. When the Chief Justice refuses, the Prince "giueth him a boxe on the eare." The Chief Justice then commits the Prince to the Fleet. There follows a "play extempore" between Dericke and John Cobler.]

DER. Sownds maisters, heres adoo,
When Princes must go to prison:
Why *Iohn*, didst euer see the like?
IOHN. O *Dericke*, trust me, I neuer saw the like.
DER. Why *Iohn* thou maist see what princes be in choller,
A Iudge a boxe on the eare, Ile tel thee *Iohn, O Iohn*,
I would not haue done it for twentie shillings.
IOHN. No nor I, there had bene no way but one with vs,
We should haue bene hangde.
DER. Faith *Iohn*, Ile tel thee what, thou shalt be my
Lord chiefe Iustice, and thou shalt sit in the chaire,
And ile be the yong prince, and hit thee a boxe on the eare,
And then thou shalt say, to teach you what prerogatiues
Meane, I commit you to the Fleete.
IOHN. Come on, Ile be your iudge,
But thou shalt not hit me hard.
DER. No, no.
IOHN. What hath he done?
DER. Marry he hath robd *Dericke*.
IOHN. Why then I cannot let him go.
DER. I must needs haue my man.

IOHN. You shall not haue him.
DER. Shall I not haue my man, say no and you dare:
How say you, shall I not haue my man?
IOHN. No marry shall you not.
DER. Shall I not *Iohn*?
IOHN. No *Dericke*.
DER. Why then take you that till more come,
Sownes, shall I not haue him?
IOHN. Well I am content to take this at your hand,
But I pray you, who am I?
DER. Who art thou, Sownds, doost not know thy self?
IOHN. No.
DER. Now away simple fellow,
Why man, thou art *Iohn* the Cobler.
IOHN. No, I am my Lord chiefe Iustice of England.
DER. Oh *Iohn*, Masse thou saist true, thou art indeed.
IOHN. Why then to teach you what prerogatiues mean
I commit you to the Fleete.
DER. Wel I will go, but yfaith you gray beard knaue,
Ile course you.

Enter the yoong PRINCE, *with* NED *and* TOM.

HEN. 5. Come away sirs, Gogs wounds *Ned*,
Didst thou not see what a boxe on the eare
I tooke my Lord chiefe Iustice?
TOM. By gogs blood it did me good to see it,
It made his teeth iarre in his head.

Enter sir Iohn Old-Castle.

HEN. 5. How now sir *Iohn Old-Castle*,
What newes with you?
IOH. OLD. I am glad to see your grace at libertie,
I was come I, to visit you in prison.
HEN. 5. To visit me, didst thou not know that I am a Princes son, why tis inough for me to looke into a prison, though I come not in my selfe, but heres such adoo now adayes, heres prisoning, heres hanging, whipping, and the diuel and all: but I tel you sirs, when I am King, we will haue no such things, but my lads, if the old king my father were dead, we would be all kings.
IOH. OLD. Hee is a good olde man, God take him to his mercy the sooner.
HEN. 5. But *Ned*, so soone as I am King, the first thing
I wil do, shal be to put my Lord chief Iustice out of office,
And thou shalt be my Lord chiefe Iustice of England.
NED. Shall I be Lord chiefe Iustice?
By gogs wounds, ile be the brauvest Lord chiefe Iustice
That euer was in England.

HEN. 5. Then *Ned*, ile turne all these prisons into fence Schooles, and I will endue thee with them, with landes to maintaine them withall: then I wil haue a bout with my Lord chiefe Iustice, thou shalt hang none but picke purses and horse stealers, and such base minded villaines, but that fellow that will stand by the high way side couragiously with his sword and buckler and take a purse, that fellow giue him commendations, beside that, send him to me and I will giue him an anuall pension out of my Exchequer, to maintaine him all the dayes of his life.

IOH. Nobly spoken *Harry*, we shall neuer haue a mery world til the old king be dead.

NED. But whither are ye going now?

HEN. 5. To the Court, for I heare say, my father lies verie sicke.

TOM. But I doubt he wil not die.

HEN. 5. Yet will I goe thither, for the breath shal be no sooner out of his mouth, but I wil clap the Crowne on my head.

IOCKEY. Wil you goe to the Court with that cloake so full of needles?

HEN. 5. Cloake, ilat-holes, needles, and all was of mine owne deuising, and therefore I wil weare it.

TOM. I pray you my Lord, what may be the meaning thereof?

HEN. 5. Why man, tis a signe that I stand vpon thorns, til the Crowne be on my head.

IOC. Or that euery needle might be a prick to their harts that repine at your doings.

HEN. 5. Thou saist true *Iockey*, but thers some wil say, the yoong Prince will be a well toward yoong man and all this geare, that I had as leeue they would breake my head with a pot, as to say any such thing, but we stand prating here too long, I must needs speake with my father, therefore come away.

Enter the KING, *with the* LORD OF EXETER.

HEN. 4. And is it true my Lord, that my sonne is alreadie sent to the Fleete? now truly that man is more fitter to rule the Realme then I, for by no meanes could I rule my sonne, and he by one word hath caused him to be ruled. Oh my sonne, my sonne, no sooner out of one prison, but into an other, I had thought once whiles I had liued, to haue seene this noble Realme of England flourish by thee my sonne, but now I see it goes to ruine and decaie.

He wepeth.

Enters LORD OF OXFORD

OX. And please your grace, here is my Lord your sonne,
That commeth to speake with you,
He saith, he must and wil speake with you.

HEN. 4. Who my sonne *Harry*?
OXF. I and please your Maiestie.
HEN. 4. I know wherefore he commeth,
But looke that none come with him.
OXF. A verie disordered company, and such as make
Verie ill rule in your Maiesties house.
HEN. 4. Well let him come,
But looke that none come with him.

He goeth.

Enters the PRINCE *with a dagger in his hand.*

HEN. 4. Come my sonne, come on a Gods name,
I know wherefore thy comming is,
Oh my sonne, my sonne, what cause hath euer bene,
That thou shouldst forsake me, and follow this vilde and
Reprobate company, which abuseth youth so manifestly:
Oh my sonne, thou knowest that these thy doings
Wil end thy fathers dayes.

He weepes.

I so, so, my sonne, thou fearest not to approach the presence of thy sick father, in that disguised sort, I tell thee my sonne, that there is neuer a needle in thy cloke, but it is a prick to my heart, & neuer an ilat-hole, but it is a hole to my soule: and wherefore thou bringest that dagger in thy hande I know not, but by coniecture.

He weepes.

HEN. 5. My cõscience accuseth me, most soueraign Lord, and welbeloued father, to answere first to the last point, That is, whereas you coniecture that this hand and this dagger shall be armde against your life: no, know my beloued father, far be the thoughts of your sonne, sonne said I, an vnworthie sonne for so good a father: but farre be the thoughts of any such pretended mischiefe: and I most humbly render it to your Maiesties hand, and liue my Lord and soueraigne for euer: and with your dagger arme show like vengeance vpon the bodie of that your sonne, I was about [to] say and dare not, ah woe is me therefore, that your wilde slaue, tis not the Crowne that I come for, sweete father, because I am vnworthie, and those vilde & reprobate company I abandon, & vtterly abolish their company for euer. Pardon sweete father, pardon: the least thing and most desire: and this ruffianly cloake, I here teare from my backe, and sacrifice it to the diuel, which is maister of al mischiefe: Pardõ me, sweet father, pardon me: good my Lord of *Exeter* speak for me: pardon me, pardõ good father, not a word: ah he wil not speak one word: A *Harry*, now thrice vnhappie *Harry*. But what shal I do? I wil go take me into some solitarie place, and there lament my sinfull life, and when I haue done, I wil laie me downe and die.

Exit.

HEN. 4. Call him againe, call my sonne againe.
HEN. 5. And doth my father call me again? now *Harry*,
Happie be the time that they father calleth thee againe.
HEN. 4. Stand vp my son, and do not think thy father,
But at the request of thee my sonne, I wil pardon thee,
And God blesse thee, and make thee his seruant.
HEN. 5. Thanks good my Lord, & no doubt but this day,
Euen this day, I am borne new againe.
HEN. 4. Come my son and Lords, take me by the hands.

Exeunt omnes.

[The remaining two-thirds of the play is chiefly concerned with Henry the Fifth's victory at Agincourt and his acquisition of Katharine, daughter of Charles VI of France, as his wife.]

CRITICISM

James L. Sanderson's original 1962 Norton Critical Edition provides a comprehensive selection of critical essays on *1 Henry IV* up to that year; his second edition of 1969 updates the volume and includes eight additional essays. This revised edition, while retaining certain of Professor Sanderson's choices, aims to provide a representative range of criticism up to the present (2002). The critical state of play has changed substantially since the 1960s (just as the universities from which criticism generally emerges have changed substantially since then), most notably with the rise and dominance in early modern literary studies of feminist criticism and of the New Historicism (along with its British cousin, Cultural Materialism).

1 Henry IV, as it happens, is the textual focus of the essay which brought New Historicism to a wide readership—Stephen Greenblatt's "Invisible Bullets"—and the play has been closely associated with major critical developments over the decades. I initially thought that I would probably not include "Invisible Bullets" because it has been so widely anthologized elsewhere, but then decided to reprint it because of its particular significance in the play's critical history; because for the intended readership of this edition—a substantial proportion of whom will be undergraduates in all probability coming to the play for the first time—it will not be at all familiar; and simply because it is a very fine piece of writing.

The essays chosen by Professor Sanderson in 1962 and 1969 are typical of their time in their focus on analysis of and speculation about character, in their insistence upon aesthetic unity as the principal criterion for literary achievement, in their quest for satisfying and coherent patterns of imagery, and in their dependence upon the idea of a fixed and unquestioned "Elizabethan world picture." They touch only briefly on the "stage history" of the play, and they emphasize above all the characterization of Falstaff. I have incorporated several of Professor Sanderson's choices here: if I were asked to recommend just one, it would be J. Dover Wilson's essay, which is beautifully written, exuberant, and informative, and which rises above the relentless formalism of most other essays of its time in its insistent and imaginative historicizing. The new essays I have chosen for this revised edition are, I hope, characteristic of the developments in Shakespeare criticism—and specifically in the criticism of Shakespearean history—that have unfolded between the 1970s and the present (though of course I have had to omit, for reasons of space, many fine essays on the play). Primarily this involves in various ways the impact of literary theory on the study of Shakespeare, from feminism to performance history, from new textualism to queer theory, from film and media studies to dialogic criticism. The diversity of this work—despite the attempts by the decreasing number of anti- or pre-theorists to caricature such material as limited and one-dimensional—is astonishing, and the potential range of engagement for students of Shakespeare of differing backgrounds and creeds seems to me both immense and exciting. I hope you find it so too.

Line-number citations in the following essays and extracts have, wherever possible, been keyed to the text of the play as given in the present volume.

JOHN DRYDEN

The Composition of a Character†

A character, or that which distinguishes one man from all others, cannot be suppos'd to consist of one particular Virtue, or Vice, or passion only; but 'tis a composition of qualities which are not contrary to one another in the same person: thus the same man may be liberal and valiant, but not liberal and covetous; so in a Comical character, or humour, (which is an inclination to this, or that particular folly) *Falstaff* is a lyar, and a coward, a Glutton, and a Buffon, because all these qualities may agree in the same man; . . . 'Tis one of the excellencies of *Shakespear*, that the manners of his persons are generally apparent; and you see their bent and inclinations. . . . [O]ur *Shakespear*, having ascrib'd to *Henry the Fourth* the character of a King, and of a Father, gives him the perfect manners of each Relation, when either he transacts with his Son, or with his Subjects.

SAMUEL JOHNSON

[Falstaff]†

None of *Shakespeare*'s plays are more read than the first and second parts of *Henry* the fourth. Perhaps no authour has ever in two plays afforded so much delight. The great events are interesting, for the fate of kingdoms depends upon them; the slighter occurrences are diverting, and, except one or two, sufficiently probable; the incidents are multiplied with wonderful fertility of invention, and the characters diversified with the utmost nicety of discernment, and the profoundest skill in the nature of man.

The prince, who is the hero both of the comick and tragick part, is a young man of great abilities and violent passions, whose sentiments are right, though his actions are wrong; whose virtues are obscured by negligence, and whose understanding is dissipated by levity. In his idle hours he is rather loose than wicked, and when the occasion forces out his latent qualities, he is great without effort, and brave without tumult. The trifler is roused into a hero,

† From John Dryden, *Troilus and Cressida, or, Truth found too late. A Tragedy, by John Dryden*. 1679. Preface (The Grounds of Criticism in Tragedy), a4r-v.
† From *The Plays of William Shakespeare* (London, 1765) 4.355–6.

and the hero again reposes in the trifler. The character is great, original, and just.

Piercy is a rugged soldier, cholerick, and quarrelsome, and has only the soldier's virtues, generosity and courage.

But *Falstaff* unimitated, unimitable *Falstaff*, how shall I describe thee? Thou compound of sense and vice; of sense which may be admired but not esteemed, of vice which may be despised, but hardly detested. *Falstaff* is a character loaded with faults, and with those faults which naturally produce contempt. He is a thief, and a glutton, a coward, and a boaster, always ready to cheat the weak, and prey upon the poor; to terrify the timorous and insult the defenceless. At once obsequious and malignant, he satirises in their absence those whom he lives by flattering. He is familiar with the prince only as an agent of vice, but of this familiarity he is so proud as not only to be supercilious and haughty with common men, but to think his interest of importance to the duke of *Lancaster*. Yet the man thus corrupt, thus despicable, makes himself necessary to the prince that despises him, by the most pleasing of all qualities, perpetual gaiety, by an unfailing power of exciting laughter, which is the more freely indulged, as his wit is not of the splendid or ambitious kind, but consists in easy escapes and sallies of levity, which make sport but raise no envy. It must be observed that he is stained with no enormous or sanguinary crimes, so that his licentiousness is not so offensive but that it may be borne for his mirth.

The moral to be drawn from this representation is, that no man is more dangerous than he that with a will to corrupt, hath the power to please; and that neither wit nor honesty ought to think themselves safe with such a companion when they see Henry seduced by *Falstaff*.

ELIZABETH MONTAGU

[Hal, Falstaff, and Taste]†

Our author is so little under the discipline of art, that we are apt to ascribe his happiest successes, as well as his most unfortunate failings, to chance. But I cannot help thinking, there is more of contrivance and care in his execution of this play, than in almost any he has written. It is a more regular drama than his other historical plays, less charged with absurdities, and less involved in confusion. It is indeed liable to those objections which are made to tragicom-

† From Elizabeth Montagu, *An Essay on the Writings and Genius of Shakespear, Compared with the Greek and French Dramatic Poets* (London, 1769), 100–108.

edy. But if the pedantry of learning could ever recede from its dogmatical rules, I think that this play, instead of being condemned for being of that species, would obtain favour for the species itself, though perhaps correct taste may be offended with the transitions from grave and important, to light and ludicrous subjects, and more still with those from great and illustrious, to low and mean persons. . . . From some peculiar circumstances relating to the characters in this piece, we may, perhaps, find a sort of apology for the motley mixture thrown into it. We cannot but suppose, that at the time it was written, many stories yet subsisted of the wild adventures of this Prince of Wales, and his idle companions. His subsequent reformation, and his conquests in France, rendered him a very popular character. It was a delicate affair to expose the follies of Henry V. before a people proud of his victories, and tender of his fame, at the same time so informed of the extravagancies and excesses of his youth, that he could not appear divested of them with any degree of historical probability. Their enormity would have been greatly heightened, if they had appeared in a piece entirely serious and full of dignity and decorum. How happily therefore was the character of Falstaffe introduced, whose wit and festivity in some measure excuse the Prince for admitting him into his familiarity, and suffering himself to be led by him into some irregularities. There is hardly a young hero, full of gaiety and spirits, who, if he had once fallen into the society of so pleasant a companion, could have the severity to discard him, or would not say, as the Prince does,

> He could better spare a better man.

How skillfully does our author follow the tradition of the Prince's having been engaged in a robbery, yet make his part in it a mere frolic to play on the cowardly and braggart temper of Falstaffe! The whole conduct of that incident is very artful: he rejects the proposal of the robbery, and only complies with playing a trick on the robbers; and care is taken to inform you, that the money is returned to its owners.——The Prince seems always diverted, rather than seduced by Falstaffe; he despises his vices while he is entertained by his humour: and though Falstaffe is for a while a stain upon his character, yet it is of a kind with those colours, which are used for a disguise in sort, being of such a nature as are easily washed out, without leaving any bad tincture. And we see Henry, as soon as he is called to the high and serious duties of a king, come forth at once with unblemished majesty. The disposition of the hero is made to pierce through the idle frolics of the boy, throughout the whole play; for his reformation is not effected in the last scene of the last act, as is usual in our comedies, but is prepared from the very beginning of the play. The scene between the Prince and Francis, is low and ridiculous, and seems one of the greatest indecorums in the piece; at the same time the attentive spectator will find the purpose of it is to shew him, that Henry was studying human nature, in all her variety of tempers and faculties. I am now, says he, acquainted with all humours, (meaning dispositions) since the days of good man Adam to the present hour. In the play of Henry V. you are told, that in his youth he had been sedulously observing mankind; and from an apprehension, perhaps, how difficult it was to acquire an intimate knowledge of men, whilst he kept up the forms his rank prescribed, he waved the ceremonies and decorums of his situation, and familiarly conversed with all orders of society.——The jealousy his father had conceived of him would probably have been increased, if he had affected such a sort of popularity as would have gained the esteem and love of the multitude.

Whether Henry in the early part of his life was indulging a humour that inclined him to low and wild company, or endeavouring to acquire a deeper and more extensive knowledge of human nature, by a general acquaintance with mankind, it is the business of his historians to determine. But a critic must surely applaud the dexterity of Shakespear for throwing this colour over that part of his conduct, whether he seized on some intimations historians had given of that sort, or, of himself imagined so respectable a motive for the Prince's deviations from the dignity of his birth. This piece must have delighted the people at the time it was written, as the follies of their favourite character so managed, that they rather seemed foils to set off its virtues, then stains which obscured them.

Whether we consider the character of Falstaffe as adapted to encourage and excuse the extravagancies of the Prince, or by itself, we must certainly admire it, and own it to be perfectly original.

The professed wit, either in life or on the stage, is usually severe and satirical. But mirth is the source of Falstaffe's wit. He seems rather to invite you to partake of his merriment, than to attend to his jest; a person must be ill-natured, as well as dull, who does not join in the mirth of this jovial companion, who is in all respects the best calculated to raise laughter of any that ever appeared on a stage.

He joins the finesse of wit with the drollery of humour. Humour is a kind of grotesque wit, shaped and coloured by the disposition of the person in whom it resides, or by the subject to which it is applied. It is oftenest found in odd and irregular minds: but this peculiar turn distorts wit, and though it gives it a burlesque air, which excites momentary mirth, renders it less just, and consequently less agreeable to our judgments. Gluttony, corpulency, and cowardice, are the peculiarities of Falstaffe's composition, they render him ridiculous without folly, throw an air of jest and festivity about him, and make his manners suit with his sentiments, without giving to his understanding any particular bias. As the contempt attendant on these vices and defects is the best antidote against any infection that might be caught in his society, so it was very skilful to make him as ridiculous as witty, and as contemptible as entertaining. The admirable speech upon humour would have been both indecent and dangerous from any other person. We must every where allow his wit is just, his humour genuine, and his character perfectly original, and sustained through every scene, in every play, in which it appears.

As Falstaffe, whom the author certainly intended to be perfectly witty, is less addicted to quibble and play on words, than any of his comic characters, I think we may fairly conclude, our author was sensible it was but a false kind of wit, which he practised from the hard necessity of the times: for in that age, the professor quibbled in his chair, the judge quibbled in the pulpit, the statesman quibbled at the council-board; nay even majesty quibbled on the throne.

MAURICE MORGANN

[The Courage of Falstaff]†

The ideas which I have formed concerning the Courage and Military Character of the Dramatic Sir *John Falstaff*, are so different from those which I find generally to prevail in the world, that I shall take the liberty of stating my sentiments on the subject.

I do not clearly discern that Sir *John Falstaff* deserves to bear the character so generally given him of an absolute Coward; or, in other words, that I do not conceive *Shakespeare* ever meant to make Cowardice an essential part of his constitution. . . . Cowardice *is not* the *Impression* which the *whole* character of *Falstaff* is calculated to make on the minds of an unprejudiced audience; tho' there be, I confess, a great deal of something in the *composition* likely enough to puzzle, and consequently to mislead the Understanding. It is not to the *Courage* only of *Falstaff* that we think these observations will apply: No part whatever of his character seems to be fully settled in our minds; at least there is something strangely incongruous in our discourse and affections concerning him. We all like *Old Jack*; yet, by some strange perverse fate, we all

† From *An Essay on the Dramatic Character of Sir John Falstaff* (London, 1777), reprinted from *Eighteenth Century Essays on Shakespeare*, ed. D. Nichol Smith (Glasgow, 1903), 218–231.

abuse him, and deny him the possession of any one single good or respectable quality. . . . It is strange then that it should now be a question, whether *Falstaff* is or is not a man of Courage; and whether we do in fact contemn him for the want, or respect him for the possession of that quality: And yet I believe the reader will find that he has by no means decided this question, even for himself.—If then it should turn out that this difficulty has arisen out of the Art of *Shakespeare*, who has contrived to make secret Impressions upon us of Courage, and to preserve those Impressions in favour of a character which was to be held up for sport and laughter on account of actions of apparent Cowardice and dishonour, we shall have less occasion to wonder, as *Shakespeare* is a Name which contains All of Dramatic artifice and genius. . . . Perhaps, after all, the *real* character of *Falstaff* may be different from his *apparent* one; and possibly this difference between reality and appearance, whilst it accounts at once for our liking and our censure, may be the true point of humour in the character, and the source of all our laughter and delight. We may chance to find, if we will but examine a little into the nature of those circumstances which have accidentally involved him, that he was intended to be drawn as a character of much Natural courage and resolution; and be obliged thereupon to repeal those decisions which may have been made upon the credit of some general tho' unapplicable propositions. . . . With respect to every infirmity, except that of Cowardice, we must take him as at the period in which he is represented to us. If we see him dissipated, fat,—it is enough;—we have nothing to do with his youth, when he might perhaps have been modest, chaste, *"and not an Eagle's talon in the waist."* But *Constitutional Courage* extends to a man's whole life, makes a part of his nature, and is not to be taken up or deserted like a mere Moral quality. It is true, there is a Courage founded upon *principle*, or rather a principle independent of Courage, which will sometimes operate in spite of nature; a principle which prefers death to shame, but which always refers itself, in conformity to its own nature, to the prevailing modes of honour, and the fashions of the age.—But Natural courage is another thing: It is independent of opinion; It adapts itself to occasions, preserves itself under every shape, and can avail itself of flight as well as of action. . . . That Courage which is founded in nature and constitution, *Falstaff*, as I presume to say, possessed; * * *—The truth is that he had drollery enough to support himself in credit without the point of honour, and had address enough to make even the preservation of his life a point of drollery. The reader knows I allude . . . to his fictitious death in the battle of Shrewsbury. This incident is generally construed to the disadvantage of *Falstaff*: It is a transaction which bears the external marks of Cowardice. . . . Whatever there may be of dishonour in *Falstaff*'s conduct, he neither does or says any thing on this occasion which indicates terror or disorder of mind: On the contrary, this very act is a proof of his having all his wits about him, and is a stratagem, such as it is, not improper for a buffoon, whose fate would be singularly hard, if he should not be allowed to avail himself of his Character when it might serve him in most stead. We must remember, in extenuation, that the executive, the destroying hand of *Douglas* was over him: *"It was time to counterfeit, or that hot termagant Scot had paid him scot and lot too."* He had but one choice; he was obliged to pass thro' the ceremony of dying either in jest or in earnest; and we shall not be surprised at the event, when we remember his propensities to the former.—Life (and especially the life of *Falstaff*) might be a jest; but he could see no joke whatever in dying: To be chopfallen was, with him, to lose both life and character together: He saw the point of honour, as well as every thing else, in ridiculous lights, and began to renounce its tyranny. Such, I think, is the true character of this extraordinary buffoon; and from hence we may discern for what special purposes *Shakespeare* has given him talents and qualities, which were to be afterwards obscured, and perverted to ends opposite to their nature; it was clearly to furnish out a Stage buffoon of a peculiar sort; a kind of Game-bull which would stand the baiting thro' a hundred Plays, and produce equal sport, whether he is pinned down occasionally by *Hal* or *Poins*, or tosses such mongrils as *Bardolph*, or the Justices, sprawling in the air. There is in truth no such thing as totally demolishing Falstaff. * * *

JOHN DOVER WILSON

The Falstaff Myth†

* * *

The site of the Boar's Head tavern in Eastcheap is now as deep-sunk in the ooze of human forgetfulness as that of the palace of Haroun. But it was once a real holstelry, and must have meant much to Londoners of the reigns of Elizabeth and James. Records are scanty, but the very fact that Shakespeare makes it Falstaff's headquarters suggests that it was the best tavern in the city. And

† From John Dover Wilson, "The Falstaff Myth," chapter 2 of *The Fortunes of Falstaff* (Cambridge: Cambridge University Press, 1943), 24–34. Reprinted by permission of the publisher.

the further fact that he avoids mentioning it directly, though quibbling upon the name more than once, suggests, on the one hand, that he kept the name off the stage in order to escape complications with the proprietors of the day, and on the other that he could trust his audience to jump to so obvious an identification without prompting. In any event, no other tavern in Eastcheap is at all likely to have been intended, and as Eastcheap is referred to six times in various scenes, there can be little real doubt that what Falstaff once calls 'the king's tavern' [2.2.49] is the famous Boar's Head, the earliest known reference to which occurs in a will dating from the reign of Richard II.[1] Whether there is anything or not in Skeat's conjecture that the Glutton in *Piers Plowman* made it the scene of his exploits like Falstaff, it was a well-known house of entertainment more than two hundred years before Shakespeare introduced it into his play, and had come therefore by his day to be regarded as a historic hostelry, for which reason it was probably already associated in popular imagination with the floating legends of the wild young prince.[2] What, however, seems to have escaped the attention of modern writers is that the house, with a name that symbolized good living and good fellowship above that of any other London tavern, was almost certainly even better known for good food than for good drink.

Eastcheap, there is plenty of evidence to show, was then, and had long been, the London centre at once of butchers and cookshops. Lydgate, writing in the reign of Henry V, puts the following words in the mouth of his *London Lyckpenny*:

> Then I hyed me into Estchepe;
> One cryes 'rybbes of befe and many a pye';
> Pewter pots they clattered on a heap;
> There was a harp, pype, and minstrelsy.

The street was famed, in short, not only for meat and drink, but also for the 'noise' of musicians, which belonged to 'the old Tauerne in Eastcheap' in *The Famous Victories*, and which 'Mistress Tearsheet would fain hear' in Part II of *Henry IV* [2.4.11–12]. As for 'rybbes of befe', though we never see or hear of Falstaff eating, or desiring to eat, anything except Goodwife Keech's dish of prawns [*2H4*, 2.1.94] and the capon, anchovies and halfpenny worth of bread recorded with an 'intolerable deal of sack' in the bill found

1. See "East Cheap" in Sugden's *Topographical Dictionary to the Works of Shakespeare* (Manchester: University of Manchester, 1925). The designation "king's tavern" perhaps implies a claim to royal patronage on the proprietor's part, possibly connected with the quasi-historical incident known as the Hurling in Eastcheap, an affray which rose among their retinue while Hal's brothers, the princes John and Thomas, wre taking supper at a tavern (unnamed) in Eastcheap, on St. John's Eve, 1410, as is related by Stow.
2. See W. W. Skeat, ed., *Piers Plowman* (Oxford: Clarendon Press, 1886), Passus v, 313.

upon him while asleep [2.4.485], Shakespeare none the less contrives to associate him perpetually with appetizing food by means of the imagery that plays about his person. For the epithets and comparisons which Hal and Poins apply to him, or he himself makes use of, though at times connected with his consumption of sack, are far more often intended to recall the chief stock-in-trade of the victuallers and butchers of Eastcheap, namely meat of all kinds, and meat both raw and roast.

Falstaff is once likened to a 'huge bombard' [2.4.402], once to a 'hogshead' [*2H4*, 2.4.59], once to a 'tun' [2.4.399], and twice to a 'hulk', that is, to a cargo-boat; the nature of the cargo being specified by Doll, who protests to Mistress Quickly, 'There's a whole merchant's venture of Bourdeaux stuff in him, you have not seen a hulk better stuffed in the hold' [*2H4*, 2.4.59–61]. But beyond these there is little or nothing about him in the vintner's line. When, on the other hand, Shakespeare promises the audience, through the mouth of his Epilogue in Part II, to continue the story, with Sir John in it, 'if you be not too much cloyed with fat meat', the phrase sums up the prevailing image, constant in reference though ever-varying in form, which the physical characteristics of Falstaff presented to his mind's eye, and which he in turn was at pains to keep before the mind's eye of his public. Changes in London, and even more, changes in the language, have obliterated all this for the modern reader, so that what was intended, for the first, as little more than a kind of shimmering half-apprehended jest playing upon the surface of the dialogue, must now be recovered as a piece of archaeology, that is, as something long dead. The laughter has gone out of it; yet I shall be disappointed if the reader does not catch himself smiling now and again at what follows.

'Call in Ribs, call in Tallow' [2.4.101] is Hal's cue for Falstaff's entry in the first great Boar's Head scene; and what summons to the choicest feast in comedy could be more apt? For there is the noblest of English dishes straightaway: Sir John as roast Sir Loin-of-Beef, gravy and all. 'Tallow', a word often applied to him, generally in opprobrium, is not rightly understood, unless two facts be recalled: first, that it meant to the Elizabethans liquid fat, as well as dripping or suet or animal fat rendered down; second, that human sweat, partly owing perhaps to the similarity of the word to 'suet', was likewise thought of as fat, melted by the heat of the body. The most vivid presentation of Falstaff served up hot, so to say, is the picture we get of him sweating with fright in Mistress Page's dirty linen basket, as it was emptied by her servants into the Thames; and though *The Merry Wives* does not strictly belong to the Falstaff canon, the passage may be quoted here, as giving the clue to passages in *Henry IV* itself. For however different in character the

Windsor Falstaff may be from his namesake of Eastcheap, he possesses the same body, the body that on Gad's Hill 'sweats to death, and *lards* the lean earth, as he walks along' [2.2.95–96].

'And then', he relates to the disguised Ford,

> to be stopped in, like a strong distillation, with stinking clothes that fretted in their own grease! Think of that, a man of my kidney! think of that—that am as subject to heat, as butter; a man of continual dissolution and thaw; it was a miracle to 'scape suffocation. And in the height of this bath, when I was more than half stewed in grease, like a Dutch dish, to be thrown into the Thames, and cooled, glowing-hot, in that surge, like a horse-shoe. Think of that—hissing hot: think of that, Master Brook! [*MWW*, 3.5.103–12]

The 'greasy tallow-catch' [2.4.206], again, to which the Prince compares him, much to the bewilderment of commentators, betokens, I believe, nothing more mysterious than a dripping-pan to catch the fat as the roasting joint turned upon the spit before the fire. Or take the following scrap of dialogue:

> *L. Chief Justice*. What, you are as a candle, the better part burnt out.
>
> *Falstaff*. A wassail candle, my lord, all tallow—if I did say of wax, my growth would approve the truth.
>
> *L. Chief Justice*. There is not a white hair on your face, but should have his effect of gravity.
>
> *Falstaff*. His effect of gravy, gravy, gravy. [2H4, 1.2.155–61]

Falstaff's repeated 'gravy' is a quibble, of course. But it is not just a feeble jest upon his table manners, as seems to be usually assumed: it follows upon the mention of 'tallow' and refers to the drops of sweat that never cease to stand upon his face. In fact, to use a seventeenth-century expression, applicable to one bathed in perspiration, he may be said perpetually to 'stew in his own gravy'.[3]

Indeed, he glories in the fact. Was it not, according to the physiological notions of the time, the very warrant of his enormous vitality? Never is he more angered to the heart than when the Prince likens him one day to a dry withered old apple-john. His complexion is merely sanguine; heat and moisture mingle to form the element he movers in; except in moods of mock-repentance he leaves to baser earth the cold and dry of melancholy.[4]

Once we have the trick of it, all sorts of other allusions and playful terms of abuse are seen to belong to the same category, while

3. See *OED* "gravy."
4. See "Shakespeare's Universe," *Edinburgh University Journal* (Summer 1942), 224.

the analogy between that vast carcase, as a whole or in its parts, and roasts of various kinds is capable of almost infinite elaboration. 'Chops', for instance, as he is twice called [1.2.118; *2H4*, 2.4.211], carries the double significance of 'fat cheeks' and 'cutlets'; 'guts', the Elizabethan word for 'tripe', is an epithet that occurs no less than five times [2.4.205, 233, 403; 3.3.136, 138]; and 'sweet beef' as a term of endearment requires no explaining. Nor is he only served up as beef; pork, still more appropriate to the Boar's Head, though brought in less often, provides some magnificent examples. The term 'brawn' [2.4.99], which means a large pig fattened for the slaughter, is applied to him on two occasions, on his return from Wales the Prince, enquiring of Bardolph, 'Is your master here in London? . . . Where sups he? doth the old boar feed in the old frank?' [*2H4*, 2.2.143] refers to the familiar inn-sign; Falstaff himself declares that he walks the street followed by the diminutive page 'like a sow that hath overwhelmed all her litter but one' [*2H4*, 1.1.11–12]; last, and best of all, when Doll salutes him between her 'flattering busses' as her 'whoreson little tidy bartholomew boar-pig' [*2H4*, 2.4.224–25], she is alluding to the tender sweet-fleshed little sucking-pigs which formed the chief delicacy at Bartholomew Fair.

The mention of Bartholomew Fair, the most popular annual festivity of Elizabethan and Jacobean London, may be linked with two other comparisons, which take us beyond the confines of Eastcheap and help to bestow on Falstaff that 'touch of infinity' which Bradley discovers in him, associating him, as they do, with feasting on a vast and communal scale. The first, already quoted above, is the Prince's description of him as a 'Manningtree ox with the pudding in his belly' [2.4.403–04], in other words, as an ox roasted whole and stuffed with sausages, after the fashion of the annual fairs at Manningtree, an Essex town famed for the exceeding fatness of its beasts. But the extremest inch of possibility is reached by Poins when he asks Bardolph 'How doth the Martlemas, your master?' [*2H4*, 2.2.100] Martlemas, or the feast of St Martin, on 11 November, was in those days of scarce fodder the season at which most of the beasts had to be killed off and salted for the winter, and therefore the season for great banquets of fresh meat. Thus it had been for centuries, long before the coming of Christianity, and thus it remained down to the introduction of the cropping of turnips in the eighteenth century.[5] In calling him a 'Martlemas' Poins is at once likening Falstaff's enormous proportions to the

5. See E. K. Chambers, *The Medieval Stage*, 2 vols. (Oxford: Oxford University Press, 1903), ch. 11, "The Beginning of Winter."

prodigality of fresh-killed meat which the feast brought, and acclaiming his identity with Riot and Festivity in general.[6] But perhaps the best comment upon Falstaff as Martlemas comes from Spenser's possession of the seasons in the Book of Mutabilitie. His November might almost be Falstaff himself, though the dates prove that the two figures must be independent:

> Next was November, he full grosse and fat,
> As fed with lard, and that right well might seeme;
> For, he had been a fatting hogs of late,
> That yet his browes with sweat did reek and steem.
> And yet the season was full sharp and breem.[7]

One might go to the other end of the scale and point out that the objects Falstaff chooses as a contrast to his person, objects excessively thin, wizened or meagre, are likewise often taken from the food-shops. There is, for instance, the shotten herring, the soused gurnet, the bunch of radish, the rabbit-sucker or poulter's hare, and wittiest of all perhaps, the carbonado—the rasher of bacon, we should say—which he will only allow Hotspur to make of him, if he is foolish enough to come in his way [5.3.56]. But enough to have shown that by plying his audience with suggestions of the choicest food that London and Eastcheap had to offer, whenever the person of Falstaff is mentioned, Shakespeare lays as it were the physical foundations of his Falstaff myth.

The prodigiously incarnate Riot, who fills the Boar's Head with his jollity, typifies much more, of course, than the pleasures of the table. He stands for a whole globe of happy continents, and his laughter is 'broad as ten thousand beeves at pasture'.[8] But he is Feasting first, and his creator never allows us to forget it. For in this way he not only perpetually associates him in our minds with appetizing images, but contrives that as we laugh at his wit our souls shall be satisfied as with marrow and fatness. No one has given finer expression to this satisfaction than Hazlitt, and I may fitly round off the topic with words of his:

> Falstaff's wit is an emanation of a fine constitution; an exuberance of good-humour and good-nature; an overflowing of his love of laughter and good-fellowship; a giving vent to his heart's ease, and over-contentment with himself and others. He would not be in character, if he were not so fat as he is; for there is the greatest keeping in the boundless luxury of his

6. I owe this point to the late Lord Ernle: writing in *Shakespeare's England* (I: 356), he notes: 'To Shakespeare's mind the prodigious plenty of Martlemas suggested Falstaff in its proportions.'
7. Edmund Spenser, *The Faerie Queene*, Book 7, canto 7, stanza 40.
8. George Meredith, *The Spirit of Shakespeare*.

imagination and the pampered self-indulgence of his physical appetites. He manures and nourishes his mind with jests, as he does his body with sack and sugar. He carves out his jokes, as he would a capon or a haunch of venison, where there is *cut and come again*; and pours out upon them the oil of gladness. His tongue drops fatness, and in the chambers of his brain 'it snows of meat and drink'. He keeps perpetually holiday and open house, and we live with him in a round of invitations to a rump and dozen. . . . He never fails to enrich his discourse with allusions to eating and drinking, but we never see him at table. He carries his own larder about with him, and is himself 'a tun of man'.[9]

Monsieur Remorse

Like all great Shakespearian characters Falstaff is a bundle of contradictions. He is not only Riot but also Repentance. He can turn an eye of melancholy upon us, assume the role of puritan sanctimony, and when it pleases him, even threaten amendment of life. It is, of course, *mock*-repentance, carried through as part of the untiring 'play extempore' with which he keeps the Prince, and us, and himself, entertained from beginning to end of the drama. And yet it is not mere game; Shakespeare makes it more interesting by persuading us that there is a strain of sincerity in it; and it almost completely disappears in Part II, when the rogue finds himself swimming on the tide of success. There is a good deal of it in Part I, especially in the earliest Falstaff scenes.

> But, Hal, I prithee, trouble me no more with vanity. I would to God thou and I knew where a commodity of good names were to be bought.
>
> Thou hast done much harm upon me, Hal—God forgive thee for it: before I knew thee, Hal, I knew nothing, and now am I, if a man should speak truly, little better than one of the wicked: I must give over this life, and I will give it over: by the Lord, an I do not, I am a villain. I'll be damned for never a king's son in Christendom. [1.2.69–72, 79–84]

One of his favourite poses is that of the innocent, beguiled by a wicked young heir apparent; he even makes it the burden of his apologia to the Lord Chief Justice at their first encounter. It serves too when things go wrong, when resolute men who have taken £1000 on Gad's Hill are left in the lurch by cowardly friends, or when there's lime in a cup of sack:

9. William Hazlitt, *Characters of Shakespeare's Plays* in Hazlitt, *Works*, ed. A. R. Waller and A. Glover, 13 vols. (London: Dent, 1902), 1:278.

> The is nothing but roguery to be found in villainous man, yet a coward is worse than a cup of sack with lime in it. A villainous coward! Go thy ways, old Jack, die when thou wilt, if manhood, good manhood, be not forgot upon the face of the earth, then am I a shotten herring. . . . There lives not three good men unchanged in England, and one of them is fat, and grows old. God help the while! a bad world, I say. I would I were a weaver—I could sing psalms or anything. [2.4.111–19]

But beside this talk of escaping from a wicked world and the toils of a naughty young prince, there is also the pose of personal repentance. At his first entry Poins hails him as Monsieur Remorse, an indication that this is one of his recognized roles among Corinthians and lads of mettle. And we may see him playing it at the opening of act 3, scene 3, when there is no Hal present to require entertaining.

> Well, I'll repent, and that suddenly, while I am in some liking. I shall be out of heart shortly, and then I shall have no strength to repent. An I have not forgotten what the inside of a church is made of, I am a peppercorn, a brewer's horse. The inside of a church! Company, villainous company, hath been the spoil of me.

Such passages, together with the habit of citing Scripture, may have their origin, I have said, in the puritan, psalm-singing, temper of Falstaff's prototype—that comic Lollard, Sir John Oldcastle in the old *Henry IV*. But, if so, the motif, adapted and developed in Shakespeare's hands, has come to serve a different end. In this play of the Prodigal Prince it is Hal who should rightly exhibit moods of repentance; and on the face of it, it seems quite illogical to transfer them to Falstaff, the tempter. Yet there are reasons why Hal could not be thus represented. In the first place, as already noted, repentance in the theological sense, repentance for sin, is not relevant to his case at all, which is rather one of a falling away from political virtues, from the duties laid upon him by his royal vocation. And in the second place, since Henry V is the ideal king of English history, Shakespeare must take great care, even in the days of his 'wildness', to guard him from the breath of scandal. As has been well observed by a recent editor: 'His riots are mere frolics. He does not get drunk and is never involved in any scandal with a woman.'[1] And there is a third reason, this time one of dramatic technique not of morals, why the repentance of the Prince must be kept in the background

1. See William Shakespeare, *1 Henry IV*, ed. G. L. Kittredge (Boston: Ginn, 1936), xi. I fancy Hal is just a little tipsy at the beginning of Part 1, 2.4; but the point is, in general, sound enough, and the more striking that the chronicles do not hide the fact that Prince Henry was given to sexual intemperance.

as much as possible, viz. that as the only satisfactory means of rounding off the two parts, it belongs especially to the last act of the play.

Yet Monsieur Remorse is a good puppet in the property-box of the old morality, and may be given excellent motions in the fingers of a skilful showman, who is laying himself out, in this play especially, to make fun of the old types. Why not shape a comic art out of it, and hand it over to Falstaff, who as the heir of traditional medieval 'antics' like the Devil, the Vice, the Fool, Riot and Lord of Misrule, may very well manage one more? Whether or not Shakespeare argued it out thus, he certainly added the ingredient of melancholy, and by so doing gave a piquancy to the sauce which immensely enhances the relish of the whole dish. If only modern actors who attempt to impersonate Falstaff would realize it!

Falstaff, then, came to stand for the repentance, as well as the riotous living, of the Prodigal Son. And striking references to the parable, four of them, seem to show that his creator was fully aware of what he was doing. 'What, will you make a younker of me? shall I not take mine ease in mine inn but I shall have my pocket picked?' [3.3.69–70][2] Sir John indignantly demands of Mistress Quickly, on discovering, or pretending to discover, the loss of his grandfather's seal-ring. The word 'younker' calls up a scene from some well-known representation of the parable, in picture or on the stage, a scene to which Shakespeare had already alluded in the following lines from *The Merchant of Venice*:

> How like a younker or a prodigal
> The scarfèd bark puts from her native bay,
> Hugged and embracèd by the strumpet wind!
> How like a prodigal doth she return,
> With over-weathered ribs and ragged sails,
> Lean, rent, and beggared by the strumpet wind!
> [*Merchant*, 2.6.14–19]

Equally vivid is Falstaff's description of the charge of foot he led into battle at Shrewsbury as so 'dishonourable ragged' that 'you would think that I had a hundred and fifty tattered prodigals, lately come from swine-keeping, from eating draff and husks' [4.2.28–32]. And seeing that he calls them in the same speech 'slaves as ragged as Lazarus in the painted cloth, where the Glutton's dogs licked his sores', we may suppose that, here too, he is speaking right painted cloth, from whence he had studied his Bible, an inference which seems borne out by his third reference, this

2. See Richmond Noble, *Shakespeare's Biblical Knowledge* (London: SPCK, 1935): 'The alternative title for the Prodigal Son was the "younger," as the alternative for the good brother was the "elder" ' (277).

time from Part II.[3] Having, you will remember, already honoured Mistress Quickly by becoming indebted to her for a hundred marks, that is for over £65, he graciously condescends to borrow £10 more from her. And when she protests that to raise the sum she must be fain to pawn both her plate and the tapestry of her dining-chambers, he replies: 'Glasse, glasses, is the only drinking—and for thy walls, a pretty drollery or the story of the Prodigal or the German hunting in waterwork is worth a thousand of these bed-hangers and these fly-bitten tapestries [*2H4*, 2.1.143–47]. This is not just the patter of the confidence-trickster; Falstaff, we must believe, had a real liking for the Prodigal Son story, or why should that tactful person, mine Host of the Garter Inn, have gone to the trouble of having it painted, 'fresh and new', about the walls of the chamber that he let to the greasy philanderer who assumed the part of Sir John, in Windsor. Not being a modern critic, the good man could not know that his guest was an impostor.

* * *

ARTHUR C. SPRAGUE

Gadshill Revisited†

For about a hundred and eighty years after Sir John Falstaff for the first time ran roaring from Gadshill, the fact of his cowardice was taken for granted. Falstaff was immensely popular with readers and playgoers alike. In the seventeenth century, allusions to him are far more numerous, by actual count, than those to any other Shakespearian character,[1] and the terms in which he is referred to are quite unambiguous. "A thrasonical puff, and emblem of mock valour," Tom Fuller calls him;[2] and Dryden, not, I think, inaccurately, describes him as "old, fat, merry, cowardly, drunken, amorous, vain, and lying." Yet Falstaff's individuality, as Dryden perceived, lay elsewhere:

> That wherein he is singular is his wit, or those things he says . . . unexpected by the audience; his quick evasions, when you expect him surprised, which, as they are extremely diverting of themselves, so receive a great addition from his person.[3]

3. Cf. *As You Like It*, 3.2.271: 'I answer you right painted cloth, from whence you have studied your questions.'

† From *Shakespeare Quarterly*, IV (April 1953), 125–37. Reprinted by permission of the author and the Shakespeare Association of America. Originally a paper read at the Shakespeare Conference at Stratford-on-Avon in August 1951.

1. G. E.Bentley, *Shakespeare and Jonson* (Chicago [1945]), chap. vii.
2. Thomas Fuller, *The History of the Worthies of England*, ed. P. Austin Nuttall (London, 1840), II, 455.
3. John Dryden, "An Essay of Dramatic Poesy," in *Dramatic Essays*, "Everyman's Library," 43.

And Dr. Samuel Johnson, agreeing with Dryden, pronounces Falstaff a coward and defines his wit as consisting "in easy escapes and sallies of levity."[4]

It was not until 1777 that heresy began. In that year appeared a long essay of a good deal of subtlety, and even charm, *On the Dramatic Character of Sir John Falstaff*, by Maurice Morgann. Morgann, a middle-aged civil servant of "uncommon powers," acknowledges that his book was written on a dare, and he dreads that it might be taken, as, indeed, it was by many, as a mere exercise in paradox. He recognizes "how universally the contrary opinion prevails"; and that "the appearances" in this case are all against him. Falstaff is involved, almost immediately, "in circumstances of apparent dishonour"; he is called a coward; is seen "in the very act of running away," and "betrayed into those *lies* and *braggadocioes*, which are the usual concomitants of cowardice in military men, and pretenders to valour." What was more, these things are "thrust forward, pressed upon our notice as the subject of our mirth."[5] The grounds for his own belief that Sir John was no coward were of quite another sort, and he asks patience of the reader while he sets forth what "lies so dispersed, is so latent, and so purposely obscured" [Morgann, 4]—the "secret impressions upon us of courage" [Morgann, 3].

Though Morgann's ideas were to prevail, they were not unopposed in his own day. A carefully reasoned reply by Richard Stack appeared in *The Transactions of the Royal Irish Academy*. Dr. Johnson's opinion was twice asked and given. "Why, Sir," Boswell quotes him as saying, "we shall have the man come forth again; and as he has proved Falstaff to be no coward, he may prove Iago to be a very good character."[6] Thomas Davies, too, the actor and bookseller, spoke out, and the point he made was, I think, a telling one: "If the knight is proved to be a man of courage, half the mirth he raises is quite lost and misplaced."[7] What is more curious, Falstaff on the stage remained unregenerate. As he had once been, in this matter of cowardice, so he has remained right down to the present—though such fine actors as Sir Ralph Richardson and (at Stratford) Mr. Anthony Quayle and the late Roy Byford, have dispensed with most of the traditional buffoonery which once disfigured the role.

We have come, indeed, to a parting of ways, the actors keeping straight on as they had been going, the critics, with few exceptions,

4. *The Plays of William Shakespeare*, ed. Johnson (London, 1765), IV, 356.
5. Maurice Morgann, *An Essay on the Dramatic Character of Sir John Falstaff* (London, 1820), 2, 3.
6. James Boswell, *Life of Samuel Johnson*, ed. G. B. Hill and L. F. Powell (Oxford, 1934), IV, 192 note.
7. Thomas Davies, *Dramatic Miscellanies* (London, 1784), I, 272.

straying obscurely to the left. Nor was Morgann, with his notion of appearance and reality, his "secret impressions" of courage, a safe guide. Thus, William Lloyd would have Falstaff's delightfully spontaneous rejoinder to the Prince's "Where shall we take a purse to-morrow, Jack?" "Zounds, where thou wilt, lad! I'll make one," a bit of crafty duplicity, with the speaker fully conscious of the incongruity of what he says.[8] And Hazlitt fancies that Falstaff's bill, with its "out-of-the-way charge for capons and sack with only one half-penny-worth of bread," may have been planted for the Prince to find.[9] (One might question, with equal propriety, whether at the moment of the reading of the bill Sir John, for all his snoring, was really asleep!)

The starting point for such divagations remains the denial of what in the theater seems obvious, the fact of cowardice. Yet Bradley and even Kittredge are among those who have denied it. Bradley, indeed, is not without misgivings. The manner of Falstaff's flight at Gadshall troubles him, if only in a footnote: "It is to be regretted . . . that in carrying his guts away so nimbly he 'roared for mercy'; for I fear we have no ground for rejecting Henry's statement to that effect."[1] He grants, too, that "Falstaff sometimes behaves in what we should generally call a cowardly way." But conduct is not a certain indication of character. "If the word [coward] means a person who feels painful fear in the presence of danger, and yields to that fear in spite of his better feelings and convictions, then assuredly Falstaff was no coward" [Bradley, 266]. As for Kittredge, strangely, as it always seemed to me, he had no doubts whatsoever. Even the roaring at Gadshill he denied, or explained away. For once, dramatic evidence went by the board with him, and his Falstaff was *sans peur*, if not quite *sans reproche*.

Among the minority-critics who have held out for cowardice (and John Bailey was one), the foremost is, of course, Professor Stoll. Time after time he has returned to the question, bringing to it his broad knowledge of popular drama and its enduring conventions.[2] Thus, he shows that Falstaff's behavior on the battlefield—his cracking jokes, for instance, or capturing a prisoner of his own, the redoubtable Colevile of the Dale—cannot be taken as evidence of courage, since the mere type-cowards and comic butts of earlier and cruder plays do the like. Sir John's ancestors are a shabby lot,

8. William Lloyd, *Essays on Shakespeare* (1858), in *1 Henry IV*, Furness Variorum Edition, 135.
9. James Hazlitt, *Characters of Shakespeare's Plays*, Bohn ed. (1892), 135.
1. A. C. Bradley, *Oxford Lectures on Poetry* (London, 1909), 268 note.
2. E. E. Stoll, "Recent Shakespeare Criticism," *Shakespeare Jahrbuch*, 74 (1938); *Shakespeare and Other Masters* (Cambridge [Massachusetts], 1940); *From Shakespeare to Joyce* (New York, 1944); "Symbolism in Shakespeare," *Modern Language Review*, 42 (1947).

but their existence may as well be acknowledged. In fact, a latecomer to this controversy, who has convinced himself that Falstaff was no braver than he should be, is likely to discover that many of his best arguments have already been used, somewhere, by Mr. Stoll. That they have been so largely disregarded is a little puzzling.

Finally, Professor J. Dover Wilson, though he repeatedly invokes the authority of Johnson in combatting the Romantic critics, is ambiguous on this matter of timidity; or, rather, as it seems to me, he would have it both ways. Falstaff, during the overpowering of the travelers at Gadshill, is described as "dancing with rage, on the fringe of the scuffle," and his subsequent flight becomes as ignominious as the older actors were accustomed to make it. Indeed, if the Gadshill Scene stood alone, Mr. Wilson is satisfied that the audience would accept Sir John as "an absolute coward"—which he will not admit.[3] The representation of cowardice by the right sort of comedian will (he thinks) have produced an effect upon us very different from what might be expected—affection, even, rather than a "jeering contempt" [Wilson, 47]. The impression of cowardice is dissolved in the mirth of the Tavern Scene. Falstaff, sensing the plot against him, deliberately exaggerates, winking to the audience at the moment he begins to do so. The groundlings might miss the point; there would be others to whom the question of cowardice was left open to debate. And Falstaff's "magnificent display of stoutness of heart" when the Sheriff comes to arrest him, is "the final answer to the Prince's slanderous story of the events on Gad's Hill, and to our own receding impressions" [Wilson, 58].

Yet as we pass to still later episodes, it is curious to find Mr. Wilson taking issue repeatedly with the contentions of the Morgann school. Falstaff's presence in the thick of battle is no longer accepted as evidence of valor. His "military reputation is not only complete bogus, but one of the best jokes in the whole drama" [Wilson, 89]. Had Colevile of the Dale resisted, "we may surmise that another sham death would have followed the exchange of a few blows" [Wilson, 87]. Even the turning out of poor swaggering Pistol is left to Bardolph, "while Falstaff, sword in hand, follows up at a discreet distance behind" [Wilson, 107].

On this whole question of cowardice, then, the earlier critics, and the actors, are on one side; the later critics, with few exceptions, on the other. Either, that is to say, Falstaff is an egregious coward; or he is—here there is some want of agreement—a veteran soldier, usually, and a realist in war; trusted, and not wholly undeserving of trust; wily, and of great presence of mind; no Hotspur, of course but just as certainly, not a coward. The chief arguments of

3. J. Dover Wilson, *The Fortunes of Falstaff* (Cambridge and New York, 1944), 44, 45.

Morgann and his followers, the arguments against cowardice, are familiar—Morgann, himself, thought up most of them—and I shall present them only summarily, though I hope with fairness.

There is, first of all, Morgann's bold challenge to the impartial reader: "We all like *Old Jack*" though we so constantly abuse him! But could we like him, vicious as he is, were he actually a coward? Cowardice seems incompatible with our impression of the character as a whole. Our feeling toward Falstaff is altogether different from our feeling toward, say, the cowardly Parolles in *All's Well that Ends Well.*

From impressions and their analysis we pass to inference. Falstaff's military reputation is pointed to with confidence as evidence of desert. Thus, in the dark days before Shrewsbury, the Prince himself entrusts him with the command of a company of foot. Falstaff is present at the King's Council of War; and in the premature account of the outcome of the battle is prominently mentioned among the casualties—"And Harry Monmouth's brawn, the hulk Sir John, Is prisoner" [*2H4*, 1.1.19–20]. Later we hear of "a dozen Captains" searching anxiously for him while he sups with Mistress Tearsheet. Then, too, a rebel of some note, a knight, Colevile of the Dale, surrenders at once upon hearing who his antagonist is: "I think you are Sir John Falstaff, and in that thought yield me" [*2H4*, 4.3.16–17].

Much is made, also, of a relatively inconspicuous episode at the close of the great Tavern Scene in *1 Henry IV.* Bardolph rushes in, with a good deal of nasal clamor, to interrupt the play which Falstaff and Prince Hal are acting: "O, my lord, my lord! the sheriff with a most monstrous watch is at the door" [2.4.434–38]—looking of course, for certain thieves. Falstaff, it is urged, might well be expected to show alarm at this, or even terror. On the contrary, he merely takes hiding behind the arras, where he is presently discovered, not quaking with fear but asleep, and "snorting like a horse" [2.4.473–74].

Later in the same play we have Sir John on the field of battle—and in time, too! He tells us in soliloquy that he has led his poor soldiers where they were slaughtered. He finds himself in the very thick of the fight. Hotspur contends with Prince Hal in single combat. The terrible Douglas suddenly attacks Falstaff. Whereupon Falstaff, no match of course for such an adversary, but never losing his coolness and presence of mind, has recourse to a brilliant stratagem by which he escapes: lives, as is hopefully said of him, to fight another day. As no coward could have slept, earlier, so no coward could now have outwitted death by seeming to die!

The complicated happenings at Gadshill, Morgann takes up last of all, and he admits the possibility that Falstaff in this single instance yielded to a momentary and quite understandable terror (even Bradley, as we saw, was troubled by Sir John's *roaring* as he ran). For an uncompromising defense of the fat hero at this point, one goes to Kittredge. Falstaff, he urges, is under no sort of obligation to fight it out. On the contrary, as a thief caught in the act, it behooves him to take to his heels. "How the fat rogue roar'd!" [2.2.98] says Poins, at the end of the Gadshill Scene. But this refers to Falstaff's "vociferous swaggering"—his "Down with them . . . whoreson caterpillars" and so on—as he set upon the travellers—or encouraged poor Bardolph and the others to set upon them! And when the roaring is again mentioned and its precise character specified ("and, Falstaff, you carried your guts away as nimbly . . . and roar'd for mercy, and still run and roar'd, as ever I heard bullcalf" [2.4.232–34]), it is the "only departure from accuracy in Prince Hal's story."

These, then, are the principal arguments which have been used by those who deny that Falstaff was a coward, despite those circumstances of "apparent dishonour" and appearances "singularly strong and striking" which Morgann recognized as likely to sway the judgment of a simple reader. They are arguments which vary a good deal in force; but each of them can, I think, be fairly met.

There is Morgann's argument, first of all, that we could not like "plump Jack" as we do if to his other failings, and quite tipping the balance, were added cowardice. But this is to leave out of account Sir John's years, and it might be added his corpulence. He is obviously disqualified as a combatant—"blasted with antiquity" [*2H4*, 1.2.207]. To expect valor of him is, indeed, to expect too much! And in the Play Scene when, speaking in the person of Prince Hal, he has occasion to praise himself, he makes a point of this: "But for sweet Jack Falstaff, kind Jack Falstaff, true Jack Falstaff, valiant Jack Falstaff, and therefore more valiant being, as he is, old Jack Falstaff. . . ." Nor need the argument remain hypothetical. For it is quite obvious that Dr. Johnson liked Falstaff, though recognizing the rogue's numerous vices and insisting upon his cowardice.

As for his military reputation, I am tempted merely to repeat Professor Dover Wilson's comprehensive description of it as "complete bogus" and "one of the best jokes in the whole drama." Colevile of the Dale has only to learn who his antagonist is, and yields without striking a blow. (His alacrity in yielding does not, indeed, escape comment: "It was more, his courtesy than your deserving," says Prince John to Falstaff, unpleasantly enough.) But if Pistol, the complete coward, is able to take a prisoner on the field of battle, why not his old master, the better man of the two? And Colevile, though his words are not abject like those of Pistol's Frenchman, seems scarcely formidable. Falstaff speaks of him with suspicious emphasis as "a most furious knight and valorous enemy" and of his own "pure and immaculate valour" in taking such a prisoner. Perhaps, the first tribute is as unsubstantial as the second?

But the Prince entrusted Falstaff with the command of a company shortly before Shrewsbury? And this same company, it might be answered, will afford occasion for one of Sir John's happiest monologues; is fully justified, in terms of dramatic economy, by the use made of it! The Prince, too, seems to take the matter lightly. "I'll procure this fat rogue a charge of foot," he says, adding, not I think without relish, "and I know his death will be a march of twelve score." He wants to see Falstaff larding the lean earth once more! Meanwhile, there will be the pleasure of telling him the news:

> I have procured thee, Jack, a charge of foot.
> *Falstaff.* I would it had been of horse. [3.3.165–66]

Later, by the way, Hal entrusts dispatches of obvious importance to—of all messengers—Bardolph!

He slept behind the arras—slept soundly and snored. Now this fact has been taken as incontestable proof of high fortitude on the snorer's part. But is it? I would not so far belittle Sir John's sagacity as to believe that what even a minor member of the gang (Gadshill) recognized would not have been perceived by Falstaff—that on this particular expedition they stole "as in a castle, cocksure" [2.1.78]. The Prince of Wales, deeply involved as he is, himself, must needs "(if matters should be look'd into) for [his] own credit sake make all whole." Falstaff might well sleep soundly, and, sleeping, contribute to the forwarding of the plot by allowing his pockets to be picked. What is natural in itself has reason as well in the economy of the play as a whole; most of dramatic technique (as I have come to believe) consisting in a playwright's ability to kill more than one bird with a single stone.

Falstaff's behavior at Shrewsbury and Gadshill remains to be considered. At Shrewsbury, then, he led his ragamuffins where they were peppered; is found, himself, where the fighting is fiercest, and escapes death by means of a quite legitimate stratagem. The passing allusion to the destruction of the ragamuffins is impressive when taken out of context. Nor would I impute a sinister motive to old Jack and believe that the securing of their death pay was his object here.[4] Were this so, one would expect some intimation of it in the text. They fell, in any case, almost to a man—and it is convenient for the playwright certainly, and perhaps for Sir John, to have them out of the way. Meanwhile, the soliloquy in which we hear of their fate is worth examining. "Though I could scape shot-free at

4. Cf. J. W. Fortescue, in *Shakespeare's England*, I, 123.

London," Falstaff begins, "I fear the shot here." Then, starting at the sight of one who has paid his score—"There's honour for you!" "I am as hot as molten lead," he mutters, "and as heavy too. God keep lead out of me! I need no more weight than mine own bowels." For an Elizabethan audience—for, I think, any popular audience—the character of the speech will already have been determined. It is addressed to them, designed for their amusement—a comic monologue spoken by one who does, indeed, "fear the shot" and who will have recourse to whatever shifts he can devise to save that precious carcass of his. * * *

"Enter *Douglas*. He fighteth with *Falstaff*, who falls down as if he were dead." I recall a very good performance of *1 Henry IV* at an American repertory theater before a small audience. In the row behind me were two very young girls who clearly had not read the play but, as clearly, were greatly enjoying it. And the happy comment of one of them, wholly spontaneous as it was, delighted me: "He's playing possum!" It came, as I noted, a moment or two after Sir John's descent. To her, as to a good many in that first audience of long ago, he must have seemed to have died indeed. And when, upon the talk of embowelling, Falstaff rose, there came amusement and relief. Though the expedient he practiced was, as an eighteenth-century critic stated, "very natural to a coward,"[5] and one which an unfortunate fat man of the same name repeats in *The Merry Wives of Windsor*, it is not, I should say, conclusive evidence of cowardice any more than it is of valor. Relief and amusement come first, and beyond such feelings I doubt if the ordinary spectator goes. Long ere this, he will have made up his mind on the matter of cowardice and will interpret this episode accordingly. And if we, away from the theater, disputing as we do over niceties, are in need of further enlightenment, it comes in the speech immediately following. "The better part of valour is discretion," Falstaff rationalizes. Then, as he looks about him, come thoughts of another sort. "Zounds, I am afraid of this gunpowder Percy, though he be dead. How if he should counterfeit too, and rise?" And, accordingly, to "make him sure," he will thrust his sword into the dead body. If, he adds as an afterthought, he takes upon himself the glory of having slain Hotspur, he may succeed in brazening it out. "Why may not he rise as well as I?" he repeats. There is a double incentive for what he does—fame, yes, but caution as well. Tom Davies who, knowing as he did a great deal about the practical theater, remained undazzled by the brilliance of Maurice Morgann, gave this passage the emphasis it deserves: "If any proof of [Falstaff's] timidity be yet wanting, we have, in this scene, such as bids defiance to

5. Richard Stack, in *1 Henry IV*, Furness Variorum Edition, 417.

all question; for Falstaff, not satisfied with seeing the dead body of Percy before him, to make all sure, wounds the corpse in the thigh."[6]

The circumstances of the Gadshill robbery Morgann, for obvious reasons, examined last of all. In the play, it is of some consequence, however, that the episode comes very early. Shakespeare's practice in matters of exposition is remarkably consistent. Facts and impressions, once imparted, are rarely contradicted, and then in quite unmistakable terms. Even Iago, who for a few moments may appear to have something of a case against his master, a still unknown Moor, is soon shown in his true colors as a designing villain. What is more, the cowardice of Falstaff is not lightly referred to, or joked about; it receives in the Gadshill episode what amounts, in dramatic terms, to demonstration.

As Poins outlines the plan, he and the Prince are to set upon Falstaff, Bardolph, Peto, and Gadshill, and rob them of their newly acquired booty. The Prince, not unnaturally, wonders whether "they will be too hard for us"—four men against two. But Poins reassures him:

> Well, for two of them, I know them to be as true-bred cowards as ever turn'd back; and for the third, if he fight longer than he sees reason, I'll forswear arms. The virtue of this jest will be the incomprehensible lies that this same fat rogue will tell us when we meet at supper: how thirty, at least, he fought with; what wards, what blows, what extremities he endured; and in the reproof of this lies the jest. [1.2.158–64]

Thus, two things are promised: that Falstaff, to translate understatement by understatement, is not likely to do much fighting; and that, in keeping with his timidity and making it truly diverting, his tales of prowess afterwards will be infinite ("incomprehensible"). Hal is satisfied—and, indeed, Poins knows his man!

At Gadshill, Falstaff has first to endure the distress of being deprived of his horse—that unfortunate animal!—but being Falstaff is soon able to play upon the familiar theme of his own bulk quite as happily as his tormenters. He hears that the travelers are numerous. "Zounds," he cries, "will they not rob us?" And the Prince: "What, a coward, Sir John Paunch?" "Indeed," he answers, "I am not John of Gaunt, your grandfather; but yet no coward, Hal." "Well, we leave that to the proof" [2.2.57–61]. And the proof is soon forthcoming. The travelers, easing their legs by walking down the hill, are pounced upon and relieved of their money, Falstaff setting up a prodigious clamor while this is going on. Once more, to keep these complicated happenings clear, the prince comments:

6. *Dramatic Miscellanies*, I, 273.

> The thieves have bound the true men. Now could thou and I rob the thieves and go merrily to London, it would be argument for a week, laughter for a month, and a good jest for ever. [2.2.81–84]

But Falstaff, returning with the booty, is full of satisfaction:

> Come, my masters, let us share, and then to horse before day. An the Prince and Poins be not two arrant cowards, there's no equity stirring. There's no more valour in that Poins than in a wild duck. [2.2.86–89]

It is the note he will sound insistently at the beginning of the Tavern Scene. They are the cowards, not he! He may even believe it, himself. Then,

> *as they are sharing, the Prince and Poins set upon them. They all run away, and Falstaff, after a blow or two* [he is, of course, less nimble than the rest], *runs away too, leaving the booty behind them.*
>
> PRINCE. Got with much ease. Now merrily to horse.
> The thieves are scattered, and possess'd with fear
> So strongly that they dare not meet each other.
> Each takes his fellow for an officer.
> Away, good Ned. Falstaff sweats to death
> And lards the lean earth as he walks along.
> Were't not for laughing, I should pity him.
> POINS. How the fat rogue roar'd! [2.2.92–98]

So in *A Midsummer Night's Dream*, Bully Bottom's companions had fled in panic at sight of the ass's head.

George Bartley, a distinguished Falstaff of the early years of the last century and for a long time stage-manager at Covent Garden Theatre, is described as "a courteous, discreet gentleman." He had, nevertheless, a very low opinion of the intelligence of audiences.

> "Sir," he would say . . . , "you must first tell them you are going to do so and so; you must then tell them you are doing it, and then that you have done it; and then, by G-d" (with a slap on his thigh), "*perhaps* they will understand you!"[7]

Shakespeare in the present instance might almost be anticipating the precautions recommended. We are told what will happen; told, as well, what has happened. And if the actual encounter can scarcely be interpreted while it is taking place, it is, in Shakespeare's theater, no encounter of phantom-shapes, of dimly outlined silhouettes, but one clearly visible by honest daylight.

7. J. R. Planché, *Recollections and Reflections* (London, 1872), II, 208.

Misunderstanding could not well have existed. "But yet no coward, Hal. . . . Well, we leave that to the proof."

More still was promised: "the virtue of this jest . . . the incomprehensible lies." And Falstaff fairly outdoes expectation. In the study, one may forget or overlook, the visual impressiveness of his entrance. He and his followers carry battered weapons, their clothes are stained with blood ("Tell me now in earnest," the Prince asks later, "how came Falstaff's sword so hack'd?" and Peto explains, "Why, he hack'd it with his dagger, and said he would swear truth out of England but he would make you believe it was done in fight, and persuaded us to do the like" [2.4.271–75]). It is he, Sir John, who makes complaint, "A plague of all cowards, I say." Deserted, as he found himself, by those who should have fought beside him, he had yet borne himself magnificently and escaped only "by miracle." Poins had prophesied he would claim to have fought with "thirty, at least," and he reaches fifty—"two or three and fifty upon poor old Jack." Then, before the fun of the mounting figures is yet exhausted, he is led to mention casualties: "two rogues in buckram . . . pepper'd." The same two, as we recognize, who are so eagerly listening to him now, who can wait, nonetheless, and give their great fish more line, for he is surely caught!

For the actor to wink at his audience, somewhere here, as Mr. Dover Wilson would have him do, seems to me purely arbitrary. (The meaning of innumerable passages in Shakespeare could be perverted by means of extra-textual winkings, and it is to be hoped that the present vogue for imagining them does not spread to tragedy!) Arbitrary, and also confusing, dividing the audience at a moment when they should be at one and sharing their pleasure as good audiences ever do. Above all, for Sir John to appear conscious of his danger thus, is to anticipate our pleasure in his escape. Whereas, if we are to judge from the text alone, this comes as a magnificent surprise. He seems doomed.

> PRINCE. Mark now how a plain tale shall put you down. Then did we two set on you four and, with a word, outfac'd you from your prize, and have it; yea, and can show it you here in the house. And, Falstaff, you carried your guts away as nimbly, with as quick dexterity, and roar'd for mercy, and still run and roar'd, as ever I heard bullcalf. . . . What trick, what device, what starting hole canst thou now find out to hide thee from this open and apparent shame?
> POINS. Come, let's hear, Jack. What trick has thou now?
> [2.4.229–34, 236–39]

And then, and only then (and the actor will not fail to bring out the sudden and dramatic change of speed which marks the moment), Falstaff replies:

> By the Lord, I knew ye as well as he that made ye. Why, hear you, my masters. Was it for me to kill the heir apparent? Should I turn upon the true prince? Why, thou knowest I am as valiant as Hercules; but beware instinct. The lion will not touch the true prince. [2.4.240–44]

Falstaff, as Davies recognized, "is never in a state of humiliation; he generally rises superior to attack, and gets the laugh on his side in spite of truth and conviction."[8] Nevertheless, it is the Prince who recurs to this episode with enjoyment, still gloating over it in *The Second Part of Henry the Fourth.* And Falstaff, having outdone himself with his glorious lion and a prince whose legitimacy is *now*, he says, established (as if there might have been some slight reason to doubt it before!) significantly changes the subject:

> Gallants, lads, boys, hearts of gold, all the titles of good fellowship come to you! What, shall we be merry? Shall we have a play extempore?
> PRINCE. Content—and the argument shall be thy running away.
> FALSTAFF. Ah, no more of that, Hal, an thou lovest me!
> [2.4.249–53]

As Professor Waldock asked in *The Review of English Studies* some years ago, "What point would there be in such a reply . . . if Falstaff had had the laugh on them all along?"[9] He has extricated himself—"in spite of truth and conviction"—and we in the audience are glad of it. Yet Poins and Prince Hal were right; and for them Gadshill will be, as prophesied, "argument for a week, laughter for a month, and a good jest for ever."

It will be seen, if we look back, that the arguments of those who have denied that Falstaff was a coward are of many different sorts. For the most part, they are suggestive of the study rather than the playhouse. Some, indeed, are abstract, or even syllogistic, like Morgann's *We do not like cowards; we like Falstaff; therefore, Falstaff is not a coward.* Some, again, are based on inferences, sound enough, perhaps, in real life, but untrustworthy in the case of popular drama, as that a coward is unlikely to be found in the thick of the fighting. Often, it is as if the critics were determined to impose their own sense of naturalness on what, in the theater, is the more effective for being extreme—Falstaff's "incomprehensible" lying, for example. Yet Bradley himself perceived that "Shakespeare's comic world" was one of make-believe, "not merely as his tragic world is, but in a further sense—a world in which gross improbabilities are accepted with a smile. . . ."[1]

8. *Dramatic Miscellanies*, I, 237, 238.
9. A. J. A. Waldock, "The Men in Buckram," *Review of English Studies*, 23 (1947), 19.
1. A. C. Bradley, *Oxford Lectures on Poetry*, 270.

It remains possible, of course, that with this great character Shakespeare was not contented to work on a single level; so that at one instant we may be back with the Clowns of primitive drama and at another are not far from the amiable philosopher of the romantic critics. Thus, the soliloquy on honor seems to me something more than a very witty apology for the speaker's cowardice—though is it not that, as well? We read of an American actor whose fame is associated with this role:

> the shudder with which Hackett spoke the words about Honor, "Who hath it? he that-*died*-o'Wednesday," with its obvious revulsion from even the thought of death, was wonderfully expressive of *Falstaff's* animal relish of life, and also it was supremely comic.[2]

For the cowardice of Falstaff as a comic assumption gives added point to speech after speech, and to deprive the actors of it is to deprive them of a constant source of merriment. "Where," as John Bailey asked, "would be the humour of 'a plague of all cowards' if the speaker were a brave man? Where would be the fun of the 'plain tale' that put his preposterous boastings down if, as we are told, he never meant to be believed?"[3] I would not defend the farcical enormities which have been committed in Falstaff's name by unworthy comedians. Descriptions of the older stage business, whether at Gadshill or Shrewsbury, are sometimes far from edifying. But suppose, merely for the sake of argument, that Sir John *was* a coward—a fat, old, witty, boastful coward. * * *

Finally, I would suggest that even single lines and phrases may take on an unexpected impressiveness for us if we return to the earlier conception of the character: to a Falstaff of dexterous evasions and miraculous escapes, lawless in his exaggerations, redoubtable only in repute, and the funnier for being fat and old and a coward. So, in the theater, I have heard Ned Poins lay a sudden emphasis upon two words, just before the Gadshill robbery: "Sirrah Jack, thy horse stands behind the hedge. When thou need'st him, there thou shalt find him. Farewell and *stand fast*"; and their portentousness was of exactly the sort that Sir Toby Belch, sometimes, imparts to a phrase in Sir Andrew's letter: "Fare thee well, and *God have mercy upon one of our souls!*" I conceive, too, of a glint in Falstaff's eye, a certain morbid insistence in his voice, as, at another time, he dwells on the strength of the rebels.

> But tell me, Hal, art not thou horrible afeard? Thou being heir apparent, could the world pick thee out three such enemies

2. William Winter, *Shakespeare on the Stage: Third Series* (New York, 1916), 359.
3. John Bailey, *Shakespeare* (London, New York, and Toronto, 1929), 128.

> again as that fiend Douglas, that spirit Percy, and that devil Glendower? Art thou not horribly afraid? Doth not thy blood thrill at it? [2.4.325–29]

A veteran talking to a young soldier, you may say of the passage—and perhaps it is merely that. Just before Shrewsbury they are talking in a somewhat similar vein.

> FALSTAFF. Hal, if thou see me down in the battle and bestride me, so! 'Tis a point of friendship. [5.1.121–22]

It is delivered with a flourish—almost as if in imagination he saw the Prince of Wales standing over and defending a gallant old soldier wounded (at any rate, *fallen*) in battle. Hal's quibbling reply gives him cold comfort: "Nothing but a Colossus can do thee that friendship. Say thy prayers, and farewell." And Falstaff: "I would 'twere bedtime, Hal, and all well" [5.1.123–25].

The last instance I shall give is from a soliloquy, in which the Elizabethan actor, standing in the midst of his hearers, would have directly and familiarly addressed them. Falstaff speaks of Prince John, who does not appreciate him and cannot be made to laugh. No wonder, he says, for "this same young sober-blooded boy" does not drink as he should:

> There's never none of these demure boys come to any proof; for thin drink doth so over-cool their blood, and making many fish-meals, that they fall into a kind of male greensickness; and then, when they marry, they get wenches. They are generally fools and cowards—which some of us should be too, but for inflammation. [*2H4*,4.2.81–86]

For an instant, the joke has become one between Falstaff and ourselves. He pauses after "cowards"; then, "which some of us" (Sir John himself, no less!) would certainly be too, except (triumphantly) for the effects of drinking sack! And who could accuse him of negligence in that regard? *You thought I was confessing, did you?*

I would not seem to attach an undue importance to these passages. They can be reconciled, each of them, with the Morgann Falstaff. "Would 'twere bedtime, Hal, and all well" is a sentiment which can be responded to by plenty of soldiers on a level quite different from that of comic cowardice. And the loss to the actor—though there is loss—will not be irreparable. On the other hand, it may be that the consensus among early readers and critics deserves more emphasis than I have given it. The burden of proof, as even Morgann recognized, rests upon those who deny cowardice. Samuel Johnson, as I said earlier, referred twice to Morgann's *Es-*

say. On the second occasion, when it is Malone who records the Doctor's words, they are splendidly comprehensive: "all he shd. say, was, that if Falstaff was not a coward, Shakespeare knew nothing of his art."[4]

E. M. W. TILLYARD

The Second Tetralogy†

However large the apparent differences in style between *Richard II* and *Henry IV*, these plays are connected with a network of cross-references. On the other hand, although *Richard II* may have been written not long after *King John*, the connexions are fitful and unimportant. *Richard II* looks forward; and Shakespeare conceived his second tetralogy as one great unit.

The matter is important and calls for substantiation.

First and most important, Richard and Prince Hal are deliberately contrasted characters; Richard being the prince in appearance rather than in reality, Hal being the prince in reality whose appearance at first obscures the truth. Richard's emblem was the sun of royalty emerging from a cloud, a piece of symbolism to which Bolingbroke refers when Richard appears on the walls of Flint Castle:

> See, see, King Richard doth himself appear
> As doth the blushing discontented sun
> From out the fiery portal of the east,
> When he perceives the envious clouds are bent
> To dim his glory and to stain the track
> Of his bright passage to the occident. [*R2*, 3.3.62–67]

But Richard did not live up to his emblem, for he allowed the clouds, his evil advisers, to obscure his proper glory. It is Prince Hal who adopts and justifies in himself the emblem, according to his own declaration at the end of the second scene of *1 Henry IV*:

> Yet herein will I imitate the sun,
> Who doth permit the base contagious clouds
> To smother up his beauty from the world,
> That, when he please again to be himself,
> Being wanted he may be more wonder'd at
> By breaking through the foul and ugly mists
> Of vapours that did seem to strangle him. [1.2.170–76]

4. James Boswell, *Life of Johnson*, iv, 515.
† From E. M. W. Tillyard, *Shakespeare's History Plays* (London: Chatto & Windus, 1944; reprinted Penguin, 1962), 240–43, 275–77, 279–82, 323, 324. Reprinted by permission of the Estate of E. M. W. Tillyard.

If this were the one possible cross-reference between *Richard II* and *1 Henry IV* we might doubt its authenticity; being one of many it can hardly not be intentional.

Secondly, the whole theme of insurrection and civil war as developed in the plays is continuous, as if conceived as a whole. Carlisle's speech in Westminster Hall, for instance, prophesying civil war if Bolingbroke is crowned proclaims its sequel in future plays:

> My Lord of Hereford here, whom you call king,
> Is a foul traitor to proud Hereford's king.
> And if you crown him, let me prophesy:
> The blood of English shall manure the ground,
> And future ages groan for this foul act;
> Peace shall go sleep with Turks and infidels,
> And in this seat of peace tumultuous wars
> Shall kin with kin and kind with kind confound;
> Disorder horror fear and mutiny
> Shall here inhabit, and this land be call'd
> The field of Golgotha and dead men's skulls. [*R2*, 4.1.134–44]

If these lines in the first play of the tetralogy look forward, Henry's prayer before Agincourt in the last one, that God should not visit on him the death of Richard, looks right back.

Thirdly, the Percies figure in *Richard II* in a way that suggests that they will figure even more prominently in the future. Northumberland is the main executant of Henry's rise; and Richard, informed by Northumberland that he must go to Pomfret Castle, warns him that one day he will think no reward sufficient for his services:

> Northumberland, thou ladder wherewithal
> The mounting Bolingbroke ascends my throne,
> The time shall not be many hours of age
> More than it is, ere foul sin gathering head
> Shall break into corruption. Thou shalt think,
> Though he divide the realm and give thee half,
> It is too little, helping him to all;
> And he shall think that thou, which know'st the way
> To plant unrightful kings, will know again,
> Being ne'er so little urg'd, another way
> To pluck him headlong from the usurped throne. [*R2*, 5.1.55–65]

When Hotspur is airing his grievances to Blunt before the battle of Shrewsbury he recalls Bolingbroke's promise that he had returned from exile for no further purpose than to claim the Duchy of Lancaster. This was the promise conveyed by Northumberland to Richard in Flint Castle in the previous play:

> His coming hither hath no further scope
> Than for his lineal royalties and to beg
> Enfranchisement immediate on his knees,
> Which on thy royal party granted once,
> His glittering arms he will commend to rust. [*R2*, 3.3.112–16]

A casual remark made by Green to the queen that Worcester (Northumberland's brother, who does not figure in *Richard II* in person) has broken his staff of office and resigned his stewardship is caught up in *1 Henry IV*, when before Shrewsbury Worcester tells Henry IV

> For you my staff of office did I break
> In Richard's time. [5.1.34–35]

Lastly, to cut short an argument that could easily be prolonged, King Henry in 2 *Henry IV* actually quotes from *Richard II*. He reminds Warwick of the words Richard spoke to Northumberland when about to be taken to Pomfret, and proceeds to quote some of them:

> 'Northumberland, thou ladder by the which
> My cousin Bolingbroke ascends my throne,'
> (Though then, God knows, I had no such intent,
> But that necessity so bow'd the state
> That I and greatness were compell'd to kiss)
> 'The time shall come,' thus did he follow it,
> 'The time will come, that foul sin gathering head
> Shall break into corruption'; so went on,
> Foretelling this same time's condition
> And the division of our amity. [*2H4*, 3.1.70–79]

Shakespeare would never have quoted from the History Play before last unless he had thought his sequence an organic whole. That he misquotes (as can be seen by comparing the original passage from *Richard II* just quoted) shows that he was more mindful of big than of little things.

If then the plays of the second tetralogy are so closely connected, we must treat them as a single organism. Confronted with different styles in *Richard II* and *Henry IV*, we shall have to refrain from calling the first archaic and the second suddenly and miraculously mature, but shall be forced to admit that Shakespeare knew what he was doing from the start and deliberately planned this stylistic contrast. Once we accept this compulsion we shall be the gainers, finding that the plays form a great symphonic scheme. * * *

* * *

The Prince as depicted in *Henry IV* (and what follows has no reference whatever to Henry V in the play which goes by that name) is a man of large powers, Olympian loftiness, and high sophistication, who has acquired a thorough knowledge of human nature both in himself and in others. He is Shakespeare's studied picture of the kingly type: a picture to which his many previous versions of the imperfect kingly type lead up: the fulfilment of years of thought and of experiment. Shakespeare sets forth his character with great elaboration, using both direct description and self-revelation through act and word. Though all the subtlety is confined to the second, there is no important discrepancy between the two versions. And first for the Prince's character as described from without.

At the end of the first scene in which he appears the Prince assumes the function of chorus to comment on himself: in the soliloquy beginning 'I know you all'. Here he pronounces his knowledge of his present companions and of what they are worth and the studied deliberateness of his present conduct. For his kingly style there is Vernon's description of him to Hotspur,

> As full of spirit as the month of May,
> And gorgeous as the sun at midsummer, [4.1.101–02]

and of the godlike ease 'like feather'd Mercury' with which he vaults fully armed onto his horse. His father recognizes the comprehensiveness of his mind and passions, when, late in the second part of the play (4.4), he exhorts his son Thomas of Clarence to cherish his place in the Prince's affections so that he may 'effect offices of mediation' between the Prince's 'greatness' and his other brothers:

> For he is gracious, if he be observ'd.
> He hath a tear for pity, and a hand
> Open as day for melting charity.
> Yet notwithstanding, being incens'd, he's flint;
> As humorous as winter and as sudden
> As flaws congealed in the spring of day.
> His temper, therefore, must be well observ'd.
> Chide him for faults and do it reverently,
> When you perceive his blood inclin'd to mirth;
> But, being moody, give him line and scope,
> Till that his passions, like a whale on ground,
> Confound themselves with working. [*2H4*, 4.4.30–41]

But the king is pessimistic. Through the very abundance of his nature the Prince is as subject to excessive evil as to excessive good—

> Most subject is the fattest soil to weeds—

and he thinks the signs are that evil will prevail. But Warwick disagrees, arguing for the power of the Prince's deliberate and sophisticated nature and his appetite for knowledge:

> The prince but studies his companions
> Like a strange tongue, wherein, to gain the language,
> 'Tis needful that the most immodest word
> Be look'd upon and learn'd; which once attain'd,
> Your highness knows, comes to no further use
> But to be known and hated. So, like gross terms,
> The prince will in the perfectness of time
> Cast off his followers; and their memory
> Shall as a pattern or a measure live,
> By which his grace must mete the lives of others,
> Turning past evils to advantages. [*2H4*, 4.4.68–78]

Something indeed has to be allowed for in all these testimonies. The Prince in his choric self-comment is concerned first of all with justifying to an Elizabethan audience this apparent degradation of royalty: hence the powerful emphasis on the rich compensation for such degradation—

> My reformation, glittering o'er my fault,
> Shall show more goodly and attract more eyes
> Than that which hath no foil to set it off. [1.2.186–88]

Henry not only describes his son but gives the general version of the princely nature, as can be seen by comparing his words with Belarius's description of the two princes in *Cymbeline*:

> Thou divine Nature, how thyself thou blazon'st
> In these two princely boys. They are as gentle
> As zephyrs, blowing below the violet
> Not wagging his sweet head; and yet as rough,
> Their royal blood enchaf'd, as the rud'st wind
> That by the top doth take the mountain pine
> And make him stoop to the vale. [4.2.170–76]

Warwick is preparing for the rejection of Falstaff as well as describing the Prince's character. But, for all these reservations, the speakers do combine to testify to the comprehensiveness of the Prince's mind and the deliberateness of his actions.

External testimony, however, is of small account compared with what is revealed by action and speech; and we must now consider what sort of person the Prince shows himself. This means speaking of his relations to some of the other characters, principally Falstaff. Those who cannot stomach the rejection of Falstaff assume that in some ways the Prince acted dishonestly, that he made a friend of Falstaff, thus deceiving him, that he got all he could out of him and then repudiated the debt. They are wrong. The Prince is aloof and Olympian from the start and never treats Falstaff any better than his dog, with whom he condescends once in a way to have a game.

It is not the Prince who deceives, it is Falstaff who deceives himself by wishful thinking. The most the Prince does is not to take drastic measures to disabuse Falstaff; doing no more than repeat the unkind truths he has never spared telling. His first speech to Falstaff ('Thou art so fat-witted . . . ') is, as well as much else, a cool statement of what he thinks of him. And the epithet 'fat-witted', so plainly the very opposite of the truth in most of its application, is brutally true of Falstaff's capacity for self-deceit. The Prince has a mind far too capacious not to see Falstaff's limitations. In the same scene he plays with him (and with a coolness in full accord with the rejection), when he refers to the gallows. Falstaff dislikes the subject, but the Prince will not let him off. And when later Falstaff tries to attach the Prince to him with 'I would to God thou and I knew where a commodity of good names were to be bought,' he gets not the slightest encouragement. The Prince just watches and tells the truth. And not in this place alone: it is his habit. He also relishes the ironic act of telling the truth in the assurance that he will thereby deceive. * * *

* * *

* * * His comprehensive nature comes out most brilliantly in an episode that is usually taken as trivial if not positively offensive: the foolery of the Prince and Poins with Francis and the other drawers in the Eastcheap tavern, before Falstaff arrives from the Gadshill robbery. It is a difficult scene, for the editors have not been able to find any meaning in it that at all enriches the play, and the sense of one or two sentences remains obscure. But the general drift should be clear from the Prince's satirical account of Hotspur killing 'six or seven dozen of Scots at a breakfast' at the end of the incident and from his own reference to 'honour' at the beginning. After what Hotspur has said already of honour earlier in the play it is impossible that there should not be a connexion between Hotspur and honour here. The Prince has been drinking and making friends with the drawers of the tavern. He has won their hearts and learnt their ways:

> To conclude, I am so good a proficient in one quarter of an hour that I can drink with any tinker in his own language during my life. I tell thee, Ned, thou hast lost much honour that thou wert not with me in this action. [2.4.15–19]

In other words the Prince has won a signal victory and great honour in having mastered this lesson so quickly. It was Johnson who perceived that the Prince's satire on Hotspur is logically connected with what goes before and not a mere unmotivated outburst. But later critics have not given due weight to that perception. Poins and the Prince have just had their game with Francis, Poins being as ignorant of the Prince's true meaning as he was in the scene from the second part just examined.

> *Poins.* But hark ye; what cunning match have you made with this jest of the drawer? Come, what's the issue?
> *Prince.* I am now of all humours that have showed themselves since the old days of goodman Adam to the pupil age of this present twelve o'clock at midnight.
> *Re-enter* Francis.
> What's o'clock, Francis?
> *Fran.* Anon, anon, sir. *Exit.*
> *Prince.* That ever this fellow should have fewer words than a parrot, and yet the son of a woman! His industry is upstairs and downstairs; his eloquence the parcel of a reckoning. I am not yet of Percy's mind, the Hotspur of the north. . . . [2.4.82–93]

Johnson saw that the reference to Hotspur connects with the Prince's declaration that he is 'now of all humours', the entry and exit of Francis with the Prince's comment being a mere interruption. The Prince's wealth of humours is contrasted with the single humour of Hotspur. Once again the Prince says just what he means but in words that will bear another meaning. On the face of it his words mean that he is greatly excited, being ruled simultaneously by every human motive that exists; but he also means that having learnt to understand the drawers he has mastered all the springs of human conduct, he has even then completed his education in the knowledge of men. We can now understand his earlier talk of honour: he has won a more difficult action than any of Hotspur's crudely repetitive slaughters of Scotsmen. Bearing this in mind, we may perceive things at the beginning of the episode which can easily be passed over. To Poins's question where he has been the Prince answers:

> With three or four loggerheads among three or four score hogsheads. I have sounded the very base string of humility. Sirrah, I am sworn brother to a leash of drawers and can call them all by their christen names, as Tom, Dick, and Francis. They take it already upon their salvation that though I be but Prince of Wales yet I am the king of courtesy. [2.4.4–9]

When the Prince speaks of sounding the base string of humility he uses a musical metaphor. He means in one sense that he has touched the bottom limit of condescension. But he means something more: he is the bow that has got a response from the lowest string of the instrument, namely the drawers. We are to think that he has sounded all the other human strings already: he has now completed the range of the human gamut; he is of all humours since Adam. Now the idea of the world as a complicated musical harmony was a cosmic commonplace, which would evoke all the other such commonplaces. The drawers are not only the base or lowest string of the instrument; they are the lowest link in the human portion of the chain of being and as such nearest the beasts. And that is why the Prince directly after compares them to dogs by calling them 'a leash of drawers'. At the risk of being accused of being over-ingenious I will add that 'sounding' and 'base' suggest plumbing the depths of the sea as well as playing on a stringed instrument and that there is a reference to Hotspur's boast earlier in the play that he will

> dive into the bottom of the deep,
> Where fathom-line could never touch the ground,
> And pluck up drowned honour by the locks. [1.3.203–05]

It is not for nothing too that the Prince says the drawers think him the king of courtesy. As I shall point out later this is precisely what Shakespeare makes him, the *cortegiano*,[1] the fully developed man, contrasted with Hotspur, the provincial, engaging in some ways, but with a one-track mind.

* * *

At a time when so much has been said about the principle of order and of the hierarchies in English literature of the Renaissance tradition, it is not likely that anyone will question my conclusion that Shakespeare's Histories with their constant pictures of disorder cannot be understood without assuming a larger principle of order in the background. * * *

* * *

* * * First, Shakespeare turned the Chronicle Play into an independent and authentic type of drama, and no mere ancillary to the form of tragedy. He did this largely because he grasped the potentialities of the old Morality form, never allowing the personalities of his kings to trespass on the fundamental Morality subject of Respublica. In the total sequence of his plays dealing with the subject matter of Hall he expressed successfully a universally held and still comprehensible scheme of history: a scheme fundamentally religious, by which events evolve under a law of justice and under the ruling of God's Providence, and of which Elizabeth's England was the acknowledged outcome. The scheme, which, in its general outline, consisted of the distortion of nature's course by a crime and its restoration through a long series of disasters and suffering and struggles, may indeed be like Shakespeare's scheme of tragedy; but

1. Italian: courtier; one fully versed in the courtly arts.

it is genuinely political and has its own right of existence apart from tragedy. But in addition to this concatenated scheme, Shakespeare in *Richard II* and *1* and *2 Henry IV* gave us his version, which I have called epic, of what life was like in the Middle Ages as he conceived them and in his own day. This version was entirely successful and presents not even a parallel to the form of tragedy. It is one of Shakespeare's vast achievements and it stands unchallengeable: something entirely itself without a jot of suspicion that it ought to be, or ought to lead up to, something else; an achievement sufficient to put Shakespeare among the world's major poets.

* * *

HENRY ANSAGAR KELLY

[Providence and Propaganda]†

In previous analyses of the historical treatments of fifteenth-century England (it is particularly Professor Tillyard's that is in question here), a number of themes have been studied simultaneously, and used to supplement each other in formulating the basic patterns of thought involved in these writings. The political and providential aspects of discord and unity have been especially stressed. But a certain amount of distortion has resulted from the failure to consider each element in its own right, and too often lacunae in the pattern postulated for both themes are filled by inferences illegitimately drawn from one theme alone.[1]

Specifically, the political theme of discord beginning with the usurpation of Henry IV and ending with the marriage of Henry VII and Elizabeth of York (or with the reign of their offspring, Henry VIII), which is formulated most clearly in Hall's preface, has been taken as the primary analogue of an over-all metahistorical pattern that involves not only the human element of sin and its effects, in terms of suffering and further sins in reaction to the suffering, but also the divine dimension of the providential rule of all created being. To correspond precisely to the political theme of Hall, the role of Providence in this period of history would have to be conceived of in terms of a divine curse laid upon the land and its people for the sins committed in deposing and killing Richard II, so that from this point of view all the disturbances and injustices that followed

† From Henry Ansagar Kelly, *Divine Providence in the England of Shakespeare's Histories* (Cambridge, MA: Harvard University Press, 1970), 297–99, 304–06, 214–22. Reprinted by permission of the publisher.

1. A similar analysis could be made for the themes of order and hierarchy in Tillyard's *Elizabethan World Picture.*

would be somehow regarded as God's punishment not only of the guilty persons but of the innocent as well, until he finally took pity upon the people and relented from his wrath by sending peace in the person and dynasty of Henry Tudor. And the fact that this theme was never expressed in this way has been taken to mean that everyone assumed the whole when referring to the parts, just as references to planets presupposed the rest of the cosmos, or just as tangible objects were considered by Plato to participate in and express the reality of the Ideas, but only in fragmentary and incomplete ways.

However, it would seem that the providential aspect of the Tudor myth as described by Mr. Tillyard is an ex post facto Platonic Form, made up of many fragments that were never fitted together into a mental pattern until they felt the force of his own synthesizing energy. This judgment is not meant to detract from the valuable insights that his undertaking has produced and inspired; and he himself indicated that many of the large vistas which he discovered and described could profit from a more minute attention to individual details.

In tracing the development of providential interpretations in the chronicles of the fifteenth century, we saw that myths or mystiques tended to develop along the political lines of the immediate present, enveloping favorite sons with an aura of personal integrity and divine support, and supplying appropriately evil motives and cosmically based troubles for the members of the opposition. Thus there developed a Lancastrian God who overshadowed for a long time the comparatively feeble efforts of the opposing divinity that favored Richard. But as time went on God developed decided Yorkist tendencies and reversed much of the work he had done as the protector of the house of Lancaster. But soon the God of Henry Tudor appeared on the scene, and the religion of later Lancastrianism was revived.

When Polydore Vergil[2] came to England from Italy, it was the Tudor view of history that he found ready at hand, and it was this that he first incorporated into his comprehensive history. He accepted the representation of his patron as having been sent by God to put down usurpation and tyranny in the person of Richard III and to bring peace to England. But later, in preparing the early rough draft of his work for publication, he meditated upon the lessons that could be taught from the events of earlier years, and supplemented with new insights the occasional providential interpretations he had previously obtained from writings inspired by the numinous influences of Lancaster and York. However, Vergil's views of those

2. Historian and friend of Henry VII, who commissioned him to write the history of England; 1470–1555 [*Editor's note*].

early times were not politically motivated or grounded, and he attempted to arrive at the providential cause for certain events on the basis of absolute justice, whereby sin is punished and virtue tested and rewarded.

And because of the nature of the circumstances concerning the Lancastrian usurpation and the failure of its dynasty three generations later, he seemed to accept as a real possibility that the reason for its failure was the working of divine justice, which deprived that family of the realm and restored it to its proper owner. But he also maintained that the troubles that happened to the saintly heir of the Lancasters, Henry VI, were providentially beneficial to him, and that he found at least as much favor with God as did his glorious father, Henry V.

Vergil also reflected upon the sins committed by Edward IV in securing the crown and maintaining it, and since he died an apparently natural death, whereas his two sons were cruelly murdered, Vergil invoked the early biblical notion of the sins of the father being visited upon the children, and considered it likely that the death of his sons constituted a divine punishment upon Edward; however, Edward's brothers, Clarence and especially Richard, were punished for their sins in their own persons. At the same time, the divine element in Henry Tudor's accession was noticeably lessened, perhaps because Vergil felt that the peace it brought in the person of his son was not developing in directions entirely pleasing to God.

Edward Hall inherited Vergil's providential interpretations and adopted most of them without much critical evaluation, and also accepted, in an equally uncritical way, many similar and dissimilar interpretations from other sources. As a result he often upset the already precarious balance of reason and justice in Vergil's account of God's workings. Holinshed made a new synthesis of previous ideas concerning providential retribution in this century, one in some ways more satisfactory than Vergil's. But once again his balance was upset by the clumsy additions of Abraham Fleming.[3]

In all these accounts it is the guilty persons who suffer divine punishment. But in some rare cases, the punishment falls upon their children or grandchildren; the punishment as such, however, never extends beyond the immediate family circle. * * *

Shakespeare's great contribution was to unsynthesize the syntheses of his contemporaries and to unmoralize their moralizations. His genius for sounding the realities of human passion and action, which are the components and raw materials of historical reflections, enabled him to sort out the partisan layers that had been combined in rather ill-digested lumps in Hall and Holinshed and to

3. Historian who helped to revise and add information to Holinshed's chronicles; 1552–1607 [*Editor's note*].

distribute them to appropriate spokesmen. Thus the sentiments of the Lancaster myth are spoken by Lancastrians, and opposing views are voiced by anti-Lancastrians and Yorkists. And the Tudor myth finds its fullest statement in the mouth of Henry Tudor. In this way Shakespeare often reproduces by instinct the viewpoints of fifteenth-century documents which for the most part were either completely unavailable to him or present only in their assimilated forms in the large compilations which he drew upon.

This characterization of Shakespeare's histories is not completely verified throughout, of course, since he often accepts the moral portraitures of the chronicles which were originally produced by political bias, and has his characters commit or confess to the crimes which their enemies falsely accused them of.

There were, obviously, elements of dramatization in all the sources before Shakespeare, in the contemporary as well as in the sixteenth-century histories; and Vergil, More, Redmayne, Hall, and Daniel (and also, in a sense, the authors of the *Mirror for Magistrates*) added to the given historical scenes by composing their own orations in the spirit of the various historical characters that they portrayed. But in these authors the sentiments of the characters are usually weighed in the balance of a pedagogical absolute morality in order that suitable lessons might be extracted for public consumption.

Shakespeare, however, as a playwright, completely dramatized the characters, and so eliminated all the purportedly objective providential judgments made by the histories upon historical characters, the kind of reflection which would be valid or pertinent only if made by God himself. All such judgments were placed where they belonged and where many of them originated—in the mouths of the characters themselves. Here these judgments, which reflect belief in God's providential control of all things and all events, are expressed in terms of petitions and aspirations to God (which may or may not be answered), of prayers of thanksgiving to God for some favor (though the reason ascribed to him may not have entered into his motives at all), and of providential attributions that are obviously based on personal viewpoints.

And though this kind of characterization involves making moral judgments on the motives of the characters for their own actions, it eliminates simplistic evaluations of complex moral situations, and leaves the question open as to how God would distribute praise and blame and sanctions for good and evil in these instances. There are, certainly, exceptional cases, like those of Henry V and Richard III, where Shakespeare seems to reinforce his play as a whole with the unanimous expression of divine approval or disfavor towards individuals. But even in these cases Shakespeare's opinion is not ventured as his own.

Shakespeare's individual characterizations of men and their moral attitudes change from play to play, which indicates that he is not concerned with the absolute fixing of praise and blame in the historical characters; but he does ordinarily take pains to achieve a general consistency within each play or each scene. That is, Shakespeare was primarily a dramatist and not a historian—though many of his changes in characterization must be blamed upon the faulty inconsistencies of the historians and moralists before him. For this reason, the moral conflicts of each play must be taken on the terms of the play and not supplemented from the other plays, or from his sources, or from general principles, without extreme caution. Each play creates its own moral ethos and mythos, and though the details may vary from those established in other plays concerning the same characters and events, still each view can serve as a valid hypothesis to demonstrate the springs of human and cosmic action from a world of bygone events whose inner causes are essentially lost and irretrievable.

* * *

The First Part of Henry the Fourth opens with the king discussing the preparations for the crusade he desires to lead to Jerusalem. And since *Richard II* closed with a similar expression of desire to go to the Holy Land, it has often been assumed that Shakespeare intended the motive that Henry named in *Richard II* to carry over into *1 Henry IV.* But it is not at all clear that such an assumption is justified. If Shakespeare had meant Henry to envision his crusade as a work of reparation for Richard's death, it is almost inconceivable that he would not have brought this motive explicitly to the fore, instead of relying entirely upon the recollection of those in the audience who had seen *Richard II.*

It seems much more likely that if Shakespeare assumed any knowledge in his audience of the historical events he was dramatizing, it would be the knowledge that they could have derived from the chronicle accounts of these events. It also seems highly probable that Shakespeare himself consulted the chronicles once more before writing *1 Henry IV.* It is significant therefore that he dramatizes Henry as expressing only those intentions specified in the Vergil-Hall-Holinshed account of his motivations for the crusade, except that Shakespeare does not extend the notion of strife among Christians to include anything but the troubles of England; one reason for this is that he does not cover the French conflicts of Henry IV's reign; furthermore, he has Henry project the crusade early in his reign, before most of the rebellions against him take place.

According to the chronicles, Henry was motivated by sorrow at seeing Christians oppose one another, and also by his zeal to recover the Holy Land from the hands of the infidel. Similarly, in the first act of the play, Shakespeare has Henry say that there will be no more civil war in England. No more will those eyes, which "like the meteors of a troubled heaven" are bred of one nature and substance, oppose each other, but everyone will march in one direction. "Therefore, friends," he continues:

> As far as to the sepulchre of Christ,
> Whose soldier now, under whose blessed cross
> We are impressed and engaged to fight,
> Forthwith a power of English shall we levy,
> Whose arms were moulded in their mother's womb
> To chase these pagans in those holy fields
> Over whose acres walked those blessed feet
> Which fourteen hundred years ago were nailed
> For our advantage on the bitter cross. [1.1.19–27]

Preparations for the crusade are still in the planning stage, and Henry has called this meeting to discuss what is to be done. But the immediate needs of the Welsh and Scottish wars force him to set aside his "holy purpose" for a while.

No other motives are given for the crusade here, and this is also true of *2 Henry IV,* except in the deathbed scene, where, as we shall see, Henry alleges a more selfish interest for his expedition. But the motive of reparation for Richard's death is never returned to in this context, nor does Henry express the least remorse or show any signs of guilt for his treatment of Richard in the whole of *1 Henry IV.* In fact, quite the opposite is true. He regards himself as the rightful king, supported by human and divine right against rebellion. And this is the viewpoint of the chroniclers in general, especially Walsingham, Vergil, and Hall, for the events covered in this play.

This characterization of Henry is made very evident in his dealings with his son. When he calls him in to give an account of himself, the king addresses him as follows:

> I know not whether God will have it so,
> For some displeasing service I have done,
> That, in his secret doom, out of my blood
> He'll breed revengement and a scourge for me;
> But thou dost in thy passages of life
> Make me believe that thou art only marked
> For the hot vengeance and the rod of heaven
> To punish my mistreadings. Tell me else,
> Could such inordinate and low desires,
> Such poor, such bare, such lewd, such mean attempts,
> Such barren pleasures, rude society,

As thou art matched withal and grafted to,
Accompany the greatness of thy blood
And hold their level with thy princely heart? [3.2.4–17]

In this remarkable speech we are told that Henry is not conscious of any sin that God could be punishing him for. Furthermore, the audience is well aware that he is completely mistaken in his analysis of God's dispositions toward him as far as the prince is concerned; he has not bred revenge for him in his son; if anything he has blessed him with the most glorious son and successor that a king ever had.

Of course, it could be held that Shakespeare introduced the providential theme here for its rhetorical effectiveness in its immediate context, in spite of the fact that it goes counter to a larger theme in the play. Shakespeare rather frequently employs this kind of rhetorical abstraction from the plot of his plays; for instance, he has Hamlet declare that no one ever returns to this world from the dead, just after he has received a rather convincing visitor from the other world in the person of his own father. But the evidence for a "greater theme" of the providential punishment of Henry IV is completely lacking in this play. And if we are to assume that the theme is wholly taken for granted on Shakespeare's part, we must protest that a speech like this one of Henry's would practically negate such an implied theme, unless one were to postulate an extraordinarily subtle kind of irony in the king's words.

A more plausible interpretation is that Shakespeare indeed introduced the providential theme for its rhetorical effect, but that it contradicts no other theme. It is simply Henry's way of saying that his son's conduct is absolutely inexplicable. It may be that he says this in despair of ever seeing him reformed, or that he is using these strong words to convince the prince of his error.

On the other hand, if irony were intended, the audience would be expected to believe that Henry is really suffering the pangs of a remorse he always feels but never acknowledges, even in soliloquy, and that he knows or suspects that God is punishing him for his crimes against Richard, in allowing or forcing his son to follow his disastrous course. Perhaps one could even make a case for saying that God is actually punishing Henry in allowing him to believe that his son is on the path to destruction; there is no doubt that the king does suffer much in this regard. But if so, we must also admit that God very shortly calls a halt to this punishment, for Henry realizes his mistake when the prince answers him. He now realizes what the audience already knows, that his son will turn out well, and that therefore God is not punishing him as he feared; the prince will have fulfilled his promise abundantly by the end of the play.

Furthermore, the theory that Henry is meant to be afflicted with remorse for his offenses against Richard throughout the play is decisively refuted in this very scene. The king is clearly thinking of the way he acquired the crown, but it is in terms precisely the opposite of remorse. He recalls his achievement with pride, and he chides his son for not imitating the deportment that enabled him to succeed as he did; he compares the prince's actions with Richard's and warns that a fall like Richard's may be his lot as well.[2]

Henry goes on not only to compare Prince Henry to Richard, but to liken Hotspur to himself when he landed at Ravenspurgh; and he adds:

> Now, by my scepter and my soul to boot,
> He hath more worthy interest to the state
> Than thou, the shadow of succession.
> For of no right, nor color like to right,
> He doth fill fields with harness in the realm,
> Turns head against the lion's armed jaws,
> And, being no more in debt to years than thou,
> Leads ancient lords and reverend bishops on
> To bloody battles and to bruising arms. [3.2.97–105]

Once more, then, we see that Henry considers himself the legitimate king, and that the rising against him has no right whatsoever to commend it. He completely ignores or disallows the reasons brought up by the Percys, which in the sources derive from the Yorkist chroniclers like Hardyng, who wrote in the latter part of Henry VI's reign. In other words, Shakespeare has once again distributed the moral and providential judgments of the sources according to their political components; in this play, the Lancastrians speak from the viewpoint of the Lancaster myth, and their opponents voice the anti-Lancastrian objections assimilated into the York myth.

If Henry manifests no guilt about Richard's deposition and death, the Percys do—or at least Northumberland does; he prays God to

2. *1H4*, 3.2.29–88. As has been indicated, the audience realizes that there is no danger at all of this, for they have heard the prince explain his course of action (1.2.218–40). It is interesting to remark that although Hal uses different means from those employed by his father, his concept of government is the same—to base his rule upon an intimate knowledge of the popular mind and its reactions, and to maintain authority by an impressive demeanor. M. M. Reese, *The Cease of Majesty: A Study of Shakespeare's History Plays* (New York, 1961), 315, thinks that Prince Hal refused complicity in Henry IV's ideas of statecraft in *1–2 Henry IV*. But though the prince's policies differ from his father's, it is not evident that Shakespeare means to have the prince regard his father's career as objectionable in any way. It is only in *Henry V*, in his prayer before Agincourt, that Henry refers to anything sinful in his father, and here he is speaking of his acquisition of the throne, not his methods in holding it (at least, not after the death of Richard II).

pardon their part in his wrongs.[3] From this phrase, we can gather that Northumberland hopes to be pardoned by God for the crimes he committed against Richard, as did Henry at the end of *Richard II*. However, none of the three Percys is really thinking in terms of guilt and repentance, but rather in terms of dishonor and revenge.[4]

As for Henry's statement that Hotspur was taking to the field against him with no shadow of right, Hotspur does pretend to a right in the person of his brother-in-law Mortimer, who was named by Richard as his heirs.[5] We are told this in a rather awkward piece of exposition, in which Hotspur professes complete ignorance of Mortimer's title, although, as we find out later, Hotspur's wife knows well enough about it, and so do the elder Percys.

There was no mention of Mortimer in *Richard II*, and after *1 Henry IV*, he drops out of the picture again; and the existence of another claimant to the throne besides the Henrys is never again alluded to in this tetralogy, which constitutes Shakespeare's last words upon the subject. * * *

* * * Henry never admits that Mortimer has any valid claim to the throne. In the chronicles it is conjectured that Henry deliberately wished Mortimer dead because of his prior right to the crown; but Shakespeare transforms this editorial view into a supposition made by Hotspur.[6] Further, the conviction of the chroniclers that Henry fabricated the charge of conspiracy against Mortimer is not at all clear in Shakespeare. In point of fact there is a conspiracy already under way, as Worcester later informs Hotspur.[7] And though it is not obvious from Worcester's account that Mortimer was in on the plot from the beginning, the fact that he has already married Glendower's daughter would seem to indicate this (Henry points this out), as would Kate Percy's suspicion that he is agitating for his title.[8] Furthermore, any appearance of right the Percys might have had in supporting Mortimer is rather decisively counteracted by their plan to divide the kingdom into three and to rule one of the sections themselves.[9] On the other hand, Hotspur's ridicule of Glendower's pretensions to magic and his interpretations of por-

3. 1.3.149. The text reads: "Whose wrongs in us God pardon!" It could conceivably be referring to the wrongs Richard did to them, but this seems a less likely interpretation than the one adopted here.
4. This is evident from their words in 1.3.153–86.
5. Richard's heir was Roger Mortimer, whose son, Edmund, was considered to have been named heir on Roger's death in 1398; the Edmund Mortimer who was Hotspur's brother-in-law was Roger's younger brother.
6. 1.3.158–59. Shakespeare, of course, does make it obvious that Henry fears Mortimer and would like to be rid of him. We may take Hotspur's word for it that the king paled at the mention of Mortimer's name (1.3.141–44).
7. See 1.3.188–299.
8. See 1.3.84–85; 2.3.76–78. Cf. Charles Fish, "Henry IV: Shakespeare and Holinshed," *Studies in Philology* 61:208 (1964).
9. See 3.1.1–139.

tents has the effect of undermining any serious significance that might be attached to other allusions of this sort, not only in Falstaff's jocular view[1] but also in Henry IV's reference to him as "that great magician, damned Glendower."[2] And it certainly goes counter to the providential implications Hall found in their misfortunes, which he viewed as the result of divine punishment for believing in false prophecies, since Glendower is the only one who believes in them. Shakespeare does, however, make functional use of this theme of prophecy later, for he explains Glendower's failure to appear at Shrewsbury by his being overruled by prophecies.[3]

It is evident that Worcester does not have the highest estimation for the righteousness of their cause, when he expresses his fears that the people will construe Northumberland's absence as his disapproval of them; he says:

> For well you know we of the offering side
> Must keep aloof from strict arbitrament,
> And stop all sight-holes, every loop from whence
> The eye of reason may pry in upon us. [4.1.69–72]

This sense of the unlawful nature of their rising is reinforced by Blunt's response to Hotspur's wish to have him on their side instead of having him stand against them as an enemy:

> And God defend but still I should stand so,
> So long as out of limit and true rule
> You stand against anointed majesty. [4.3.38–40]

And of the motives of the "well beloved" Archbishop of York, that "noble prelate," we hear only the one related by Vergil and Hall, namely, revenge; for, according to Worcester, he "bears hard / His brother's death at Bristol, the Lord Scrope."[4]

The charges Hotspur and Worcester bring against Henry before the battle of Shrewsbury are in substance those reported by Hardyng and transmitted by Hall, concerning the king's rise to power in violation of his oath, his destruction of Richard, and his depriving the true heir, Mortimer, of the kingship; but it was Henry's bad treatment of the three Percys, Hotspur says, that caused them to raise this power for their own protection, and to examine his title, which they find "too indirect for long continuance."[5]

Worcester makes similar accusations later[6] but it is evident that

1. See 2.4.327–29.
2. See 1.3.83.
3. See 4.4.18.
4. See 1.3.265–68. Hotspur says, however, that the archbishop commends the general course of the action [2.3.17–18], and this would no doubt include the formulation of the charges brought against Henry before Shrewsbury.
5. See 4.3.52–105.
6. See 5.1.30–71.

the Percys are not being completely honest in the declaration of their motives, for they do not mention the tripartite pact; and Henry does not answer their charges but exposes what he takes to be their true motive—they publish these reasons to give some appearance of justice to their rebellion, in order to attract the malcontents who welcome every change.[7]

The heavy emphasis upon the Percys as rebels is strengthened still more by Henry's prayer to God to befriend his side, because of the justice of his cause.[8] It is true that Hotspur also assures his men that their own cause is just,[9] but just before this his uncle Worcester characterized their action as treason.[1] It is evident that Shakespeare has put the burden of blame for this rebellion and the losses suffered in the battle upon Worcester, and no doubt Henry's closing sentiments are to be taken as an honorable summation of the play's events, especially since they reflect Prince Henry's victory and vindication as well as his own.

When therefore Henry speaks the *Mirror for Magistrates* maxim, "thus ever did rebellion find rebuke"[2] (his own career is a glaring exception), we are to interpret it to mean that right has triumphed, and perhaps also to see in it an implicit claim of divine aid. Henry rebukes Worcester and tells him that if he had reported the truth of his offer like a Christian, many would still be alive;[3] and we are to believe, it would seem, that he was sincere in his offer of pardon before the battle. And his concluding words confirm the approval we are to give him:

> Rebellion in this land shall lose his sway,
> Meeting the check of such another day;
> And since this business so fair is done,
> Let us not leave till all our own be won. [5.5.41–44]

Shakespeare no doubt meant these words to indicate to the audience that Henry did succeed within a short time in putting down all further rebellion. And if he meant to imply divine support for any person in the play, in the light of the play's ending we must conclude that that person is Henry IV if it is anyone at all. * * *

7. See 5.1.72–82.
8. See 5.1.120. Henry's appeal to God here has much the same flavor as that found in the accounts of Walsingham and Hall.
9. See 5.2.87–88.
1. See 5.2.1–11.
2. See 5.5.1.
3. See 5.5.2–10.

GRAHAM HOLDERNESS

[Tillyard, History, and Ideology]†

Virtually all modern critical accounts of Shakespeare's historical drama, including the various types of theoretically informed and 'poststructuralist' criticism—New Historicism, poststructuralism, feminism, cultural materialism—represented in this anthology, take their bearings from E. M. W. Tillyard's *Shakespeare's History Plays*, published in 1944. That continual orientation back towards so early a source of interpretation is an unusual critical relationship, particularly given that Tillyard's work, together with other related studies of Shakespeare and of the history plays deriving from that same period, are so firmly rooted in precisely the kinds of conservative, nationalistic and authoritarian ideology contemporary criticism has sought comprehensively and systematically to challenge. In Tillyard's study the sequence of plays from *Richard II* to *Henry V* were constituted as a central chapter in the great nationalistic 'epic' of England (an American critic subsequently even found a name for this epic narrative—the *Henriad*). The plays are interpreted as a linked and integrated series, revealing a broad and complex panorama of national life, unified and balanced into a coherent aesthetic 'order' mirroring the political order of the Elizabethan state. The central action of the plays is the education of a prince, the perfect ruler, Henry V, who is shown learning the wisdom of experience, undergoing trials of chivalry and morality, and achieving a perfect balance of character as a preliminary to establishing a perfectly balanced state. The plays were presented by Tillyard as operating between public and private dimensions, linking the formation of a perfect monarch to the unification of England as an ideal kingdom. Tillyard's study thus reproduces the plays as parables of political order, or as what some of the critics represented here would prefer to call strategies of legitimation, cultural forms by means of which the dominant ideology of the Tudor state validated its own moral and political power, through the voluntary intervention and commitment of a loyal and talented subject, Shakespeare.

The general case made by Tillyard was that the historical ideas informing Shakespeare's plays were to be located within a world-view dominated by the heritage of medieval Christianity. In this philosophical (or rather metaphysical) system the state or 'body

† From Graham Holderness, ed., *Shakespeare's History Plays: "Richard II" to "Henry V,"* "New Casebooks" (Basingstoke: Macmillan, 1992), 1–7, 9–10.

politic' was not considered merely sociologically, as a particular form of civil organisation, but metaphysically, as one of the functions of a universal order, created and supervised by God, and governed directly by divine providence. In this hierarchical model of universal relations human beings occupied an intermediate position with God and the angels above, and the animal and plant kingdoms below. The structure of a well-ordered state was a microcosm of the hierarchical cosmos, containing within itself (as it was in turn contained within) a 'chain of being', stretching from the monarch at the head, through the various gradations of social rank down to the lower orders. The ruler of a body politic possessed power which reflected, but was also subject to, that of God; a king therefore ruled by divine right. The natural condition of a state, like the natural condition of the cosmos, was 'order', defined primarily in terms of the maintenance of this rigid hierarchy. Since the state was a function of the divine order, any rupturing of this pattern must to contemporary witnesses have appeared not as legitimate social change, but as disorder or 'chaos', a disruption of a divine and natural order incurring the inevitable displeasure of God. The extreme forms of such disruption, such as the deposition of a legitimate king and the usurpation of a throne (the action of *Richard II*), would constitute a gross violation of order, inevitably punished by the vengeance of God, working through the machinery of providence.

This account of Elizabethan intellectual and cultural history as the dominance of a single unified philosophical system was initially developed by Tillyard in *The Elizabethan World Picture* (1943), and then subsequently applied specifically to the functioning of the political state within the universal order in *Shakespeare's History Plays*. Here the whole sequence of Shakespeare's English chronicle dramas becomes a grand illustration of the operation of divine providence in human affairs, with the deposition and murder of Richard II initiating a disruption of the universal order, a century of social chaos and civil war, the eventual punishment of those responsible and their descendants by the exercise of divine wrath—a process ended only by the 'succession' of Henry VII, the first Tudor monarch, to the English throne. The plays are read as offering a unified historical narrative expressing a politically and morally orthodox monarchist philosophy of history, in which the Tudor dynasty is celebrated as a divinely sanctioned legitimate regime, automatically identifiable with political stability and the good of the commonwealth. This ideology is in Tillyard's argument derived from a system already developed by the great Tudor historical writers, particularly Edward Halle in his *Union of the Noble and Illustrious Houses of Lancaster and York* (1548), and was continually hammered into the popular consciousness by various forms of loyalist political discourse, notably the homilies against rebellion and disobedience appointed to be read in churches.

Tillyard's version of the history plays as loyal celebrations of Tudor power, functioning within the context of a general ideology in which that power was conceived as an element of an inclusive natural order, became a strong and powerful critical position dominating discussion of the plays for many years. Essentially similar approaches to these plays were put forward in the 1940s by Lily B. Campbell and by G. Wilson Knight. They were then promulgated more widely to different publics by J. Dover Wilson, through the popular revised 'complete works' the *New Shakespeare* (1953), and through his influential study *The Fortunes of Falstaff* (1964); and by critics of the *Scrutiny* movement such as D. A. Traversi in *Shakespeare from 'Richard II' to 'Henry V'* (1957), and (with a more independent perspective) L. C. Knights.

Constitutive to the release and formation of modern critical possibilities was the interrogation of this authoritarian critical stance. Gradually and from a range of different perspectives, critical, scholarly and historical, other writers demonstrated that these early critics had constructed their model of Elizabethan culture from a narrow and highly selective range of sources, drawing the ideological framework they described from works of contemporary government propaganda and Tudor apology, or arbitrarily stripping loyalist and orthodox details from sources (such as Holinshed's *Chronicles of England, Scotland and Ireland* [1577, 2nd edition 1587]) which, when examined more comprehensively, delivered much more complex and interesting accounts of the history they were reconstructing. Where Tillyard emphasised Shakespeare's indebtedness to Edward Halle, regarded as the most orthodox of the contemporary historians, later critics proposed a more significant reliance on Holinshed, or a more eclectic frequentation of a wider range of sources reflecting many different political and ideological perspectives. Where Tillyard asserted that the Machiavellian school of historical research and political science had no impact whatsoever on English culture, later critics found in Shakespeare's plays a secular and ironic investigation of the processes of political change curiously akin to the understanding of Machiavelli.

It is not that the ideology Tillyard described did not exist, nor even that it was not, as he affirms, a dominant ideology. The key questions raised by post-Tillyard criticism of the history plays pertained to the status of this ideology within Elizabethan culture and society, and to its relationship with the historical drama. Was this Christian and politically apologetic 'Tudor myth' really a universal mode of understanding the world in the later sixteenth century?

And is it the case that Shakespeare's plays embody and express that myth, thus forming a constitutive element (to shift into more modern terminology) of the cultural apparatus of Tudor state propaganda?

Being in essence a historical interpretation of literature, Tillyard's work was in turn reliant on the picture of Elizabethan society to be found in the pages of particular historians, notably Trevelyan's *History of England.* This dependence of literary criticism on historical scholarship naturally entailed a vulnerability to change in that discipline as well as shifts within the methodologies of literary criticism itself, and to the general ideological shifts influencing all intellectual activity, which as it happens were in this period (at the end of the Second World War) enormous and far-reaching. Subsequent to the work of pre-war historians, historical scholarship researched more deeply into the cultural and ideological context of Tudor and Elizabethan England, and demonstrated that Tillyard's 'Elizabethan world-picture', powerful and influential though it may have been, was only one dimension of Renaissance ideology: an official, orthodox, conservative world-view, imposed and preached by church and state through executive government, legislation and the voices of an organic establishment intelligentsia. Not every Elizabethan could have accepted the state's official explanation of things: there were within the culture intellectual divisions over matters of religion, politics, law, ethics; there were Catholics and Protestants and Puritans, monarchists and republicans, believers in the divine right of kings and defenders of the common law and the rights of the subject. In the Tillyardian view political thought in the 1590s was dominated by an almost superstitious belief in the significance of the political settlement of 1485 when, over a century before Shakespeare's history plays were composed, the civil wars (the 'Wars of the Roses') were ended by the accession of the first Tudor monarch, Henry VII. Yet only 50 years subsequent to the production of these plays, the entire kingdom of Britain was divided by a Civil War of much greater consequence, in the course of which the people found it legally and morally possible to execute the king and declare a republic. The killing of kings, by secret murder or open battle, was virtually a national sport in the fourteenth and fifteenth centuries (Richard II, Henry VI, Richard III all died violently at the hands of their powerful rivals): but the execution of Charles I by decision of the people in their representative assembly, parliament, was a strikingly new form of 'deposition', indicating a new constitutional situation quite different from the traditional late-medieval pattern of aristocratic competition and baronial struggle. Acrimonious debates foreshadowing the bitter ideological divisions of the mid-seventeenth century were already to be heard in the early parliaments of James I, who succeeded Elizabeth in 1603—and indeed even earlier, albeit in a muted and coded form, in the later years of Elizabeth's own reign. It would be difficult indeed to explain how Tillyard's unified organic society of the 1590s could have collapsed so quickly and easily into the most extreme form of political crisis.

The critique of Tillyard and his school involved more, however, than combating his historical interpretation of Elizabethan culture and politics. It was necessary also to engage with the ideological inflection of Tillyard's own intervention of 1944, and to situate his critical views within the ideological crisis of British nationalism as the war drew to a close, and as the imperialism built on British nationalism entered its last, terminal phase. One of the key features of contemporary theoretically informed criticism is its loss of faith in the traditional values of objectivity in criticism and disinterestedness in the critic. At some distance both from the events of the 1940s and from their historical repercussions and persuasive rhetorical strategies, it became possible to recognise that Tillyard, Wilson Knight and Dover Wilson all found in Shakespeare's history plays a ruling ideology of order because that is precisely what they wanted to find. Their real ideological commitment (suppressed and implicit in Tillyard, frequently overt and declamatory in Wilson Knight and Dover Wilson) was only indirectly to the order of a vanished historical state, and directly to the political and ideological problems of Britain in the late 1930s and 1940s. The Elizabethans, Tillyard asserted, believed implicitly in 'order', hated the idea of 'disorder', and had no use for a philosophy such as Machiavelli's which proposed disorder, rather than order, as the natural condition of existence.

> Such a way of thinking was abhorrent to the Elizabethans (as indeed it always has been and is now to the majority) who preferred to think of order as the norm to which disorder, though lamentably common, was yet the exception.

The parenthesis quietly affirms a continuity between the conservatism of the Elizabethans and the instinctive conservatism of the modern-day 'majority'. Yet the single most obvious shift in post-war (post-Depression, post-Empire, post-Hiroshima, post-Holocaust) culture was an immediate preference for systems of thought offering a principle of 'disorder' rather than a metaphysic of 'order' as the most convincing explanation of the universe. Unsurprisingly, within a decade or so after Tillyard, critics were beginning to find in Shakespeare's political vision a distinct strain of Machiavellian scepticism. Tillyard's traditional patriotism must already have seemed distinctly old-fashioned to the generation who returned from the war to vote in a Labour government in the election of 1945.

Nonetheless, Tillyard's study remains the critical text which above all others framed and shaped the subsequent and continuing debate over the history plays largely because, as Alan Sinfield and Jonathan Dollimore have pointed out, Tillyard positioned the plays firmly within a context in which the terms history, historical evidence, historiography, must be regarded as indispensable theoretical factors in the activity of interpretation. Tillyard's approach was based on a 'historicist' methodology quite distinct from the traditional forms of 'literary history' that preceded him. Literary history presented the history of literature as an independent realm of art and thought, a sequence of great writers producing major works which then constituted the literary 'tradition'. Historicist approaches such as those of G. W. F. Hegel (1770–1831) or Thomas Carlyle (1795–1881) substituted a broader, more inclusive totality of cultural development, in the form of a concept of 'history' of which literature was an essential component. Here 'literature' became identified as the 'voice' or 'spirit' of an age or a society. Tillyard's work embodied a Hegelian analysis of literature as the expression of a common spirit of the age. In some ways Tillyard's study must be acknowledged as revolutionary (just as Marx acknowledged the revolutionary significance of Hegel), since both the critical orthodoxy it established and the counter-currents it provoked assume the historical as a basic premise, and therefore open up the debate for some of the characteristic concerns of contemporary criticism.

Tillyard's thesis was in its cultural moment radical and controversial, and it was opposed almost immediately by critical positions which looked backward to other traditional certainties, as well as forward to more recent critical interventions. What Tillyard was proposing was a particular relationship between the writer and (what we would now call) ideology, which proved quite unacceptable to critics committed to a more traditional notion of art as free from the constrictions of ideology or the determinants of history. Such critics as Irving Ribner in *The English History Play in the Age of Shakespeare* and A. P. Rossiter in some influential lectures delivered in the 1950s and published in *Angel with Horns* [1961] accepted the historicism of Tillyard's position, but denied his contention that Shakespeare held and expressed the orthodox thought of his time. Such an affirmation of ideological complicity with a dominant system of thought challenged the traditional post-romantic concept of the writer as a free imagination, liberal of sympathy and pluralist in ideas. Ribner, for example, proposed that the ideological 'frame' into which Tillyard located Shakespeare was far too narrow for his myriad-minded genius:

> What Tillyard says of Shakespeare is largely true, but by limiting the goals of the serious history play within the narrow framework of Halle's particular view, he compressed the wide range of Elizabethan historical drama into entirely too narrow a compass. There were other schools of historiography in Elizabethan England. The providential history of Halle, in fact, represents a tradition which, when Shakespeare was writing, was already in decline.

Employing the same metaphor of Tillyard's historicist thesis as a 'frame', Rossiter argued that Shakespeare's particular genius consisted in a refusal to work within the parameters of ideological orthodoxy: the 'frame' of Tudor historical thought is always in Shakespeare's work qualified and questioned by a supreme intelligence playing freely around the underlying issues.

* * *

* * * In the course of the 1970s and 1980s a whole range of new critical approaches to Shakespeare's history plays emerged, capable of a much more comprehensive and systematic exposure and demystification of the ideological character of Tillyard's thesis. Prominent among them was a 'new historicism' which offered to reconstitute the chronicle plays in different and politically oppositional ways. 'New Historicism', a critical movement originating in America and strongly influenced by the work of the radical historian and psychological theorist Michel Foucault, and the Marxist theoretician Louis Althusser, started from the same point as Tillyard, with a will to grasp the relationships between literature and the larger cultural totality of 'history'. Where the old historicism relied on a basically empiricist form of historical research, confident in its capacity to excavate and define the events of the past, New Historicism drew on poststructuralist theory, and accepted 'history' only as a contemporary activity of narrating or representing the past. It follows from this that New Historicism dismisses the claims of traditional scholarship to objectivity and disinterestedness: historians reconstruct the past in the light of their own ideological preoccupations and constraints. New Historicism rejects the conception of unified historical periods (such as the 'England of Elizabeth'), replacing what it regards as a propagandist myth by the alternative notion of different, contradictory and discontinuous 'histories' experienced by the various groups within a society; so the history of the Elizabethan aristocracy is not the same as that of the Elizabethan peasantry, and the history of women cannot be sub-

sumed into the history of men. Lastly, for New Historicism there can be no privileging of 'literature' as an ahistorical body of achievement standing out from a historical 'background'. All writing is equally historical, and occupies its own foreground. The texts conventionally designated as 'literature' need therefore to be read in relation to other texts not so prioritised.

These theoretical principles produced an entirely different historical method from that employed by Tillyard. New Historicism began to examine Renaissance drama as a functional 'discourse' in which the ideological conflicts and material power-struggles of the age would be fought out in more or less overt forms. If history is always a contemporary narrative, then what Tillyard saw as the intellectual spirit of an age becomes merely that story the Tudor government wished to have told about its own rise to power and continuing dominance; and it becomes legitimate for a modern critic to refashion that story otherwise, to disclose a different range of meanings and values. If the notion of historical totality needs to be replaced by the alternative concept of a fragmentary and discontinuous series of historical differences, then the drama should be able to speak of diverse and contradictory ideologies. If the kinds of writing traditionally separated off as 'literature' need to be restored to their intertextual relations with other kinds of writing, then new methods of inquiry and explication become appropriate.

* * *

SIGURD BURCKHARDT

[Symmetry and Disorder]†

* * *

Dialectics is an ordering device; it orders by arranging disorder symmetrically. We do not resort to it as long as we know, or think we know, where and wherein order resides; we resort to it when we do not know, or pretend not to know, where our quest for order is taking us. The dialectician acts as though he had fully accepted the challenge of disorder and were seriously engaged in meeting it. What he forgets, or chooses to ignore, is that dialectical conflict is a question-begging device. Whatever victories are won in this way are won by prearrangement.

There are various possible images of order; traditionally, that of the Christian West has been the triad. Unlike the circle (the image

† From Sigurd Burckhardt, *Shakespearean Meanings* (Princeton: Princeton University Press, 1968), 145–49. Reprinted by permission of the publisher.

of divine order), the triad allows for discord, as any image of human order must; the base points are seen as potentially or actually in conflict. But at the same time it provides the apex where conflict can be arbitrated and resolved. For any level where conflict can arise there is a next higher level of appeal—the whole forming a pyramid, with God or some other absolute as the supreme arbiter.

If this is our image of order, it is natural that we should think of disorder as a triad minus the apex—as conflict where there is no higher court of appeal. Dialectics undertakes to reconstruct the apex from the base points, once the former can no longer be assumed as known. But the fact is that the apex *is* known; it is given by the symmetry of the image. Dialectical conflict is an instance not so much of disorder as of order *manqué*. It is a duel, trial by combat. A duel differs from normal, "orderly" trials only in that the court speaks through the outcome rather than *in propria persona.*[1] This may not be very consoling to the losing combatant, who may be so unreasonable and dialectically unenlightened as to feel that *he* was in the right and should have won. But it is most reassuring to the observing dialectician, who can persuade himself that once again disorder has brought forth order. If it had, the birth would be miraculous; in fact it is simply a *petitio principii.*[2]

All this may seem an odd preamble to an interpretation of Shakespeare's Prince Hal plays. But I hope to show that in these plays Shakespeare took a much more searching look at the problem of disorder than he had in the earlier histories. He had long since discovered that the apex had disappeared or become inaccessible; he now finds that even the remnant is more than he can safely take for granted.

Symmetry is so satisfying an arrangement because it gives scope to our secret lust for combat and disorder even while reassuring us that we are ultimately safe. We may think as we wish of Hal's famous soliloquy in *1 Henry IV*—"I know you all, and will a while uphold"—we *are* reassured by it. Between rebellion and misrule, between hot pride and slippery wit, sword-edged honor and fat-bellied self-indulgence, we know there is an axis of symmetry and a *tertius ridens.*[3] Order will emerge in the end, not necessarily because it has proved its superior title but because the two kinds of disorder will kill and cancel each other.

1 Henry IV seems to reach this point of satisfying resolution when Hal stands between what he assumes to be the corpses of

1. Latin idiom: i.e., justice is served by the duel's outcome rather than by a physical judge [*Editor's note*].
2. Latin idiom: the truth of the conclusion is assumed by the premise [*Editor's note*].
3. Latin idiom, literally "he who laughs third": the one who has seen the joke behind the joke [*Editor's note*].

Hotspur and Falstaff and speaks over each the appropriate obsequies. If the stage were simply a mirror of reality, its order and disorders, here the ordering would seem achieved. But of course it is not; no sooner has Hal walked off than disorder arises in massive palpability:

> 'Sblood, 'twas time to counterfeit. . . . Counterfeit? I lie, I am no counterfeit. To die is to be a counterfeit, for he is but the counterfeit of a man who hath not the life of a man; but to counterfeit dying when a man thereby liveth, is to be no counterfeit, but the true and perfect image of life indeed. . . . I am afraid of this gunpowder Percy though he be dead. How, if he should counterfeit too and rise? By my faith, I am afraid he would prove the better counterfeit. Therefore I'll make him sure; yea, and I'll swear I killed him. Why may not he rise as well as I? [5.4.111–23]

Not only *may* Hotspur rise but he *will*—as soon as the scene is ended and his "body" has been lugged off the stage. Like other leading actors in tragedies and histories, he makes a living by counterfeit dying, and to do so "is to be no counterfeit, but the true and perfect image of life indeed." Falstaff's rising destroys all kinds of reassuring symmetries, the first being that of stage and world. *Sub specie realitatis*,[4] his claim to being Hotspur's killer is exactly as good, or bad, as Hal's, just as his pretense of having died on the field of honor is exactly as good, or bad, as Hotspur's. Simply by refusing to submit to the agreeable fiction that there is an axis of symmetry between on-stage and off-stage and that reality and its representation correspond to each other in perfect balance, Falstaff throws us and the play back into dizzying confusion.

The confusion is covered up—at a price. In order to reestablish the stage-world balance, Hal lures—not to say bribes—Falstaff back into fictionality:

> Come, bring your luggage nobly on your back,
> For my part, if a lie may do thee grace,
> I'll gild it with the happiest terms I have. [5.4.150–52]

He manages to sound magnanimous about it, but is he doing more than making a virtue of necessity? For the "truth," in this confusion of counterfeits, is with Falstaff; he is the only one at this point who is not a "double man":

> Falstaff: No, that's certain; I am not a double man. . . . There is Percy. If your father will do me any honor, so; if not, let him kill the next Percy himself. . . .

4. Latin: in reality [*Editor's note*].

Hal: Why, Percy I killed myself, and saw thee dead.
Falstaff: Didst thou? Lord, Lord, how this world is given to lying! I grant you I was down and out of breath, and so was he. . . .

[5.4.134–42]

Falstaff is ready to split the credit for Hotspur's killing: if Hal supports him in his "lie," he will sustain Hal in Hal's "lie." And this bargain does represent some sort of truth, or at least of justice. For no matter who has run his sword through Hotspur in the make-belief of the stage, dramatically and morally it is Falstaff's role to kill him and to be killed by him; in the dialectic of the play's structure, he is a hero, while Hal is the *tertius ridens.* Strangely, it is he, the creature of Shakespeare's imagination rather than of history, who in the end asserts himself as the reality principle incarnate, reminding us that disorder is not slain as neatly and inexpensively as the calculated symmetrics of dialectics would have us believe. Very likely his creator planned him as Hal means to use him: as a foil, with Hotspur as a counterfoil. But he would not stay so corseted; he outgrew his preassigned measure and function. In the end, while he does not seriously disquiet us—Shakespeare, when he has need, is a master at letting us have our cake and eat it—Falstaff *remains*, the bulky remainder of a division which was calculated at 2÷2=1, but which would not come out even.

JOHN WILDERS

[Knowledge and Misjudgement]†

The episode in Glendower's castle in *Henry IV Part I* gives a fresh interest to the middle of the play by introducing a vividly eccentric new character. It also introduces a different kind of comedy from that of the tavern scenes, created by the incompatibility of Glendower and Hotspur. Their temperamental differences are obvious from the moment when the leaders sit down to their conference: Hotspur ridicules Glendower's claim that his birth was accompanied by supernatural portents, and when Glendower reveals that he was once a poet, Hotspur derides the whole art of poetry. For all his chivalric idealism, Hotspur's contempt is that of a rationalist for a romantic and, during Glendower's absence from the conference table, he confides to Mortimer how much the Welshman infuriates him:

† From John Wilders, *The Lost Garden: A View of Shakespeare's English and Roman History Plays* (London: Macmillan, 1978), 79–80, 85–91. Printed by permission of the publisher.

O, he is as tedious
As a tired horse, a railing wife;
Worse than a smoky house; I had rather live
With cheese and garlic in a windmill, far,
Than feed on cates and have him talk to me
In any summer house in Christendom. [3.1.157–62]

Mortimer, however, has a quite different opinion of his father-in-law and he tactfully protests that Glendower is learned, courageous, 'wondrous affable' and, moreover, has the highest regard for Hotspur. The two opinions are not inconsistent but, since Glendower appears only in this one scene, we have no means of knowing which estimate is the more just, though one suspects Hotspur of prejudice: it is the penalty he pays for having such a vital personality of his own.

These conflicting opinions and partial judgements are typical of *Henry IV*; indeed the action of many of Shakespeare's plays depends on the fact that our knowledge of other people must necessarily be not absolute but subjective, and that it is impossible for one man totally to know another. The consequences can be amusing, as in the clashes between Hotspur and Glendower, or tragic as in Othello's misconception of Desdemona. The absurdities of *The Comedy of Errors* derive from the belief by most of the characters that, because one man looks like another, he must necessarily be another, and the agonies of Lear derive from his assumption that his daughters really mean what they say.

* * *

By this stage in his career Shakespeare had become interested in man as 'a "reflective" being: self-picturing, self-deceiving, and acutely aware of the regard of others', as Iris Murdoch says of Sartre's view of human nature.[1] The inescapable tendency of men to create their own world-views, to see themselves and others not in absolute, objective terms but subjectively according to their own characters and situations was dramatised fully by Shakespeare for the first time in *Richard II*. The conflict between different ways of perceiving the same situation put him in mind of the kind of pictures known as 'perspectives', which are painted on a corrugated surface and present different subjects depending on whether they are viewed from the left or the right, but looked at from the front appear confused. This is used metaphorically by Bushy in his attempt to console the Queen:

Each substance of a grief hath twenty shadows,
Which shows like grief itself, but is not so;
For sorrow's eye, glazed with blinding tears,

1. Iris Murdoch, *Sartre* (Cambridge, 1953), 56.

Divides one thing entire to many objects,
Like perspectives which, rightly gaz'd upon,
Show nothing but confusion—ey'd awry,
Distinguish form. So your sweet Majesty,
Looking awry upon your lord's departure,
Find shapes of grief more than himself to wail;
Which, look'd on as it is, is nought but shadows
Of what it is not. (*R2*, 2.2.14–24)

As things turn out it is, of course, Bushy who perceives things mistakenly. In this play men are not deceived by appearances, like the characters in *The Comedy of Errors*, but instinctively create a world of appearances with which to surround themselves. It is therefore difficult to decide which is the 'correct', objective version of the events which the play portrays. We are left to weigh up at least two conflicting versions, Richard's and Bolingbroke's, and form our own opinion; the plays which succeed it, the two parts of *Henry IV*, contain yet more versions of the deposition as it was seen by Worcester, Hotspur, and Henry in his later years. This mode of presentation also allows Shakespeare to incorporate into the play the conflicting interpretations of the historians, for Richard is seen within the play both as an incompetent tyrant (Northumberland's view) and as a royal martyr (Richard's view of himself). As H. A. Kelly has shown, some of the characters give a 'Lancastrian' and others a 'Yorkist' version of events within the same play.[2] Shakespeare seems to have realised that our inability to perceive absolute truth extends to our judgement of the dead: his view of history includes the idea that we can never know what history really consists of.

The irreconcilable conflict between people's individual conceptions of one another is also a feature of the comedies and is fully developed in *The Merchant of Venice*, a play written about a year after *Richard II*. In the figure of Shylock Shakespeare created a character who was to become controversial for this very reason. A member of an unjustly persecuted race in his own eyes, and a predatory monster in the eyes of people like Gratiano, he voices his own subjective impression of the play so eloquently that, since the beginning of the eighteenth century, the critics have been in constant disagreement as to whether his or the Christians' is the authentic version: the play is a tragedy or a comedy depending on whether you see it through Shylock's eyes or those of the Christians.[3] Shylock is obviously the most vital and imposing character

2. H. A. Kelly, *Divine Providence*, 205.
3. In his *Account of the Life of Mr. William Shakespeare* (1709), Nicholas Rowe remarks: 'Tho' we have seen that Play Receiv'd and Acted as a Comedy, and the Part of the Jew perform'd by an Excellent Comedian, yet I cannot but think it was design'd Tragically by the Author'; Shakespeare, *Works*, 6 vols. (London, 1709), vol. 1, xix–xx.

in this play, but Shakespeare's next history play, *Henry IV Part I*, abounds with independent, idiosyncratic, energetic characters such as Hotspur, Falstaff, Hal, the King, and a host of vividly realised minor people, all reluctant to be governed, tending to see the world in their own terms and to dictate their terms to other people. The play has scarcely begun before there is a clash of wills between the King and Hotspur which takes the form of an argument about the true character and conduct of Mortimer. To Henry, Mortimer is a traitor who has betrayed his troops to the enemy; to Hotspur, Mortimer is a loyal subject who has proved his faithfulness in violent combat against Glendower. Henry's reaction to Hotspur's report of this encounter is to call him a liar, and Hotspur's reaction is to accuse Henry of misrepresenting the truth for his own purposes, for Mortimer has a strong claim to the throne. Neither allows the other to be right, and their disagreement, incidentally, allows Shakespeare to incorporate into his play the uncertainty be found in Holinshed, who wrote that 'whether by treason or otherwise . . . the English power was discomfited, the earle taken prisoner, and above a thousand of his people slaine in the place'. What actually happened we can never know: the mild, affable man who appears later in the play seems neither treacherous nor a warrior. It should be noticed, however, that the row over Mortimer helps to spark off the Percys' rebellion: it propels Hotspur into the arms of his already mutinous uncle and we must conclude that the impulse which encouraged Hotspur to ally himself with the rebels resulted from a possible misjudgement of the facts.

We have already noticed the tendency of Bolingbroke and Richard to regard each other as objects in their own subjective worlds, but the action of *Henry IV* is distributed between different physical worlds or locations, each dominated by a unique and uniquely demanding character. The court is dominated by Henry, solitary and obsessed with affairs of state, the tavern by Falstaff, gregarious and devoted to the satisfaction of his appetites, and the rebel camp by Hotspur, independent and preoccupied by the desire for fame in battle. Each world is vividly real but is also an image of the character who dominates it (in a manner reminiscent of the 'houses' of medieval allegory) and each of the major protagonists sees the others subjectively as aids or impediments to the achievement of success within his own individual world. There is, in particular, a wide variety of opinion about Prince Hal, who plays a crucial role in all three worlds. To Hotspur, Hal is a mere playboy, 'the sword and buckler Prince of Wales', but also, however trivial, a threat to his ambition to be the unrivalled champion of chivalry. As he dies on the battlefield, Hotspur is galled to think that, far from winning honour by the defeat of Hal, he has actually contributed to Hal's reputation by falling at his hands:

> I better brook the loss of brittle life
> Than those proud titles thou has won of me:
> They wound my thoughts worse than thy sword my flesh.
> [5.4.77–79]

Whereas Hotspur regards the Prince as a threat to his reputation and is nettled by Vernon's eulogy of him, the King fears Hal as a threat to the succession and the stability of the country to which he has laboriously devoted his reign. In Henry's eyes, Hal is a dangerous profligate whose accession will initiate a further period of political chaos, whereas Hotspur is an ideal son whose character and achievements overshadow Hal's. Hotspur, as Henry tells his son,

> hath more worthy interest to the state
> Than thou the shadow of succession. [3.2.98–99]

In spite of Hal's display of loyalty at the Battle of Shrewsbury, the King, almost up to the moment of his death, continues to see his son as a danger to the state. When Hal, towards the end of the *Second Part*, moved by the thought of the immense responsibilities he is about to assume, takes the crown from his father's pillow, Henry interprets his gesture as a confirmation of his worst suspicions about his son:

> Thou has stol'n that which, after some few hours,
> Were thine without offence; and at my death
> Thou hast seal'd up my expectation.
> Thy life did manifest thou lov'dst me not,
> And thou wilt have me die assur'd of it. [*2H4*, 4.5.102–06]

To the King, Hal is a character in his own tragedy.

Falstaff shares with Hotspur and the King the impression that Hal is a profligate, and, in spite of the Prince's continual protests to the contrary, persists in seeing him as a lifelong ally in crime. Whereas Henry foresees Hal's accession as the ruin of his aspirations, Falstaff foresees it as the realisation of his hopes, and he rides off to London convinced that the young King is sick for him. To each of these three people, Hal is a character in his own private drama, a subjective impression created in his own mind. Each regards him as a creature to be used. It does not, apparently, occur to any of them that Hal may be using them. The Prince shares this secret only with the audience who are allowed to learn that his association with Falstaff is a deliberately assumed appearance of profligacy, designed to 'falsify men's hopes' in order that his well-timed public 'reformation' may compel the admiration of his subjects. To his mind he is the sun, the centre of a universe in which Falstaff is not an ally but a mere 'base contagious cloud' which he permits, for the moment, to obscure his own beauty, a 'foil' with which he will eventually dispense [1.2.168–90]. Hal regards Falstaff, as Falstaff regards Hal, as an instrument in his own ascent to power. The rejection scene portrays the inevitable collision of these two views in which Hal's prevails, not because it is the truer but because Hal has the necessary power to enforce it. It is only then that Falstaff discovers not simply that he has no future but that he is no more than a disgusting idea in the mind of Henry V:

> I have long dreamt of such a kind of man,
> So surfeit-swell'd, so old and so profane;
> But, being awak'd, I do despise my dream. (*2H4*, 5.5.50–52)

At that moment, Falstaff begins to wake from his dream too.

The lives of all these characters are shown to have been built upon conjectures which are unavoidable and in most cases lead to disaster. Hotspur builds his hopes on the illusion that the Prince is a shallow profligate, easily disposed of, Falstaff on the illusion that Hal's seeming loyalty will ensure his future, and, though the King's fears of Hal are luckily dispelled just before he dies, nevertheless he wastes the night hours dreading his son's accession.

The rebellion against Henry is likewise motivated by conjectures. Worcester, its instigator, simply assumes that the King will continue to be embarrassed by his former dependence on the Percys, that he will expect them to trade on this dependence and will therefore find an excuse to be rid of them:

> For, bear ourselves as even as we can,
> The King will always think him in our debt,
> And think we think ourselves unsatisfied,
> Till he hath found a time to pay us home. [1.3.282–85]

It is on this projection of his own fears into what he imagines to be the mind of Bolingbroke that Worcester initiates the rebellion. Even when, immediately before the crucial battle, Henry offers them an amnesty, Worcester is unable to take him at his word:

> It is not possible, it cannot be,
> The King should keep his word in loving us;
> He will suspect us still, and find a time
> To punish this offence in other faults. [5.2.4–7]

On this conjecture, he deliberately conceals the King's offer of peace from Hotspur who, as we are later told, leads his men into battle on the false assumption that his strength will be sufficient to overcome the enemy:

> [He] lin'd himself with hope,
> Eating the air and promise of supply,
> Flatt'ring himself in project of a power
> Much smaller than the smallest of his thoughts;
> And so, with great imagination
> Proper to madmen, led his powers to death
> And, winking, leapt into destruction. (*2H4*, 51.2.27–33)

Hotspur's death, like the defeat of Falstaff's hopes, is caused by a failure of perception. He misconstrues everything.

One consequence of this tendency to misjudgement is that the characters constantly accuse one another of lying. Henry IV accuses Hotspur and Hotspur accuses the King of lying about Mortimer; the Prince accuses Falstaff of lying about the Gadshill robbery; Worcester refuses to believe in the King's offer of an amnesty and deliberately lies about it to Hotspur; Falstaff claims the credit for killing Hotspur and observes how subject old men like Shallow are to this vice of lying. Appropriately the Second Part of the play is introduced by the figure of Rumour, 'painted full of tongues'. Another manifestation of this subjectivity is the prominence of episodes in which characters impersonate one another: Prince Hal gives an impersonation of breakfast-time at Warkworth which does not quite correspond to the behaviour of Hotspur and his wife which we have witnessed in the previous scene [*1H4*, 2.3], and, although we are denied the promised pleasure of seeing Falstaff play Lady Percy, we do see him, together with Hal, in a charade of the Prince's forthcoming interview with the King. Such mimicry reveals as much about the attitudes of the performers as it does about the characters they impersonate. The winner in this game of deception is Hal, who deliberately impersonates the prodigal son and feigns the false impression he knows his subjects have formed of him in order that, eventually, they will be convinced by his equally contrived reformation. Only he succeeds in an imperfect world by ingeniously exploiting its imperfections. Yet it is doubtful whether Hal himself knows wholly what he is doing: his assurances, in his first soliloquy, that his profligacy is merely a sham, may be an attempt to justify his actions to himself, and his later confession to the Lord Chief Justice that he is a reformed character presupposes that he was formerly corrupt.[4] Just as we can never be sure of Bolingbroke's motives for returning from exile, we can never absolutely know Hal's motives for frequenting the tavern. The two parts of *Henry IV* are almost as open to our own sub-

4. This was Johnson's interpretation of the soliloquy, which he described as 'a natural picture of a great mind offering excuses to itself, and palliating those follies which it can neither justify nor forsake'; Arthur Sherbo (ed.), *Johnson on Shakespeare*, 2 vols. (Yale edition, 1968), vol. 1, 458.

jective interpretations as they are to those of the protagonists; hence the continual critical discussion about their 'real' meaning.

* * *

STEPHEN GREENBLATT

[Theater and Power]†

In his notorious police report of 1593 on Christopher Marlowe, the Elizabethan spy Richard Baines informed his superiors that Marlowe had declared, among other monstrous opinions, that 'Moses was but a juggler, and that one Heriots, being Sir Walter Ralegh's man, can do more than he'.[1] The 'Heriots' cast for a moment in this lurid light is Thomas Harriot, the most profound Elizabethan mathematician, an expert in cartography, optics, and navigational science, an adherent of atomism, the first Englishman to make a telescope and turn it on the heavens, the author of the first original book about the first English colony in America, and the possessor throughout his career of a dangerous reputation for atheism.[2] In all of his extant writings, private correspondence as well as public discourse, Harriot professes the most reassuringly orthodox religious faith, but the suspicion persisted. When he died of cancer in 1621, one of his contemporaries, persuaded that Harriot had challenged the doctrinal account of creation *ex nihilo*,[3] remarked gleefully that 'a *nihilum* killed him at last: for in the top of his nose came a little red speck (exceeding small), which grew bigger and bigger, and at last killed him'.[4]

Charges of atheism levelled at Harriot or anyone else in this period are extremely difficult to assess, for such accusations were smear tactics, used with reckless abandon against anyone whom the accuser happened to dislike. At a dinner party one summer evening in 1593, Sir Walter Ralegh teased an irascible country parson named Ralph Ironside and found himself the subject of a state investigation; at the other end of the social scale, in the same Dorsetshire parish, a drunken servant named Oliver com-

† Stephen Greenblatt, "Invisible Bullets" in Jonathan Dollimore and Alan Sinfield, eds., *Political Shakespeare: New Essays in Cultural Materialism* (Manchester: Manchester University Press, 1985), 18–47. Reprinted by permission of the author.

1. John Bakeless, *The Tragicall History of Christopher Marlowe*, 2 vols. (Cambridge, Mass.: Harvard University Press, 1942), I, 111.
2. On Harriot see especially *Thomas Harriot, Renaissance Scientist*, ed. John W. Shirley (Oxford University Press, 1974); also Muriel Rukeyser, *The Traces of Thomas Harriot* (New York: Random House, 1970), and Jean Jacquot, 'Thomas Harriot's Reputation for Impiety', *Notes and Records of the Royal Society*, 9 (1952), 164–87.
3. Latin: from nothing [*Editor's note*].
4. John Aubrey, *Brief Lives*, ed. Andrew Clark, 2 vols. (Oxford University Press, 1898), I, 286.

plained that in the Sunday sermon the preacher had praised Moses excessively but had neglected to mention his fifty-two concubines, and Oliver too found himself under official scrutiny.[5] Few if any of these investigations turned up what we would call atheists, even muddled or shallow ones; the stance that seems to come naturally to the greenest college freshman in late twentieth-century America seems to have been almost unthinkable to the most daring philosophical minds of late sixteenth-century England.

The historical evidence, of course, is unreliable; even in the absence of substantial social pressure, people lie quite readily about their most intimate beliefs. How much more must they have lied in an atmosphere of unembarrassed repression. Still, there is probably more than politic concealment involved here. After all, treason was punished as harshly as atheism, and yet, while the period abounds in documented instances of treason in word and deed, there are virtually no professed atheists. If ever there were a place to confirm the proposition that within a given social construction of reality certain interpretations of experience are sanctioned and others excluded, it is here, in the boundaries that contained sixteenth-century scepticism. Like Machiavelli and Montaigne, Thomas Harriot professed belief in God, and there is no justification, in any of these cases, for a simple dismissal of the profession of faith as mere hypocrisy.

I am not, of course, arguing that atheism was literally unthinkable in the late sixteenth century; rather that it was almost always thinkable only as the thought of another. This is, in fact, one of its attractions as a smear; atheism is one of the characteristic marks of otherness. Hence the ease with which Catholics can call Protestant martyrs atheists, and Protestants routinely make similar charges against the Pope.[6] The pervasiveness and frequency of these charges then does not signal the probable existence of a secret society of freethinkers, a School of Night, but rather registers the operation of a religious authority that, whether Catholic or Protestant, characteristically confirms its power in this period by disclosing the threat of atheism. The authority is secular as well as religious; hence at Raleigh's 1603 treason trial, Justice Popham solemnly warned the accused not to let 'Harriot, nor any such Doctor, persuade you there is no eternity in Heaven, lest you find an eternity of hell-torments'.[7] Nothing in Harriot's writings suggests that he held the position attributed to him here, but of course the charge does not depend upon evidence: Harriot is invoked as the

5. For the investigation of Ralegh, see *Willobie His Avisa* (1594), ed. G. B. Harrison (London: John Lane, 1926), appendix 3, 255–71.
6. See, for example, *The Historie of Travell into Virginia Britania* (1612), ed. Louis B. Wright and Virginia Freund (London: Hakluyt Society, 2nd. ser., no. 103, 1953), 101.
7. Jacquot, 'Thomas Harriot's Reputation for Impiety', 167.

archetypal corrupter. Achitophel seducing his glittering Absolom.[8] If he did not exist, he would have to be invented.

Yet atheism is not the only mode of subversive religious doubt, and we cannot entirely discount the persistent rumors of Harriot's heterodoxy by pointing to his perfectly conventional professions of faith and to the equal conventionality of the attacks upon him. Indeed I want to suggest that if we look closely at *A Brief and True Report of the New Found Land of Virginia*, the only work Harriot published in his lifetime and hence the work in which he was presumably the most cautious, we can find traces of exactly the kind of material that could lead to the remark attributed to Marlowe, that 'Moses was but a juggler, and that one Heriots, being Sir Walter Ralegh's man, can do more than he'. Further, Shakespeare's Henry plays, like Harriot in the New World, can be seen to confirm the Machievellian hypothesis of the origin of princely power in force and fraud even as they draw their audience irresistibly toward the celebration of that power.

The apparently feeble wisecrack attributed to Marlowe finds its way into a police file because it seems to bear out one of the Machiavellian arguments about religion that most excited the wrath of sixteenth-century authorities: Old Testament religion, the argument goes, and by extension the whole Judeo-Christian tradition, originated in a series of clever tricks, fraudulent illusions perpetrated by Moses, who had been trained in Egyptian magic, upon the 'rude and gross' (and hence credulous) Hebrews.[9] This argument is not actually to be found in Machiavelli, nor does it originate in the sixteenth century; it is already fully formulated in early pagan polemics against Christianity. But it seems to acquire a special force and currency in the Renaissance as an aspect of a heightened consciousness, fuelled by the period's prolonged crises of doctrine and church governance, of the social function of religious belief.

Here Machiavelli's writings are important, for *The Prince* observes in its bland way that if Moses's particular actions and methods are examined closely, they do not appear very different from those employed by the great pagan princes, while the *Discourses* treat religion as if its primary function were not salvation but the achievement of civic discipline and hence as if its primary justification were not truth but expediency. Thus Romulus's successor, Numa Pompilius, 'finding a very savage people, and wishing to reduce them to civil obedience by the arts of peace, had recourse to religion as the most necessary and assured support of any civil soci-

8. The Second Book of Samuel, chapters 13–19, recounts how King David's favorite son Absolom is persuaded by his false friend Achitophel to rebel against his father [*Editor's note*].
9. See for instance Richard Baines's version of Marlowe's version of this argument: C. F. Tucker Brooke, *The Life of Marlowe* (London: Methuen, 1930), appendix 9, 98.

ety'.[1] For although 'Romulus could organize the Senate and establish other civil and military institutions without the aid of divine authority, yet it was very necessary for Numa, who feigned that he held converse with a nymph, who dictated to him all that he wished to persuade the people to' (147). In truth, continues Machiavelli, 'there never was any remarkable lawgiver amongst any people who did not resort to divine authority, as otherwise his laws would not have been accepted by the people' (147).

From here it was only a short step, in the minds of Renaissance authorities, to the monstrous opinions attributed to the likes of Marlowe and Harriot. Kyd, under torture, testified that Marlowe had affirmed that 'things esteemed to be done by divine power might have as well been done by observation of men', and the Jesuit Robert Parsons claimed that in Ralegh's 'school of Atheism', 'both Moses and our Savior, the Old and the New Testament, are jested at'.[2] On the eve of Ralegh's treason trial, some 'hellish verses' were lifted from an anonymous tragedy written ten years earlier and circulated as Ralegh's own confession of atheism. (The movement here is instructive: the fictional text returns to circulation as the missing confessional language of real life.) At first the earth was held in common, the verses declare, but this golden age gave way to war, kingship, and property:

> Then some sage man, above the vulgar wise,
> Knowing that laws could not in quiet dwell,
> Unless they were observed, did first devise
> The names of Gods, religion, heaven, and hell . . .
> Only bug-bears to keep the world in fear.[3]

Now Harriot does not give voice to any of these speculations, but if we look attentively at his account of the first Virginia colony, we find a mind that seems interested in the same set of problems, a mind indeed that seems to be virtually testing the Machiavellian hypotheses. Sent by Ralegh to keep a record of the colony and to compile a description of the resources and inhabitants of the area, Harriot took care to learn the North Carolina Algonkian dialect and to achieve what he calls a 'special familiarity with some of the priests'.[4] The Indi-

1. Niccolò Machiavelli, *Discourses*, trans. Christian Detmold (New York: Random House, 1950), 146. See also *The Prince* in *Tutte le opere di Niccolò Machiavelli*, ed. Francesco Flora and Carlo Cordiè, 2 vols. (Rome: Arnoldo Mondadori, 1949), I, 18.
2. Kyd is quoted in Brooke, *Life of Marlowe*, appendix 12, 107; Parsons in Ernest A. Strathmann, *Sir Walter Ralegh* (New York: Columbia University Press, 1951), 25.
3. Quoted in Jean Jacquot, 'Ralegh's "Hellish Verses" and the "Tragicall Raigne of Selimus" ', *Modern Language Review*, 48 (1953), I.
4. Thomas Harriot, *A Briefe and True Report of the New Found Land of Virginia* (1588), in *The Roanoke Voyages, 1584–1590*, ed. David Beers Quinn, 2 vols. (London: Hakluyt Society, 2nd ser., no. 104, 1955), 375. (Quotations are modernised here.) On the Algonkians of southern New England see Bruce G. Trigger, ed., *Handbook of North American Indians*: vol. 15, *Northeast* (Washington, D.C.: Smithsonian, 1978).

ans believe, he writes, in the immortality of the soul and in other-worldly punishments and rewards for behaviour in this world; 'What subtlety soever be in the *Wiroances* and Priests, this opinion worketh so much in many of the common and simple sort of people that it maketh them have great respect to their Governors, and also great care what they do, to avoid torment after death and to enjoy bliss' (374). The split between the priests and the people implied here is glimpsed as well in the description of the votive images: 'They think that all the gods are of human shape, and therefore they represent them by images in the forms of men, which they call Kewasowal. . . . The common sort think them to be also gods' (373).

We have then, as in Machiavelli, a sense of religion as a set of beliefs manipulated by the subtlety of the priests to help ensure social order and cohesion. To this we may add a still more telling observation not of the internal function of native religion but of the impact of European culture upon the Indians: 'Most things they saw with us', Harriot writes, 'as mathematical instruments, sea compasses, the virtue of the loadstone in drawing iron, a perspective glass whereby was showed many strange sights, burning glasses, wildfire works, guns, books, writing and reading, spring clocks that seem to go of themselves, and many other things that we had, were so strange unto them, and so far exceeded their capacities to comprehend the reason and means how they should be made and done, that they thought they were rather the works of gods then of men, or at the leastwise they had been given and taught us of the gods' (375–76). The effect of this delusion, born of what Harriot supposes to be the vast technological superiority of the European, is that the savages began to doubt that they possessed the truth of God and religion and to suspect that such truth 'was rather to be had from us, whom God so specially loved than from a people that were so simple, as they found themselves to be in comparison of us' (376).

What we have here, I suggest, is the very core of the Machiavellian anthropology that posited the origin of religion in a cunning imposition of socially coercive doctrines by an educated and sophisticated lawgiver upon a simple people. And in Harriot's list of the marvels—from wildfire to reading—with which he undermined the Indians' confidence in their native understanding of the universe, we have the core of the claim attributed to Marlowe: that Moses was but a juggler and that Ralegh's man Harriot could do more than he. It was, we may add, supremely appropriate that this hypothesis should be tested in the encounter of the Old world and the New, for though vulgar Machiavellianism implied that all religion was a sophisticated confidence trick, Machiavelli himself saw that trick as possible only at a radical point of origin: 'if any one wanted to establish a republic at the present time', he writes, 'he would find it much easier with the simple mountaineers, who are almost without any civilization, than with such as are accustomed to live in cities' (*Discourses*, 148).

In Harriot then we have one of the earliest instances of a highly significant phenomenon: the testing upon the bodies and minds of non-Europeans or, more generally, the non-civilised, of a hypothesis about the origin and nature of European culture and belief. Such testing could best occur in this privileged anthropological moment, for the comparable situations in Europe itself tended to be already contaminated by prior contact. Only in the forest, with a people ignorant of Christianity and startled by its bearers' technological potency, could one hope to reproduce accurately, with live subjects, the relation imagined between Numa and the primitive Romans, Moses and the Hebrews. And the testing that could then take place could only happen once, for it entails not detached observation but radical change, the change Harriot begins to observe in the priests who 'were not so sure grounded, nor gave such credit to their traditions and stories, but through conversing with us they were brought into great doubts of their own' (375). I should emphasise that I am speaking here of events as reported by Harriot. The history of subsequent English–Algonkian relations casts doubts upon the depth, extent, and irreversibility of the supposed Indian crisis of belief. In the *Brief and True Report*, however, the tribe's stories begin to *collapse* in the minds of their traditional guardians, and the coercive power of the European beliefs begins to show itself almost at once in the Indians' behaviour: 'On a time also when their corn began to wither by reason of a drought which happened extraordinarily, fearing that it had come to pass by reason that in some thing they had displeased us, many would come to us and desire us to pray to our God in England, that he would preserve their corn, promising that when it was ripe we also should be partakers of the fruit' (377). If we remember that, like virtually all sixteenth-century Europeans in the New World, the English resisted or were incapable of provisioning themselves and were in consequence dependent upon the Indians for food, we may grasp the central importance for the colonists of this dawning Indian fear of the Christian God.[5] As Machiavelli understood, physical compulsion is essential but never sufficient; the survival of the rulers depends upon a supplement of coercive belief.

The Indians must be persuaded that the Christian God is all-powerful and committed to the survival of his chosen people, that he will wither the corn and destroy the lives of savages who dis-

5. Cf. Richard Hakluyt, *The Principal Navigations, Voyages, Traffiques, & Discoveries of the English Nation*, 12 vols. (Glasgow: James Maclehose, 1903–5), X, 54, 56.

please him by disobeying or plotting against the English. We have then a strange paradox: Harriot tests and seems to confirm the most radically subversive hypothesis in his culture about the origin and function of religion by imposing his religion—with all of its most intense claims to transcendence, unique truth, inescapable coercive force—upon others. Not only the official purpose but the survival of the English colony depends upon this imposition. This crucial circumstance is what has licensed the testing in the first place; it is only as an agent of the English colony, dependent upon its purposes and committed to its survival, that Harriot is in a position to disclose the power of human achievements—reading, writing, gunpowder and the like—to appear to the ignorant as divine and hence to promote belief and compel obedience.

Thus the subversiveness which is genuine and radical—sufficiently disturbing so that to be suspected of such beliefs could lead to imprisonment and torture—is at the same time contained by the power it would appear to threaten. Indeed the subversiveness is the very product of that power and furthers its ends. One may go still further and suggest that the power Harriot both serves and embodies not only produces its own subversion but is actively built upon it: in the Virginia colony, the radical undermining of Christian order is not the negative limit but the positive condition for the establishment of the order. And this paradox extends to the production of Harriot's text: *A Brief and True Report*, with its latent heterodoxy, is not a reflection upon the Virginia colony nor even a simple record of it—not, in other words a privileged withdrawal into a critical zone set apart from power—but a continuation of the colonial enterprise.

By October 1586, there were rumours in England that there was little prospect of profit in Virginia, that the colony had been close to starvation, and that the Indians had turned hostile. Harriot accordingly begins with a descriptive catalogue in which the natural goods of the land are turned into social goods, that is, into 'merchantable commodities': 'Cedar, a very sweet wood and fine timber; whereof if nests of chests be there made, or timber thereof fitted for sweet and fine bedsteads, tables, desks, lutes, virginals, and many things else, . . . [it] will yield profit' (329–30).[6] The inventory of these commodities is followed by an inventory of edible plants and animals, to prove to readers that the colony need not starve, and then by the account of the Indians, to prove that the colony could impose its will upon them. The key to this imposition, as I have argued, is the coercive power of religious belief, and the

6. On these catalogues, see Wayne Franklin, *Discoverers, Explorers, Settlers: the Diligent Writers of Early America* (University of Chicago Press, 1979), 69–122.

source of this power is the impression made by advanced technology upon a 'backward' people.

Hence Harriot's text is committed to record what we have called his confirmation of the Machiavellian hypothesis, and hence too this confirmation is not only inaccessible as subversion to those on whom the religion is supposedly imposed but functionally inaccessible to most readers and quite possibly to Harriot himself. It may be that Harriot was demonically conscious of what he was doing—that he found himself situated exactly where he could test one of his culture's darkest fears about its own origins, that he used the Algonkians to do so, and that he wrote a report on his findings, a coded report, of course, since as he wrote to Kepler years later, 'our situation is such that I still may not philosophize freely'.[7] But we do not need such a biographical romance to account for the phenomenon: the subversiveness, as I have argued, was produced by the colonial power in its own interest, and *A Brief and True Report* was, with perfect appropriateness, published by the great Elizabethan exponent of missionary colonialism, the Reverend Richard Hakluyt.

Yet it is misleading, I think, to conclude without qualification that the radical doubt implicit in Harriot's account is *entirely* contained. Harriot was, after all, hounded through his whole life by charges of atheism and, more tellingly, the remark attributed to Marlowe suggests that it was fully possible for a contemporary to draw the most dangerous conclusions from the Virginia report. Moreover, the 'Atlantic Republican Tradition', as Pocock has argued, does grow out of the 'Machiavellian moment' of the sixteenth century, and that tradition, with its transformation of subjects into citizens, its subordination of transcendent values to capital values, does ultimately undermine, in the interests of a new power, the religious and secular authorities that had licensed the American enterprise in the first place. What we have in Harriot's text is a relation between orthodoxy and subversion that seems, in the same interpretive moment, to be perfectly stable and dangerously volatile.

We can deepen our understanding of this apparent paradox if we consider a second mode of subversion and its containment in Harriot's account. Alongside the *testing* of a subversive interpretation of the dominant culture, we find the *recording* of alien voices or, more precisely, of alien interpretations. The occasion for this recording is another consequence of the English presence in the New World, not in this case the threatened extinction of the tribal religion but the threatened extinction of the tribe: 'There was no town where

7. Quoted by Edward Rosen, 'Harriot's Science: the Intellectual Background', in *Thomas Harriot*, ed. Shirley, 4.

we had any subtle device practiced against us', Harriot writes, 'but that within a few days after our departure from every such town, the people began to die very fast, and many in short space; in some towns about twenty, in some forty, in some sixty and in one six score, which in truth was very many in respect of their numbers. The disease was so strange, that they neither knew what it was, nor how to cure it; the like by report of the oldest man in the country never happened before, time out of mind' (378).[8] Harriot is writing, of course, about the effects of measles, smallpox, or perhaps simply the common cold upon people with no resistance to them, but a conception of the biological basis of epidemic disease lies far, far in the future. For the English the deaths must be a moral phenomenon—the notion is for them as irresistible as the notion of germs for ourselves—and hence the 'facts' as they are observed are already moralised: the deaths only occurred 'where they used some practice against us', that is, where the Indians conspired secretly against the English. And, with the wonderful self-validating circularity that characterises virtually all powerful constructions of reality, the evidence for these secret conspiracies is precisely the deaths of the Indians.

Now it is not surprising that Harriot seems to endorse the idea that God is protecting his chosen people by killing off untrustworthy Indians; what is surprising is that Harriot is interested in the Indians's own anxious speculations about the unintended but lethal biological warfare that was destroying them. Drawing upon his special familiarity with the priests, he records a remarkable series of conjectures, almost all of which assume—correctly, as we now know—that their misfortune was linked to the presence of the strangers. 'Some people', observing that the English remained healthy while the Indians died, 'could not tell', Harriot writes, 'whether to think us gods or men'; others, seeing that the members of the first colony were all male, concluded that they were not born of women and therefore must be spirits of the dead returned to mortal form (an Algonkian 'Night of the Living Dead'). Some medicine men learned in astrology blamed the disease on a recent eclipse of the sun and on a comet—a theory Harriot considers seriously and rejects—while others shared the prevailing English interpretation and said 'that it was the special work of God' on behalf of the colonists. And some who seem in historical hindsight eerily prescient prophesied 'that there were more of [the English] generation yet to come, to kill theirs and take their places'. The supporters of this theory even worked out a conception of the disease that in some features uncannily resembles our own: 'Those that were im-

8. Cf. Walter Bigges's account of Drake's visit to Florida in 1586, in *The Roanoke Voyages*, I, 306.

mediately to come after us [the first English colonists], they imagined to be in the air, yet invisible and without bodies, and that they by our entreaty and for the love of us did make the people to die . . . by shooting invisible bullets into them' (380).

For a moment, as Harriot records these competing theories, it may seem to a reader as if there were no absolute assurance of God's national interest, as if the drive to displace and absorb the other had given way to conversation among equals, as if all meanings were provisional, as if the signification of events stood apart from power. This impression is intensified for us by our awareness that the theory that would ultimately triumph over the moral conception of epidemic disease was already at least metaphorically present in the conversation. In the very moment that the moral conception is busily authorising itself, it registers the possibility (indeed from our vantage point, the inevitability) of its own destruction.

But why, we must ask ourselves, should power record other voices, permit subversive inquiries, register at its very centre the transgressions that will ultimately violate it? The answer may be in part that power, even in a colonial situation, is not perfectly monolithic and hence may encounter and record in one of its functions materials that can threaten another of its functions; in part that power thrives on vigilance, and human beings are vigilant if they sense a threat; in part that power defines itself in relation to such threats or simply to that which is not identical with it. Harriot's text suggests an intensification of these observations: English power in the first Virginia colony *depends* upon the registering and even the production of such materials. 'These their opinions I have set down the more at large', Harriot tells the 'Adventurers, Favorers, and Wellwishers' of the colony to whom his report is addressed, 'that it may appear unto you that there is good hope they may be brought through discrete dealing and government to the embracing of the truth, and consequently to honor, obey, fear, and love us' (318). The recording of alien voices, their preservation in Harriot's text, is part of the process whereby Indian culture is constituted as a culture and thus brought into the light for study, discipline, correction, transformation. The momentary sense of instability or plenitude—the existence of other voices—is produced by the monological power that ultimately denies the possibility of plenitude, just as the subversive hypothesis about European religion is tested and confirmed only by the imposition of that religion.

We may add that the power of which we are speaking is in effect an allocation method—a way of distributing resources to some and denying them to others, critical resources (here primarily corn and game) that prolong life or, in their absence, extinguish it. In a remarkable study of how societies make 'tragic choices' in the allocation of scarce resources (e.g. kidney machines) or in the determination of high risks (e.g. the military draft), Guido Calabresi and Philip Bobbitt observe that by complex mixtures of approaches, societies attempt to avert 'tragic results, that is, results which imply the rejection of values which are proclaimed to be fundamental'. These approaches may succeed for a time, but it will eventually become apparent that some sacrifice of fundamental values has taken place, whereupon 'fresh mixtures of methods will be tried, structured . . . by the shortcomings of the approaches they replace'. These too will in time give way to others in a 'strategy of successive moves' that comprises an 'intricate game', a game that reflects the simultaneous perception of an inherent flaw and the determination to 'forget' that perception in an illusory resolution.[9] Hence the simple operation of any systematic order, any allocation method, will inevitably run the risk of exposing its own limitations, even (or perhaps especially) as it asserts its underlying moral principle.

This exposure is at its most intense at moments in which a comfortably established ideology confronts unusual circumstances, moments when the moral value of a particular form of power is not merely assumed but explained. We may glimpse such a moment in Harriot's account of a visit from the colonists' principal Indian ally, the chief Wingina. Wingina was persuaded that the disease decimating his people was indeed the work of the Christian God and had come to request the English to ask their God to direct his lethal magic against an enemy tribe. The colonists tried to explain that such a prayer would be 'ungodly', that their God was indeed responsible for the disease but that, in this as in all things, he would only act 'according to his good pleasure as he had ordained' (379). Indeed if men asked God to make an epidemic he probably would not do it; the English could expect such providential help only if they made sincere 'petition for the contrary,' that is, for harmony and good fellowship in the service of truth and righteousness.

The problem with these assertions is not that they are self-consciously wicked (in the manner of Richard III or Iago) but that they are highly moral and logically coherent; or rather, what is unsettling is one's experience of them, the nasty sense that they are at once irrefutable ethical propositions and pious humbug designed to conceal from the English themselves the rapacity and aggression that is implicit in their very presence. The explanatory moment manifests the self-validating, totalising character of Renaissance political theology—its ability to account for almost every occurrence, even (or above all) apparently perverse or contrary occur-

9. Guido Calabresi and Philip Bobbitt, *Tragic Choices* (New York: Norton, 1978), p. 195. The term *tragic* is, I think, misleading.

rences—and at the same time confirms for us the drastic disillusionment that extends from Machiavelli to its definitive expression in Hume and Voltaire. In his own way, Wingina himself clearly thought his lesson in Christian ethics was polite nonsense. When the disease had in fact spread to his enemies, as it did shortly thereafter, he returned to the English to thank them—I presume with the Algonkian equivalent of a sly wink—for their friendly help, for 'although we satisfied them not in promise, yet in deeds and effect we had fulfilled their desires' (379). For Harriot, this 'marvelous accident', as he calls it, is another sign of the colony's great expectations.

Once again a disturbing vista—a sceptical critique of the function of Christian morality in the New World—is glimpsed only to be immediately closed off. Indeed we may feel at this point that subversion scarcely exists and may legitimately ask ourselves how our perception of the subversive and orthodox is generated. The answer, I think, is that 'subversive' is for us a term used to designate those elements in Renaissance culture that contemporary authorities tried to contain or, when containment seemed impossible, to destroy and that now conform to our own sense of truth and reality. That is, we locate as 'subversive' in the past precisely those things that are *not* subversive to ourselves, that pose no threat to the order by which we live and allocate resources: in Harriot's *Brief and True Report*, the function of illusion in the establishment of religion, the displacement of a providential conception of disease by one focused on 'invisible bullets', the exposure of the psychological and material interests served by a certain conception of divine power. Conversely, we identify as the principle of order and authority in Renaissance texts things that we would, if we took them seriously, find subversive for ourselves: religious and political absolutism, aristocracy of birth, demonology, humoral psychology, and the like. That we do not find such notions subversive, that we complacently identify them as principles of aesthetic or political order, is a version of the process of containment that licensed what we call the subversive elements in Renaissance texts: that is, our own values are sufficiently strong for us to contain almost effortlessly alien forces. What we find then in Harriot's *Brief and True Report* can best be described by adapting a remark about the possibility of hope that Kafka once made to Max Brod: There is subversion, no end of subversion, only not for us.

I want now to consider the relevance of what I've been saying to our understanding of more complex literary works. It is tempting to focus such remarks on Shakespeare's *Tempest* where Caliban, Prospero's 'salvage and deformed slave' enters cursing the expropriation of his island and exits declaring that he will 'be wise hereafter, /

And seek for grace.[1] What better instance, in the light of Harriot's Virginia, of the containment of a subversive force by the authority that has created that force in the first place: 'This thing of darkness', Prospero says of Caliban at the close, 'I acknowledge mine.'

But I do not want to give the impression that the process I have been describing is applicable only to works that address themselves directly or allusively to the New World. Shakespeare's plays are centrally and repeatedly concerned with the production and containment of subversion and disorder, and the three modes that we have identified in Harriot's text—testing, recording, and explaining—all have their recurrent theatrical equivalents. I am speaking not solely of plays like *Measure for Measure* and *Macbeth*, where authority is obviously subjected to open, sustained, and radical questioning before it is reaffirmed, with ironic reservations, at the close, but of a play like *1 Henry IV* in which authority seems far less problematical. 'Who does not all along see', wrote Upton in the mid-eighteenth century, 'that when prince Henry comes to be king he will assume a character suitable to his dignity?' My point is not to dispute this interpretation of the prince as, in Maynard Mack's words, 'an ideal image of the potentialities of the English character',[2] but to observe that such an ideal image involves as its positive condition the constant production of its own radical subversion and the powerful containment of that subversion.

We are continually reminded that Hal is a 'juggler', a conniving hypocrite, and that the power he both serves and comes to embody is glorified usurpation and theft; yet at the same time, we are drawn to the celebration of both the prince and his power. Thus, for example, the scheme of Hal's moral redemption is carefully laid out in his soliloquy at the close of the first tavern scene, but as in the act of *explaining* that we have examined in Harriot, Hal's justification of himself threatens to fall away at every moment into its antithesis. 'By how much better than my word I am', Hal declares, 'By so much shall falsify men's hopes' [1.2.183–84]. To falsify men's hopes is to exceed their expectations, and it is also to disappoint their expectations, to deceive men, to turn their hopes into fictions, to betray them. Not only are the competing claims of Bolingbroke and Falstaff at issue but our own hopes, the fantasies continually aroused by the play of absolute friendship and trust, limitless playfulness, innate grace, plenitude. But though all of this is in some sense at stake in Hal's soliloquy and though we can perceive at

1. V.i.295–6. All citations of Shakespeare are to *The Riverside Shakespeare*, ed. G. Blakemore Evans (Boston: Houghton Mifflin, 1974).
2. John Upton, *Critical Observations on Shakespeare* (1748), in *Shakespeare: the Critical Heritage*, ed. Brian Vickers, vol. 3: *1733–1752* (London: Routledge, 1975), p. 297; Maynard Mack, introduction to Signet Classic edition of *1 Henry IV* (New York: New American Library, 1965), xxxv.

every point, through our own constantly shifting allegiances, the potential instability of the structure of power that has Henry IV at the pinnacle and Robin Ostler, who 'never joy'd since the price of oats rose' [2.1.11], near the bottom, Hal's 'redemption' is as inescapable and inevitable as the outcome of those practical jokes the madcap prince is so fond of playing. Indeed, the play insists, this redemption is not something toward which the action moves but something that is happening at every moment of the theatrical representation.

The same yoking of the unstable and the inevitable may be seen in the play's acts of *recording*, that is, the moments in which we hear voices that seem to dwell in realms apart from that ruled by the potentates of the land. These voices exist and have their apotheosis in Falstaff, but their existence proves to be utterly bound up with Hal, contained politically by his purposes as they are justified aesthetically by his involvement. The perfect emblem of this containment is Falstaff's company, marching off to Shrewsbury: 'discarded unjust servingmen, younger sons to younger brothers, revolted tapsters, and ostlers trade-fall'n, the cankers of a calm world and a long peace' [4.2.25–27]. These are, as many a homily would tell us, the very types of Elizabethan subversion—masterless men, the natural enemies of social discipline—but they are here pressed into service as defenders of the established order, 'good enough to toss,' as Falstaff tells Hal, 'food for powder, food for powder' [4.2.59–60]. For power as well as powder, and we may add that this food is produced as well as consumed by the great.

Shakespeare gives us a glimpse of this production in the odd little scene in which Hal, with the connivance of Poins, reduces the puny tapster Francis to the mechanical repetition of the word 'Anon':

> *Prince*. Nay, but hark you, Francis: for the sugar thou gavest me, 'twas a pennyworth, was't not?
> *Francis*. O Lord, I would it had been two!
> *Prince*. I will give thee for it a thousand pound. Ask me when thou wilt, and thou shalt have it.
> *Poins*. [*Within*] Francis!
> *Francis*. Anon, anon.
> *Prince*. Anon, Francis? No Francis; but tomorrow, Francis; or, Francis, a' Thursday; or indeed, Francis, when thou wilt.
> [2.4.52–60]

The Bergsonian comedy in such a moment resides in Hal's exposing a drastic reduction of human possibility: 'That ever this fellow should have fewer words than a parrot,' he says at the scene's end, 'and yet the son of a woman!' [2.4.90–91]. But the chief interest for us resides in the fact that Hal has himself produced the reduction he exposes. The fact of this production, its theatrical demonstration, implicates Hal not only in the linguistic poverty upon which he plays but in the poverty of the five years of apprenticeship Francis has yet to serve: 'Five year!' Hal exclaims, 'by'r lady, a long lease for the clinking of pewter' [2.4.40–41]. And as the Prince is implicated in the production of this oppressive order, so is he implicated in the impulse to abrogate it: 'But, Francis, darest thou be so valiant as to play the coward with thy indenture, and show it a fair pair of heels and run from it?' [2.4.41–43]. It is tempting to think of this peculiar moment—the Prince awakening the apprentice's discontent—as linked darkly with some supposed uneasiness in Hal about his own apprenticeship,[3] but if so the momentary glimpse of a revolt against authority is closed off at once with a few words of calculated obscurity designed to return Francis to his trade without enabling him to understand why he must do so:

> *Prince*. Why then your brown bastard is your only drink! for look you, Francis, your white canvas doublet will sully. In Barbary, sir, it cannot come to so much.
> *Francis*. What, sir?
> *Poins*. [*Within*] Francis!
> *Prince*. Away, you rogue, dost thou not hear them call?
> [2.4.67–72]

If Francis takes the earlier suggestion, robs his master and runs away, he will find a place for himself, the play implies, as one of the 'revolted tapsters' in Falstaff's company, men as good as dead long before they march to their deaths as upholders of the crown. Better that he should follow the drift of Hal's deliberately mystifying words and continue to clink pewter. As for the prince, his interest in the brief exchange, beyond what we have already sketched, is suggested by his boast to Poins moments before Francis enters: 'I have sounded the very base-string of humility. Sirrah, I am sworn brother to a leash of drawers and can call them all by their christen names, as Tom, Dick, and Francis' [2.4.5–8]. The prince must sound the basestring of humility if he is to know how to play all of the chords and hence to be the master of the instrument, and his ability to conceal his motives and render opaque his language offers assurance that he himself will not be played on by another.

I have spoken of such scenes in *1 Henry IV* as resembling what in Harriot's text I have called *recording*, a mode that culminates for Harriot in a glossary, the beginnings of an Algonkian–English dictionary, designed to facilitate further acts of recording and hence

3. See S. P. Zitner, 'Anon, Anon: or, a Mirror for a Magistrate', *Shakespeare Quarterly*, 19 (1968), 63–70.

to consolidate English power in Virginia. The resemblance may be seen most clearly perhaps in Hal's own glossary of tavern slang: 'They call drinking deep, dyeing scarlet: and when you breathe in your watering, they cry "hem!" and bid you play it off. To conclude, I am so good proficient in one quarter of an hour that I can drink with any tinker in his own language during my life' [2.4.13–17]. The potential value of these lessons, the functional interest to power of recording the speech of an 'under-skinker' and his mates, may be glimpsed in the expressions of loyalty that Hal laughingly recalls: 'They take it already upon their salvation that . . . when I am King of England I shall command all the good lads in Eastcheap' [2.4.8–13].

There is, it may be objected, something slightly absurd in likening such moments to aspects of Harriot's text; *1 Henry IV* is a play, not a tract for potential investors in a colonial scheme, and the only values we may be sure that Shakespeare had in mind, the argument would go, were theatrical values. But theatrical values do not exist in a realm of privileged literariness, of textual or even institutional self-referentiality. Shakespeare's theatre was not isolated by its wooden walls, nor was it merely the passive reflector of social and ideological forces that lay entirely outside of it: rather the Elizabethan and Jacobean theatre was itself a *social event*. Drama, and artistic expression in general, is never perfectly self-contained and abstract, nor can it be derived satisfactorily from the subjective consciousness of an isolated creator. Collective actions, ritual gestures, paradigms of relationship, and shared images of authority penetrate the work of art, while conversely the socially overdetermined work of art, along with a multitude of other institutions and utterances, contributes to the formation, realignment, and transmission of social practices.

Works of art are, to be sure, marked off in our culture from ordinary utterances, but this demarcation is itself a communal event and signals not the effacement of the social but rather its successful absorption into the work by implication or articulation. This absorption—the presence within the work of its social being—makes it possible, as Bakhtin[4] has argued, for art to survive the disappearance of its enabling social conditions, where ordinary utterance, more dependent upon the extraverbal pragmatic situation, drifts rapidly toward insignificance or incomprehensibility.[5] Hence art's genius for survival, its delighted reception by audiences for whom it was never intended, does not signal its freedom from all other do-

4. Mikhail Bakhtin (1895–1975), Russian literary theorist [*Editor's note*].
5. See V. N. Volosinov, *Freudianism: a Marxist Critique*, trans. I. R. Titunik, ed. Neal H. Bruss (New York: Academic Press, 1976), 93–116; the book was written by Bakhtin and published under Volosinov's name.

mains of life, nor does its inward articulation of the social confer upon it a formal coherence independent of the world outside its boundaries. On the contrary, artistic form itself is the expression of social evaluations and practices.

One might add that *1 Henry IV* itself insists that it is quite impossible to keep the interests of the theatre hermetically sealed off from the interests of power. Hal's characteristic activity is playing or, more precisely, theatrical improvisation—his parts include his father, Hotspur, Hotspur's wife, a thief in buckram, himself as prodigal and himself as penitent—and he fully understands his own behaviour through most of the play as a role that he is performing. We might expect that this role-playing gives way at the end to his true identity—'I shall hereafter', Hal has promised his father, 'be more myself' (3.2.92–93)—but with the killing of Hotspur, Hal clearly does not reject all theatrical masks but rather replaces one with another. 'The time will come', Hal declares midway through the play, 'That I shall make this northern youth exchange / His glorious deeds for my indignities' (3.2.144–46); when that time *has* come, at the play's close, Hal hides with his 'favours' (that is, a scarf or other emblem, but the word also has in the sixteenth century the sense of 'face') the dead Hotspur's 'mangled face' [5.4.95], as if to mark the completion of the exchange.

Theatricality then is not set over against power but is one of power's essential modes. In lines that anticipate Hal's promise, the angry Henry IV tells Worcester, 'I will from henceforth rather be myself, / Mighty and to be fear'd, than my condition' (1.3.5–6). 'To be oneself here means to perform one's part in the scheme of power as opposed to one's natural disposition, or what we would normally designate as the very core of the self. Indeed it is by no means clear that such a thing as a natural disposition exists in the play as anything more than a theatrical fiction; we recall that in Falstaff's hands 'instinct' itself becomes a piece of histrionic rhetoric, an improvised excuse when he is confronted with the shame of his flight from the masked prince: '[B]eware instinct—the lion will not touch the true prince. Instinct is a great matter; I was now a coward on instinct. I shall think the better of myself, and thee, during my life; I for a valiant lion, and thou for a true prince' [2.4.243–47]. Both claims—Falstaff's to natural valour, Hal's to legitimate royalty—are, the lines darkly imply, of equal merit.

Again and again in *1 Henry IV* we are tantalised by the possibility of an escape from theatricality and hence from the constant pressure of improvisational power, but we are, after all, in the theatre, and our pleasure depends upon the fact that there is no escape, and our applause ratifies the triumph of our confinement. The play then operates in the manner of its central character, charming us with its visions of breadth and solidarity, 'redeeming' itself in the end by betraying our hopes, and earning with this betrayal our slightly anxious admiration. Hence the odd balance in this play of spaciousness—the constant multiplication of separate, vividly realised realms—and claustrophobia—the absorption of all of these realms by a power at once vital and impoverished. The balance is almost eerily perfect, as if Shakespeare had somehow reached through in *1 Henry IV* to the very centre of the system of opposed and interlocking forces that held Tudor society together.

When we turn, however, to the plays that continue the chronicle of Hal's career, *2 Henry IV* and *Henry V*, not only do we find that the forces balanced in the earlier play have pulled apart—the claustrophobia triumphant in *2 Henry IV*, the spaciousness triumphant in *Henry V*—but that from this new perspective the familiar view of *1 Henry IV* as a perfectly poised play must be revised. What appeared as 'balance' may on closer inspection seem like radical instability tricked out as moral or aesthetic order; what appeared as clarity may seem now like a conjurer's trick concealing confusion in order to buy time and stave off the collapse of an illusion. Not waving but drowning.

2 Henry IV makes the characteristic operations of power less equivocal than they had been in the preceding play: there is no longer even the lingering illusion of distinct realms, each with its own system of values, its soaring visions of plenitude, and its bad dreams. There is manifestly a single system now, one based on predation and betrayal. Hotspur's intoxicating dreams of honour are dead, replaced entirely by the cold rebellion of cunning but impotent schemers. The warm, roistering sounds overheard in the tavern—sounds that seemed to signal a subversive alternative to rebellion—turn out to be the noise of a whore and bully beating a customer to death. And Falstaff, whose earlier larcenies were gilded by fantasies of innate grace, now talks of turning diseases to commodity (*2H4*, 1.2.234–35).

Only Prince Hal seems, in comparison to the earlier play, less meanly calculating, subject now to fits of weariness and confusion, though this change serves less, I think, to humanise him (as Auerbach argued in a famous essay[6]) than to make it clear that the betrayals are systematic. They happen to him and for him. He needn't any longer soliloquise his intention to 'Falsify men's hopes' by selling his wastrel friends: the sale will be brought about by the structure of things, a structure grasped in this play under the twinned names of time and necessity. So too there is no longer any need for heroic combat with a dangerous, glittering enemy like Hotspur

6. Erich Auerbach, "The Weary Prince" in *Mimesis: The Representation of Reality in Western Literature* (1968) [*Editor's note*].

(the only reminder of whose voice in this play is Pistol's parody of Marlovian swaggering); the rebels are deftly if ingloriously dispatched by the false promises of Hal's younger brother, the primly virtuous John of Lancaster. To seal his lies, Lancaster swears fittingly 'by the honour of my blood'—the cold blood, as Falstaff observes of Hal, that he inherited from his father.

The 'recording' of alien voices—the voices of those who have no power to leave literate traces of their existence—continues in this play, but without even the theatrical illusion of princely complicity. The king is still convinced that his son is a prodigal and that the kingdom will fall to ruin after his death—there is a certain peculiar consolation in the thought—but it is no longer Hal alone who declares (against all appearances) his secret commitment to disciplinary authority. Warwick assures the king that the prince's interests in the good lads of Eastcheap are entirely what they should be:

> The Prince but studies his companions
> Like a strange tongue, wherein, to gain the language,
> 'Tis needful that the most immodest word
> Be look'd upon and learnt, which once attain'd,
> Your Highness knows, comes to no further use
> But to be known and hated. So, like gross terms,
> The Prince will in the perfectness of time
> Cast off his followers, and their memory
> Shall as a pattern or a measure live,
> By which his Grace must mete the lives of other,
> Turning past evils to advantages. (*2H4*, 4.4.68–78)

At first the language analogy likens the prince's low-life excursions to the search for proficiency: perfect linguistic competence, the 'mastery' of a language, requires the fullest possible vocabulary. But the darkness of Warwick's words—'to be known and hated'—immediately pushes the goal of Hal's linguistic researches beyond proficiency. When in *1 Henry IV* Hal boasts of his mastery of tavern slang, we are allowed for a moment at least to imagine that we are witnessing a social bond, the human fellowship of the extremest top and bottom of society in a homely ritual act of drinking together. The play may make it clear, as I have argued, that there are well-defined political interests involved, but these interests may be bracketed, if only briefly, for the pleasure of imagining what Victor Turner calls 'communitas'—a union based on the momentary breaking of the hierarchical order that normally governs a community.[7] And even when we pull back from this spacious sense of union, we are permitted for much of the play to take pleasure at the

7. See, for example, Victor Turner, *Drama, Fields, and Metaphors: Symbolic Action in Human Society* (Ithaca: Cornell University Press, 1974).

least in Hal's surprising skill, the proficiency he rightly celebrates in himself.

To learn another language is to acknowledge the existence of another people and to acquire the ability to function, however crudely, within its social world. Hal's remark about drinking with any tinker in his own language suggests, if only jocularly, that for him the lower classes are virtually another people, an alien tribe—immensely more populous than his own—within the kingdom. That this perception extended beyond the confines of Shakespeare's play is suggested by the evidence that middle- and upper-class English settlers in the New World regarded the American Indians less as another race than as a version of their own lower classes: one man's tinker is another man's Indian.[8]

If Hal's glossary initially seems to resemble Harriot's, Warwick's account of Hal's practice quickly drives it past the functionalism of the word-list in the *Brief and True Report*, with its Algonkian equivalents for fire, food, shelter, and toward a different kind of glossary, one more specifically linked to the attempt to understand and control the lower classes. I refer to the sinister glossaries appended to sixteenth-century accounts of criminals and vagabonds. 'Here I set before the good reader the lewd, lousy language of these loitering lusks and lazy lorels', announces Thomas Harman, as he introduces (with a comical flourish designed to display his own rhetorical gifts) what he claims is an authentic list, compiled at great personal cost.[9] His pamphlet, *A Caveat for Common Cursitors*, is the fruit, he declares, of personal research, difficult because his informants are 'marvellous subtle and crafty'. But 'with fair flattering words, money, and good cheer', he has learned much about their ways, 'not without faithful promise made unto them never to discover their names or anything they showed me' (82). Harman cheerfully goes on to publish what they showed him, and he ends his work not only with a glossary of 'peddlar's French' but with an alphabetical list of names, so that the laws made for 'the extreme punishment' of these wicked idlers may be enforced.

It is not at all clear that Harman's subjects—upright men, doxies, Abraham men, and the like—bear any relation to social reality, any more than it is clear in the case of Doll Tearsheet or Mistress Quickly. Much of the *Caveat*, like the other cony-catching pamphlets of the period, has the air of a jest book: time-honoured tales of tricksters and rogues, dished out cunningly as realistic observation. (It is not encouraging that the rogues' term for the stocks in

8. See Karen Ordahl Kupperman, *Settling with the Indians: the Meeting of English and Indian Cultures in America, 1580–1640* (Totawa, N.J.: Rowman and Littlefield, 1980).
9. Thomas Harman, *A Caveat of Warening, for Commen Cursetors Vulgarely Called Vagabones* (1566), in Gāmini Salgādo, ed., *Cony-Catchers and Bawdy Baskets* (Harmondsworth: Penguin, 1972), 146.

which they were punished, according to Harman, is 'the harmans'.) But Harman is quite concerned to convey at least the impression of accurate observation and recording—clearly, this was among the book's selling points—and one of the principal rhetorical devices he uses to do so is the spice of betrayal: he repeatedly calls attention to his solemn promises never to reveal anything that he has been told, for his breaking of his word serves as an assurance of the accuracy and importance of what he reveals.

A middle-class Prince Hal, Harman claims that through dissembling he has gained access to a world normally hidden from his kind, and he will turn that access to the advantage of the kingdom by helping his readers to identify and eradicate the dissemblers in their midst. Harman's own personal interventions—the acts of detection and apprehension he proudly reports (or invents)—are not enough: only his book can fully expose the cunning sleights of the rogues and thereby induce the justices and shrieves to be more vigilant and punitive. Just as theatricality is thematised in the *Henry IV* plays as one of the crucial agents of royal power, so in the *Caveat for Common Cursitors* (and in much of the cony-catching literature of the period in England and France) printing is represented in the text itself as a force for social order and the detection of criminal fraud. The printed book can be widely disseminated and easily revised, so that the vagabonds' names and tricks may be known before they themselves arrive at an honest citizen's door; as if this mobility weren't quite tangible enough, Harman claims that when his pamphlet was only half-way printed, his printer helped him apprehend a particularly cunning 'counterfeit crank'—a pretended epileptic. In Harman's account the printer turns detective, first running down the street to apprehend the dissembler, then on a subsequent occasion luring him 'with fair allusions' (116) and a show of charity into the hands of the constable. With such lurid tales Harman literalises the power of the book to hunt down vagabonds and bring them to justice.

The danger of such accounts, of course, is that the ethical charge will reverse itself: the forces of order—the people, as it were, of the book—will be revealed as themselves dependent on dissembling and betrayal, and the vagabonds either as less fortunate and well-protected imitators of their betters or, alternatively, as primitive rebels against the hypocrisy of a cruel society. Exactly such a reversal seems to occur again and again in the rogue literature of the period, from the doxies and morts who answer Harman's rebukes with unfailing if spare dignity to the more articulate defenders of vice elsewhere who insist that their lives are at worst imitations of the lives of the great:

> Though your experience in the world be not so great as mine [says a cunning cheater at dice], yet am I sure ye see that no man is able to live an honest man unless he have some privy way to help himself withal, more than the world is witness of. Think you the noblemen could do as they do, if in this hard world they should maintain so great a port only upon their rent? Think you the lawyers could be such purchasers if their pleas were short, and all their judgements, justice and conscience? Suppose ye that offices would be so dearly bought, and the buyers so soon enriched, if they counted not pillage an honest point of purchase? Could merchants, without lies, false making their wares, and selling them by a crooked light, to deceive the chapman in the thread or colour, grow so soon rich and to a baron's possessions, and make all their posterity gentlemen?[1]

Yet though these reversals are at the very heart of the rogue literature, it would be as much of a mistake to regard their final effect as subversion as it would be to regard in a similar light the comparable passages—most often articulated by Falstaff—in Shakespeare's histories. The subversive voices are produced by the affirmations of order, and they are powerfully registered, but they do not undermine that order. Indeed as the example of Harman—so much cruder than Shakespeare—suggests, the order is neither possible nor fully convincing without both the presence and perception of betrayal.

This dependence on betrayal does not prevent Harman from levelling charges of hypocrisy and deep dissembling at the rogues and from urging his readers to despise and prosecute them. On the contrary, Harman's moral indignation seems paradoxically heightened by his own implication in the deceitfulness that he condemns, as if the rhetorical violence of the condemnation cleansed him of any guilt. His broken promises are acts of civility, necessary strategies for securing social well-being. The 'rowsy, ragged rabblement of rakehells' has put itself outside the bounds of civil conversation; justice consists precisely in taking whatever measures are necessary to eradicate them. Harman's false oaths are the means of identifying and ridding the community of the purveyors of false oaths. The pestilent few will 'fret, fume, swear, and stare at this my book' in which their practices, disclosed after they had received fair promises of confidentiality, are laid open, but the majority will band together in righteous reproach: 'the honourable will abhor them, the worshipful will reject them, the yeomen will sharply taunt them, the husbandmen utterly defy them, the labouring men bluntly

1. Gilbert Walker?, *A manifest detection of the moste vyle and detestable use of Diceplay* (*c.* 1552), in Salgădo, *Cony-Catchers*, 42–43.

chide them, the women with clapping hands cry out at them' (84). To like reading about vagabonds is to hate them and to approve of their ruthless betrayal.

'The right people of the play', a gifted critic of *2 Henry IV* observes, 'merge into a larger order; the wrong people resist or misuse that larger order'.[2] True enough, but like Harman's happy community of vagabond-haters, the 'larger order' of the Lancastrian State seems, in this play, to batten on the breaking of oaths. Shakespeare does not shrink from any of the felt nastiness implicit in this sorting out of the right people and the wrong people; he takes the discursive mode that he could have found in Harman and a hundred other texts and intensifies it, so that the founding of the modern State, like the founding of the modern prince, is shown to be based upon acts of calculation, intimidation, and deceit. And the demonstration of these acts is rendered an entertainment for which an audience, subject to just this State, will pay money and applaud.

There is throughout *2 Henry IV* a sense of constriction that the obsessive enumeration of details—'Thou didst swear to me upon a parcel-gilt goblet, sitting in my Dolphin chamber, at the round table by a sea-coal fire, upon Wednesday in Wheeson week. . . .'—only intensifies. We may find, in Justice Shallow's garden, a few twilight moments of release from this oppressive circumstantial and strategic constriction, but Falstaff mercilessly deflates them—and the puncturing is so wonderfully adroit, so amusing, that we welcome it: 'I do remember him at Clement's Inn, like a man made after supper of a cheese-paring. When 'a was naked, he was for all the world like a forked radish, with a head fantastically carv'd upon it with a knife' (*2H4*, 3.2.308–12).

What is left is the law of nature: the strong eat the weak. Yet this is not quite what Shakespeare invites the audience to affirm through its applause. Like Harman, Shakespeare refuses to endorse so baldly cynical a conception of the social order; instead actions that should have the effect of radically undermining authority turn out to be the props of that authority. In this play, even more cruelly than in *1 Henry IV*, moral values—justice, order, civility—are secured paradoxically through the apparent generation of their subversive contraries. Out of the squalid betrayals that preserve the State emerges the 'formal majesty' into which Hal at the close, through a final, definitive betrayal—the rejection of Falstaff—merges himself.

There are moments in *Richard II* in which the collapse of kingship seems to be confirmed in the discovery of the physical body of the ruler, the pathos of his creatural existence:

2. Norman N. Holland, in the Signet Classic edition of *2 Henry IV* (New York: New American Library, 1965), xxxvi.

> . . . throw away respect,
> Tradition, form, and ceremonious duty,
> For you have but mistook me all this while.
> I live with bread like you, feel want,
> Taste grief, need friends: subjected thus,
> How can you say to me I am a king? (*R2*, 3.2.172–77)

By the close of 2 *Henry IV* such physical limitations have been absorbed into the ideological structure, and hence justification, of kingship. It is precisely because Prince Hal lives with bread that we can understand the sacrifice that he and, for that matter, his father, have made. Unlike Richard II, Henry IV's articulation of this sacrifice is rendered by Shakespeare not as a piece of histrionic rhetoric but as a private meditation, the innermost thoughts of a troubled, weary man:

> Why rather, sleep, liest thou in smoky cribs,
> Upon uneasy pallets stretching thee,
> And hush'd with buzzing night-flies to thy slumber,
> Than in the perfum'd chambers of the great,
> Under the canopies of costly state,
> And lull'd with sound of sweetest melody? (*2H4*, 3.1.9–14)

Who knows? perhaps it is even true; perhaps in a society in which the overwhelming majority of men and women had next to nothing, the few who were rich and powerful did lie awake at night. But we should understand that this sleeplessness was not a well-kept secret: the sufferings of the great are one of the familiar themes in the literature of the governing classes in the sixteenth century. Henry IV speaks in soliloquy, but as is so often the case in Shakespeare his isolation only intensifies the sense that he is addressing a large audience: the audience of the theatre. We are invited to take measure of his suffering, to understand—here and elsewhere in the play—the costs of power. And we are invited to understand these costs in order to ratify the power, to accept the grotesque and cruelly unequal distribution of possessions: everything to the few, nothing to the many. The rulers earn, or at least pay for, their exalted position through suffering, and this suffering ennobles, if it does not exactly cleanse, the lies and betrayals upon which this position depends.

As so often Falstaff parodies this ideology, or rather—and more significantly—presents it as humbug *before* it makes its appearance as official truth. Called away from the tavern to the court, Falstaff turns to Doll and Mistress Quickly and proclaims sententiously: 'You see, my good wenches, how men of merit are sought after. The undeserver may sleep when the man of action is called on' (*2H4*, 2.4.374–77). Seconds later this rhetoric—marked out as something with which to impress whores and innkeepers to whom one owes money one does not intend to pay—recurs in the speech, and by convention of the soliloquy, the innermost thoughts of the king.

At such moments 2 *Henry IV* seems to be testing and confirming an extremely dark and disturbing hypothesis about the nature of monarchical power in England: that its moral authority rests upon a hypocrisy so deep that the hypocrites themselves believe it. 'Then (happy) low, lie down! / Uneasy lies the head that wears a crown' (*2H4*, 3.1.30–31): so the old pike tells the young dace. But the old pike actually seems to believe in his own speeches, just as he may believe that he never really sought the crown, 'But that necessity so bow'd the state / That I and greatness were compell'd to kiss' (*2H4*, 3.1.72–73). We who have privileged knowledge of the network of State betrayals and privileged access to Falstaff's cynical wisdom can make this opaque hypocrisy transparent. And yet even in 2 *Henry IV*, where the lies and the self-serving sentiments are utterly inescapable, where the illegitimacy of legitimate authority is repeatedly demonstrated, where the whole State seems—to adapt More's phrase—a conspiracy of the great to enrich and protect their interests under the name of commonwealth, even here the audience does not leave the theatre in a rebellious mood. Once again, though in a still more iron-age spirit than at the close of *1 Henry IV*, the play appears to ratify the established order, with the new-crowned Henry V merging his body into 'the great body of our state', with Falstaff despised and rejected, and with Lancaster—the cold-hearted betrayer of the rebels—left to admire his still more cold-hearted brother: 'I like this fair proceeding of the King's' (5.5.97).

The mood at the close remains, to be sure, an unpleasant one—the rejection of Falstaff has been one of the nagging 'problems' of Shakespearean criticism—but the discomfort only serves to verify Hal's claim that he has turned away his former self. If there is frustration at the harshness of the play's end, the frustration is confirmation of a carefully plotted official strategy whereby subversive perceptions are at once produced and contained:

> My father is gone wild into his grave;
> For in his tomb lie my affections,
> And with his spirits sadly I survive,
> To mock the expectation of the world,
> To frustrate prophecies, and to rase out
> Rotten opinion. . . . (*2H4*, 5.2.123–28)

The first part of *Henry IV* enables us to feel at moments that we are like Harriot, surveying a complex new world, testing upon it dark thoughts without damaging the order that those thoughts would seem to threaten. The second part of *Henry IV* suggests that we are still more like the Indians, compelled to pay homage to a system of beliefs whose fraudulence somehow only confirms their power, authenticity, and truth. The concluding play in the series, *Henry V*, insists that we have all along been both coloniser and colonised, king and subject. The play deftly registers every nuance of royal hypocrisy, ruthlessness, and bad faith, but it does so in the context of a celebration, a collective panegyric to 'This star of England', the charismatic leader who purges the commonwealth of its incorrigibles and forges the martial national State.

By yoking together diverse peoples—represented in the play by the Welshman Fluellen, the Irishman Macmorris, and the Scotsman Jamy, who fight at Agincourt alongside the loyal Englishmen—Hal symbolically tames the last wild areas in the British Isles, areas that in the sixteenth century represented, far more powerfully than any New World people, the doomed outposts of a vanishing tribalism. He does so, obviously, by launching a war of conquest against the French, but his military campaign is itself depicted as carefully founded upon acts of what I have called 'explaining'. The play opens with a notoriously elaborate account of the king's genealogical claim to the French throne, and, as we found in the comparable instances in Harriot, this ideological justification of English policy is an unsettling mixture of 'impeccable' reasoning[3] (once its initial premises are accepted) and gross self-interest. The longer the Archbishop of Canterbury continues to spin out the public justifications for an invasion he has privately said would relieve financial pressure on the Church, the more the audience is driven toward scepticism. None of the subsequent attempts at explanation and justification offers much relief: Hal continually warns his victims that they are bringing pillage and rape upon themselves by resisting him, but from the head of an invading army these arguments lack a certain moral force. Similarly, Hal's meditation on the sufferings of the great—'What infinite heart's ease / Must kings neglect that private men enjoy!'—suffers a bit from the fact that he is almost single-handedly responsible for a war that by his own account and that of the enemy is causing immense civilian misery. And after watching a scene in which anxious, frightened troops sleeplessly await the dawn, it is difficult to be fully persuaded by Hal's climactic vision of the 'slave' and 'peasant' sleeping comfortably, little knowing 'What watch the King keeps to maintain the peace' (*H5*, 4.1.283).

This apparent subversion of the glorification of the monarch has led some recent critics to view the panegyric as bitterly ironic or to argue, more plausibly, that Shakespeare's depiction of Henry V is

3. So says J. H. Walter in the New Arden edition of *Henry V* (London: Methuen, 1954), xxv.

radically ambiguous.[4] But in the light of Harriot's *Brief and True Report*, we may suggest that the subversive doubts the play continually awakens serve paradoxically to intensify the power of the king and his war, even while they cast shadows upon this power. The shadows are real enough, but they are deferred—deferred until after Essex's campaign in Ireland, after Elizabeth's reign, after the monarchy itself as a significant political institution. Deferred indeed even today, for in the wake of full-scale ironic readings and at a time in which it no longer seems to matter very much, it is not at all clear that *Henry V* can be successfully performed as subversive. For the play's enhancement of royal power is not only a matter of the deferral of doubt: the very doubts that Shakespeare raises serve not to rob the king of his charisma but to heighten it, precisely as they heighten the theatrical interest of the play; the doubt-less celebrations of royal power with which the period abounds have no theatrical force and have long since fallen into oblivion.

The audience's tension then enhances its attention; prodded by constant reminders of a gap between real and ideal, facts and values, the spectators are induced to make up the difference, to invest in the illusion of magnificence, to be dazzled by their own imaginary identification with the conqueror. The ideal king must be in large part the invention of the audience, the product of a will to conquer which is revealed to be identical to a need to submit. *Henry V* is remarkably self-conscious about this dependence upon the audience's powers of invention. The prologue's opening lines invoke a form of theatre radically unlike the one that is about to unfold: 'A kingdom for a stage, princes to act, / And monarchs to behold the swelling scene!' (*H5*, Prologue, 3–4). In such a theatre-State there would be no social distinction between the king and the spectator, the performer and the audience; all would be royal, and the role of the performance would be to transform not an actor into a king but a king into a god: 'Then should the warlike Harry, like himself, / Assume the port of Mars' (*H5*, Prologue, 5–6). This is in effect the fantasy acted out in royal masques, but Shakespeare is intensely aware that his theatre is not a courtly entertainment, that his actors are 'flat unraised spirits,' and that his spectators are hardly monarchs—'gentles all', he calls them, with fine flattery. 'Let us', the prologue begs the audience, 'On your imaginary forces work . . . For 'tis your thoughts that now must deck our kings' (*H5*, Prologue, 18, 28). This 'must' is cast in the form of an appeal and an apology—the consequence of the miserable limitations of 'this unworthy scaffold—but the necessity extends, I suggest, beyond

4. See the illuminating discussion in Norman Rabkin, *Shakespeare and the Problem of Meaning* (University of Chicago Press, 1981), 33–62.

the stage: all kings are 'decked' out by the imaginary forces of the spectators, and a sense of the limitations of king or theatre only excites a more compelling exercise of those forces.

To understand Shakespeare's whole conception of Hal, from rakehell to monarch, we need in effect a poetics of Elizabethan power, and this in turn will prove inseparable, in crucial respects, from a poetics of the theatre. Testing, recording, and explaining are elements in this poetics that is inseparably bound up with the figure of Queen Elizabeth, a ruler without a standing army, without a highly developed bureaucracy, without an extensive police force, a ruler whose power is constituted in theatrical celebrations of royal glory and theatrical violence visited upon the enemies of that glory. Power that relies upon a massive police apparatus, a strong, middle-class nuclear family, an elaborate school system, power that dreams of a panopticon in which the most intimate secrets are open to the view of an invisible authority,[5] such power will have as its appropriate aesthetic form the realist novel;[6] Elizabethan power, by contrast, depends upon its privileged visibility. As in a theatre, the audience must be powerfully engaged by this visible presence while at the same time held at a certain respectful distance from it. 'We princes', Elizabeth told a deputation of Lords and Common in 1586, 'are set on stages in the sight and view of all the world.'[7]

Royal power is manifested to its subjects as in a theatre, and the subjects are at once absorbed by the instructive, delightful, or terrible spectacles, and forbidden intervention or deep intimacy. The play of authority depends upon spectators—'For 'tis your thoughts that now must deck our kings'—but the performance is made to seem entirely beyond the control of those whose 'imaginary forces' actually confer upon it its significance and force. These matters, Thomas More imagines the common people saying of one such spectacle, 'be king's games, as it were stage plays, and for the more part played upon scaffolds. In which poor men be but the lookers-on. And they that wise be will meddle no farther'.[8] Within this theatrical setting, there is a remarkable insistence upon the paradoxes, ambiguities, and tensions of authority, but this apparent production of subversion is, as we have already seen, the very condition of power. I should add that this condition is not a theoretical necessity of theatrical power in general but an historical phenomenon, the

5. In Michel Foucault's discussions of a hegemonic society, a panopticon is an idealized prison in which all prisoners may be observed at all times [*Editor's note*].
6. For a brilliant exploration of this hypothesis, see D.A. Miller, 'The Novel and the Police', *Glyph*, 8 (1981), 127–47.
7. Quoted in J. E. Neale, *Elizabeth I and her Parliaments, 1584–1601*, 2 vols. (London: Cape, 1965), II, 119.
8. *The History of King Richard III*, ed. R. S. Sylvester, in *The Complete Works of St. Thomas More*, vol. 3 (New Haven: Yale University Press, 1963), p. 80.

particular mode of this particular culture. 'In sixteenth century England', writes Clifford Geertz, comparing Elizabethan and Majapahit royal progresses, 'the political centre of society was the point at which the tension between the passions that power excited and the ideals it was supposed to serve was screwed to its highest pitch. . . . In fourteenth century Java, the centre was the point at which such tension disappeared in a blaze of cosmic symmetry.'[9]

It is precisely because of the English form of absolutist theatricality that Shakespeare's drama, written for a theatre subject to State censorship, can be so relentlessly subversive: the form itself, as a primary expression of Renaissance power, contains the radical doubts it continually provokes. There are moments in Shakespeare's career—*King Lear* is the greatest example—in which the process of containment is strained to the breaking point, but the histories consistently pull back from such extreme pressure. And we are free to locate and pay homage to the plays' doubts only because they no longer threaten us. There is subversion, no end of subversion, only not for us.

SCOTT MCMILLIN

[Performing *1 Henry IV*]†

One decisive change marks the stage history of *1 Henry IV*, and it occurred in the twentieth century. What had been a 'Falstaff' play or, on occasion, a 'Hotspur' play—a play about one or both of the most flamboyant characters—came in the twentieth century to be seen as a study of political power with Prince Hal as the central character. That change of emphasis required a change of format. It takes both parts of *Henry IV* followed by *Henry V* to make Prince Hal into a fully-fledged hero, or anti-hero, and it was not until the mid-twentieth century that an influential cycle of these plays—influential enough to be imitated in later productions—was staged in the English theatre.

When it was first performed, in about 1596, *1 Henry IV* was immediately a Falstaff play. The fat knight was being quoted as though everyone knew his lines. 'Honour pricks them on,' says a

9. Clifford Geertz, 'Centers, Kings and Charisma: Reflections on the Symbolics of Power', in *Culture and its Creators: Essays in Honour of Edward Shils*, ed. Joseph Ben-David and Terry Nichols Clark (University of Chicago Press, 1977), 160.

† From Scott McMillin, *Henry IV, Part One,* "Shakespeare in Performance" series (Manchester: Manchester University Press, 1991), 1–13, 115–122. Reprinted by permission of the author.

letter of 1598 about a military venture of the day, 'and the world thinks that honour will quickly prick them off again'.[1] In the same year, which is also the year the play was first published, the Earl of Essex made a joke about a friend's sister being married to Sir John Falstaff, and before long the Countess of Southampton was making an unkind remark about Falstaff being the father of someone's child.[2] No other Shakespearian character can be found circulating in social discourse so soon after appearing on the stage or in print.

Some of the early notoriety probably stemmed from the controversy over Falstaff's name (for he was originally meant to be Sir John Oldcastle, a comic version of the famous Protestant martyr, and Shakespeare was apparently pressured to write in a new name), but the stage character was famous in his own right. The title page of the first edition does not mention Prince Hal and promises more of a battle 'between the King and Lord Henry Percy' than actually takes place at Shrewsbury, but with an eye for the trade it names the comic element accurately enough: 'With the humorous conceits of Sir John Falstaff.' Queen Elizabeth is said to have requested a play showing 'Sir John in love', and it is sometimes thought this is how *The Merry Wives of Windsor* came to be written. The existence of the rumour, not its veracity, illustrates the character's popularity. At the court of James I, the two *Henry IV* plays were sometimes known as 'Falstaff, Parts One and Two'.

Part One was one of the most popular Shakespeare plays after the Restoration, and the list of actors who played Falstaff and Hotspur includes almost every famous male performer in the history of the English-speaking theatre. To follow the more luminous names to 1900, Hotspur was undertaken by Thomas Betterton, Barton Booth, David Garrick (not successfully), J. P. and Charles Kemble, R. W. Elliston, William Macready, Edmund and Charles Kean, and Henry Wallack; Falstaff by William Cartwright, Betterton, James Quin, Stephen and Charles Kemble, Elliston, Samuel Phelps, James Hackett, and Beerbohm Tree. These are not generally regarded as good roles for women, but Ludia Webb played Falstaff in 1786 (*New York Times*, 29 June 1990). So long as *Part One* is staged by itself, Falstaff ends at the peak of his renown, full of resiliency. For a moment it seems the fat knight is dead at Shrewsbury, but then he gets to his feet—a comic adventure in itself sometimes—and claims for his own the victory Hal has earned over Hotspur. For nearly three centuries, with *Part One* usually being played by itself, the plot ended with Hotspur defeated and Falstaff claiming victory. It is no wonder that the play was regarded both as

1. William Shakespeare, *1 Henry IV*, ed. David Bevington (Oxford, 1987), 2.
2. Samuel B. Hemingway, ed., *New Variorum Edition of Henry IV, Part 1* (Philadelphia, 1936), 446.

historical romance with Hotspur as its centre of heroic pathos and as a comedy with Falstaff as its presiding spirit.

Part Two was occasionally performed in the same repertory as *Part One* during the seventeenth and eighteenth centuries, but the change of emphasis that makes Prince Hal the central character requires *Henry V* as well, and there is no evidence that the three plays were performed as a sequence during the first 250 years of their existence. The first recorded cycle of Shakespearian histories was produced by the nineteenth-century German director Franz Dingelstedt, who began with *1 Henry IV* in Munich in 1851 and gradually built up a connected series of seven histories over the next thirteen years.[3] Dingelstedt had moved to Weimar by the time his series was complete, and there the 1864 tercentenary celebration of Shakespeare's birth was centred on something the English theatre would not attempt for another 100 years (and then most of the English would think they were first), a series of *seven* successive Shakespearian histories played in rotation, the entire cycle taking a week to perform.

The English began with smaller cycles. If we define 'cycle' as three or more connected plays, the first recorded one in England was staged by Frank Benson at Stratford-upon-Avon in 1905–06. But Benson cut and rearranged the plays severely and even left *1 Henry IV* out of the fullest version of the series, preferring *Part Two* as a link between *Richard II* and *Henry V.* The Benson cycles—there were several combinations, sometimes including Marlowe's *Edward II*—certainly drew attention, and W. B. Yeats left behind an admiring comment that is still cherished at the Shakespeare Centre in Stratford about how one play supports another. But Benson's idea did not spread into the English theatre at large, and it cannot be deemed influential. The next notable history series occurred thirty years later in Pasadena, California, where the Community Playhouse staged successive productions of all *ten* English history plays in 1935, with one play closing before the next opened. That heroic effort probably deserves a book to itself, but if we are searching for the first virtually uncut cycle on the model of repeatable sequences, as Wagner's *Ring* cycle is staged by the boldest opera companies, the first example we find in England is Stratford's contribution to the Festival of Britain in 1951, where *Richard II*, the two parts of *Henry IV*, and *Henry V* were staged on a single set by a single company in repertory fashion. That is the production that brought about the modern change in our understanding of the plays and made Prince Hal/Henry V the central character. Since then, the most in-

3. Simon Williams, *Shakespeare on the German Stage*, vol. 1 (Cambridge, 1990), 153–54; Robert K. Sarlos, "Dingelstadt's Celebration of the Tercentenary: Shakespeare's Histories as a Cycle," *Theatre Survey* 5 (1964), 117–31.

fluential productions of *1 Henry IV* have belonged to sequences in which the Prince, an apparent rapscallion, attains a well-planned maturity at the Battle of Shrewsbury, passes beyond his victory over Hotspur to the reconciliation with his father and the rejection of Falstaff in *Part Two,* then establishes further proof of royal authority in the unexpected victory over France at Agincourt in *Henry V.*

One result of the modern emphasis on cycles is that the importance of Prince Hal/Henry V in Shakespeare's writing has become apparent. I am not sure it has been noted before that Shakespeare wrote more lines for this character than for any other—more than for Hamlet, more than for Richard III, more than for Falstaff (who comes second). But those lines for Hal/Henry V are stretched over three plays which were not seen together in the days of 'Falstaff' or 'Hotspur' attractions, and it required the staying-power and financing of twentieth-century institutional theatre to take on the task of staging history plays in cycles that would make Shakespeare's most extensive study of political characterisation fully evident.

The question necessarily arises: did Shakespeare plan things this way? Did he set out to write a cycle of plays on English history? Did he discover the opportunity for such a cycle somewhere in the course of writing the individual plays? Or—a heretical thought today—did he remain unconcerned about a cycle all along, leaving the whole idea to be discovered 300 to 400 years later under the pressures of Germanic bardolatry, scholarly study, and Festivals of Britain? Not for an instant should it be thought that these questions can be answered. The producers of the modern cycles have claimed they were following Shakespeare's intentions, but the earlier producers of the individual 'Falstaff' and 'Hotspur' plays were sure of his intentions too, and so were most scholars through the ages—Shakespeare's 'intentions' being a hyperuranian lucky-bag that one can dip into for a boost of confidence on any occasion. As with most matters before he drew up his will (and even that raises problems), Shakespeare left no record of his intentions—certainly none about the 'cycle'.

In the absence of the facts, scholars have been able to speak freely about the implications of the plays themselves. Some have found a grand design connecting not only *Part One* to *Part Two* but also this two-part play to *Richard II* before it and *Henry V* after it. This is the series staged at Stratford in 1951 and it has become known as the 'second tetralogy' among cycle advocates, the other 'tetralogy' being the three parts of *Henry VI* and *Richard III*, which Shakespeare wrote earlier. In 1964, when the Royal Shakespeare Company celebrated the 400th anniversary of Shakespeare's birth, they caught up with the Weimar example of 100 years earlier by staging both tetralogies, the eight plays being boiled down to seven thanks to some shrewd cutting and rewriting in the earlier pieces. Behind these cycles of 1951 and 1964 lay a work of scholarship that was influential in forming the 'grand design' theory, E. M. W. Tillyard's *Shakespeare's History Plays.* Behind *that* lay something more profound, the real source of the scholarly and theatrical 'grand design' thinking in England. I refer to the English experience of the Second World War and the desire to assert the continuing dominance of the nation's culture after the devastation of the German bombings.

This combination of nationalism, scholarship, and theatre production has left a deep impression. It is virtually impossible for a major London company to stage *1 Henry IV* today without at least wishing to connect that play to something besides itself and make a cycle of some sort. Moreover, the ambition to perform history cycles has spread to North America. It is a sign of the change I am discussing that Stratford, Ontario performed a major cycle of the histories between 1964 and 1967 in celebration of the Canadian centenary; that Ashland, Oregon connected *Richard II* and the two parts of *Henry IV* over three seasons between 1970 and 1972; that the CSC Repertory Company in New York did the same three plays in one season in 1979; and that the US Naval Academy reduced those three plus *Henry V* into two plays in 1984. Cycle-thinking has been on the upswing. Although recent scholarly opinion has rejected Tillyard's broader claims about the design of the two tetralogies, the general opinion remains tilted towards a belief that if the author's intentions could be known, they would show Shakespeare to have been something of a cycle-thinker too, albeit one who discovered some of the connections as he went along.

Shakespeare's own acting company probably did not stage anything like a cycle. Even two-part plays, of which there were many in the Elizabethan period, were not always performed on successive days. Such evidence as remains about the day-by-day Elizabethan repertory—none of it from Shakespeare's company, incidentally—shows that two-part plays such as Marlowe's *Tamburlaine* were staged in tandem less often than as separate pieces. Nothing from the Elizabethan theatre suggests that the better part of a week of a busy commercial repertory would have been given over to a series of plays in one vein. Variety was the hallmark of the repertory system. Whatever we claim about the intentions of the author, it is unlikely that Shakespeare's company ever gave him a first or second tetralogy in successive performances. What has happened to the *Henrys* in the institutional theatre since 1951 is probably a true English innovation (the producers do not seem to have known of the German examples), and our nervous claims about following Shakespeare's intentions might as well give way to an admission that the modern Shakespearian theatre has been branching out on its own.

In the theatre of the Restoration and eighteenth century, it was hard not to approve of Falstaff. The moral earnestness by which the modern age has come to regard him as dangerous and wicked may be a return to Elizabethan thinking, as some scholars maintain, but the ages in between found him funny and sometimes grand. Joseph Addison approved of him in 1711 because 'he turns the ridicule on him that attacks him', Corbyn Morris in 1744 because 'he is happy himself and makes you happy', Samuel Johnson in 1765 because 'his licentiousness is not so offensive but that it may be borne for his mirth', although there is an additional Johnsonian note that 'neither wit nor honesty ought to think themselves safe with such a companion' (Hemingway, 404–5). In the later eighteenth century Maurice Morgann wrote the first extended study of a Shakespearian character, the first in the mode of psychological essays that treat characters as though they are real persons. He did not inquire whether Hamlet was able to make up his mind or Lady Macbeth was obsessed with infantile guilt. He inquired if Falstaff was truly a coward—and found that he was vigorous, amiable, and courageous. Actors knew well enough not to bother with this deeper consideration, and they went on portraying Falstaff as a coward, albeit one confident enough to turn cowardice to his advantage. At the end of *Part One*, when he converts his battlefield fears into a stolen reputation for bravery and becomes the hero of the Battle of Shrewsbury, it is hard not to agree that such panache deserves admiration. Even Prince Hal seems a bit appreciative. So long as *1 Henry IV* was staged by itself, there was certainly little reason to think that someone so adept and amusing should be *rejected*.

The history cycles staged since the Second World War, however, have been rife with rejection for Falstaff. Turning the old man aside is a key manoeuvre in Hal's growth to political power. The actual rejection occurs in *Part Two*, but the *Part One* play-acting scene at the Boar's Head, where Falstaff and Hal take turns acting the role of King, is one of the fixing-points for productions today, because the eventual rejection is being prefigured as Hal takes the mock crown from Falstaff and mounts the mock throne. In the 1951 cycle, Richard Burton's Hal grew vehement and intense as he hurled the series of epithets against Falstaff, 'that trunk of humours, that bolting-hutch of beastliness, that swollen parcel of dropsies', and so on, to 'wherein villainous, but in all things? Wherein worthy, but in nothing?' [2.4.401–02, 408–09]. The rejection was virtually occurring already in Burton's growing seriousness of tone, and it is now standard in the theatre to use the final lines of the exchange—Hal's

'I do, I will' in answer to Falstaff's 'Banish plump Jack and banish all the world'—as a profound moment of realisation, on everyone's part, that Falstaff will suffer rejection when the moment is ripe for Hal's royal personality to be declared.

The theatre of the eighteenth and early nineteenth centuries greeted this profound episode by cutting it entirely. The tavern scene 'is vastly too long', declared the acting version published in 1773, which goes back to James Quin's version of the earlier eighteenth century on this point: 'therefore it is curtailed of a mock trial the author introduced; which rather checked and loaded the main business, notwithstanding a vein of pure comedy runs through it'.[4] In other words, it is funny but not funny enough, and what stands in the way of the comedy is the play-acting, which we find the centre of importance. The King's role also suffered major cuts in the early eighteenth century. Betterton's version of 1700, for example, reduced the opening speech to ten lines, and forty-five of the King's lines were cut from his later interview with Prince Hal (3.2; Hemingway, 502). These political elements were gradually restored during the first half of the nineteenth century, although it is reported that Abraham Lincoln, for one, still wondered why the play-acting scene should be cut.[5]

The other major episode to be reduced during much of the eighteenth and nineteenth centuries was the Welsh scene [3.1] in which the rebel leaders argue over the division of the kingdom and things are brought to a calmer close by the singing of Lady Mortimer. The Betterton version of 1700 kept the quarrel between the men but ended the scene before the entrance of the women, thus avoiding the need to write the Welsh dialogue and song for Lady Mortimer, but also avoiding one of the few decent moments for actresses in the entire play. The 1773 edition cut the entire Glendower episode, calling it 'a wild scene . . . which is properly rejected in the representation' (Odell, 2:41). To a modern way of thinking, again, such an opinion is hard to credit. The Welsh scene fleshes out the rebellion by showing how its leaders act when they are apart from the King and free to be themselves, but its true brilliance is the elaborate confidence of the writing, especially when the women come in. To introduce Lady Mortimer and the issue of her Welsh language may be unnecessary to the narrative, but it deepens the characterisation and ideas of the rebel side. Then to pursue that elaboration to the interlude of the song—where Welsh takes over the theatre in music and word, putting rebellion to rest for a minute—is to let an inner voice sound against the main busi-

4. George C. D. Odell, *Shakespeare from Betterton to Irving*, 2 vols. (New York, 1966), 2:41.
5. A. C. Sprague, *Shakespeare's Histories: Plays for the Stage* (London, 1964), 62–63.

ness of political scheming. It is a difficult scene to stage, with its music, its call for a distinct female role which does not appear elsewhere, the ability in Welsh that is required. Life in the theatre is easier without these inner voices, but not as good. What I have called the confidence of the writing is actually confidence in a theatre company. I take this scene as a sign that Shakespeare's company was very certain of itself and its audience by the later 1590s, and the elimination of the Welsh scene during the thriving theatre of the eighteenth century may indicate how unusual it is to reach that stage of company development.

The earlier nineteenth century gradually restored the text of these scenes and added a new element to the play. Falstaff and Hotspur were still the main roles, but now they were joined by the astonishing technology that developed in the theatre and was capable of drawing audiences for its own sake. A production at Covent Garden in 1824 was advertised by a listing of the scenery one would surely go out of one's way to see (Odell, 2:174). 'Shrewsbury from the Field of Battle' was one of these—a distant view of Shrewsbury itself in perspective behind the battle that bears its name. (The Old Vic production of 1945 * * * was still using such a view, although in other respects it had been freed of elaborate scenery.) The victory over Hotspur would be concluded by an impression of sunset in the Victorian theatre, although this was not as stunning as the other major lighting opportunity, moonlight for the Gadshill robbery. Stages were enlarged to serve as arenas for these visual effects, and for episodes like the Battle of Shrewsbury enormous crowd scenes became the fashion. For the 1864 London tercentenary celebration, with *Part One* being done by itself, the Drury Lane stage filled with what looked like real armies by the fifth act: 'The Shrewsbury battle-field was divided by a long ridge, and the numerous combatants, arrayed in bright armour, were concealed under its shelter, until, rising from the ambush, they filled the stage with their glittering figures, all in vivid action and stirring conflict' (*Illustrated London News*, 2 April 1864). By this time, the Welsh scene and the play-acting segment had been restored, so it was virtually the full text that was being treated to such sumptuousness.

The twentieth-century theatre brought a reaction against Victorian pictorialism. Scenic realism and large-scale archaeological reconstructions were found to be cloying, and research into the original conditions of Elizabethan theatres showed that Shakespeare wrote for a relatively unadorned stage on which scenes could follow one another at rapid pace. Scenic effects were recognised to be in the language of the plays. The technology of the previous age was retained, of course, but it now served the interests of streamlined and supple designs which allowed directors and designers to create non-realistic environments for their productions. Quickening the pace of Shakespearian staging also opened the way for the combined performances of the two parts of *Henry IV* on the same day—not quite up to a cycle but pointing the way. Barry Jackson staged the two parts of *Henry IV* on the same day at the Birmingham Repertory Theatre in 1921, and the Stratford Memorial company performed the two parts in matinée–evening combination in 1932 to celebrate the opening of their new theatre. These double-bills were special events, but they indicate an increasing tendency in modern repertory companies to include *Part Two* in the same repertory as *Part One*.

* * * John Burrell's [production] for the Old Vic in 1945 reflects these twentieth-century developments: a simplified stage design (apart from Shrewsbury) and the inclusion of *Part Two* in repertory with *Part One*. Ralph Richardson's performance as Falstaff became legendary, especially because of the dimension *Part Two* gave him: he could combine the traditional comedy of *Part One* with forebodings of the rejection to follow in the next play. While this was a modern production in design and directorial conception, however, it also belonged to the centuries-old tradition of centring on famous actors in the roles of Hotspur and Falstaff. Laurence Olivier as Hotspur and Richardson as Falstaff drew most of the attention, although they were in fact surrounded by a first-rate Old Vic ensemble. Prince Hal did not attract much comment.

The giant step to a cycle was taken by the Shakespeare Memorial Theatre Company in 1951, which staged the second tetralogy, running from *Richard II* through *Henry V*, under the direction of Anthony Quayle. This is the production which established the cycle format as the modern mode for the histories [and was followed by] the 1964 Stratford cycle of seven histories, which raised Peter Hall's new Royal Shakespeare Company to world-wide influence. * * * Terry Hands' 1975 four-play cycle (three *Henrys* plus *The Merry Wives of Windsor*) for a scaled-down Royal Shakespeare Company * * * emphasised the psychological anxieties that might be thought to obtain between a royal father and a royal son. That series hardly brought the Royal Shakespeare Company's engagement with history cycles to a close, but some signs of strain apparent in the institutional surroundings of the 1975 production suggest that the excitement and fresh thinking of 1951 and 1964 could not be expected to last forever in one organisation.

* * * Orson Welles' [film] *Chimes at Midnight* of 1966 * * * usefully contradicts the expansionist tendency of the cycles by condensing the Falstaff plays into one two-hour viewing. This may look like a return to the Falstaff-centred productions of the past, but by my interpretation Welles is actually displacing Falstaff through cin-

ematic technique, and by anyone's interpretation the film matters more for its wordless episodes than for its portrayal of any one character. Its achievement concerns the film medium *per se*: * * * the BBC television version of 1979 * * * seems to me a failure because it refuses to do what Welles did so well, use the potential of the medium. The best feature of the BBC version is its preservation of Anthony Quayle's Falstaff, for Quayle had also played the role in the 1951 cycle, and by the time the BBC version was made, his was one of the most settled and assured Falstaffs of which we have any record at all.

* * * A new company in the mid-1980s, the English Shakespeare Company, offered an irreverent version of the cycle. Beginning from conditions that could hardly promise success—no theatre of their own, for example—this troupe opened with a *1 Henry IV* that brushed the usual pieties about Shakespeare and history into the dustbin. This was part of a cycle of *1 and 2 Henry IV* plus *Henry V* from the start, but within a year of their initial success, the company expanded the cycle to seven plays, each of them disturbing the usual notions of how these pieces should be staged. Thus they were covering the same immense territory that the Royal Shakespeare Company covered in 1964—eight of Shakespeare's histories performed as seven plays—but they were doing the entire cycle on the road, venturing across large portions of the world, and shattering some of the settled images of English history. I fancy that in touring foreign countries with their own account of English history they were imitating Henry V more closely than the anti-royalist outlook of their productions should have allowed them to do, but they also retained an admirable sense of Eastcheap attitudes: they were still without a theatre of their own, for example, and were still ready to overturn settled opinions. That is to say, *they* hadn't rejected Falstaff and his point of view even while they employed something of Henry V's overseas ambitions.

A word should be added here about the theatre as an institution * * *. The Old Vic production of 1945 was connected to efforts behind the scenes to turn the Richardson—Olivier—Burrell company into the nucleus of the long-sought National Theatre. The Stratford cycle of 1951 was part of the transformation that was brought about at the Shakespeare Memorial Theatre after the war. The 1963–64 cycle brought a new Royal Shakespeare Company out of the Stratford organisation and helped it become the most influential English company of the 1960s. The 1975 cycle served to resolve a financial crisis in the same company. I have not hesitated to refer to the institutional politics discernible behind productions of our play, although my primary concern is to describe what happened on stage and how that was received in the audience. The play's the thing, to be sure, although Hamlet's famous line goes straight on to a remark about the conscience of the King; and that alignment of the theatrical and the political is worth retaining.

The politics of the institutional theatre are not exactly remote from the politics in *1 Henry IV.* The modern subsidised theatre helps cycles be staged, and cycles make Falstaff a figure to be rejected. That is what happens to *1 Henry IV* in its modern cycle-oriented treatments: the Prince grows into royal authority by turning aside the old fat man, and it is government subsidy that provides the wherewithal—some of the wherewithal, because it is never enough—to let this lesson be dramatised.

Theatre people will know that this cannot be the final word. The theatre is too subversive for that. For one thing, the shift to cycle-thinking that has occurred in the institutional theatre has not caused isolated productions of *1 Henry IV* to dwindle among smaller companies. *1 Henry IV* continues to be performed as a single play throughout the English-speaking world, and I would imagine that most readers of this book first encountered it that way—without the actual rejection of Falstaff, and without the Prince becoming a King. I saw my first production—and worked on it, too—in an American university in the 1950s. We took on *1 Henry IV* because it was a great challenge. The play requires a larger capable company than do most of the comedies and tragedies, but it also requires what the comedies and tragedies always require, something special at the top, in this case a Falstaff who can live up to the reputation of the role, the reputation that was built up by Betterton, Quin, and the other famous Falstaffs over the long course of the English stage. We tried to stress the political roles of Prince Hal and Henry IV, for we knew what Stratford had done in 1951. Our director had read Tillyard and in part believed it. More to the point, he *played* Henry IV, and was not interested in marginalising himself. Our Falstaff was well-read too. He tried to subordinate his performance to the political design. After all, this was a university.

But Falstaff still stole the show—and he stole it because of the way the play comes to an end, with Falstaff's comic survival at the Battle of Shrewsbury and his outrageous trick of stealing Prince Hal's victory over Hotspur. That is not quite the ending, of course, but the final lines about further rebellion and so on did not make us think we ought to be staging *Part Two* as well and even looking ahead to *Henry V.* That is for the institutional theatre. Our production was complete with the closure Falstaff gave it, and I think this must still be the experience of many theatregoers. I have checked the American Shakespeare productions listed in *Shakespeare Quarterly* over recent years, and I find that *1 Henry IV* has been staged by itself in New Hampshire, Maine, Vermont, Massachusetts, California, Colorado, Washington, North Carolina, Illinois, Texas, Ohio, New Jersey, Alabama, Utah, Oregon, New York, Connecticut, Indiana, Pennsylvania, and the District of Columbia. The list is bound to be incomplete. Every one of the United States has surely had this play on the boards in the past quarter-century, and this is not exactly North American subject matter. I would not begin to count the productions staged in the provincial repertory companies, university drama departments, and local theatres of the nation whose history Shakespeare was actually writing about, let alone the rest of the English-speaking world.

* * * Falstaff cannot be rejected so emphatically as cycle-thinkers, including Shakespeare if he was one, would ask us to believe he should. * * * Orson Welles was practising some Falstaffian ruses as producer of *Chimes at Midnight* * * * and I believe the extraordinary visual rhythm of the film comes from an artistic imagination that resembles Falstaff's way of seeing the world. His rejection by Prince Hal is dutifully shown (again and again, as it turns out), but the Falstaffian way of seeing, if I am right about it, is inherent in the technique of the film and cannot be eliminated. As for the English Shakespeare Company, another aspect of Falstaff lies behind the iconoclasm of their version of English history, but I also have in mind the interaction between the director, Michael Bogdanov, and John Woodvine, who played Falstaff. I believe my impression is shared by others that these two were not a perfect match, the one an actor experienced in the classics, the other a director antagonistic to classicism; and the wonderful Falstaff that resulted had an air of negotiation about him, as though good theatre could be produced by people who learn from one another without losing their individuality. This Falstaff was rejected in the cycle too, of course, but it was too late. He had already arrived to stay in the planning stages, as an attitude of risk-taking and anti-establishment thinking that directors and actors can build on. It is a pleasure to let this survey of *1 Henry IV* come to a close with a company that carried a scandalous version of English history the world over—cultural imperialists to be sure, but impious ones, prepared to act as though Jack Falstaff and the theatre could still co-operate in the spirit of Misrule.

* * *

* * * The Falklands War was recent history when this production took shape, and some early rehearsals were held at the Mountbatten RAF base near Plymouth, where real troopers in camouflage—minor imitations of Falstaff—were preparing for war rehearsals in the Channel.[6] Anti-imperialism was a strong and consistent theme

6. Marianne Ackerman, "Mirvish, Marx, and Shakespeare," *Canadian Theatre Review* 50 (1987), 64.

in this version of Hal's 'development' into the warrior-King of Agincourt.

The interview scene between father and son was a study of unpredictability. Hal's first response to his father's rebuke, a speech in which he is supposed to 'beg' extenuation, was delivered as a mock set-piece, the sort of cynicism with which he has been driving his father wild for years. Probably the father has replied with the same lecture before: you are just like Richard II, you mingle too easily with popularity, you don't know how to stage yourself sparingly as a King must do. On and on he went in this vein, and Pennington's Hal was ready to twiddle his thumbs. He knew all about staging himself—his first soliloquy was an essay in how he would stage himself when the time was right—and the lecture he was hearing was really a demonstration of how little the father knew his son.

But something snapped in Hal when the King compared him to Hotspur. This is where the battle will really be fought, Hal thought—the battle for his father's admiration as well as the battle for his own authority—and Pennington opened himself to his father in a fury, vowing to 'tear the reckoning' from Percy's heart (3.2.152). That Hal could reveal himself to his father only in terms of violence seemed true and frightening. The hero of Agincourt was making himself apparent, his future greatness taking shape here in the anger of a son whose father does not know him, and a son who lacks the maturity to let himself be known.

From here it would have been easy to end the interview on a note of reconciliation, but this production rarely settled for something easy. The text makes it look as though the father and son are in harmony, as they exchange hyperboles:

> *Hal*. And I will die a hundred thousand deaths
> Ere break the smallest parcel of this vow.
> *King*. A hundred thousand rebels die in this! (3.2.158–60)

But Pennington rejected the King's embrace on 'a hundred thousand rebels', as though he could not let his father close the circle. They were no closer at the end than at the beginning of this brilliant, unsettling scene. How little Hal would give to this rigid father was stunningly clear, as was the violence that would erupt in the kingdom from their refusal to understand each other.

Part of the shock of this encounter was Hal's costume, for to this interview with his Victorian-clad father he wore torn blue jeans. This father and son were so far out of touch they came from different periods. But a mixture of period styles ran through the entire production. Bogdanov's trademark is Shakespeare in modern dress, but even he thought the single combat between Hal and Hotspur at

Shrewsbury required armour and swords. Rather than give in to period costuming throughout, Bogdanov and his costumer Stephanie Howard held back on their decisions and let the actors have something to say as they worked into their roles. Most productions begin with the actors looking at costume designs which have already been laid out for them, but in this case the costume decisions were left open while the company spent their early rehearsals listening to Bogdanov talk about Shakespeare and history, then 'putting the scenes on the floor' to see how they might look. The intention was to observe the images given off by the actors as they rehearsed and to let the costuming reflect those images. Pennington himself felt that denim and hiking boots were right for Hal in the Eastcheap scenes (he told me in an interview). This would set the Prince's adolescence apart from the punk and leather attitudes of the other young people there. It would also, Pennington said, reflect something of his own observations of adolescence. Blue jeans on the Prince of Wales were one of the images the critics found shocking, but there is no doubt that holding costume decisions open until well along in rehearsals helped create the charged immediacy of Pennington's performance.

Bogdanov and Stephanie Howard gradually worked out visual ideas for each group: the northern rebels wore bits and pieces picked from the rail, in a 'pot-pourri of rebellion through the ages' (Stephanie Howard's phrase, in an interview with me), while the King and courtiers needed something more consistent, as befits power on display. Bogdanov favoured modern business suits at first, as part of his career-long campaign to stereotype the bureaucrat, but Stephanie Howard and the actors wanted formal dress from the past, and it was finally agreed to use Victorian frock-coats and scarlet tunics as a way of giving a 'layering' of period to the power image. The decision was important. It broadened the reference to power, for these ministers of state in the opening scene, for example, looked like Victorians while using the media technology of today (the microphone) to present what were, after all, fifteenth-century political references. This took the 'heart' out of the King's opening complaint in 'So shaken as we are . . . and supplied a political point instead. His confessional mode on guilt and the hope for repentance now became a media presentation: Henry IV and Richard Nixon had something in common, and they looked like Gladstone.[7]

7. Making the King's opening speech into a press-conference had been done in a modern-dress production at Santa Cruz, California, in 1984. For a full account of this version, see Mary Judith Dunbar, '*Henry IV* and *The Tempest* at Santa Cruz,' *Shakespeare Quarterly* 35 (1984), 475–76 and Alan Dessen, 'Staging Shakespeare's History Plays in 1984: A Tale of Three Henrys," *Shakespeare Quarterly* 36 (1985), 71–79. Costuming from various periods was used in Joan Littlewood's production for the Edinburgh Festival in 1964 and in the Indiana Repertory Theatre's production at Indianapolis in 1984.

The different periods of dress offended those who favour proper history. Giles Gordon complained that 'the crucial hierarchical distinctions of fifteenth century England go for nothing' (*London Daily News*, 23 March 1987), Michael Billington found the effect 'reductive and confusing' (*Guardian*, 23 March 1987), and Irving Wardle thought the sense of history had been lost (*The Times*, 23 March 1987). Even those who praised the production wondered at the 'anything goes' spirit, with Robin Ray comparing Bogdanov to 'a berserk chef' whipping up a stir-fry and 'using anything and everything available' (*Punch*, 8 April 1987). One of the intentions of the production was liable to be lost in such complaints, for the costuming at its best was more than a *mélange* and did have a logic to it.

Take the tavern scenes, for example. Everyone saw the modern costuming: Hal in blue jeans danced with a punked-up Doll Tearsheet (Jenny Quayle in black leather bustier, mini-skirt, torn fishnet tights, and ankle boots). The on-stage band, 'Sneak's Noise', was amplified. But the drawers and background customers were out of the nineteenth century: waistcoats, britches, long dresses. If Hal and Doll were rocking in an East End pub of today, the others were Dickensian. Falstaff, in his outrageously loud checked trousers, was in a world of his own. Where was this tavern? When? There was no way to answer those questions, but the consistency within the layers and the contrast between them—the punk layer set against the nineteenth-century layer—made the questions impossible to disregard. This was not an 'anything goes' timelessness. It was instead an England of partial consistencies, the elements refusing to fit with one another but refusing to collapse into randomness either. Hal's job would be to whip this diversity into a shape of his own design as the cycle of plays progressed; but here in the tavern scenes, while he was still looking for opportunities and finding his way, something valuable was on display. This variegated England was not polite, and certainly not wealthy, but it was, of all things, when one stopped to consider it, civilised.

Of course Hal paused in the middle of 'I do, I will.' He was not discovering something spontaneously, as Richard Burton had done. He had seen the opportunity coming, had planned it a little ahead: a chance to practise the role he would later take on. This Hal could freeze the heart at moments, and if it is accurate to call the layered tavern scenes 'civilised' even with their disreputability and unruliness, one also has to admit that the Hal who can reject what he does not find useful and force the rest into an instrument of overseas destruction is despicable. The taunting of Francis, the drawer, illustrates the point. Hal was a little drunk by this time, and was being utterly malicious. Even Poins thought this joke pointless. But

John Tramper's delicately etched Francis loved the Prince no matter what games were being played. His 'anon, anon' to Poins was not the cry of a servant torn in two directions, but the acknowledgment of a small nuisance named Poins off to the side. Who is this man to be bothering me—the Prince is here! Francis was magnetised by Hal even as he was being manipulated. This kind of allegiance can be beneficial if the authority be sound and confident, but Hal had to twist it to his own neurotic ends, building it through jingoism and manipulation into the psychology of mob-hooliganism that would eventually produce victory at Agincourt. In *Henry V* the actor of Francis played the Boy killed at Agincourt, and the visual reminder was unmistakable.

That is what eventually happened. But in the tavern scenes the ruthless Hal was only momentarily apparent. He had his civilised side too. To protect Falstaff from the authorities who enter at the end of the first tavern scene, Hal summoned an astonishing Gadshill to play a Mozartian tune on his flute. Gadshill had his head shaved bald, except for an enormous Mohican plume that arose from his skull. He was aggressively punk—strong men would cross the King's Road to avoid him. (The same actor, Andrew Jarvis, would play Richard III when the cycle was complete.) But in the world of this tavern, he could improvise ravishing melodies on his flute. When the Lord Chief Justice himself came after Falstaff (there was no Sheriff in this production, and the Chief Justice's role in *Part Two* was being established here), he was confronted by a Prince tipped back in his chair, eyes closed in rapture, waving his finger in accompaniment to a classical flute played by a Mohawked punk bully-boy in a tavern that might have been in Eastcheap, Dickens, or Stepney-heath. There was nothing a Chief Justice could do in such circumstances. He just stood there. Power cannot gain a foothold in the face of such incongruity. To make power wait until the comedy and the beauty are played out is what I mean by calling the tavern scenes 'civilised,' and the Hal who had just chilled everyone with his treatment of Francis and his 'I do, I will' to Falstaff now looked like he had humorous and humane possibilities after all.

Hotspur appears in 2.4 reading a letter about the rebellion. Olivier, standing with one foot on the ground, the other on a chair, so that his doublet was riding high and his tight-fitted legs could be seen, played this moment for its statuesque effect. Who has ever read a letter with one foot on a chair? But he looked good, especially in his neatly trimmed ginger beard. In Bogdanov's production John Price read the letter stripped to the waist, shaving, his face covered with lather. Not many letters have been read that way either, but shaving put Hotspur into motion from the beginning, and in motion he remained. Price was a vibrant, physical Hotspur, full of energy and a bit thick, the sort who might actually dive in and try to pluck up drowned honour by the locks. Only one person was a physical match for him, and that was Lady Percy (played with marvellous energy by Jennie Stoller). Their 'argument' scene was a rough-and-tumble delight. Against this roistering Hotspur, however, it was clear that Pennington's Hal, cringing from physical contact, would not stand up in single combat.

Indeed, when it came to single combat at the Battle of Shrewsbury, Hotspur had the fight won. Pennington played the only Hal who actually lost the single combat. Hotspur was stronger and more of a fighter. He knocked the sword and shield out of Hal's hands and forced him to his knees. It was all over for the Prince of Wales, who was cowering and praying to some unknown deity, waiting for the fatal blow to strike from behind. He was saved by his opponent's chivalry—Hotspur would not kill an unarmed man. There was no trace of Merrie-England nostalgia about this chivalry. It was a code of honour long past its prime and vulnerable to the political manipulations of the other rebel leaders (Worcester and Northumberland could get Hotspur to do anything they wanted by heating his blood over a question of honour). Now, with Hal down and helpless in the single combat, chivalry intervened as a piece of stupidity. Hotspur bent over to slide Hal's sword back to him, and within an instant Hal was driving that sword into him from behind.

This was the moment the 1945 Old Vic production had immortalised when Hal completed Hotspur's stutter on 'worms'. Pennington's Hal had no interest in such formality. He stole the line away from Hotspur as he again drove his sword into the back of his enemy's neck. This was the Hal who vowed he would 'tear the reckoning' from Hotspur's heart, and he was being true to his promise. What that truth indicated for England, however, was hard to name. Hotspur's code of chivalry, outdated though it was, at least had recognisable standards of behaviour, but Hal's victory asserted nothing but his own determination to gain credit before a society and a father who refused to take him as seriously as he took himself. So, with luck, he used violence to establish his credibility, and it did not work. Hal was staging himself without an audience, and his violence looked like a back-alley killing. That oddly private part of the battlefield where Shakespeare sets the single combat could now be understood. Virtually no one sees the single combat in which Hal thinks to emerge a hero. The unseen theatrical performance is superfluous, as Falstaff knows. Nothing *remains* superfluous in the presence of Falstaff (his huge girth is a metaphor of that), and as John Woodvine stole the corpse away then returned with it in the next scene when an audience was available, to present 'his' prize before the King, one realised that Hal—having rubbed out the system of chivalry in killing Hotspur—was now being outdone by the system that has taken over in modern politics, the system of theatrical publicity.

Hal was left virtually alone at the end of this production. His father had stalked away thinking him a liar, Falstaff had walked off with the honours of Shrewsbury, his brother (Prince John) had seized the opportunity to sneer at him once more, and that sneer represented the attitude of the ruling class whose leader he was supposed to become. As Hal exited alone, he raised his sword over his head in an odd gesture of bitterness. The same gesture had been made earlier by a character with whom Hal should have little in common—the rebel Douglas. Douglas is no future king. The bald Andrew Jarvis played him as the last Scotsman on the face of the earth, kilted and stripped to the waist, overcoming his vulnerability by sheer fury. He would raise his swords (for he fought with two swords and no shield) over his head in a sort of Highlands Kung Fu gesture of individualism. Douglas had no father, no family, no crown to strive for, no commitment beyond the combat of the moment. For Hal to reflect Douglas for a second was a sign of his isolation and the futility of his design for heroism. No future King was evident at the end of *Part One*.

As Hal exited, a figure stood to the side of the stage, playing a mournful melody on a flute. It was, of all people, Douglas. Or, to put it more exactly, it was Andrew Jarvis still dressed as Douglas, the Andrew Jarvis who appeared in various roles when flute music was needed. He had been Gadshill, outrageously punked, playing the flute in the tavern scene, and he had been one of the Welsh musicians at Glendower's castle. His flute music was always quiet and mournful, in contrast to the amplified Christian chorales and fugues sponsored by the royal family. The flute was the sound of societies being wiped out by the dynasty—the Eastcheap world, the Welsh world, the Douglas world, rebels all of them, and unlike the royal family capable of hearing something subtle and natural—ragtag people, capable of violence but also capable of preserving the culture. This final image of Hal's isolated exit with the flute heard off to the side suggested the thoughtful care that lay behind this production. Hal's gesture made one think of Douglas and his simple fury, a sign of adolescent failure, but Douglas himself was standing to the side, without a sword now, playing a flute, the flute being played by the actor who had threaded his sad music through Eastcheap, Wales, and now Shrewsbury, the music of a rebellion that had the remnants of real culture within it. This is what Hal had to destroy. Not that it was particularly worth saving. The Eastcheap people were crooked, the Welsh unreliable, the Percies a bit stupid. Flute melodies can only go so far in building a culture. As I have mentioned, this production ruled out the sentimental possibilities. Its combination of iconoclasm and intelligence provided something that sentimentality can never approach, however—an opportunity to think beyond the staged moment to other parts of the production, and beyond those to other royal families, other rebellions, other authorities whose power is based on insecurity and the use of force. By refusing to dress 'England' in any one period, Bogdanov and the company portrayed a nation whose variegation was still distinct but threatened by the establishment of a centralised government with no strength beyond publicity and violence. That this government arose in the fifteenth century was no more certain than that it was arising today—and both possibilities were certain enough to dislodge the Shakespeare history plays from the national pride they often serve and make them a source of watchful anger instead.

DAVID SCOTT KASTAN

"The King Hath Many Marching in His Coats," or, What Did You Do in the War, Daddy?†

> Out of many, one: a logical impossibility; a piece of poetry, or symbolism; an enacted or incarnate metaphor; a poetic creation.
>
> —Norman O. Brown, *Love's Body*

If *1 Henry IV* can be said to be "about" anything, it is about the production of power, an issue as acute in the early years of the reign of Henry IV as in the final years of the aging Elizabeth when the play was written. Henry has, of course, the problem of how to consolidate and maintain his authority, having deposed Richard who ruled by lineal succession. Elizabeth inherited her crown, but, in the complex religio-political world of post-Reformation England, her ability to succeed her Catholic half-sister was in some consid-

† David Scott Kastan, " 'The King Hath Many Marching in His Coats,' or What Did You Do in the War, Daddy?" in Ivo Kamps, ed., *Shakespeare Left and Right* (New York: Routledge, 1991), 241–58. Reprinted by permission of Routledge, Inc., part of The Taylor & Francis Group.

I would like to thank David Bevington, Barbara Bono, Art Efron, and Coppélia Kahn for generously arranging occasions on which parts of this paper were delivered and discussed. In addition to the valuable responses I received on those occasions, the comments and criticism of Jean Howard, James Shapiro, Peter Saccio, and Peter Stallybrass have continually pointed me toward the essay I should be writing.

erable doubt until the day before her accession, and, like Henry, she would rule over a divided country and similarly face a rebellion of Northern nobility led by the Percy family.[1]

Understandably "shaken" and "wan with care" (1.1.1),[2] Henry recognizes the fragility of his delegitimized political position. In deposing Richard, exposing the insubstantiality of the assertions of sacred majesty, Henry's own claims of rightful authority ring hollow. His access to the powerful ideology of order is necessarily limited, as his presence on the throne reveals its tendentiousness. "Thus ever did rebellion find rebuke" (5.5.1), Henry chides Worcester, asserting the inevitability of the victory of legitimacy, but certainly Henry's own rebellion found no such "rebuke," as he successfully opposed Richard's legitimate kingship.

Henry rules over a nation whose boundaries are insecure and whose integrity is under attack from within. He is at war with the Scots in the North, the Welsh in the West, and the very nobles that helped him to power now oppose his rule. Henry's discussion of his intended crusade is then both an understandable fantasy of national unity and a strategy for its production. The national identity torn by civil war would be reformed in common purpose. The unitary state, "All of one nature, of one substance bred" (1.1.11), would be produced in opposition to an alien and barbaric "other," almost precisely the way an idea of an orderly and coherent English nation was fashioned in Elizabethan England largely by reference to the alterity and inferiority of the Irish.[3] Henry promises

> To chase these pagans in those holy fields
> Over whose acres walk'd those blessed feet
> Which fourteen hundred years ago were nail'd
> For our advantage on the bitter cross. (1.1.24–27)

Henry would construct through the agency of the holy war the national unity he desperately seeks. The nation that

1. Lily B. Campbell has called attention to the ways in which Shakespeare's presentation of the events of the reign of Henry IV necessarily recalled for "an English audience of the last years of the sixteenth century" recent English history and contemporary concerns (229–44). While her sense of the political meanings of Shakespeare's play seems to me unduly prescriptive, her reconstruction of the contemporary resonances of the events of the reign of Henry IV provides a useful corrective to almost exclusive focus of historical critics on the parallel provided by Elizabeth's notorious "I am Richard II, know ye not that?"
2. All quotations are from the Arden editions of the plays: *1 Henry IV* (ed. A. R. Humphreys), 2 *Henry IV* (ed. A. R. Humphreys), *Richard II* (ed. Peter Ure), *Henry V* (ed. J. H. Walter), *The Merchant of Venice* (ed. John Russell Brown), and *Hamlet* (ed. Harold Jenkins).
3. Recently a number of studies of English colonialism have insisted that "the cultural products which celebrated the supremacy of Englishness were based upon differences and discrimination and ensure that the positional superiority of the English was produced through the 'otherness' and inferiority of alien people of which the Irish were one" (Cairns and Richards 7).

> Did lately meet in the intestine shock
> And furious close of civil butchery,
> Shall now, in mutual well-beseeming ranks,
> March all one way. . . . (1.1.12–15)

Henry knows, of course, that in fact his nation does not "march all one way," but is sharply divided by class loyalties, ethnic conflicts, and regional concerns, differences purposefully organized in hierarchies of inequality. The reality of his kingdom—of any kingdom—is that it is multiple and heterogeneous, a loose aggregation of individuals, families, counties, etc., all with local and sectarian interests and commitments. The desire to undertake the crusade articulates a familiar fantasy of political incorporation, a utopian solution to the problems of difference; but Henry must acknowledge it as a fantasy denied by present circumstance:

> But this our purpose now is twelve month old,
> And bootless 'tis to tell you we will go. (1.1.28–29)

A similar insistence upon an imaginary unity marked the production of power in Elizabethan England. The familiar political metaphors of the well-ordered body or the patriarchal family articulate the would-be absolutist state's desire for an integral wholeness, and the multiple historical and mythological typologies of Elizabeth did the same. Elizabeth, the Tudor Rose, representing the unification of aristocratic factions, was also Deborah, uniting secular and divine authority, and Diana, expressing in her chastity the inviolability of the Queen's body and the body politic.[4] A nation that since mid-century had experienced five forms of official religion, endured four changes of monarch, the reign of each marked by a significant rebellion, and that now faced further instability as Elizabeth ruled without an heir and over a country whose traditional social and economic structures were changing with the pressures and possibilities of a nascent capitalism, no doubt demanded the various tropes of the integrity of the virgin Queen and the sovereign nation for which she stood. In the prologue of Dekker's *Old Fortunatus* (1599), an old man speaks of Eliza: "Some call her Pandora, some Gloriana, some Cynthia, some Belphoebe, some Astraea, all by several names to express several loves. Yet all those names make but one celestial body, as all those loves meet to create but one soul." And, if almost hysterically, Nicholas Breton, in his "Character of Queen Elizabeth," similarly finds a radical unity in the representations of the Queen:

> was shee not as she wrote herself *semper eadem* alwaies one? zealous in one religion, believinge in one god, constant in one

4. For extensive discussion of these mythological identifications, see Elkin Calhoun Wilson's *England's Eliza* (*passim*), as well as Frances A. Yates's *Astraea* (88–111).

> truth, absolute vnder god in her self, one Queene, and but one Queene; for in her dayes was no such Queene; one Phoenix for her spiritt, one Angell for her person, and one Goddesse for her wisedome; one alwayes in her word, one alwayes of her word, and one alwaies, in one word ELIZABETHA βασιλεθέα, a princelie goddesse, Elizabeth a deliverer of godes people from their spiritual thraldome and a provider for their rest: one chosen by one god to be then the one and onlie Queene of this one kingdome, of one Isle. . . . (Breton 2, n.p.)

Not least of the inadequacies of this is that the "one isle" contained in fact *two* kingdoms: England and Scotland, as well as the conquered principality of Wales; but such fantasies of imperial unity, however attractive, always occlude the reality that their unity is constructed only through acts of exclusion and homogenization. In Elizabethan England this was achieved by ideological configuration and political repression that either violently eliminated marginal subgroups—such as gypsies, witches, vagabonds, the Irish—from the articulation of the English nation or discursively arranged them into stable and stabilizing hierarchies. In *1 Henry IV*, with the rebels routed, Henry orders his forces to follow up their advantage and extinguish the remaining pockets of resistance:

> Rebellion in this land shall lose his sway,
> Meeting the check of such another day,
> And since this business so far is done,
> Let us not leave till all our own be won. (5.5.41–44)

The homonymic pun (inexact but recognizable in late sixteenth-century London English) between "won" and "one" exactly enacts the political process of unification, verbally reconciling what can only be coerced. "Winning" is "oneing," we might say, but the processes of incorporation involve always a more violent repression of difference than can be admitted. In complex society, only what is "won" is "one."

The play registers its unreconciled social disjunctions generically. The comic plot voices what the unitary state would repress, indeed exactly what the unitary *plot* would repress. Criticism has delighted in demonstrating the play's aesthetic unity by showing how the comic plot "serves" the historical plot, functions as a *sub*plot clarifying the "main" plot. But the play seems to me less coherent—not therefore less interesting or good, but less willing to organize its disparate voices into hierarchies—than such demonstrations of its putative unity would allow. The formal coherence that critics have demanded from the play can be achieved only by subordinating subplot to main plot, commoners to aristocrats, comedy to history—by imposing, that is, the same hierarchies of privilege and power that exist in the slate upon the play. But the play does not so readily subordinate its comedy. Though Thomas Fuller in 1662 objected that Falstaff was merely "the property of pleasure" for Hal "to abuse" (408), the fat knight resists all efforts completely to subjugate him to the prince's desires or designs. "The humorous conceits of Sir John Falstaff" in fact share the title page of the 1598 Quarto with "the battell at Shrewsburie . . ." as the most notable aspects of *The History of Henrie the Fourth.* And indeed throughout the seventeenth century, the play was as likely to be called *Falstaff* as *Henry IV.* On New Year's Night in 1625, for example, the play entitled *The First Part of Sir John Falstaff* was presented before the Prince at Whitehall.

If this striking inversion of the traditional relationship of history and comedy perhaps overestimates the domination of Falstaff, it does reveal the inadequacy of the familiar critical demonstrations of the play's unity. Certainly the comic plot gives voice to what is silent in the historical plot. I don't mean by this merely that the comic plot includes social elements absent from the "main" plot or even that the comic plot speaks the reality of class differentiation and domination that the aristocratic historical plot ignores or idealizes, though no doubt Hal's arrogant joking at the expense of Francis, for example, does do this. I mean something more radical: that the very existence of a comic plot serves to counter the totalizing fantasies of power, to expose and disrupt the hierarchies upon which they depend. History is displayed as something other—something more extensive, however less stable—than merely the history of what Renaissance historians characteristically called "matters of slate." The play, however, insists that history is not identical with state politics, indeed that the history of state politics inevitably and purposefully erases other histories—histories of women or of the poor, for example—histories whose very existence contests the story that the hegemonic state would tell of itself.

To find in the play the ready subordination of comedy to history that has become the norm of formalist accounts of *1 Henry IV* is to accept Hal's version of events for Shakespeare's, or rather, it is to *behave* as Hal, to presume that the Tavern world exists only for the production of aristocratic pleasure and value. Yet most accounts of the unity of the play's two plots do exactly this. They analyze the comic plot's thematic relation to the "main" plot, finding that it parallels or parodies the historical action. In either case, the analysis reproduces the priority and privilege of aristocratic history. The comedy is seen to exist primarily to clarify the meaning of the serious plot, thus unwittingly performing a formalist version of Stephen Greenblatt's elegant demonstration of the containment of subversion in the play and in Renaissance England.

For Greenblatt, as he argues in his influential article, "Invisible Bullets," the play, like the culture of Renaissance England, contains, in both senses of the world, the potential subversions of its counter-cultures. The play's comic energies are never able effectively to challenge the claims and claimants of power: "The subversiveness which is genuine and radical . . . is at the same time contained by the power it would appear to threaten. Indeed the subversiveness is the very product of that power and furthers its ends" (Greenblatt, *Negotiations,* 30).[5] Thus, the actions and values of the Tavern world are denied any disruptive effect; they serve to legitimate and consolidate political power rather than to contest it. Hal is seen as a master actor, merely playing at prodigality to achieve a purchase on rule. "The unyoked humour of [his] idleness" (1.2.191), which seems a potential subversion of Hal's political destiny and desire, is revealed instead to be a "product" of that desire, designed to further "its ends," a carefully calculated intemperance designed to make his "reformation" the more extraordinary. Hal's insistent role-playing, which finds its essential form in the Tavern, Greenblatt concludes, is then not opposed to power but rather "one of power's essential modes" (46); and the comic plot is, therefore, not an alternative to the monological voice of aristocratic history but finally its justification.

This discussion of what could be called Hal's power play leads to Greenblatt's argument that the play enacts precisely the forms of power that dominated Elizabethan England. Certainly Elizabeth's rule was marked by an insistent theatricality, as perhaps it had to be in the absence of effective agencies of coercive control. Sir Robert Naunton said that he knew

> no prince living that was so tender of honor and so exactly stood for the preservation of sovereignty, that was so great a courter of her people, yea, of the commons, that stooped and descended lower in presenting her person to the public view as she passed in her progresses and perambulations. . . . (44)

From the moment her accession to the throne was assured, Elizabeth was almost compulsively concerned with "presenting her person to the public view," that is, with representing herself, aware that her rule could be—and perhaps could *only* be—constituted and confirmed theatrically.

While certainly we need to recognize the relationship between Shakespeare's dramatic practices and Elizabethan political condi-

5. Compare C. L. Barber's argument that "misrule works . . . to consolidate rule" (205), and Leonard Tennenhouse's assertion that in the history plays "the figures of carnival will play a particularly instrumental role in the idealizing process that proves so crucial in legitimizing political power" (83).

tions if ever we are to historicize our understanding of his plays, nonetheless, it seems important, and fortunately possible, to distinguish between the theatricalized world of Elizabethan politics and the politicized world of the Elizabethan theater. "Royal power" may be, as Greenblatt claims, "manifested to its subjects as in a theater" (65) but the simile must not be quickly collapsed into an identity as it has often been by those who see the theater merely producing and legitimizing the ideology of royal power. *Nullum simile est idem*, as was said proverbially. Royal power is not manifested to its subjects *in* the theater, only *as* in the theater. The simile would make the various modes of a culture's production homologies, occluding their uneven development that becomes a source of social contradiction, a space for the resistance to power that Greenblatt's argument precludes. The labile and unlegitimated representations of the popular theater prevent the drama, regardless of any overt political intentions of its playwrights or patrons, from simply reproducing the dominant ideology, and clearly theatrical representation was never, as the insistent governmental efforts to supervise and control its production attest, merely a vehicle for the reproduction of royal authority.

As much recent scholarship on the institution of the Elizabethan theater has demonstrated, Shakespeare's theater was oddly liminal—geographically, socially, and politically.[6] Located in the Liberties, it was both part and not part of the City, which no doubt was appropriate for the home of a commercial acting company that was both dependent and not dependent upon its aristocratic patron; and actors, deemed rogues, vagabonds, and beggars by the 1572 Poor Act, became formally members of aristocratic households, in the case of the King's men even entitled to call themselves gentlemen. These contradictions of the theater were the inescapable conditions of its playing and suggest that the spectacle of rule was not merely reproduced in its representations but redistributed and dislocated.

The modes of representation in the popular theater of Elizabethan England, as Robert Weimann has shown, refuse to privilege what is represented. Its staging practices, which shifted the action between an upstage *locus* and a downstage *plataea*, continually displace the dominant aristocratic ideology, submitting its postures and assumptions to the interrogation of clowns and commoners (*Popular Tradition*, 208–55). Both on stage and in the playhouse itself, the popular theater mixed linguistic and social consciousness. "The toe of the peasant," as Hamlet says, or, at least of the artisan,

6. See, for example, Mullaney, esp. 26–39; and Montrose, "Purpose" 53–76, each of whom provocatively discusses the contradictory institutional, social, and geographical locations of Elizabethan playing.

"comes so near the heel of the courtier, he galls his kibe" (*Hamlet* 5.1.136—38). Artisan and courtier confronted one another in the theater as they confronted one another on the stage. The public theaters thus produced the situation that Bakhtin saw as characteristic of the Renaissance itself, in which the aristocratic and the common, the sacred and the vulgar, the elite and the popular "frankly and intensely peered into each other's faces" (*Rabelais* 465).[7] Diverse accents and dialects, styles and values sounded, clashed, and sometimes blended, the polyphony challenging the homogenizing and unifying pressure of the theater of state: a drama that in presenting the spectacle of power reveals the fantasy of univocality that must be exposed and modified by the heterogeneity it anxiously denies.

But in the public theater that heterogeneity found full expression, its diverse social and formal modalities expressed in the generic hybrids that came to dominate the stage. John Florio, in his *Second Frutes*, includes a dialogue about the state of the English theater which holds that the plays are "neither right comedies, nor right tragedies," but "representations of histories, without any decorum" (Sig. D4[r]). Florio, of course, is echoing Sidney, who had grumbled that the native drama contained "neither right tragedies, nor right comedies, mingling kings and clowns, not because the matter so carrieth it, but thrust in the clown by head and shoulders to play a part in majestical matters with neither decency nor discretion, so as neither the admiration and commiseration, nor the right sportfulness, is by their mongrel tragi-comedy achieved" (114). Words like "mongrel," "mingle-mangle," "gallimaufrey" appear again and again to describe, or at least to protest, these increasingly common miscegenated forms. In 1597, probably the year *1 Henry IV* was first performed, Joseph Hall, in his *Virgidemiarum*, complained about what he termed the "goodly *hoch-poch*" that results "when vile *Russetings* / Are match't with monarchs, & with mighty kings" (*The Poems*, 15). But in the popular theater, and certainly in *1 Henry IV*, kings and clowns did mingle; disparate languages and conventions regularly—or better, irregularly—shared the stage, com-peting for attention and control.

But this brings us back to Falstaff. No doubt it must be said of him, in Sidney's words, that he plays "his part in majestical matters with neither decency nor discretion." Indeed Hal does say it, as he upbraids Falstaff on the battlefield for having a bottle of sack instead of his pistol: "What, is it a time to jest and dally now?" (5.3.55). But Falstaff refuses to privilege "majestical matters" any

7. Cf. Annabel Patterson's suggestive account of the "complex social phenomenon" that was the popular theater, comparing it to the cafe-concerts in the Paris of Napoleon III: both were "scandalous in their apparent jumble of classes, itself a result of new social mobilities; and, more subtly, this very social mélange was itself a form of theater, a two-way impersonation" (18).

more than the play does. Hal privileges them. They provide the telos of his Prodigal Son play, but not of Shakespeare's mingle-mangle. Falstaff's lack of decency and discretion is the sign of the play's resistance to the totalizations of power, massive evidence of the heterogeneity that will not be made one. His exuberance and excess will not be incorporated into the stabilizing hierarchies of the body politic.

Revealingly, when he imagines his life in the impending reign of Henry V, he thinks in terms of his social role:

> let us be Diana's foresters, gentlemen of the shade, minions of the moon; and let men say we be men of good government, being governed as the sea is, by our noble and chaste mistress the moon. . . ." [1.2.22]

This is the exact fantasy of social order in the England of Elizabeth, the virgin Queen. She of course was Diana in one of the familiar political mythologies that surrounded her, and her loyal subjects would be "men of good government, being governed . . . by our noble and chaste mistress." But for Falstaff this is not a submission to authority but an authorization of transgression; he serves not the monarch whose motto, as Nicholas Breton insisted, was "*semper eadem* alwaies one," but only the changeable moon, "under whose countenance we steal" [1.2.25].

Falstaff, then, is one of "the moon's men" [1.2.27], endlessly ebbing and flowing instead of filling a fixed place in a stable social hierarchy. He resists incorporation either into the hierarchical logic of the unitary state or that of the unified play. Nonetheless, Hal attempts to fix him. However much the Prince enjoys his banter with Falstaff, it is clear that Hal is using the fat knight to construct his own political identity. Hal is only a temporary inhabitant of the underworld of Eastcheap, and that only to make his inevitable assumption of responsibility the more remarkable and desired:

> I . . . will awhile uphold
> The unyok'd humour of your idleness.
> Yet herein will I imitate the sun,
> Who doth permit the base contagious clouds
> To smother up his beauty from the world,
> That, when he please again to be himself,
> Being wanted he be more wonder'd at. . . . [1.2.168–74]

This is, of course, exactly the political strategy of King Henry, though the King mistakes his son's behavior for real rather than a carefully managed prodigality. In act 3, scene 2, when he rebukes Hal for his "inordinate and low desires," the King worries that Hal has put his authority at risk. Henry is not worried about the state of

Hal's soul but about Hal as the soul of the state. Clearly the issues are political not moral; what is at stake is the production of power.

> Had I so lavish of my presence been,
> So common-hackney'd in the eyes of men,
> So stale and cheap to vulgar company,
> Opinion, that did help me to the crown,
> Had still kept loyal to possession. . . . (3.2.39–43)

Henry would turn his aristocratic aloofness into a political asset: "By being seldom seen, I could not stir / But like a comet I was wonder'd at . . ." (3.2.46–47). Henry anticipates Edward Forset's assertion in 1606 that "seeing that both God and the Soule, working so vnlimitably, be yet vndiscerned, in their essence, as hidden and concealed from the eyes of men; it may seeme to stand more with maieste, and to work more regarding, more admiring, and more adoring if (howsoeuer their power doth shew it selfe) yet their presence be more sparing & lesse familiarly vouchsafed" (Sig. E1[r]). No doubt Forset here reflects King James's particular imperial style, his distaste for, as opposed to Elizabeth's apparent delight in, the theatricalizations of power by which it is constituted. But James, no less than Elizabeth, knew that it was precisely in the ability of the monarch to "work more regarding, more admiring, and more adoring" that sovereign authority resides. The spectacular presence of rule is the very condition of its power.

Certainly it is Henry's understanding that power is not merely confirmed but actually constituted theatrically that leads him to fear that Hal has alienated opinion with his "rude society" (3.2.14). Hal seems to Henry too much like Richard, who

> Grew a companion to the common streets,
> Enfeoff'd himself to popularity
> . . . .
> So, when he had occasion to be seen,
> He was but as the cuckoo is in June,
> Heard, not regarded; seen, but with such eyes
> As, sick and blunted with community,
> Afford no extraordinary gaze,
> Such as is bent on sun-like majesty
> When it shines seldom in admiring eyes. . . . (3.2.68–69, 74–80)

In his carousing, Hal has become similarly familiar, a "common sight" (3.2.88), affording no "extraordinary gaze" to the people and so apparently derogating his authority as Richard had his own: "thou hast lost thy princely privilege / With vile participation" (3.2.86–87).

Though obviously his father misrecognizes Hal's behavior, what is interesting is that for Henry, "participation" is "vile," "community" sickens, "popularity" enslaves. The familiar watchwords of modern democracy sound dangerously to the King who in deposing Richard has brought power into range of popular contestation or control. Nonetheless, in spite of the distinction Henry draws between a "common sight" and an "extraordinary gaze," his conception of majesty as what Hobbes resonantly termed "visible Power" (129),[8] silently demands and authorizes an audience of commoners as a condition of its authority. If a spectacular sovereignty would construct power in its "privileged visibility" (Greenblatt, *Negotiations* 64), it risks, as Christopher Pye has written, reducing "the sovereign to the object of the spectator's unseen and masterfully panoptic gaze" (43). However reluctantly, a spectacular sovereignty must acknowledge the people's constitutive role even as it seeks to constrain, if not deny, it. "Opinion did help [him] to the crown," Henry knows, but it is a hypostatized "Opinion" that he acknowledges, erasing the agency of the people who must hold it.

Similarly, in his emphasis upon the "extraordinary gaze," Henry seeks to escape the destabilizing political implications of the subjection of the sovereign to the "admiring eyes" of his subjects. The unacknowledgeable power of the viewing subject is registered in Henry's disgust that Richard was "daily swallow'd by men's eyes" (3.2.70), and his own escape from the threat of this power is achieved through verbal magic: "My presence, like a robe pontifical, / [was] Ne'er seen but wondered at. . . . " (3.2.56–57). Most immediately, of course, this means that each time he was seen he was an object of wonder, but the lines must also mean that he was "ne'er seen" at all, only wondered at. This is the strategy by which spectacular sovereignty denies that its viewing subjects are the source of its power. The king is never seen, never subjected to the gaze of his subjects; he is only wondered at, subjecting them to his spectacular presence. The spectacle of the monarch must dazzle those it would captivate. Sidney calls Elizabeth "the only sun that dazzeleth their eyes" (52), and, with a similar understanding, in *Henry V*, Hal, now King, promises to unleash his power in France:

> I will rise there with so fully a glory
> That I will dazzle all the eyes of France,
> Yea, strike the Dauphin blind to look on us. (*H5*, 1.2.278–80)

But the English monarch must first "dazzle all the eyes of" England, eyes that are at once constitutive of and captivated by his

8. Christopher Pye has brilliantly applied Hobbes to the problem of political and theatrical representation in the Renaissance, finding in Hobbes's account of the constitution of sovereignty a means to explore "the vulnerability and the terrifying power of the monarch's visible presence" (43–81). * * *

spectacular sovereignty, and strike them "blind" that they not recognize their productive power; and it is this fundamental contradiction—unacknowledged and unresolved—underwriting the notion of spectacular authority that leads Henry IV to identify the legitimate Richard with the apparent political liabilities of Hal, and his own course with the rebel Hotspur.

> As thou art to this hour was Richard then
> When I from France set foot at Ravenspurgh,
> And even as I was then is Percy now. (3.2.94–96)

No doubt, in part this represents a residual class loyalty. Hotspur's aristocratic ambition would hold an inevitable appeal for the man who, in returning from exile to reclaim his ducal inheritance and achieving the crown, similarly asserted aristocratic privilege against the absolutist assertions of the King. But Henry has always been attracted to Hotspur, earlier admitting his envy of Northumberland and his hope that "some night-tripping fairy had exchang'd / In cradle-clothes our children where they lay, / And call'd mine Percy, his Plantagenet!" (1.1.86–88). But however much Hotspur is the child of Henry's desire, clearly Hal is the child of his loins. Henry's hope is only a displacement of his knowledge of the illegitimacy of his rule. His identification with Hotspur is his unintended acknowledgment that his conception of sovereignty opens a space for resistance, empowering precisely those whom it would subject.

Henry's unnecessary advice to Hal is based on the idea that the destabilizing potential glimpsed in the conception of spectacular sovereignty can be kept under control by carefully managing its representation, by controlling what is made available to "admiring eyes" to ensure that it dazzles. But the play recognizes a similar instability lurking in the representations themselves, and nowhere more obviously than in act 5, in scenes 3 and 4. There the play explicitly becomes a representation *of* representation, as the rebels at Shrewsbury encounter various nobles "semblably furnish'd like the King himself" (5.3.21). Holinshed reports that Douglas "slew Sir Walter Blunt and three other appareled in the King's suit and clothing, saying, I marvell to see so many kings thus suddenlie arise one in the necke of an other." But Holinshed's narrative of the battle immediately goes on to emphasize the King's own actions: "The king in deed was raised, & did that daie manie a noble feat of armes, for as it is written, he slue that daie with his owne hands six and thirtie persons of his enimies" (Sig. Eee2^{r}).

Shakespeare's dramatic account of Shrewsbury, however, erases the King's powerful and decisive intervention in the battle. Royal power appears in the play exclusively in represented form, and where the King is present on the battlefield, he must be saved in his confrontation with Douglas by the intervention of the Prince. In a sense the multiple representations of the King at Shrewsbury (literally his lieu-tenants, his place-holders) can be seen not to weaken the idea of sovereign power but to literalize its operations; the state depends upon the authority of the sovereign being successfully communicated in acts of representation in various modalities. Power is both the effect of representation and its authorization. Nonetheless, the scene reveals the inevitable contradiction of representation. It is always an agent both of production and loss. If it communicates sovereign authority, it is necessary only in the absence of that authority; in standing as surrogate it cannot help calling attention to what is not there. Representation thus at once constructs and subverts authority, at once enables it and exposes its limitation.

This doubleness is what Derrida calls, in another context, the "risk of *mimesis*" (241), the risk that any form of figuration will reveal the gap between the representing agent and what is represented, will admit their relation to be arbitrary and fragile, will expose the emptiness that it would fill. Representations mark the absence of a presence that is never fully available in and of itself, and they are, therefore, always more mobile, both less legitimate and legitimating, than theories of cultural dominance allow. Douglas, when he sees yet another representation of the King in the field at Shrewsbury, says with weary irritation: "They grow like Hydra's heads" (5.4.24), ironically using the familiar figure of rebellion to describe the replications of sovereignty he encounters, but thus articulating exactly the destabilizing potential, the possibility of a chaotic reproduction, that resides in the very notion of representation. At best, then, power might be understood as the effect of its representations; at worst, power might be seen actively to be undone by them.

Seeking the King, Douglas encounters a surplus of royal representations that he believes can brutally be dispatched to reveal their authorizing presence.

> Now, by my sword, I will kill all his coats;
> I'll murder all his wardrobe, piece by piece,
> Until I meet the King. (5.3.26–28)

Yet, although he works his way through the King's wardrobe with murderous efficiency, he is unable to recognize royalty when he finally confronts it. In *The Merchant of Venice*, Portia confidently asserts that "A substitute shines brightly as a King / Until a king be by" (5.1.94–95), but when Douglas does at last "meet the King," Henry shines no more brightly than any of the substitutes Douglas has killed.

Douglas: What art thou
That counterfeit'st the person of a king?
Henry: The King himself, who, Douglas, grieves at heart
So many of his shadows thou hast met,
And not the very King. . . .
Douglas: I fear thou art another counterfeit. . . .
(5.4.26–30, 34)

The language of difference here—"shadows" and "counterfeit"—clearly implies an authentic regal presence against which these imperfect representations can be measured; however, on the battlefield at Shrewsbury the King cannot be distinguished from his representations. Henry's majesty can be effectively mimed. Though Douglas admits to Henry that "thou bearest thee like a king" (5.4.35), royal bearing proves no guarantee of royalty. But the implications of the episode are not merely that Henry unheroically, if prudently, adopts a strategy in the interests of his safety, that appearances are manipulated to disguise the king. They are far more disturbing: that kingship itself is a disguise, a role, an action that a man might play. Even Henry can bear himself only "*like* the king"; he has no authentic royal identity prior to and untouched by representation. In dispossessing Richard from his throne, Henry, no less than Blunt, has only a "borrow'd title" (5.3.23), but he must manipulate the verbal and visual symbols of authority as if they were rightfully his own.

Yet the play perhaps registers even a deeper skepticism about the nature of authority: that Henry's inability to partake of an authentic majesty is not merely a result of his usurpation of Richard's crown but is indeed a condition of rule. To counterfeit "the person of the king" is always to counterfeit a counterfeit, for "person," as Hobbes observes, derives from the Latin *persona*, which "signifies the disguise or outward appearance of a man, counterfeited on the stage; and sometimes more particularly that part of it, which disguiseth the face, as a mask or vizard" (125). The "person of the king" is, then, always already a representation, unstable and ungrounded, and not the immanent presence of what Henry calls the "very King."

The language of Renaissance absolutism, responding to the same crisis of authority, attempted to resolve the regress of representation by locating authority finally in God. Thus Henry VIII in the Act of Succession of 1534 insisted upon the "grants of jurisdiction given by God immediately to Emperors, kings and princes in succession to their heirs." If the monarch knew that to rule was to be "like the King," he (or she, in the case of Mary and Elizabeth) knew also that to be "like the king" was to be, in the system of hierarchical homologies that organized experience, like God; the monarch rules in God's name and in His manner. James, in his treatise on rule, *Basilikon Doron*, claimed that

> God gives not Kings the stile of *Gods* in vaine,
> For on his Throne his Scepter doe they swey. (3)

However, the appeal to divine authority is itself unsatisfying without a convincing account of how this sanction is transmitted and transferred. The King "by birth . . . commeth to his crowne" (69), as James familiarly put it, but the principles of patrilineal inheritance providing for the succession of the eldest son occlude the question of origin. Even in an unbroken line of rule somewhere there must be an originating act which, except perhaps in the case of Saul in *1 Samuel* in the Old Testament, is something other than an immediate ordination by God. Sovereignty would construct itself upon a vertical axis of authorization, a synchronic principle of divine authority. But however much the state wishes to conceive of itself as timeless, permanently existing, the discontinuities of history must be acknowledged. The crown exists also upon a horizontal, diachronic axis of coercive power. Bodin held that "Reason, and the verie light of nature, leadeth vs to beleeue very force and violence to haue giuen course and beginning vnto Commonweals" (Sig. E6^{r}). Even James had to admit the coercive origin of monarchical rule. In part to escape the dangerous implications of what has been recently called translation theory, the idea that monarchy begins with a transfer of power from the people, James acknowledged that the authority of the Scottish crown derived directly from the conquest of the Irish King, Fergus, though James attempted to defuse the potentially destabilizing implications of grounding authority in power by insisting that the "people willingly fell to him" and that, in any case, the country was "scantly inhabited" (61–62).

But if authority must concede these coercive origins, the distinction between, for example, Richard II's legitimate rule and Henry IV's usurpation soon begins to blur. What is the difference in legitimacy between the rule of a usurper and the rule of a usurper's heir? English monarchs habitually based their authority "on the goodness of the cause of William the Conqueror, and upon their lineal, and directest descent from him," as Hobbes notes, but, as he wryly continues, "whilst they needlessly think to justify themselves, they justify all the successful rebellions that ambition shall at any time raise against them, and their successors" (506). Deriving legitimacy from conquest risks, however, not merely authorizing rebellion but delegitimizing rule itself. William Segar in 1590 skeptically wrote that "Kings, Princes, and other soveraign commanders did (in the beginning) aspire unto greatness by puissance and force:

of which Cain was the first" (Sig. S6r). And once authority acknowledges its customary origins in "puissance and force," recognizing the mark of Cain upon the throne, the distinction between legitimate and usurped rule no longer can be made absolute. If authority is grounded only in power and sanctioned only by custom then all titles are merely "borrowed" rather than in any significant sense rightfully belonging to those who hold them.

Lacan notoriously asserted that the man who believes himself king is no more mad than the *king* who believes himself king,[9] that is, it is madness to believe that kingship resides magically in the person of the king rather than in the political relations that bind, even create, king and subject. But this is precisely Hal's enabling knowledge, the authorization of his impressive improvisations. He never confuses the charismatic claims of kingship with the political relations they would accomplish. In 2 *Henry IV*, King Henry anxiously admits the "indirect, crooked ways" by which he achieved the crown, but for Hal the matter is almost comically simple, untouched by political irony or moral complexity:

> You won it, wore it, kept it, gave it me;
> Then plain and right must my possession be. . . .
> (*2H4*, 4.5.221–22)

Hal knows that the crown is always illegitimate, that is, always an effect of social relations and not their cause, and therefore must (and can) endlessly be legitimated by the improvisations of each wearer. Legitimacy is something forged, no less by kings in Westminster than by Falstaff in the Boar's Head. The king's state, scepler, and crown have no more intrinsic link to sovereignty than Falstaff's chair, dagger, and cushion. All are props in the representation of rule. If "the raised place of the stage" continuously refers to "the raised place of power," as Raymond Williams has said (15), the reference works to materialize and thus demystify the gestures of authority, exposing their theatricality in its own. Puttenham speaks of "the great Emperour who had it usually in his mouth to say, *Qui nescit dissimulare nescit regnare*" (Sig. X4r).[1] But rather than an admission of the necessary tactics of rule, this is an acknowledgment of its inescapable nature. Certainly Hal knows how to dissemble, is able and willing to "falsify men's hopes" [1.2.184]. If Falstaff insists on the distinction between "a true piece of gold"

9. " . . . *si un homme qui se croit un roi est fou, un roi qui se croit un roi ne l'est pas moins*" (Lacan 170). See also the discussion by Slavoj Žižek, who invokes Lacan in considering the "fetishistic misrecognition" by both king and subject that the "the king is already in himself, outside the relationship to his subjects" (25).

1. Sir Anthony Weldon claimed disparagingly in his "Court and Character of King James" that this, along with the more familiar *Beati pacifici*, was actually the King's motto (Scott 1, 421).

and "a counterfeit" [2.4.439–40], Hal blurs the difference. He is always aware that kingship is only a role, however much a major one; and he is well-prepared to play it, to "monarchize" (*Richard II*, 3.2.165), in Richard II's shocking word, with the same authority that Hal has played heir-apparent. He is indeed what Henry terms him scornfully, "the shadow of succession" (3.2.99), not in the sense that Henry intends "shadow"—that, unlike Hotspur, Hal is a weak and unworthy successor—but in a more characteristic Renaissance colloquial sense of "actor." And Hal will successfully *act* his succession.

Indeed he literally does act it, in the "play extempore" in act 2, scene 4. He deposes Falstaff from the "joint-stool" that is the throne, instantly capable of the language and gestures of sovereignty, and more, instantly aware that rule depends on the exclusion of what resists the incorporation of the unitary state. "Banish plump Jack, and banish all the world," Falstaff warns, and the future is chillingly etched in Hal's "I do, I will."

But it really isn't that simple. Hal will, of course, banish Falstaff in *2 Henry IV*, but the popular energy of comic misrule is not so easily excluded or contained. At the end of *2 Henry IV*, the victory over misrule is announced as a linguistic purification, a triumph of the monoglot aristocratic hegemony: "all are banish'd till their conversations / Appear more wise and modest to the world" (5.5.101–02). But although, as Bakhtin says, the monological voice of authority always "pretends to be the *last word*" (*Poetics,* 318), in *2 Henry IV* the "wise and modest" aristocratic voice does not have the final say; literally that belongs to the epilogue—and to the clown, I would argue, who has played Falstaff.[2] And *his* speech, like the dance that concludes it, exuberantly undermines both the unifying fantasies of charismatic kingship and the coherence and closure of the represented history that such kingship appropriates for its authorization, insisting precisely on the social, ideological, linguistic, and aesthetic multiplicity that both the unitary state and the unified play would deny.

2. See David Wiles's excellent account of Falstaff and clowning, esp. 116–35. Wiles argues that Falstaff's role "is structurally the clown's part" and that the part was written specifically for Kemp (116). The epilogue, or jig, Wiles sees as part of a convention of clowning which when understood would force us "to discard the old critical notion of the unity of the text, and seek instead the unity of the theatrical experience" (56). Recently John Cox has also suggestively recognized Falstaff as the dramatic heir of the stage clown, particularly Tarlton (121–24).

C. L. BARBER

[Mingling Kings and Clowns]†

The fascination of Falstaff as a dramatic figure has led criticism, from Morgann's essay onward, to center *1 Henry IV* on him, and to treat the rest of the play merely as a setting for him. But despite his predominating imaginative significance, the play is centered on Prince Hal, developing in such a way as to exhibit in the prince an inclusive, sovereign nature fitted for kingship. The relation of the Prince to Falstaff can be summarized fairly adequately in terms of the relation of holiday to everyday. As the non-historical material came to Shakespeare in *The Famous Victories of Henry the Fifth*, the prince was cast in the traditional role of the prodigal son, while his disreputable companions functioned as tempters in the same general fashion as the Vice of the morality plays. At one level Shakespeare keeps this pattern, but he shifts the emphasis away from simple moral terms. The issue, in his hands, is not whether Hal will be good or bad but whether he will be noble or degenerate, whether his holiday will become his everyday. The interregnum of a Lord of Misrule, delightful in its moment, might develop into the anarchic reign of a favorite dominating a dissolute king. Hal's secret, which he confides early to the audience, is that for him Falstaff is merely a pastime, to be dismissed in due course:

> If all the year were playing holidays,
> To sport would be as tedious as to work;
> But when they seldom come, they wish'd-for come . . .
> [1.2.177–79]

The prince's sports, accordingly, express not dissoluteness but a fine excess of vitality—"as full of spirit as the month of May"—together with a capacity for occasionally looking at the world as though it were upside down. His energy is controlled by an inclusive awareness of the rhythm in which he is living: despite appearances, he will not make the mistake which undid Richard II, who played at saturnalia until it caught up with him in earnest. During the battle of Shrewsbury (when, in Hotspur's phrase, "Doomsday is near"), Hal dismisses Falstaff with "What! is it a time to jest and dally now?" [5.3.53]. This sense of timing, of the relation of holiday to everyday and doomsday, contributes to establishing the prince as a sovereign nature.

† From C. L. Barber, *Shakespeare's Festive Comedy: A Study of Dramatic Form and its Relation to Social Custom* (Princeton: Princeton University Press, 1959), 195–214. Reprinted by permission of the publisher.

But the way Hal sees the relations is not the way other people see them, nor indeed the way the audience sees them until the end. The holiday-everyday antithesis is his resource for control, and in the end he makes it stick. But before that, the only clear-cut definition of relations in these terms is in his single soliloquy, after his first appearance with Falstaff. Indeed, it is remarkable how little satisfactory formulation there is of the relationships which the play explores dramatically. It is essential to the play that the prince should be misconstrued, that the king should see "riot and dishonor stain" (1.1.85) his brow, that Percy should patronize him as a "nimble-footed madcap" [4.1.95] who might easily be poisoned with a pot of ale if it were worth the trouble. But the absence of adequate summary also reflects the fact that Shakespeare was doing something which he could not summarize, which only the whole resources of his dramatic art could convey.

It is an open question, throughout *Part One*, as to just who or what Falstaff is. At the very end, when Prince John observes "This is the strangest tale that ever I heard," Hal responds with "This is the strangest fellow, brother John" [5.4.148–49]. From the beginning, Falstaff is constantly renaming himself:

> Marry, then, sweet wag, when thou art king, let not us that are squires of the night's body be called thieves of the day's beauty. Let us be Diana's Foresters, Gentlemen of the Shade, Minions of the Moon; and let men say we be men of good government . . . [1.2.20–24]

Here Misrule is asking to be called Good Government, as it is his role to do—though he does so with a wink which sets real good government at naught, concluding with "steal":

> . . . men of good government, being governed as the sea is, by our noble and chase mistress the moon, under whose countenance we steal. [1.2.23–25]

* * * The witty equivocation Falstaff practices, like that of Nashe's Bacchus and other apologists for folly and vice, alludes to the very morality it is flouting. Such "damnable iteration" is a sport that implies a rolling-eyed awareness of both sides of the moral medal; the Prince summarizes it in saying that Sir John "was never yet a breaker of proverbs. He will give the devil his due" [1.2.103–04]. It is also a game to be played with cards close to the chest. A Lord of Misrule naturally does not call himself Lord of Misrule in setting out to reign, but takes some title with the life of pretense in it. Falstaff's pretensions, moreover, are not limited to one occasion, for he is not properly a holiday lord, but a *de facto* buffoon who makes his way by continually seizing, catch as catch can, on what names

and meanings the moment offers. He is not a professed buffoon—few buffoons, in life, are apt to be. In Renaissance courts, the role of buffoon was recognized but not necessarily formalized, not necessarily altogether distinct from the role of favorite. And he is a highwayman: Shakespeare draws on the euphemistic, mock-chivalric cant by which "the profession" grace themselves. Falstaff in *Part One* plays it that he is Hal's friend, a gentleman, a "gentleman of the shade," and a soldier; he even enjoys turning the tables with "Thou hast done much harm upon me, Hal . . . I must give over this life, and I will give it over . . . I'll be damn'd for never a king's son in Christendom" [1.2.79–84]. It is the essence of his character, and his role, in *Part One*, that he never comes to rest where we can see him for what he "is." He is always in motion, always adopting postures, assuming characters.

That he does indeed care for Hal can be conveyed in performance without imposing sentimental tableaux on the action, provided that actors and producer recognize that he cares for the prince after his own fashion. It is from the prince that he chiefly gets his meaning, as it is from real kings that mock kings always get their meaning. We can believe it when we hear in *Henry V* that banishment has "killed his heart" (*H5*, 2.1.92). But to make much of a personal affection for the prince is a misconceived way to find meaning in Falstaff. His extraordinary meaningfulness comes from the way he manages to live "out of all order, out of all compass" by his wit and his wits; and from the way he keeps reflecting on the rest of the action, at first indirectly by the mock roles that he plays, at the end directly by his comments at the battle. Through this burlesque and mockery an intelligence of the highest order is expressed. It is not always clear whether the intelligence is Falstaff's or the dramatist's; often the question need not arise. Romantic criticism went the limit in ascribing a God-like superiority to the character, to the point of insisting that he tells the lies about the multiplying men in buckram merely to amuse, that he knew all the time at Gadshill that it was with Hal and Poins that he fought. To go so far in that direction obviously destroys the drama—spoils the joke in the case of the "incomprehensible lies," a joke which, as E. E. Stoll abundantly demonstrates, must be a joke *on* Falstaff. On the other hand, I see no reason why actor and producer should not do all they can to make us enjoy the intellectual mastery involved in Falstaff's comic resource and power of humorous redefinition. It is crucial that he should not be made so superior that he is never in predicaments, for his genius is expressed in getting out of them. But he does have genius, as Maurice Morgann rightly insisted though in a misconceived way. Through his part Shakespeare expressed attitudes towards experience which, grounded in a saturnalian reversal of values, went beyond that to include a radical challenge to received ideas.

Throughout the first three acts of *Part One*, the Falstaff comedy is continuously responsive to the serious action. There are constant parallels and contrasts with what happens at court or with the rebels. And yet these parallels are not explicitly noticed; the relations are presented, not formulated. So the first scene ends in a mood of urgency, with the tired king urging haste: "come yourself with speed to us again." The second scene opens with Hal asking Falstaff "What a devil hast thou to do with the time of day?" The prose in which he explains why time is nothing to Sir John is wonderfully leisurely and abundant, an elegant sort of talk that has all the time in the world to enjoy the completion of its schematized patterns:

> Unless hours were cups of sack, and minutes capons, and clocks the tongues of bawds, and dials the signs of leaping houses, and the blessed sun himself a fair hot wench in flame-colored taffeta, I see no reason why thou shouldst be so superfluous to demand the time of day. [1.2.6–10]

The same difference in the attitude towards time runs throughout and goes with the difference between verse and prose mediums. A similar contrast obtains about lese majesty. Thus at their first appearance Falstaff insults Hal's majesty with casual, off-hand wit which the prince tolerates (while getting his own back by jibing at Falstaff's girth):

> And I prithee, sweet wag, when thou art king, as God save thy Grace—Majesty I should say, for grace thou wilt have none—
>
> *Prince*. What, none?
>
> *Falstaff*. No, by my troth; not so much as will serve to be prologue to an egg and butter.
>
> *Prince*. Well, how then? Come, roundly, roundly. [1.2.13–19]

In the next scene, we see Worcester calling into question the grace of Bolingbroke, "that same greatness to which our own hands / Have holp to make so portly" [1.3.12–13]. The King's response is immediate and drastic, and his lines point a moral that Hal seems to be ignoring:

> Worcester, get thee gone; for I do see
> Danger and disobedience in thine eye.
> O, sir, your presence is too bold and peremptory,
> And majesty might never yet endure
> The moody frontier of a servant brow. (1.3.15–19)

Similar parallels run between Hotspur's heroics and Falstaff's mock-heroics. In the third scene we hear Hotspur talking of "an easy leap / To pluck bright honor from the pale-face'd moon"

(1.3.201–02). Then in the robbery, Falstaff is complaining that "Eight yards of uneven ground is threescore and ten miles afoot for me," and asking "Have you any levers to lift me up again, being down?" [2.2.21–22, 30.] After Hotspur enters exclaiming against the cowardly lord who has written that he will not join the rebellion, we have Falstaff's entrance to the tune of "A plague of all cowards" [2.4.103]. And so on, and so on. Shakespeare's art has reached the point where he makes everything foil to everything else. Hal's imagery, in his soliloquy, shows the dramatist thinking about such relations: "like bright metal on a sullen ground, / My reformation, glitt'ring o'er my fault" [1.2.185–86].

Now it is not true that Falstaff's impudence about Hal's grace undercuts Bolingbroke's majesty, nor that Sir John's posturing as a hero among cowards invalidates the heroic commitment Hotspur expresses when he says "but I tell you, my lord fool, out of this nettle, danger, we pluck this flower, safety" [2.3.7–9]. The relationship is not one of a mocking echo. Instead, there is a certain distance between the comic and serious strains which leaves room for a complex interaction, organized by the crucial role of the prince. We are invited, by the King's unfavorable comparison in the opening scene, to see the Prince in relation to Hotspur. And Hal himself, in the midst of his Boars Head revel, compares himself with Hotspur. In telling Poins of his encounter with the drawers among the hogsheads of the wine-cellar, he says "I have sounded the very bass-string of humility," goes on to note what he has gained by it, "I can drink with any tinker in his own language during my life," and concludes with "I tell thee, Ned, thou hast lost much honour that thou wert not with me in this action" [2.4.5–6, 17–18]. His mock-heroic way of talking about "this action" shows how well he knows how to value it from a princely vantage. But the remark cuts two ways. For running the gamut of society *is* an important action: after their experiment with Francis and his "Anon, anon, sir," the Prince exclaims

> That ever this fellow should have fewer words than a parrot, and yet the son of a woman! . . . I am not yet of Percy's mind, the Hotspur of the North; he that kills me some six or seven dozen of Scots at a breakfast, washes his hands, and says to his wife, "Fie upon this quiet life! I want work." "O my sweet Harry," says she, "how many hast thou kill'd to-day?" "Give my roan horse a drench," says he, and answers "Some fourteen," an hour after, "a trifle, a trifle." I prithee call in Falstaff. I'll play Percy, and that damn'd brawn shall play Dame Mortimer his wife.
>
> [2.4.90–100]

It is the narrowness and obliviousness of the martial hero that Hal's mockery brings out; here his awareness explicitly spans the distance between the separate strains of the action; indeed, the distance is made the measure of the kingliness of his nature. His "I am not *yet* of Percy's mind" implies what he later promises his father (the commercial image he employs reflects his ability to use, after his father's fashion, the politician's calculation and indirection):

> Percy is but my factor, good my lord,
> To engross up glorious deeds on my behalf . . .
> (3.2.147–48)

In the Boars Head Tavern scene, Hal never carries out the plan of playing Percy to Falstaff's Dame Mortimer; in effect he has played both their parts already in his snatch of mimicry. But Falstaff provides him with a continuous exercise in the consciousness that comes from playing at being what one is not, and from seeing through such playing.

Even here, where one world does comment on another explicitly, Hotspur's quality is not invalidated; rather, his achievement is putting an enormous pressure on the comedy to resolve the challenge posed by the ironic perceptions presented in his historical action.

The process at work, here and earlier in the play, can be made clearer, I hope, by reference now to the carrying off of bad luck by the scapegoat of saturnalian ritual. We do not need to assume that Shakespeare had any such ritual patterns consciously in mind; whatever his conscious intention, it seems to me that these analogues illuminate patterns which his poetic drama presents concretely and dramatically. After such figures as the Mardi Gras or Carnival have presided over a revel, they are frequently turned on by their followers, tried in some sort of court, convicted of sins notorious in the village during the last year, and burned or buried in effigy to signify a new start. In other ceremonies described in *The Golden Bough*,[2] mockery kings appear as recognizable substitutes for real kings, stand trial in their stead, and carry away the evils of their realms into exile or death. One such scapegoat figure, as remote historically as could be from Shakespeare, is the Tibetan King of the Years, who enjoyed ten days' misrule during the annual holiday of Buddhist monks at Lhasa. At the climax of his ceremony, after doing what he liked while collecting bad luck by shaking a black yak's tail over the people, he mounted the temple steps and ridiculed the representative of the Grand Llama, proclaiming heresies like "What we perceive through the five senses is no illusion.

2. *The Golden Bough* by Sir James George Frazer (1854–1941) was originally published in two volumes in 1890, went through several revised versions, and was eventually edited into one volume in 1922. In this seminal work, Frazer explores the anthropology of magic, mythology, and folklore across several cultures. While many of Frazer's descriptions and theories have been discounted in recent decades, *The Golden Bough* stands as a remarkable literary achievement [*Editor's note*].

All you teach is untrue." A few minutes later, discredited by a cast of loaded dice, he was chased off to exile and possible death in the mountains.[3] One cannot help thinking of Falstaff's catechism on honor, spoken just before another valuation of honor is expressed in the elevated blank verse of a hero confronting death: "Can honour . . . take away the grief of a wound? No. . . . What is honour? a word. What is that word, honour? Air" [5.1.130–34]. Hal's final expulsion of Falstaff appears in the light of these analogies to carry out an impersonal pattern, not merely political but ritual in character. After the guilty reign of Bolingbroke, the prince is making a fresh start as the new king. At a level beneath the moral notions of a personal reform, we can see a nonlogical process of purification by sacrifice—the sacrifice of Falstaff. The career of the old king, a successful usurper whose conduct of affairs has been sceptical and opportunistic, has cast doubt on the validity of the whole conception of a divinely-ordained and chivalrous kingship to which Shakespeare and his society were committed. And before Bolingbroke, Richard II had given occasion for doubts about the rituals of kingship in an opposite way, by trying to use them magically. Shakespeare had shown Richard assuming that the symbols of majesty should be absolutes, that the names of legitimate power should be transcendently effective regardless of social forces. Now both these attitudes have been projected also in Falstaff; he carries to comically delightful and degraded extremes both a magical use of moral sanctions and the complementary opportunistic manipulation and scepticism. So the ritual analogy suggests that by turning on Falstaff as a scapegoat, as the villagers turned on their Mardi Gras, the prince can free himself from the sins, the "bad luck," of Richard's reign and of his father's reign, to become a king in whom chivalry and a sense of divine ordination are restored.

But this process of carrying off bad luck, if it is to be made *dramatically* cogent, as a symbolic action accomplished in and by dramatic form, cannot take place magically in Shakespeare's play. When it happens magically in the play, we have, I think, a failure to transform ritual into comedy. In dealing with fully successful comedy, the magical analogy is only a useful way of organizing our awareness of a complex symbolic action. The expulsion of evil works as dramatic form only in so far as it is realized in a movement from participation to rejection which happens, moment by moment, in our response to Falstaff's clowning misrule. We watch Falstaff adopt one posture after another, in the effort to give himself meaning at no cost; and moment by moment we see that the meaning is specious. So our participation is repeatedly diverted to laugh-

3. See James G. Frazer, *The Scapegoat* (London, 1914), 218–23.

ter. The laughter, disbursing energy originally mobilized to respond to a valid meaning, signalizes our mastery by understanding of the tendency which has been misapplied or carried to an extreme.

Consider, for example, the use of magical notions of royal power in the most famous of all Falstaff's burlesques:

> By the Lord, I knew ye as well as he that made ye. . . . Was it for me to kill the heir apparent? Should I turn upon the true prince? Why, thou knowest I am as valiant as Hercules; but beware instinct. The lion will not touch the true prince. Instinct is a great matter. I was now a coward on instinct. I shall think the better of myself, and thee, during my life—I for a valiant lion, and thou for a true prince. But, by the Lord, lads, I am glad you have the money. Hostess, clap to the doors: watch to-night, pray to-morrow. (2.4.242–51)

Here Falstaff has recourse to the brave conception that legitimate kingship has a magical potency. This is the sort of absolutist appeal to sanctions which Richard II keeps falling back on in his desperate "conjuration" (*R2*, 3.2.23) by hyperbole:

> So when this thief, this traitor, Bolingbroke, . . .
> Shall see us rising in our throne, the East,
> His treasons will sit blushing in his face,
> Not able to endure the sight of day . . .
> The breath of worldly men cannot depose
> The deputy elected by the Lord.
> For every man that Bolingbroke hath press'd
> To lift shrewd steel against our golden crown,
> God for his Richard hath in heavenly pay
> A glorious angel. (*R2*, 3.2.47, 50–52, 56–61)

In Richard's case, a tragic irony enforces the fact that heavenly angels are of no avail if one's coffers are empty of golden angels and the Welsh army have dispersed. In Falstaff's case, the irony is comically obvious, the "lies are like the father that begets them; gross as a mountain, open, palpable" (2.4.249–50). Hal stands for the judgment side of our response, while Falstaff embodies the enthusiastic, irrepressible conviction of fantasy's omnipotence. The Prince keeps returning to Falstaff's bogus "instinct"; "Now, sirs . . . You are lions too, you ran away upon instinct, you will not touch the true prince; no—fie!" (2.4.29–34). After enjoying the experience of seeing through such notions of magical majesty, he is never apt to make the mistake of assuming that, just because he is king, lions like Northumberland will not touch him. King Richard's bad luck came precisely from such an assumption—unexamined, of course, as fatal assumptions always are. Freud's account of bad luck, in *The Psychopathology of Everyday Life*, sees it as the expression of unconscious motives which resist the conscious goals of the personality. This view helps to explain how the acting out of disruptive motives in saturnalia or in comedy can serve to master potential aberration by revaluing it in relation to the whole of experience. So Falstaff, in acting out this absolutist aberration, is taking away what might have been Hal's bad luck, taking it away not in a magical way, but by extending the sphere of conscious control. The comedy is a civilized equivalent of the primitive rite. A similar mastery of potential aberration is promoted by the experience of seeing through Falstaff's burlesque of the sort of headlong chivalry presented seriously in Hotspur.

In order to put the symbolic action of the comedy in larger perspective, it will be worth while to consider further, for a moment, the relation of language to stage action and dramatic situation in *Richard II*. That play is a pioneering exploration of the semantics of royalty, shot through with talk about the potency and impotence of language. In the first part, we see a Richard who is possessor of an apparently magical omnipotence: for example, when he commutes Bolingbroke's banishment from ten to six years, Bolingbroke exclaims:

> How long a time lies in one little word!
> Four lagging winters and four wanton springs
> End in a word: such is the breath of kings.
> (*R2*, 1.3.213–15)

Richard assumes he has such magic breath inevitably, regardless of "the breath of worldly men." When he shouts things like "Is not the king's name twenty thousand names? / Arm, arm, my name!" he carries the absolutist assumption to the giddiest verge of absurdity. When we analyze the magical substitution of words for things in such lines, looking at them from outside the rhythm of feeling in which they occur, it seems scarcely plausible that a drama should be built around the impulse to adopt such an assumption. It seems especially implausible in our own age, when we are so conscious, on an abstract level, of the dependence of verbal efficacy on the social group. The analytical situation involves a misleading perspective, however; for, whatever your assumptions about semantics, when you have to *act*, to *be* somebody or become somebody, there is a moment when you have to have faith that the unknown world beyond will respond to the names you commit yourself to as right names.[4] The Elizabethan mind, moreover, generally assumed that one played one's part in a divinely ordained pageant where each man *was* his name and the role his name implied. The expression of

4. I am indebted to my colleagues Professor Theodore Baird and Professor G. Armour Craig for this way of seeing the relation of names to developing situations.

this faith, and of the outrage of it, is particularly drastic in the Elizabethan drama, which can be regarded, from this vantage, as an art form developed to express the shock and exhilaration of the discovery that life is not pageantry. As Professor Tillyard has pointed out, *Richard II* is the most ceremonial of all Shakespeare's plays, and the ceremony all comes to nothing.[5] In Richard's deposition scene, one way in which anguish at his fall is expressed is by a focus on his loss of names: he responds to Northumberland's "My Lord—" by flinging out.

> No lord of thine, thou haught insulting man,
> Nor no man's lord. I have no name, no title—
> No, not that name was given me at the font—
> But 'tis usurp'd. Alack the heavy day,
> That I have worn so many winters out
> And know not now what name to call myself!
> O that I were a mockery king of snow,
> Standing before the sun of Bolingbroke
> To melt myself away in water-drops!
> (*R2*, 4.1.253–62)

His next move is to call for the looking glass in which he stares at his face to look for the meaning the face has lost. To lose one's meaning, one's social role, is to be reduced to mere body.

Here again the tragedy can be used to illuminate the comedy. Since the Elizabethan drama was a double medium of words and of physical gestures, it frequently expressed the pathos of the loss of meaning by emphasizing moments when word and gesture, name and body, no longer go together, just as it presented the excitement of a gain of meaning by showing a body seizing on names when a hero creates his identity. In the deposition scene, Richard says "mark me how I will undo myself" (4.1.203). Then he gives away by physical gestures the symbolic meanings which have constituted that self. When at last he has no name, the anguish is that the face, the body, remain when the meaning is gone. There is also something in Richard's lines which, beneath the surface of his self-pity, relishes such undoing, a self-love which looks towards fulfillment in that final reduction of all to the body which is death. This narcissistic need for the physical is the other side of the attitude that the magic of the crown should altogether transcend the physical—and the human:

> Cover your heads, and mock not flesh and blood
> With solemn reverence. Throw away respect,
> Tradition, form, and ceremonious duty;

5. See *Shakespeare's History Plays* (New York, 1946), pp. 245 ff.

> For you have but mistook me all this while.
> I live with bread like you, feel want, taste grief,
> Need friends. Subjected thus,
> How can you say to me I am a king?
> (*R2*, 3.2.171–77)

In expressing the disappointment of Richard's magical expectations, as well as their sweeping magnificence, the lines make manifest the aberration which is mastered in the play by tragic form.

The same sort of impulse is expressed and mastered by comic form in the Henry IV comedy. When Richard wishes he were a mockery king of snow, to melt before the sun of Bolingbroke, the image expresses on one side the wish to escape from the body with which he is left when his meaning has gone—to weep himself away in water drops. But the lines also look wistfully towards games of mock royalty where, since the whole thing is based on snow, the collapse of meaning need not hurt. Falstaff is such a mockery king. To be sure, he is flesh and blood, of a kind: he is tallow, anyway. He "sweats to death / And lards the lean earth as he walks along." Of course he is not just a mockery, not just his role, not just bombast. Shakespeare, as always, makes the symbolic role the product of a life which includes contradictions of it, such as the morning-after regrets when Falstaff thinks of the inside of a church and notices that his skin hangs about him like an old lady's loose gown. Falstaff is human enough so that "Were't not for laughing, . . . [we] should pity him." But we do laugh, because when Falstaff's meanings collapse, little but make-believe has been lost:

> *Prince*. Thy state is taken for a join'd-stool, thy golden sceptre for a leaden dagger, and thy precious rich crown for a pitiful bald crown. [2.4.338–40]

Falstaff's effort to make his body and furnishings mean sovereignty is doomed from the start; he must work with a leaden dagger, the equivalent of a Vice's dagger of lath. But Falstaff does have golden words, and an inexhaustible vitality in using them. He can name himself nobly, reordering the world by words so as to do himself credit:

> No, my good lord. Banish Peto, banish Bardolph, banish Poins; but for sweet Jack Falstaff, kind Jack Falstaff, true Jack Falstaff, valiant Jack Falstaff, and therefore more valiant being, as he is, old Jack Falstaff, banish not him thy Harry's company, banish not him thy Harry's company. Banish plump Jack, and banish all the world! [2.4.422–28]

I quote such familiar lines to recall their effect of incantation: they embody an effort at a kind of magical naming. Each repetition of "sweet Jack Falstaff, kind Jack Falstaff" aggrandizes an identity which the serial clauses caress and cherish. At the very end, in "plump Jack," the disreputable belly is glorified.

In valid heroic and majestic action, the bodies of the personages are constantly being elevated by becoming the vehicles of social meanings; in the comedy, such elevation becomes burlesque, and in the repeated failures to achieve a fusion of body and symbol, abstract meanings keep falling back into the physical. "A plague of sighing and grief! it blows a man up like a bladder" [2.4.295–96]. The repetition of such joking about Falstaff's belly makes it meaningful in a very special way, as a symbol of the process of inflation and collapse of meaning. So it represents the power of the individual life to continue despite the collapse of social roles. This continuing on beyond definitions is after all what we call "the body" in one main meaning of the term: Falstaff's belly is thus the essence of body—an essence which can be defined only dynamically, by failures of meaning. The effect of indestructible vitality is reinforced by the association of Falstaff's figure with the gay eating and drinking of Shrove Tuesday and Carnival. Whereas, in the tragedy, the reduction is to a body which can only die, here reduction is to a body which typifies our power to eat and drink our way through a shambles of intellectual and moral contradictions.

So we cannot resist sharing Falstaff's genial self-love when he commends his vision of plump Jack to the Prince, just as we share the ingenuous self-love of a little child. But the dramatist is ever on the alert to enforce the ironies that dog the tendency of fantasy to equate the self with "all the world." So a most monstrous watch comes beating at the doors which have been clapped to against care; everyday breaks in on holiday.

* * *

In *Part One*, Falstaff reigns, within his sphere, as Carnival; *Part Two* is very largely taken up with his trial. To put Carnival on trial, run him out of town, and burn or bury him is in folk custom a way of limiting, by ritual, the attitudes and impulses set loose by ritual. Such a trial, though conducted with gay hoots and jeers, serves to swing the mind round to a new vantage, where it sees misrule no longer as a benign release for the individual, but as a source of destructive consequences for society.[6] This sort of reckoning is what *Part Two* brings to Falstaff.

But Falstaff proves extremely difficult to bring to book—more difficult than an ordinary mummery king—because his burlesque and mockery are developed to a point where the mood of a moment

6. The ritual of Carnival in Italy and its relation to Italian comedy has recently been exhibited in Professor Paolo Toschi's *Le origini del teatro italiano* (Torino, 1955) with a fullness and clarity made possible by the rich popular Italian heritage.

crystallizes as a settled attitude of scepticism. * * * [I]n a static, monolithic society, a Lord of Misrule can be put back in his place after the revel with relative ease. The festive burlesque of solemn sanctities does not seriously threaten social values in a monolithic culture, because the license depends utterly upon what it mocks: liberty is unable to envisage any alternative to the accepted order except the standing of it on its head. But Shakespeare's culture was not monolithic: though its moralists assumed a single order, scepticism was beginning to have ground to stand on and look about—especially in and around London. So a Lord of Misrule figure, brought up, so to speak, from the country to the city, or from the traditional past into the changing present, could become on the Bankside the mouthpiece not merely for the dependent holiday scepticism which is endemic in a traditional society, but also for a dangerously self-sufficient everyday scepticism. When such a figure is set in an environment of sober-blooded great men behaving as opportunistically as he, the effect is to raise radical questions about social sanctities. At the end of *Part Two*, the expulsion of Falstaff is presented by the dramatist as getting rid of this threat; Shakespeare has recourse to a primitive procedure to meet a modern challenge. * * *

* * *

MICHAEL D. BRISTOL

[The Battle of Carnival and Lent]†

* * * It has frequently been implied, or suggested, that individual plays, and in the case of Shakespeare's 'tetralogies' whole cycles of plays, are organized in accordance with strategies similar to those of official pageantry. They consist of extended political antimasques eventually routed by the appearance of a legitimate king. In such a project, disorder or misrule is a politically marginal impulse or tendency, a temporary and merely contingent rift or hiatus in the plenitude of social and cosmic harmony. C. L. Barber, in discussing this problem as it applies to the two parts of *Henry IV*, argues that 'the dynamic relation of comedy and serious action is saturnalian rather than satiric. . . . the misrule works, through the whole dramatic rhythm, to consolidate rule.'[1] This view of conflict

† From Michael D. Bristol, *Carnival and Theatre: Plebeian Culture and the Structure of Authority in Renaissance England* (New York: Methuen, 1985), 198–202, 204–7. Reprinted by permission of the author.

1. C. L. Barber, *Shakespeare's Festive Comedies: A Study of Dramatic Form and Its Relation to Social Custom* (New York: Meridian Books, 1963), 205.

recuperates the marginal experience of misrule by making it the instrument whereby rule, order or domination might be better defended and secured. This humanistic account of the history plays is part of a much wider cultural and political theodicy, variously articulated in respect to Shakespeare as 'the universe's hospitality to life' (Barber); a 'background of order' that gives meaning to 'pictures of civil war and disorder' (Tillyard); 'the unresolvable complexity of life [present to] the fullest human consciousness' (Rabkin).

Analysis of Shakespeare's plays that proceeds in accordance with one of these strategies will certainly appreciate structural complexity and will even take note of the failure of certain represented actions to conform with the norms of an ordered universe and a correspondingly ordered civil society. Nevertheless, conflict and misrule are interpreted as relatively small and localized turbulence that in the end cannot be permitted to expand beyond certain limits. This interpretive strategy is predicated on a commitment to order and to authority, as the necessary conditions for individual and collective well-being.

The hierarchical opposition order/disorder or rule/misrule coincides with certain explicitly political assumptions. Most prominent among these is the critical presupposition that the nation-state is the natural and necessary political form emerging from some kind of archaic disorder and consolidating itself against marginal forms of residual feudal anarchy or popular resistance. The English nation and the consolidation of its state apparatus were certainly substantially accomplished and very much part of the objective conditions of social life at the time Shakespeare's plays were written. In general, critics have argued from the implicit premise that it is definitely better for the state to exist than for it not to exist, even though the state is not the only form that civil society can take. Given this presupposition, that orderly collective life is only possible within the nation-state, interpretation of the plays may proceed to such secondary but consequential problems as 'the specialty of rule', the precarious historical transitions from ceremonially based kingship to practical and administratively based kingship, and the compelling urgency of Lear's division of the kingdom. Each of these questions is a way of thematizing the conviction that the state is a plenitude and, in fact, the only plenitude that could ever exist in the sphere of political life. A united kingdom is implicitly—and sometimes explicitly—asserted to be the exclusive guarantor of safety and of peace. The only legitimate purpose of any political activity, including kingship, therefore, is to sustain that united kingdom against all local and marginal initiatives and resistances.

Rule against misrule, the state against civil war, correspond to two additional hierarchized oppositions—everyday life/holiday and serious speech/jesting speech. Both of these distinctions correspond to governing categories of a real, substantive order, objectified in the state, and marginal disorder, objectified in disparate and disunited fragmentary social practices. The reintegration of the marginal term through such conceptions as 'saturnalian clarification', 'complementary perspective', 'burlesque or jesting counterpoint to a serious discourse', nevertheless insists on a subordinate and purely instrumental role for the marginal term. Thus to speak of 'clownish inversions' clearly implies that the *un*clownish version is right side up. And even the argument that folk festivals and popular theater are 'skeptical and anti-authoritarian' concedes that such activities are already peripheral to authority and to real political life.[2]

The characteristic dramatic images of political life iterated throughout chronicle history plays and tragedies include scenes of exaggerated, grotesque and often farcical violence; the suffering and abjection of a royal victim; treachery, usurpation and assassination, together with civil butchery, as the preferred means and as the inevitable consequence of every succession. As texts, many of these plays seem inversive in respect to the relationship between rule and misrule. Misrule and disorder are the pervasive, objective conditions of political life that correspond to the disunited fullness of the production, distribution and exchange of social wealth. Misrule and localized conflict on a small scale may be perfectly compatible with a general condition of relative social well-being; and the overthrow and abjection of the royal victim an acceptable and sometimes enjoyable element of business as usual.

The critical recognition of misrule and Carnival provides an alternative to a political theodicy of the nation-state. Misrule is not a merely negative idea, however, as in Jan Kott's conception of an absurd 'Grand Mechanism'.[3] The rhythmic succession of Carnivalesque uncrowning and renewal, the 'pathos of radical change', is the 'second life' of the people, a form of real politics, an ethos, a 'mode of production' existentially prior to the state and its administrative apparatus. This second life is lived in the public squares and also in the theater as a public space; it is mimetically represented in the forms of political drama. Bakhtin elaborates this 'second life' in his account of 'the folkloric bases of the Rabelaisian Chronotope', describing it as an alternative experience of time.

> This time is collective, that is, it is differentiated and measured only by the events of *collective* life; everything that exists in this time exists solely for the collective. The progression of

2. Michael Hattaway, *Elizabethan Popular Theatre: Plays in Performance* (London: Routledge & Kegan Paul, 1982), 2.
3. Jan Kott, *Shakespeare Our Contemporary* (New York: Anchor Books, 1966), 3–57.

> events in an individual life has not yet been isolated (the interior time of an individual life does not yet exist, the individuum lives completely on the surface, within a collective whole). Both labor and the consuming of things are collective.
>
> This is the time of labor. Everyday life and consumption are not isolated from the labor and production process. Time is measured by labor events. . . . This sense of time works itself out in a collective battle of labor against nature. . . .
>
> This is the time of productive growth. It is a time of growth, blossoming, fruit-bearing, ripening, fruitful increase, issue. The passage of time does not destroy or diminish but rather multiplies and increases the quantity of valuable things. . . . [The] single items that perish are neither individualized nor isolated; they are lost in the whole growing and multiplying mass of new lives. . . .
>
> This time is profoundly spatial and concrete. It is not separated from the earth or from nature. It, as well as the entire life of the human being, is all on the surface.[4]

The culture of common people or plebeians in its political, social, philosophical and artistic manifestations is already everywhere; government and the nation-state as institutional forms are latecomers. Holiday, or holy-day, Carnival and misrule are not isolated episodes in a uniform continuum of regularly scheduled real-life: the experience of holiday pervades the year and defines its rhythm.[5]

The theater in its 'mature' or 'developed form' is an institution 'invented' by Jonson and by many others to oppose and displace a theater already practiced and appreciated throughout plebeian culture. Jonson, as the exemplary 'institution maker' proceeds by making a series of exclusions, redefining activities characteristic of traditional theatricality as aberrant and marginal. This project is carried out against the background of a very much larger and even more protracted struggle, in which the centralized authority of the state comes into being against social and political life already lived, and by means of traditionally dispersed, collective authority. One of the many engagements in that struggle concerns the local tradition of midsummer watches in London.

> This midsummer watch was thus accustomed yearly, time out of mind, until the year 1539, the 31st of Henry VIII, in which year, on the 8th of May, a great muster was made by the citizens of the Mile's End, all in bright harness, with coats of white silk, or cloth and chains of gold, in three great battles, to

4. Mikhail Bakhtin, *The Dialogic Imagination*, trans. Michael Holquist and Caryl Emerson (Austin: University of Texas Press, 1981), 206–8.
5. Claude Gaignebet, "Le Combat de carnaval et de carême de P. Breughel (1559)," *Annales: Economies, Sociétés, Civilizations* 27 (1972), 313–43; Keith Thomas, "Work and Leisure in Pre-Industrial Society," *Past and Present* 29 (1964), 67–84.

> the number of fifteen thousand. . . . King Henry, then considering the great charges of the citizens for the furniture of this unusual muster, forbade the marching watch provided for at Midsummer for that year, which being once laid down was not raised again till the year 1548.[6]

The midsummer watch was, among other things, a procession of armed citizenry organized at the initiative of the common people. It was suppressed once in 1539, and again after the term of office as Lord Mayor of Sir John Gresham, during the reign of Edward VI. The initiative for this practice did not die out entirely, however, and, according to Stow, attempts were made to revive it during Elizabeth's reign. The antiquity and the scope of participation of such a manifestly powerful and independent urban politics could not in the end be compatible with the coalition of interests that support the centralized state, whose representatives find reasons quietly to discourage such activities. But the political life of plebeian culture is not effaced by these tactics; it persists in other popular festive events, in processional life, and in the theatrical performance of dramatic texts where elements of a 'second life' in the pattern of misrule provide the organizing scheme for exemplary, mimetic actions. A central instance of this Carnival or popular festive structuration of politically significant narrative is the use of characteristic festive personae and the festive agon or Battle of Carnival and Lent as a narrative scheme governing both comic and serious actions. The festive agon reinterprets political succession, and other transitional procedures, as the double and reciprocal thrashing and expulsion of the Carnivalesque and Lenten tendencies.

* * *

The Battle of Carnival and Lent is an explicit structuring device in the two parts of *Henry IV*. These plays are seriocomic, anachronistic recreations of epically distanced chronicle history within the familiar *mise-en-scène* of the streets and taverns of contemporary London. Falstaff's girth, his perpetual drinking and eating, his disrespect of time, place and person are typical features of Carnival as a festive persona. His companion and Lenten antagonist, a character known variously as Hal, Harry Monmouth and the Prince of Wales, is a 'stockfish' who continually chastises Falstaff and admonishes him in respect of a less abundant future. Falstaff, like Carnival, is an ambivalent and grotesque figure. Hal, miming his own father, characterizes Falstaff as a vicious and decaying fat old man.

> PRINCE. There is a devil haunts thee in the likeness of an old fat man, a tun of man is thy companion. Why dost thou converse with that trunk of humors, that bolting hutch of beastli-

6. John Stow, *Survey of London*, ed. H. B. Wheatley (London: Dent, 1956), 115.

> ness, that swollen parcel of dropsies, that huge bombard of sack, that stuffed cloak bag of guts, that roasted Manningtree ox with the pudding in his belly. [*1H4*, 2.4.398–404]

This denunciatory language, in which Falstaff is mainly described as a series of large vessels or containers filled with vile, excremental matter, is suddenly interrupted with an image of savory, festive abundance. This is the language Bakhtin identifies as belonging to 'lower bodily stratum', in which degraded excremental images coexist with images of the digestive organs that consume food—dead meat—and turn it into 'beastliness' which is both living flesh and bodily waste.[7]

Falstaff is socially as well as ethically ambivalent. He is Sir John, but prefers to name himself Jack, the most versatile and familiar name for every nameless hero of plebeian culture, including, paradoxically, Jack-a-Lent.

> Of Jack-an-apes I list not to indite
> Nor of Jack Daw my goose's quill shall write;
> Of Jack of Newbury I will not repeat,
> Nor Jack of both sides, nor of Skip-Jack neat.
> To praise the turnspit Jack my Muse is mum,
> Nor of the entertainment of Jack Drum
> I'll not rehearse: nor of Jack Dog, Jack Date,
> Jack fool, or Jack-a-Dandy, I relate:
> Nor of black Jacks at gentle buttery bars,
> Whose liquor oftentimes breeds household wars:
> Nor Jack of Dover that grand jury Jack,
> Nor Jack Sauce (the worst knave amongst the pack).
> (*Iacke-a-Lente*, 3)[8]

As Falstaff's apology for himself suggests, his iniquitous conduct is typical of a wider world where 'every man jack' has to make his way in the best way he can manage.

> FAL. . . . If to be old and merry be a sin, then many an old host that I know is damned. If to be fat be to be hated, then Pharaoh's lean kine are to be loved. No, my good lord. Banish Peto, banish Bardolph, banish Poins. But for sweet Jack Falstaff, kind Jack Falstaff, true Jack Falstaff, valiant Jack Falstaff, and therefore more valiant, being as he is, old Jack Falstaff, banish not him thy Harry's company, banish not him thy Harry's company. Banish plump jack, and banish all the world. [*1H4*, 2.4.420–28]

7. Mikhail Bakhtin, *The Dialogic Imagination*, 171–92; Bakhtin, *Rabelais and His World*, trans. Hélène Iswolsky (Cambridge, MA: MIT Press, 1968), 369–437.
8. John Taylor, *Iacke-a-Lente, His Beginning and Entertainment*, in Charles Hindley, ed., *The Works of John Taylor the Water Poet* (London, 1872).

Falstaff multiplies and refracts his identity to blend with 'every man jack'; his plea is also an admonition. To proscribe Carnival is the undoubtedly fatal project of 'banishing all the world', a consolidation of rule by the ruthless and permanent suppression of misrule. As Falstaff hints, however, misrule is the amoral and ungovernable pattern of social life itself.

Falstaff's companionable antagonist and eventual 'successor' as Carnival king is Hal, the exemplary embodiment of Lenten civil policy. Both Carnival and Lent are grotesque, double-valued personae who enjoy temporary and limited sovereignty and who submit to thrashing and to abjection. Hal's project, however, is eventually to break the rhythmic alternation between the abundance of the material principle embodied in Carnival and the abstemious social discipline embodied in Lent by establishing a permanent sovereignty of Lenten civil policy. This project is very much out in the open, publicly acknowledged in respect of the contemporaneous space-time of the performance, as Hal informs the audience of his overall intentions.

> PRINCE. I know you all, and will a while uphold
> The unyoked humor of your idleness. . . .
> If all the year were playing holidays,
> To sport would be as tedious as to work.
> But when they seldom come, they wished-for come,
> And nothing pleaseth but rare accidents.
> [1.2.168–69, 177–80]

Under the supervision of a comprehensive social discipline, a holiday will be an isolated episode, a limited release that is all the more appreciated for its rarity. This is the social discipline that Hal undertakes to establish. His project is, in respect of the represented, epically distanced narrative action, covert and unacknowledged. To secure the conditions of Lenten civil policy, Hal plays out his role of Jack-a-Lent, the festive, transgressive and feasting side of the Lenten reality. He wins support from 'all the lads in east cheap', a constituency that certainly includes a number of butcher's apprentices. In the politics of authoritarian populism, 'Lenten butchery' emerges as a sanctioned response to a putative need for social order. The 'Lenten butcher with a license to kill' emerges from an ambiguous and obscure status to become the necessary instrument of prudential political foresight. The civil state arrogates to itself the authority both to proscribe 'Lenten butchery' and to sanction it for the sake of larger social purposes. In order to accomplish this comprehensive administrative project, it is not sufficient merely to thrash Carnival and misrule. All competing local authority or suspensions of authority must be either permanently abolished or incorporated into the machinery of civil policy and the administration of social discipline. Hal's success in accomplishing this project—revealing himself to be the true prince—is ominous in the context of a wider world. He has evaded his obligation to submit to compensatory thrashing and abjection. The rhythm that requires Lenten civil policy to be ceremonially expelled in the mock-trial of Jack-a-Lent is a piece of unfinished cultural and political business in the celebratory imagery of the final scenes of each of the *Henry IV* plays.

* * *

SAMUEL CROWL

[Welles and Falstaff]†

One of the richest debates in the history of Shakespearean criticism focuses upon Falstaff's role in the second tetralogy. In our time we have been rewarded with a variety of provocative interpretations of Shakespeare's most famous comic creation. To mention only some of the more familiar and recent, we have Falstaff as Braggart Soldier and Vice (J. Dover Wilson), Falstaff as Saturnalian Lord of Misrule (C. L. Barber), Falstaff as Emblem of Supreme Charity (W. H. Auden), Falstaff as Parodist and Holy Fool (Roy Battenhouse), and Falstaff as Centaur (Douglas J. Stewart).[1] The vigor of the continuing dialogue is witness to the power the second tetralogy exercises for modern readers. It is therefore surprising that our age has not produced a series of stage interpretations to match the wit and intelligence of the critical exchange about Falstaff's central importance to the plays which give him life. What makes it all the more paradoxical is that we live at a time when directors, particularly in England, have been highly receptive to translating the insights and methods of literary critics and scholars into imaginative production strategies.

The most recent staging of *1* and *2 Henry IV* and *Henry V* by the Royal Shakespeare Company in 1975 found its interpretive center in Alan Howard's development of Hal rather than in Brewster Mason's portrayal of Falstaff. The great production in the trio was *Henry V*, which was justifiably applauded by international audi-

† Samuel Crowl, "The Long Good-Bye: Welles and Falstaff," *Shakespeare Quarterly* 31 (1980), 369–80. Reprinted by permission of The John Hopkins University Press.

1. *The Fortunes of Falstaff* (Cambridge: Cambridge Univ. Press, 1943); *Shakespeare's Festive Comedy* (Princeton: Princeton Univ. Press, 1959); *The Dyer's Hand* (New York: Random House, 1962); "Falstaff as Parodist and Perhaps Holy Fool," *PMLA*, 90 (January 1975), 32–52; and "Falstaff the Centaur," *Shakespeare Quarterly*, 28 (Winter 1977), 5–21.

ences and critics. Significantly, it was also the first of the three plays to be performed at Stratford, though Alan Howard has indicated that "when we began rehearsals we worked on *Henry V* for one half the day, and *Henry IV, Part One* for the other half. And gradually one began to see that the whole question of acting, of assuming roles, which is so central to the early Hal, is carried through into *Henry V*."[2] Howard makes no mention of what Hal may have learned about "assuming roles" from his master teacher, Protean Falstaff. Stratford Festival Canada's productions of *1* and *2 Henry IV* in the 1979 season followed the pattern set by the RSC, magnifying Hal's relationship with his father while minimizing the importance of his imaginative invigoration when in Falstaff's company.

Several concrete examples from the two productions will help to illustrate what I'm exploring. In Terry Hands's direction for the RSC the blocking emphasis in *1 Henry IV* was far more thoughtful and interesting in the scenes between Hal and his father than in the Hal-Falstaff exchanges, so much so that 3.2 emerged as more subtle and complex than its wonderful parody in 2.4. Hal entered brandishing a tankard, a prop he continued to use with effect at moments intended to remind his father that he was determined to be his own man. In contrast, Emrys James's King made several faltering and embarrassed moves to embrace his son early in the scene but repeatedly pulled back when confronted with Hal's insistence on keeping a wary distance. The only furniture in the scene was the King's chair positioned at center stage, and the two men did a delicate dance around it, ending up in it together in a loving embrace on Hal's promise to "die a hundred thousand deaths / Ere break the smallest parcel of this vow" (3.2.158–59). Both leapt up to regain composure and control on Blunt's entrance (which received the intended laughter), but their pact was further sealed (and their identities were merged) when Henry IV took Hal's tankard and downed its contents as he delivered "A hundred thousand rebels die in this" (3.2.160). For those fortunate enough to see all three productions (once given on a single Saturday in March 1976), a stroke of casting became further evidence of the productions' intention to create a vital, living relationship between father and son, King and Prince. Hands cast Emrys James as the Chorus in *Henry V*. If one saw that production in close sequence with *1* and *2 Henry IV*, one was given the quite remarkable impression that the old King had been rewarded miraculously with his own deep wish: "Not an eye / But is a-weary of thy common sight, / Save mine, which hath desir'd to see thee more" [3.2.87–89].

2. *The Royal Shakespeare Company's Production of Henry V*, ed. Sally Beauman (Oxford: Pergamon Press, 1976), p. 53.

In Peter Moss's Canadian Stratford production of *1 Henry IV* the father-son relationship was again heightened and resolved in a fashion which led one to believe that their reunion was both a fitting climax and extension of Hal's tavern frolic. In this instance the comparison between Falstaff and Henry IV was made manifest by the casting and costuming of Lewis Gordon as Falstaff and Douglas Rain as King. Gordon is physically slight and even with the appropriate padding was not measurably larger than Rain's Henry. The resemblance between the two was further strengthened by having both characters sport nearly identical grey-white beards. When the two were both present on stage in Act 5 and enlarged by their armor they might have been mistaken for brothers! Moss underlined his efforts to create a bond twixt father and son by some damaging surgery to the concluding lines of the play. In the aftermath of Shrewsbury, after Falstaff has waddled in with his prize, Henry turns to Hal for a report on the day's success: "How goes the field?" Hal replies with his graphic description of Douglas' reaction to seeing his men scurry for safety on the "foot of fear":

> The noble Scot, Lord Douglas, when he saw
> The fortune of the day quite turn'd from him,
> The noble Percy slain, and all his men
> Upon the foot of fear, fled with the rest,
> And falling from a hill, he was so bruis'd
> That the pursuers took him.
> (5.5.17–22)

Hal and Henry share a boisterous laugh at Douglas' sad fall and exit arm and arm as the lights fall. The production sacrificed a great deal to end on that shared laughter, for it obliterated Hal's generous pardon, his expression of a noble charity to a worthy warrior-opponent, and his demonstrated political graciousness soon to be contrasted with his brother John's cold-blooded actions at Gaultree Forest in *2 Henry IV.* These are but a few examples of the ways in which both productions dramatized fresh approaches to Hal's relationship with his father, but failed to discover equally arresting strategies for exploring Falstaff's importance to these plays.

I

An important exception to the present trend to diminish Falstaff in order to underscore other values can be found in Orson Welles's critically neglected film, *Chimes at Midnight*, retitled *Falstaff* for its American release in 1966. The recent burst of intelligent essays on films based on Shakespeare's plays has not produced a single thorough analysis of this richest of Welles's film adaptations of Shakespeare. It is true that Jack Jorgens has a solid chapter on the film in his excellent book, *Shakespeare on Film*, and Daniel Seltzer offers enlightening comments about it in his pioneering essay describing how several productions of Shakespeare took liberties with the text in ways which enlarged rather than impoverished our understanding of the plays.[3] And of course there are numerous chapters on the film in books exclusively devoted to Welles's career as a film director. Most of these, however, view the film solely on cinematic grounds, uninterested to explore it as an interpretation of Shakespeare.

Critical inattention to the film can be traced to its lack of availability rather than to its merits. Prints of *Chimes at Midnight* are expensive and difficult to locate—a situation underlined by *New York Times* film critic Vincent Canby in a 1975 column devoted to Welles on the occasion of his being honored with the American Film Institute's Life Achievement Award: "Some of Welles's achievements are already easily recognized (*Citizen Kane* and *The Magnificent Ambersons*) but some spend most of their time in vaults, films like *Falstaff-Chimes at Midnight*, which may be the greatest Shakespeare film ever made, bar none."[4]

Like Canby, I believe that Welles's *Chimes at Midnight* is an excellent contemporary contribution to our understanding of Falstaff—and a work that has not received the close attention it warrants.

Welles is working, of course, with his own integration and dramatization of material lifted from the second tetralogy. His major emphasis is on *1* and *2 Henry IV*, with brief borrowings from *Richard II* and *Henry V*. He uses short selections from Holinshed as a narrative device to link this material together. I do not propose to delineate the exact manner in which Welles has organized and rearranged specific scenes, brief exchanges, or individual lines from Shakespeare's four plays in the making of his film, for such material is readily available in Jack Jorgens' indispensable summary of that material.[5] I wish merely to explore how Welles captures Hal's emergence from the two fathers who threaten to submerge his own unique identity, either through guilty rule or guilded license, with particular emphasis on Welles's treatment of Falstaff. Daniel Seltzer's synopsis of Welles's achievement is instructive:

> Welles's movie is essentially a kaleidoscopic revisualization of Shakespeare's two plays. Scenes are set in new sequence,

3. Jack Jorgens, *Shakespeare on Film* (Bloomington and London: Indiana Univ. Press, 1977), and Daniel Seltzer, "Shakespeare's Texts and Modern Productions," in *Reinterpretations of Elizabethan Drama: Selected Papers from the English Institute*, ed. Norman Rabkin (New York: Columbia Univ. Press, 1969), 89–115.
4. *The Sunday New York Times*, 2 March 1975, 17.
5. Jorgens, 268–72.

> many of them cut entirely, others formed of the original text intact but with lines from elsewhere in the plays inserted for conceptual emphasis—either ironic or corroborative, some of the characters eliminated, but those remaining never destructively over-simplified. Amazingly, into two and a half hours of film time, Welles has set forth the psychological reality of these plays, taking as his dynamic center the same core of deep human emotion that energizes Shakespeare's texts—the struggle within Prince Hal simultaneously to love, resist, and to survive two parents, one his father and the other a surrogate, and to choose from among several life styles one that is uniquely and triumphantly his.[6]

I agree with Seltzer: *Chimes at Midnight* is a compelling contemporary attempt to capture Shakespeare's resonances, not a self-aggrandizing effort to reshape Shakespeare's plays into a bastardization celebrating Welles's cinematic genius. Seltzer is mistaken, however, when he declares that Welles "has placed his emphasis where it is in Shakespeare, and so often is not in modern productions—upon the prince himself. The King, Falstaff, and Hotspur move about him, come tangent to him, but never do we forget what these scenes are about."[7] Welles's two titles, if nothing else, point to the centrality of Falstaff, not Hal. The original title (*Chimes at Midnight*) explicitly places the passing of Falstaff at the heart of his interpretation.

II

Welles's interest in Falstaff and the Henry plays dates from 1938, when, at the age of 23, he and John Houseman mounted an ambitious but unsuccessful stage production of this material, entitled *Five Kings*, for the Theater Guild. In his fascinating book on Welles's stage career, Richard France offers this account: "Central to Welles's understanding of the chronicle plays was his use of the character of Falstaff to dominate the stage completely. He was for Welles the production's major expressive element. While enlarging the stature and importance of Falstaff, Welles reduced the character of Prince Hal."[8] Twenty-eight years later Welles had not changed his mind about the need to focus on Falstaff. In an interview conducted just prior to the film's release, Welles indicated that "you discover in the making of the film that the death of the King, and the death of Hotspur, which is the death of chivalry, and Falstaff's poverty and Falstaff's illness run all throughout the play.

6. Seltzer, 103–4.
7. Seltzer, 104–5.
8. *The Theater of Orson Welles* (Lewisburg and London: Bucknell Univ. Press, 1977), 161.

Comedy can't really dominate a film made to tell this story, which is all in dark colors."[9] When asked if he agreed that his film could be seen as a lament for Falstaff, he replied, "Yes, that may be true. I would like to think that."[1] Seltzer's description of Welles's portrayal of Falstaff—"jovial he can be, but predominantly he is sad"—is a perceptive comment on Welles's performance.[2] What Seltzer fails to realize is that such a reading extends beyond Welles's interpretation of the character to cast a cold eye on the entire film. An analysis of several crucial scenes in the film will demonstrate, I hope, that Welles's overriding visual and structural emphasis is to signal farewell, to say a long goodbye to Falstaff, rather than to celebrate Hal's homecoming to princely right reason and responsible rule.

III

The opening shot of the film shows Welles's way of organizing his own shaping fantasy of Shakespeare's material. The camera peers from a ridge over a snow-covered landscape; there we pick out two figures slowly working their way through the snow toward an ancient and imposing oak tree, equidistant between our vantage-point and the travelers. The composition of the shot is arresting; and its quality of stark black and white, coupled with its immediate evocation of landscape as symbolic and psychological territory (years past Macbeth's sere and yellow leaf), owes as much to Bergman as it does to Shakespeare. We follow the figures as they move toward and around the oak, and then we cut to a medium close-up as they enter a heavy-beamed and timbered room and settle themselves before an immense roaring fire. The two figures are in striking contrast: one huge and placid, the other frail and nervous. The camera shoots between them to the warmth of the fire as Alan Webb's Shallow rasps, "Jesus, Sir John, the days that we have seen."

The frame through which Welles presents his film, then, is not Shakespeare's "so shaken as we are, so wan with care," with its focus on Henry IV's burden and political dilemma; it is the personal filter of the play's other Olympian pretender, Falstaff. The intention of this partial, open-ended frame is to create the impression of a flashback. Its effect is to allow us to see that this is Falstaff's story. We are to witness the glory of his days and to partake in the sorrow of their passing. The winter landscape, the two stoic figures seeking the warmth of the blazing fire, the scene of slow, uphill struggle culminating in stasis—all speak profoundly to Welles's observation that by focusing on Falstaff his Shakespearean material leads him

9. Juan Cobos and Miguel Rubio, "Welles and Falstaff," *Sight and Sound*, 35 (Autumn 1966), 159.
1. Cobos and Rubio, 159.
2. Seltzer, 105.

into dark colors; it is Falstaff's winter which dominates the texture of the film, not Hal's summer of self-realization.

IV

Though I think the atmosphere of loss and lament can be identified throughout the film, I would now like to describe five key scenes which most fully embody the farewell atmosphere of Welles's interpretation.

Welles stresses the importance of leave-taking in his conception of the relationship between Hal and Falstaff: "I directed everything, and played everything, with a view of preparing for the last scene. The relationship between Falstaff and the Prince is not a simple comic relationship . . . but always a preparation for the end. And as you see, the farewell is performed about four times during the movie, foreshadowed four times."[3] I do not deny that Welles's view of Falstaff is a sentimental one, but it does not indulge in the hyperbolic though memorable excesses of Falstaff's romantic apologists from Morgann to Auden to Battenhouse. Because Welles is intelligent enough to let us see Falstaff's cowardice as well as his discretion, he manages to avoid misleading us into regarding his fat knight as no more than a harmless comedian spinning his anti-establishment jests for any well-paying dispensation. Welles has said that he regards Falstaff as more witty than funny, and his film squares with that assessment.[4] For Welles's Falstaff is a threat as well as a treat, and our sorrow at his rejection is tempered but not supplanted by the film's consistent awareness of that fact.

After the opening sequence, the credits are rolled against a background of marching troops and jaunty martial music, giving a vigorous pace to these shots in significant contrast to the tempo and landscape of the Falstaff-Shallow beginning. The film then moves to Westminster and the clash between Henry IV (beautifully played by John Gielgud) and Northumberland, Worcester, and Hotspur. Gielgud's elevated presence (captured by the actor's tone and haughty demeanor and by the camera's low-angle perspective) in the Spanish cathedral at Cardonna, with the light streaming in from the clerestories in carefully divided segments and his breath flowing visibly forward in the same cold divisions, is a remarkable visual achievement. At once we grasp all the textual images associated with Henry IV and his rule: care, division, distance, concern,

3. Cobos and Rubio, 159. Jack Jorgens enumerates these farewell moments, but does not examine their implications in detail, being content to allow his listing to conclude with the following sweeping observation: "Welles portrays people alienated, people driven apart by death and the forces of history, people betraying each other" (114). I trust it is no betrayal of Jorgens' fine analysis to insist that more attention needs to be given to the significance of the ways in which Welles's film says farewell to Falstaff.
4. "Welles on Falstaff," *Cahiers du Cinema in English*, 11 (September 1967), 7.

austerity, calculation, emotional repression. When the film cuts from Westminster to the Boar's Head, our focus is immediately upon Falstaff snoring in his bed (the two fathers, thus, at once placed and defined).[5] The horseplay between Hal and Falstaff which follows is enlivened by the camera's careening progress as it tracks Falstaff in pursuit of Hal. Falstaff thunders down a narrow, twisting staircase into the tavern's great room, arched by giant beams and filled with long tables. Every time the camera is in this setting, it is alive with the energy of festive motion. Tracking, cutting, rapid shifts of angle: the camera's activity becomes a metaphor for the frenetic pleasure this locale releases in its celebrants. But the significant movement, repeated three times in the film, is Hal's progress *through* the tavern atmosphere, trailed by a cajoling Falstaff, out into its courtyard. In this first pass through the Boar's Head the tavern is empty, but Hal's desire to escape is paramount.

Once we are outside, Welles provides us with a dual landscape. In the foreground we have the entrance to the tavern proper, at mid-distance are the gates opening out from the inn-yard, and in the extreme background we see the imposing ramparts of a castle. Welles chooses to shoot the opening of Hal's "I know you all" soliloquy from a medium long shot in which we see (a) the castle ramparts, (b) Hal poised at the inn-yard's gates, and (c) Falstaff (slightly out of focus) framed in the Boar's Head entrance, looking quizzically toward the heir-apparent.

Welles's strategy here is both disconcerting and revealing. Hal is speaking directly into the camera—to us—but our perspective is complicated because we also see Falstaff over his shoulder. Here the landscape provides meaning. Hal is literally poised between the tavern and the castle, as his soliloquy makes metaphorically manifest. He is speaking to us, not to Falstaff; and thus we are associated with the castle in the foreground, incorporated into the drama as that audience who demand an explanation for his riotous behavior. Hal thus separates us from Falstaff, making us members of the Prince's party by confiding to us his regard for the past and his plans for the future. The moment is further enriched, and our sense of being suspended with Hal enlarged, by the way in which

5. Terry Hands's production for the RSC made another interesting attempt to capture spatially the two-fathers theme. The opening scene was played on a bare platform with only stage right lit by spots; as Henry received the reports of the civil disturbances within the kingdom, the audience gradually became aware of two figures stationed on stage left. One was lying down covered with a blanket. The other stood upstage center equidistant from the busy King and the slumbering body. As the play shifted into its second scene, we became aware that the standing figure was Hal, who approached the covered body and began to try and rouse it, unsuccessfully, by a series of buzzing noises. Finally, Hal uncorked a bottle of wine and began to pour it into a huge tankard resting beside the sleeper. The sound of wine, of course, roused Falstaff into action, and the play had its first laugh before the fat knight had spoken a word.

Welles has Keith Baxter break up the concluding couplet of the soliloquy. The penultimate line "I'll so offend to make offense a skill" is delivered with Hal pivoting to face Falstaff, and "offend" is underlined by Baxter's wink, which draws a smile from the old misleader of youth. Then Baxter turns back to the camera and to us to confess, *sotto voce*, "Redeeming time when men least think I will." In Welles's strategic use of topography and spatial relationships, Hal here stands caught between the tavern and the castle, between Falstaff's inviting smile and the bleak landscape leading toward the fortifications of responsibility. As Hal leaves, he moves through the innyard gates shouting his farewell to Falstaff, whose mind is absorbed, not with the implications of this leave-taking, but with the morning's promised "offensive" at Gad's Hill. The camera cuts between Hal riding off and Falstaff planted at the threshold of his domain, accepting the first of his long goodbyes.

The farewell motif is repeated in a minor, but wildly comic, key in the Gad's Hill robbery scene—one of the film's most beautiful visual moments. Shot in Madrid's El Retiro park, the scene's ground is covered with leaves, and narrow trees stand tall and bare in late autumn's austere beauty. The invention and pace of Welles's tracking shots become an integral part of the comic zest and jest exploding from the multiple collisions of this pack of fellow travelers. Falstaff and crew have adorned themselves in the voluminous folds of hooded, white terry-cloth robes, and they approach their prey in the guise of prayerful supplicants. Hal and Poins wear romantic capes and broad-brimmed black hats as they swoop down to rob the robbers of their booty. (This scene in film and text works in ironic counterpoint with the later battle at Shrewsbury, where it is Falstaff who proves the counterfeit and robs Hal of his purse-y.) At Gad's Hill, Hal says goodbye by simply showing Falstaff his backside as he scurries away, remarking to Poins:

> Falstaff sweats to death,
> And lards the lean earth as he walks along.
> Were't not for laughing I should pity him.
> [2.2.95–97]

This mixture of tough-mindedness and sentiment prefigures the tone and stance Hal will adopt in his famous (and mistaken) eulogy of his fat friend delivered at Shrewsbury:

> What, old acquaintance, could not all this flesh
> Keep in a little life? Poor Jack, farewell!
> I could have better spar'd a better man:
> O, I should have a heavy miss of thee
> If I were much in love with vanity:

Death hath not struck so fat a deer today,
Though many dearer, in this bloody fray.
(5.4.101–7)

When the film returns to the Boar's Head, it is to capture Act 2, scene 4, the celebrated tavern scene where Hal and Falstaff exuberantly mock rebels and rivals, kings and kingdoms, vanities and vices, and, most significantly, fathers and sons. In one great intuitive sweep, Shakespeare here accomplishes the dream of every comic writer—to give us the parody before the reality. Welles's Falstaff, firmly planted atop a tavern table with a tin saucepan for a crown, literally becomes, through the camera's low-angle perspective, a titanic figure well deserving of Hal's hyperbolic slander—the roasted manning-tree ox with the pudding in his belly. This is the moment, in both play and film, when Falstaff is at his zenith: Auden's emblem of life and laughter-giving charity. But that moment fades as soon as Hal sees which way Falstaff's wind is blowing. Hal insists that they change places and parts, thus displacing his surrogate father at the very instant that he assumes the mock *persona* of his real father. Now the camera provides us with repeated overhead angles: Hal-Henry admonishes Falstaff-Hal for the villainous company he keeps. Welles holds the climactic moment—"Banish plump Jack and banish all the world." "I do. I will."—for several beats before that monstrous watch comes banging at the door. This frozen moment works in spite of our awareness that Hal's threat must be interrupted before it can be absorbed by Falstaff, because the camera catches on Welle's face the same quizzical expression that we witnessed peering at us in the background of the "I know you all" soliloquy.

Here Welles's critical intelligence captures an important dimension of Shakespeare's meaning, a dimension that frequently escapes other interpreters of Falstaff. For all of Falstaff's Orwellian alertness to the sham hollowness of political rhetoric, for all his ability to see through and comically explode the pieties of power, the one person he does not see through is his own pupil, Hal—the most powerfully shrewd character in the play. In that suspended moment, Welles makes us see Falstaff's inability to comprehend Hal's projected threat of banishment. When the watch does come knocking on the door, however, the screen is filled with activity and the camera bursts into motion as the Boar's Head patrons race for cover from the law's intrusion. In the text, Hal instructs Falstaff to hide behind the arras, but Welles has him disappear through a trapdoor (a neat stage analogy) into the tavern's bowels. This scene becomes a perfect foreshadowing of the eventual rejection scene, where King Hal sends Falstaff toward that grave which "gapes for him thrice wider than for other men."

Adroitly, Welles now cuts directly to 3.3 as though it were the following morning with all its marvelous otter play with Mistress Quickly and the debate over Hal's supposed indebtedness of £1,000 to Falstaff. There is great poignance in Falstaff's rejoinder that Hal owes him his love, which is surely worth a million. Hal is drawn into a gigantic bear-hug on this line, illustrating the exuberant and warm tactile relationship Falstaff and Hal share in the film, an aspect of Hal's behavior that is skillfully contrasted with the aloof and distanced space Henry IV insists on keeping even in his fondest exchanges with his son. When, during that companionable embrace, we get the exchange concerning Falstaff's jest that he fears Hal only as he fears "the roaring of the lion's whelp," Hal asks, "And why not as the lion?" The camera closes in on Falstaff, who responds: "The king himself is to be feared as the lion: dost thou think I'll fear *thee* as I fear thy *father*?" With Falstaff's question left swaying in the unanswered air, the camera slowly pulls back to a medium close shot. Falstaff then collapses into a chair, where his ample lap is quickly filled by Doll Tearsheet (another skillful interpolation from *2 Henry IV*), come to mourn his imminent departure to recruit his charge of foot. Tearsheet is played by Jeanne Moreau, and as this remarkable French actress puts her inviting pout into framing Shakespeare's words we are treated to a marvelous, and I'm sure unintentional, reward of international casting. As she caresses Welles and coos to him Shakespeare's loving "Ah, Jack you whoreson tidy Bartholomew boar-pit," Moreau's "whoreson" emerges distinctly as "Orson."

When Hal moves to take his second leave from Falstaff and the tavern world, he passes through the central room, now alive with customers whose festive presence repeatedly impedes his attempts at exit and release. Once he has emerged from the labyrinth of revelry, he is framed by the same landscape we witnessed earlier in his first departure. This time Hal turns and shouts back at Falstaff: "Farewell thou latter spring, all-hallown summer!" As Hal makes this second exit from Falstaff and his tavern rule, he is not riding to soothe a ruffled father but to confront a fiery rival—Hotspur. If the first farewell was an indication that Hal was called upon to move in other worlds than the tavern, the second reminds us that if those other worlds pose a threat to Falstaff ("Should I fear thee as I fear thy father?"), they also present a threat and a challenge, in the person of Hotspur, to Hal. As Hal departs now we know that he isn't simply taking leave of Falstaff but is moving irrevocably toward engagement in his father's world of political responsibility. Nevertheless the film's focus is on Hal's sad goodbye to the Boar's Head and Falstaff rather than on a jaunty welcome (represented in the text by

Vernon's hyperbolic description of Hal in arms, but cut in Welles's film) to honor's battlefield.

The Shrewsbury battle scene is one of the film's justly celebrated visual achievements, and Pauline Kael is right to see it as belonging with sequences from Eisenstein, D. W. Griffith, Kurosawa, and John Ford.[6] From a Shakespearean's viewpoint, it corresponds directly with Jan Kott's chilling, middle-European reading of the history plays as dramas re-enacting not the sanctity of hierarchy but the brutality of armed aggression: The Grand Mechanism. There is little doubt that Welles meant to endow his Shrewsbury with a very different tone and atmosphere from the romantic and stirring version of Agincourt Olivier achieved in his justly-admired film of *Henry V.* Shakespeare presents multiple perspective on Shrewsbury's significance: Worcester's cold Machiavellianism, Henry IV's shrewd military strategy, Hotspur's heady intemperance, Douglas' exasperated professionalism, Falstaff's knowing cynicism, and Hal's practical assurance that this is his day to seize. Abandoning Shakespeare's multiplicity, Welles concentrates on a modern extension of Falstaff's understanding that war's appetite is fed by "mortal men," that war can make all of us "food for powder." Welles attempts to capture what war is like for the men in the trenches rather than for those mounted on dashing chargers gliding athletically toward their opponents. If Olivier's film version of Agincourt was a patriotic evocation of Hal's unsullied triumph (all lines revealing his darker side having been cut, including "Kill all the prisoners"), shot in a manner to highlight his vitality and pluck, Welles's treatment of Shrewsbury is a slow, painful, exhausting depiction of mud-laden soldiers enacting some primal destructive rite.[7]

When asked how he managed the intense blow-by-blow effect of the battle scene, Welles responded:

> On the first day I tried to do very short pieces, but I found that extras didn't work as well unless they had a longer thing to do. They didn't seem to be really fighting until they had time to warm up. That's why the takes were long, since there was no way of beginning the camera later and cutting. But I knew I was only going to use very short cuts. For example, we shot with a very big crane very low to the ground, moving as fast as

6. *Kiss Kiss Bang Bang* (New York: Bantam Books, 1969), 247.
7. Perhaps the finest compliment to Welles's capturing of ignorant armies clashing by day can be illustrated by a personal example. When I first taught this film several years ago, my daughter and son (then ages 9 and 7) joined me for one of its screenings. During the unfolding of the Hal-Falstaff relationship prior to the battle scene I was repeatedly bombarded with questions about "who," "what," and "why"? Once the battle sequence began there was a period of long silence. When my daughter finally offered an observation, she was met with an intense "Shhhhhhhh" from her younger brother, who had become completely engrossed in Welles's surreal landscape.

> it could be moved against the action. What I was planning to do—and did—was to intercut the shots in which the action was contrary, so that every cut seemed to be a blow, a counter blow, a blow received, a blow returned. Actually it takes a lot of time for the crane to move over and back, but everything was planned for this effect and I never intended to use more than a small section of the arc in each case.[8]

Welles's battle is stunning in its horror, and the camera clearly sympathizes with Falstaff's comic cowardice as he scurries in and out of harm's way looking like a giant armadillo in his ill-fitting armor. The clash between Hal and Hotspur is not prolonged. Both men are exhausted, their swords as heavy to their arms as a boxer's fists become in the fifteenth round of a title fight, and Hal outlasts his spirited rival because he has husbanded his energies more resourcefully than Hotspur. The battle world Welles gives us represents Falstaff's perspective on war and honor, just as Olivier's Agincourt sprang from his understanding of Henry V's daring determination.

After Falstaff has counterfeited death back into life, Welles jumps us into 2 *Henry IV* and creates a post-Shrewsbury scene which contains the third of our leave-takings, this time in a new landscape and with an interesting reversal of perspective.

For the first time in the film we see Hal, his father, and Falstaff together. When Falstaff drags the body of Hotspur into the camp where father and son, King and Prince, are congratulating themselves on their victory, Welles has Gielgud give Falstaff a disdainful glare as the King moves away from the crowd gathering to admire Falstaff's prize. The sky is filled with large, somber clouds moving elegantly across the horizon. A camp wagon, holding a butt of wine, is positioned in the center of the frame. The composition of this shot is reminiscent of countless John Ford and Howard Hawks western scenes. In fact, the roll of the clouds across the sky here mirrors the famous graveyard scene in Hawks's *Red River*, where, as the story goes, Hawks had instructed John Wayne to speed up his lines so that the camera could capture the cloud which was passing overhead on patrol. In an interview I conducted several years ago with Hawks, I asked him if he thought Welles's scene was derivative (Welles has repeatedly stressed his indebtedness to both Hawks and Ford), and his charming reply was "Yep. I always thought Orson was just using Shakespeare to disguise the fact he was making a western in that picture."[9] What Welles draws on by employing this particular setting is a sense of post-battle camaraderie as the men

8. Cobos and Rubio, 161.
9. Hawks made this remark during a television interview with me in April 1976. Hawks was in Athens, Ohio, to be honored by the Athens International Film Festival, and had a seemingly inexhaustible supply of stories, which he liberally shared with all. The interview was televised on WOUB-TV, the local PBS station, on 14 May 1976.

gather for refreshment and tale-telling (as in the campfire scenes which conclude days on the cattle drive in westerns), a setting ideally suited to Falstaff's talents. Now that the actual danger has passed, the setting seems to say, Falstaff is ready to usurp the center of attention by dramatizing his version of the day's events. He moves eagerly toward the wagon and a waiting cup of sack and then turns to deliver his famous disquisition on the inventive powers of sherris-sack. This speech is, of course, a soliloquy in Shakespeare's text; but Welles presents it with Hal poised in the background, in a stunning reversal of their positions in the two Boar's Head tavern farewell scenes we have already examined. This is an incredibly full moment in the film. One father, Henry IV, has exited on the arrival of his surrogate. As Falstaff reaches the brilliant climax of his essay—"If I had a thousand sons, the first human principle I would teach them would be to forswear thin potations and addict themselves to sack" (*2H4*, 4.3.121–23)—Hal drops his tankard on the barren ground and moves off to follow his father's path. Falstaff is left to search for an audience and a reaction in an empty landscape. This third goodbye is an unspoken one, but once again it leaves the camera focused on Falstaff's uncomprehending face, perplexed by Hal's failure to be overwhelmed by his performance.

The fourth goodbye is, of course, the one which both plays move toward, the coronation scene where Hal accepts the role of his public father and rejects the threat of his private one. Welles's visual construction of the scene is, again, based on a reversal of the pattern established in Hal's earlier farewells at the Boar's Head. If earlier it was Hal who had to push his way through the tavern crowd (those foul and ugly mists which did seem to strangle him), now it is Falstaff who has to fight his way through an imposing congregation of soldiers, armed with long pikes, to confront his son-king. To reach the lion's whelp, Falstaff must pick his way through a labyrinth of pomp and power. As he falls to his knees to receive the tap which will put the laws of England at his command (as well as those resources necessary to repay the £1,000 he has conjured out of Shallow), the camera pulls back to shoot Hal's austere "I know thee not old man . . . " through the interstices of the pikes of power. When the procession has passed on and over our large supplicant, Falstaff makes a resigned recovery for his expectant companions and then, in the company of his page, moves away from us down a long, tunnel-like passageway, slowly diminishing in size. This is the last shot we have of this vast physical presence—moving away from the audience he had courted and entertained, swallowed by the shadows.

The final scene of the film returns to the Boar's Head innyard where Mistress Quickly, Bardolph, Pistol, and Falstaff's page are positioned at the same tavern entrance where we witnessed Falstaff responding to Hal's initial farewell. Now the scene is funereal. The camera closes in on Margaret Rutherford as she blubbers her way through one of the most memorable eulogies in the history of literature. "And then I felt to his knees, and so upward and upward, and all was cold as any stone." Bardolph, Pistol, and the other pallbearers move away to an immense cart upon which rests the largest coffin in the history of film. Slowly and with great effort, they begin to push it out through the gates. Once again the castle ramparts define and limit the upper edge of the frame. This is the film's final long goodbye: the camera lingers over the laborious procession wheeling away the body "that when it did contain a spirit, a kingdom for it was too small a bound." As we participate in this sad farewell to Falstaff, Holinshed's words (in the voice of Ralph Richardson) emerge to proclaim a bitterly ironic contrast to what our eyes are telling us: "Thus began the reign of King Henry V, famous to the world in all ways." As the new dispensation proclaims itself, the coffin rumbles on its inexorable path to the grave. The new King is headed for France, and Citizen Falstaff is dead.

V

I hope my analysis has demonstrated that Welles builds his film around his conception of Falstaff. Fully aware that great works of narrative art construct a necessary and significant relationship between their central characters and the landscape they inhabit, Welles says:

> The people must live in their world. It is a fundamental problem for the filmmaker, even when you are making apparently the most ordinary modern story. But particularly when you have a great figure of myth like Quixote, like Falstaff, a silhouette against the sky of all time . . . you can't simply dress up and *be* them, you have to make a world for them.[1]

From our first view of Falstaff working his way through a wintry landscape, to the horrors of the combat at Shrewsbury, to the titanic coffin making its way to the grave, Welles's images all contribute to the creation of a world enriched by Falstaff's presence and diminished by his loss.

Kenneth Tynan has written in admiration of Welles that "Orson coming into a room is like the sunrise."[2] In *Chimes at Midnight,* we do see a son rise, but our last and lingering image—a silhouette against the sky of all time—is of a great genius being carted off to the grave.

1. Cobos and Rubio, 159.
2. *The Sound of Two Hands Clapping* (New York: Holt, Rinehart and Winston, 1975), 170.

PATRICIA PARKER

[Falstaff]†

* * *

One Shakespearean "fat lady" is ostensibly no lady at all—old Jack Falstaff, whose corpulence, in the *Henriad*, in some sense embodies Prince Hal's delay, a Prodigal Son plot in which the completed movement of reformation and return to the father takes not one but two long and prodigally copious plays to effect. This "hill of flesh" [2.4.219] "lards the lean earth as he walks along" [2.2.95–96]. But he is even more tellingly imaged in the series of hierarchized oppositions we have already encountered. His fat body is specifically a "*globe* of sinful continents" (*2H4*, 2.4.285). The second and completing half of the two plays also evokes in both comic and more serious contexts that "Jordan" to be crossed before entrance into the Promised Land, before its own culminating "Jerusalem." It is, we remember, the Chief Justice, representative of both the father and the Law he evades, who warns Falstaff that his "waste"—manifested in his expanding waist—is "great" (*2H4*, 1.2.141). And the Hal who from the beginning of the two extended plays forecasts to the audience that his own tarrying and prodigality, with this "fat rogue" and the other "tattered prodigals," will be of only a "holiday" or temporary nature, ends that promise of reformation with an echo of the text in Ephesians on redeeming the time ("Redeeming time when men think least I will"; [1.2.190]), leaving Falstaff with the other "Ephesians" or "boon companions" as the counterpart of the unredeemed Ephesus before the "partition" between Old and New is crossed.

Falstaff in these plays, as Hal puts it, is "my sweet creature of bumbast" [2.4.291] in both punning senses—the padding that stuffs a body out and its verbal equivalent. His fat is linked not just with "harlotry" (*2H4*, 2.4.41)—including perhaps that of Mistress Quickly's malapropped "harlotry players" [2.4.352]—but with verbal *copia* as well, with that "throng of words" (*2H4*, 2.1.112) which, even in these two prodigally copious plays, "cannot," as Falstaff says of himself, "last forever" (*2H4*, 1.2.214). Falstaff's own decision to repent his wasted life (with more punning on his expanded waist or girth) is, we might note, accompanied by references to his dwindling size, as if this movement to closure,

† From Patricia Parker, *Literary Fat Ladies: Rhetoric, Gender, Property* (London: Methuen, 1987), 20–22. Reprinted by permission of the author.

reformation, and repentance involved a literal relation between the body of this prodigal play and its physically fat emblem (*1H4*, 3.3.1–2: "Bardolph, am I not fall'n away vilely since this last action? Do I not bate? Do I not dwindle?").

Falstaff himself is, of course, not a woman but a man. But he actually appears as a fat lady in *The Merry Wives of Windsor.* When he does, in a scene of transvestitism which perhaps suggests what Falstaff has all along been missing, explicit embodiment is given to his effeminate associations throughout the other plays in which he figures. Here, as a "fat woman," he takes refuge in the chamber associated with an "Ephesian" Host (4.5.18) and "painted about with the story of the Prodigal" (4.5.7–8). And the play links references to "Fat Falstaff" with figures of "mirth . . . so larded with . . . matter" and of recounting "at large" (4.6.14–18). In *Henry IV, Parts 1* and 2, fat itself is compared to the image of the pregnant earth, filled with wind (Falstaff punningly attributes his great size to his "sighs" or wind). Falstaff's fat is repeatedly associated with the copiousness or dilation of discourse, with avoiding the summons of the law through various counterparts of the "dilatory plea," and with the wombs and tongues of women ("I have a whole school of tongues in this belly of mine, and not a tongue of them all speaks any other word but my name. . . . My womb, my womb, my womb undoes me"; *2H4*, 4.3.18–23).

But his expanded "waste" is a womb which in a sense never delivers the "issue" and which is therefore left behind in what, after all, is the drama of a return to the father, or genealogical succession. Falstaff's belly full of tongues links him, as do his tavern hostesses, Mistress Quickly and Doll Tearsheet, with the proverbially unstoppable female tongue. But Hal, in his only temporary prodigality and delay, merely "studies his companions / Like a strange tongue," in order to master or "gain the language," so, "like gross terms" (with Falstaff visibly the grossest), he can "cast" them "off" in "the perfectness of time" (*2H4*, 4.4.68–78). If, in seasonal terms, Falstaff's fatness suggests the autumnal plenty of "martlemas" before the coming of winter (*2H4*, 2.2.97), in genealogical and political terms, he is, together with the languages or "tongues" to be gained by the young prince, finally a sign of the prodigiousness and teleology of mastery. Though technically androgynous, Falstaff ends up, in this movement to kingship which banishes and effectively "kills" him, subject to that law of categorization in which, in relation to the exclusively male, even the androgyne remains on the side of the female. And "[b]anish plump Jack, and banish all the world" [2.4.427–28] leaves fat Falstaff, in relation to the fabled leanness of a king descended from a "John of *Gaunt*," in the same textual space, so to speak, in this movement to ending, as that of the globular Nell in *The Comedy of Errors*.

As the "fat woman of Brainford" (*MWW*, 4.2.75), Falstaff is not only a harlot or "queen" but a Circean "witch" as well (4.2.172). The fact, however, that this figure associated both with "fat" and with a Ciceronian copia of words is not actually female but effeminized male is in itself revealing. The gendered oppositions at work here—the ones that produced another Renaissance text entitled "Women are words, men deeds," which goes on to treat not of wordy women but of the monstrous third possibility of wordy men, including by implication what Greene called the "babbling" of poets—are by no means stable. The opposition male/female often masks anxieties surrounding the figure of the feminized or effeminate male, just as in the misogynist diatribes against the female tongue the generative power inhabiting and generating the very discourse of misogyny often becomes the female loquacity which is its animating subject.

* * *

COPPÉLIA KAHN

[Masculine Identities]†

* * *

Richard II portrays a loss of identity through a loss of kingship; the *Henry IV* plays, an identity won through kingship. The story of how Henry and his son reciprocally validate each other as father and son, king and prince, begins in the last act of *Richard II*, when Henry cries, "Can no man tell me of my unthrifty son?" (5.3.1). Henry's anxiety about Hal is complexly related to his two last actions in the play: pardoning Aumerle's treason and arranging for the murder of Richard. The two actions are depicted so as to present a spectrum of attitudes toward the father-son bond. Though York at first defends Richard as the divinely appointed king who rules by successive right, he finally opts for loyalty to Henry as *de facto* king, but not without misgivings. In accusing his own son of treason, he acts on this new loyalty but violates the blood tie between himself and his son—the tie that, the Duchess argues, far outweighs any other. Surprisingly, Henry pardons Aumerle and goes against his own characteristic alle-

† From Coppélia Kahn, *Man's Estate: Masculine Identity in Shakespeare* (Berkeley & Los Angeles: University of California Press, 1981), 69–74. Reprinted by permission of the publisher.

giance to patriarchal order by failing to punish a man who would betray both father and king. Henry gives no explanation for his action except to say, "I pardon him as God shall pardon me" (5.3.129). Since this scene is followed by the scene in which Exton pins the responsibility for Richard's murder on Henry, we may infer that Henry pardons Aumerle's treason because he already feels guilty for his own. In order to be king, he kills the king, his brother-cousin, and must suffer Cain's guilt. Henry regards Hal as his punishment long before he explicitly admits (in *2 Henry IV*) having committed any crime. He who righteously invoked the principle of succession even as his troops massed before Richard at Flint Castle, and claimed to seek only his "lineal royalties," is appropriately punished by his own son's seeming unfitness to inherit the crown.

In the course of the two *Henry IV* plays, Shakespeare presents a conception of the father-son bond and its part in the formation of a masculine identity vastly different from that in the first tetralogy. In place of the emphasis on repetition and the past there, with its taut emulation of the father and inflexible vendettas, Shakespeare conceives of a relationship with some give to it, literally some free play, some space for departure from paternal priority and for experiences fundamentally opposed to it. In place of the failures in transition from sonship to fatherhood represented by Henry VI, John Talbot, Young Clifford, and Richard III, he tries to portray a successful passage negotiated, paradoxically, as lawful rebellion and responsible play. He makes Hal the stage manager of his own growing up, the embodiment of a wish to let go—but to let go only so far, without real risks. In the end, Falstaff's regressive appeal is so dangerously strong for Shakespeare that he cannot afford to integrate it into Hal's character, and must, to Hal's loss, exclude it totally.[1] From the sonnets to *The Winter's Tale*, the idea of remaining "boy eternal" exerts a powerful pull on Shakespeare's imagination that he strenuously resists. At the same time, however, he discovers new

1. Interpreters of the Henry IV plays divide into two camps: those who find Hal's rejection of Falstaff a limitation of Hal's character and/or of Shakespeare's breadth of sympathy, and those who justify it in terms of a moral theme unifying the plays. I line up behind those in the first camp, including C. L. Barber, "Rule and Misrule in Henry IV," in his *Shakespeare's Festive Comedy: A Study of Dramatic Form and Its Relation to Social Custom* (Princeton: Princeton University Press, 1959), 192–218; Jonas Barish, "The Turning Away of Prince Hal," *Shakespeare Studies* 1 (1965): 9–17; A. C. Bradley, "The Rejection of Falstaff," reprinted in *Shakespeare, Henry IV, Parts I and II: A Casebook*, ed. G. K. Hunter (London: Macmillan, 1970), 55–72; J. A. Bryant, "Prince Hal and the Ephesians," *Sewanee Review* 67 (1959): 204–19. However, John Dover Wilson, *The Fortunes of Falstaff* (Cambridge: Cambridge University Press, 1943), argues that the morality structure, in which Falstaff is the Vice, necessitates his rejection; and Sherman Hawkins, "Virtue and Kingship in Shakespeare's *Henry IV*," *English Literary Renaissance* 5 (Autumn 1975): 313–342, holds that the tradition of the four kingly virtues also dictates the rejection. Both convincingly show that these doctrines are at work in the plays. I maintain, however, that Shakespeare's purpose is to show in Hal the tension between Falstaff's encompassing humanity and the moral and political imperatives of rule, not to justify the latter at the expense of the former.

dimensions in the lifelong process of becoming a man; he begins to see how the father's identity is shaped by his son, as well as the son's by his father. In Henry and Hal he uses the renewal of the principle of succession as a way to validate Henry's kingship as much as Hal's; identity becomes a reciprocal process between father and son.

The relationship between the two men has three focal points of overdetermined needs and signals at which crises are defined or resolved. The first is the Boar's Head and Hal's reign there as madcap prince under the tutelage of Falstaff, who is usually seen as anti-king and anti-father, standing for misrule as opposed to rule.[2] But he is also the opposite of the king in the sense of being his predecessor psychologically, the king of childhood and omnipotent wishes, as Henry is king in the adult world of rivalry and care. Franz Alexander describes Falstaff as the personification of "the primary self-centered narcissistic libido of the child," commenting that

> the child in us applauds, the child who knows only one principle and that is to live. . . . Since the child cannot actually overcome any external interferences, it takes refuge in fantastic, megalomaniac self deception.[3]

"Banish plump Jack, and banish all the world!" Falstaff cries. Because of his sophisticated adult wit, however, he makes social capital out of his megalomania; men love his gloriously ingenious lies better than their own truth. Falstaff is a world unto himself, shaped like the globe and containing multitudes of contradictions as the world itself does; fat and aging in body, but ever young in spirit and nimble in wit; a shape-shifter in poses and roles, yet always inimitably himself; a man with a curiously feminine sensual abundance.

A fat man can look like a pregnant woman, and Falstaff's fatness is fecund; it spawns symbols. In the context of Hal's growing up, its feminine meaning has particular importance.[4] As W. H. Auden says, it is "the expression of a psychological wish to withdraw from sexual competition and by combining mother and child in his own person, to become emotionally self-sufficient."[5] Falstaff is said to be fond of hot wenches and leaping-houses, but he is no Don Juan even in Part 2 when his sexual relations with Doll Tearsheet and

2. Notably, by Ernst Kris, "Prince Hal's Conflict," in *The Design Within: Psychoanalytic Approaches to Shakespeare* [Jason Aronson, 1976], 389–407, who takes Hal's friendship with Falstaff as an outlet for and defense against his hostility toward his father. Kris's case depends too heavily on the hypothesis that Hal had a previous friendship with Richard II, and on reading a parricidal urge into Hal's taking of the crown, however evident it is that Falstaff is a father-figure.
3. Franz Alexander, "A Note on Falstaff," *Psychoanalytic Quarterly* 2 (1933): 392–406.
4. Suggested subtly and convincingly by Sherman Hawkins in "Falstaff as Mom," a talk given at the Special Session on Marriage and the Family in Shakespeare, at a meeting of the Modern Language Association. Chicago, December 30, 1977.
5. W. H. Auden, "The Prince's Dog," in his *The Dyer's Hand* (New York: Random House), 196.

Mistress Quickly are made more explicit. They are fond of him rather than erotically drawn to him. It is not only tactful regard for Hal's legendary dignity as the perfect king that keeps Shakespeare from compromising him by making Falstaff a lecher. Rather, Falstaff represents the wish to bypass women; he has grown old, but remains young, and yet in terms of women has "detoured manhood," as Harold Goddard says.[6] In the first tetralogy Shakespeare avoided treating the woman's part in male development by making women witches or helpless victims. In the second tetralogy he again treats the feminine obliquely, through its absence, as Falstaff's avoidance of sexual maturity. The fat knight desires food and drink more than he desires women. And though women are devoted to him, he cheats and deceives them, giving his own deepest affections to a boy. No wonder that, for Hal, Falstaff incarnates his own rebellion against growing up into a problematic adult identity.

Hal himself is unaware that his affinity for the fat knight constitutes rebellion; he conceives it, rather, as part of his long-term strategy for assuming a proper identity as king. That strategy reveals his likeness to his father, his ability to think and act in the same terms of political image-building as his father, his fitness for the very role he seems to be rejecting. Many parallels between Hal's first soliloquy (1.2) and the king's long admonitory speech to him (3.2) reveal the essential similarities between father and son. Both speeches dwell on the proper management of one's political visibility and the importance of avoiding overexposure. Hal pictures himself as the sun obscured by clouds and therefore more "wonder'd at" when he reappears, while Henry compares himself to a comet "wonder'd at" because it is "seldom seen." He implies that his is that "sun-like majesty" that, when it "shines seldom," wins an "extraordinary gaze," and Hal says that his reformation "shall show more goodly, and attract more eyes" because of his fault. Both use clothing imagery to denote a kingliness they put on or off at will; Hal says he can "throw off this loose behaviour," and Henry says that he too dressed himself in humility, then donned his "presence like a robe pontifical." Hal's soliloquy implies that the Hal we have just seen with Falstaff is no more genuine and spontaneous than the self he will assume as king, and it is immediately followed by Henry addressing the Percys in equally ambiguous terms:

> I will from henceforth rather by myself,
> Mighty and to be fear'd, than my condition. . . .[7]
> (1.3.5–6)

6. Harold C. Goddard, "*Henry IV*," in his *The Meaning of Shakespeare*, 2 vols. (Chicago: University of Chicago Press, 1951), vol. 1, 184.
7. A. R. Humphreys, editor of the new Arden text, glosses *condition* as "natural disposition."

Neither man can freely express his true self, whatever that is, because each has something to hide. For reasons to be explained shortly, Hal hides his sympathy with his father, while Henry hides his guilt over the deposition and murder of Richard. Nonetheless, that guilt is revealed in the way he splits his son into two contending images: the bad son, Hal the wastrel; and the good son, Hotspur the king of honor. For Hal to become his father's son personally (to be loved) and politically (to be trusted as fit to succeed his father), he must restore his reputation as heir apparent, triumph over Hotspur, and assume Hotspur's identity as the model of chivalric manhood in England. This he obediently promises and economically does, in the sum-zero terms of heroic combat:

> Percy is but my factor, good my lord,
> To engross up glorious deeds on my behalf
> And I will call him to so strict account
> That he shall render every glory up,
> Yea, even the slightest worship of his time,
> Or I will tear the reckoning from his heart.
> (3.2.147–52)

Thus Shrewsbury is the second focal point of the father-son relationship, and constitutes Hal's and Henry's first mutual reaffirmation of identity.

* * *

GUS VAN SANT

[*My Own Private Idaho*]†

GUS VAN SANT: [I]n fashioning *My Own Private Idaho,* there were a number of scripts that I was writing. The original script was written in the seventies when I was living in Hollywood. * * *

* * * I was writing this thing about Mike, who had a friend named Scott. In the script, I made him a rich kid, although he wasn't in reality. Although I think there were rich kids like that on the streets, I didn't fully know who he was until I saw Orson Welles's *Chimes at Midnight.* Seeing that, I realized that Shakespeare's *Henry IV* plays had this gritty quality about them. They had the young Henry, Prince Hal, who is about to become king,

† Gus Van Sant, extracts from "Gus Van Sant: Swimming Against the Current," an interview by Graham Fuller, and from the screenplay of *My Own Private Idaho* (1989) from Gus Van Sant, *Even Cowgirls Get the Blues & My Own Private Idaho* (London and Boston: Faber, 1993), xxiii–xxv, xxxvii–xliii, 145–50. Text copyright © 1993 by Graham Fuller and Gus Van Sant. Text copyright © 1993 by Gus Van Sant. Reprinted by permission of Faber and Faber, Inc., an affiliate of Farrar, Straus, and Giroux, LLC.

slumming on the streets with his sidekick. The young Henry seemed to be Scott and the sidekick seemed to be Mike, so I adapted the Shakespeare story to modern Portland. It was called *In a Blue Funk* or *Minions of the Moon*; it had a lot of different titles. At that time I had, through *Mala Noche*, gotten an agent, and I showed the script to somebody at 20th Century-Fox who liked Shakespeare. Eventually we toned the Shakespeare down and made the language more modern. But at the time it was literally, from beginning to end, a restructuring of the *Henry IV* plays.

I was also working on this short story called *My Own Private Idaho* which I intended to film. * * *

GRAHAM FULLER: *When you wrote the* Henry IV *scenes for* Idaho, *did you actually go back to the text of the plays or was your reference point* Chimes at Midnight?

GVS: I tried to forget the Welles film because I didn't want to be plagiaristic or stylistically influenced by it, even though it had given me the idea. So I referred to the original Shakespeare. When *My Own Private Idaho* was shown at the Venice Biennale someone put together a comparative study of the Shakespeare scenes that I'd used and the same scenes from a different text of the play. I started to realize that there were many different versions of Shakespeare.

GF: *Kenneth Branagh's* Henry V *also imported the Falstaff scenes from* Henry IV, Part I.

GVS: Yes, the flashbacks—we used some of the same scenes actually.

GF: *Why did you cut down on the scenes with Jane Lightwork—your version of Mistress Quickly—in the film?*

GVS: There were a couple of different characters that got slimmed down because the Shakespeare scenes were becoming like a movie within the movie. It was interesting up to a point, but in the editing room we were still trying to figure out whether or not it would fly. There was a whole contingent of people at New Line—the domestic distributors—who were totally against the Shakespeare scenes and wanted us to cut them all out. The foreign distributors wanted as much Shakespeare in there as we could get. In the end, we cut out one long scene between Scott and Bob [William Reichert], who are Prince Hal and Falstaff, when they put on a play and Falstaff does this mock-deposing of the king. It was nice, but it went on too long.

* * *

Scott comes from a wealthy family and his father is mayor because Prince Hal came from royalty, and that was the closest thing I could find to royalty in Portland. I think the film might have suffered a little bit from that because there is a difference between being a king and being the mayor's son. The reason Scott's like he is is because of the Shakespeare, and the reason the Shakespeare is in the film is to transcend time, to show that those things have always happened, everywhere.

* * *

[From *My Own Private Idaho*]

Alleyway. Night.

SCOTTIE *is helping Bob with a disguise, putting on pants over a large belly, with medallions around the neck.*

SCOTT How long has it been, Bob, since you could see your own feet?

BOB About four years, Scottie. Four years of grief. It blows a man up like a balloon.

MIKE *and* BUDD *appear, running, with costumes on. There are two others behind them.*

MIKE There's rock and roll money walking this way!

BUDD And they're drunk as skunks.

MIKE This is going to be easy. We can do it lying down.

SCOTT But don't fall asleep, now, Mike.

BUDD Shh!! Here they come!

SCOTT You four should head them off there!

BOB We four? How many are walking with them?

MIKE About six.

BOB Huh, shouldn't *they* be robbing *us*?

SCOTTIE *laughs.* BOB *waddles along the side of the alleyway, stepping on a curb, then in a pothole losing his balance. Another accomplice whistles from atop a building. We* SEE *the group of* ROCK AND ROLL PROMOTERS.

BOB *walks further from* MIKE *and* SCOTTIE.

SCOTTIE If they escape from you, we'll get them here.

BOB *struggles as he walks.*

BOB Eight feet of cobblestones is like 30 yards of flat road with me.

MIKE *and* SCOTT *run off, laughing at him.*

BOB I can't see a damned thing in here.

BUDD Jesus, will you shut up! And keep on your toes!

BUDD *sees the promoters coming and waves to* BOB *as he lies down on the ground.*

BUDD Lie down!!
BOB Lie down!?
BUDD Lie down and stay quiet until they round the corner and we'll ambush them.
BOB Have you got a crane to lift me up again?

BUDD *laughs.*

MIKE They're coming!!

Down the way, the ROCK AND ROLL PROMOTERS *are approaching, having no knowledge of the buffoonery at the other end of the tunneling alleyway. They are drunk.*

VICTIM 1 Come along neighbor, Tommy will lead the way. I've lost track of time . . . (*burp*)

At the other end of the alley:

BOB *and* THREE OTHERS *are marching in procession, chanting, a facsimile of Rashneesh,*[1] *but a bad act.*

The ROCK PROMOTERS *approach, smashing a bottle.*

VICTIM 1 Who are these jokers?
VICTIM 2 Rashneesh, listen!
VICTIM 1 They're chanting. . . .

SCOTTIE *and* MIKE *hide behind garbage cans, laughing.*

The ROCK PROMOTERS *circle the group of chanting Rashneesh.*

VICTIM 3 I thought that all you Rashneesh had up and left . . .

VICTIM 1 *pours a beer on one of their heads. Just as he does this* BOB *pulls out two long pistols, almost heavy enough that he cannot hold them straight, barrels parallel.*

BOB Aha! One move and I'll blow you away, you silly scumbags, up against that wall!

One of the victims falls down and begins to run away. One of Bob's men starts after him. A lockbox that he was carrying falls to the around. BOB *spies it.*

BOB No! Let him go!

BOB *aims one pistol at the running figure as he keeps the others against the wall with the other pistol. He fires three times. One of Bob's boys grabs the lockbox.*

1. Followers of Bhagwan Shree Rashneesh, an eccentric, wealthy, Hindu guru, whose eponymous religious community flourished in the 1970s and 1980s [*Editor's note*].

A VIEW *of the running figure, bullets cutting around him.*

BOB Look at him go!

VICTIM 2 Don't shoot us!

BOB *winks at the lockbox and shoots the gun in the air.*

All the ROCK PROMOTERS *go running.* BOB *charges after them, firing the gun twice more in the air, then once at the lockbox, breaking it open.*

BOB The valise is open. Let's see what we got.

MIKE *and* SCOTTIE *hiding behind trashcans.*

SCOTTIE Where are our disguises?

MIKE *runs to his stash and finds two large capes and large hats. They put these on.*

BOB *finds wads of money and receipts.*

BOB Ticket anyone? To next week's show?

He throws these on the ground and the boys fall over themselves for the tickets. BOB *wads the money and puts it back in the box, laughing to himself.*

MIKE *and* SCOTTIE *sneak closer to the group still hiding, long flowing capes concealing their identity.*

BOB Scott and Mike have disappeared, did the shots scare them away?

They sneak closer. MIKE *lights a big firecracker and waits.*

BOB . . . maybe we should get the hell out of here. But, are they such chickens?

A LOUD EXPLOSION!

MIKE *and* SCOTTIE, *disguised, jump out with large silver baseball bats, swinging them and making as much noise as they can, knocking over a set of garbage cans, flashing flashlights into* BOB *and the others' eyes.*

Frightened, BOB *drops the lockbox and runs, the others follow,* MIKE *and* SCOTTIE *hitting them with the bats as they go.*

BOB Get the box! Oh, fuck!

MIKE *swings the bat at* BOB, *it grazes the side of a building and sparks fly from it.* BOB *wheezes from the run.*

SCOTTIE *chases the others in the same direction.*

They stand, kicking garbage cans and watching them run, convulsing with laughter.

SCOTTIE The thieves scatter!
MIKE Bob Pigeon will sweat to death!

JACK FAVOR *enters the Governor's* CHAMBERS[;] *day.*

JACK Can anyone tell me about my son?

He walks across the room.

JACK It's been a full three months since I last saw him. Where is my son Scott?
AID We don't know, sir.
JACK Ask around in Old Town, in some of the taverns there. Some say he frequently is seen down there drinking with street denizens. Some who they say even rob our citizens and store owners. I can't believe that such an effeminate boy supports such "friends."

* * *

SUSAN WISEMAN

[Shakespeare in Idaho]†

[1]

Where is "Shakespeare" in *My Own Private Idaho*? Who, what or where is the work undertaken by the bard or the shadows of the bard? This is the question this essay poses. The director, Gus Van Sant, has asserted that "the reason Scott's like he is is because of the Shakespeare, and the reason Shakespeare is in the film is to transcend time, to show that these things have always happened, everywhere"[1] This seems more like a retrospective claim for the transcendent qualities of Shakespeare than a consideration of the specific place of the *Henry IV* plays in the film. What place do

† Susan Wiseman, "The Family Tree Motel: Subliming Shakespeare in *My Own Private Idaho*," in Lynda E. Boose and Richard Burt, eds., *Shakespeare, The Movie: Popularizing the Plays on Film, TV, and Video* (London: Routledge, 1997), 225–239. Reprinted by permission of Routledge, Inc., part of The Taylor & Francis Group.

1. Graham Fuller, "Gus Van Sant: Swimming against the Current, an interview by Graham Fuller," in *Even Cowgirls Get the Blues* and *My Own Private Idaho* (London: Faber, 1993), xlii.

the Shakespearean sections claim, and what implications do they have for the way the film organizes its subjects and viewers? In finding Shakespeare in the film this essay aims to tease out some of the implications of the film, concentrating on paternity and the family tree, visual versus verbal signifiers and the uncanny/sublime as these are deployed through the narrative.

It does not take much probing to find that *Idaho* is dealing with—or stylishly commodifying—some of the Big Questions of contemporary culture; questions around the family, paternity, place, home, maternity, sexuality, status and all the elements of the masculine filmic *Bildungsroman*. Since the fatal overdose of one of the film's two stars, the twenty-three year old River Phoenix, it is as if Phoenix and the film have become reciprocally "about" one another. Phoenix's death, as well as his acting style, his work on the script (Van Sant describes him working "furiously" on the fireside scene) and the improvised style of the scenes where the groups of boys discuss their lives seem to refer the film back to a social world and to substantiate Van Sant's claim that those parts of the film "come directly from a number of people that I've known", "I'm not being analytical" (Fuller, xli).

But *Idaho* is also full of textual markers and pointers; "Shakespeare" is far from the only cultural marker in the film. It is richly intertextual—not to say overbearingly knowing—in its deployment of cultural references from popular culture to quasi-Freudian symbolism (for example the "family metaphor" that Van Sant speaks of in interview [Fuller, xxxix]). "Narcolepsy", glossed for us in a precredit sequence, is the symptom which the film takes as the key to or metaphor for the irresolubility of violent trauma. It opens in the middle of America, in Idaho—the private, agoraphobic, landscape of the B52s song, but also the haunted place of mining ghost towns, migrant farmworkers, salmon rivers.[2] The visuals of empty farmhouses suggest the ghostly presences of Idaho's past and, in the present, the psychic importance of the farming crisis in the mid-80s (Duncan Webster reminds us of the 1986 Democratic Party slogan: "It wasn't just a farm. It was a family"; though in this case, it is more than a family—incestuous—but less than a farm; more of a migrant's trailer).[3] The film prompts nostalgia for other social forms and gestures towards the life of the cowboy—always loved, always leaving, always single—in references including the song "Cattle Call", a cowboy statue at a diner, and Mike's friend's disturbed parody of a quick draw. These remind us of other models of lonely, but still possible, masculinity.

2. See Donald C. Miller, *Ghost Towns of Idaho* (Colorado: Pruett, 1976).
3. Duncan Webster, *Looka Yonder: The Imaginary America of Populist Culture* (London: Routledge, 1988), 28.

In its focus on men in early adulthood, gangs, pairs or couples, even in its use of Portland, Oregon and the gang leader called Bob, the film recycles Van Sant's obsessions from *Drugstore Cowboy* (1989). *Idaho*, however, uses a script generated from many sources rather than one novel and deploys layered visual and literary references. Van Sant has commented on the origins of Scott, "I didn't fully know who he was until I saw Orson Welles's *Chimes at Midnight*" (Fuller, xxiii). But the central figures are also reminiscent of other American narratives. Mikey and Scott's journey is, as José Arroyo notes, reminiscent of road and buddy movies as well as *The Wizard of Oz*.[4] It even replays the drifting narrative of Twain's Huck and Jim, with Huck/Scott opting out of all those things Jim/Mikey can never have (Webster, 118). And the film ends on (apparently) the same road with a replay of the story of the Good Samaritan. Indeed, *My Own Private Idaho* is a film that advertises its cultural claims. But the title also raises the question, what would it mean to live in one's own private Idaho, an internal, "private", terrain of loss and repetition, a past that can never be revistited but which, figured in spatial terms in the memory, can never be escaped either?

Amongst a plethoric and sometimes literary referentiality two elements occupy dominant and perhaps competing positions in the text: quasi-Freudian images of the past and a Shakespearean narrative of the transition to adult masculinity. As far as the Henry plays are concerned, the film seems to build on the words of Hal/Henry once he is king "I'll be your father and your brother too" (*2H4*, 5.2.57) to make an oedipal drama of fathers and brothers, past, present, and future. The ghostly presence of the Henry plays is also used to address the two adolescents' need for a path to adulthood. Even as the film carnivalizes or cannibalizes Shakespeare's texts, it uses them as a cultural anchor. In doing so, the film sets the "Shakespearean" text not only in but against the perilous journey Michael Waters (River Phoenix) makes towards resolving an impossible oedipal tangle. It would be overschematic to say that the film offers two versions of oedipal narrative, Mike's story inviting reading as a version of the Freudian uncanny in terms of the family tree and Scott's using the *Henry IV* plays to chart Scott's rise to power. But these twin trajectories do allow us to begin to analyse the place of "Shakespeare" in the text, and how and why the film ties "Shakespeare" to a contemporary America in a way that announces both the seriousness of the text and its hipness.

The knowingness of the film, its setting among the street-boy

4. See José Arroyo, "Death, Desire and Identity: The Political Unconscious of 'New Queer Cinema,' " in Joseph Bristow and Angelica R. Wilson, eds., *Activating Theory: Lesbian, Gay, Bisexual Politics* (London: Lawrence & Wishart, 1993).

hustlers of Portland, Oregon, and its evident desire to slum it with Freud and Shakespeare—even as it offers viewers the pleasures of having their cultural markers in place (and I shall come back to this at the end of the essay)—also interrogates sexuality and masculinity in late eighties America. Like Steve MacLean's first feature, *Postcards From America* (1994), *Idaho* analyses abuse and paternity in contemporary America. As MacLean has commented, "You look at the white male backlash in America at the moment, it is all about . . . fears of disenfranchisement".[5] Both *Postcards From America* and *My Own Private Idaho* are concerned with disenfranchisement and marginality, both use visual style to associate the disenfranchised with a version of the American landscape steeped in the associations of the American sublime. *Idaho* does this through analepses using different visual orders—home movies, landscape, time-lapse photography.

Although the Scott Favor narrative is the section of the film which rereads *Henry IV*, the film opens and closes on the story of Mike Waters; the rise of Favor and the fall of Waters are clearly parallel stories but it is arguably the Waters narrative which the audience follows. The story is, more or less, as follows: Mikey and Scott seem to be friends (Mike is in love with Scott) and each hang out, working as prostitutes and sharing the life of underclass adolescents in urban America. Scott is the son of the wheelchair-bound mayor of Portland, Oregon (no visible mother), whereas Mike is the product of no "ordinary family"—his "father" seems to have drowned himself and later he seems to actually be the son of his brother, Dick. Where Scott turns tricks for money only, Mike identifies as gay; where Scott's father searches for him and makes a contract with him for the son's reform and inheritance, Mike is attempting to untangle an impossible family tree by searching for his mother. The narrative follows first a trip back to Idaho (like a salmon returning upstream to the source of its life) to visit his brother–father, then a trip to the Family Tree Motel to search for his mother and then a trip to Italy in search of her, before ending on the return of Scott with an Italian wife to a new life in Portland. Here we have the rejection of Bob Pigeon/Falstaff in a restaurant peopled by the Portland City establishment and then the twin funerals—of Bob, conducted by street boys, and of Scott Favor's father, attended by Scott.

Such a film cannot really be considered as an adaptation of Shakespeare. It borrows from the bard, from Freudian and other narratives. Mike has a past, whereas Scott has a future and Mike's

5. Lizzie Francke, "Postcards from the Edgy," *The Guardian*, 6 April 1995, 7.

story is given a quasi-Freudian mediation, Scott's a Shakespearean. In the next sections I aim to elucidate and complicate these alliances and to end by returning to my question—what work *is* Shakespeare doing in *Idaho*?

[2]

HANS: Where do you want to go?
MIKEY: I want to go home.

SCOTT: Where shall we go?
MIKEY: To visit my brother.

My Own Private Idaho opens with what turns out to be Mikey on a road, in Idaho. Voice and visuals are split: in a voice-over Mike tells us that he has been there before, on this road "like a fucked-up face". As he finishes his thought the camera turns to the road, then to the sky and then switches to a fantasy/flashback from Mikey's point of view. These flashbacks are repeated throughout the film; characteristically they feature flimsy, uninhabited buildings—first the shed which, in this first sequence, is blown onto the road and smashed, then we see an abandoned gothic-style wooden bungalow, then the flimsy sixties bungalow which seems to have been Mikey's home in his childhood and next to which his brother—father Dick lives in a caravan. The habitations seem to become increasingly transient, migratory, as they move towards Mikey's homeless present.

Van Sant's *Drugstore Cowboy* featured visions of flying, cartwheeling, buildings, trees, animals, hats. In this later film the visions are at the core of the conundrum which they both pose and partially explain. During a flashback in Rome, the "home-movie" footage of Mikey's childhood with his mother and pubertal father–brother leads our eye to the door of the house where, in wrought metalwork, we find the H that stands for home. In his visions, Mikey goes "home" to his mother's house. What might in other circumstances be read as an emphasis on the homely qualities takes on richer connotations in association with other issues in the film. The link to sexuality and desire is made clear when, early in the film, Mike has a client who pays to suck him off. We see what Mikey sees behind closed eyes: an empty house or building is taken up as in a twister, and destroyed. In part this gestures towards *The Wizard of Oz*; it is after this that his quest begins. But in terms of thematics, Mikey is presented as attempting to escape from an impossible oedipal situation through a search for his mother and desire for his brother–lover, Scott, thwarted by Scott's desire for Carmilla.

These visuals, flashbacks, reveal a problematic past—in Freud's terms, the secret "known of old and long familiar".[6] The Mikey section of the narrative takes us back to what should have been hidden; during the trip to Idaho the story of Mikey's paternity is replayed in his encounter with his brother–father. In these scenes "Dick"—the (comic?) name of Mikey's brother—offers various versions of what might be interpreted as the primal scene. First, he shows Mikey a photo of "Me, you and mom": but this turns out to be mother–father–child, as well as a mother with two sons.

Inside the caravan where Dick lives surrounded by his paintings of individuals and families, Dick and Mike propose different versions of Mike's paternity. Dick claims that Mike's father was "a lowlife cowboy fuck", shot at the cinema by their mother during a performance of the Howard Hawkes western, *Rio Bravo*: "*Rio Bravo* on the big screen, John Wayne on his horse riding through the desert . . . " But Mikey interrupts: "I know who my real dad is . . . Richard, you are my dad. I know that." In refusing the elective/screen paternity of the "lowlife cowboy fuck" and by displaced association, John Wayne, Mikey is left with the literal incestuous situation, the uncanny doubling of father and brother.

Richard's elaborate story, in which an elective father is proposed by a real father, is interrupted by both Mikey's narcoleptic moments—figured for the audience as a combination of the sublime and memories of his childhood as if seen in a home movie—and by Mikey's refusals of the fantasy father in favour of the scandalous "truth". The clear narrative implication is that the narcoleptic visions, to which we also are given access, are the compensatory mechanism activated by the impossibility of any kind of successful negotiation of such a traumatic paternity.

Further signifies suggest that the film itself may joke about the family drama, its secrecy and determining nature, in quasi-Freudian terms. When Mike and Scott leave Dick Waters (the father–brother) they are sent by their clue—a postcard—to the Family Tree Motel. Here Mikey is to begin his search to find his mother among the impossibly tangled and fused branches of his own family tree. But this is not all. As he and Scott arrive at the hotel, who should turn up but Hans. They met Hans earlier, after an evening with a female client, and he had offered Michael a lift in his car. This is Hans Klein, whose name coincidentally seems to translate as Little Hans—one of Freud's youngest patients, with whom he communicated through the parents, especially the father.[7] During the

6. Sigmund Freud, "The Uncanny," in *The Standard Edition of the Complete Psychological Works*, ed. James Strachey (London: Hogarth, 1955), vol. 17: 217–53.
7. Sigmund Freud, "Analysis of a Phobia in a Five Year Old Boy," in *The Standard Edition of the Complete Psychological Works*, ed. James Strachey (London: Hogarth, 1955), vol. 10: 145.

interview with the brother–father "Dick" and at other points—such as at the meeting with Hans at the Family Tree Motel and in Hans's interest in forms of transport and mothers—the film jokily, and apparently seriously, advertises its commitment to "the family metaphor" or Freudian narratives.

Reading the film in these terms involves a negotiation between two types of interpretation; one finds oneself at a mid-point between making a reading of the film which laboriously reads into it/makes explicit a subtextual narrative dynamic and a tracing of clues or jokes already highly thematized and framed as textual pointers. If the Shakespeare section is self-conscious in its use of *Henry IV* as a version of the family romance, then the Mike section might, too, be seen as deliberately narrating a version of the family story. The two stories *are* sharply distinguished and set apart in the viewer's experience by their contrasting uses of visual codes and styles versus Shakespeareanized language.

What Mike's narrative teases out, visually, seems to be the impossibility of escape from the scandal of being fathered by his brother, a past for which he is not responsible but which leaves him without any place in a social world. His meaning is made in the past, in the conjunction of too many and contradictory meanings in the place of the "H", a home on which too many meanings home in. So what about that wrought metalwork "H" that we (and apparently also Mike) see during his visions? The sequence, as we focus on it, evidently names "home"—the house where he lived as a child, the place where he tells the German dealer in (car?) parts that he wants to go (Where do you want to go? I want to go home). In terms derived from Freudian discussion, though, we can also see Mike's visions, activated at moments of stress, as emerging from a genealogical crisis in terms of his exclusion from a place in American society, an exclusion which the café scene, a scene central to placing Mike's narrative in the context of his peers, indicates is part of a more pervasive disenfranchisement. In such terms, the "H" names the "homely" place from which Mike emerged. Freud discusses the fantasy of return to "the former . . . home of all human beings", the womb, reporting a joke in which " 'Love is homesickness' " and Van Sant, too, describes Mike as "trying to find the place where he was conceived" (Fuller, xliii; Freud, "Uncanny," 245). "H" names Mike's home, but also his history or genealogy. Accordingly, one narrative structure of the film takes us back into Mike's past, giving his impossible oedipus as a "source" for the things which prevent him from finding a full place in the social world.

In his visions, Mike and we, apparently from his point of view, see the home—bungalow or house—he lived in with his mother in his childhood. Mother's body and that signifier of mother's body, "home", are both present in the visions. These analepses also interrupt the forward movement of the narrative, providing a quite different aesthetic and visual texture, without words. These silent interludes appear when Mike's present experiences touch on events from the past, events which are too traumatic to be integrated into the social/cultural narrative of life, but yet determine identity.

Mike's paternity and his relationship with his mother, as in Freud's version of the uncanny, return to haunt him. The association, for Mike, between the female body, desire for the mother, or desired and feared return to an intimate maternity, is made clear in two incidents early in the film. He sees a woman who reminds him of his mother in the street; he collapses. He has a narcoleptic turn, too, when he is picked up by a female client. When Mike sees her he says, "This chick is living in a new car ad"; once at *her* home we and Mike are shown a luminous stained-glass panel of Virgin Mary and infant Jesus (the film offers us no chance to miss the point). When she tries to have sex with him, he sleeps. To be sure, later in the film Mike falls into a narcoleptic sleep when he is picked up in Italy; it is not solely the possibility of the return of the maternal that the film proposes as insurmountable. Nevertheless, these elements are present and enable—even, perhaps, invite—an audience to read Mike's predicament in terms of the specific "family metaphor" of the Freudian uncanny.

The experiences of repression and lapse are elaborated in Freud's writing on the traumatic moment when something "secretly familiar" emerges (Freud, "Uncanny, 245). Freud plays, as the film itself appears to, on the way the German word *heimlich/unheimlich* tends to collapse into itself in such a way as the domestic, secure, familiar is also simultaneously dangerous and strange. Freud associates this feeling with the adult response to the childhood wish to return to "intra-uterine existence" and to questions of the resolution of Oedipus (Freud, "Uncanny," 244). The homely/unhomely implications of the mother's body, for Mikey are redoubled, as it were, because of the tortuous and traumatic relations between his mother, himself, and his brother–father. This cultural confounding and excessive doubling of roles is figured in the text at the level of plot as a narcoleptic reaction to impossible stress and trauma.

This is signalled visually: the spectator sees a vision of landscape, the sublime hallucination of the barn in the wind. The "narcoleptic" gaps in the narrative are inhabited by visions which could be characterized as an aestheticization of crisis as the sublime. Such interruptions of the present by the partially repressed forces of the past are discussed by Mladen Dolar in terms of a refusal to relinquish the past.[8] Dolar's reformulation of Freud offers a way to read Mike's quest for his mother in terms of just such a feared and desired return to the past. The quest is doomed but is also apparently Mike's motivating purpose. The present—adulthood, desire and ironically economic exchange—is interrupted either by narcoleptic moments figured as sublime or by the heterosexual union of Scott and Carmilla at the time and place when Mike hopes to find his mother.

Idaho offers a case study in this aspect of the Freudian family romance, twice: in Scott's rigid "success" and Mike's apparent failure. The constant interruption of Mike's present by the past is contrasted with the other oedipal drama; Scott's election of an "unknown, greater" father in Bob. Whereas Mike is unable to escape the paralyzing knowledge that his father is his brother, when Scott's father dies he inherits massive social and economic power, some of which is in any case destined for him on his twenty-first birthday. After the boys leave the Family Tree Motel the separation of the destinies of the two boys becomes increasingly clear; the motel, with its contradictory name, only temporarily houses both boys and the contrasting, narratives which they inhabit.

[3]

The name, the Family Tree Motel, suggests the permanent inescapability of the family tree—however scandalous. But a "motel" is a quintessentially postmodern transient location. The name combines the film's contradictory interests in what Jean Baudrillard has called "the lyrical [American] nature of pure circulation. As against the melancholy of European analyses".[9] Yet as Baudrillard's comparison suggests, the two chains of association—circulation/surface and analysis/depth—imply each other, and so in a similar way to the pairing of the Michael and Scott narratives. They are buddies, almost siblings, almost lovers, and Mike's narrative of the psyche contrasts with Scott's ability to turn situations to his advantage.

Where Mikey is made socially placeless by a traumatic paternity which cannot be overcome, Scott is bound in to paternity and inheritance but also free to select amongst possible fathers. Through drifting he acquires the necessary accessories of his future rule. We see Scott as initially having a complicated relationship with his biological father, the mayor ("My dad doesn't know I'm just a kid. Thinks I'm a threat") and the narrative implies that it is the unsat-

8. Mladen Dolar, " 'I Shall Be With You On Your Wedding Night': Lacan and the Uncanny," *October* 58 (1991), 59.
9. Jean Baudrillard, *America*, trans. Chris Turner (London: Verso, 1986), 27; Fuller, xliv.

isfactory nature of this paternity which has propelled him into street life and rebellion.

The pairing of the narratives uses specific aspects of the Henry plays. In Mike and Scott's distinct careers *Idaho* also reworks those of Hal and Hotspur. When the film opens, Scott Favor is indeed the opposite of the Percy described in *Henry IV* as "the theme of honour's tongue" [1.1.81]—but he, like Hal, is "Fortune's minion" (1.1.83). Scott's narrative of succession is set out in terms of the Hal/Falstaff/Henry relationships of the Henry plays and like Prince Hal, Scott is a cold pragmatist. He is on the street but not of it, because from the start, he is going to inherit. And, as in the Henry plays, the question of merit and money is foregrounded in Scott's unearned inheritance of his father's status. We know he is going to inherit and that he plans to transform his life; for the audience, the question is how and when this will happen.

It is through Scott's transition to adulthood that Shakespeare's history plays resonate in *Idaho* as the film reworks the play's thematization of father–son and peer relations. In Portland City we see him choosing street baron Bob Pigeon as his "real father". This is no uncomplicated paternal electivity; Scott tells Mike, that Bob "was fucking in love with me". But soon after, in a monologue to camera that explicitly parallels Hal's "I know you all" first soliloquy in *1 Henry IV,* Scott vows to reform in a way which implies his eventual rejection of Bob:

> PRINCE HAL: I know you all, and will awhile uphold
> The unyoked humour of your idleness.
> . . .
> So when this loose behaviour I throw off,
> And pay the debt I never promised,
> By how much better than my word I am.
> By so much shall I falsify men's hopes.
> [1.2.168–69, 181–84]

Or, in the *Idaho*/Reeves version: "All my bad behaviour I will throw away to pay a debt". Scott's comedic election of fathers, both dead by the end of the film, contrasts with the incestuous nightmare inflicted on and implicitly determining Mike. Not only does Scott get to choose fathers, but—perhaps the ultimate triumph in oedipal struggle—when he rejects them they die.

Both Scott's fathers are flawed—the mayor has money and power but no body (he is in a wheelchair) and Bob is all body, like Falstaff, but has nothing else. In questioning paternal potential *Idaho* reworks the paternal drama of Hal/Henry/Falstaff. The arrival of Bob in Portland, Oregon (where Scott's father is mayor, and therefore, ostensibly "greater") is accompanied by Scott's election of Bob as his "real" father. However, we hear Bob describing himself as Scott's dependant: he needs Scott for a "ticket out" of street life. Bob's status as a father is predicated on a reversal of oedipal relations with "father" as suitor to son: Scott's possession of all the powerful cards in the relationship makes him partly self-fathering or self-produced. For him, fathers are a matter of temporary choice, a feature which emphasizes his potential to switch from rent boy to king, but also contrasts with Mike's paternal narrative.

Idaho presents a disintegration of economic structures into psychic and social chaos, and this differently marks the paternal and filial bodies and psyches it presents. Bob's boys, his "family" of street boys, act as an index of impossible identities being forged beyond the social margins—in economic as much as sexual terms. And the boys' clients, generationally the same as Scott's fathers and, like him, notionally part of a functioning society, are figured as parasitic upon the position of these outcasts. This is explored in the café scene in Portland where the boys tell their stories, and in the interludes in which Mikey services clients. The street offers the boys no social potential beyond prostitution; their carnival world is delimited by money and clients. Through these scenes, the film's dominant interest in the canny/uncanny sexualized buddy (and sibling) narratives of Mike and Scott is connected to a more general questioning of the economics of masculinity in contemporary America.

A superficially similar range of issues is articulated in the *Henry IV* plays in terms of the relations of usurpers to feudal lords, states to servants, fathers to sons. Both parts of *Henry IV* are set against a background of rebellion and social unrest; in 2 *Henry IV*, Act 4 the Earl of Westmoreland describes rebellion's proper (true) appearance as "boys and beggary", and the film suggests this, as do specific scenes (*2H4*, 3.2; the Gads Hill episode; the rejection of Falstaff). The Shakespearean section of the film is (tenuously) connected to social critique because Bob represents the leader of the boys, and it is with Bob that the Shakespeare-derived style and dialogue arrive.

Bob first appears staggering and swaying out from beneath a network of flyovers when the boys have reached Portland, Oregon. The reworking of 2 *Henry IV* 3.2 also echoes the opening (and indeed the title) of Welles's *Chimes at Midnight*. His comment, "Jesus, the days we have seen", simultaneously signals Welles, Shakespeare and the hard life of the streets. Bob's arrival inserts a Shakespearean linguistic presence into the colony of boys as the figures he speaks with are drawn into pastiche "Shakespeare". The new rhetoric "Shakespeareanizes" the hotel, making Bob's scenes there significant because of their attatchment to Shakespeare, perhaps, but without "Shakespeare" ever being the language in which the boys discuss their own situation. The hotel scenes use Falstaff's relations to his boon companions to code them, in part, as a social space beyond the bounds and rule of law; but in its organization at this point the story is not of the rent boys, but scenes from Shakespeare as reworked and improvised. In a sense, one doesn't need to "know Shakespeare" to read them as intertextual. Indeed, during the editing, Van Sant cut some Shakespeare sections because, he claimed they were "becoming like a movie within a movie" (Fuller, xxxviii).

Bob (landless knight) may be King of the Street, but the street is dangerous; it involves the boys making themselves vulnerable in cars, rooms, houses, and offers no status or income. The film interrogates the difficulty of crossing the threshold from adolescence into adulthood, gay or straight, in a moment when models of mature masculinity have vanished with cowboys and the only route to power, even safety, is through inheritance. In figuring the failure of masculinity in terms of the underworld of the *Henry IV* plays the film is far from "imperial Shakespeare".[1] To this extent the film could be said to be using Shakespeare to make a political point, or to ask, where is the place of the young male in America, now? But the boys themselves get few Shakespearean lines, and the Shakespearean dialogue tends to have a life of its own—as "Shakespeare".

Where the sublime impossibility of Mikey's situation is rendered visually, the *Henry IV* plays enter the film as stylized rather than improvised talking, dialogue, drama and as "Shakespeare": they do seem to introduce "a movie within a movie", or to produce two cohabiting styles one dominated by visuals, the other by voice.[2] Jack Jorgens wrote of early Shakespeare silents "struggling to render great poetic drama in dumb show", but *Idaho* replaces visuals with talk: the scenes slow down and give themselves over to words.[3] Shakespeare marks the text as a demand that the audience transfer attention to the spoken, Shakespearean, word. The film's contrasting of visual and verbal signifiers and sequences organizes, too, the differentiation of the narratives of the doomed Michael Waters and the rising Scott Favor; Michael's past is signalled in visions, Scott's control of the situation is shown in his Prince Hal-like control of dialogue and its placement in relation to Shakespeare. Unlike Mikey, who can barely speak, Scott talks to the camera on several occasions, in a *gestus* when the boys are covers for porn mags, and in the soliloquy when he explains that he will give up this course of

1. Robert F. Wilson, "Recontextualising Shakespeare on Film," *Shakespeare Bulletin* 10 (1992), 24–37.
2. See Kate Chedgzoy, *Shakespeare's Queer Children* (Manchester: Manchester University Press, 1995).
3. Jack Jorgens, *Shakespeare on Film* (Bloomington: Indiana University Press, 1977), 1.

life. He talks: to other characters, to us, to Carmilla in Italy. Indeed, the volte-face predicted in his address to the camera has an important linguistic aspect to it. He returns to Portland leaving Mikey in Italy, a country whose language he cannot understand but which is figured as potentially maternal (he has gone in search of his mother).

To summarize: we can see the film as inviting empathy and producing Mike as the central emotional focus of the film; as José Arroyo points out, "the homosexuality that *Idaho* values the most is Mike's". Mike is the audience's empathetic focus (the fact that his narrative opens and closes the film, style of acting, the fact that we get "inside his head" rather than Scott's monologues to camera all contribute to this); the Scott–Carmilla heterosexual coupling replaces Mike's quest for maternity; and Scott plays a self-interested pragmatist against Michael's romantic hero. Indeed, such a reading is suggested by the popularity of the film, and as Arroyo notes, posters from the film, in gay circles (Arroyo). However, the place of Shakespeare in all this is complicated, even troubling, in its connection primarily to the Scott story. The question of which of the twin narratives should dominate was, it seems, hotly debated during the production of the film. Van Sant has claimed that New Line, the independent American distributors, were "totally against the Shakespearean scenes" but the foreign distributors wanted as much Shakespeare in there as we could get" (Fuller, xxxviii).

As Van Sant's comments indicate, the film has a metarelationship to Shakespeare. Even as it thematizes the struggles between fathers and sons, and to an extent offers a social critique of these issues, *Idaho* could be figured as in an oedipal relationship to the material out of which it produces itself, particularly "Shakespeare", and to be articulating its relation to "Shakespeare" in a way which invites closer analysis. How does the putting of the play through "Shakespeare", or the self-fathering of the narrative upon "Shakespeare" work in the text which narrates the failed and successful adventures in self-paternity and/or family romancing of the two boys? The film both fathers itself upon Shakespeare's text and uses the text as a moment to intervene in the question of fatherhood, and of begetting and growing up a modern (or postmodern) man.

Marjorie Garber traces the uncanny return of Shakespeare in the way "his" ghosts haunt "our" present; she analyses Shakespeare's uncanny returns, suggesting that "he" is used in various cultural actings-out of the family romance. As she puts it: "For some . . . 'Shakespeare' represents . . . a monument to be toppled . . . A related phenomenon follows the pattern of Freud's family romance, which involves the desire to subvert the father, or to replace a known parent with an unknown, greater one".[4] At first sight, it seems that this is how "Shakespeare" is working here; that, just as Derek Jarman's reworking of *Edward II* radicalizes the play's potential for a late twentieth-century audience, so putting *Idaho* through Shakespeare "radicalizes" Shakespeare, giving Shakespeare's texts new meanings in a modern world. We could see "Shakespeare" as claimed for a set of non-dominant values, wrested back from the theatre audiences and returned; the conservative Shakespeare toppled, the film sets about putting a new "radical" version into place. However, as Richard Burt has argued, the only intermittent adaptation of Shakespeare's play is itself part of the film's "critique of the repressiveness of oedipalization".[5] It refuses to be fathered, exactly, but borrows and reworks.

Moreover, a reading of *Idaho* as turning Shakespeare towards a critique of sexual and economic disenfranchisement becomes more problematic when we consider the precise placing of the dialogue pastiche from the Henry plays, rather than a more general effect. Bob Pigeon speaks in "Shakespeare", and those involved in prolonged conversation with him are drawn into it. Mike, though, is not drawn into it. Nor is Bob present when the boys are telling their stories; the desperate side of the underworld is either untouched by Shakespearean language or, when it is, this results in an annexation of the Portland hotel to Shakespeare's scenes, not vice versa. The entry of "Shakespeare" into the text produces, or emphasizes, the visual/verbal split and initiates the "movie within a movie" effect derived as much from the way "Shakespeare" as a cultural anchor takes over the text as by the text's carnivalizing or radicalizing of Shakespeare.

Indeed, Mike's story is the one which might be seen as more strongly expressing social critique, and his story—although it is the centre of our attention and empathy—is isolated from Shakespeareanized language. Rivers is given few Shakespearean lines and in the scenes where he plays against Scott and Bob not only do they have most of the dialogue but though they are together visually and acting ensemble, it is as if there is a line down the script dividing the types of speech offered to each. Indeed, in these scenes, Mikey is virtually an audience to the exchanges of Bob and Scott.

Moreover, on a larger scale, the pairing of the two narratives of Scott and Michael tends to undermine the sense that the Henry

4. Marjorie Garber, *Shakespeare's Ghost Writers* (London: Methuen, 1987), 7.
5. Richard Burt, "Baroque Down: The Trauma of Censorship in Psychoanalysis and Queer Film Re-Visions of Shakespeare and Marlowe," in Michael Hattaway, Boika Sokolova, and Derek Roper, eds., *Shakespeare in the New Europe* (Sheffield: Sheffield Academic Press, 1994), 338.

plays are radicalized by the things they are linked to. Even though most of the parts used by *Idaho* are comic scenes suggesting the subversion of dull order, the acting-out of a joyous subversiveness does not seem to be how Shakespeare is being used in *Idaho*. Where Welles—who played Falstaff—commented "Comedy can't really dominate a film made to tell this story, which is all in dark colours," there is little sense in *Idaho* that we are invited to laugh at the comic scenes, even at Bob's deception over the robbery, though these are the scenes incorporated into the film from the plays.[6] Rather than failing to be comedy (a criticism levelled at the Welles film) even the comic moments of *1 Henry IV* and *2 Henry IV* are incorporated in *Idaho* in order to generate seriousness and to tie the film to the "classic" narrative of Shakespeare; the comic scenes are there to be recognizably Shakespeare; Shakespearicity, not comedy, is their function.

The Henry plays do not only outline the shape of a society in crisis, they also delineate the transfer of power and control to Henry V, perhaps augmented and deepened by his knowledge of street life. It is this contrast that *Idaho* seizes upon to open up the question of what it means to be a man in contemporary America, fusing the mythic pasts of *Henry IV* and the cowboy community to raise the question of the possibility not only of any fulfilling resolution of Oedipus but of finding any kind of place—to live, let alone work. It retells the *Bildungsroman* of masculine achievement both ways: once in Scott's transition to power, and again in the failed paternity of Bob and the rigorous exclusion of not only Bob but Mike from Scott/Hal's transformation in the final scenes. (This worked rather differently in the script for the film, where it was explicitly stated that in the final scene, "Scott is driving the car" [Fuller, 187].) And when we look at the work done by Shakespeare in the light of the pairing of the two narratives, a rather different pattern is suggested.

Scott gets to choose Bob Pigeon as his father in a paternal/sexual relationship. And then he is allowed to dispose of him—along with his own father—at the end of the film. Of course, the use of the dialogue from and referring to Shakespeare's *Henry IV* plays underlines Scott's coldness, his pragmatic princehood, and the Machiavellian utilization of experience of the underworld/underclass in making a successful entry into a "political career". Nevertheless, his trajectory is contrasted by the film with Mike's in terms which imply that, in attaining the world of money, politics, restau-

6. Roberta E. Pearson and William Uricchio, " 'How Many Times Shall Caesar Bleed in Sport': Shakespeare and the Cultural Debate about Moving Pictures," *Screen* 31 (1990), 250; Juan Cobos and Miguel Rubio, "Welles and Falstaff," *Sight and Sound* 35 (1966), 60.

rants, Scott is making some kind of superficially "successful" transition to adulthood. The mediation of his "coming of age" through the chosen key moments in the Henry narratives—the scenes in the hotel, the robbery, the rejection—underline the unearned, inherited, and therefore arbitrary, nature of his rise from street boy to public power. However, the use of the Henry plays at these moments also serves to mark them out as tracing a rising and socially sanctioned trajectory.

The contrasting narrations of the stories of Mike and Scott are further emphasized by the way in which Mike's being locked into adolescence is figured by a verbal non- or pre-linguistic realm. His narcoleptic visions are not accompanied by dialogue; in that sense they are virtually "silent". Moreover, the trauma marks Mike's speech which, though meaningful (in both senses), is tangential, fragmentary. We find out about his story—the past—through visual materials; Scott's narrative, tied to the future, is worked out through dialogue-heavy scenes and through a formal, set-piece, rejection or murder of Bob Pigeon. This contrasting of chains of association can, at a cost, be put schematically:

> visual / silent / homosexual / adolescent (storyline: family romance with echoes of Freud)
>
> versus
>
> verbal / dialogue / heterosexual(?) / adult (storyline: family romance from Shakespeare).

Such an organization of significances troubles an understanding—which the film simultaneously seems to invite—of the film's emphasis on the centrality of the figure of Mike. It invites empathy for Mike, whose story takes up much of the film. Moreover, though vulnerable, he is still alive at least and taking his chances at the end of the film. More particularly, though, such associative links, combined with the splitting-off of the Shakespeareanized sections of the film, suggest that, although the film does address the issue of sexual identity and disenfranchisement in post-rural and post-industrial America, and does produce an ending for Mike which, in its reworking of the story of the Good Samaritan leaves the future of that narrative open to some extent, it does not use the Shakespeare sections of dialogue and performance to do so.

In the light of these layered connections, the place occupied by "Shakespeare" in *Idaho* can be reassessed. On the one hand, and this is registered in the initial response of critics, the film seems to be bringing out a subtextual or latent amusing perversity in the plays. In terms of its general use of the *Henry IV* plays the film can be said to be reworking relationships in terms of a greater indeterminacy. Certainly, *Idaho* points up the potentially sexual charge of boy gangs and makes explicit the homoerotic potential to be found throughout the Henriad. And it appears to be using the most carnivalesque, anti-authoritarian, potentially *politically* subversive moments of the Shakespeare texts.

But this questioning use of Shakespeare at a general level in the film is not precisely underpinned or reproduced in its detail. Our understanding of *Idaho*'s use of Shakespeare changes when we concentrate on the twin details of the actual use of Shakespearean language and the twinning of the narratives. For all that elsewhere in the text the film seems to be bringing to the surface subtextual sexual implications from the Henry plays—"boys and beggary"—the specific work of Shakespeare is to mark out the narrative of Hal's rise and to give it the cultural weight of "Shakespeare". Combined with the associations traced above, for all the questioning attitudes suggested by the rest of the film, this puts "Shakespeare" in an anchoring position; tying interpretation of the film back to cultural (intertextual) knowledge, it conserves and separates the storyline of Scott's transition from prince to King. The other Shakespearean figure, Bob/Falstaff, dies, thereby removing any "alternative" Shakespearean route. By way of micro-conclusion, the film may indeed present a critique of modern life and of the disenfranchisement of sexual identity, and one in which the future is left open. But it is not Shakespeare's language that it uses to do so; Shakespeare in *Idaho* stands by the heterosexual potential of the Henry plays and is kept separate from and contrasted with Mike's oedipal narrative.

[4]

My argument so far has been about the place of Shakespeare in a particular filmic text, not about the use of Shakespeare in film in any general sense. In 1910, Shakespeare on film was described thus: "it elevates and improves the literary taste and appreciation of the great mass of the people" (*Moving Picture World,* February 1910, 257, quoted in Pearson and Uricchio). Shakespeare began his film career by making film respectable. Was Shakespeare rendered quintessentially American by film or was America's link with Englishness reaffirmed and enriched by contact with Shakespeare? How was Shakespeare to be appropriated as cultural capital?

Obviously, the answer would depend on film and audience, but it is a question that recurs in a range of films that are not adaptations of Shakespeare but that use Shakespeare as a cultural marker. I have argued for a specific use of Shakespeare in *Idaho* but another context for this film is an emerging arthouse/mainstream narrative cinema about male homosexuality. These films—from *Philadelphia* to more avant-garde expositions such as *Postcards From America*—are working with a problematic cultural capital and weaving tropes, songs, images into a set of patterns which do have generic relationships. Moments and tropes include the sublime American landscape, country music, fashion—all the elements that the first round of critics identified as "stylish" in *Idaho*; this emergent style and use of cultural capital is a wider context for the claiming and deployment of Shakespeare as cultural capital in *Idaho*.

JEAN E. HOWARD AND PHYLLIS RACKIN

[Gender and Nation]†

In the last moments of his life, Richard [II] follows his loving queen's injunction to emulate the royal lion, who thrusts out his paw in noble resistance at the moment of his death (5.1.29–34). Behaving, for once, like the warrior kings who were his ancestors, he kills two of his assassins with his own hands, and he uses his dying breath to reassert his status as king and to reclaim the land as his kingdom: "Exton, thy fierce hand / Hath with the King's blood stain'd the King's own land" (5.5.109–10). In the Henry IV plays, England is no longer a kingdom, but an aggregate of heterogeneous people and places. Geographical space replaces allegiance to monarchial authority as the defining principle of English-ness, but England is not yet a unified nation, for it is divided by endless civil wars.

Shakespeare's history plays are primarily monarchial in orientation. Other history plays, such as Heywood's *Edward IV* (*c.* 1599), focus a great deal of attention on the city of London, its citizen classes, and its mercantile culture. Shakespeare, by and large, does not. Rather than focusing on the city of London and the relations between the king and the city, his history plays foreground struggles between English kings and foreign monarchs and between English kings and the heads of the country's great feudal families. But there is a subterranean tension, especially in the second tetralogy, between the idea of a borderless state centered on the body of the monarch and a chorographic focus on the land and people of England, including the city of London, as defining the nation. This tension is implied even in *Richard II*, of all Shakespeare's English

† Jean E. Howard and Phyllis Rackin, "Gender and Nation: The Henry IV Plays," in *Engendering a Nation: A Feminist Account of Shakespeare's English Histories,"* Feminist Readings of Shakespeare" series (London: Routledge, 1997), 160–85. Reprinted by permission of Routledge, Inc., part of The Taylor & Francis Group.

histories the play most insistently focused on the monarch; but in the Henry IV plays it becomes fully manifest in the social heterogeneity of the characters and the geographical heterogeneity of the settings. No longer confined to the elevated domain of court and battlefield, the world of Henry IV includes a variety of vividly detailed contemporary settings, ranging, like a disordered chorographic "perambulation," from Shallow's bucolic Gloucestershire to an innyard on the road to London, to Falstaff's bustling, urban Eastcheap.

The coronation procession at the end of *Henry IV, Part II* returns to the chronicles to impose in retrospect a teleological order on the plot of the two plays, culminating in patrilineal succession. A show of state, the coronation procession stages the restoration of the hierarchical, patriarchal order that has been disrupted both by the preceding action and in its representation. As Lawrence Manley explains, a state procession constructed "a model of society . . . segmented in graduated degrees" that "form a syntagmatic chain . . . leading upward toward . . . elite patriarchal leadership."[1] Up to this point, however, the dramatic structure of the two plays has constructed a model of a fragmented society. The linear, causal plot of *Richard II,* centered on the king, is replaced by a proliferation of subplots tenuously connected by the spatial principles of analogy, parody, juxtaposition and contrast. Structured by the spatial form of chorography, the subplots interrupt the chronicle narrative of diachronic royal succession for a synchronic perambulation of the landscape, moving from royal council chamber and battlefield to borderland and alehouse and country orchard.[2] The displacement of chronicle by chorography in the Henry IV plays transforms the temporality of the narrative from past to present, not only because chorography was a newer form of historiographic representation but also because chronicle, by its very nature, is set in the past tense, while chorographical descriptions, although they typically began with the history of a place, focused on contemporary life rather than the ancient past. Shakespeare's anachronistic, contemporary Eastcheap, like his anachronistic representation of Shallow's country home in Gloucestershire, recalls the present temporality of chorographic description.

1. Lawrence Manley, "From Matron to Monster: Tudor-Stuart London and the Languages of Urban Description," in Heather Dubrow and Richard Strier, eds., *The Historical Renaissance: New Essays on Tudor and Stuart Literature and Culture* (Chicago: University of Chicago Press, 1983), 360.
2. Cf. Manley's description of the second half of John Stow's *Survey of London*: Conducting a "street-by-street perambulation of the wards, a technique he seems to have borrowed from William Lambarde's 1572 *Perambulation of Kent,*" the prototypical chorography, Stow "transformed what was . . . essentially a blazon or at best a triumphal procession of the city's attributes into an extended *voie* or exploration of the landscape" (Manley, 363).

No longer the center of dramatic action, the king also lacks both patrilineal right and providential warrant. His desire to recuperate the sacramental authority of a medieval crusader king by leading a pilgrimage to Jerusalem is endlessly deferred and finally discredited as a mask for a secular domestic political agenda—"To lead out many to the Holy Land, / Lest rest and lying still might make them look / Too near unto my state" (*2H4*, 4.5.210–12). The model of a self-made theatrical man, Henry conceives his reign as a drama and theatrical performance as the basis of royal authority. In *Part I* he lectures his son on the arts of calculated public self-presentation, without which, he says, "Opinion, that did help me to the crown / Had still kept loyal to possession, / And left me in reputeless banishment / A fellow of no mark nor likelihood" (3.2.42–44). By the end of *Part II,* the king acknowledges the failure of his performance, but he still uses theatrical language to describe it: his entire reign, he says, has been "but as a scene / Acting" an "argument" of usurpation and domestic disorder (4.5.197–98). Hal, he now recognizes, will put on a better show.

Hal's promise as heir apparent is based, from the beginning of *Henry IV, Part I,* on his superior performative power, but although performance provides a necessary basis for royal authority, it is not represented as sufficient. As Barbara Hodgdon has observed, the spectacle of many men marching in the king's coats at Shrewsbury "recirculates the question of the true king's identity, the central issue behind the Hotspur–Northumberland rebellion."[3] This practice had ample historical precedent (Holinshed, in fact, records the presence of decoys "apparelled in the kings sute" at Shrewsbury), but its foregrounding in Shakespeare's representation of the battle draws on antitheatrical sentiment to offer an implicit critique of Henry's reliance upon theatrical performance to secure his authority. For although costume and performance are indeed sufficient to make a king in a theatrical production, their proliferation here is staged in a way to remind an audience that off the stage costume is not everything: who is wearing the coat really does make a difference. As Douglas says in *Part I,* after killing Blunt, "A borrowed title hast thou bought too dear . . . I will kill all his coats . . . / Until I meet the King" (5.3.23–28).

Dynastic authority is even more explicitly discredited by its association with the forces of rebellion and national disunity. The alliance between the rebel leaders is cemented by the traditional bonds of dynastic alliances (Mortimer is married to Glendower's daughter, Hotspur to Mortimer's sister), and they rationalize their rebellion in terms of patrilineal right, since Mortimer is the lineal

3. Barbara Hodgdon, *The End Crowns All: Closure and Contradiction in Shakespeare's History* (Princeton: Princeton University Press, 1991), 158.

heir to Richard II. But the rebel cause is discredited, not only or even chiefly because it defies the authority of the monarch, but because it threatens to dismember the body of the land, a threat that is graphically illustrated when the rebel leaders haggle over the map of Britain and agree finally to have the river Trent turned from its natural course in the interest of their "bargain" (3.1.137).

Patrimonial inheritance no longer legitimates royal authority, but in this play, unlike *Richard III* and *Richard II,* neither does matrimony. There are no women at Henry's court and only two brief references to Henry's queen, both, significantly, in the form of irreverent jokes at the Eastcheap Tavern. The first is when Hal is informed that a nobleman has come from the court with a message from his father. Hal's flippant response—"Give him as much as will make him a royal man, and send him back again to my mother" [2.4.259–60]—defies the authority of his father, expresses his disrespect for nobility and conflates the names of hereditary entitlement with the names of coins. The second comes in the form of theatrical parody when Falstaff assumes the role of king in the play extempore. Expert in theatrical performance, Falstaff evokes delighted exclamations from Mistress Quickly, but he immediately redefines her response to cast her in the stereotypical role of his weeping queen, thus providing himself with a token of royal authority that Henry never manages to achieve [2.4.348–51]. The same association between a king's authority and that of a husband—along with a reminder that Henry never manages to achieve either—provides the basis for the Archbishop of York's description of the king's inability to govern: the land, he says, is like "an offensive wife / That hath enrag'd him on to offer strokes, / As he is striking, holds his infant up / And hangs resolv'd correction in the arm / That was uprear'd to execution" (*2H4*, 4.1.208–12). Significantly, the Archbishop's metaphor is the only place in the text where Henry himself is cast in the role of a husband.

As Barbara Hodgdon notes, in *Part I* "only the rebel leaders—Hotspur and Lord Mortimer—have wives" (155); but in both cases the wives pose a threat to their husbands' public success. Hotspur, for example, must leave his wife because, as he explains, "This is no world / To play with mammets and to tilt with lips" [2.3.85–86]. When there is a kingdom to be won, the sexual warfare of the bedroom can only be a distraction. Mortimer stays home with his wife, but the home he stays in is hers, and it is located in the alien world of Wales; once Mortimer decides to stay there he loses his claim to royal authority and his place in English history. Here, as in the Henry VI plays, a man's desire for his wife is represented as a source of potential danger and disempowerment.

The heterogeneous, decentered world of the Henry IV plays includes marginal spaces where female characters regain some of the subversive power they had in the first tetralogy. Here, as in *Richard III* and *Richard II,* women are excluded from court and battlefield, but they play dominant roles in Eastcheap and Wales.[4] Both Eastcheap and Wales are separated from the central scenes of English historical representation, and both, like the commercial theaters in Shakespeare's England, are represented as sexualized domains of idleness and play. The location of the female characters in Eastcheap and Wales also recalls the places that real women occupied in the public theaters; for although English women never appeared on stage, they did appear in the playhouses as paying customers, and French and Italian companies, which included women, did occasionally perform in England.[5]

Mistress Quickly's tavern in Eastcheap is a plebeian, comic, theatrical—and strikingly contemporary—place that mirrors the disorderly push and shove of the playhouse itself. The women in the tavern are theatergoers, entrepreneurs, and purveyors of commercial sex. Their portraits are unexpectedly modern. The name of Quickly's tavern is not specified in the text, but its traditional identification as the Boar's Head is suggested in *Henry IV, Part II* (2.2.146–47), and it seems appropriate in a number of ways. One critic has made the intriguing suggestion the name was a spoonerism for "whore's bed."[6] Historically associated with Sir John Fastolfe, Falstaff's real-life namesake, the Boar's Head was also the name of at least six real taverns in Shakespeare's London, one of them used for a theater.[7] Shakespeare's anachronistically modern tavern is both a playhouse and a bawdy house. Frequented, like the playhouse, by a disorderly, socially heterogeneous crowd, it is also the scene of play-acting. Falstaff pretends to be Hal; Hal pretends to be Falstaff; and both degrade the dignity of royalty by playing the part of the reigning king. The pleasures of the Boar's Head are illicit, and they are also dangerous. The disreputable crowd the

4. A suggestive gloss to the marking of Eastcheap as a feminine space is provided by Lawrence Manley's observation that cities were gendered feminine. He cites examples ranging from "the book of Revelation's contrast between Jerusalem, the bride of Christ, and Rome, the whore of Babylon" (Manley, 355) to "the feminine personages who mark the towns on the maps in Michael Drayton's *Polyolbion*" (371, *n.* 37). He points out that "London was almost invariably personified as a woman in the city's annual mayoral pageants" and that when Ben Jonson, in his text for the coronation pageant of James I represented the Genius of the City as a man, Jonson's collaborator, Dekker, felt obliged to object (371 *n.* 37).

5. Stephen Orgel, "Nobody's Perfect: Or Why Did the English Stage Take Boys for Women?" *South Atlantic Quarterly* 88 (1989), 9 and 28, *n*2.

6. James Black, "*Henry IV*: A World of Figures There," in Press, C. McGuire and D. A. Samuelson (eds), *Shakespeare: The Theatrical Dimension* (New York: AMS Press, 1979), 167.

7. S. B. Hemingway, ed., *A New Variorum Edition of Henry the Fourth Part I* (Philadelphia: Lippincott, 1936), 124–25; E. K. Chambers, *The Elizabethan Stage,* 4 vols. (Oxford: Clarendon Press, 1923), 2:443–45.

tavern attracts is given to every sort of transgression, from drunkenness and brawling to thieving and prostitution. Here, as in the antitheatrical tracts, the dangers of the playhouse are most prominently represented by women and sexuality. Like the prostitutes who looked for customers in the theater audiences, Doll Tearsheet infects her customers with venereal disease; and at the end of *Henry IV, Part II,* when Doll and the hostess are arrested, we learn that "there hath been a man or two kill'd about her" (*2H4*, 5.4.5–6). Whether "her" means Doll or the hostess and whether "about" means "concerning" or "near," clearly the women are a source of danger. A. R. Humphreys, the editor of the Arden edition, glosses this line with a quotation from Dekker's *Honest Whore*: "O how many thus . . . have let out / Their soules in Brothell houses . . . and dyed / Just at their Harlots foot" (3.3.77–80).

Although the tavern is clearly marked as a feminized, theatrical space, the most memorable inhabitant of that space—and of the Henry IV plays generally—is not the hostess, or any other woman, but Falstaff. Physically a man and a womanizer, Falstaff is nonetheless characterized in feminine terms.[8] In *The Merry Wives of Windsor,* one of the punishments for his sexual pursuit of Mistress Ford is a beating in women's clothes, which recalls the rough punishments meted out in early modern English villages to uxorious men who failed to conform to the conventions of patriarchal marriage.[9] Falstaff's contempt for honor and military valor, his incompetence on the battlefield, his inconstancy, his lies, his gross corpulence, and his sensual self-indulgence all imply effeminacy within the system of analogies that separated spirit from body, aristocrat from plebeian, and man from woman in early modern England.[1] Contemplating what he thinks is Falstaff's corpse at the end of the battle of Shrewsbury, Hal asks, "What, old acquaintance! could not all this flesh / Keep in a little life?" [5.4.101–02]. Falstaff himself, in a usage that would have been clearly intelligible to Shakespeare's audience, refers to his fat belly as a "womb" (*2H4*, 4.3.22: "My womb,

8. Valerie Traub, *Desire and Anxiety: Circulations of Sexuality in Shakespearean Drama* (London: Routledge, 1992), 50–70.
9. See David Underdown, "The Taming of the Scold: The Enforcement of Patriarchal Authority in Early Modern England," in Anthony Fletcher and J. Stevenson, eds., *Order and Disorder in Early Modern England* (Cambridge: Cambridge University Press, 1985).
1. [Phyllis Rackin, "Historical Difference/Sexual Difference," in Jean Brik, ed., *Privileging Gender in Early Modern Britain* (Kirksville, MO.: Sixteenth-Century Journal Publishers, 1992), 3.] It is generally agreed that Falstaff was originally named Sir John Oldcastle. A historical figure who lived during the reign of Henry IV, Oldcastle was often viewed as an early Protestant martyr. His descendents included the powerful Brooke family, who may have objected to the fact that Shakespeare's dissolute knight had been given this name, with the result that "Oldcastle" was changed to "Falstaff" in the quarto texts of *Henry IV, Part I* published in 1598, although there remains a reference to Falstaff as "my old lad of the castle" (1.2.41–42). In the epilogue to *Henry IV, Part II,* however, Shakespeare is at pains to declare, "Oldcastle died [a] martyr, and this is not the man" (Epi.32).

my womb, my womb undoes me"); and he compares himself to a "sow that hath overwhelm'd all her litter but one" (*2H4*, 1.2.11–12).

Like Richard III and Richard II, Falstaff is both empowered and discredited by his appropriation of the woman's part, especially by its theatricality. However, Falstaff's "female" theatricality, unlike theirs, is inscribed in the degraded register of comedy. Hal appropriates Falstaff's theatrical power for his own use, as indeed he must, since the power of theatrical performance is a requisite for royal authority in the modernized world of the second tetralogy.[2] However, just as Hal's robbery of the Gadshill robbers serves to distance him from the taint of criminality that attends the initial theft and just as his victory over Hotspur at Shrewsbury appropriates the dead rebel's honor without the personal and political defects that attend it, this appropriation, sanitized by Hal's final rejection of Falstaff, produces a theatrical power purged of its feminine pollution.

Falstaff, like the queen in *Richard II* and Katherine in *Henry V*, is thus ultimately conscripted into the hegemonic project of affirming the authority of a true king. Nonetheless, throughout most of the Henry IV plays he exercises a subversive theatrical power and performs a subversive role in the represented action, both of which are articulated in his threat to "beat [Hal] out of [his] kingdom with a dagger of lath" [*1H4*, 2.4.122–23]. Like Joan in *Henry VI, Part I*, Falstaff discredits the aristocratic shibboleths of martial valor and chivalric honor; like Margaret, he threatens to dominate and effeminate the heir to the English throne, for the fat knight is not only feminized; he also threatens the virility of other men. *Henry IV, Part I* ends with the spectacle of Falstaff mutilating Hotspur's corpse [5.4.124–25]. Wounding the dead hero's thigh, he reenacts the female threat to manhood and military honor symbolized in the opening scene by a report that the women of Wales have inflicted some unspeakably shameful mutilation on the corpses of English soldiers (1.1.43–46).

The parallel between the two veiled references to castration suggests an analogical relationship between the world of Eastcheap and that of Wales, both associated with the loss of masculine honor. Analogy, however, is not identity. Although both settings are clearly marked as comic and theatrical and thus as opposed to history, the low comic scenes in the Boar's Head Tavern recall the disorderly scene of present theatrical performance, while the scene in Wales, with its emphasis on magic and romantic love and its exotic setting, recalls the Shakespearean genre of romantic comedy. The women in the tavern are too familiar to enter history, too much like

2. Jean E. Howard, *The Stage and Social Struggle in Early Modern England* (London: Routledge, 1994), 139–53.

the disorderly women in the theater audience. The woman in Wales, by contrast, is marked as an exotic creature from another world, like the French and Italian actresses who occasionally appeared on the English stage, or the heroine of a narrative romance or romantic comedy.

Or, perhaps, like Queen Elizabeth herself. In this connection, the epilogue to *Henry IV, Part II* is revealing. In the preceding scene, the representation of the great historical moment when the wild Prince Hal of popular legend takes his historical place as Henry V, no female characters are present. The epilogue is rarely performed today, perhaps because it problematizes the closing representation of patriarchal historical order. The epilogue is set apart from the prior action in the folio text of the play, where it is printed on a separate page, marked off by colophon devices. As Barbara Hodgdon points out, "other Epilogues are not so separated, in either Quarto or Folio texts" (Hodgdon, 285, n. 73). Some critics have suggested that the banished Falstaff—or the actor who played his part—returned to speak the epilogue (Hodgdon, 181–82); but whoever its speaker, the epilogue serves to reconstitute the preceding action—and the action to come—as comic entertainment. It promises the restoration of Falstaff, and of female characters—to "continue the story, with Sir John in it, and make you merry with fair Katherine of France" (27–29); and it contains two additional references to women. One recalls the world of Eastcheap as it acknowledges the presence of women—and of sexual transactions between men and women—in the theater audience: "All the gentlewomen here have forgiven me," he says, and "if the gentlemen will not, then the gentlemen do not agree with the gentlewomen, which was never seen in such an assembly" (22–25). The other acknowledges the presence of a woman on the English throne, kneeling "to pray for the Queen" (17).

This is the only reference to Elizabeth in the history plays Shakespeare wrote during her lifetime, but the ideological contradiction she embodied hovers just beyond the horizon of the historical world they project. The presence of a woman on the English throne, like the matter of Wales, haunts the borders of Shakespeare's Lancastrian histories. Both evoked powerful, and related, anxieties for a patriarchal culture ruled by a female monarch who traced her hereditary right to a Welsh grandfather who had turned to the dim mists of Welsh antiquity to buttress his tenuous genealogical authority, incorporating the red dragon of Cadwallader in the royal arms and giving his eldest son the name of Arthur. Wales was both a necessary origin for Tudor monarchial legitimacy and a place of dangerous difference. The Welsh troops, mentioned but never seen, mark the transmission of royal power in *Richard II* when they desert Richard's army, "gone to Bullingbrook, dispers'd and fled" (*R2*, 3.2.74). Throughout the two parts of *Henry IV*, the audience is reminded of Hal's title as Prince of Wales, and even in *Henry V*, the king's Welsh origins are a subject of repeated emphasis. Nonetheless, the only history play in which Shakespeare actually takes the audience to the wild country just beyond the English border is *Henry IV, Part I*.

An alien world of witchcraft and magic, of mysterious music, and also of unspeakable atrocity that horrifies the English imagination, Shakespeare's Wales is inscribed in the same register that defined the dangerous power of women. In addition to the liminal location at England's geographical border that makes Wales a constant military threat and the liminal attributes that make it psychologically disturbing, Wales is also the place where the hereditary heir to the throne is sequestered.[3] This is the case not only in *Henry IV, Part I* but also in *Cymbeline*, a much later play which is also based on Holinshed and also centers on issues of English national identity. A land of miracles and music and also of mortal danger, the Wales in *Cymbeline* is also the place where the true heirs to the British throne (disguised with the historically resonant names of Polydore and Cadwal) are hidden from sight of the court.

The double association of Wales with savagery and with female power had a precedent as ancient as Geoffrey of Monmouth's *Historia Regum Britanniae,* which records that the name *Welsh* derives "either from their leader Gualo, or from their Queen Galaes, or else from their being so barbarous."[4] It also had a contemporary context in anxieties about English colonists who married native women and became assimilated to the culture of the savage places they had been sent to domesticate.[5] As Christopher Highley points out, Mor-

3. Effeminated by sexual passion, Mortimer nonetheless remains a frightening figure. Long before Mortimer appears on stage, we witness the king's agitated response to Hotspur's demand that he be ransomed and brought home (1.3), but the threat of an alternative royal line with a better claim to the throne is also dramatized in Mortimer's association with the dangerously seductive Welsh woman. By her sex and by her nationality, she both represents and threatens the true legitimacy that the Tudor sovereigns, as well as their male subjects, always needed to claim but could never truly have.
4. Geoffrey of Monmouth (c. 1136), *Historia Regum Britanniae,* translated as *The History of the Kings of Britain,* trans. L. Thorpe (Harmondsworth: Penguin Books, 1966), 284.
5. The threefold association of female power, foreignness, and atrocity appears to be a persistent feature of early modern colonialist discourse. Ralegh's *Discoverie of Guiana* (1596) reports that Amazons "are said to be very cruel and bloodthirsty" (quoted in Louis A. Montrose, "The Work of Gender is the Discourse of Discovery," *Representations* 33 (1991), 26). Even more suggestive is a late sixteenth-century travel narrative quoted by Stephen Greenblatt, which reports that "near the mountains of the moon there is a queen, an empress of all these Amazons, a witch and a cannibal who daily feeds on the flesh of boys. She ever remains unmarried, but she has intercourse with a great number of men by whom she begets offspring. The kingdom, however, remains hereditary to the daughters, not to the sons" [Stephen J. Greenblatt, *Renaissance Self-Fashioning: From More to Shakespeare* (Chicago: University of Chicago Press, 1980), 181]. What is especially interesting for our argument is that this account, like Fleming's account of the female atrocities in Wales, comes to its readers doubly mediated. It is recorded in the diary

timer's "capitulation to Glendower replays the process of 'going native' whereby English colonists in Ireland were assimilated to Gaelic society", a process that Spenser identified in his *View of the Present State of Ireland* (1596) as "degendering" and exemplified by, among others, "the great Mortimer, who forgetting how great he was once in England, or English at all, is now become the most barbarous of them all."[6]

At the beginning of *Henry IV, Part I,* the Earl of Westmerland comes to the English court with bad news from a Welsh battlefield: Mortimer's army has been defeated in battle, Mortimer captured by Owen Glendower, a thousand of his soldiers killed. Westmerland also reports that after the battle, the Welsh women committed some "beastly shameless transformation" upon the bodies of the dead English soldiers—an act, he says, "as may not be / Without much shame retold or spoken of" (1.1.43–46). Refusing to describe the act, Shakespeare follows Holinshed, who anxiously reported, "The shameful villanie used by the Welshwomen towards the dead carcasses, was such, as honest eares would be ashamed to heare, and continent toongs to speake thereof."[7] In Shakespeare's historical source as in his play, Wales is identified as the scene of emasculation and female power—and also as the site of a repression in the English historical narrative.

Told in the English court, Shakespeare's account of the Welsh women reproduces Holinshed's anxious repressions, but the unspeakable threat of castration returns and proliferates throughout the play. It surfaces in Kate's playful threat to break Hotspur's "little finger" [2.3.82] and in Falstaff's desecration of Hotspur's corpse. Most insistently, however, the threat of emasculation returns in Act III, when Shakespeare moves beyond the boundary of

of Richard Madox, an English traveler in Sierra Leone, but Madox claims that he heard the story from a Portuguese trader. Carroll Smith-Rosenberg has found still another account of female savagery, most closely resembling Fleming's in *The Columbian Magazine and Monthly Miscellany* I (Philadelphia, 1787), 549. This account is also represented as doubly mediated (told to the writer by an unnamed "gentleman" met "near Alexandria, in Virginia, in 1782"). In this report, a surveyor named Colonel Crawford, captured by Indians, "was delivered over to *the women,* and being fastened to a stake, in the centre of a circle, formed by the savages and their allies, the female furies, after the preamble of a war song, began by tearing out the nails of his toes and fingers, then proceeded, at considerable intervals, to cut off his nose and ears; after which they stuck his lacerated body full of pitch pines, large pieces of which they inserted (horrid to relate!) into his private parts; to all of which they set fire, and which continued burning, amidst the inconceivable tortures of the unhappy man, for a considerable time. After thus glutting their revenge, by arts of barbarity, the success of which was repeatedly applauded by the surrounding demons, they cut off his genitals, and rushing in upon him, finished his misery with their tomohawks, and hacked his body limb from limb."

6. Christopher Highley, "Wales, Ireland, and *1Henry IV,*" *Renaissance Drama* 21 (1990), 97.

7. Raphael Holinshed, *Chronicles of England, Scotland, and Ireland* (1587), reprinted, 6 vols. 2nd ed. (1808), 3:20.

English historical narration to stage a scene in Wales. Westmerland's horrified report of Welsh barbarism is replaced by the glamour of Glendower's poetry and his daughter's singing, the castrating savages of the battlefield with the seductive allure of the lady in the castle. What makes this replacement interesting is that Glendower's daughter is also associated with the Welsh women who intruded on the masculine space of the battlefield to deprive the English soldiers of their manhood and honor. Unwilling to part with her amorous companion, she resolves, ominously, that "She'll be a soldier too, she'll to the wars" (3.1.193). Like the weeping queens in *Richard II* and *Richard III,* Glendower's daughter is a devoted wife, bathed in tears at the prospect of her husband's departure for battle. Like the women in the Boar's Head Tavern, however, she resists domestication. The inhabitant of a marginal place, she speaks a language that announces her otherness, and she embodies a dangerous sexuality that disables the man who succumbs to its temptation.

Holinshed's passing reference to Mortimer's marriage refuses to specify Mortimer's motivation, but it identifies the union in traditional medieval terms, as a contract between men designed to secure a treaty: "Edmund Mortimer earle of March, prisoner with Owen Glendouer, whether for irksomnesse of cruell captiuitie, or feare of death, or for what other cause, it is vncerteine, agreed to take part with Owen, against the king of England, and tooke to wife the daughter of the said Owen" (Holinshed, 3:21). In Shakespeare's play, however, Mortimer is motivated—and emasculated—by sexual passion for his wife. Although Shakespeare emphasizes Mortimer's lineal claim to the English throne, we see him agreeing to a treaty that will divide the land, and we hear him identify that division as "gelding" the portion that will be left for him [3.1.110]. His manhood lost to female enchantment, Shakespeare's Mortimer prefers what he calls the "feeling disputation" (3.1.203) of kisses with his wife to military battle in pursuit of his patriarchal right. He is "as slow / As hot Lord Percy is on fire to go" [3.1.259–60] to join the battle that will decide the future of the English kingdom.[8]

Shakespeare's Welsh interlude replaces the unspeakable horror of castration with the theatrical performance of seduction. A similar displacement seems to characterize Shakespeare's relation at this point to his historical source. The love scene in Wales has no historical precedent, but its structural position in Act III of the play is similar to that of a passage inserted by Abraham Fleming in the 1587 edition of Holinshed's *Chronicles* (the edition Shakespeare

8. Matthew H. Wikander, *The Play of Truth and State: Historical Drama from Shakespeare to Brecht* (Baltimore: The Johns Hopkins University Press, 1986, 14–25.

used). Fleming interrupts the account of a later battle to insert a detailed account of the act Holinshed had refused to describe:

> The dead bodies of the Englishmen, being above a thousand lieng upon the ground imbrued in their owne bloud . . . did the women of Wales cut off their privities, and put one part thereof into the mouthes of everie dead man, in such sort that the cullions hoong downe to their chins; and not so contented, they did cut off their noses and thrust them into their tailes as they laie on the ground mangled and defaced.
>
> (Holinshed, 3:20, 34)

Fleming seems delighted with the grisly story, introducing it with numerous references to gory atrocities committed by women against men in classical times, but he also feels constrained to defend his decision to write the problematic material into the English historical record. He notes the precise location in Thomas Walsingham's Latin chronicle where he found it, and he explains,

> though it make the reader to read it, and the hearer to heare it, ashamed: yet bicause it was a thing doone in open sight, and left testified in historie; I see little reason whie it should not be imparted in our mother toong to the knowledge of our owne countrimen, as well as unto strangers in a language unknowne.
>
> (3:34)

Fleming's belated account of the atrocities performed by the Welsh women seems to lie behind Shakespeare's deferred Welsh scene. Both interrupt the historical narrative for a belated supplement to Holinshed's account, but Shakespeare transvalues the terms of Fleming's gruesome description. Fleming's account of bloody corpses lying on the ground, their organs of bottom and top horribly transposed, becomes the lady's seductive invitation to Mortimer to lie down upon the "wanton rushes"—his head luxuriously resting in her lap, while she sings "charming [his] blood with pleasing heaviness," a delicious languor like the state " 'twixt wake and sleep" (3.1.211–16). The strange tongue from which Fleming translated his gruesome story becomes the sweet babble of the lady's Welsh, a sound that Shakespeare represents by repeated stage directions, *"The lady speaks in Welsh."*

Although the lady cannot speak English, she expresses her love in tears, in kisses, and in music. She wishes, her father explains, to sing "the song that please[s]" Mortimer (3.1.213); and even her speech reminds her besotted husband of "ravishing" music "Sung by a fair queen in a summer's bow'r" (3.1.207–8). Music, as Shakespeare's Orsino tells us, was considered the "food of love." Philip Stubbes, well known for his warnings against the dangerous consequences of theater-going, also warned that music could corrupt "good minds, [making] them womanish and inclined to all kinds of Whoredom and mischief."[9] In fact, the spectacle of a woman singing was widely regarded in Shakespeare's time as an incitement to lust.[1]

Like the historical record of the Welshwomen's barbarism, and like the French that Katherine speaks in *Henry V,* Glendower's daughter speaks in a language that requires translation. In *The Famous Victories of Henry the Fifth* the French princess speaks the same good English as the men. Shakespeare, however, departs from theatrical convention to write the women's lines in foreign tongues, thus excluding them from the linguistic community that includes all the male characters—French and Welsh as well as English—along with his English-speaking audience. The incomprehensible speech that masks the lady's meaning is doubly the language of the Other—the language of England's enemies and also the language of women and of love. The difference, however, is that while Katherine learns English in order to communicate with Henry, Mortimer proposes to learn Welsh. Bewitched and enthralled in Wales, he desires to abandon the King's English, the discourse of patriarchal authority, for the wordless language of love. He looks beyond words to communicate with his lady—"I understand thy looks," he says, "I understand thy kisses, and thou mine" (3.1.198, 202)—and he resolves to learn Welsh, the language of England's barbarous enemies, the incomprehensible discourse of the alien world that lies beyond the bounds of English historical narration.[2] Geographically and dramatically isolated, Shakespeare's representation of Mortimer in Wales interrupts the progress of the English historical plot to depict the dangerous allure of a world that is both feminine and effeminating. The Welsh scenes thus serve a double purpose. They discredit Mortimer's lineal claim to the English throne by aligning him with what in this play is represented as non-English, the territory and language of Wales. At the same time, they demonstrate the degrading uxoriousness that is the dangerous aspect of spousal affection. If in the first tetralogy

9. Stubbes sig. D4^r, quoted in L. Austern, " 'Sing Againe Syren': Female Musicians and Sexual Enchantment in Elizabethan Life and Literature," *Renaissance Quarterly* 42 (1989), 424.

1. See Austern; see also Laurie E. Maguire, " 'Household Kates': Chez Petruchio, Percy and Plantagenet," in Susan P. Cerasano and Marion Wynne-Davies, eds., *Gloriana's Face: Women, Public and Private, in the English Renaissance* (Detroit: Wayne State University Press, 1992), 144.

2. Mullaney points out that although Henry VIII had outlawed Welsh in 1535, the alien language ("nothing like, nor consonant to the natural Mother Tongue within this realm") consistently defied English efforts "to control or outlaw it." Resisting repeated "pressures of assimilation and suppression . . . Welsh remained a strange tongue, a discomfiling reminder that Wales continued to be a foreign and hostile colony, ruled and to an extent subjected but never quite controlled by Tudor power" [Steven Mullaney, *The Place of the Stage: License, Play, and Power in Renaissance England* (Chicago: University of Chicago Press, 1988), 77, 162 *n.* 47].

women threaten to disrupt the men's genealogical authority by adultery, here they threaten to disable their husbands for the public achievements required by a performative conception of male authority by drawing them to private sensual pleasures.

Significantly, these pleasures are also represented as theatrical. When Glendower calls his daughter "a peevish self-will'd harlotry" (3.1.196), he uses a word that associates her with the women in the Boar's Head Tavern, and also with the playhouse itself. The only other time that word appears in the *Henry IV* plays is in the immediately preceding scene, when Mistress Quickly praises Falstaff's acting: "he doth it as like one of these harlotry players as ever I see!" [2.4.352–53]. The term "harlotry players" makes explicit the association between the dangers (and the pleasures) of sexual indulgence and those of the playhouse which also informs the scene in Glendower's castle. Shakespeare's representation of Mortimer in Wales enacts contemporary beliefs that excessive sensuality would make a man effeminate, but it also recalls the antitheatrical arguments that the theater encouraged idleness and lechery. And it anticipates his representation of Cleopatra's Egypt, another exotic, alien nation where, as Caesar complains, Antony "is not more manlike / Than Cleopatra; nor the queen of Ptolemy / More womanly than he" (1.4.5–7).[3] Like the Romans' contempt for Cleopatra's feminine wiles and the luxurious idleness of Antony's Egyptian life, the bickering between Hotspur and Glendower recalls the charges that the theater encouraged idleness and lechery, the denunciations that associated dramatic impersonation with sorcery and deception, and the condemnations of the playhouse as Satan's synagogue. Hotspur is impatient at the waste of time in Wales. Glendower identifies himself as a magician; like Prospero, he claims he can "call spirits from the vasty deep" (3.1.52). Hotspur calls Glendower a liar and denounces magic as the work of the devil. Nonetheless, when Glendower declares that he will summon musicians who "hang in the air a thousand leagues from hence" to play for his guests, Shakespeare's text supports Glendower's project—and his claim to magical power—with the stage direction "*The music plays*" (3.1.224, 228). In fact, Shakespeare seems in this scene to be complicit with the Welsh magician. Together they detain—and entertain—their audiences with an idyllic interlude that interrupts the progress of the historical plot.

Endlessly repeated in antitheatrical polemics, the charge that

3. Cf. Stephen Greenblatt's exposition of the ways the allurements of the Bower of Bliss threaten the "civilization—which for Spenser is achieved only through renunciation and the constant exercise of power" and the analogies he draws between European responses to the natives of Africa and North America and English colonial struggles in Ireland (Greenblatt 173–4, 179–92). In these accounts * * * contact with native people results in a loss of masculinity.

theatrical performance corrupted its audiences with incitements to sexual lust—often accompanied by supporting anecdotes—attests to an attraction as powerful as the anxiety it produced.[4] The lush, theatrical scene that depicts Mortimer's Welsh idyll has a similar ambivalence. Replacing historical narrative with dramatic enactment and Westmerland's horrified report with the sensual beauty of Glendower's poetry and his daughter's singing, it moves the audience from the austere English court to an outlandish world of idleness and illicit pleasure. It uses the seductive art—the music—of theatrical performance to represent the dangerous female power that was present in the playhouse and in the world but could never be "retold or spoken of" in the discourse of patriarchal history.

The scene in Wales is a brief interlude in *Henry IV, Part 1*. The numerous scenes in Eastcheap, however, threaten to take over both parts of the play. The epilogue to *Henry IV, Part II,* acknowledges their prominence and relies on their appeal for the theater audience to advertise a sequel: "If you be not too much cloy'd with fat meat, our humble author will continue the story, with Sir John in it" (26–28). The quarto title pages for both plays also advertise Falstaff, and the second adds a reference to "swaggering Pistoll" as well. Moreover, even in *Richard II,* there is a passage that looks very much like an advertisement for the tavern scenes in the play to come, when the new king, Henry IV, worries about his wayward son who has been absent from court for three months:

> Inquire at London, 'mongst the taverns there,
> For there, they say, he daily doth frequent,
> With unrestrained loose companions,
> Even such, they say, as stand in narrow lanes
> And beat our watch and rob our passengers,
> Which he, young wanton and effeminate boy,
> Takes on the point of honor to support
> So dissolute a crew.
>
> (2*H*4,5.3.5–12)

This speech announces in advance two important features of Hal's characterization: the fact that his chosen companions are exactly the sort of people that antitheatrical writers claimed constituted the majority of the audience in the commercial theaters, and the fact that the king regards those associations as symptoms of effeminacy. It also serves as a good advertisement for the Henry IV plays, where all the scandalous behavior the king describes will be enacted on stage for the pleasure of the theater audience.

4. See Ann Jennalie Cook, " 'Bargaines of Incontinencie': Bawdy Behavior in the Playhouses," *Shakespeare Studies* 10 (1977), 271–90; see also Laura Levine, *Men in Women's Clothing: Anti-theatricality and Effeminization, 1579–1642* (Cambridge: Cambridge University Press, 1994).

The tavern is a pivotal locale in the Henry IV plays. For the prince, as for the audience, it offers the attractions as well as the dangers of the playhouse. For Hal, it is the place of liberty and experimentation where he escapes from his princely responsibilities to fleet the time in play-acting, jokes, and revelry. For the audience, it is a place of transgressive entertainment. The Boar's Head, however, is not only a timeless, Saturnalian space, but also the very specific world of contemporary London. In the Boar's Head Tavern, the historical prince meets unhistorical characters who drink anachronistic cups of sack and wear anachronistic ruffs and peach-colored silk stockings (Rackin, 139). Here the realities of sixteenth-century urban life—its theatricality and its commercial vigor—interrupt, impede, and parody a historical narrative detailing the monarchial history of fifteenth-century England.

The fear of social indifferentiation hangs heavy over the heterogeneous world of the Henriad.[5] At the inn, a carrier complains, "This house is turn'd upside down since Robin ostler died" (2.1.10–11). In the countryside, Justice Shallow's servant Davy o'ermasters his master; in the city, Falstaff flouts the authority of the Chief Justice, and Hal assumes the roles of highwayman and then serving-man in an Eastcheap tavern. Hal threatens to betray his patriarchal lineage by making the lawless Falstaff his parent and Ned Poins his brother. Falstaff even accuses Poins of giving it out that Hal will marry Poins's sister (*2H4*, 2.2.127–29). Shrinking from court and longing for small beer, the prince seems to be out of love with his greatness (*2H4*, 2.2.6–12). The endings of both Parts of *Henry IV* seem attempts to allay this specter of indifferentiation. At Shrewsbury, Hal differentiates himself from the cowardly Falstaff and emerges as a chivalric hero; at the end of *Part II* Hal embraces first his own father and then the Chief Justice, casting off his false father, Falstaff. Similarly, the prince casts aside his tavern brothers to embrace his blood brothers in a fellowship founded on their assumed difference from both the English lower orders and the French others.

Significantly, no female characters are present in either of these scenes. The last scene in *Part II,* however, is preceded by a brief interlude in which Quickly and Doll Tearsheet are hustled off to prison (5.4). The scene is only thirty-one lines long, it is unhistorical, and there is no explicit connection between the women's arrest and the transformation of the wild prince Hal into the model King Henry V. The two are connected, however, by the same logic of displacement that entails the representation of the tavern women as criminalized and comic figures upon whom anxieties about social

5. See Laurie E. Osborne, "Crisis of Degree in Shakespeare's *Henriad,*" *Studies in English Literature, 1500–1900* 25 (1985), 337–59.

disorder could be conveniently displaced. While Hal's dereliction of duty threatened to make monarchy "common" and to undo all forms of social hierarchy, some of the anxiety occasioned by his behavior is displaced onto the tavern women. Through prostitution, it is suggested, these women erase distinctions between man and man, and Quickly's pervasive malapropisms erase, as well, distinctions between one word and another. Nonetheless, the very act of representing Quickly and Tearsheet as internal threats to the nation, as the criminal underbelly of the commonwealth, opens the door to registering their theatrical vitality and their links to the commercial world where the players plied their own trade. These women may be socially marginal and the roles their prototypes played in their nation's history may be elided, but on the stage, players they most definitely are. Their presence calls attention to the gap between official history and the social domains it must exclude to constitute itself.

In *Henry IV, Part I* and *Part II* Quickly's presence fractures the hermetically sealed world of aristocratic, masculine history to confront London playgoers—both men and women—with a representation of contemporary life in which a woman runs a tavern, both uses and defies the law, exists for a time without a husband, and with her friend Doll Tearsheet probably participates in the sale of sex. This "public" woman hardly conforms to dominant codes of acceptable femininity, and nothing more clearly signals her ideological volatility than the play's ambivalent representation of her status as wife, for a woman's marital status was a crucial component of her identity in early modern England. As *The Lawes Resolutions of Womens Rights,* published in 1632, explicitly states, "all [women] are understood either married, or to be married.[6]"

A notable exception to the wholesale domestication of female characters that began in *Richard III,* Quickly is not easily assimilated to the institution of marriage. In the course of the Henry IV plays, in fact, her marital status becomes increasingly ambiguous. In *Henry IV, Part I* Quickly is identified as the "wife" of "an honest man" (3.3.93, 119). Mr Quickly, however, never appears on stage, and the hostess seems to preside by herself over a domain that is clearly connected with lawlessness as well as the freedom of play. It is in her tavern that the prince and Falstaff elude the law after the Gadshill robbery and there that the two of them turn kingship into a role a "harlotry player" might perform (2.4.395–96). The feminized, theatrical world of the tavern is set in clear opposition to the world of masculine power and duty symbolized by Henry IV and his court. At the Boar's Head, disorder and carnival freedom reign.

6. T. E., *The Lawes Resolutions of Womens Rights* (London, 1632), sig. B3ᵛ.

Even Quickly's deformed speech—her cheerfully rendered malapropisms and double entendres—underscore her social marginality and disorderliness. Not even the King's English—let alone the king's son—is safe in her hands. When Falstaff says of her, "She's neither fish nor flesh, a man knows not where to have her," she replies, "Thou art an unjust man in saying so. Thou or any man knows where to have me, thou knave, thou!" [*1H4*, 3.3.112–15]. Attempting to establish her integrity, Quickly inadvertently announces her sexual availability.

Part II intensifies the sense of lawlessness, anarchy and disease not only in Henry IV's kingdom but also in Nell Quickly's tavern. Now joined on stage by her prostitute friend Doll Tearsheet, Quickly seems to lose her tenuous place in the marriage system. The figure of the prostitute is a potent symbol in this text. As rebellion threatens to fracture the unity of the nation and as Hal's disaffection from the duties of kingship threatens further debasement of the institution of monarchy, the prostitute comes to embody the general breakdown of order and social distinctions. Not the exclusive property of one man, Doll Tearsheet sleeps with many, rendering them interchangeable. And she does so for profit, leaving her partners, it is suggested, bonded in a gruesome fraternity of disease. As Falstaff intones, "We catch of you, Doll, we catch of you" (*2H4*, 2.4.45–46).

Especially intriguing in this text, however, is the way Quickly gradually becomes assimilated into the discourse of prostitution surrounding Doll, and the way Quickly's status as wife becomes increasingly ambiguous. In an example of what we might call the disappearing husband syndrome, Mistress Quickly seems to lose her husband at exactly the time she acquires Doll as a companion. In *Part II* there is no more talk of the hostess's good husband: rather, Quickly insistently pursues Falstaff to make good on his promise to marry her.

> Thou didst swear to me upon a parcel-gilt goblet, sitting in my Dolphin chamber, at the round table by a sea-coal fire, upon Wednesday in Wheeson week, when the Prince broke thy head for liking his father to a singing-man of Windsor, thou didst swear to me then, as I was washing thy wound, to marry me and make me my lady thy wife. (*2H4*, 2.1.86–92)

The playscript offers no corroborating evidence for the Chief Justice's assumption that Falstaff has "made her [Quickly] serve your uses both in purse and in person" (*2H4*, 2.1.115–16). Quickly's own uncertain control of the English tongue and the double entendres that dance through her speech, make determining her degree of sexual activity all the more difficult. To the Chief Justice, she says, "take heed of him! He stabb'd me in mine own house, most beastly, in good faith.' A cares not what mischief he does, if his weapon be out. He will foin like any devil, he will spare neither man, woman, nor child" (*2H4*, 2.1.13–17). It is not quite clear what "weapon" Falstaff has been brandishing. Whatever the "truth" of Quickly's sexual involvement with Falstaff, certainly her close association with Doll Tearsheet colors the audience's perception both of her and of the tavern, now not only a refuge for male criminals and a wayward prince but a place as well for female criminality: prostitution and violence against a man. In the last scene Quickly and Doll are accused of having, with Pistol, beaten a man to death, perhaps an unruly male consumer of Doll's sexual wares (*2H4*, 5.4.16–17). The women of the tavern are increasingly presented as preying on the commonwealth, endangering its (male) citizens and diverting its wealth from authorized purposes.

Interestingly, the sexualizing and criminalizing of Quickly in *Part II* seems to coincide with an increasing emphasis on her economic well-being. Once one begins to notice them, signs of her economic independence litter the text. Here, as in *Part I,* she has employees, such as the hapless apprentice Francis, under her control. In the first act of *Part II,* she calls in the law to make Falstaff pay his debts to her, an indication that she has been able to lend him money. And he insists she has the means, if she wishes, to supply his present needs as he sets off for war. We now discover that she has plate and tapestries to sell or pawn for more cash (*2H4*, 2.1.140–42), and, if the beadle in 5.4 is to be believed, she also has a dozen cushions for the seats in her tavern, one of which has been used to pad Doll Tearsheet's stomach to fake a pregnancy in order to avoid punishment for her various crimes (*2H4*, 5.4.14–15).

The tavern world in *Part II,* rendered as a sexualized scene of female entrepreneurship, becomes the locus for the play's anxiety about a levelling lawlessness. Doll, the sexually independent woman, and Quickly, the economically independent woman, form a threatening combination. They challenge both gender ideology and the system of social stratification distinguishing man from man. Predictably, the punishment meted out to these women is severe. Unlike Falstaff, they are not simply banished from the king's presence; rather, they are sent off to prison to be whipped. As Barbara Hodgdon observes, when Doll and Quickly are arrested in 5.4, "The potential threats Carnival represents are displaced on the play's women," who are now "demonized as corrupt, set aside and excluded from the commonwealth" (1991, 172). It is not clear what place, if any, they will possibly have in the reordered state that is about to follow from Hal's assumption of the throne. Hardly good wives, these women become the detritus of official history.

The closing scenes of *Henry IV, Part II,* which include the imprisonment of Doll and Quickly, look forward to *Henry V,* where the king attempts to construct a renewed sense of national identity and purpose. The success of this project depends in part on casting out of the commonwealth all those who do not assent to the king's logic, a logic that makes the interests of some men—king, aristocrat, and churchman—the interests of all. Men like Bardolph, Nym, and Pistol who put their own material interests ahead of the king's are excluded from the band of brothers. The place of women in the renewed nation is also precarious. While there is a space for Katherine in the marriage arranged between Henry and the French king, the old inhabitants of the tavern fare less well. Criminalized at the end of *Henry IV, Part II,* Quickly remarkably emerges at the beginning of *Henry V* once more a wife—but now she is wed neither to some unseen "good husband" nor to Falstaff but to the disreputable Pistol. As *his* wife, her entrepreneurial activities threaten to move her ever deeper into illicit territory. At one point she laments, "we cannot lodge and board a dozen or fourteen gentlewomen that live honestly by the prick of their needles but it will be thought we keep a bawdy house straight" (*H5*, 2.1.32–35). Perhaps the lady protests too much. Her comment raises the possibility that she does indeed now keep a bawdy house and that while her husband is being a horseleech abroad, she is being one at home. It is therefore not too surprising when the last thing we hear of Quickly is that she died a whore's death. Or is it really Doll who dies this death? The humiliated Pistol says,

> News have I that my Doll is dead i' th' spittle
> Of a malady of France,
> And there my rendezvous is quite cut off.
> (*H5*, 5.1.81–83)

Textual editors have a variety of ways of explaining the "curious reference" to Doll Tearsheet which, to quote the Riverside editors, "properly should be to Mistress Quickly, Pistol's wife."[7] But the momentary textual conflation of the two women—whatever its source—underscores the symbolic conflation of the two types of "public women," the entrepreneurial tavern keeper and the prostitute, that has been underway since *Henry IV, Part II.* Quickly cannot simply be a "good man's" wife, because her visibility, her volubility, and her economic independence clash with patriarchal imperatives regarding wifely behavior. Quickly's remarkably unsteady relationship to the marriage state signals the gender trouble

7. G. B. Evans *et al.*, eds., *The Riverside Shakespeare* (Boston: Houghton Mifflin, 1974), 972.

she embodies. There seems, finally, no way for the entrepreneurial urban woman to exist in the Shakespearean history play except on terms of criminality. Quickly exits the play as a common whore.

In the second tetralogy, the Eastcheap tavern is the only place where non-aristocratic women enter the Shakespearean history play, but Quickly's degradation implies that they can do so only on sexualized and criminalized terms. It is as if the playwright, gesturing nervously toward the famed independence of the women of contemporary London, can acknowledge their existence only by transforming that independence into sexual licentiousness and criminality. And yet, this is only half the story. While the playwright does criminalize Quickly and Doll, he also endows them, intentionally or not, with remarkable theatrical vitality. Quickly's speech, in particular, is a source of enormous comic pleasure, and it introduces—along with Pistol's bombastic swagger and the dialects of Jamy, Fluellen, and Macmorris—a sense of the linguistic and social differences that the dominant language of the court cannot eradicate or homogenize.

At the beginning of Act II of *Henry IV, Part II,* for example, Quickly urges two officers of the law, Fang and Snare, to lay hands on the fat knight, Falstaff, and bring him to justice:

> I am undone by his going. I warrant you, he's an infinitive thing upon my score. Good Master Fang, hold him sure. Good Master Snare, let him not scape. 'A comes [continuantly] to Pie-Corner (saving your manhoods) to buy a saddle, and he is indited to dinner to the Lubber's Head in Lumbert street, to Master Smooth's the silk-man. I pray you, since my exion is ent'red and my case so openly known to the world, let him be brought in to his answer. A hundred mark is a long one for a poor lone woman to bear, and I have borne, and borne, and borne, and have been fubb'd off, and fubb'd off, and fubb'd off, from this day to that day, that it is a shame to be thought on. There is no honesty in such dealing, unless a woman should be made an ass and a beast, to bear every knave's wrong.
>
> *Enter* SIR JOHN [FALSTAFF] *and* BARDOLPH *and the Boy* [PAGE]
>
> Yonder he comes, and that arrant malmsey-nose knave, Bardolph, with him. Do your offices, do your offices, Master Fang and Master Snare, do me, do me, do me your offices.
>
> (*2H4*, 2.1.23–42)

This is quite a piece of language, so plain and yet so mystifying to those who seek in the King's English a standard of authoritative communication. In Quickly's world there is on the one hand an absolute correspondence between people and the concrete objects and occupations by which they are known. A silk merchant is named Smooth; officers of the law are called Snare and Fang; Falstaff is an infinitive thing upon Quickly's score. Yet as that troubling word, *infinitive*, suggests, there is static in the communicative circuit, a potential doubleness, in a great many of the things Quickly says. When she calls Falstaff an "infinitive" thing upon her score, the playgoer probably silently translates *infinitive* to *infinite*, thus imaging Falstaff as an endless series of chalk markings on a board on which Quickly keeps track of credit extended. But at the same time, the grammatical term *infinitive* is not simply wiped from consciousness; it has its own resonances, pointing exactly to a domain—that of grammar—where Quickly is no master and in which, in fact, she can be read as comically deficient by those who "know better."

The same doubleness subtends the rest of her speech, making its reception unpredictable. Falstaff is *indited* to supper, the domain of hospitality entangled in Quickly's speech with the domain of legal punishment, social fact and Quickly's desire running together indiscriminately. He has been *invited*, but Quickly would like him to be *indicted*. Similarly, even as she calls for the law to vindicate her rights as tavern keeper and virtuous woman, one who will not be "an ass and a beast, to bear every knave's wrong," her iterations, "do me, do me, do me your offices," make her the unintentional solicitor of sexual favors, so that her status as victim seeking legal redress for wrongs done her is made uncertain by the way her speech continually sexualizes her, suggesting that she is a loose woman and so perhaps herself deserving of legal correction rather than assistance. Quickly's malapropisms jam the communicative networks by which the law does its work of making distinctions and hierarchies, separating criminals from honest men and women, whores from wives, winners from losers, legitimate kings from their theatrical imitations.

Quickly's language is, of course, a means of marking her social unimportance and transforming her into an object of fun. In the Henry IV plays and *Henry V,* the distance of various characters from the culture's center of power and importance is marked by their linguistic distance from perfect command of the King's English. Many of those who inhabit Quickly's tavern are marked as outsiders by their deformed speech. Francis has "fewer words than a parrot" [*1H4*, 2.4.90–91]; Pistol's bombastic swagger makes his language incomprehensible even to the other characters in the play. In *Henry IV, Part II,* in fact, Falstaff has to tell him to deliver his news "like a man of this world" (5.3.97–98). In *Henry V,* the regionals—Fluellen, Jamy and Macmorris, sturdy officers in Henry's army—become the butts of a mildly deprecating humor because of their dialects. In *Henry IV, Part I* Hotspur rebukes his wife for using language that makes her sound like "a comfit-maker's wife" who never walks "further than Finsbury" (a London district popular with ordinary citizens): "Swear me, Kate, like a lady as thou art / A good mouth-filling oath, and leave 'in sooth,' / And such protest of pepper-gingerbread / To velvet-guards and Sunday-citizens" (3.1.248, 252–56). In short, linguistic difference is used in the service of social stratification. The women of the tavern enter the national history play on sexualized and criminalized terms, and they also enter by means of a language that infantilizes, others, and culturally disempowers them.

This is not the whole story, however. To become the butts of linguistic humor, figures such as Mistress Quickly have to be brought into the circuits of representation. Mistress Quickly's speech renders her comic, but it also pluralizes the language of the play and denaturalizes the authority and automatic primacy of the speech of dominant groups. The carnivalized rhetoric of Quickly's first-act conversation with the Chief Justice, like Dogberry's malapropisms in *Much Ado About Nothing* and Elbow's in *Measure for Measure,* provides material resistance to the operations of the law and the hegemony of its official language. Before the law, a woman is either a virtuous wife or widow and so worthy of the law's support, or she is a whore and subject to the law's force. Quickly's speech importuning the Chief Justice for aid in apprehending Falstaff makes it difficult to determine just which she is. Eventually the law makes a determination, and both Quickly and Doll are hauled off to prison, but for much of *Henry IV, Part II* the hostess's sexual, legal, and marital status remains wonderfully ambiguous.

It is not necessary, in fact it would be unwise, to impute to Mistress Quickly an oppositional, politicized consciousness. She is a fictional creation written to be a humorous butt. But her speech, in the tradition of carnival foolery, makes available a logic and language that can provide an alternative to the logic and language of dominant groups. In the public theater, with its socially mixed audiences, it is not clear how such speech would have been received. Men who wrote against the theater worried that the stage would foster unruliness and licentiousness among its socially diverse auditors. Certainly the linguistic and social variety in these plays enhances the possibilities for "unauthorized" acts of reception. Toward the end of her time on stage, Quickly makes a speech about the death of Falstaff that suggests the disruptive potential of the alternative world view made available through her troubling language:

> Nay sure, he's not in hell; he's in Arthur's bosom, if ever man went to Arthur's bosom. 'A made a finer end, and went away

> and it had been any christom child.' A parted ev'n just between twelve and one, ev'n at the turning o'th'tide; for after I saw him fumble with the sheets, and play with flowers, and smile upon his finger's end, I knew there was but one way; for his nose was as sharp as a pen, and 'a [babbled] of green fields. "How now, Sir John?" quoth I, "what, man? be a' good cheer." So 'a cried out, "God, God, God!" three or four times. Now I, to comfort him, bid him 'a should not think of God; I hop'd there was no need to trouble himself with any such thoughts yet. So 'a bade me lay more clothes on his feet. I put my hand into the bed and felt them, and they were as cold as any stone; then I felt to his knees, and so up'ard and up'ard, and all was as cold as any stone. (*H5*, 2.3.9–26)

This speech again fractures the logic of authority by which this jester was banished as a vice. Quickly gives Falstaff a home in Arthur's bosom, calling in question not only Falstaff's damnation but Hal's exclusive right to the legacy of this mythic Welsh forefather. Moreover, here and in subsequent lines, Quickly's language celebrates Falstaff's sensuality—his handling of women, his love of sack, all of which seem in her jumbled speech to qualify him for a holy death. In the language of this common woman the sensual and the spiritual interpenetrate, as do the recording of sin and the promise of salvation, carnivalizing, inverting, and mixing categories elsewhere strictly hierarchized and held in separation. This is very different from the speech and logic of Henry V, King of England, who knows what makes a man an offender and has no hesitation in ordering the death of his old friend Bardolph because, as he says, "We would have all such offenders so cut off" (*H5*, 3.6.107–8). Quickly's presence in the play makes possible an alternative understanding of what would constitute "justice."

Quickly's presence is important for yet another reason, having this time to do with the presence of women in the audience watching the play. As Andrew Gurr has made clear, women of all classes went to the public theater.[8] In the Boar's Head Tavern too, women are spectators to theatrical entertainment. When Hal and Falstaff undertake "The Arraignment of the Prodigal Son," Quickly proves an avid and involved auditor. As Falstaff prepares to take a turn at playing the king, Hal's father, she cries out, "O Jesu, this is excellent sport, i' faith!" and a moment later compliments Falstaff on his performance: "O Jesu, he doth it as like one of these harlotry players as ever I see!" (2.4.390, 395–96). Quickly knows something of playing, at least enough to have a standard by which to compare Falstaff's performance.

8. Andrew Gurr, *Playgoing in Shakespeare's London* (Cambridge: Cambridge University Press, 1988), 59–64.

Shakespeare's representation of Owen Glendower's daughter as an exotic, eroticized object of desire and anxiety is a projection of male fantasies, but it is tempting to imagine real-life counterparts for Doll and Quickly in the audience to the Henry IV plays; for, as the epilogue to *Henry IV, Part II* explicitly recognizes, that audience included women as well as men. However, the form that recognition takes—"All the gentlewomen here have forgiven me; if the gentlemen will not, then the gentlemen do not agree with the gentlewomen, which was never seen in such an assembly" (22–25)—makes all the women in the audience into "gentlewomen," thus distancing them from any imputation that they are Mistress Quicklys or Doll Tearsheets. The epilogue's acknowledgement of the women's presence is still significant, however, because it also constitutes an implicit acknowledgement that the theater constituted a "public" that consisted of more than the elite players of chronicle history. As Heywood was to argue in his *Apology for Actors,* the theater was one of the most noteworthy London institutions, an ornament to the city, a magnet for foreign visitors, a source of edification for England's people. That theater—communal, inclusive, and dedicated to the mutual pursuit of profit and play—bears more resemblances to Quickly's tavern than to the king's court. Officially denigrated as the seat of vice and disorder, the theater, like the tavern, let foolery thrive, situating the official discourses of chronicle history alongside the less decorous languages of swaggerer, prostitute, and tosspot. In the outrageous voice of Quickly—"Do me, do me, do me your offices—is embodied the contradictions of this place, devoted to the pieties of dominant history and giving voice, simultaneously, to social forces which challenge that hegemony, among which we must include the entrepreneurial energies of the women in the tavern and the women in the theater audience.

CHRISTOPHER HIGHLEY

[Defining the Nation]†

[I]

In May of 1603, several weeks after the death of Queen Elizabeth, and following his surrender to Lord Mountjoy, the Irish rebel chieftain Hugh O'Neill, earl of Tyrone, traveled to London to receive his

† Christopher Highley "Wales, Ireland and *1 Henry IV*," *Renaissance Drama* 21 (1990), 91–114. Reprinted by permission of Northwestern University Press.

pardon from the new king.[1] Part of Tyrone's journey led through Wales, where he was greeted by the enraged women of that country, who, as Fynes Moryson relates, flung "durt and stones at the Earle as he passed, and . . . revil[ed] him with bitter words." Historians have accepted Moryson's own reading of the encounter, assuring us that in this act of scapegoating the women were avenging themselves upon Tyrone for the "Husbands and Children" they had lost in the recent wars and expressing their solidarity with the English cause.[2] But it is equally conceivable that the attack was motivated by a different set of loyalties, and that the women targeted Tyrone not because they were sharing in English hostility but because they looked upon him as the failed and discredited leader of a cause they had themselves supported.

Although Moryson does not censure the women's action, his account registers a certain unease with their lack of respect for Lord Mountjoy, in whose company Tyrone travels. Unlike Moryson, who suppresses the potentially ambiguous motives behind the attack, other writers were convinced that the common people of Wales were sympathetic toward and in collusion with the Irish rebels. This was certainly the view of a group of loyal Welsh gentry who in January 1599 wrote to the Privy Council about Tyrone's local popularity and of a sympathetic bond uniting the subject people of Wales and Ireland. "No Welshmen," they warned, "should be used in service against the Irishmen, because they were not to be trusted.[3]

English suspicions of complicity between the lower orders of Wales and the Irish rebels may have been a logical outgrowth of the general identification of the two countries. In the sixteenth century, such a link was routinely established by invoking the English conquest and settlement of Wales as an example to guide and justify current colonial policy in Ireland. English officials there treated this earlier conquest as a model to be imitated, and urged that the policies used in subduing the Welsh be revived in Ireland. Applauding the appointment of Sir Henry Sidney as Lord Deputy in Ireland, and punning on his previous title of Lord President of the

1. I wish to thank the Stanford Humanities Center, where this essay was begun, as well as Susan Kneedler and Stephen Orgel for their many suggestions.

2. Fynes Moryson, *The Itinerary of Fynes Moryson,* 4 vols. (Glasgow: MacLehose, 1908), 3:336; see also Glanmor Williams, *Recovery, Reorientation, and Reformation: Wales, c. 1415–1642* (Oxford: Clarendon Press, 1987); Cyril Bentham Falls, *Mountjoy: Elizabethan General* (London: Odhams, 1955); and Sean O'Faolain, *The Great O'Neill: A Biography of Hugh O'Neill, Earl of Tyrone, 1550–1616* (London: Longmans, 1942).

3. [*Calendar of State Papers Relating to Ireland,* ed. Hans Claude Hamilton, *et al.,* 11 vols. (London, 1860–1912), *1598–99,* 461–62.] When quoting the Irish state papers I have mostly relied on the printed calendar, although in some instances I have consulted the original manuscripts in the Public Record Office, London (P.R.O.). From 1585 on, as Cyril Falls notes, the calendars are virtually complete transcriptions of the originals. [See Falls, *Elizabeth's Irish Wars* (London: Methuen, 1950), 347–48.]

council in the marches of Wales, William Gerard told the Privy Council that "A better president [precedent] . . . colde not be founde then to imitate the course that reformed Walles."[4]

The association of Ireland and Wales, however, was not simply based on a recognition of the similar struggle each country had waged against English rule. Conceptually, the English organized their Celtic neighbors through a network of flexible and shifting relationships that allowed the English to both distinguish and, where appropriate, make strategic connections between them. While the respective genealogies of the Irish and Welsh distinguished them on the basis of ethnicity, the two peoples were conflated in the English mind by the perceived affinities between their languages. Hotspur's claim in *1 Henry IV*, that he would "rather hear Lady, my brach [i.e., bitch], howl in Irish," than "the lady sing in Welsh" [3.1.233–34], is a virulently misogynist variation on the commonplace identification of Welsh and Irish as equally bestial languages.[5]

Hotspur's gibe is one of several allusions to Ireland in a play that coincides with a critical juncture in Elizabeth's Irish campaign. While it cannot be dated precisely, *1 Henry IV* was most likely written and first performed between August 1596 and 25 February 1598, when it was entered in the Stationers' Register. It was at this time that reports of the imminent collapse of English rule in Ireland became more frequent and shrill. In February 1597, for example, Maurice Kyffin reported that Elizabeth's army was in a state of disarray, and the country approaching anarchy: "our soldiers die wretchedly in the open streets and highways; the native subjects spoiled and brought to extreme beggary; no service in war performed; no military discipline or civil justice exercised; briefly, the whole kingdom ruined and foraged" (*C.S.P. Ireland 1596–97*, 233). With the proliferation of newsletters and the circulation of political gossip, a general—if not necessarily accurate—awareness of events and conditions in Ireland spread beyond the council chamber to a much broader audience.[6] That Shakespeare was himself familiar with these conditions is suggested by the compelling affinities between the "pitiful rascals" impressed by Falstaff in both parts of

4. [Quoted in Penry Williams, "The Welsh Borderland under Queen Elizabeth," *Welsh History Review* 1 (1960), 31.] See also Nicholas P. Canny, *The Elizabethan Conquest of Ireland: A Pattern Established, 1565–76* (Hassocks: Harvester, 1976), 97–99, on the utility of the Welsh analogy and Sir Henry Sidney's policy of establishing Welsh-style provincial presidencies in Ireland.
5. On the issue of language, Ann Rosalind Jones mentions Thomas Coryat's ironic coupling of "the Welch and the Irish" as among "the best and most learned languages of the world" [quoted in Jones, "Italians and Others: Venice and the Irish in *Coryat's Crudities* and *The White Devil*," *Renaissance Drama* 18 (1987), 113].
6. See H.S. Bennett, *English Books and Readers, 1558–1603* (Cambridge: Cambridge University Press, 1965), on the early development of a news service in Elizabethan England (220–47).

Henry IV, and the wretched state of Elizabeth's malnourished, largely conscript, army in Ireland [4.2.58].[7]

Underlying the crisis was an escalation in Irish resistance to English rule. Earlier in the century, Irish opposition to the private plantation schemes of English adventurers had generally been local and uncoordinated.[8] In Ulster, traditionally the most intractable and rebellious province, the maintenance of English control had since 1567 hinged upon the cooperation of Hugh O'Neill, second earl of Tyrone. But after his provocative decision to accept the outlawed Gaelic title of The O'Neill in 1595, Tyrone's usefulness and loyalty to the crown became increasingly vexed and uncertain.[9] Following his first direct attack upon English forces, Tyrone was declared a traitor in June 1595. Although he was to reassert his loyalty to the crown and to receive a temporary pardon a year later, Tyrone had now set upon a course of galvanizing native resistance to the English and transforming it into a nationalist struggle for independence.[1]

In their letter of January 1599 to the Privy Council, the Welsh authors disclosed that the local people had proclaimed Tyrone Prince of Wales and King of Ireland. The authors claimed that "Tyrone had in his service 500 Welshmen" and "that he had friends in Wales, that looked for him, as he was both favourable and bountiful to Welshmen." Furthermore, Tyrone's Welsh sympathizers made the intriguing assertion that their hero was "descended of Owyne Clyne Dore, who had interest both in Ireland and Wales . . . [and] that there was a prophecy the Earl of Tyrone should prevail against the English nation" (*C.S.P. Ireland 1598–99* 462). Previously unnoted by critics of *1 Henry IV,* the putative genealogical link between Owyne Clyne Dore (a variant spelling of Owen Glendower) and Tyrone prompts an interpretation of Glendower and his part in the Percy rebellion as a displaced actualization of Tyrone's contemporaneous rebellion in Ireland.

7. For a vivid account of these conditions that also mentions their pertinence to both parts of *Henry IV* and to *Henry V,* see O'Faolain, 154–59.* * *
8. The major exception to this was the Munster rebellion led by James Fitzmaurice Fitzgerald in 1569. As Nicholas P. Canny explains, "from the beginning Fitzmaurice's rebellion assumed a wider dimension than any of the others as he identified with the Counter-Reformation against the heretic English" (*Elizabethan Conquest,* 147).
9. Originally Baron Dungannon, Tyrone was elevated to the peerage as the second earl of Tyrone in 1585 (see G.A. Hayes-McCoy, "The Completion of the Tudor Conquest, and the Advance of the Counter-Reformation, 1571–1603," in T. W. Moody, F. X. Martin, and F. J. Byrne, eds., *A New History of Ireland,* 9 vols. (Oxford: Clarendon Press, 1976), 117–18.
1. Hayes-McCoy, 121. Tyrone drifted into indirect opposition to the English by first supporting the disturbances of his kinsmen and allies (Hayes-McCoy, 118–22). The period between June 1595 and June 1598, when open hostilities resumed, was generally one of sporadic fighting, treaties, pardons, and duplicities on both sides: see Falls, *Elizabeth's Irish Wars,* ch. 15. On the chronology of Tyrone's rebellious career also see Steven G. Ellis, *Tudor Ireland: Crown, Community, and the Conflict of Cultures, 1470–1603* (London: Longman, 1985), 298–312, esp. 303–7 for Tyrone and a nationalist confederacy.

II

When Glendower informs Hotspur of his education in England—"I can speak English, lord as well as you; / For I was trained up in the English court" [3.1.120–21]—the play's first audiences could have recalled Tyrone's similar upbringing in England. Sir Henry Sidney had taken the nine-year-old Hugh as his ward in 1559 and sent him to England, where he was educated in the reformed faith under the patronage of Sidney and Leicester in preparation for his later strategic reinsertion into Irish society. Both Glendower and Tyrone had experienced the "civilizing" effect of English culture and both had served English authority: Glendower as a follower of Henry Bolingbroke, Tyrone as an ally of Elizabeth. With both men, though, familiarity with English ways had only bred a latent resentment, and upon returning to their respective homes they had rebelled against their former English benefactors and masters.[2]

Biographical affinities between Glendower and Tyrone represent one straightforward form of topicality. But since Ireland is a pervasive subtext in *1 Henry IV*, contemporary events and conditions there are also registered in more diffuse and complex ways.[3] For instance, in its general configuration the rebel alliance simulates the underlying structure and dynamics of Irish resistance. The play's rebel alliance is underwritten by kinship ties just as the rebellion in Ireland was based upon a coalition of various families and factions. G. A. Hayes-McCoy observes that, "since the Maguires, O'Donnells, and O'Neills were interrelated, the developing confederacy of the Ulster lords has the quality of a family compact" (118). Mortimer's marriage to Glendower's daughter completes a triangular alliance that through the marriage of Mortimer's sister to Hotspur also includes the powerful Percy family. To the king, Mortimer's marriage into a rebellious Welsh family is a provocative crossing of national and racial boundaries that equips his rival with a power base; to the rebels, on the other hand, it represents an invaluable exogamic alliance that unites the north of the realm with both the west and Wales in a bond of consanguinity against the king.

In order to prevent the formation of larger groupings against their rule in Ireland, the English promoted competition and hostil-

2. On Glendower's training and service in England, see Herbert V. Fackler, "Shakespeare's 'Irregular and Wild' Glendower: The Dramatic Use of Source Materials," *Discourse: A Review of the Liberal Arts* 13 (1970), 311–12 and J. E. Lloyd, *Owen Glendower* (Oxford: Clarendon Press 1931).

3. Some of the problems associated with an older historicism that I have tried to avoid are set forth by David Bevington [*Tudor Drama and Politics: A Critical Approach to Topical Meaning* (Cambridge, MA: Harvard University Press, 1968), esp. 1–26], while the sort of multilayered topical approach I have attempted is positively laid out by Leah S. Marcus [in her *Puzzling Shakespeare: Local Reading and its Discontents* (Berkeley: University of California Press, 1988), esp. 32–43].

ity between and within the clans and septs that constituted tribal society. Edmund Spenser recalled how the English had originally "set up" Tyrone, "then called Baron of Dongannon," to "beard" his rival and predecessor "Turlagh Lenagh." But the plan backfired when Tyrone turned the power invested in him by Elizabeth against the English.[4] Unlike his predecessors, Tyrone largely succeeded in foiling the English strategy of divide and conquer, and through cultivating connections with other families he was able to establish a nearly unified front of opposition: "All Ulster," declared an English tract of 1598, "is now joined together in Rebellion against the Quene, saving the Countie of Louth . . . all the Captens of Countries are bound to the Earle of Tyrone, either by Affinitie or Consanguinitie or duetie."[5] During the parley between Tyrone and an English delegation in December 1597, the latter were taken aback by Tyrone's willingness to push demands on behalf of other septs and Gaelic leaders. Thomas Jones, the English recorder of the interviews, saw in Tyrone's audacity an attempt by the "crafty traitor" to enlarge his constituency by adopting the grievances of groups he had previously ignored: "His demand made now for the Moores and Connors, and for Edmund Gerald [Kavanagh], of whom he made no mention in his treaty with Sir John Norreys, may induce us to think that, the longer he is suffered, the further will he extend his power" (*C. S. P. Ireland 1596–97*, 488–89). Even more alarming to the English delegation was Tyrone's demand for liberty of religion, a claim he made, according to Jones, in order "to become popular amongst this idolatrous people" (490). By December 1597, then, the English faced in Tyrone a rebel leader of national standing whose aspirations must have appeared uncannily similar to those of his precursor Glendower some two centuries earlier.[6]

Tyrone's status as the single unrivaled head of Irish resistance certainly does not correspond with the place of Glendower in the structure of the play's rebel alliance. Glendower is one component of a remarkably heterogeneous rebellion that brings together an array of groups that were each capable in their own right of challenging or destabilizing the authority of the Tudor state. Ranged against the king by the end of act 1 are the Welsh, the Scots (who as mercenaries fought alongside Tyrone in Ireland), a dissident group of clergy, and a rebellious fraction of the English aristocracy. Shakespeare thus accentuates the threat from the Celtic fringe by compounding it with these other threats, particularly the internal threat

4. Edmund Spenser, *A View of the Present State of Ireland*, ed. W. L. Renwick (Oxford: Clarendon Press, 1970), 113.
5. Edmund Hogan, ed., *The Description of Ireland . . . in Anno 1598* (London, 1878), 33.
6. Sean O'Faolain discusses the parley of December 1597; he sees Tyrone's demands as effectively formulating the rights of an "emergent Irish nation" (196). See Lloyd on the Glendower rebellion.

of a factious nobility led by the Percies.[7] The Percies of *1 Henry IV* are the ancestors of Thomas Percy, seventh earl of Northumberland, who in 1572 had been executed for the leading part he had played in the abortive Northern Rebellion, a regional uprising that had aimed at restoring Catholicism and establishing Mary Stuart as Elizabeth's successor.[8] Thomas's brother Henry had pursued the same objectives, and in 1585 he died in the Tower, suspected of plotting against Elizabeth's life (*DNB*). In reviving memories of an independent recusant family, the Percy presence in *1 Henry IV* helps foreground the continuing struggle between crown and aristocracy. The Northern Rebellion may have been the last of the great feudal uprisings against the crown, but its failure did not signal the demise of the "overmighty subject" whose private armies and fortified houses continued throughout Elizabeth's reign to deny the crown a monopoly on either violence or allegiance.

Glendower is Tyrone's main analogue in the play, but he is not the only character that the first audiences might have identified with the Irish "arch-traitor" (*C.S.P. Ireland 1598–99,* 162). In the early seventeenth century, the attorney-general for Ireland, Sir John Davies, invoked Mortimer as an equivalent figure to Tyrone.[9] Offering parallels to Tyrone from England's own past, Davies observed that

> when England was full of tenants-at-will our barons were then like the mere Irish lords, and were able to raise armies against the crown; and as this man was O'Neal in Ulster, so the Earl of Warwick was O'Nevill in Yorkshire, and the Bishopric and Mortimer was the like in the Marches of Wales.[1]

Mortimer, in fact, sets off a series of topical resonances in relation to Ireland. In particular, his marriage to Glendower's daughter brings to the surface a collection of cultural anxieties about the attraction of native society for English settlers in Ireland. Mortimer's obscure capitulation to Glendower replays the process of "going native" whereby English colonists in Ireland were assimilated to Gaelic society. The earliest Old English settlers were the group most associated with this lapse from civility. Discussing them in *A View of the Present State of Ireland* (1596), Spenser noted that,

7. I have found Jonathan Dollimore and Alan Sinfield's discussion of these various threats as they appear in *Henry V* to be especially helpful. [See their "History and Ideology: The Instance of *Henry V*," in John Drakakis, ed., *Alternative Shakespeares* (London: Methuen, 1985), 206–27.]
8. J. E. Neale, *Queen Elizabeth I* (New York: Doubleday-Anchor, 1957), ch. 11.
9. Shakespeare, like Holinshed before him, confuses Sir Edmund de Mortimer with his nephew Edmund Mortimer, the fifth earl of March [see William Shakespeare, *1 Henry IV,* ed. David Bevington (Oxford: Clarendon Press, 1987), 287–88].
1. Cited in Nicholas P. Canny, "The Ideology of English Colonization: From Ireland to America," *William and Mary Quarterly* 30 (1973), 591.

through intermarriage and promiscuous contact generally, they had "degenerated and grown almost mere Irish, yea and more malicious to the English than the very Irish themselves" (48). Significantly, Spenser includes among the Old English families who "have degendered from their ancient dignities," "the great Mortimer, who forgetting how great he was once in England, or English at all, is now become the most barbarous of them all, and is called Macnemarra" (66). In his search for support from all available quarters, Tyrone had appealed successfully to the Old English " 'gentlemen of Munster' to join the Ulster confederacy and to 'make war with us' " (Hayes-McCoy, 123). The Glendower-Mortimer bond, by refiguring the much-feared collusion between England's Gaelic and Old English enemies in Ireland, contributes yet another dimension to the topical nuances of the play's rebel alliance.

If we accept the king's view in 1.2 that Mortimer has defected to the enemy voluntarily, then we can also connect him with the English soldiers and officers who deserted to the Irish, and who in some cases are reported to have helped train Tyrone's army.[2] Also, as a regional commander who starts out loyal to his monarch but later turns traitor, Mortimer conveys the unease with which Elizabeth and her government viewed the post of Lord Deputy in Ireland, a post that was notoriously sensitive and dangerous for both parties. For Elizabeth, investing power in regional commanders was always a calculated gamble because that power could readily be abused and possibly turned against a vulnerable central government. This problem was especially acute in Ireland, where the local administration was always out of sight—if never out of mind—of the queen and her advisers, and in touch with the court via slow and unreliable lines of communication. Elizabeth complained repeatedly of the lack of regular and reliable news from the wars; a "regular postal service to Ireland" was not established until late 1598 (Falls, *Elizabeth's Irish Wars*, 228).

It was not uncommon for Elizabeth's Lord Deputies to be accused of exploiting their office for personal gain, but on occasion more serious charges of the kind the king levels at Mortimer were also made (1.3.77–92). In 1592, for instance, after his return to England, Sir John Perrot was tried for high treason. Perrot, it seems, was guilty of little more than slandering the queen; but through the efforts of his rivals he was also charged with conspiring with the Spanish to overthrow Elizabeth. These charges may have proven unduly alarming to the government because of the fact that

2. Nicholas P. Canny, "The Permissive Frontier: The Problem of Social Control in English Settlements in Ireland and Virginia, 1550–1650," in K. R. Andrews, Nicholas P. Canny and P. E. H. Hair, eds., *The Westward Enterprise: English Activities in Ireland, the Atlantic and America, 1480–1650* (Liverpool: Liverpool University Press, 1978), 23–24; A. L. Rowse, *The Expansion of Elizabethan England* (London: Macmillan, 1955), 417.

Perrot was reputed to be Henry VIII's bastard son and half-brother to Elizabeth; in *1 Henry IV*, Mortimer is a blood relation of the king and pretender to the throne.[3]

In the process of unraveling its dense and overlapping webs of topical significance, we need to consider how the play works upon these materials for ideological purposes. Whether we speak of Shakespeare's deliberate intentions or of the play's "political unconscious," *1 Henry IV* constitutes an intervention in the discursive field of Anglo-Irish relations. In both reproducing and critically reshaping prevailing cultural and political realities, the play undertakes a form of "social *work*."[4] As part of its ideological design, the play handles Glendower in a way designed radically to curtail the anxiety-causing potential of the Celtic chieftain and of Tyrone in particular. To this end, the play initially sets up an image of Glendower as both hostile and admirable, an image that is fully congruent with ambivalent English depictions of Tyrone and his fellow Irish chiefs.[5]

The descriptions of Glendower that precede his appearance at 3.1 characterize him as a figure of formidable power. Westmorland sees Glendower as "irregular and wild," an uncivilized outlaw whose "rude hands" have defeated and taken Mortimer captive (1.1.40–41). For Hotspur, he is the "great Glendower," a "valiant combatant" in his fight with Mortimer (1.3.101, 107). Sounding a more sinister note, the king ascribes Glendower's strength not to physical valor but to witchcraft. Henry calls him "that great magician, damned Glendower" (1.3.83), epithets that resonate suggestively with Tyrone's reputation as "the Great Divill."[6] Through a similar collection of tropes, Tyrone was constructed as a potent adversary of English rule and transformed into something of a mythical entity, more animal or demon than mortal man. The assorted labels applied to him by Lord Deputy Burgh—the Running Beast, the Great Bear, the Northern Lucifer, and Beelzebub—collectively suggest a strange blend of elusiveness, boldness, and inscrutable evil (O'Faolain, 191).

In the only scene in which he actually appears, however, Glendower turns out to bear little resemblance either to the early de-

3. Spenser, 109; Mona L. Schwind, " 'Nurse to All Rebellions': Grace O'Malley and Sixteenth-Century Connacht,' *Eire-Ireland* 131 (1978), 40–61; *DNB*.
4. This is a phrase Jean E. Howard uses in her lucid account of the methodologies and practices of so-called new historicist Renaissance critics: see Howard, "The New Historicism in Renaissance Studies," *English Literary Renaissance* 16 (1986), 35.
5. Patricia Fumerton and David B. Quinn discuss a more general English ambivalence toward Ireland which oscillates between admiration and revulsion. [See Fumerton, "Exchanging Gifts: The Elizabethan Currency of Children and Poetry," *English Literary History* 53 (1986), 256; Quinn, *The Elizabethans and the Irish* (Ithaca: Cornell University Press, 1966), 61.]
6. Quoted in O'Faolain, 182. And compare "the great Devil of the North" (*C.S.P. Ireland 1598–99*, 505). At [2.4.329], Falstaff calls him "that devil Glendower."

scriptions of him in the play or to those in Shakespeare's main sources. Glendower acts as courteous host to his fellow rebel-lords, boasts of his proficiency in English and musical composition, shows a civilized self-restraint, and even yields to Hotspur over the issue of land distribution [3.1.134]. But even as Shakespeare domesticates Glendower, invalidating his frightening reputation, he turns the chieftain into a figure of ridicule. Falstaff's satirical vignette of Glendower mastering the forces of Hell [2.4.300–01] lays the ground for Hotspur's demystification of Glendower's prodigious self-image and magical pretensions. The exposure of Glendower as a hoax is all the more devastating precisely because his principal accuser is one of Glendower's own allies. And behind Glendower's preoccupation with prophecies and astrological signs we can perhaps detect a more general disdain for the superstitions that Protestant Englishmen associated with the popular Catholicism of both Wales and Ireland.

After his humiliation by Hotspur, Glendower does not appear again. The disarming of Glendower seems complete when, discouraged by unfavorable prophecies, he fails to appear for the crucial battle (4.1.125–27, 4.4.16–18). Shakespeare emphasizes Glendower's absence by evacuating the Welsh altogether from the battle of Shrewsbury. In this, he follows his source in Daniel and not Holinshed, for whom "Welshmen" are present although Glendower himself is not.[7] The particular explanation for Glendower's absence is Shakespeare's own invention, and its inclusion has the effect of nullifying Glendower's alleged "magic"—transforming it from a potential source of opposition to the state into a rationale for inaction.[8]

Glendower's fate, moreover, is extended to the rebel alliance as a whole, which dissolves before its full military impact is felt. After a planning session marked by personal rivalries and arguments over the distribution of land, the rebel alliance unravels internally and spontaneously as if in confirmation of the continuing trust placed by the English in the policy of undermining the cohesion of the Irish forces. Despite Tyrone's acknowledged success at bonding the native community, one English observer remained confident that "many [Irish families], which now shadow themselves under the cloak of Tyrone's villainies, will yield great means, and plot good courses for Tyrone's ruin and overthrow, if they might see Her Majesty fully resolved to prosecute war against them" (*C.S.P. Ireland 1598–99,* 169).

7. See Raphael Holinshed, *Holinshed's Chronicles of England, Scotland, and Ireland* (1587), 6 vols. (London, 1807–8), vol. 3, 25.
8. Sheldon P. Zitner, "Staging the Occult in *1 Henry IV,*" in J. C. Gray, ed., *Mirror Up to Shakespeare: Essays in Honour of G. R. Hibbard* (Toronto: University of Toronto Press, 1984), 145.

In the deterioration of Glendower from a principal scourge of the English to charlatan and palpable absence—and in the parallel fate of the alliance generally—the play can be seen as disempowering the figure of the Celtic chieftain by literally wishing him away. Theatrical magic imaginatively assuages English anxieties about his modern counterparts in Ireland. *Henry IV, Part 1* was not unique in offering this kind of wish-fulfillment. Between 1596 and 1597, at the same time the Chamberlain's Men were playing *1 Henry IV,* the Admiral's Men at the Rose were performing *The History of the Life and Death of Captain Thomas Stuckeley,* a play that directly confronts the issue of Irish rebellion by setting an early scene in Ireland at the time of Shane O'Neill's revolt. The murder of Shane by his own Scottish associates and the spectacle of his severed head offered vicarious satisfaction to all who sought the overthrow of the present O'Neill.[9]

III

In one of the more curious metaphors imposed on Tyrone by the English, Lord Deputy Burgh, notifying Robert Cecil in July 1597 of his plans to march against and defeat Tyrone, vowed "to 'beat the Diana' in the proud traitor's fort, which he hath made upon the ford" (*C.S.P. Ireland 1596–97,* 340). On the surface, Burgh's analogy can be taken as a commonplace attempt to disarm Tyrone by effeminizing him, just as Hotspur emasculates Glendower by likening the Welshman's garrulousness to that of "a railing wife" [3.1.157]. But the analogy, which rests upon the association of Tyrone and Diana as forest dwellers, also demonizes Tyrone by linking him to a goddess whom the Renaissance portrayed from one perspective as a dangerous and uncontained figure, an Amazon who existed outside and in defiance of established, male, power structures.[1]

Burgh's assimilation of Tyrone to this figure of female misrule alerts us to the part played by women in both the Irish rebellion and in the Welsh rebellion of *1 Henry IV.* Glendower's daughter is the only Welshwoman to appear in the play but not the only one mentioned. Mortimer, in fact, only falls into her hands after first coming perilously close to other, less gentle, ones. In the play's opening scene, Westmorland tells the king how

> the noble Mortimer,
> Leading the men of Herefordshire to fight
> Against the irregular and wild Glendower,

9. Richard Simpson, ed., *The School of Shakespeare,* 2 vols. (New York: Bouton, 1878), 1:207–09.
1. This version of Diana can be found in Richard Beacon's *Solon His Follie* (Oxford, 1594), 3–4, as well as in the first of Spenser's *Two Cantos of Mutabilitie* (c. 1596).

> Was by the rude hands of that Welshman taken,
> A thousand of his people butcherèd—
> Upon whose dead corpse there was such misuse,
> Such beastly shameless transformation
> By those Welshwomen done as may not be
> Without much shame retold or spoken of.
> (1.1.38–46)

This, the play's only allusion to the incident, is a teasing hint of an account contained in Shakespeare's principal source, Holinshed's *Chronicles*. When Holinshed confronts the incident he is just as reticent as Westmorland, and refuses to relate it fully lest the "honest eares" and "continent toongs" of the decorous English readers be scandalized (20). Only when the women repeat their atrocity after a later battle does Abraham Fleming, the editor of the second (1587) edition of the *Chronicles*, add a less inhibited account.

> The dead bodies of the Englishmen, being above a thousand lieng upon the ground imbrued in their owne bloud, was a sight (a man would thinke) greevous to looke upon, and so farre from exciting and stirring up affections of crueltie; that it should rather have mooved the beholders to commiseration and mercie: yet did the women of Wales cut off their privities, and put one part thereof into the mouthes of everie dead man, in such sort that the cullions [testicles] hoong downe to their chins; and not so contented, they did cut off their noses and thrust them into their tailes as they laie on the ground mangled and defaced. (34)

Since England's Celtic borderlands could be cognitively mapped along one axis as symbolically continuous and interchangeable, it follows that in their wider provenance the castrating energies of Fleming/Shakespeare's Welshwomen evoke the dangers of native, Celtic women generally. In fact, the Welshwomen's atrocities have their counterparts in reports from Ireland that deal with the fate of English settlers and soldiers there, reports that were more an index to what the English wished to believe than to what had actually occurred. In October 1598, for example, the Chief Justice of Munster, William Saxey, told Robert Cecil about the mutilations inflicted by the rebels on the English dead: "some with their tongues cut out of their heads, others with their noses cut off" (*C.S.P. Ireland 1598–99,* 300). And the first earl of Essex alleged that it was the practice of the rebels "to cut off their [English victims'] privy parts, set up their heads and put them in their mouths" (qtd. in Canny, *Elizabethan Conquest* 139).

Both play and social text, then, imagine the threat from the Celtic fringe in terms of the overthrow of a masculine English identity through castration. Spenser, likewise, referred to the Old English settlers who had turned native as having "degendered," a term that implied both general devolution and sterility.[2] Fleming's uncensored version of the atrocity presents the Welshwomen's violence as a kind of ritual performance that turns the human body into a text upon which gender and power relations are symbolically contested. First the soldier is castrated and the "privities" stuffed in his mouth; then the nose—a surrogate phallus—is removed and stuffed in the anus. By cutting and transposing the soldiers' noses and "privities" the Welshwomen invert and parody an "official" notion of bodily integrity and hierarchy, conflating and joining in carnivalesque fashion the lower regions with the higher. The gesture of blocking the mouth is both an expression of gender conflict—it symbolically transfers to men the stipulation of silence enjoined by society upon women—and an evocation and rejection of English attempts to impose their language upon the people of Wales and Ireland.

If the acts of cutting and gagging related by Fleming and Essex are familiar components in an imaginary repertoire of colonial violence constructed by the English, Fleming's account of the sodomizing of the soldiers, on the other hand, has no apparent precedent. The women consummate their performance with what the Renaissance regarded as the ultimate sexual transgression. Penetrating the soldiers with their victims' own noses, the women assume the kind of sexual dominance that the culture reserved for men while making it appear as if their male victims are sodomizing themselves. In short, the women's act of silent ventriloquism destroys the soldiers' last vestigial claims to manhood.

Although the atrocities in Fleming/Shakespeare have a basis in contemporary allegations of Irish brutality, those same allegations do not specifically ascribe the atrocities to women. Fleming/Shakespeare's identification of the crimes as female-specific can be taken as symptomatic of the period's drive to criminalize women, a process that was most marked on the fringes of the nation-state and that tended to focus on the most vulnerable and powerless kinds of women. Christina Larner argues in her study of the relations between Scottish state-building and witch-hunting in the sixteenth century that masterless or lower-class women were typically constructed and targeted as the final embodiments of resistance to

2. [Edmund Spenser, *The Faerie Queene*, ed. A.C. Hamilton (London: Longman, 1977), 527.] The fiction of national identity as male and virile made much of the Saxon origins of the English people because the Saxons were considered the masculine race *par excellence*. A rhetoric of Saxon-Englishness in the sixteenth century is especially marked in works arguing for the vigorous independence of England from Continental hegemony (see, for example, John Aylmer, *An harborowe for faithfull and trewe subjectes, agaynst the late blowne blaste concerninge the governmēnt of wemen* [London, 1559]) and in patriotic celebrations of English overseas expansion (Shakespeare's *Henry V*).

the expansionist and "civilizing" thrust of the nation-state (199). As Fynes Moryson's account of the Welshwomen's attack on Tyrone suggests, English ethnographic knowledge of the Welsh also tended to identify women as most adept at avoiding containment or moral cleansing. This assumption persisted in Wales long after the Renaissance, for when a royal inquiry was conducted into the state of education and manners in Wales in the mid-nineteenth century, it was "the backwardness and immortality" of the women that the commissioners singled out for censure.[3]

But Fleming/Shakespeare's castrating women are also conceived in response to the specific anxieties aroused by Celtic, and especially Irish, women. A particularly well-documented anxiety concerned their role as wet nurses to the children of Old English settlers. Like many of the English, Spenser believed that in taking the nurse's milk, the child internalized her "nature and disposition," thus subverting its potential to achieve a civilized English identity.[4] In general, the Irishwoman was supposedly unimpressed by patriarchal authority and the other institutional props of the "godly" society. This was adduced from her indifference to the proscriptions that banned English and other "civilized" women from war. The scandalous appearance of Shakespeare's Welshwomen on the field of battle, in fact, recalls the English claim that Irishwomen played a crucial part in promoting rebellion. Among his neighbors and allies Tyrone numbered "O'Donnell's Ineen Duv—she whom the Four Masters describe as a woman 'like the mother of Machabees who joined a man's heart to a woman's thought' " (O'Faolain 121). Another Irish Amazon was the legendary Grace O'Malley, "a great feminine sea captain" of Connaught, as Sir Henry Sidney called her in 1583 (qtd. in Schwind 45). At times cooperating with the English, at times defying them, she was, according to Lord Justice Drury, "a woman that hath impudently passed the part of womanhood and been a great spoiler, and chief commander and director of thieves and murderers at sea," while in 1593 Sir Richard Bingham characterized her as that "notable traitoress and nurse to all rebellions in the province for forty years" (qtd. in Chambers 93, Schwind 43).

Not all rebel women were as conspicuous and individually powerful as Grace O'Malley. Sir Geoffrey Fenton complained in January 1601 of "the witches of that country (which aboundeth with witches), [who] are all set on work to cross the service [English campaign] by extraordinary unseasonable weather" (qtd. in Rowse 417). Support for the rebels was also forthcoming, as Humphrey Gilbert

3. Prys Morgan, "From a Death to a View: The Hunt for the Welsh Past in the Romantic Period," in Eric Hobsbawm and Terence Ranger, eds., *The Invention of Tradition* (Cambridge: Cambridge University Press, 1983), 92.

4. Spenser, *View*, 67–68; see Stephen J. Greenblatt, *Renaissance Self-Fashioning: From More to Shakespeare* (Chicago: University of Chicago Press, 1980), 185.

pointed out, from the "churls and 'Calliackes' [*cailleacha*, old women], or women who milked their [the rebels'] 'Creates' [*creacha*, herds] and provided their victuals and other necessaries." Therefore, reasoned Gilbert, "the killing of [the women] by the sword was the way to kill the men of war by famine" (qtd. in Quinn 127).

Henry IV, Part 1 also presents two distinct classes of Celtic women. Glendower's daughter is clearly of a different social standing from her sister Welshwomen, whose collective action marks them as an all-female version of the many-headed monster so feared by the propertied and privileged of Tudor England. What she shares with them, though, is a desire to enter male space and cross gender boundaries: "She'll be a soldier too, she'll to the wars," is how Glendower translates his daughter's Welsh words as the rebels prepare to leave for battle [3.1.193]. Together, Glendower's daughter and her plebeian Welsh sisters exemplify the double-construction of the native woman within English colonial discourse as eroticized enchantress and/or fierce Amazon. Contemporary writing on Ireland typically alternates between eroticizing and demonizing native women, offering them as objects for voyeuristic inspection and degrading them as hags, cannibals, or infanticides. The English traveler Luke Gernon neatly encapsulates this binary vision in his remark that the women of Ireland "are wemen at thirteene, and olde wives at thirty. I never saw fayrer wenches nor fowler calliots, so we call the olde wemen."[5]

The central danger embodied in Glendower's daughter is her ability to entrap male onlookers. She is described as "Charming [Mortimer's] blood with pleasing heaviness" [3.1.215], effectively overpowering the English war lord with her bewitching—and unintelligible—Welsh words and songs. And her obscure attraction is confirmed in the revealing wish of the anti-lover Hotspur to occupy "the Welsh lady's bed" [3.1.240]. Seduction was a form of symbolic castration also feared by the English in Ireland. When direct means failed, the rebels allegedly employed the wiles of native women to entrap the settlers. During the siege of an English town in Limerick, for example, the Irish earl of Desmond "sent a fair young harlot as a present to the [English] constable, by whose means he hoped to get the house; but the constable, learning from whence she came, threw her . . . with a stone about her neck, into the river."[6]

5. Luke Gernon, "A Discourse of Ireland, Anno 1620," in C. Litton Falkiner, ed., *Illustrations of Irish History and Topography, Mainly of the Seventeenth Century* (London: Longman, 1904), 357.
6. Edwin Greenlaw *et al.*, eds., *The Works of Edmund Spenser: A Variorum Edition*, 10 vols. (Baltimore: Johns Hopkins University Press, 1932–49), 5:174.

IV

In *1 Henry IV*, our encounter with the castrating Welshwomen could hardly be more fleeting. Textually, the women are twice removed or doubly mediated, since Westmorland's report of the atrocity to the king is based on the prior report made to Westmorland by a "post from Wales" (1.1.37). The very brevity of Westmorland's report and the king's puzzling failure to respond to it seem designed to minimize the transgressive import of the incident. Yet the result of such reticence is to make the incident more enigmatic and disturbing. The surrounding narrative in Fleming's account at least provides a context for the violence by offering precedents of female cruelty from antiquity, whereas in the play its very obscurity is a cause for speculation. The Welshwomen's violation seems to be raised only to be immediately repressed, but as I shall argue, it remains in the play's memory as a problem that must be returned to and later resolved.

Responsibility for symbolically overcoming or canceling this violation falls to Prince Hal. His pivotal role in the recovery of a masculine English identity that has been specifically lost to women depends upon his own conspicuous insulation from them. As Peter Erickson sees it, the essential characteristic of the Englishman in such Shakespearean figures as Talbot (*1 Henry VI*) and Henry V is an "approved image of manhood based on resistance to women and on allegiance to men."[7] Hal's possession of what Erickson calls "self-contained masculine purity" (124) effectively denies the determining and contaminating power of women over men, the kind of power readily associated with the nursing and fostering roles of Irishwomen.

Prince Hal's combat with "this northern youth" (3.2.145) Hotspur thus becomes a pivotal moment in the play's rehearsal of the subversion and recovery of a masculine and militant English identity. Their confrontation in the Welsh borderlands recalls us to the scene of an earlier heroic encounter

> When on the gentle Severn's sedgy bank,
> In single opposition, hand to hand,
> [Mortimer] did confound the best part of an hour
> In changing hardiment with great Glendower.
> (1.3.98–101)

The later fight effects a substitution of one set of "valiant combatants" (1.3.107) for another, projecting onto Hotspur the oppositional energies originally invested in Glendower. Hotspur becomes

7. Peter Erickson, "Fathers, Sons, and Brothers in *Henry V*," in Harold Bloom, ed., *William Shakespeare's* Henry V (New York: Chelsea, 1988), 125.

a final attenuated image of Tyrone in the play, the scapegoat who must bear off Tyrone's residual danger. In Hal's single combat with Hotspur, Shakespeare triumphantly re-presents the protracted and inconclusive warfare in Ireland as a chivalrous conflict that is simple, direct, and final.

Against his great rival, Hal asserts and achieves a vigorous male sexuality. Vernon's famous description of Hal in battle dress evokes the energy of the prince and his company in specifically sexual terms and likens Hal's skill at horsemanship—he "vaulted with such ease into his seat" [4.1.107]—to sexual mastery over women. As the battle of Shrewsbury approaches, images of sexual vitality and erection turn into a kind of phallic competitiveness between Hal and Hotspur. Before the battle, Hotspur imagines their imminent encounter as a blend of homoerotic camaraderie and violence: "I will embrace him with a soldier's arm, / That he shall shrink under my courtesy"; but afterward it is Hal who proclaims victoriously over Hotspur's corpse "how much art thou shrunk" [5.2.73–74, 5.4.87]. Similarly, the struggle between Tyrone and his English male adversaries was represented in terms of a genital rivalry. In his "Happy Farewell to the fortunate and forward most Noble Earle of Esex," Thomas Churchyard wrote,

> When *Mars* shal march, with shining sword in hand,
> A craven cock cries creak, and hangs down wing,
> Will run about the shraep and daer not stand.
> When cocks of gaem coms in to give a bloe,
> So false *Tyroen* may faint when he would fight,
> Thogh now alowd on dunghill duth he croe.[8]

Churchyard's put-down of Tyrone as flaccid and impotent works by simply contradicting the pervasive English recognition of the earl's enviable strength and virility: "He is the best man of war of his nation, having had his education in our discipline, and being naturally valiant," thought Sir George Carewe (*C.S.P. Ireland 1592–96*, 231). Hal's desire to kill Hotspur, while capturing and internalizing his rival's accumulated stock of personal chivalric capital, offers a way of channeling the opposed impulses of hatred and admiration that the English felt for Tyrone.

As we have already noted, the play's climactic showdown returns us to the same liminal space between two realms in which Mortimer is captured and the Welshwomen commit their atrocity. More precisely, the final battle takes place on the outskirts of Shrewsbury, a town strategically situated on the margins of English territory in the marches of Wales. Forming a corridor of land on either side of

8. John Nichols, ed., *The Progresses and Public Processions of Queen Elizabeth,* 3 vols. (London, 1823), 3:434.

the English-Welsh border, the marches of Wales had traditionally been divided into a series of miniature principalities, each governed by its own marcher lord. Equipped with their own private armies and observing only their own laws, these local magnates were synonymous with political autonomy and resistance to the crown. It was only with the shiring of the marches and the introduction of English legal and administrative procedures in 1536 as part of the first Act of Union that the crown finally curtailed the anomalous powers of these magnates and so took control of the region (Penry Williams 20–21, Glanmor Williams ch. 11). Yet long after their pacification and political incorporation the Welsh borderlands were still perceived as a locus of disorder and instability on the fringes of the nation-state.[9] At the same time, the whole of Gaelic Ireland beyond the English pale was also referred to as an extended march or borderland. The pale itself, as J. H. Andrews argues, was thought of not so much as a fixed physical area but as "a moving 'colonial' frontier."[1] To enlarge its extent was a major goal of English officials, who hoped thereby to convert the Gaelic borderland into civil shire ground.

The victory of the king's forces over the rebels in this highly charged territory, then, signifies an act of boundary-marking in which the political center of the nation physically and symbolically asserts control over its volatile and vulnerable borders. And in resecuring the border between England and Wales, Hal enacts the metaphorical reintegration of the corpses of the English soldiers. For as Mary Douglas argues, in a variety of cultures "the body is a model which can stand for any bounded system. Its boundaries can represent any boundaries which are threatened or precarious."[2]

Writing with the benefit of hindsight and from a later position of English security in Ireland, Sir John Davies argued that Ireland's systemic problems could be attributed to "the absence of our Kings, three of them only since the Norman conquest have made royal journeys into this land."[3] For Davies, Edward III's success in gov-

9. Dramatic representations helped perpetuate this view of the marches as lawless territory. *1 Sir John Oldcastle* (1599), for example, opens with an affray between Lords Herbert and Powis and their followers in the border town of Hereford. Recent work by Steven Mullaney and Leah S. Marcus has explored the symbolic connotations of urban boundaries in the early modern period, emphasizing the process by which communal fears were projected into the Liberties and suburbs of Elizabethan and Jacobean London.
1. J. H. Andrews, "Geography and Government in Elizabethan Ireland," in Nicholas Stephens and Robin E. Glasscock, eds., *Irish Geographical Studies* (Belfast: Queen's University of Belfast, 1970), 182.
2. Mary Douglas, *Purity and Danger: An Analysis of the Concepts of Pollution and Taboo* (London: Ark, 1985), 115.
3. Sir John Davies, *A Discovery of the True Causes Why Ireland Was Never Entirely Subdued, Nor Brought Under Obedience of the Crown of England, until the Beginning of His Majesty's Happy Reign* (1612), in James P. Myers, Jr., ed., *Elizabethan Ireland: A Selection of Writings by Elizabethan Writers on Ireland* (Hamden, CT: Archon, 1983), 166.

erning Ireland was due to the "personal presence of the King's son as a concurrent cause of this Reformation, because the people of this land, both English and Irish, out of a natural pride, did ever love and desire to be governed by great persons" (165). *Henry IV, Part 1* offers the fantasy-remedy outlined by Davies of an activist male heir visiting the fringes of the realm and virtually single-handedly banishing rebellion. What made the fantasy both more compelling and more hollow, however, was the reality it belied of an aging woman ruler, who had never set foot in Ireland, and who stubbornly resisted all discussion of a successor.

While Hal is conceived on the one hand as an antidote to Elizabeth's inadequacies and failures, he is also drawn as an ideal successor to the long parade of men whom Elizabeth had appointed to govern in Ireland. At a later stage in Hal's career, Shakespeare explicitly likens Henry V on his victorious return from France to Elizabeth's own "General" returning from Ireland with "rebellion broachèd on his sword" (*Henry V,* 5.0.25–35). Critics have almost unanimously taken these lines to be a reference to the earl of Essex, Elizabeth's penultimate and ill-fated Lord Deputy in Ireland, yet the "General" in question could conceivably be his successor, Lord Mountjoy (Bevington, *Tudor Drama,* 290). Although *1 Henry IV* dates from the time when the young and charismatic Essex was first being linked with the Irish post, there is no reason to assume that Hal represents anything more than a general pattern of the kind of decisive and single-minded leadership required in Ireland.[4] Between 1596 and March 1599 the Irish command was in a state of flux, with two Lord Deputies and three interim justices in turn occupying the chief position (Ellis, 330). The arrival of the aggressive Thomas, Lord Burgh, as deputy in May 1597 had occasioned considerable confidence that Tyrone would soon be defeated, but less than five months later Burgh was dead of typhus (Hayes-McCoy, 123–24).

When Hal pronounces Hotspur's epitaph and observes the "fair rites of tenderness" (5.4.97) toward Hotspur's corpse, he reconstitutes a code of battlefield honor that the Welshwomen had so outrageously violated in this same territory. Yet even after Hal's consummation of his victory, the memory of that initial act of female castration still haunts the action. In a gesture that critics have long puzzled over, Falstaff, acting out his own genital rivalry with Hotspur ("Why may not he rise as well as I?" [5.4.122–23]), mutilates the corpse by stabbing it in the thigh. With that strategically

4. The allusion to Essex in *Henry V* only occurs in the Folio version of the play. See Annabel Patterson, "Back by Popular Demand: The Two Versions of *Henry V*," *Renaissance Drama* 19 (1988), 29–62.

placed blow, the repressed returns, disrupting the play's mechanisms of reintegration and resolution.[5] In the last lines of the play, a second eruption follows, when the king announces his plan to march "towards Wales, / To fight with Glendower and the Earl of March" (5.5.39–40). The sudden reintrusion of Glendower and Mortimer transforms the effect of closure from a reassuring completion into a postponement, the deferral of a threat apparently dismissed earlier.

That the play's ideological design should finally falter is hardly surprising, for in Ireland at this time Tyrone remained threatening and uncontained. "He is now become impotent to contayne himself within his bounds; but Seeketh to Usurpe the whole province," declared an exasperated English observer in 1598 (Hogan, 33). Only in December 1601 at the decisive battle of Kinsale were Tyrone's forces finally routed. In the meantime, Elizabeth's commanders argued about Tyrone's intentions and how to deal with them. Unable to fix on a consistent course of action, the English first declared him a traitor, then pardoned him and parleyed with him, then attacked him and tried to trick him with such "shiftes and subtelties," as the Privy Council put it, "tyll tyme serve to use more forcible meanes to reduce him to other manner of obedience."[6]

BARBARA HODGDON

[Endings]†

Taking Falstaff's part, A. C. Bradley begins "The Rejection of Falstaff" (1902) by asking, "Now why did Shakespeare end his drama with a scene which, though undoubtedly striking, leaves an impression so unpleasant?" Eventually, he concludes that *Henry IV*'s "chief hero" is the "wild" Prince Henry, who, in order to emerge "as a just, wise, stern, and glorious King," must, together with Bradley himself, banish Falstaffian plenitude.[1] Like Bradley, Orson Welles, a later Falstaffian conjuror, also begins with the end: discussing his

5. Gayle Whittier has a helpful discussion of Falstaff's stabbing of Hotspur. She sees it as symbolically replicating the assault "wrought by the barbaric Welshwomen upon dead warriors' bodies," and as an indication of Falstaff's submerged androgyny. [See Whittier, "Falstaff as a Welshwoman: Uncomic Androgyny," *Ball State University Forum* 20 (1979), 32–33.]
6. J.R. Dasent, ed., *Acts of the Privy Council of England, 1596–97* (London: 1902), 26:422.

† From Barbara Hodgdon, *The End Crowns All: Closure and Contradiction in Shakespeare's History* (Princeton: Princeton University Press, 1991), 151–66. Reprinted by permission of the publisher..

1. See A. C. Bradley, "The Rejection of Falstaff," 1902; reprinted in *Henry the Fourth, Parts I and II,* ed. David Bevington (New York, 1986), 81, 96.

1966 film, *Chimes at Midnight,* an adaptation of *1* and *2 Henry IV* with traces of *Richard II, Henry V,* and *The Merry Wives of Windsor,* he comments, "I directed everything, and played everything, with a view to preparing for the last scene."[2] The close of his film, however, not only readdresses Bradley's question from a diametrically opposed position but, by staging Falstaff's body as its primary site of spectacle, turns *Henry IV's* royal narrative, as in Hotspur's phrase, "topsy-turvy down" (*1H4*, 4.1.82).

In the cathedral space where Henry V is crowned, Welles's film articulates the rejection in a shot–reverse shot exchange consisting primarily of low- and high-angle close-ups and mid-close-ups in which two shots are especially striking. In the first, as Henry says "I know thee not, old man," he stands with his back to a Falstaff he clearly knows so well he does not even need to look at him; in the second, as the new King finally turns away from the "surfeit-swelled" old man to walk between massed banners toward the light, the film cuts to a mid-close-up of Falstaff, whose gaze registers pride in the splendid figure of his "sweet boy." When soldiers carrying lances bar his view of Hal, Falstaff moves slowly to stand alone next to a column, speaks with Shallow and, finally, moves out of the shot. As Shallow calls to him, a series of extreme long shots details his own procession as he walks away from the camera toward the darkened castle ramparts, his bulk growing smaller and smaller in the frame until, against deep, empty foreground space, his tiny silhouette disappears through a lit archway. As in Shakespeare's playtext, the Lords—here, the Bishop, Prince John, and the Lord Chief Justice—remark on the King's "fair proceeding"; but then Welles's textual rearrangements counterpose that judgment with its "fair" results: Doll is arrested, calling for Falstaff, who is ordered to the Fleet; his tiny Page, squirming through the crowd, tells Pistol that Falstaff is sick; and Bardolph comments, "The King is a good king, but it must be as it may." Before the castle battlements, Henry proclaims "Now, Lords, for France" and orders Falstaff released from prison—"We consider / It was excess of wine that set him on."

Now the camera pans right to follow Poins as he walks past the empty tavern "throne" where Falstaff and Hal had both played Henry IV and into the innyard, where he stops beside a huge coffin, resting on a rude cart: "Falstaff?" "Falstaff is dead," says the page; and, after Mistress Quickly speaks his epitaph (*H5*, 2.3.9–24), she watches while the three men push the enormous coffin through the innyard gates across a snow-speckled landscape bounded by the distant castle walls. The camera slowly booms up to offer an om-

2. Quoted in Juan Cobos and Miguel Rubio, "Welles and Falstaff," 1966; reprinted in *Chimes at Midnight*, ed. Bridget Gellert Lyons (New Brunswick, N.J., 1988), 261.

niscient perspective that traps this procession, in a high-angle extreme long shot, between tavern and court, and Ralph Richardson's authoritatively impersonal voice speaks a pastiche from Holinshed: "The new king, even at first appointing, determined to put on him the shape of a new man. This Henry was a captain of such prudence and such policy that he never enterprised anything before it forecast the main chances that it might happen. So humane withal, he left no offense unpunished nor friendship unrewarded. For conclusion, a majesty was he that both lived and died a pattern in princehood, a lodestar in honor, and famous to the world alway." Over a slow-motion film loop of a row of soldiers, nobles, and clerics, armed and ready for war, standing against the side wall of a church, pennon lances waving in the breeze, muffled drums beat out a rhythm that replaces his words.[3]

Rejected from the court by the King and from the tavern by Death, Falstaff's body inhabits a no-man's-land between the two spaces over which the voice of "history" presides, circumscribing and displacing Quickly's report of the fat knight's death with excerpts from Henry V's chronicle epitaph. Finally, the film reconstitutes the body, and the hierarchy, of the kingdom in an image that repeats itself endlessly, like the drums that simultaneously sound Falstaff's death knell and presage the coming war. If Welles's pseudo-Aristotelian complicity with tragedy generates a "finer end" (the Hostess's phrase), it also remaps the traditional territory[4] framed by "I know you all" and "I know thee not, old man" onto Falstaff's body to call Henry V's "carefully plotted official strategy" as well as the spectacle of rule into question. Strikingly, Welles's film is responsive not only to Bradley's praise, echoed by other readers, for Falstaff and his overreaching creator, "caught up in the wind of his own genius"—"It is not a misfortune that happens to many authors, nor is it one we can regret, for it costs us but a trifling inconvenience in one scene"[5]—but also to more recent configurations of the *Henry IV* plays as an ideal testing ground for examining the relations between plebian and patrician discourses, the carnivalesque and the theater as sites of subversion that work,

3. For discussions of Welles's film, see Jorgens, *Shakespeare on Film,* 106–21; Samuel Crowl, "The Long Goodbye: Welles and Falstaff," *Shakespeare Quarterly* 31 (1980): 369–80; and Dudley Andrew, *Film in the Aura of Art* (Princeton, 1984), 152–71.

4. Sherman H. Hawkins reviews, judges, and extends the two-century-old debate over the plan, structure, and aesthetic unity of the plays, which ranges from Dr. Johnson and Malone to Harold Jenkins, in "*Henry IV*: The Structural Problem Revisited," *Shakespeare Quarterly* 33 (1982): 278–301. See also Calderwood, *Metadrama in Shakespeare's Henriad,* especially III–16, and Berry, *Patterns of Decay,* 109. Giorgio Melchiori posits an "original" one-part play (based on *The Famous Victories*) comprising *1* and *2 Henry IV* and *Henry V,* rejected because of the Oldcastle controversy and later divided into three ("Reconstructing the *Ur-Henry IV,*" in *Essays in Honour of Kristian Smidt,* ed. Peter Bilton, Lars Hartveit, Stig Johansson, and Arthur O. Sandved [Oslo, 1986], 59–77).

5. Bradley, "Rejection of Falstaff," 97.

ultimately, to authorize the state.[6] Indeed Welles himself envisioned his film, not as a "lament for Falstaff, but for the death of Merrie England . . . a myth, which has been very real to the English-speaking world . . . the age of chivalry, of simplicity, of Maytime and all that."[7] When Steven Mullaney writes, of Falstaff's rejection, that "what surprises is not the event itself but the fact that the world being cast off has been so consummately rehearsed: so fully represented to us, and consequently, so fully foreclosed,"[8] he identifies quite precisely the rupture between "play" and "history" that shapes *2 Henry IV*'s close, a contradiction Welles's film reveals in the disjuncture between image and sound—the one recording what history excludes to hollow out the voice of official memory.

However split between a "prodigally lavish" Falstaffian economy and one of royal legitimation, between subversion and its containment, critical narratives of the *Henry IV* plays as well as late twentieth-century theatrical practice so consistently link its two parts into one that Falstaff's banishment becomes an end that indeed "crowns all." In fact, *Henry IV*'s "master narrative" not only subsumes *1 Henry IV*'s ending but absorbs the insistently coded closural gestures of *1* and *2 Henry IV*—what Samuel Crowl, writing on Welles's film, calls "The Long Goodbye"—into a pattern that arches over both plays to (always already) expel Falstaff. Reading *1* and *2 Henry IV*'s multiple endings from a "double vantage," I want not only to raise questions concerning their late sixteenth-century representation and reception but, by looking at several of their latter-day theatrical configurations, to examine how these reproduce or refashion, arrange or rearrange, social meaning as theatrical meaning. And I want to begin by describing *1 Henry IV*'s close in a version that, complete within itself, forecloses, so to speak, on the need for a second play.

Beerbohm Tree's 1895 *1 Henry IV*[9] constructs a highly idealized

6. See, for instance, C. L. Barber, *Shakespeare's Festive Comedies* (New York: Meridian Books, 1966), 18–47; Greenblatt, "Invisible Bullets," in Jonathan Dollimore and Alan Sinfield, eds., *Political Shakespeare: New Essays in Cultural Materialism* (Manchester: Manchester University Press, 1985), 265; Graham Holderness, *Shakespeare's History* (New York: St. Martin's Press, 1985), 88–95; Michael Bristol, *Carnival and Theatre: Plebeian Culture and the Structure of Authority in Renaissance England* (New York: Methuen, 1985), 180–83, 204–7; C. L. Barber and Richard P. Wheeler, *The Whole Journey: Shakespeare's Power of Development* (Berkeley: University of California Press, 1986), 198–217; Leonard Tennenhouse, *Power on Display: The Politics of Shakespeare's Genres* (New York: Methuen, 1986), 83–84; and Steven Mullaney, "Strange Things, Gross Terms, Curious Customs: The Rehearsal of Cultures in the Late Renaissance," in Stephen Greenblatt, *Representing the English Renaissance* (Berkeley: University of California Press, 1988), 82–89.
7. Quoted in Cobos and Rubio, "Welles and Falstaff," 262.
8. Mullaney, "Strange Things," 87.
9. Prompt copy in the Beerbohm Tree Collection, the University of Bristol Theatre Collection.

resolution of the play's contradictory, oppositional father-son relations. Omitting Hal's rescue of his father, Tree cuts from Falstaff's exit, taking a quick drink from the bottle Hal has just refused, to Hotspur's entrance, effecting a double exchange: rival son for rival father, true chivalry for its lack. As Hal and Hotspur recognize one another, the prompt copy indicates a trumpet flourish, followed by a pause and "picture" before an orchestral tremolo signals Falstaff's reentry to confront the Douglas. After the fights, Hal places a battle standard over Hotspur's body, turns briefly to address Falstaff, salutes Hotspur, and, with a sigh, exits. As the stage lights dim to an "evening effect," Falstaff glances over his shield; to the offstage clashing of swords, "very piano," he slowly rises and takes another drink from his bottle; but rather than taking up Hotspur's body, he falls to his knees and is about to lie down again when, seeing Hal and Prince John enter, he tries to creep away on his hands and knees. Helping Falstaff to his feet, Hal laughs, as Hotspur had done earlier in disbelief at his own death, and willingly gilds Falstaff's lie before proclaiming "the day is ours," at which a "15th and Final Flourish" sounds, backed by "hurrahs." Tree cuts Falstaff's promise to reform and moves directly to a mass entrance that fills the stage with soldiers, who frame a central tableau in which King Henry and Prince Hal embrace, surrounded by waving banners and triumphant "Huzzahs." Not only does Hotspur's body remain on the stage to figure the rebels' defeat and Hal's victory but, since Tree himself played Falstaff and since the prompt copy indicates no exit for him,[1] this close gives Hal two fathers and celebrates his reconciliation with both amidst a splendid military spectacle.

Its pictorial realization reminiscent of eighteenth and nineteenth-century commemorative paintings of famous battles, this sort of grand finale, its power greatly enhanced by the practice then common of playing the national anthem at the end of each performance, caps *1 Henry IV*s well into the 1950s.[2] While some performance texts, like Tree's, simply substitute military spectacle for the play's final scene, others, such as Bridges-Adams's for the Shakespeare Memorial Theatre in 1932,[3] by retaining King Henry's sentence of Worcester and Vernon, punish treason against the state and heal filial "treason" with the image of a Hal who kneels to his

1. Because Tree played Falstaff, he probably remained onstage, since common stage practice licensed actor-managers' presences at significant moments, especially at curtain, regardless of the playtext's stage directions. Whether or not his presence undercut the embrace between father and son is impossible to gauge. Although 5.5 was apparently returned at a later time (perhaps for the 1906 production), a second, less thoroughly marked, prompt copy for this production also highlights the Battle of Shrewsbury conceived as a spectacular tableau.
2. For example, in Anthony Quayle's 1951 Shakespeare Memorial Theatre production; prompt copy at the Shakespeare Centre Library.
3. Prompt copy at the Shakespeare Centre Library.

father at the final victory declaration. So transformed into moral myth, closure becomes a nostalgic fantasia in which rebellion has indeed lost its sway, mastered by heroism and military might embodied in a unitary spectacle that authenticates the relations between past and present cultures along a trans-historical continuum of idealized national and familial values.

In taking on such contours, these *1 Henry IV*s push to extremes the resolution of a story familiar to Elizabethans—the parable of the prodigal son, one well-known through two models, the biblical narrative and the equally mythologized tales, dramatized in the anonymous play, *The Famous Victories of Henry V*, of what Henry IV calls his son's "vile participation" (3.2.87).[4] In both versions, it is an exclusively male narrative directed toward working through father-son antagonisms and, in the case of the parable only, those between a dutiful elder son and his wastrel brother. Also in both, it is not the prodigal son's legitimacy that is in question but the need to establish his authenticity in relation to patriarchal law. Drawing on these paradigms as well as on chronicle materials, Shakespeare's play constructs a highly mythologized economy, structured through binary oppositions—court/tavern, honor/dishonor, time/timelessness, everyday/holiday, word/body, serious history/comic–popular discourse—in which the first term represents the desirable ideal, the second its inversion. As the only figure who can move flexibly between their boundaries, Hal encompasses their contradictions, for which Shrewsbury—represented on the one hand as history, and on the other as a purely theatrical invention—is the ideal testing ground.

Unlike Shakespeare's earlier histories, where conflict centers on genealogical descent in a struggle for the crown's rightful ownership, *1 Henry IV* positions the Percy-Northumberland rebellion against the state so that it serves Hal's mimetic rivalry with Hotspur as well as that between his authentic and counterfeit fathers, Henry IV and Falstaff.[5] In this extremely limited gender economy, structured by a desire for the male other that takes the form of aggression, women are positioned at history's margins: unnecessary to prove or deny Hal's or Hotspur's legitimacy (as, for instance, in *King John*), they simply delay historical time. Only the rebel leaders—Hotspur and Lord Mortimer—have wives, whose presence functions primarily to separate

4. Richard Helgerson, *The Elizabethan Prodigals* (Berkeley, 1977). See also Mullaney, "Strange Things," 83.
5. In reading the substitutions and replacements in these character relations, I draw from V. I. Propp, *Morphology of the Folktale* (1928); reprint, trans. Laurence Scott (Austin, 1958); A. J. Greimas, "Elements of a Narrative Grammar" (1969), reprinted in *Diacritics* 7 (1977): 23–40; and Barthes, *S/Z*. See also my "Falstaff: History and His Story," *Iowa State Journal of Research* 53, no. 3 (1979): 185–90. For an analysis based on René Girard's concept of sacred mythic difference, see Laurie E. Osborne, "Crisis of Degree in Shakespeare's *Henriad*," *Studies in English Literature* 25 (1985): 337–59. On morality elements, see Alan C. Dessen, *Shakespeare and the Late Moral Plays*, 55–90.

public from private domains and, by proving their husbands' heterosexuality, deflects the homoerotic into the homosocial; says Hotspur, "This is no world / To play with mammets or to tilt with lips" [2.3.85–86] nor has he time to listen to the Welsh lady sing (3.1.234). In their resistance to the male chivalric project, Kate Percy and Glendower's daughter are kin to Falstaff, a more substantial image of feminine "misrule," who lies within the tavern space, together with thieves, swaggerers, a Hostess-landlady, and "gentlewomen" who it is said, "live honestly by the prick of their needles" (*H5*, 2.1.31–32). Although within the Oedipal narrative, Falstaff figures as Hal's surrogate father, he is coded in feminine, maternal terms:[6] his fat belly is the masculine counterpart of the pregnant woman; his Rabelaisian excesses of food and drink make him the Carnival antithesis to Henry IV's ascetic Lenten identity and his world of religious penance, bent as Henry IV is on expiating personal as well as national guilt with a crusade. It is Falstaff who accuses Hal of being the king's bastard son, and Hal, too, imagines him as female when, just before baiting Falstaff about his Gadshill cowardice and with Hotspur circulating in his mind and in his talk, he thinks himself into playing Percy and "that damned brawn" into "Dame Mortimer his wife" (2.4.104–5). That "play extempore" is then transformed into one where the roles of king and son become interchangeable, shared between Falstaff and Hal, and where women have no place: Falstaff's first "command" as "father-king" is "convey my tristful queen" (2.4.375).

But perhaps the most telling of Falstaff's multiform female guises of misrule is his association with Queen Elizabeth's virgin identity: "Let us be Diana's foresters, gentlemen of the shade, minions of the moon; and let men say we be men of good government, being governed as the sea is, by our noble and chaste mistress the moon" (1.2.23–27).[7] Desiring to undertake something like Essex's role in the annual Accession Day Tourneys that celebrated Elizabeth's powerfully mythic, theatricalized presence, his fantasy of social order would steal and invert Essex's chivalric image—echoed in Hotspur's "easy leap / To pluck bright honor from the pale-faced moon" (1.3.201–2)—in order to recode his own body. Chivalry's daytime, however, cannot admit an aging, corpulent "squire of the night's body," whose *2 Henry IV* counterpart, mentioned in passing, is Shallow's "bona roba," Jane Nightwork (3.2.188). Even Hal, "a

6. On Falstaff's "curiously feminine sensual abundance," see Coppélia Kahn, *Man's Estate: Masculine Identity in Shakespeare* (Berkeley: University of California Press, 1981) 72. See also Valerie Traub, "Prince Hal's Falstaff: Positioning Psychoanalysis and the Female Body," *Shakespeare Quarterly* 40 (1989): 456–74. On the *Henriad* as an Oedipal narrative, see Ernst Kris, "Prince Hal's Conflict," *Psychoanalytic Quarterly* 17 (1948): 487–506. See also Richard Wheeler, *Shakespeare's Development and the Problem Comedies* (Berkeley, 1981), 158–67.
7. Marcus also notes the connection (*Puzzling Shakespeare: Vocal Reading and Its Discontents* [Berkeley: University of California Press, 1988], 94.

truant to chivalry" and the "shadow" of his father's succession (5.1.94), must transform himself to look the part of a May lord, "Ris[ing] from the ground like feathered Mercury . . . / As if an angel dropped down from the clouds," in order to confront Hotspur, a "Mars in swaddling clothes," the "king of honor" (4.1.106–8; 3.2.112; 4.1.10).[8] And although Sir John's body is also capable of metamorphosis, his transformations, and the codes he serves, work precisely to expose such glorious disguises.

Elizabethan spectators would have still other figures for Falstaff, and for his fluid gender identity, including his guise of eternal youth, that are distant from present-day readers and spectators. Spectators at *1 Henry IV*'s first performances, when Falstaff was called Oldcastle, would connect him not only with the character of the same name in *The Famous Victories* but also with a historical Sir John Oldcastle, a martyr celebrated in Foxe's *Actes and Monuments* and sentenced to death for treason by Henry V. Certainly some observers, the sixteenth-century Oldcastle descendants, Sir William Brooke and his son, the seventh and eighth Lord Cobhams, objected to such libel of the family name. And their objections had considerable weight, for Sir William was the Lord Chamberlain, with oversight responsibilities for the Master of Revels and the licensing of plays: given such sensitivity in high places, Shakespeare changed the name, and though traces of it remain in *1 Henry IV, 2 Henry IV*'s Epilogue offers a public disclaimer that "Oldcastle died martyr, and this is not the man" (Ep., 27–28).[9] The subject of anecdotes, letters, and rival plays, the Oldcastle-Falstaff issue may well have been fueled by the character's impersonator, the famous clown, Will Kemp, whom Nashe described as "jestmonger and Vice-gerent general to the ghost of Dick Tarlton" and who "succeeded" Tarlton as a favorite of Queen Elizabeth as well as the general public.[1] David Wiles argues persuasively that the Oldcastle-Falstaff role was written with Kemp in mind and that Kemp's particular skills helped to shape it, especially his ability to produce the illusion, in speaking scripted words, of spur-of-the-moment improvisation. And the conventions that coded a clown's role—ambiguous social status and semi-androgynous identity, freedom to separate himself from the play's role and plot structure,

8. See Tennenhouse, *Power on Display,* 83–84.
9. On the Oldcastle connection, see Alice Lyle Scoufos, *Shakespeare's Typological Satire* (Athens, Oh., 1979). See also *Henry the Fourth, Part I,* ed. David Bevington (Oxford, 1987), 3–10. Gary Taylor argues for returning Old castle's name to the playtext ("The Fortunes of Falstaff," *Shakespeare Survey* 38 [1985]: 95–100). Holderness positions the Oldcastle controversy in relation to *The True and Honourable History of the Life of Sir John Oldcastle* and to Puritan risings (*Shakespeare's History,* 107–12).
1. *Almond for a Parrat* (1590); *Apology for Actors* (1612); both quoted in David Wiles, *Shakespeare's Clown* (Cambridge, 1987), II.

metamorphosis and final exclusion[2]—rather precisely figure the attributes of Falstaff, who is both thief and knight, gentleman and marginal reveller, mother as well as father and giant "Power Baby,"[3] separate from but also central to the historical rebellion, protean liar, the excluded other. Throughout, but most especially at Shrewsbury, all of these images of his theatrical abundance come into play.

To "thrust in clowns by head and shoulders"[4] or, in this case, belly first, at Shrewsbury is, of course, Shakespeare's invention. The official chronicle sources record a battle in which the chief actors are Henry IV, Hotspur, and the Douglas, and position Hal simply as his father's helper, "a lusty young gentleman" who, though wounded, refuses to withdraw and continues to "fight where the battle was most hot."[5] And it is entirely possible to extract, from Shakespeare's own fictional account in *1 Henry IV*—in which his major additions to its royal plot are Hal's offer to oppose Hotspur "in single fight," his rescue of his father, his combat with Hotspur, his freeing of the Douglas, and the presence of Prince John—a "decent" version of Shrewsbury that avoids the "mingling [of] kings and clowns" that Sidney so deplores.[6] Indeed, these particular alterations are sufficient to reshape the chronicle record as a test of feudal and familial values, similar to those dramatized in the closing battles of the *Henry VI* plays. Selectively retold, such a decorously perfected narrative might begin as the King, with unexpected concern for his wounded son, begs him to retire; following Hal's refusal, both Henry IV and Hal praise John's valor in "hold[ing] Lord Percy at the point"—an event that gives Hal a second rival, his "true" brother. And when Hal's "fair rescue" of his father "redeem[s] his lost opinion, he dispels his "loose behavior" and supposed treachery—and with it the filial aggression dramatized in *The Famous Victories*[7]—as a rumor perpetrated by others: "they did me too much injury / That ever said I heark'ned for your death" (5.4.50–51). So prepared for, the Hal-Hotspur combat—what Graham Holderness calls "a vivid poem of feudal romance and chivalric adventure"[8]—is an exchange of "glorious deeds" for "indignities"

2. See Wiles, *Shakespeare's Clown,* 116–20.
3. I borrow Beverle Houston's apt phrase, "Power and Dis-Integration in the Films of Orson Welles," *Film Quarterly* 35 (Summer 1982): 2.
4. Sidney, *A Defence of Poetry,* 77. On the clown's "disorder," see David Scott Kastan, " 'Clownes Should Speake Disorderlye': Mongrel Tragicomedy and the Unitary State," unpublished paper, Shakespeare Association of America, 1989.
5. Holinshed, *Chronicles,* 521/1/74, reproduced in Bullough, *Narrative and Dramatic Sources,* 4:191.
6. Sidney, *A Defence of Poetry,* 77.
7. See Holinshed's report of Hal coming to his father strangely attired (538/2/74, reproduced in Bullough, *Narrative and Dramatic Sources,* 4:193).
8. Holderness, *Shakespeare's History,* 122. See also Gerard H. Cox, " *'Like a Prince Indeed'*: Hal's Triumph of Honor in *1 Henry IV,*" in David M. Bergeron, ed., *Pageantry in the Shakespearean Theater* (Athens: University of Georgia Press, 1985) 133, 135–47; and

that, with the death of the rival (rebel) son, ensures Hal's place as Henry IV's "authentic" heir. Finally, in the play's last scene, with the rebels vanquished and punished, Henry IV acknowledges that authenticity: Hal, granted leave by his father to dispose of the Douglas, not only redeems his prisoner, and so takes on the Hotspur-like qualities his father had so admired, but, in recognition of John's valor, transfers the "honorable bounty" to his brother just before his father, for the first time, and in the play's concluding speech, calls him "son Harry" (5.5.39).

In that Falstaff is kept apart from his kingly other, Shakespeare's fiction of Shrewsbury approaches this decorous ideal: during the battle, he appears only with Hal or alone on the stage and, in conformity with convention, is absent from its final "official" ending. Yet, curiously enough, Shakespeare's "double reading" of the chronicle takes license for Falstaff's appearance at Shrewsbury from details that, in keeping with his fictional status as a Lord of Misrule, are introduced as hearsay:

> (as some write) the earl of Douglas struck [Henry IV] down, and at that instant slew sir Walter Blunt, and three other, apparelled in the kings suit and clothing, saying: I marvel to see so many kings thus suddenly arise one in the neck of an other. The king in deed was raised, & did that day many a noble feat of arms, for as it is written, he slew that day with his own hands six and thirty persons of his enemies. The other on his part encouraged by his doings, fought valiantly, and slew the lord Percy, called sir Henry Hotspur.[9]

In *1 Henry IV*'s Shrewsbury, many also walk in the King's coats: indeed, Shrewsbury begins by killing the king, later recognized by Hotspur as Blunt, and so recirculates the question of the true king's identity, the central issue behind the Hotspur-Northumberland rebellion (5.3). Having others march in the King's armor represents the King's body both as powerfully doubled and redoubled in his subjects and as an empty lie; it also questions whether counterfeiting, dying as one's self or in another's guise, is honorable when put at the king's service, dishonorable when put into play by a Falstaffian subject.

For in *1 Henry IV*, it is Falstaff, not the King, who "rises," and the ambiguous "other on his part" becomes Hal who, as in Daniel's *Civil Wars*, saves his father's life.[1] While Holinshed represents the king father's body as a multiform illusion, in *1 Henry IV*, it is Fal-

---

Derek Cohen, "The Rite of Violence in *1 Henry IV*," *Shakespeare Survey* 38 (1985), especially 82.

9. Holinshed, *Chronicles*, reproduced in Bullough, *Narrative and Dramatic Sources*, 4:191.
1. Daniel, *Civil Wars*, 4:110–11, reproduced in Bullough, *Narrative and Dramatic Sources*, 4:214.

staff—whose "lying" nature the play codes in his body as well as his voice—who calls such illusion, and the omnipresence of fatherly law, into question. If, like the Douglas, the play's first, or first-time, spectators assume that, in killing Blunt, he has killed the king, they could also imagine that the Douglas does indeed kill Falstaff, especially since their attention is, so to speak, doubled, for the encounter occurs at the same time as Hal's mythic combat with Hotspur, Shrewsbury's most heroic event for which Falstaff is, at first, an observer:

> *They fight. Enter Falstaff*
> FALST. Well said, Hal, to it Hal. Nay you shall find no boys' play here I can tell you.
> *Enter Douglas, he fighteth with Falstaff, he falls down as if he were dead, the Prince killeth Percy.* (5.4.74–75)

When, later, Hal speaks double epitaphs—one for Hotspur's "stout" heart, one over Falstaff's stout body—the conventions alone dictate resolution, neatly rounded off in perfect, and perfectly accidental, closure that dispenses with both rival son and rival parent, throwing the rivals into relationship, joining anthithetical perspectives on honor that the play has kept separate but parallel, restoring order in the play's most politically significant systems: father-son relations, the threatened division of the kingdom, and Hal's authenticity. Indeed, since the last six lines of Hal's eulogy on Falstaff even fall into rhyme, it is possible for spectators as well as readers to hear these "last words" as the end of the play. In present-day theatrical configurations of the scene, the pause that invariably follows Hal's exit certainly invites spectators to believe in both deaths: even when "Falstaff riseth up" to falsify the illusion, it is only his ability to speak, proclaiming himself "no counterfeit, but the true and perfect image of life indeed," that codes the moment as something other than a curtain call where, eventually, the two other bodies onstage—the players of Hotspur and Blunt, dressed in armor that counterfeits the King—would also rise to acknowledge spectators' applause.

Most present-day critical configurations of this moment claim that Falstaff's resurrection invites readers and spectators, first, to be complicit with him, welcoming his surprise return from death, and then reject him when he stabs Hotspur and leaves to claim Hal's glory as his own.[2] But in fact the playtext makes none of these

2. See, for instance, Edward Pechter, "Falsifying Men's Hopes: The Ending of *1 Henry IV*," *Modern Language Quarterly* 41 (1980): 227–28. See also Barber, *Shakespeare's Festive Comedy*, 204–6; James Black, "*Henry IV*: A World of Figures Here," in McGuire and Samuelson, *Shakespeare*, 173–80; and Calderwood, *Metadrama in Shakespeare's* Henriad, 83–84, 119, 174. In Welles's film, Hal sees breath rising like steam from the kettle of Falstaff's armadillo-like armor, which turns his "Embowelled will I see thee by-and-by" (5.4.108) into a threatening joke.

moralistic judgments; rather, the only "moral work" is Falstaff's own, and it constitutes a riff on the infinite possibilities of theatrical dying (5.4.114–17). Here again, *1 Henry IV*'s Elizabethan spectators would have other options. For those who knew the character as Oldcastle, the fat knight's "rising" might take on specific topical resonances and be read as a lampoon on Oldcastle's alleged dying promise that he would "rise from death to life again, the third day."[3] And when his "killing" of Hotspur is read through the conventions associated with the clown, Falstaff's weapon takes on particular meaning. His sword first appears at Gadshill as a property that figures him as both Vice and adolescent, for the Vice's traditional weapon was a dagger of lath, similar to the wooden "waster" used by apprentices in the Sunday evening fights allowed them by their masters.[4] "Hacked like a handsaw" by Falstaff himself after the robbery, it is clearly a toy sword as well as a figure for his name—a "false staff" that, in figuring his lack of a potent phallus, is an emblematic weapon well chosen to represent his ineffectiveness in chivalry's, so to speak, metallic world. And it is this same child's toy with which he gives Hotspur a "new wound in [his] thigh" (5.4.127), an injury Shakespeare seems to transfer from the chronicler's Douglas—who "brake one of his cullions" in a fall and, having so lost his manliness, was pardoned by Henry IV[5]—to Hotspur. For all its insistent mythologizing of the heroic, Shrewsbury's battle is, finally, just what Falstaff claimed it was not: "boys' play."[6] And what gives it the lie and refutes its chivalric signs, making them serve his own interests, is the clown's interventionary presence. A creature who draws his own authenticity from the suspect realm of theatrical shadows, he, more than any other, is well aware that the counterfeit—the reproduced image of the authentic—has no value until it is put into circulation and exchanged.[7]

Curiously enough, it is the rupture within Hal's own chivalry—his failure to take favors from Hotspur and, instead, to give him his own—that enables Falstaff to recirculate Hotspur's body and claim for himself the father's honor. While it is usual to displace Hal's "fault" onto Falstaff and to read Falstaff as one who takes meaning from Hal, present-day theatrical configurations in which Hal demonstrates less than chivalric tactics in the fight show him sharing in Falstaff's brand of honor, a choice that can turn his gilding of Falstaff's lie into a kind of self-justification. Even more important,

3. See Stow's account, taken from Walsingham; quoted in Scoufos, *Shakespeare's Typological Satire,* 109.
4. See Wiles, *Shakespeare's Clown,* 120–22.
5. See Holinshed, *Chronicles*, quoted in Bullough, *Narrative and Dramatic Sources,* 4:191.
6. Wiles also notes this (*Shakespeare's Clown,* 123).
7. For a pertinent discussion of counterfeit images, see Sharon Willis, "Disputed Territories: Masculinity and Social Space," *Camera Obscura* 19 (1989): 5–23.

however, is Falstaff's ability to steal meaning from Henry IV. As he leaves the stage to "follow . . . for reward" [5.4.156] promising dietary reform, it looks as though Carnival will indeed yield to Lent and so, perhaps, create a new fiction of a Falstaff who can insert his transformed body into history. His words sound final—sound, that is, like the end of his role—and *1 Henry IV*'s final scene excludes him from its image of a reconstituted, rebellion-free royal hierarchy. Elizabethan spectators would recognize these moves as entirely "decorous," for the clown's final metamorphosis and his absence from the play's last scene were conventions of his role, and he would, in most cases, return to perform the traditional jig finale.[8] In the play's representational economy, convention works to dismantle narrative closure. By the last scene, Shakespeare seems to revert to reading the chronicle "straight": Henry IV never has knowledge of precisely which "other on his part"—whether Hal or Falstaff—has killed Hotspur. It is only Falstaff who, at least in some sense, has witnessed the event and turned it to imagined future advantage. And when, at the close, the King looks forward to "such another day," he reads into Shrewsbury's official account what *2 Henry IV* will, at first, record as a lie destined for the ears of Hotspur's "crafty-sick" father and, then, as the means to reinstate a newly costumed, newly titled "valiant Jack Falstaff," and so to further transform *1 Henry IV*'s "mingle" of king and clown.

From the mid-1950s forward, theatrical configurations of *1 Henry IV*'s close for the most part avoid the seamless, unitary discourse of spectacle characteristic of late nineteenth- and earlier twentieth-century versions and so not only "play out the play" but extend its boundaries, though not, except in one case, in order to say more on Falstaff's behalf (2.4.460–61). In that it so clearly articulates patterns of substitution and replacement among rival sons and fathers, Terry Hands's 1975 Royal Shakespeare Company *1 Henry IV* draws the closing scenes into what might be called a structuralist's dream.[9] In the Hal-Hotspur combat, Hotspur disarms Hal, who then seizes Hotspur's sword and aims two blows at his shield and a third at his stomach, which brings him to his knees; Hal then removes Hotspur's helmet and slashes his face with a dagger. On "I better brook the loss of brittle life," Hotspur grabs Hal and slowly stands, to die in his arms. To further cement their brotherhood, Hal lays Hotspur's body down and, kneeling beside it, enacts a series of ceremonial gestures: after wiping Hotspur's blood onto his own face, he places Hotspur's sword on his chest, crosses the dead hands over it, takes a red cloth from his own dagger to cover Hot-

8. See Wiles, *Shakespeare's Clown*, 110–15.
9. Prompt copy at the Shakespeare Centre Library.

spur's eyes, and finally stands and removes his own helmet while he praises his dead rival. In contrast, he pauses just long enough to see Falstaff and speak his epitaph but does not touch his body. When Falstaff returns to life, he not only performs a sequence of actions—speaking a few lines before rising to his knees and, finally, standing—that echo Hotspur's but repeats Hal's tactics by stabbing Hotspur with his own sword; linking him to both, his mimicry also calls the value of such gestures into question and, when he drags Hotspur's body offstage, subverts them completely. To further the transformed value of Hotspur's body, Hands repeats the image—not once but twice. As Falstaff exits, Hal reenters with John[1] and registers surprise at seeing neither Hotspur nor Falstaff; then Falstaff returns, dragging Hotspur's body behind him to hear a bemused Hal "gild" his lie. Left alone after Hal and John exit together, Falstaff again drags Hotspur's body out, undercutting his final promise to "live cleanly as a nobleman should do." Although this staging replaces Falstaff with John as Hal's companion, neither Hal's bond to Falstaff nor his to Hal is severed: indeed, this Hal seems to accept Falstaff's lie in order to accept his own counterfeiting self.

Hands's final stage images trace a further range of substitutions. Led in on ropes, Worcester and Vernon flank King Henry's central figure, while Westmoreland stands directly upstage of Henry, with Clarence and Humphrey at either side of him. Deliberately enforcing military justice, Henry drops, first, Worcester's rope and, after a pause, Vernon's. When Westmoreland and Humphrey exit with the prisoners, Henry moves downstage where, as Hal kneels at his right, asking for leave to dispose of the Douglas, and John moves to his father's left, both sons replace Worcester and Vernon, the traitors. On "ransomless and free," Hal stands, as Hotspur had earlier when Henry questioned him about his prisoners (1.3); and the echo of one son replacing another persists when Henry calls Hal "son Harry," puts an arm on his shoulder, and draws him toward a prominent downstage position before, pausing as though in doubt, he speaks his final line, "Let us not leave till all our own be won," which cues music filled with expectant drumbeats.[2] Hands's staging reconstitutes the initial image of Henry surrounded by roped prisoners as a Plantagenet family portrait: Clarence and John stand in

1. Hands replaces 5.4.18–19 so that these lines cap Hal's praise of John—"Before I loved thee as a brother, John, / But now I do respect thee as my soul"—and gives Hal John's "But soft, what have we here?"
2. In Michael Edward's 1984 *1 Henry IV* at Santa Cruz, Hal "avoided the simple notion that Hal returns to the role his father offered him—deliberately refusing . . . to resolve the many-sided, partly contradictory aspects of the part 'into an overall theory about Hal.' " See Mary Judith Dunbar, "Shakespeare at Santa Cruz," *Shakespeare Quarterly* 35 (1984): 477.

Vernon and Worcester's positions, Humphrey directly upstage of King Henry, Westmoreland up left, and Hal, now the "authentic" heir, directly downstage of Henry. As in Hand's closing images for the *Henry VI* plays, this final tableau figures a hard-won stability and predicts the "true" successor. And if replacing traitors with sons and cousins also refigures rebellion as a family matter, freeze-framing the close not only suppresses such potential contradictions but makes them unreadable, masked by an image of exclusive familial hierarchy that perfectly expresses the self-regarding gaze of legitimated royal power.

While the formal satisfactions of Hands's close fix Shrewsbury's moment within time, the close of Trevor Nunn's 1982 *1 Henry IV*, again for the Royal Shakespeare Company,[3] goes beyond its limits to reread its victory through Henry IV's eyes. The final image rhymes with the opening spectacle, where a flickering candlelight procession of monks, all in white robes and cowls, moves slowly downstage, while the rest of the company fills the dimly lit boxlike rooms, walkways, and turrets of the set—watchers as well as participants assembled to sing a haunting *Te Deum*. There, the King, dressed in a gold-embroidered ceremonial white cope, emerges from the procession to stand at its head, encompassed by the symbolic weight of his costume; here, the close diminishes the full panoply of that opening tableau. Bare to the waist and wearing a large crucifix, King Henry kneels in a tunnel of light, a shadowy kingdom of men and women standing in darkness behind him to observe his solitary, agonized penance. Drawing on Henry's opening wish to undertake a pilgrimage, Nunn's ending positions Shrewsbury's victory as a tainted substitute for and displacement of Henry's desire to lead a crusade that will expiate his guilt. It is an image that can be doubly read. If read backwards through *Richard II*'s ending and forward through the King's speech on the crown (*2H4*, 4.5.178–219), the image sharply focuses Henry's private angst and, by showing him surrounded by onstage spectator-subjects, all eyes turned toward the King, enhances his vulnerability and, as in *Richard II*'s close, figures not royal power but its lack. But the image can also be read through the schematic opposition of rival fathers: although it is Falstaff who promises reform, here it is Henry IV who performs his Shrewsbury penance.

Only once in *1 Henry IV*, at the parley just before Shrewsbury's battle (5.1), do King Henry and Falstaff share the stage, within a

3. The prompt copy at the Shakespeare Centre Library provides practically no directions for the close. I rely on notes taken at an August 1982 performance. See also R. L. Smallwood, "*Henry IV, Parts 1 and 2* at the Barbican Theatre" (1983; reprinted in Bevington, *Henry the Fourth, Parts I and II*, 423–30). Tree's 1895 production also opened with a procession accompanied by a Gregorian chant (prompt copy in the Beerbohm Tree Collection, the University of Bristol Theatre Collection).

context that flirts with equating carnival and rebellion. When the King asks Worcester how he came to rebel, Falstaff answers for him, "Rebellion lay in his way, and he found it," and Hal quickly silences him—"Peace, chewet, peace!" [5.1.28–29]. Whether Henry IV either does not hear or simply chooses to ignore Falstaff's remark, he never addresses him; Falstaff himself does not speak again until, following Hal's offer to "Try fortune with [Hotspur] in a single fight" and the King's offer of amnesty for the rebels, he is alone with Hal and asks for "friendship": "Hal, if thou seest me down in the battle . . . " (5.1.121). But although the playtext denies the support of language to the moment, this does not rule out the possibility of a silent exchange between Falstaff and the King, and both Hands's and Nunn's performance texts took this opportunity to sketch in their rivalry. In Hands's staging, both the King and Falstaff start to leave, and when Falstaff turns back to plead with Hal, the King pauses to watch their encounter, as though to satisfy himself that Hal will indeed keep his promise to "redeem all this on Percy's head" rather than revert to playing holiday with Falstaff. And Nunn's Henry IV, caught between envy and contempt for Falstaff, turns away, his shoulders sagging in defeat as Hal jokes with Falstaff.[4] Emrys James, who played Henry IV in Hands's production, remarked in an interview with Michael Mullin that "one can conceive a marvelous scene being written about [Henry and Falstaff]—a meeting between them."[5] Two other performance texts—Welle's *Chimes at Midnight* and Michael Bogdanov's 1987 English Shakespeare Company *1 Henry IV*—provide such a meeting, though not, perhaps, the one James may have had in mind.

Welles's film extends Hands's and Nunn's exchange of speaking looks to read Shrewsbury's victory as a record of personal loss and, by including Falstaff in its final moves, changes the relations between history and carnival, between the official version of Shrewsbury and Falstaff's account. When Falstaff throws Hotspur's body to the ground, Hal kneels in the mud and turns the body over on its back; in a mid–long shot of Hal, seen across Hotspur's body, a figure enters the frame at left, only the bottom of his robe visible, and the camera, rising with Hal, moves left to reveal King Henry, facing his son, his back to the camera. In a tightly edited sequence of close-ups—Henry's anguished face; Hal's look, caught between his two fathers; Falstaff's glow of self-pleasure; Hal meeting his father's gaze—the film links the three figures in an ambiguous web of doubt, betrayal, and dishonor in which Falstaff's expectant "I look to be either earl or duke, I assure you" cancels what Hal wants to

4. See Smallwood, "*Henry IV, Parts 1 and 2*," 425.
5. Quoted in an interview with Michael Mullin, "On Playing Henry IV," *Theatre Quarterly* 7, no. 27 (1977): 31.

say but cannot: that he has killed Hotspur. In a long shot, father and son face each other across the dead body before the King walks past Hal, strides into the background, and, in the next several shots, mounts his horse, collapses over the saddle in anguish, and, recovering, raises his arm in salute as the camera pans right to follow rows of horsemen. The next sequence reveals Falstaff, surrounded by his entire crew of ragged soldiers, a huge wine keg in the background; as though the previous confrontation had not occurred, he speaks a truncated version of his dissertation on sherris-sack (*2H4*, 4.3.83–119) and offers a tankard to Hal, who takes it and drinks, his forced smile suddenly becoming serious as he turns away from Falstaff, not sharing in the general laughter. As Falstaff's own smile turns quizzical and disappears, Hal, seen in an extreme long shot, walks away across the smoke-filled battlescape, dropping the tankard: the sound track registers only the wind's empty roar, and the shot fades out. Restating father-son oppositions, Welles's film deepens and sharply triangulates them to entrap a doubly orphaned Hal between his rival fathers—cut off by his father's gaze and rejecting Falstaff's sack-nurturing maternity himself—and, in eclipsing the image of Falstaff's bulk with that of Hal's receding figure, points forward to Sir John's ultimate rejection.

Deliberately quoting Welles's film, Michael Bogdanov's *1 Henry IV* not only reorders the play's final events but figures a more radical disjuncture between historical event and Falstaffian intervention than either *Chimes at Midnight* or Shakespeare's play.[6] In this eclectically dressed production, where costume ranges from Hal's blue jeans and open-necked shirt to nineteenth-century military uniform for Henry IV to commandolike garb for the rebels and camouflage gear for Falstaff, Hal and Hotspur wear tabards and chain mail for their mythic combat on a bare stage—bare, that is, except for the rounded hill of Falstaff's body. Toward the end of a long fight with heavy broadswords, Hal loses his and curls into a fetal position, as though overcome with infantile fear. With a grin, Hotspur slides the sword across to him; recovering immediately, Hal comes at him, slices across his gut in an ugly sweep, and then plunges the sword down from the shoulder, crosswise under the tabard, to his heart. Standing behind Hotspur and cradling his body, he stabs him once more, this time from the rear, on Hotspur's "And food for . . ."—an unnecessary overkill, this Hal's deliberate revenge on his father's obvious preference for Hotspur, as well as a coup de grace in tribute to Hotspur's bravery. As Hal returns his sword to the scabbard, he starts to exit, and then, seeing Falstaff,

6. My account combines details from a June 1987 performance in Toronto and a May 1988 performance in Chicago. In a September 1988 interview, Bogdanov indicated that his rearranged ending indeed drew from Welles's film, which he much admires.

dismissively speaks his epitaph. When, after removing a NO ENTRY sign from his shirt, Falstaff rises, he uses a child's toy sword to saw at Hotspur's thigh before heaving him onto his back as he leaves the stage.

Now the King, Worcester, Westmoreland, Prince John, and Hal return for the play's final scene, but as Henry concludes his last speech, Falstaff enters with Hotspur's body and unceremoniously plunks it down center, in front of Hal (fig. 13). His "I look to be either earl or duke, I assure you" is spoken half to Henry IV, half to Hal; positioned between the two, his bulk separating father and son, he recounts his version of Shrewsbury. Henry IV crosses to the body, looks down at it and then up at Hal, silently accusing him, before turning away to exit upstage center; after a self-righteous smirk at his brother, John follows his father, and an angry Hal smashes his sword to the floor with both hands. Pulling a cart piled with dead bodies, a soldier enters to circle the stage, weaving around Hal and Falstaff, stopping briefly at Hotspur's body before he exits. Now Hal bends over Hotspur's body, takes back the neckerchief he had worn in the earlier tavern scenes and had tied around the dead Hotspur's neck, and replaces it jerkily around his own—a mark of his kill through which he reaccepts the rivalry separating father and son. As though attempting to placate him, Falstaff delivers his promise to leave sack and live cleanly to a Hal who, without looking at him, orders him to "bring your luggage *nobly* on your back," an irony this Falstaff shrugs off as he exits, once again bearing Hotspur's body. Alone, Hal raises his sword with both hands straight over his head, turns upstage, and, his back rigid, exits toward his father into the gathering dark to the accompaniment of crashing brasses.

Like Welles's ending for Shrewsbury, Bogdanov's rewritten close sharply focuses Hal's entrapment. Although similar to Welles's strategy in catalyzing Hal's guilt through an exchange of gazes to turn him back into an unredeemed son, Bogdanov's close also more sharply calls the limits of counterfeiting into question. This *1 Henry IV* not only restores the father-son opposition but refuses to exclude a Falstaff who imagines his lie a Shrewsbury joke not unlike Henry IV's "shadows" marching in armor. By omitting Hal's gilding of Falstaff's lie, Bogdanov's rearranged ending permits Falstaff to take revenge for Hal's exposure of his Gadshill cowardice. And its final emphases rest not on Hal's rejection of Falstaff but on Hal's own exclusion, his need to prove himself once more and also, perhaps, to seek revenge against the father who, doubting his true son, believes the boastful lie of another, counterfeit, father.

* * *

Selected Bibliography

• indicates works included or excerpted in this Norton Critical Edition.

FILM/TELEVISION PERFORMANCES

Chimes at Midnight (also known as *Campanadas a medianoche* and *Falstaff*), prod and dir. Orson Welles. 115 min., Alpine Films and Internacional Films Española, 1965.

Henry IV, Part I, prod. Cedric Messina, dir. David Giles. British Broadcasting Corporation (BBC) and Time-Life Television Productions Inc., 1979.

Henry IV, prod. Annie Castledine, dir. John Caird. BBC2, 1995.

Wars of the Roses (including *1 Henry IV*), prod. John Paul Chapple and Andy Ward, dir. Michael Bogdanov. English Shakespeare Company, 1989.

• *My Own Private Idaho* (based loosely on *1 Henry IV*), prod. Laurie Parker, dir. Gus Van Sant. 102 min., New Line Cinema, 1991, videocassette.

AUDIO RECORDINGS

Henry the Fourth, Part I, performed by the Shakespeare Recording Society, dir. Peter Wood. New York: Caedmon Records, 1964. Caedmon AR 22881, audio discs.

Henry IV Part One, performed by Julian Glover, Jamie Glover, Timothy West, Jonathan Keeble, and Prunella Scales, dir. Gordon House. BBC, 1998, audiocassette.

Henry IV Part One, performed by Julian Glover, Jamie Glover, and others, prod. Bill Shepherd and Tom Treadwell, dir. Clive Brill. New York: Penguin Audiobooks (Arkangel Complete Shakespeare), 1999, audiocassette.

CRITICISM

Anderegg, Michael. "*Chimes at Midnight:* Rhetoric and History." In Anderegg, *Orson Welles, Shakespeare, and Popular Culture,* 123–40. New York: Columbia Univ. Press, 1999.

Auden, W. H. "The Prince's Dog." In Auden, *The Dyer's Hand,* 182–208. New York: Random House, 1962.

• Barber, C. L. *Shakespeare's Festive Comedy: A Study of Dramatic Form and Its Relation to Social Custom.* Princeton: Princeton Univ. Press, 1959.

Barish, Jonas A. "The Turning Away of Prince Hal." *Shakespeare Studies,* no. 1, 9–17. 1965.

Bennett, Robert B. "Four Stages of Time: The Shape of History in Shakespeare's Second Tetralogy." *Shakespeare Studies,* no. 19, 61–85. 1987.

Berger, Harry, Jr. "Food for Words: Hotspur and the Discourse of Honor." In Berger, *Making Trifles of Terrors: Redistributing Complicities in Shakespeare,* 251–87. Stanford: Stanford Univ. Press, 1997.

Berry, Edward. "Twentieth-Century Shakespeare Criticism: The Histories." In *The Cambridge Companion to Shakespeare Studies,* ed. Stanley Wells, 249–56. Cambridge: Cambridge Univ. Press, 1986.

Black, James. "Henry IV's Pilgrimage." *Shakespeare Quarterly,* no. 34, 18–26. 1983.

Blanpied, John W. *Time and the Artist in Shakespeare's English Histories.* Newark: Univ. of Delaware Press, 1983.

- • Bradley, A.C. "The Rejection of Falstaff." In Bradley, *Oxford Lectures on Poetry*, 245–75. London: Macmillan, 1909.
- • Bristol, Michael D. *Carnival and Theatre: Plebeian Culture and the Structure of Authority in Renaissance England.* New York: Methuen, 1985.

Bullough, Geoffrey, ed. *The Narrative and Dramatic Sources of Shakespeare.* 8 vols. London: Routledge Kegan Paul, 1958. 1957–73.

Bulman, J. C. and H. R. Coursen, eds. *Shakespeare on Television: An Anthology of Essays and Reviews.* Hanover, NH: Univ. Press of New England, 1988.

- • Burckhardt, Sigurd. *Shakespearean Meanings.* Princeton: Princeton Univ. Press, 1968.

Calderwood, James L. *Metadrama in Shakespeare's* Henriad: Richard II *to* Henry V. Berkeley: Univ. of California Press, 1979.

Campbell, Lily B. *Shakespeare's "Histories": Mirrors of Elizabethan Policy.* San Marino, CA: Huntington Library Publications, 1947.

Champion, Larry S. *"The Noise of Threatening Drum": Dramatic Strategy and Political Ideology in Shakespeare and the English Chronicle Plays.* Newark: Univ. of Delaware Press, 1990.

Champion, Larry S. *Perspectives in Shakespeare's English Histories.* Athens, GA: Univ. of Georgia Press, 1980.

Corbin, Peter and Douglas Sedge, eds. *The Oldcastle Controversy: "Sir John Oldcastle, Part I" and "The Famous Victories of Henry V."* In "The Revels Plays Companion Library." Manchester: Manchester Univ. Press, 1991.

Cox, Gerard H. " 'Like a Prince Indeed': Hal's Triumph of Honor in *1 Henry IV.*" In *Pageantry in the Shakespearean Theater,* ed. David M. Bergeron, 130–49. Athens, GA: Univ. of Georgia Press, 1985.

Cox, John. *Shakespeare and the Dramaturgy of Power.* Princeton Univ. Press, 1989.

Crane, Mary Thomas. "The Shakespearean Tetralogy." *Shakespeare Quarterly,* no. 36, 282 99. 1985.

- • Crowl, Samuel. "The Long Good-Bye: Welles and Falstaff." *Shakespeare Quarterly,* no. 31, 369–80. 1980.

Dawson, Anthony B. *Watching Shakespeare: A Playgoer's Guide.* London: Macmillan, 1988.

Dessen, Alan. "Staging Shakespeare's History Plays in 1984: A Tale of Three Henrys." *Shakespeare Quarterly,* no. 36, 71–79. 1985.

Findlay, Heather. "Renaissance Pederasty and Pedagogy: The Case of Shakespeare's Falstaff." *Yale Journal of Criticism,* no. 3, 229–38. 1989.

Fischer, Sandra K. " 'He means to pay': Value and Metaphor in the Lancastrian Tetralogy." *Shakespeare Quarterly,* no. 40, 149–64. 1989.

Garber, Marjorie. " 'What's past is prologue': Temporality and Prophecy in Shakespeare's History Plays." in *Renaissance Genres: Essays on Theory, History, and Interpretation,* ed. Barbara Lewalski, 301–31. Cambridge, MA: Harvard Univ. Press, 1986.

Goldberg, Jonathan. "The Commodity of Names: 'Falstaff' and 'Oldcastle' in *1 Henry IV.*" In *Reconfiguring the Renaissance: Essays in Critical Materialism,* ed. Jonathan Crew, 76–88. Bucknell: Bucknell Univ. Press, 1992.

Goldberg, Jonathan. "Rebel Letters: Postal Effects from *Richard II* to *Henry V.*" *Renaissance Drama,* no. 19, 3–28. 1988.

- • Greenblatt, Stephen J. "Invisible Bullets." In *Political Shakespeare: New Essays in Cultural Materialism,* ed. Jonathan Dollimore and Alan Sinfield, 18–47. Manchester: Manchester Univ. Press, 1985.

Hapgood, Robert. "*Chimes at Midnight* from Stage to Screen: The Art of Adaptation." *Shakespeare Survey,* no. 39, 39–52. 1987.

Hawkins, Sherman H. "*Henry IV*: The Structural Problem Revisited." *Shakespeare Quarterly,* no. 33, 278–301. 1982.

Hemingway, S. B., ed. *A New Variorum Edition of Henry the Fourth Part I.* Philadelphia: Lippincott, 1936.

- • Highley, Christopher. "Wales, Ireland and *1 Henry IV.*" *Renaissance Drama,* no. 21, 91–114. 1990.
- • Hodgdon, Barbara. *The End Crowns All: Closure and Contradiction in Shakespeare's History.* Princeton: Princeton Univ. Press, 1991.
- • Holderness, Graham, ed. *Shakespeare's History Plays: "Richard II" to "Henry V."* In "New Casebooks." Basingstoke: Macmillan, 1992.

Honigmann, E. A. J. "Sir John Oldcastle: Shakespeare's Martyr." In *"Fanned and Winnowed Opinions": Shakespearean Essays Presented to Harold Jenkins,* ed. John W. Mahon and Thomas A. Pendleton, 118–32. London: Methuen, 1987.

- • Howard, Jean E., and Phyllis Rackin. "Gender and Nation: The Henry IV Plays." In *Engendering a Nation: A Feminist Account of Shakespeare's English Histories,* 160–85. "Feminist Readings of Shakespeare" series, London: Routledge, 1997.

Howlett, Kathy M. "Utopian Revisioning of Falstaff's Tavern World." In Howlett, *Framing Shakespeare on Film,* 149–77. Athens, OH: Univ. of Ohio Press, 2000.
Hunter, G. K. "*Henry IV* and the Elizabethan Two-Part Play." *Review of English Studies,* no. 5, 236–48. 1954.
Jackson, MacDonald P. "The Wars of the Roses: The English Shakespeare Company on Tour." *Shakespeare Quarterly,* no. 40, 208–12. 1989.
• Kahn, Coppélia. *Man's Estate: Masculine Identity in Shakespeare.* Berkeley & Los Angeles: Univ. of California Press, 1981.
• Kastan, David Scott. " 'Killed with Hard Opinions': Oldcastle and Falstaff and the Reformed Text of *1 Henry IV.*" In Kastan, *Shakespeare After Theory,* 93–106. New York: Routledge, 1999.
• Kastan, David Scott. " 'The King hath many marching in his Coats,' or What did you do in the War, Daddy?" In *Shakespeare Left and Right,* ed. Ivo Kamps, 241–58. New York: Routledge, 1991.
• Kelly, Henry Ansagar. *Divine Providence in the England of Shakespeare's Histories.* Cambridge, MA: Harvard Univ. Press, 1970.
Lindenberger, Herbert. *Historical Drama: The Relation of Literature and Reality.* Chicago: Univ. of Chicago Press, 1975.
MacDonald, Ronald R. "Uneasy Lies: Language and History in Shakespeare's Lancastrian Tetralogy." *Shakespeare Quarterly,* no. 35, 22–39. 1984.
Maguire, Laurie E. " 'Household Kates': Chez Petruchio, Percy and Plantagenet." In *Gloriana's Face: Women, Public and Private, in the English Renaissance,* ed. Susan P. Cerasano and Marion Wynne-Davies, 129–65. Detroit: Wayne State Univ. Press, 1992.
Manheim, Michael. "The English History Play on Screen." In *Shakespeare and the Moving Image: The Plays on Film and Television,* ed. Anthony Davies and Stanley Wells, 121–45. Cambridge: Cambridge Univ. Press, 1994.
• McMillin, Scott, *Henry IV, Part One.* "Shakespeare in Performance" series, Manchester: Manchester Univ. Press, 1991.
Melchiori, Georgio. "Reconstructing the *Ur-Henry IV.*" In *Essays in Honour of Kristian Smidt,* ed. Peter Bilton *et al.,* 59–77. Oslo: Oslo Univ. Press, 1986.
Moseley, C. W. R. D. *Shakespeare's History Plays: Richard II to Henry V, the Making of a King.* New York: Penguin, 1991.
Mullaney, Steven. "The Rehearsal of Cultures." In Mullaney, *The Place of the Stage: License, Play and Power in Renaissance England,* 60–87. Ann Arbor: Univ. of Michigan Press, 1995.
Novy, Marianne, ed. *Transforming Shakespeare: Contemporary Women's Re-Visions in Literature and Performance.* New York: Palgrave Macmillan, 1999.
Ornstein, Robert, *A Kingdom for a Stage; The Achievement of Shakespeare's History Plays.* Cambridge, MA: Harvard Univ. Press, 1972.
Osborne, Laurie E. "Crisis of Degree in Shakespeare's *Henriad.*" *Studies in English Literature, 1500–1900,* no. 25, 337–59. 1985.
• Parker, Patricia. *Literary Fat Ladies: Rhetoric, Gender, Property.* London: Methuen, 1987.
Patterson, Annabel. *Reading Holinshed's Chronicles.* Chicago: Univ. of Chicago Press, 1994.
Phillips, Stephen. "Telling the Story: Shakespeare's Histories in Performance." *New Theatre Quarterly,* no. 6, 207–14. 1990.
Pilkington, Ace G., *Screening Shakespeare from* Richard II *to* Henry V. Newark, DE: Univ. of Delaware Press, 1991.
Prior, Moody E. "Comic Theory and the Rejection of Falstaff." *Shakespeare Studies,* no. 9, 159–71. 1976.
Rackin, Phyllis. *Stages of History: Shakespeare's English Chronicles.* Ithaca: Cornell Univ. Press, 1990.
Reese, M. M. *The Cease of Majesty: A Study of Shakespeare's History Plays.* London: Arnold, 1961.
Ribner, Irving. *The English History Play in the Age of Shakespeare.* Princeton: Princeton Univ. Press, 1957; rep. New York: Octagon Books, 1979.
Scoufos, Alice-Lyle. *Shakespeare's Typological Satire: A Study of the Falstaff-Oldcastle Problem.* Athens, OH: Ohio Univ. Press, 1979.
Shaw, Catherine M. "The Tragic Substructure of the *Henry IV* plays." *Shakespeare Survey,* no. 38, 61–67. 1985.
Simmons, J. L. "Masculine Negotiations in Shakespeare's History Plays: Hal, Hotspur, and 'the Foolish Mortimer.' " *Shakespeare Quarterly,* no. 44, 440–63. 1993.
Smidt, Kristian. *Unconformities in Shakespeare's History Plays.* Atlantic Highlands, NJ: Humanities Press, 1982.
• Sprague, Arthur Colby. "Gadshill Revisited." *Shakespeare Quarterly,* no. 4. 1953.
Sprague, A[rthur] C[olby]. *Shakespeare's Histories: Plays for the Stage.* London: The Society for Theatre Research, 1964.

• Taylor, Gary. "The Fortunes of Oldcastle." *Shakespeare Survey,* no. 38, 85–100. 1985.

Tillyard, E.M.W. *The Elizabethan World Picture.* London: Chatto & Windus, 1943; rep. Penguin, 1963.

• Tillyard, E.M.W. *Shakespeare's History Plays.* London: Chatto & Windus, 1944; rep. Penguin, 1962.

Traub, Valerie. "Prince Hal's Falstaff: Positioning Psychoanalysis and the Female Reproductive Body." *Shakespeare Quarterly,* no. 40, 456–74. 1989.

Traversi, Derek A. *Shakespeare: From* Richard II *to* Henry V. Stanford: Stanford Univ. Press, 1957.

Wikander, Matthew H. *The Play of Truth & State: Historical Drama from Shakespeare to Brecht.* Baltimore: Johns Hopkins Univ. Press, 1986.

• Wilders, John. *The Lost Garden: A View of Shakespeare's English and Roman History Plays.* London: Macmillan, 1978.

Wiles, David. *Shakespeare's Clowns: Actor and Text in the Elizabethan Playhouse.* Cambridge: Cambridge Univ. Press, 1987.

Willems, Michele M. "Misconstruction in *1 Henry IV.*" *Cahiers Elisabéthains,* no. 37, 43–57. 1990.

• Wilson, John Dover. *The Fortunes of Falstaff.* Cambridge: Cambridge Univ. Press, 1943.

• Wiseman, Susan. "The Family Tree Motel: Subliming Shakespeare in *My Own Private Idaho.*" In *Shakespeare, The Movie: Popularizing the Plays on Film, TV, and Video,* ed. Lynda E. Boose and Richard Burt, 225–39. London: Routledge, 1997.

• Yachnin, Paul. "History, Theatricality, and the 'Structural Problem' in the *Henry IV* Plays." *Philological Quarterly,* no. 70, 163–79. 1991.

Yachnin, Paul. "The Powerless Theater." *English Literary Renaissance,* no. 21, 49–74. 1991.

Zitner, S.P. "Staging the Occult in *1 Henry IV.*" In *The Mirror Up to Shakespeare: Essays in Honour of G. R. Hibbard,* ed. J. C. Gray, 138–48. Toronto: Univ. of Toronto Press, 1984.